Communications
in Computer and Information Science   222

Mohammad S. Obaidat
George A. Tsihrintzis   Joaquim Filipe (Eds.)

e-Business and Telecommunications

7th International Joint Conference, ICETE 2010
Athens, Greece, July 26-28, 2010
Revised Selected Papers

 Springer

Volume Editors

Mohammad S. Obaidat
Monmouth University, Department of Computer Science
West Long Branch, NJ 07764, USA
E-mail: obaidat@monmouth.edu

George A. Tsihrintzis
University of Piraeus, Department of Informatics
Piraeus 185 34, Greece
E-mail: geoatsi@unipi.gr

Joaquim Filipe
Polytechnic Institute of Setúbal – INSTICC
Department of Systems and Informatics
Rua do Vale de Chaves - Estefanilha, 2910-761 Setúbal, Portugal
E-mail: joaquim.filipe@estsetubal.ips.pt

ISSN 1865-0929   e-ISSN 1865-0937
ISBN 978-3-642-25205-1   e-ISBN 978-3-642-25206-8
DOI 10.1007/978-3-642-25206-8
Springer Heidelberg Dordrecht London New York

Library of Congress Control Number: 2011940215

CR Subject Classification (1998): C.2, J.1, K.4.4, K.6.5, D.4.6, H.4, H.5.1

© Springer-Verlag Berlin Heidelberg 2012
This work is subject to copyright. All rights are reserved, whether the whole or part of the material is
concerned, specifically the rights of translation, reprinting, re-use of illustrations, recitation, broadcasting,
reproduction on microfilms or in any other way, and storage in data banks. Duplication of this publication
or parts thereof is permitted only under the provisions of the German Copyright Law of September 9, 1965,
in its current version, and permission for use must always be obtained from Springer. Violations are liable
to prosecution under the German Copyright Law.
The use of general descriptive names, registered names, trademarks, etc. in this publication does not imply,
even in the absence of a specific statement, that such names are exempt from the relevant protective laws
and regulations and therefore free for general use.

Typesetting: Camera-ready by author, data conversion by Scientific Publishing Services, Chennai, India

Printed on acid-free paper

Springer is part of Springer Science+Business Media (www.springer.com)

Preface

The present book includes extended and revised versions of a set of selected best papers from the 7th International Joint Conference on e-Business and Telecommunications (ICETE), which was held in July 2010, in Athens, Greece. This conference reflects a continuing effort to increase the dissemination of recent research results among professionals who work in the areas of e-business and telecommunications. ICETE is a joint international conference integrating four major areas of knowledge that are divided into six corresponding conferences: DCNET (International Conference on Data Communication Networking), ICE-B (International Conference on e-Business), OPTICS (International Conference on Optical Communication Systems), SECRYPT (International Conference on Security and Cryptography), WINSYS (International Conference on Wireless Information Systems) and SIGMAP (International Conference on Signal Processing and Multimedia).

The program of this joint conference included several outstanding keynote lectures presented by internationally renowned distinguished researchers who are experts in the various ICETE areas. Their keynote speeches contributed to heightening the overall quality of the program and significance of the theme of the conference.

The conference topic areas define a broad spectrum in the key areas of e-business and telecommunications. This wide-view reporting made ICETE appealing to a global audience of engineers, scientists, business practitioners, ICT managers and policy experts. The papers accepted and presented at the conference demonstrated a number of new and innovative solutions for e-business and telecommunication networks and systems, showing that the technical problems in these closely related fields are challenging and worthwhile approaching in an interdisciplinary perspective such as that promoted by ICETE.

ICETE 2010 received 422 papers in total, with contributions from 46 different countries, on all continents, which really shows the success and global dimension of the conference. To evaluate each submission, a double-blind paper evaluation method was used; each paper was reviewed by at least two experts from the International Program Committee, in a double-blind review process, and most papers received three reviews or even more. In the end, 122 papers were selected for oral presentation and publication, corresponding to a 28.9% acceptance ratio. Of these only 48 were accepted as full papers (11.3% of submissions) and 74 as short papers. Additionally, 60 papers were accepted for poster presentation.

We hope that you will find this collection of the best ICETE 2010 papers an excellent source of inspiration as well as a helpful reference for research in the aforementioned areas.

May 2011

Mohammad S. Obaidat
George A. Tsihrintzis
Joaquim Filipe

Organization

Conference Co-chairs

Mohammad S. Obaidat   Monmouth University, USA
George Tsihrintzis   University of Piraeus, Greece

Program Co-chairs

DCNET

Mohammad S. Obaidat   Monmouth University, USA
Jose Luis Sevillano   Universidad de Sevilla, Spain

ICE-B

David Marca   University of Phoenix, USA
Boris Shishkov   IICREST
Marten Van Sinderen   University of Twente / CTIT / IICREST,
      The Netherlands

OPTICS

Petros Nicopolitidis   Aristotle University, Greece

SECRYPT

Sokratis Katsikas   University of Piraeus, Greece
Pierangela Samarati   Università degli Studi di Milano, Italy

SIGMAP

George Tsihrintzis   University of Piraeus, Greece
Maria Virvou   University of Piraeus, Greece

WINSYS

Rafael Caldeirinha   Polytechnic Institute of Leiria, Portugal
Mohammad S. Obaidat   Monmouth University, USA

Organizing Committee

Patrícia Alves   INSTICC, Portugal
Sérgio Brissos   INSTICC, Portugal
Helder Coelhas   INSTICC, Portugal
Vera Coelho   INSTICC, Portugal
Andreia Costa   INSTICC, Portugal

Patricia Duarte	INSTICC, Portugal
Bruno Encarnação	INSTICC, Portugal
Mauro Graça	INSTICC, Portugal
Liliana Medina	INSTICC, Portugal
Elton Mendes	INSTICC, Portugal
Carla Mota	INSTICC, Portugal
Raquel Pedrosa	INSTICC, Portugal
Vitor Pedrosa	INSTICC, Portugal
Daniel Pereira	INSTICC, Portugal
Filipa Rosa	INSTICC, Portugal
Mónica Saramago	INSTICC, Portugal
José Varela	INSTICC, Portugal
Pedro Varela	INSTICC, Portugal

DCNET Program Committee

Mohiuddin Ahmed, Malaysia
Özgür B. Akan, Turkey
Julio Barbancho, Spain
Alejandro Linares Barranco, Spain
Christian Callegari, Italy
Daniel Cascado-Caballero, Spain
Tomaso De Cola, Germany
Franco Davoli, Italy
Jitender Deogun, USA
Hala ElAarag, USA
Sebastià Galmés, Spain
Jose Daniel Garcia, Spain
Katja Gilly, Spain
Mehmet Hadi Gunes, USA
Sami Habib, Kuwait
Abdelhakim Hafid, Canada
Jarmo Harju, Finland
Carlos Juiz, Spain
Helen Karatza, Greece
Randi Karlsen, Norway
Rachid El Abdouni Khayari, Germany

Michael Kounavis, USA
Zhenjiang Li, USA
Pascal Lorenz, France
S. Kami Makki, USA
Igor Margasinski, Poland
Rami Melhem, USA
Pascale Minet, France
Carlos León de Mora, Spain
Fei Nan, USA
Elena Pagani, Italy
Krzysztof Pawlikowski, New Zealand
Michal Pioro, Poland
Juan-Carlos Ruiz-Garcia, Spain
Kenji Suzuki, USA
Vicente Traver, Spain
Athanasios Vasilakos, Greece
Pere Vilà, Spain
Manuel Villen-Altamirano, Spain
Bernd E. Wolfinger, Germany
Hirozumi Yamaguchi, Japan

DCNET Auxiliary Reviewers

Jesus Bravo Alvarez, Spain
Luca Caviglione, Italy
Roman Dunaytsev, Finland
Juan S. Gonzalez, Spain

Marko Helenius, Finland
Luis Miguel Sanchez, Spain
Bilhanan Silverajan, Finland

ICE-B Program Committee

Anteneh Ayanso, Canada
Ladjel Belllatreche, France
Morad Benyoucef, Canada
Indranil Bose, Hong Kong
Christos Bouras, Greece
Stéphane Bressan, Singapore
Erik Buchmann, Germany
Rebecca Bulander, Germany
Wojciech Cellary, Poland
Dickson Chiu, China
Soon Chun, USA
Jen-Yao Chung, USA
Michele Colajanni, Italy
Rafael Corchuelo, Spain
Peter Dolog, Denmark
Khalil Drira, France
Yanqing Duan, UK
Erwin Fielt, Australia
Chiara Francalanci, Italy
Flavius Frasincar, The Netherlands
José María García, Spain
Paul Grefen, The Netherlands
Andreas Holzinger, Austria
Ela Hunt, Switzerland
Arun Iyengar, USA
Anton Lavrin, Slovak Republic
Sebastian Link, New Zealand

Liping Liu, USA
Jie Lu, Australia
David Marca, USA
Tokuro Matsuo, Japan
Gavin McArdle, Ireland
Brian Mennecke, USA
Adrian Mocan, Germany
Ali Reza Montazemi, Canada
Maurice Mulvenna, UK
Dan O'Leary, USA
Georgios Papamichail, Greece
Krassie Petrova, New Zealand
Pak-Lok Poon, China
Philippos Pouyioutas, Cyprus
Sofia Reino, UK
Ana Paula Rocha, Portugal
Gustavo Rossi, Argentina
Jarogniew Rykowski, Poland
Quah Tong Seng, Singapore
Zhaohao Sun, Australia
Thompson Teo, Singapore
Laurentiu Vasiliu, Ireland
Tomas Vitvar, Austria
Michael Weiss, Canada
Jongwook Woo, USA
Qi Yu, USA

ICE-B Auxiliary Reviewers

Emilia Cimpian, Germany
Kaouthar FakhFakh, France
Ismael Bouassida Rodriguez, France
German Sancho, France

Ricardo Seguel, The Netherlands
Jochem Vonk, The Netherlands
Xiaohui Zhao, The Netherlands

OPTICS Program Committee

Davide Careglio, Spain
Adolfo Cartaxo, Portugal
Walter Cerroni, Italy
Jitender Deogun, USA
Yi Dong, China

Christian Gaumier, Switzerland
Marco Genoves, Italy
Masahiko Jinno, Japan
Sergej Kulik, Russian Federation
Franko Küppers, USA

Cees de Laat, The Netherlands
Byoungho Lee, Republic of Korea
Zhaohui Li, China
Xavier Masip-Bruin, Spain
Amalia Miliou, Greece
John Mitchell, UK
Petros Nicopolitidis, Greece

João Rebola, Portugal
Surinder Singh, India
Salvatore Spadaro, Spain
Naoya Wada, Japan
Stuart Walker, UK
Xu Wang, UK
Xiaohua Ye, USA

OPTICS Auxiliary Reviewers

Tiago Alves, Portugal
Eva Marin-Tordera, Spain

SECRYPT Program Committee

Claudio Ardagna, Italy
Helen Ashman, Australia
Vijay Atluri, USA
Ken Barker, Canada
Mauro Barni, Italy
Giampaolo Bella, Italy
Marina Blanton, USA
Carlo Blundo, Italy
Mike Burmester, USA
David Chadwick, UK
Paolo D'arco, Italy
Anupam Datta, USA
Bart De Decker, Belgium
Josep Domingo-ferrer, Spain
Eduardo B. Fernandez, USA
Alberto Ferrante, Switzerland
Sara Foresti, Italy
Keith Frikken, USA
Steven Furnell, UK
Dieter Gollmann, Germany
Stefanos Gritzalis, Greece
Yong Guan, USA
Ragib Hasan, USA
Jiankun Hu, Australia
Michael Huth, UK
Cynthia Irvine, USA
Willem Jonker, The Netherlands

Anas Abou El Kalam, France
Maria Karyda, Greece
Stefan Katzenbeisser, Germany
Costas Lambrinoudakis, Greece
Bo Lang, China
Gyungho Lee, Republic of Korea
Albert Levi, Turkey
Javier Lopez, Spain
Wenjing Lou, USA
Manu Malek, USA
Masahiro Mambo, Japan
Antonio Maña, Spain
Konstantinos Markantonakis, UK
Evangelos Markatos, Greece
Fabio Martinelli, Italy
Sjouke Mauw, Luxembourg
Jorge Guajardo Merchan,
    The Netherlands
Chris Mitchell, UK
Marco Casassa Mont, UK
Pekka Nikander, Finland
Jose A. Onieva, Spain
Rolf Oppliger, Switzerland
Stefano Paraboschi, Italy
Gerardo Pelosi, Italy
Günther Pernul, Germany
Milan Petkovic, The Netherlands

Alessandro Piva, Italy
Joachim Posegga, Germany
Kui Ren, USA
Carlos Ribeiro, Portugal
Panos Rizomiliotis, Greece
Rodrigo Roman, Spain
Pierangela Samarati, Italy
Damien Sauveron, France
Shamik Sural, India

Willy Susilo, Australia
Angeliki Tsochou, Greece
Sabrina de Capitani di Vimercati, Italy
Lingyu Wang, Canada
Xinyuan (Frank) Wang, USA
Yang Xiang, Australia
Alec Yasinsac, USA
Justin Zhan, USA
Jianying Zhou, Singapore

SECRYPT Auxiliary Reviewers

Fenia Aivaloglou, Greece
Hayretdin Bahsi, Turkey
Jeremiah Blocki, USA
Ning Cao, USA
Alexander W. Dent, UK
Prokopios Drogkaris, Greece
Deepak Garg, USA
Dimitris Geneiatakis, Greece
Vincenzo Iovino, Italy
Jing Jin, USA
George Karopoulos, Greece
Dilsun Kaynar, USA

Hristo Koshutanski, Spain
Lukasz Krzywiecki, Poland
Ming Li, USA
Antonio Muñoz, Spain
Owen Redwood, USA
Evangelos Reklitis, Greece
Jose Francisco Ruiz Rodriguez, Spain
Daniele Sgandurra, Italy
Arunesh Sinha, USA
Nikos Vrakas, Greece
Zhenyu Yang, USA
Can Yildizli, Turkey

SIGMAP Program Committee

Harry Agius, UK
João Ascenso, Portugal
Pradeep K. Atrey, Canada
Oscar Au, Hong Kong
Arvind Bansal, USA
Adrian Bors, UK
Wai-Kuen Cham, China
Chin-Chen Chang, Taiwan
Liang-Gee Chen, Taiwan
Ryszard S. Choras, Poland
José Alfredo Ferreira Costa, Brazil
Michel Crucianu, France
Chitra Dorai, USA
Rob Evans, Australia
Marco Furini, Italy
Lorenzo Granai, Switzerland
William Grosky, USA

Malka Halgamuge, Australia
Khaled Harfoush, USA
Hermann Hellwagner, Austria
Richang Hong, Singapore
Chehdi Kacem, France
Hari Kalva, USA
Mohan Kankanhalli, Singapore
Sokratis Katsikas, Greece
Constantine Kotropoulos, Greece
Gwo Giun (Chris) Lee, Taiwan
Tayeb Lemlouma, France
Jing Li, UK
Manuel Perez Malumbres, Spain
Hong Man, USA
Tao Mei, China
Klaus Moessner, UK
Alejandro Murua, Canada

Andrew Perkis, Norway
Gang Qian, USA
Maria Paula Queluz, Portugal
Rudolf Rabenstein, Germany
Matthias Rauterberg, The Netherlands
Shin'ichi Satoh, Japan
Javier Del Ser, Spain
Xiaowei Shao, Japan
Mingli Song, China

Daniel Thalmann, Switzerland
Steve Uhlig, Germany
Zhiyong Wang, Australia
Michael Weber, Germany
Kim-hui Yap, Singapore
Hujun Yin, UK
Tianhao Zhang, USA
Ce Zhu, Singapore

WINSYS Program Committee

Vicente Alarcon-Aquino, Mexico
Novella Bartolini, Italy
Bert-Jan van Beijnum,
   The Netherlands
Luis Bernardo, Portugal
Rebecca Braynard, USA
Rafael Caldeirinha, Portugal
Cheng-Fu Chou, Taiwan
Gennaro Costagliola, Italy
Iñigo Cuiñas, Spain
Sanjay Kumar Dhurandher, India
Val Dyadyuk, Australia
David Ferreira, Portugal
Patrik Floreen, Finland
Chuan Heng Foh, Singapore
Mohammad Ghavami, UK
Matthias Hollick, Germany
Jehn-Ruey Jiang, Taiwan
Eduard Jorswieck, Germany
Abdelmajid Khelil, Germany

Thomas Kunz, Canada
Hsi-pin Ma, Taiwan
S. Kami Makki, USA
Luis Mendes, Portugal
Klaus Moessner, UK
Andreas Pitsillides, Cyprus
Nicholas Race, UK
Daniele Riboni, Italy
António Rodrigues, Portugal
Jörg Roth, Germany
Manuel García Sánchez, Spain
Christian Schindelhauer, Germany
Kuei-Ping Shih, Taiwan
Shensheng Tang, USA
George Tombras, Greece
Cesar Vargas-Rosales, Mexico
Enrique Vazquez, Spain
Dimitrios D. Vergados, Greece
Ming Yu, USA

WINSYS Auxiliary Reviewers

Josephine Antoniou, Cyprus
Reza S. Dilmaghani, UK
Dionisios Kandris, Greece

Nikolaos Pantazis, Greece
Aggeliki Sgora, Greece
Oleg Starostenko, Mexico

Invited Speakers

Ian F. Akyildiz
Petar M. Djuric
Stamatios Kartalopoulos
Nikolaos Bourbakis

Georgia Institute of Technology, USA
Stony Brook University, USA
University of Oklahoma, USA
Wright State University, USA

Table of Contents

Invited Paper

e-Business Challenges and Directions: Important Themes from the
First ICE-B Workshop   3
    David Marca, Rebecca Bulander, Cornelia Kruslin,
    Boris Shishkov, and Marten van Sinderen

Part I: Data Communication Networking (DCNET)

Static Analysis of Routing and Firewall Policy Configurations 39
    Miroslav Sveda, Ondrej Rysavy, Gayan de Silva,
    Petr Matousek, and Jaroslav Rab

Threshold Based Multipath Routing Algorithm in Mobile Adhoc and
Sensor Networks 54
    Bayrem Triki, Slim Rekhis, and Noureddine Boudriga

The Price of Security: A Detailed Comparison of the TLS Handshake
Performance on Embedded Devices When Using Elliptic Curve
Cryptography and RSA 71
    Manuel Koschuch, Matthias Hudler, and Michael Krüger

Mobile Applications Middleware for File Swapping 84
    Mario A. Gomez-Rodriguez, Victor J. Sosa-Sosa, and
    Ivan Lopez-Arevalo

Part II: e-Business (ICE-B)

Optimization of a Handwriting Recognition Algorithm for a Mobile
Enterprise Health Information System on the Basis of Real-Life
Usability Research 97
    Andreas Holzinger, Martin Schlögl, Bernhard Peischl, and
    Matjaz Debevc

A Social Location-Based Emergency Service to Eliminate the Bystander
Effect 112
    Andreas Geyer-Schulz, Michael Ovelgönne, and
    Andreas C. Sonnenbichler

Part III: Optical Communication Systems (OPTICS)

Converged Optical Networks for Multimedia Distribution and Data
Services in Hospitality Environments 133
    Iñigo Artundo, David García-Roger, and Beatriz Ortega

Part IV: Security and Cryptography (SECRYPT)

Differential Resynchronization Attacks on Reduced Round
SNOW 3G$^\oplus$ 147
    Alex Biryukov, Deike Priemuth-Schmid, and Bin Zhang

Modelling Uncertain and Time-Dependent Security Labels in MLS
Systems 158
    John A. Clark, Juan E. Tapiador, John McDermid,
    Pau-Chen Cheng, Dakshi Agrawal, Natalie Ivanic, and
    Dave Slogget

Sum Aggregation in Sensor Networks While Preserving Confidentiality
and Integrity 172
    Keith B. Frikken and Yihua Zhang

Stream Cipher-Based Hash Function and Its Security 188
    Yuto Nakano, Jun Kurihara, Shinsaku Kiyomoto, and
    Toshiaki Tanaka

Flexible Anonymous Subscription Schemes 203
    María Isabel González Vasco, Somayeh Heidarvand, and
    Jorge L. Villar

Proxiable Designated Verifier Signature 220
    Mebae Ushida, Yutaka Kawai, Kazuki Yoneyama, and Kazuo Ohta

Adaptive and Composable Non-interactive String-Commitment
Protocols 233
    Huafei Zhu, Tadashi Araragi, Takashi Nishide, and Kouichi Sakurai

Dynamic Adaptation of Security and QoS in Energy-Harvesting Sensors
Nodes 243
    Antonio Vincenzo Taddeo, Marcello Mura, and Alberto Ferrante

Threshold Discernible Ring Signatures 259
    Swarun Kumar, Shivank Agrawal, Ramarathnam Venkatesan,
    Satyanarayana V. Lokam, and C. Pandu Rangan

Universally Composable Non-committing Encryptions in the Presence
of Adaptive Adversaries... 274
  Huafei Zhu, Tadashi Araragi, Takashi Nishide, and Kouichi Sakurai

Selectively Traceable Anonymous and Unlinkable Token-Based
Transactions 289
  Daniel Slamanig and Stefan Rass

An Encryption Scheme for a Secure Policy Updating 304
  Luan Ibraimi, Muhammad Asim, and Milan Petković

Machine Learning for the Detection of Spam in Twitter Networks 319
  Alex Hai Wang

Part V: Signal Processing and Multimedia Applications (SIGMAP)

Deformable Multi-object Tracking Using Full Pixel Matching of
Image 337
  Hisato Aota, Kazuhiro Ota, Yuichi Yaguchi, and Ryuichi Oka

A Multi-sensor System for Monitoring the Performance of Elite
Swimmers.. 350
  Tanya Le Sage, Axel Bindel, Paul Conway, Laura Justham,
  Sian Slawson, James Webster, and Andrew West

Maximum a Posteriori Decoding of Arithmetic Codes in Joint
Source-Channel Coding 363
  Trevor Spiteri and Victor Buttigieg

An Ensemble Approach to Improve Microaneurysm Candidate
Extraction 378
  Bálint Antal, István Lázár, and András Hajdu

Part VI: Wireless Information Networks and Systems (WINSYS)

Modulation-Mode Assignment for SVD-Aided and BICM-Assisted
Downlink Multiuser MIMO Transmission Schemes 395
  Andreas Ahrens and César Benavente-Peces

Evaluation of the Performance of Polarization Diversity Estimated
from Measurements at One Polarization 410
  Iñigo Cuiñas and Manuel García Sánchez

Using the OTS/CafeOBJ Method to Formally Specify and Verify the
Open Mobile Alliance License Choice Algorithm 424
    *Nikolaos Triantafyllou, Iakovos Ouranos, Petros Stefaneas, and
    Panayiotis Frangos*

Extended Field Performance Evaluation of a Gbps FSO Link 439
    *J.A.R. Pacheco de Carvalho, N. Marques, H. Veiga,
    C.F. Ribeiro Pacheco, and A.D. Reis*

Author Index 447

Invited Paper

e-Business Challenges and Directions: Important Themes from the First ICE-B Workshop

David Marca[1], Rebecca Bulander[2], Cornelia Kruslin[3],
Boris Shishkov[4], and Marten van Sinderen[5]

[1] The University of Phoenix, Phoenix, U.S.A.
[2] Pforzheim University of Applied Science, Pforzheim, Germany
[3] Croatian Post and Electronic Communications Agency, Zagreb, Croatia
[4] IICREST - Interdisciplinary Institute for Collaboration and Research on
Enterprise Systems and Technology, Sofia, Bulgaria
[5] University of Twente, Enschede, The Netherlands

Abstract. A three-day asynchronous, interactive workshop was held at ICE-B'10 in Piraeus, Greece in July of 2010. This event captured conference themes for e-Business challenges and directions across four subject areas: a) e-Business applications and models, b) enterprise engineering, c) mobility, d) business collaboration and e-Services, and e) technology platforms. Quality Function Deployment (QFD) methods were used to gather, organize and evaluate themes and their ratings. This paper summarizes the most important themes rated by participants: a) Since technology is becoming more economic and social in nature, more agile and context-based application develop methods are needed. b) Enterprise engineering approaches are needed to support the design of systems that can evolve with changing stakeholder needs. c) The digital native groundswell requires changes to business models, operations, and systems to support Prosumers. d) Intelligence and interoperability are needed to address Prosumer activity and their highly customized product purchases. e) Technology platforms must rapidly and correctly adapt, provide widespread offerings and scale appropriately, in the context of changing situational contexts.

Keywords: Adaptability, agile methods, autonomic computing, business value, business-IT alignment, change management, cloud computing, collaboration, composability, context-aware computing, CRM, customer relationship management, digital native, e-Business, applications, models, enterprise ontology, enterprise engineering, e-Services, integration, intelligent user interfaces, interoperability, interoperability, mobility, physical organization, platforms, product customization, prosumer, SDLC, semantic Web, service orientation, service scalability, social CRM, social networks, societal IT, system development life cycle, ubiquity, virtual organization, virtual worlds.

1 Workshop Overview and Important Challenges

1.1 Workshop Objectives and Methodology

The International e-Business Conference (ICE-B) is one track within the International Joint Conference on e-Business and Telecommunications (ICETE). In 2010, a unique

M.S. Obaidat, G.A. Tsihrintzis, and J. Filipe (Eds.): ICETE 2010, CCIS 222, pp. 3–35, 2012.
© Springer-Verlag Berlin Heidelberg 2012

three-day interactive workshop was held for ICE-B'10. The workshop was conducted as an asynchronous collaborative consortium. The goal was to create a jointly authored paper on e-Business challenges and directions in the following subject areas: a) e-Business applications and models, b) enterprise engineering, c) mobility, d) business collaboration and e-Services, and e) technology platforms. The workshop had two venues: a) a traditional position paper presentation session, and b) an interactive forum which lasted all three days of ICE-B'10. Regarding the former, position paper authors became subject area leads for the joint paper. Regarding the latter, a very large physical display was maintained for recording: a) all themes generated by ICE-B'10 papers and presentation sessions, b) participants' research, and c) importance ratings. The method for information posting, organization and rating was directly from Quality Function Deployment [158]. On the last day of the workshop, ICETE'10 participants voted on the relative importance of posted themes. This paper reports on the most important themes, tying them back to ICE-B'10 conference papers and posters.

1.2 e-Business Applications Challenges

Economic, Technological, Societal, IT. Changes in business are usually related to the way that it must adapt to the Five Forces [131]. Nowadays, business is increasingly moving towards e-Business to stay competitive, but introducing new applications into a business may lead to a variety of problems, especially if that business is not accustomed to being supported by that technology [145]. This is particularly pronounced when a business moves from a static Web presence (i.e. a Web site or a transaction portal [30] to a dynamic Web presence (i.e. social network blog, online customer chat forum, "try before you buy" virtual experience [35] Many businesses now struggle to make Web 2.0 profitable [83].

New Technology Creates Strategic Challenges. Web 2.0 has opened up businesses to customers [66]. As a result, laggard firms are struggling to decide: how much operational transparency to provide users during an end-to-end transaction, how much investment is need to comply with new standards, how to formulate a business case that all customers can understand, and how much operation control to give up. Coupled with these decisions are dilemmas such as how much information to share, getting off the proprietary network legacy, breaking or keeping the mindset/trade-off of value versus cost, and how much product ownership to give away. In addition, traditional challenges (i.e. suppliers, new entrants, demand, etc) still exist [14].

More Agile e-Business is Needed. Application development practices from the mid-1950s to the mid-1980s concentrated on the computer. Human resistance to these applications is primarily due to bad design [21]. The practices of the mid-1980s to the mid-2000s concentrated on users, but often limited themselves to a fixed set of contexts. Resistance to using this software was due primarily to computer illiteracy or usability errors. Since the mid-2000s, user contexts are noted for being dynamic, complex, and possibly unpredictable [94]. So, e-Business applications need to have more than just interfaces and workflows that match pre-defined usage contexts [71]. Users must have the ability to design e-Business applications as they are being used.

1.3 Enterprise Engineering Challenges

Understanding and Managing the Enterprise. Enterprise engineering focuses on the technology aspects of the design, analysis, implementation and operation of all elements associated with an enterprise. Such technology aspects are closely related to the analysis and design phases of the software development process [63]. During these phases, designers aim at establishing an explicit representation of the organizational and technical system processes and infrastructures in order to increase their understanding of the enterprise and make development of automated support possible. Important notions here are Enterprise Architecture (EA) and enterprise ontology. EA is a description of the information, behavior and structure aspects of an enterprise at a business, application and infrastructure level [97]. There is no common agreement on the precise model and languages to be used for accomplishing this coverage, but the importance of EA for strategic decisions across individual projects is widely recognized. A major challenge is to maintain the integrity of EA and its consistency with the continuously changing organization [63]. More formal and prescriptive approaches may be necessary to address this challenge [76]. Also new aspects may need to be considered, such as value [60] and culture [105] in order to make EA more effective for business innovation.

Enterprise ontology is a description of the concepts and relationships that can exist for a community of people of an enterprise [44]. The description is a conceptualization of knowledge in an enterprise domain, such that knowledge can be shared among stakeholders, and, using a formal knowledge representation, automated reasoning by software agents and interoperability in distributed software applications can be supported [62]. A recognized problem in this field is the agreement of a single or intermediate ontology in B2B collaboration and the alignment of top-down and bottom-up derived ontologies [67]. Also, there is a lack of frameworks to compare the strengths and weaknesses of candidate ontologies [60].

Integration and Interoperability. A related view on enterprise engineering is the modeling and integration of various organizational and technical parts of business processes [171]. The integration problem applied to the collaboration or network aspect of enterprises leads to the identification of interoperability issues. Enterprise interoperability is necessary to achieve seamless collaboration between enterprises, and to allow new business models characterized by flexible partnerships [147]. Enterprises in several domains move from highly data-driven to more cooperative information-driven, knowledge-driven environments [122] based on standards [13].

Despite the strategic importance of interoperability, and the availability of standards and architectures, several technical, semantic and organizational issues still exist [30], [171]. Ontology-based and service-oriented approaches have been proposed here as possible solution directions [66]. Business-IT alignment contributes to the effectiveness of integrated solutions, and concerns itself with how IT can help achieve business objectives and improve business performance. Alignment implies that IT and business functions should adapt their strategies together, which is a dynamic and evolutionary endeavor [107].

1.4 Mobility Challenges

Coping with Digital Natives. e-Business needs to cope with the behavior and re-quirements of "digital natives." The generation of the digital natives grew up with the Internet and has a great degree of competence concerning the usage of Internet servic-es. Digital natives are well informed and assertive regarding products they want to buy [121]. They are continuously in contact with their community in social networks, where they express their positive as well as negative experiences with products, ser-vices and companies. These statements have a fundamental meaning for the purchase decision of the other members of the social network community. Bloggers write about the product or company in their blogs, videos are published via YouTube or similar sites, and the product is the subject of online discussions. Because of the wide-spread use of Smart phones, the digital natives are "always on". This means that a bad expe-rience of one customer can develop a huge impact on a company's reputation in a larger community. This phenomenon is similar to a chain reaction. Charlene Li and Josh Bernoff coined the term "groundswell" for this phenomenon [101]. This means companies have to: a) place their products in social networks additionally to their regular marketing activities, b) promptly respond to negative feedback, and c) create a marketing strategy that uses mobile ads to influence digital natives in a positive way.

Totally Personalized Products. According to [133], a key factor of sustainable com-petitive advantage for businesses in the future is the ability to focus on the importance of individual customer experiences and tailor products accordingly to his or her indi-vidual needs. So, the customers are able to co-create the products they want to buy. This paradigm of the customer relationship where the customer feels like they are they only one, or the most important customer of a company, is called "N = 1" [133]. To adopt this aspect to m-Business, and to create value for the customer, m-Services should be context aware and rapidly change to address user needs and environment [11]. One important context would be the current location of a user. To provide such context aware services the challenges are to: a) equip mobiles with several different and robust sensors to capture changing context (e.g., surrounding noise [23] and b) analyze, assemble and offer the right product to the user for the current situation).

Mass Adoption of m-Services. Before the introduction of the iPhone, the adoption of m-Services had been modest and focused on SMS and location based services [50]. Now, there are over 42 million iPhones [98], and so its concept has been copied and AppStores (e.g., Andriod Market, Ovi Store) offer their services to the user. Today, forecasts predict the number of mobile users accessing the Internet will surpass the number of users accessing the Internet using PCs, and some also predict a significant shift from Web use to mobile application use [7]. Beside these changes, will there be barriers from the perspective of physical, cognitive, security, economic and enter-tainment value of m-Services for mass adoption and user acceptance? According to Ervasti and Helaakoski, the utility of m-Services has a strong impact on user attitude towards mobile services [138], and this means the added value of m-Services has yet to fully to meet user needs. Another finding is that context information for personal m-Services is an important influencing factor towards user intent to buy m-Services [50]. These findings should be incorporated into the future development of m-Services.

1.5   Collaboration and e-Services Challenges

Proper Inclusion of the Digital Native Population. "Digital natives" were born after 1980, after the first social digital technologies were invented. They live much of their lives online via social mediated interaction. Their notions of making friends, creating/working, experiencing music, and sharing their lives differ from those born before 1980 [121]. Sometimes called "The Net Generation," they relate to technology differently, with reflexes tuned for speed and innovation. They want freedom, choice, and customization in everything they do and buy. They enjoy conversation, not lecture, and insist on integrity underneath communications. They want to have fun at school and work, and want to learn to think for themselves. They are very willing to electronically engage, and search online about products before buying [160]. Regardless of name, this group is global in its force, scope and nature, and operates more like a population rather than a generation [121]. Thus, e-Business needs to cope with the behavior and needs of digital natives. This means managing the groundswell and the impact of the participation of this population in the context of their social network communities [133]. Specifically: a) knowledge-intensive firms must create shared interest, b) service-oriented firms must create complementary online spaces for people to discuss shared practices, and thus discover the tacit knowledge that impacts purchases, and c) honest and open dialog between customers and the sales force [93].

Offering Fully Customized Products to Consumers. Given how digital natives think, e-Business must offer totally personalized products and adjust its customer relationships in ways so customers feel like they are the only, and most important, customer [134]. The business challenge is typically called "value co-creation" [5]. Value co-creation, is an emerging innovation, marketing and business paradigm describing how customers and users are seen as active participants in the design of personalized products, services and experiences [133], [127]. Often this participation is organized via the Internet to enable the opportunity for customers to integrate their knowledge, experience and skills into existing, modified or entirely new market offerings reflecting their personal preferences, needs and contexts [142]. For example, in the case of global software development, the platforms of electronic engagement are: a) individual connection, b) electronic Community, c) resource sharing, and thus product personalization or co-production can happen via any of these forms of engagement [159]. Therefore, e-Business must have a multi-pronged approach to digital natives and customized products. In short, it must have: a) a global strategy, b) integration of product-system-business processes, c) rapid response, d) reconfigurable manufacturing systems, e) innovative products, f) products able to be highly personalized, g) data driven operations, and h) flexible strategic alliances [176].

Matching Pragmatic Interoperability to Semantic Interoperability. Interoperability at the service level is characterized by three aspects: syntactic, semantic and pragmatic [170]. Semantic Interoperability is the ability of communicating entities (not only computers) to share unambiguous meaning [130]. Syntactic Interoperability, provided by languages such as XML, involves a common data format and protocol to organize data so that: a) information can be correctly interpreted from its structure, and b) syntactic errors can be detected [8]. However, data represented using one syntax may not be accurately translated into a different syntax [65]. Interoperability is a multifaceted problem caused by issues such as: a) organizational incompatibilities buried deep within collaborating enterprises, b) architectural mismatches, c) defective assumptions about application behavior, and d) mismatched properties within business collaboration models. Thus, pragmatic interoperability (i.e. the implementation) is hard to match to semantic interoperability (i.e. what was intended). One approach: build taxonomies of independent aspects, each being a different view of enterprise computing. A clean separation makes easier the identification interoperability requirements [140]. Ontology can aid in the construction of this taxonomy. In general, a single ontology containing every term used in every computer application is thought to be impossible, because of the speed and dynamics of how people construct business vocabulary. However, it seems possible to define a set of very primitive terms that can then be used to create concepts for applications or ontologies [43].

1.6 Technology Platforms Challenges

Technology platforms play the crucial role of enabling e-business developments, by providing the possibility for flexible service invocations. Enabling the construction of flexible and loosely coupled business applications, spanning over different networked enterprises capable of interconnecting their applications and share data by combining a set of services, service-oriented technology platforms represent an essential foundation for e-business interactions [20]. Such kind of platforms are also expected to bridge technology and real life, with regard to how technology is incorporated by real-life systems which are human-centered, taking into account that e-Business means now much more than electronic data interchange. Three key issues in this regard are Autonomy, Adaptability, and Context Awareness:

- Autonomy: how modules can maintain, in some cases, their own autonomic functioning, "deciding" on their own what to do next.
- Adaptability: how automated systems can adapt to a changing environment.
- Context-Awareness: how systems can deliver services in line with the user's situational context,
- plus the concerns of mobility, security, and collaboration.

One consideration of technology platforms relates to two desired features essentially important: service orientation and scalability.

Service Orientation. Service orientation is required for achieving a wide spread technical IT facilitations through advanced ICT platforms, unrestricted by the way the service delivering components are implemented and also by other low-level issues. Service-oriented platforms should hence allow for an easy way of pushing forward business goals through formulated requests at high level, abstracting from the underlying technical details. This can only be accomplished through "wrapping" technology and accessing it through standardized interfaces through which a platform utilizes service invocations. Although this has already been well-established as a research vision [3] it is still missing a wide practical accomplishment.

Scalability. Scalability is a significant challenge because of the open nature of most technology platforms [177], which appear as facilities often supporting interactions and/or collaboration. This means that scaling up to hundreds or thousands of users and involved organizations may be needed. In supply-chain, for instance, which much relies on e-Business facilitation [154], it is often necessary to serve hundreds of suppliers and thousands of users, allowing them to adequately profile their requests as well as to establish and maintain dynamic collaborations, relying on diverse services provided by different service-providers. To solve this, platforms are often "tempted" to enforce standards, which makes their support of limited use to many customers or they allow for dynamic, autonomic support which nevertheless handles a limited number of "scenarios." We hence need a wider degree of customization through which users would be left to shape the platform support according to their preferences, while being flexibly led in establishing this, for guaranteeing that they would only go for requests that are adequate with regard to what the platform is providing.

2   e-Business Applications Directions

Table 1. Conference Themes and Relative Importance for e-Business Applications (Scores are *relative* importance ratings. The ranking was done across all subject areas).

Area	Themes Across Area 1	Score	Rank
1	e-Business must support the convergence of producer and consumer.	26	5
1	e-Business requires needs analysis, including human "connections."	25	6
1	Business is experiencing economic, technological, societal, and IT challenges.	24	7
1	e-Business solutions have adaptive user interfaces + workflows that match user's context.	10	17
1	e-Business applications have transformed companies into global, and more trusted, providers.	10	18
1	e-Money flexibility and usability is designed into the "money" and the machines that process it.	3	30
1	Business faces strategic tensions + drivers that e-Business applications must address.	0	37
1	Validating e-Marketing agreement and its effectiveness.	0	38
1	Executives are asking engineers to build more agility into their e-Business applications.	0	39

2.1   Eliciting Context-Based Usage and Operational Requirements

Business applications are becoming easier to use, and are now being used by consumers with different technical knowledge and skills [50]. Part of this trend is due to application developers, who are improving their abilities to: a) understand how to help consumers carry out their everyday work, and b) serve the business and operational needs of producers [145].

Consumers are more and more often actively involved in the product design and development process in order to get the application that will cover all or most of their business or working needs and will be usable and understandable to them [143]. Producers as well need consumers to contextually specify the exact situations in which they will use the application, and to specify those requirements in non-technical language [71] including operational constraints. Since consumers with less technical experience usually describe their needs by giving concrete examples, involving them can provide producers with more concrete and straightforward information about the expected product [185]. The framework and the goals of existing and future application usage can be better determined if explained with concrete examples using simple language [11]. Application designers will then be able to transform those requirements into technical language, and thus implement e-Business applications with fewer errors.

The current direction of merging the producer and consumer into the so-called "prosumer" [164] brings new value to application development, especially to requirements elicitation [23]. In the end, consumers will be more satisfied with the result, such as the utility of the product or service [186] and simpler and more rational procedures for installation and use [2]. Having the prosumer actively involved in the process of e-Business development is a direction which can improve the quality of life of life for the consumer [58] and give friendlier face to the provider [84].

2.2 Positive Changes to the System Development Life Cycle (SDLC)

Improved requirements elicitation is part of a larger trend of improved practices throughout the System Development Life Cycle (SDLC) [169]. These practices start when the need for a system is recognized [105] and carry through to actual delivery and deployment of the system [186]. Here are the improved practices discussed during paper presentations at the conference:

- Project Scope and Planning: a) ontology for consistent understanding of the problem [67], b) buy versus build decisions that best meet business needs [1].
- Requirements Elicitation: a) in-depth understanding of the user's context [105] and [180] b) accurate transactional requirements [116] and [26].
- Solution Design: a) designing flexible business processes into applications [166] b) software versions of rules and standards from business models [13].
- Solution Implementation: a) implementation for interoperability [123] and [52] b) thorough and dependable testing [55] and [76].

Together, these practices address some key decision-making that occurs during the SDLC, and provide a three-way benefit to project stakeholders. First, executives are more assured that the way they designed the business and intend it to operate will actually be realized in the e-Business [14]. Second, the users will experience technology that has a higher likelihood of matching: a) the different work/leisure contexts in which they find themselves [180] b) their changing mental perspectives as their context changes [72] and c) specifics of their activities in any given work/leisure context [129]. Third, system developers spend less time in each SDLC phase on standards, rules, and agreements already decided upon by both the business and the users [59]. This win-win-win situation is the direct result of the business making an investment in better practices and tools [126] and the willingness of developers and users to collaborate during application development [145].

2.3 Widening Scope of e-Business Applications

Business Scope. While some markets continue to grow, business is attempting to resolve the sometimes conflicting requirements and constraints of the economic, technological, societal and IT perspectives [126]. In response, business models are being developed to address customer needs while also addressing industry and government standards and regulations [145]. In addition, the Internet has become part of everyday life, and in the case of "digital natives," life is lived on technology [121] The outcome of a whole population geared to electronic (versus brick and mortar) commerce means the scope of its applications must move beyond ground stores and supply chains and to the Internet. In other words, nowadays a business without an Internet presence is risking market penetration in significant ways [162]. For future success e-Business applications must be facile in social networks and with multimedia [74].

Consumer Scope. Business scope and consumer scope are intertwined. From the consumer perspective, digital natives expect anything–anywhere–anytime [118]. So, e-Business is trying to spread into every corner of the Internet, such as: blogs, wikis, portals, and social networks – in other words, e-Business must now be managed, or business will find the well-known phenomenon of "scope creep" to severely impact profitability [135]. If managed properly, consumers stand to gain many benefits; for example: a) personalized products [15], [181], b) better and simpler services [11], c) more intuitive and natural user interfaces [16], d) novel ways to transact [116] and e) application behavior sensitive to the user's current context [104].

Functional Scope. Some e-Business applications are attempting to tackle business strategy in an attempt to satisfy widening business and user scopes [53] (e.g. e-Voting, e-Health, e-Delivery, e-Careers, e-Procurement, e-Complaints, e-Banking, and e-Billing. Managing the functional scope of such applications can partially be addressed via standard: a) Web services that communicate with consumers through a generic Web-based interface using standardized information [61], b) business models [52], c) business ontology [67], and d) interoperability [123]. Clearly, growth and maturity of all these standards are a major e-Business direction.

2.4 "How Much Technology" Is a User Decision

Ultimately, the main purpose of any e-Business application is to help consumers carry out their desired activities as simply, quickly and reliably as possible [173]. As e-Business applications become more functionally rich, more adaptable, and more interactive, the user needs be put in control of just how much technology should be used in any given life context [156]. This choice is not just a simple matter of better speed, easier use, simpler process, or any other similar benefit of current e-Business applications [161]. Instead, it is a matter of user comfort with the decision-making process in whatever life context they are now experiencing [87].

While these ideas are not new, we see the next immediate generation of e-Business applications being on the tipping point of providing functions and information in ways that allows users to selectively choose, or ignore entirely, assistance and/or data at any given moment in time to at any breadth or depth. Both research and literature are not mature in this area, and we see much growth in this direction. This direction must answer the question "How much technology is really needed to make an optimal decision?" [109] A related question might be "Should e-Business applications have embedded AI technology so that they learn over time and then infer [54] to not offer assistance and/or information [49] when the user has re-entered a known life context and has previously chosen to ignore similar assistance and/or data?

We acknowledge the research and hard work of the many hundreds of scholars in the areas of participatory design [48] user-centered design [120] collaborative design [164] and many similar concepts, methods and techniques for allowing users to participate in the design of computer artifacts. Up to now, user participation has been limited to the development stage of a technology. But, with the advent of cloud computing [9], composable Web services [75], ontologies [60], and maturing of artificial intelligence technology [54], we see a potential for the e-Business application development path that allows users to design technology while it is being used. This is an interesting and an exciting direction, and we expect much growth in this area.

3   Enterprise Engineering Directions

Table 2. Conference Themes and Relative Importance for Enterprise Engineering (Scores are *relative* importance ratings. The ranking was done across all subject areas).

Area	Themes Across Area 2	Score	Rank
2	Design systems that can evolve with changing business needs.	38	1
2	Value modeling / analysis is needed in enterprise application development.	33	3
2	e-Commerce (physical to digital to virtual) is altering business economics.	14	12
2	Web 2.0 is focused on entrepreneurship as part of Enterprise 2.0.	10	19
2	Business transaction standards enable B2B interoperability.	7	21
2	Analytical CRM: discover trends + opportunities corresponding to "digital native" reqts + the social network.	7	22
2	Companies want their e-Business solutions to grow into global solutions.	6	26
2	The e-Business model must address the explicit design of culture into the solution.	4	27
2	e-Business solutions are becoming a heterogeneous collection of well-integrated components.	4	28
2	Companies are building proprietary ontologies to describe their business + how it operates.	0	40
2	Holistic business transformation framework enables physical --> digital --> virtual path.	0	41
2	Adopt a meta-design paradigm to design systems that can evolve.	0	42

3.1   Coping with Societal, Business and Technology Change

A major theme in enterprise engineering is dealing with change: business environments are continuously changing, due market or technology developments. If business organizations and their supporting IT systems do not evolve in sync, businesses would experience increasingly less effective systems. Therefore, the ability to adapt while keeping alignment between business and IT has emerged as an important factor for successful business operation. Initially, research focused on frameworks that help to understand, analyze and construct business-IT alignment. With proper alignment, the potential of IT systems is fully exploited to achieve business goals and objectives. Such frameworks have been discussed by [183], [107], Enterprise Architecture (EA) subsequently emerged as an important discipline to deal with alignment issues, next to issues of integration and complexity [188], [189].

The evolution of the Internet towards a business enabler [190] has important implications for business organizations: not only will advance IT, reduce costs, and increase productivity, it will also enable novel business models with corresponding organizational transformations. In other words, Internet developments such as electronic marketplaces, business service ecosystems and market-oriented clouds [191], [192] push business organizations to make corresponding organizational changes. These changes are not merely optional, but may be necessary to exploit these opportunities and to remain competitive or excel in their line of business.

Consequently, business-IT alignment becomes even more challenging. Organizational changes may occur more frequent, following the pace of technology development, and they will extend across organizational boundaries, due to the collaborative nature of modern ICT-based business. The role of EA remains prominent, however it is important to consider alignment as a continuous process that is addressed with an evolving EA [169]. The EA lifecycle consists of multiple improvement cycles, going through definition-implementation-execution-refinement phases, in which market and technology trends can be taken into account [193]. In order to ensure the integrity of EA across business, application and infrastructure levels, the application of model-driven approaches may be useful and should be further investigated [194], [191]. Furthermore, in order to guarantee consistency with the implemented enterprise information system, architecture reconstruction approaches [195] may be applied, acknowledging that EA cannot always enforce conforming implementations but may itself be made conformant to reality by using bottom-up knowledge.

3.2 Addressing Stakeholder Values

Many promising IT applications and services are not commercially successful due to being too much technology-biased. In order to be successful, business aspects should be carefully considered during design and implementation, leading to a clear business plan [196] with a sound value proposition [59].

Each intended partner or stakeholder will only enter a proposed collaboration for a new business service if the benefits of participation are considered to outweigh the costs. Moreover, a participant (or participant role) can be essential for the collaboration, in the sense that without this participant (role) the service cannot be introduced or provided, e.g. because of lack of budget, expertise or infrastructure. In this setting, benefits and costs are not necessarily only or directly related to monetary aspects. For example, benefits may be the increase of recognition, friendship, publicity, knowledge or ownership. Costs may be the decrease of any of these properties or assets. In any case, benefits and costs may be valued differently by different partners and stakeholders. For a business service to be successful, each participant should perceive the collaboration as being profitable, i.e. having net benefits for its particular situation and preferences. Even if a new service has clear overall benefits over an existing situation, successful introduction or operation may not occur because the distribution of benefits and costs is unbalanced: some participants benefit more than other, or some participants pay the costs while other participants enjoy the benefits. Since situations and preferences may change in time, for each individual participant, it is important to maintain value propositions in order to keep essential participants onboard.

Although this all seems obvious, in practice many technology-oriented projects still start off without considering the business case. Or, they make important design decisions without taking business aspects into account. Fortunately, the maturing of e-business technology also led to an increased interest in market exploitation opportunities, which in turn shifted attention to business models. Several frameworks for understanding and analyzing e-business models have been proposed [197], [198]. These are complemented with various accepted business modeling techniques, such as Resource-Event-Agent (REA), Business Model Ontology (BMO) and e3value. The latter focuses on value models that capture the economic value exchange in a business network, and therefore best fits the concern expressed above.

E3value has originally been proposed by [60] and since then has been extended and applied for various purposes. Since value modeling must be considered in the broader scope of enterprise engineering, value-based business-IT alignment must be addressed

[199]. This puts forward issues of consistency and transformations between the value model and various other models in the context of enterprise architecture. For example, the relationship between a value model and a goal model is studied in [200] and between a value model and a process model in [201], [199]. A systematic approach for transforming a value model into a coordination process model is proposed in [202]. Also, attention has been paid to the creating value models for business collaborations [203] and adapting B2B processes in case of changing requirements [204]. Because of the increasingly important role of service-oriented architectures for enterprise systems, value-based service analysis has been considered in [205].

3.3 Migration from Physical to Digital to Virtual

With the development of the Internet as a unified and global infrastructure for communication and access to information, commerce entered the digital era. This era is characterized by a new form of commerce – e-commerce – empowered by the Internet and associated technologies, which complement traditional, physical commerce. E-commerce facilitates the transaction of "old-fashioned" goods and services. However, it also allows new value-added services as well as fundamentally different products, namely digital products [176]. Currently, another development can be observed, which can be seen as a shift to the virtual. This shift, already foreseen more than a decade ago [206], will bring new ways of service interactions based on computer representations of people, products, processes and places. Examples are digital negotiation agents, e-stores, virtual processes for supply chains, and avatars [207].

The move to virtual is reinforced by the current phase of evolution that the Internet is undergoing, which will lead to what is being called the Future Internet [208]. The Future Internet embraces two important concepts: the Internet of Things (IoT) and the Internet of Services (IoS). The former is based on advances in pervasive computing and ambient intelligence, which allows embedded computation and communication capabilities in daily objects, making them identifiable, traceable and controllable from remote locations. This allows new monitoring and control applications, such as tracing and tracking, plus interaction between the physical world and the digital world [209]. It also enables new context-aware services [210]. These services adapt the interaction with their user environment dependent on the context –state or state changes in the physical world– that is inferred from data obtained from context sensors.

IoS entails the emergence of a global and dynamic services marketplace [211]. In the IoS vision, business services are dynamically created and adapted to match demand, supply and available partnerships [213]. Further, new deployment and delivery models can be used, enabling on-demand rapid provisioning of virtual machines, platforms and services with pay-per-use [213], [192]. E-commerce and virtual markets based on the Future Internet cause challenges for enterprise engineering. Current research provides directions to address these challenges, including: serious gaming [23], business transformation processes [84], [169], and business process flexibility [166].

4 Mobility Directions

Table 3. Conference Themes and Relative Importance for Mobility (Scores are *relative* importance ratings. The ranking was done across all subject areas).

Area	Themes Across Area 3	Score	Rank
3	e-Business needs to cope with the behavior and requirements of "digital natives."	15	8
3	e-Business must offer personalized products and adjust its customer relationships.	14	13
3	Mass adoption of m-Services requires attitude (i.e. it is useful) and intention (i.e. I will use it).	7	23
3	m-Services can adapt its solution to match changing context + location.	7	24
3	m-Business solutions provide more adaptive user interfaces + workflows to match the user's context.	4	29
3	m-Services are striving to be effortless, accessible and appealing.	3	31
3	No standard business model for solutions over wireless.	0	43
3	m-Business solutions need to recognize and acquire information in changing contexts.	0	44
3	m-Business solutions must improve their ability to locate users in "harsh environments."	0	45
3	m-Services are striving to span geography, organization and user competence.	0	46
3	Mobile e-Business is incorporating more contextual, dynamic content in support of user-to-user interaction.	0	47

4.1 Mobility and m-Services

The topic "mobility" in ICE-B focused more on the side of m-Services and mobile technology than on the side of hardware or provider networks. The term "m-Services" stands for mobile services which are services where the clients are mobile terminals (MT) and at least the access network is a wireless one. Examples for MT include cellular phones, personal digital assistants or smart phones. The ubiquitous character of MT is essential: people can carry them around with themselves most of the day in turned on state. When we use the term "mobile service" we actually mean mobile and wireless data services with added value by providing additional information for a user [38]. A thematic analysis based on ICE-B 2010 papers, ICETE 2010 keynotes and some important e-business publications has been conducted. An overview of the results of this analysis for mobility is shown in Table 3.

4.2 Context Awareness of m-Services

The term "context," with regard to mobile applications, was introduced by [144] and is a set of information that describes the current situation of a user. A context sensitive application makes use of this information to adapt itself to the needs of the user. For mobile applications this is especially important, since the terminals have a limited interface for interaction with the user, e.g., small displays or no full keyboard. Context information can be differentiated by two distinctions [22]: 1) the privacy level (public and private) and 2) the degrees of variability (static, semi-static or dynamic). One special context is the location of a user. It would be classified as "private" and "dynamic". A service that evaluates the location of at least one mobile device during execution is called "Location Based Service" (LBS) [36]. Until 2009, LBS has been one of the most popular and used services for mobile devices [50]. Since the availability of the iPhone, which has a wide variety of application services, the so-called "apps," caused other services to become more attractive [98]. An application or service is context-aware when it adapts itself according to context information, so that it offers appropriate services corresponding to the user's situation. This aspect of context awareness is very important for the private use of application services and even more for business use (e.g., for mobile sales and service representatives or mobile workers). Thus, the quality of the context information plus the analytical combination to come to the right conclusion about the user's current situation can be seen as one determining factor in the adoption process of application services [11]. Summing up, one direction in mobility will be that application services are using and combining several context services so that they can exactly adapt their services to the current context and situation of a user and offer appropriate service.

4.3 m-Services and Social Networks

It is important to note that there have been recent and significant changes in the use of media plus the overall behavior of consumers. This is affecting m-Services and their design. In short, the mobile device is not only for direct communication, but is also for real-time feedback. According to the Interone study, digital natives are using laptops and smart phones while also watching TV, in order to search for additional information or as a feedback channel to respond to quiz games or opinion surveys [78]. For companies, this means addressing this behavior when placing information and advertisements in TV shows and when offering games or surveys. Since the great success of the iPhone and the versatile offer of applications in different application stores [98], new possibilities in many ways have arrived. Here are just a few examples:

Always On. Because of being "always on" users have more flexibility and independence in planning activities with friends [41] when shopping or enjoying entertainment. This will have an impact on business models, range of coverage and types of communication [78]. Nowadays, people have new ways to interact with their environment (e.g., respond to an advertisement when passing by a shop). Virtual services enrich the user's reality with additional information. One instance of this is a new kind of navigation enriched with additional information (e.g., a city tour on a Smartphone with historical information to important buildings and nice places to have a coffee, and another option might be to get a city tour as an audio guided tour). So, because of being "always on" there are increased opportunities for mobile learning. The offer for new applications for mobile and also social learning is growing [89]. Therefore, "apps" which use context information like the location, a camera, a microphone or a motion device can realize great potential of mobile terminals [78].

"I like it" Button. Because digital natives want to be where their friends are, they primarily maintain their social contracts to friends in social networks, where they can reach them always and everywhere. In social networks they can share their preference for things with their friends or spontaneous express themselves by pressing the button "I like it". Instead of the ranking of the links the amount of clicked likes of a product now is important. Respective buying decisions these personal customer experiences are getting more and more important. Through social and mobile media the consumption of media, the communication and the shopping will come closer together [78]. This will impact product placement and advertisements. Consequently some firms already offer products in a social network.

Increase of Online Buying. Due to the personalized "reach out" to potential customers with mobile advertisement plus the improved usability of mobile devices, ads can not only be used to inform and lead to a buying decision but also lead to an online purchase. This will be positively influenced because the potential customer has the possibility to compare prices and to confirm his decision by recommendations of his friends. This can also be named as "social mobile commerce" [45], [78].

Customer Managed Relations. Due to the versatile information in social networks plus context information such as user location, completely new interconnections are possible for optimally building relationships to potential customers. A new dimension of Customer Relationship Management (CRM) is emerging due to social network users being able to converse directly with companies regarding new products and customization possibilities. Thus, Customer Managed Relations [100] is a new trend.

Online and Offline are Merging. Applying special m-Services views of real world can be expanded with information in computer generated imagery. The physical and virtual reality is merging; this is also called "augmented reality" [103]. Gartner Research identified augmented reality as one of the top ten most disruptive new technologies from 2008 to 2012 [57]. Using such an m-Service, for example using www.wikitude.org, people can track – using their smart phones – objects at a special location, called point-of-interest, thereby enriching themselves with digital information and/or reading the digital graffiti messages of other users. Digital information can be open to all or limited to the contracts of the social network of one user.

4.4   m-Service Security Gaps

Mobile-Specific Security Gaps. Mobile devices are used by a majority of people as a personal assistant, and are taken everywhere. Thus, the possibility that these devices get lost or are stolen is real. This can result in unauthorized individuals gaining large amounts of confidential data (e.g. telephone numbers, addresses, or financial data) or even access to mission-critical systems if the device contains business data. In another scenario, if an unauthorized person "borrows" an unattended mobile computer, he or she may gain access to confidential systems. Additionally, wireless data communications are much more vulnerable to attacks than conventional "wired" communication, because they use "air," thus can be more easily accessed. Since the encryption of data to ensure privacy and integrity can be cracked [39], new technologies and concepts for preventing unauthorized data access and bolstering security will be necessary.

Location Privacy Gaps. Apart from the disclosure of user location by that user – such as publishing a rectangle that contains the user's actual whereabouts – mobile devices must protect user's location and context information from unauthorized others. According to one study [37], many people do not want to be tracked by others without their knowing about it. Also, there are various ways to abuse user information. For example, one might be able to resolve a user's name based on just location information. To ensure the privacy of actual user locations, the development of approaches to prevent such location information misuse is an important direction.

5   Collaboration and e-Services Directions

Table 4. Conference Themes and Relative Importance for Collaboration and e-Services (Scores are *relative* importance ratings. The ranking was done across all subject areas).

Area	Themes Across Area 4	Score	Rank
4	An AI-based 3D friendly visual user interface.	37	2
4	Multi-media social networks.	30	4
4	e-Business needs to cope with the behavior and requirements of "digital natives."	15	9
4	e-Business must offer personalized products and adjust its customer relationships.	14	14
4	Pragmatic (i.e. implemented) interoperability must match semantic (i.e. intended) interoperability.	13	16
4	Virtual Worlds are prime candidates to become arenas for "try before you buy."	7	25
4	The semantic Web, and its applications, enable e-business solutions to grow in scope and depth.	1	33
4	Quality of Service (QoS) for e-Services is multi-dimensional, and has many specific areas of concern.	0	48
4	Ensure privacy for all queries of any individual.	0	49
4	Pragmatic (i.e. implemented) interoperability must match semantic (i.e. intended) interoperability.	0	50
4	Cloud maturity now allows for cloud-based Web services to be created.	0	51
4	Computer-mediated networks are expanding people's ability to connect and converse.	0	52
4	Business terminology model standardizes e-Services operability + its corresponding SLAs.	0	53
4	Web 2.0 --> Social Networks --> Untapped Dynamic Niche Markets.	0	54

5.1   Evolving Ubiquity and Ability of Intelligent User Interfaces

Intelligent user interfaces apply artificial intelligence to the problem of human-machine interaction [46]. As user interfaces become more aware [175], they offer people more assistance with their tasks. One kind of user interface agent is called a "wizard" [10]. These agents provide task assistance by breaking the human endeavor into an often linear series of steps and presenting the steps to a person, one at a time. Another kind of user interface agent is called a "guide" [10]. Typically, guides provide assistance by monitoring a person's interaction with their immediate environment, and then presenting appropriate information, such as: highlighted important things to now consider, a set of choices, or the next best possible steps.

Over the last ten years, wizards and guides have appeared on an increasing number of diverse of computerized devices [119]: hand-held personal digital assistants, cell phones, pagers, pens, notepads, desk and wall-size computers, and also in everyday objects. The increasing connectivity of computers, started by the World Wide Web and continuing with ubiquitous computing, bolstered this proliferation. Also, recognition-based interfaces, especially speech [132], and vision systems are now becoming available to the general public, as well the need for 3D [102], customization [148] and scripting [82].

In 2010, we see the fusion of artificial intelligence, visualization, and Web 2.0 creating interfaces not thought of ten years ago: a) recommender systems based on user preferences [106] or by the history and genealogy of the user's information [81], b) high adaptability using software ontologies [16], c) personalization governed by the user's social networks [15] or by the social tagging implied by the user's searches or Web navigation [56], d) unexpected and highly useful data generated by context-aware mashups [115] and spatial hypertext [90], and e) machine learning based on the user's evolving vocabulary [79] or the user's prior personalization choices [181]. The availability and low cost cloud computing now provides storage and processing to implement far more sophisticated approaches than the ones mentioned above.

5.2   Multimedia Social Networks Are Better Understood and Utilized

The growth of multimedia social networks on the Internet is revolutionizing content distribution and social interaction, and has led to a new research area, called social multimedia computing. Included in this area are: contextualized media understanding, cooperative multimedia networking, multimedia interaction dynamics, and social multi-media community analysis [162]. This research area is crucial to e-Business, because companies can be more successful if they know such things as: a) how social multimedia is used to discover relationships and connections, b) how identity can be reliably verified, and c) how to properly cascade authorization to view data [91]. e-Business is also in a new domain of knowledge acquisition, because traditional marketing studies do not uncover key facts about customers and buying patterns. For example, knowledge discovery in blogs is different than knowledge discovery in databases or documents: clustering, decomposition and ranking are key techniques [96].

Even simple questions do not yet have good answers. For example: Why do people connect in social networks? Is it common interest? Is it friendships? Homophily (like-mindedness) is not yet well understood [99]. We do know that connection patterns in multimedia social networks evolve. For example, communities grow quickly at the beginning of an episode. The resulting connection patterns often create "small worlds" which can affect consumer patterns. In addition, strong cultural influences can bias the final purchase. For example, in some countries, face-to-face dialog must take place after online dialog before a purchase is made [174]. However, we do have some important answers that can immediately impact e-Business design. For example, current methods for analyzing the behavior of users who share multimedia in peer-to-peer live-streaming social networks have shed light on human dynamics such as cheating, malicious activity, and attacking. As a result, strategies now exist to: a) stimulate user cooperation, b) achieve cheat free interaction, c) provide attack resistance, and d) help provide reliable services [106].

Technical directions are also promising. For example, new-generation smart phones enable learning, visualizing, and sharing data about peoples' daily activities. Through smart phones, users exchange multimedia data (e.g. video, audio, images), and wireless users in physical proximity can share these data via spontaneous social interactions triggered by user profile exchanges. Recent algorithms now exist to create fast and efficient connections and data transfers using a topology overlay [25]. Such multimedia file sharing has exploded in large-scale multimedia social network communities such as Napster, flickr and YouTube, and consumes 43% of the overall bandwidth, which is about three times of all WWW traffic. This consumption is driving innovation in efficient, scalable and robust data sharing strategies. For example, signal processing is being used to model, analyze and perform behavior forensics on multimedia social networks (i.e. fingerprinting use), for the purpose of designing more secure and personalized devices [186]. Other examples include: annotating images using personal and social network contexts [150] and event annotation [187].

5.3 Virtual Worlds for Consumer-Related Populations, Expertise and Things

Virtual worlds have become very popular, and there is a very strong trend towards larger worlds and more user generated content, including 3D content [74]. Research has shown that "try before you buy" is part of the digital native's mentality [121], and virtual worlds already provide interactive forums where potential buyers can try products or speak with product critics or evangelists, such as in Second Life [17]. Based on these experiences, there is no reason why virtual worlds in general cannot move out the gaming arena and into the e-Business arena: the connecting, interacting, and entertaining nature of Virtual Worlds makes them prime candidates to become arenas for "try before you buy" [108]. And research, such as using P2P content delivery for making real-time, multimedia content streaming more efficient [74] continues to make virtual worlds faster, and hence more life-like, for its user populations.

From a social perspective, one can envision that, as virtual worlds become interactive forums for consumerism, there could be an explosion of virtual population births. Such populations could be comprised of digital natives who would get paid for providing product/service experience/advice. A rise of "micro-nationals" around a core idea, core belief, common work task, product use, and so, may soon occur. And such populations would be just as aligned to their commonly held agreements as they are with their current nationality [149]. Understanding user behaviors in virtual worlds is also valuable for e-Business. For example, participatory sensing – the process whereby individuals and communities use ever-more-capable mobile phones and cloud computing to collect and analyze data for use in discovery [51] – can shed light on buying intent [179]. As these micro-populations are born, they become new markets, and to exploit such markets, as mentioned earlier in this Section, e-Business activities associated with the virtual community must not merely coincide with its social interactions, but be embedded within them [12].

From a technical perspective, the door is now open for virtual worlds to unite with The Internet of Things [118]. This technology merger holds great promise for e-Business. To explain: The concept of embedded interaction is very present in virtual worlds, even though "things" are not physical. No reason why virtual worlds cannot connect into the real world. Then, the current issues surrounding the Internet of Things apply [92]. And the virtual (as opposed to real) nature of the virtual world has advantages. For example: a) invisibility, interactivity, and multimodality for virtual things can be altered in real-time, b) context-aware things change their shape and/or behavior depending on user location and activity, and c) embedded computing for work or play be used in simulated contexts not suitable in the real world [118]. Many technical directions need exploration, such as the tradeoffs between embedded devices versus interaction devices, and between implicit versus explicit interaction [94].

5.4   Semantic Web Drives Standards for Smarter/Faster e-Commerce

Today, the top four technical directions for the Semantic Web are: 1) semantic-driven computation for identifying all solution possibilities and the best one, 2) automatic service composition via an orchestration model, 3) ontology-driven profiling using correct semantics for better access to solutions, and 4) semantic-driven decomposability to detect matching patterns in needs and solutions [183]. Here is a summary:

Semantic-Driven Computation. e-Commerce based on Web services allows any entity to trade with any other entity. Two frameworks are needed: a Web Services Modeling Framework (WSMF) [83] and Semantic Web Enabled Web Services (SWWS) [24]. WSMF is described below. The SWWS comprises five standards: coordination, semantics, discovery, trading, and negotiation. Future directions include: a) architecture for coordinated trading, b) semantics to mine social networks for commerce potential, c) product catalogues that suggest personalization possibilities, and d) intelligent agents for purchase negotiations [111].

Automatic Service Composition. Currently, the static Web has three key technologies: HTML, HTTP and URI for documents, and the dynamic Web three key technologies: WSDL, UDDI, and SOAP for services [83]. Today's Web Services Modeling Framework (WSMF) has four key technologies: a) ontologies, b) goal repositories, c) service descriptions, and d) mediators [83]. Future directions include: a) ontologies to define social network dynamics, b) repositories of prior successful commerce, c) an open orchestration model comprising product catalogs for personalization, and d) architecture for supporting purchases via intelligent agents [111].

Ontology-Driven Profiling. One possible future is to use "buying intention" as a new HTML anchor for tagging products to social network conversations. This tagging provides disambiguation semantics that enables more relevant ads, and simpler product discovery [125]. In this way, the strict publish-and-subscribe model of the semantic Web is augmented with buying intent history, and thus operates more along the lines of a query-for-content model [179]. Therefore, as soon as a prior buying intent is recognized, then previously used online ads can be invoked [111].

Semantic-Driven Composability. Composing Web services is a complex endeavor, and requires syntactic and semantic rules for success. Semantic composability rules include a) message, b) operation, c) qualities, and d) composition [113]. e-Business marketing exploits these rules to improve online ads: a) message = intent, b) operation = intent to buy, c) qualities = product personalization needs, and d) composition = intent plus needs matched to an offering. Such composability provides strong disambiguation semantics, and enables faster recognition of consumer buying intent [111].

6   Technology Platform Directions

A technology platform (TP) ensures optimum performance, availability, reliability, security, and intuitive data access across heterogeneous environments [20]. As such, a TP needs to adequately address the essential, desired features of current IT facilities: service orientation, support of autonomic behavior of entities, and context sensitivity [152]. We argue moreover that the actual "Cloud" direction [32] needs to be reflected as well in the current technology platform features. In the remaining of the section, we briefly outline and discuss each of these technology platform-related directions.

Table 5. Conference Themes and Importance for Technology Platforms (Scores are *relative* importance ratings. The ranking was done across all subject areas).

Area	Themes Across Area 5	Score	Rank
5	Exploitation of information fusion concepts and technologies.	15	10
5	SOA-based enterprises will evolve in service-oriented enterprises.	15	11
5	Technology platform recognizes service request patterns; manages composition + reuse.	14	15
5	Service-oriented architecture enables dynamic composition of managed and basic services.	10	20
5	Pervasive, ubiquitous computing that is intelligent + aware.	3	32
5	Adequate mechanisms for interoperability, privacy, trust, control, and self-management.	1	34
5	Data protection, encryption, integrity, corrections, publication, utility, provenance, availability + accessibility.	1	35
5	On-demand e-Service composition --> dynamic applications.	1	36
5	Grid-based applications require ways to dynamically add + remove services.	0	55
5	Wiki technology requires robust authentication, authorization, and auditing of user generated content.	0	56
5	Electronic auction applications must be designed for a variety of usage situations and rules.	0	57
5	Wiki technology provides high information availability and immediacy.	0	58
5	SENSEI Framework for middleware integration platform for horizontal B2B integration.	0	59
5	Quality of Service (QoS) attributes that drive the design of SOA components --> compliance + usability.	0	60

6.1 Service-Oriented Computing

Accommodating service orientation would require being consistent with the principles of the Service-Oriented Computing (SOC) Paradigm [146], considering the notion of "service" as a fundamental concept being nevertheless differently interpreted depending on the perspective; there are two main perspectives in this regard, namely the business perspective and the IT perspective. In a business context, a service involves the exchange of some action, performance or promise for value between a client and the provider [157]. In an IT context, a service refers to the external behavior of an IT system which behavior can be observed and experienced by the user of that system [155]. It is argued hence that considering these perspectives in combination allows SOC to bring together business and IT, by repeated aggregation of IT services into composite applications supporting business services that in turn are aggregated into business processes [168]. Thus, a SOC-inspired development of ICT applications would mean the ability to create new applications from existing services, independently of who provides these services, where they are provided, and how they are implemented [153]. Using the aforementioned, we derive the following requirements:

- Allow users to "play" with services at a high level;
- Maintain a sound link with the underlying technology;
- Reliably and flexibly establish and close connections, as needed;
- Support interoperability of full value;
- Properly handle all semantics;
- Align with advanced search facilities to enable service discovery.

6.2 Autonomic Computing

In contrast to visions for human-centered information systems [33], sometimes there are many contexts where information systems can take autonomous action [19]. Technology platforms thus need to facilitate such "autonomic" behavior, which in turn requires the need for consistency within the principles of the Autonomic Computing Paradigm [151]. From this perspective, systems should be capable of adapting to dynamic, open environments on their own, with little or no human intervention.

The Autonomic Computing Paradigm [88] has been proposed as a way to reduce the cost of maintaining complex systems, and to increase the human ability to manage these systems properly. Autonomic Computing introduces a number of autonomic properties, such as self-configuring, self-healing, self-optimizing and self-protecting. Extending and enhancing a system with these properties is an important step towards a self-management system.

At least some fundamental concepts and architectural building blocks need to be considered for constructing self-managed systems with autonomic properties. The two main building blocks of an automatic computing architecture are autonomic managers and managed resources [77]. Managed resources are hardware or software components, for example a business application, a router or a database. A managed resource is managed by an autonomic manager. This autonomic manager forms the central part of the autonomic architecture. It collects data from managed resources, which is used for diagnosing failures and other unwanted behavior. The autonomic manager formalizes and executes remedy plans for the managed resource which are intended to correct the unwanted behavior. These arguments suggest requirements:

- Properly support technical IT systems acting on their own;
- Consider autonomous action (i.e. without triggers from "outside");
- Act autonomously if the user interests would require such action;
- Yet protect users from inadequate or improper autonomic actions.

6.3 Context-Aware Computing

A key feature concerning any technology in service to human needs is its ability to adapt its behavior based on the user situation [178]. Technology platforms thus need to facilitate context-awareness, and do so consistent with the principles of the Context-Aware Computing Paradigm [152]. Their underlying logic must acknowledge that end-user needs are not static, and are partially dependent on the particular context in which the end-user is situated. Context-aware systems are thus primarily motivated by their potential to increase user-perceived effectiveness (i.e. to provide services that better suit the needs of the end-user) by taking account changing conditions. We refer to the collection of conditions which characterize an end-user's immediate surroundings, which are relevant for the system in pursuit of user-perceived effectiveness, to be "end-user context," or "context" for short, in accordance to definitions found in today's literature [40].

Context-aware systems can be somewhat effective if the end-user is mobile and uses a personal handheld device for the delivery of services. Mobility implies dynamic context, including most notably changing location. Regarding locations, different ones may have different social environments and different network access options, which offer opportunities for the provision of adaptive or value-added services based on these contexts. Especially in the mobile case, context changes are continuous, and a context-aware system may exploit this by providing near real-time adaptation during a service delivery session with its end-user. Taking the aforementioned into account, we derive the following requirements:

- Applications should be sensitive to user's entire situation;
- Applications must adapt their behavior when the situation changes;
- Platforms must guarantee adequate Quality-of-Context levels;
- Platforms support security for the end user;
- Platforms must enforce privacy of context information.

6.4 Cloud Computing

Emerging Enterprise Technologies are profoundly changing the way we think of IT. From economics and efficiency, to process and usage models, all these dimensions comprise the Cloud Computing Paradigm. Many organizations look to "externalize" IT systems and services as a potential cost-savings advantage, primarily by moving internally hosted IT services to external providers. Other organizations view "external" IT as potential disaster recovery systems, or as on-demand capacity to boost business continuity and customer service levels [80].

With regard to these issues, and considering the e-Business technology platforms directions, we need to take a closer look Cloud Computing. Most notably, we need to identify current emerging enterprise technologies, and how they might facilitate e-Business and might produce a competitive advantage. There is hence a new wave of interest in the "Externalization of IT;" for example, anything-as-a-service (e.g. Software as a Service, Infrastructure as a Service, Platform as a Service, On Demand delivery, outsourcing, and so on). Taking the above background information into account, we derive the following requirements:

- Properly mediate between Cloud services and externalized services;
- Support the utilization of externalized services;
- Enforce Quality-of-Service standards with regard to externalized services.

7 Summary and Conclusions

e-Business Applications. Today's businesses are pressured by economic, technological, societal, and IT forces. In addition, Web 2.0 creates new strategic challenges never before considered by executives. Compounding these matters are the and digital native population who are demanding highly agile e-Business and personalized products. In response to these challenges, e-Business application development methods have appeared to better elicit context-based usage and operational requirements. There have also been many improvements in the System Development Life Cycle to ensure context-awareness is properly implemented. In addition, business sees that widening the scope of e-Business applications to every corner of the Internet can prove profitable. The big direction yet to be considered is giving the user real-time decision-making on adapting e-Business application to suit his or her current context.

Enterprise Engineering. In the area of enterprise engineering, two major challenges were identified. One challenge relates to understanding and managing the enterprise, and requires further work on Enterprise Architecture and enterprise ontologies. The other challenge follows from the necessity to connect applications and the trend to collaborate in business networks and form extended enterprises. Several issues exist here, at technical, semantic and organizational level, in order to achieve seamless integration and open interoperability. We also discussed three interesting enterprise engineering directions: cope with change, address value aspects, and move to virtual. Cope with change is concerned with developments that can help to address the problem of continuous change in business environments. Addressing value aspects relates to advances in business modeling that can capture economic value exchanges between participants in a business network. Finally, move to virtual is an evolutionary development of e-commerce towards the availability of more advanced business services for virtual market places, enabled by the Future Internet and associated technologies.

Mobility. m-Services and social networks offer new possibilities in many ways. For users, they can offer more flexibility and independence in planning activities, in shopping, in communication and getting entertainment. For companies, they will need to adapt business models, advertisements, product placements, communication channels, customer relationships and business processes to address new consumer behaviors. They will need to pay special attention to, and focus on, digital natives because this population is using mobile technology in new ways. Along with the many positive effects of new mobility come the concerns of privacy. An adequate reliable protection of information is therefore necessary to ensure user privacy and data integrity.

Collaboration & e-Services. e-Business needs to recognize the groundswell of people now joining the digital native population. Part of that recognition means to reengineer the business to provide a fully customized product to each customer. In parallel, e-Business needs to be concerned with its electronic products, services and operations to ensure they all interoperate with other products, services and companies. Directionally, e-Business appears to be on a path to better understand and utilize multimedia social networks – a haven for digital natives. Thus, e-Businesses should start to see the value of virtual worlds, not only for the connection to digital natives, but also for the opportunity to offer product trials (i.e. via try before you buy demos) and advice (i.e. via product maven avatars). For products, there is growing recognition for intelligent user interfaces offering products that are highly attuned to the user's ever-changing context. Operationally, the Semantic Web is becoming more commonplace in e-Business strategies, and R&D is attempting to solve its issues and provide standards to commercial firms to enable better simplicity, reliability and speed.

Technology Platforms. In the area of technology platforms, two major challenges were rated as most important. One challenge relates to the necessity for delivering services through technology platforms in a way that hides the underlying technical complexity from the user, while at the same time keeping the vital link to the underlying technology. The second challenge relates to the need for most technology platforms to scale up when faced with the dynamic requirement of supporting a multitude of concurrent users, allowing all of them to adequately profile their requests as well as to establish and maintain dynamic collaborations. To meet these challenges, it is of essential importance to consider four relevant computing paradigms that complement each other: a) Service-Oriented Computing, b) Autonomic Computing, c) Context-Aware Computing and d) Cloud Computing. Service-Oriented Computing concerns itself with service delivery, regardless of who is providing the service. Autonomic Computing focuses on the operation of the technical system itself, which must constantly consider is autonomous action is desired, required and/or appropriate. Context-Aware Computing is simultaneously monitoring the user's ongoing changing situations, and subsequently altering the behavior of IT systems to match each situation. Cloud Computing concerns itself with the externalization of services and/or facilities through "The Cloud." To meet the aforementioned challenges, incorporating features related to each of these paradigms, in combination, is required.

Acknowledgements. The authors thank Dr. Maro Vlachopoulou from the University of Macedonia for her valuable insights on organizing workshop subject areas and their scope of concern. Thanks go to the ICETE organizing committee as well as its production team in the logistical design and delivery of the interactive workshop, which required a high amount of visual bandwidth and persistence over the three-day ICETE conference. In closing, the Conference Chairs, Dr. Joaquim Filipe and Dr. Mohammad Obaidat are to be acknowledged and thanked for their encouragement of holding this workshop at ICETE. The authors appreciate the opportunity to work with the entire conference to capture the common themes that occurred during conference dialogs, and their relative importance, for the current state of e-Business and for its possible future directions.

References

1. Abraham, P., Sikka, V., Simpson, G.: Share Vs. Own: Software Reuse using Product Platforms. In: Proc. Intl. Conf. on e-Business (ICE-B 2010) (July 2010)
2. Abrantes, S., Gouveia, L.: A Study on the Usage of Mobile Devices in Collaborative Environments: An Approach based on Flow Experience. In: Proc. Intl. Conf. on e-Business (ICE-B 2010) (July 2010)
3. ACT4SOC, Inc. (2011), http://www.icsoft.org/workshops.asp
4. Akyildiz, I.: Nanonetworks: A New Frontier in Communications. In; Proc. Intl. Conf. on e-Business (ICE-B 2010) (July 2010)
5. Allen, S., Tanev, S., Bailetti, T.: Components of Co-creation, Special Issue on Value Co-creation. Open Source Business Review Online Journal (November 2009)
6. Allen, S., Tanev, S., Bailetti, T.: Towards the Development of Research Methodology for Studying the Nature of Value Co-creation in Internet-Driven Businesses. In: Proc. 5th Intl. Conf. Software, Services & Semantic Technologies (October 2009)
7. Anderson, C., Wolff, M.: Wired Magazine: The Web is dead. Long live the Internet. Wired (September 2010), http://www.wired.com/magazine//2010/08/ff_webrip/2/ (August 18, 2010)
8. Aris, M., Ouksel, A., Sheth, A.: Semantic Interoperability in Global Information Systems. ACM SIGMOD 28(1) (1999)
9. Armbrust, M., Fox, A., Griffith, R., Joseph, A., Katz, R., Konwinski, A., Lee, G., Patterson, D., Rabkin, A., Stoica, I., Zaharia, M.: Above the Clouds: A Berkeley View of Cloud Computing. UC Berkeley Reliable Adaptive Distributed Systems Laboratory (2009), http://radlab.cs.berkeley.edu/
10. Attkinson, B., Brady, S., Gilbert, D., Levine, D., O"Connor, P., Osisek, D., Spagna, S., Wilson: IBM Intelligent Agents. In: UNICOM Seminar Proceedings (1995)
11. Badidi, E., Esmahi, L.: A Quality of Context Driven Approach for the Selection of Context Services. In: Proc. Intl. Conf. on e-Business (ICE-B 2010) (July 2010)
12. Balasubramanian, S., Mahajan, V.: The Economic Leverage of the Virtual Community. Intl. Journal of Electronic Commerce 5(3) (2001)
13. Berends, W., Folmer, E.: Assessing Business Transaction Standards and Their Adoption: A Cross Case Analysis Between the SETU and Vektis Standards. In: Proc. Intl. Conf. on e-Business (ICE-B 2010) (July 2010)
14. Berger, R.: Automotive System Integrators. University of Michigan Transportation Research Institute (2001)
15. Bernstein, M., Tan, F., Smith, G., Czerwinski, M., Horvitz, E.: Personalization via Friendsourcing. ACM Trans. Computer-Human Interaction 17(2) (2010)
16. Blumendorf, M., Lehmann, G., Albayrak, S.: Bridging Models and Systems at Runtime to Build Adaptive User Interfaces. In: EICS 2010: Proc. 2nd ACM Symposium on Engineering Interactive Computing Systems (2010)
17. Boellstorf, T.: Coming of Age in Second Life: An Anthropologist Explores the Virtually Human. Princeton University Press, United Kingdom (2008)
18. Bourbakis, N.: Information Security: The SCAN – Secure Processor with Crypto-Biometrics Capabilities. In: Proc. Intl. Conf. on e-Business (ICE-B 2010) (July 2010)
19. Brazier, F.: Self-regulation for Transformation. In: Proc. Intl. Conf. Innovative Developments in ICT (2010)
20. Brocade, Inc. (2010), http://www.brocade.com

21. Brooks, F.: No Silver Bullet: Essence and Accidents of Software Engineering. IEEE Computer 20(4) (1987)
22. Bulander, R., Decker, M., Kölmel, B., Schiefer, G.: Advertising via Mobile Terminals. In: Filipe, J., Greene, T. (eds.) Proc. Intl. Conference on E-Business and Telecommunication Networks (ICE-B 2005), Reading, UK (October 2005)
23. Bulander, R.: A Conceptual Framework of Serious Games for Higher Education: A Conceptual Framework of the Game INNOV8 to Train Students in Business Process Modelling. In: Proc. Intl. Conf. on e-Business (ICE-B 2010) (July 2010)
24. Bussler, C., Fensel, D., Maedche, A.: Conceptual Architecture for Semantic Web Enabled Web Services. SIGMOD Record 31(4) (2002)
25. Cassara, P., Melodia, T.: Optimal Overlay Construction for Wireless Multimedia Social Networks. Associazione Gruppo Telecomunicazioni e Tecnologie dell"Informazione (2010)
26. Cereci, I., Kiliç, H.: CAWP - A Combinatorial Auction Web Platform. In: Proc. Intl. Conf. on e-Business (ICE-B 2010) (July 2010)
27. Chan, K.: A Fault Taxonomy for Web Service Composition. Xian Jiaotong University Journal 40(8) (2006)
28. Chau, S., Turner, P.: A Four Phase Model of e-Business Transformation amongst Small to Medium Sized Enterprises. In: Proceedings of ACIS (2001)
29. Chen, L.: Intelligent Mobile Safety System to Educational Organization. In: Proc. Intl. Conf. on e-Business (ICE-B 2010) (July 2010)
30. Chen, L., Pu, P.: Experiments on the Preference-based Organization Interface in Recommender Systems. ACM Trans. Computer-Human Interaction 17(1) (2010)
31. Cho, S., Lee, S., Moon, K.: Fuzzy Decision Making of IT Governance. In: Proc. Intl. Conf. on e-Business (ICE-B 2010) (July 2010)
32. Cloud, About the (2010), http://www.aboutthecloud.nl
33. Cordeiro, J., Filipe, J., Liu, K.: Towards a Human-Oriented Approach to Information Systems Development. In: Proc. 3rd Intl. Workshop on Enterprise Sys. (2009)
34. Cortimiglia, M.: A Taxonomy Schema for Web 2.0 and Mobile 2.0 Applications. In: Proceedings of ICE-B 2009 (2009)
35. Debaty, P., Caswell, D.: Uniform Web Presence Architecture for People, Places, and Things. IEEE Personal Communications 8(4) (2001)
36. Decker, M.: Prevention of Location-Spoofing – A Survey on Different Methods to Prevent the Manipulation of Locating-Technologies. In: Intl. Conf. e-Business, ICE-B 2009 (2009)
37. Decker, M.: Location Privacy – An Overview. In: m-business 2008: Proc. 7th Intl. Conf. on Mobile Business (ICMB 2008) (July 2008)
38. Decker, M., Bulander, R., Schiefer, G.: A SME-friendly framework for the provision of mobile services. In: m-Business Revisited – From Speculation to Reality, 5th Intl. Conf. on Mobile Business (ICMB 2006) (2006)
39. Decker, M., Schiefer, G.: The SumoDacs-Project: Secure Mobile Data Access with a Tamperproof Hardware Token. In: Proc. of e-Challenges e-2010 Conference, IIMC, International Information Management Corporation, Warsaw, Poland (2010)
40. Dey, A., Abowd, G.D., Salber, D.: A Conceptual Framework and Toolkit for Supporting Rapid Prototyping of Context-Aware Applications. Human Comp. Int. 16(2) (2001)
41. Diplaris, S., Kompatsiaris, I., Flores, A., Escriche, M, Sigurbjornsson, B., Garcia, L.: Proc. Intl. Conf. on e-Business (ICE-B 2010) (July 2010)

42. Djuric, P.: From Nature to Methods and Back to Nature. In: Proc. Intl. Conf. on e-Business (ICE-B 2010) (July 2010)
43. Doerr, M.: The CIDOC Conceptual Reference Model: An Ontological Approach to Semantic Interoperability of Metadata. AI Magazine 24(3) (2003)
44. Dietz, J.L.G.: Enterprise Ontology – Theory and Methodology. Springer, Heidelberg (2006)
45. Drossos, D.A., Fouskas, K.: Mobile Advertising: Product Involvement and its Effect on Intention to Purchase. In: Intl. Conf. on Mobile Business, ICMB 2010 (2010)
46. Dryer, C.: Wizards, Guides, and Beyond: Rational and Empirical Methods for Selecting Optimal Intelligent User Interface Agents. In: 2nd Intl. Conf. Intel. User Interfaces (1997)
47. Dyché, J.: The CRM-Handbook. Addison-Wesley, Boston (2002)
48. Ehn, P.: Work-Oriented Design of Computer Artifacts. L. Erlbaum Associates Inc. (1990)
49. Eliassi-Rad, T., Shavlik, J.: A System for Building Intelligent Agents that Learn to Retrieve and Extract Information. Journal of User Modeling and User-Adapted Interaction 13(1-2) (2002)
50. Ervasti, M.: Adoption of Mobile Services in Finland. In: Proc. of ICE-B 2008 (2008)
51. Estrin, D.: Participatory Sensing: Application and Architecture. IEEE Internet Computing 14(1) (2010)
52. Eurich, M., Boutellier, R.: Middleware Integration Platforms: A New Challenge to Business Models of ICT Companies. Unleashing the Business Potential of Horizontalization. In: Proc. Intl. Conf. on e-Business (ICE-B 2010) (July 2010)
53. Fang, Z.: E-Government in Digital Era: Concept, Practice, and Development. Intl. Journal of The Computer, The Internet and Management 10(2) (2002)
54. Forbes Blog. Milo and Kate Live Demo (July 13, 2010), http://blogs.forbes.com/velocity/2010/07/13/milo-and-kate-live-demo-cool-creepy/
55. Frank, A.: Dependable Distributed Testing: Can the Online Proctor be Reliably Computerized? In: Proc. Intl. Conf. on e-Business (ICE-B 2010) (July 2010)
56. Fu, W., Kannampallil, T., Kang, T., He, J.: Semantic Imitation in Social Tagging. ACM Trans. Computer-Human Interaction 17(3) (2010)
57. Gartner Research: Press Release: Gartner Identifies Top Ten Disruptive Technologies for 2008 to 2012 (2008), http://www.gartner.com/it/page.jsp?id=681107 (August 18, 2010)
58. Geyer-Schulz, A., Ovelgöenne, M., Sonnenbichler, A.: Getting Help in a Crowd: A Social Emergency Alert Service. In: Proc. Intl. Conf. on e-Business (ICE-B 2010) (July 2010)
59. Gordijn, J.: Comparing Two Business Model Ontologies for Designing e-Business. In: Proceedings of the 8th BLED Conference (2005)
60. Gordijn, J., Wieringa, R.: A Value-Oriented Approach to e-Business Process Design. In: Eder, J., Missikoff, M. (eds.) CAiSE 2003. LNCS, vol. 2681, pp. 390–403. Springer, Heidelberg (2003)
61. Gottschalk, K.: Introduction to Web Services Architecture. IBM Sys. J. 41(2) (2002)
62. Gruber, T.R.: Towards principles for the design of ontologies used for knowledge sharing. International Journal of Human-Computer Studies 43(5-6) (1995)
63. Gustas, A., Gustiené, P.: Towards the Enterprise Engineering Approach for Information System Modeling Across Organizational and Technical Boundaries. In: Proc. 5th Intl. Conf. on Enterprise Info. Sys., vol. 3 (2003)

64. Hamill, L., Nigel Gilbert, N.: Social Circles: A Simple Structure for Agent-Based Social Network Models. Journal of Artificial Societies and Social Simulation 12(2) (2009)
65. Heflin, J., Hendler, J.: Semantic Interoperability on the Web. In: Conf. on Extreme Markup Languages (2000)
66. Heller, M., Allgaier, M.: Model-Based Service Integration for Extensible Enterprise Systems with Adaptation Patterns. In: Proc. Intl. Conf. on e-Business (ICE-B 2010) (July 2010)
67. Heravi, B., Bell, D., Lycett, M., Green, S., Snelling, D.: Towards Ontology Based e-Business Standards. In: Proc. Intl. Conf. on e-Business (ICE-B 2010) (July 2010)
68. Hippner, H.: CRM – Grundlagen, Ziele und Konzepte. In: Hippner, H., Wilde, K.D. (eds.) Grundlagen des CRM, pp. 13–42. Gabler, Wiesbaden (2004)
69. Hof, R.: Web 2.0 Has Corporate America Spinning. Bloomberg Business Week Online (June 5, 2006)
70. Holzinger, A., Mayr, S., Slany, W., Debevc, M.: The Influence of AJAX on Web Usability. In: Proc. Intl. Conf. on e-Business (ICE-B 2010) (July 2010)
71. Holzinger, A., Schlögl, M., Peischl, B., Debevc, M.: Preferences of Handwriting Recognition on Mobile Information Systems in Medicine: Improving Handwriting Algorithm on the Basis of Real-life Usability Research. Intl. Conf. on e-Business, ICE-B 2010 (2010)
72. Holzinger, A., Struggl, K., Debevc, M.: Applying Model-View-Controller (MVC) in design and Development of Information Systems: An Example of Smart Assistive Script Breakdown in an e-Business Application. In: Proc. Intl. Conf. on e-Business (ICE-B 2010) (July 2010)
73. Holzinger, K., Holzinger, A., Safran, C., Koiner-Erath, G., Weippl, E.: Use of Wiki Systems in Archaeology: Privacy, Security and Data Protection as Key Problems. In: Proc. Intl. Conf. on e-Business (ICE-B 2010) (July 2010)
74. Hu, S., Chen, B.: Peer-to-Peer 3D Streaming. IEEE Internet Computing 14(2) (2010)
75. Huhns, M.N.: Software Agents: The Future of Web Services. In: Kowalczyk, R., Müller, J.P., Tianfield, H., Unland, R. (eds.) NODe-WS 2002. LNCS (LNAI), vol. 2592, pp. 1–18. Springer, Heidelberg (2003)
76. Huysmans, P., Bellens, D., Nuffel, D., Ven, K.: Designing Enterprise Architectures Based on Systems Theoretic Stability. In: Proc. Intl. Conf. on e-Business (ICE-B 2010) (July 2010)
77. IBM, Inc. (2010), http://www.ibm.com
78. Interone. Interone GmbH Study: The-Age-Of-On (August 18, 2010), http://www.interone.de/iphone-studie/
79. Irmak, U., Kraft, R.: A Scalable Machine-Learning Approach for Semi-Structured Named Entity Recognition. In: Proc. 19th Intl. Conf. on the World Wide Web (2010)
80. Ivanov, I.: Emerging Utility and Cloud computing Models. In: Proc. 3rd Intl. Workshop on Enterprise Systems and Technology (2009)
81. Jensen, C., Lonsdale, H., Wynn, E., Cao, J., Slater, M., Dietterich, T.: The Life and Times of Files and Information: A Study of Desktop Provenance. In: Proc. 28th Intl. Conf. Human Factors in Comp. Sys. (2010)
82. Jin, J., Maheswaran, R., Sanchez, R., Szekely, P.: VizScript: Visualizing Complex Interactions in Multi-Agent Systems. In: Proc. 12th Intl. Conf. Intelligent User Interfaces (January 2007)
83. Kajan, E.: The Maturity of Open Systems for B2B. ACM SIGEcom Exchanges 5(2) (November 2004)

84. Kapurubandara, M., Hol, A., Ginige, A.: SMES in developed and Developing Countries treading Simial Paths Towards e-Transformation. In: Proc. Intl. Conf. on e-Business (ICE-B 2010) (July 2010)
85. Karp, S.: What If Media 2.0 Is Less Profitable Than Media 1.0? Publishing 2.0 (2006), http://publishing2.com/2006/04/23/what-if-media-20-is-less-profitable-than-media-10/
86. Kartalopoulos, S.: Chaotic Quantum Cryptography: The Ultimate for Network Security. In: Proc. Intl. Conf. on e-Business (ICE-B 2010) (July 2010)
87. Kauffman, R., Walden, E.: Economics and Electronic Commerce: Survey and Directions for Research. Intl. Journal of Electronic Commerce 5(4) (2001)
88. Kephart, J., Chess, D.: The vision of Autonomic Computing. IEEE Computer Society Press (2003)
89. Khaddage, F., Lanham, E., Zhou, W.: A Mobile Learning Model for Universities. Intl. Journal of Interactive Mobile Tech (iJIM) 3 (2009)
90. Kim, D., Shipman, F.: Interpretation and Visualization of User History in a Spatial Hypertext System. In: Proc. 21st ACM Conf. on Hypertext and Hypermedia (2010)
91. Ko, M., Cheek, G., Shehab, M.: Social-Networks Connect Services. IEEE Computer 43(8) (2010)
92. Kortuem, G., Kawsar, F., Fitton, D., Sundramoorthy, V.: Smart Object Building Blocks on The Internet of Things. IEEE Internet Computing 14(1) (2010)
93. Kosonen, M.: Knowledge Sharing in Virtual Communities. Doctoral Thesis. Lappeenranta University (2008)
94. Kranz, M., Holleis, P., Schmidt, A.: Embedded Interaction: Interacting with the Internet of Things. IEEE Internet Computing 14(2) (2010)
95. Krasonikolakis, I., Vrechopoulos, A., Pouloudi, A.: User's Personality Traits in the Context of Virtual Reality. In: Proc. Intl. Conf. on e-Business (ICE-B 2010) (July 2010)
96. Lakshmanan, G., Oberhofer, M.: Knowledge Discovery in the Blogsphere. IEEE Internet Computing 14(2) (2010)
97. Lankhorst, M., et al.: Enterprise Architecture at Work: Modeling, Communication and Analysis. Springer, Heidelberg (2005)
98. Laugesen, J., Yuan, Y.: What factors contributed to the success of Apple's iPhone? In: 9th Intl. Conf. on Mobile Business (ICMB 2010) (June 2010)
99. Lauw, H., Shafer, J., Agrawal, R., Ntoulas, A.: Homophily in the Digial World. IEEE Internet Computing 14(2) (2010)
100. Law, M., Lau, T., Wong, Y.H.: From customer Relationship Management to Customer-Managed-Relationship: Unraveling the Paradox with a Co-creative Perspective. Marketing Intelligence & Planning 21(1), 51–60 (2003)
101. Li, C., Bernoff, J.: Groundswell: Winning in a World Transformed. Social Technologies, Inc., Massachusetts (2008)
102. Li, T., Hsu, S.: An Intelligent 3D User Interface Adapting to User Control Behaviors. In: IUI 2004: Proc. 9th Intl. Conf. Intelligent User Interfaces (January 2004)
103. Liestol, G.: Situated Simulations: A Prototyped Augmented Reality Genre for Learning on the iPhone. Intl. Journal of Interactive Mobile Tech. (iJIM) 3 (2009)
104. Lin, J., Li, X., Li, L.: Integrating Mobile Agent and Context-Aware Workflow Analysis for m-Commerce Applications. In: Proc. Intl. Conf. on e-Business (ICE-B 2010) (July 2010)
105. Lin, R., Lin, C.: From Digital Archives to e-Business: A Case Study on Turning "Art" into "Business". In: Proc. Intl. Conf. on e-Business (ICE-B 2010) (July 2010)

106. Lin, W., Zhao, V., Liu, K.: Incentive Cooperation Strategies for Peer-to-Peer Live Multimedia Streaming Social Networks. IEEE Trans. on Multimedia 11(3) (April 2009)

107. Luftman, J.: Assessing Business-IT Alignment Maturity. In: van Grimbergen (ed.) Strategies for Information Technology Governance. Idea Group Inc. (2004)

108. Lugrin, J., Cavazza, M.: Making Sense of Virtual Environments: Action Representation, Grounding and Common Sense. In: Proc. Intl. Conf. on Intel. User Interfaces (January 2007)

109. Maes, P., Mistry, P.: SixthSense Demonstration (February 2009),
http://www.ted.com/talks/pattie_maes_demos_the_sixth_
sense.html

110. Manno, M., Primo, P., Passaro, G., Leggio, E., Barbera, R., Giuseppe Andronico, G., Bruno, R., Giorgio, E., Fargetta, M., Rocca, G., Monforte, S., Scardaci, D., Scibilia, F.: The COMETA e-Infrastructure: A Platform for Business Applications in Sicily. In: Proc. Intl. Conf. on e-Business (ICE-B 2010) (July 2010)

111. Marca, D.: e-Business & Social Networks: Tapping Dynamic Niche Markets Using Language-Action & Artificial Intelligence. In: Filipe, J., Obaidat, M. (eds.) e-Business and Telecommunications. Springer, Heidelberg (2010)

112. McEnvoy, G.: Using Clouds to Address Grid Limitations. In: Proc. of 6th Intl. Workshop on Middleware for Grid Computing (2009)

113. Medjahed, B.: Composing Web Services on the Semantic Web. VLDB J. 12 (2003)

114. Medjahed, B., Bouguettaya, A., Elmagarmid, A.: ComposingWeb services on the Semantic Web. VLDB J. 12 (2003)

115. Mohomed, I.: Enabling Mobile Application Mashups with Merlion. In: Proc. 11th Workshop on Mobile Comp. (2010)

116. Morimoto, S.: A Case Study of the e-Money Application in Japanese Public Transportation. In: Proc. Intl. Conf. on e-Business (ICE-B 2010) (July 2010)

117. Motta, E., Sabou, M.: Next Generation Semantic Web Applications. In: Mizoguchi, R., Shi, Z.-Z., Giunchiglia, F. (eds.) ASWC 2006. LNCS, vol. 4185, pp. 24–29. Springer, Heidelberg (2006)

118. Mulligan, G.: The Internet of Things: Here Now and Coming Soon. IEEE Internet Computing 14(1) (2010)

119. Myers, B., Hudson, S., Pausch, R.: Past, Present, and Future of User Interface Software Tools. ACM Trans. Computer-Human Interaction 7(1) (2000)

120. Norman, D., Draper, S.: User Centered System Design; New Perspectives on Human-Computer Interaction. L. Erlbaum Associates Inc. (1986)

121. Palfrey, J., Gasser, U.: Born Digital. Basic Books, Philadelphia (2008)

122. Panetto, H., Molina, A.: Enterprise Integration and Interoperability in Manufacturing Systems: Trends and Issues. Computer in Industry 59(7) (2008)

123. Papageorgiou, N., Verginadis, Y., Apostolou, D., Mentzas, G.: Semantic Interoperability on e-Services in Collaborative Networked Organizations. In: Proc. Intl. Conf. on e-Business (ICE-B 2010) (July 2010)

124. Papazoglou, M.: Service-Oriented Computing. CACM 46(10) (2003)

125. Parkhomenko, O., Lee, Y., Park, E.: Ontology-Driven Peer Profiling in Peer-to-Peer Enabled Semantic Web. In: CIKM 2003 (November 2003)

126. Parreiras, F.: E-Business Challenges and Trends. Executive Report. Nucleo de Estulos em Tecnologias para Informaceo e Conhecimento (2001)

127. Payne, A., Storbacka, K., Frow, P.: Managing the Co-Creation of Value. Journal of the Academy of Marketing Sciences 36(1) (2008)

128. Petroczi, A.: Measuring tie-Strength in Virtual Networks. Connections 27(2) (2007)
129. Plessis, C.: Mobile Marketing Communications to the Youth: An Analysis of the MXit Platform. In: Proc. Intl. Conf. on e-Business (ICE-B 2010) (July 2010)
130. Pokrae, S., Reichert, M., Steen, M., Wiering, R.: Semantic and Pragmatic Interoperability: A Model for Understanding (2005), http://www.ceur-ws.org/Vol-160/paper21.pdf
131. Porter, M.: Strategy and the Internet. Harvard Business Review 79(3) (2001)
132. Postech, G., Pan, S.: Building Ubiquitous and Robust Speech and Natural Language Interfaces. In: Proc. 12th Intl. Conf. Intelligent User Interfaces (January 2007)
133. Prahalad, C., Krishnan, M.: The New Age of Innovation. McGraw Hill, New York (2008)
134. Prahalad, C., Ramaswamy, V.: The Future of Competition: Co-Creating Unique Value with customers. Harvard Business School Press, Boston (2004)
135. Radovilsky, Z.: E-Commerce Management (2009), http://www.universityreaders.com
136. Rajkumar, B.: Cloud Computing and Emerging IT Platforms. In: Future Generation Computer Systems. Elsevier Press, Inc. (2009)
137. Robertson, B.: Enriching the Value Chain: Infrastructure Strategies. Intel Press (2004)
138. Rogers, E.M.: Diffusion of innovations, 4th edn. Free Press, New York (1995)
139. Royo, C., Rueda, J., Rugnon, O., Fuentes, B., Castro, A.: Business Terms: Model for a Telecom Operator Business View of SLA. In: Intl. Conf. on e-Business, ICE-B 2010 (2010)
140. Ruokolainen, T., Kutvonen, L.: Interoperability in Service-Based Communities. In: Bussler, C.J., Haller, A. (eds.) BPM 2005. LNCS, vol. 3812, pp. 317–328. Springer, Heidelberg (2006)
141. Sadoun, B., Saleh, B.: A Geographic Information System (GIS) to Define Indicatiors for Development and Planning in Jordan. In: Proc. Intl. Conf. on e-Business, ICE-B 2010 (2010)
142. Sawhney, M., Verona, G., Prandelli, E.: Collaborating to Create: The Internet as a Platform for Customer Engagement in Product Innovation. J. of Inter. Marketing 19(4) (2005)
143. Schauer, B., Zeiller, M., Riedl, D.: Reviewing the e-Collaboration Marketplace: A Survey of Electronic Collaboration Systems. In: Proc. Intl. Conf. on e-Business, ICE-B 2010 (2010)
144. Schilit, B.N., Adams, N.I., Want, R.: Context-Aware Computing Applications. In: Proceedings of the IEEE Workshop on Mobile Computing Systems and Applications (1994)
145. Schneider, G.: Electronic Commerce. Cengage Learning, Inc. (2009)
146. van Sinderen, M.: From Service-Oriented Architecture to Service-Oriented Enterprise. In: Proc. 3rd Intl. Workshop on Enterprise Systems and Technology (2009)
147. van Sinderen, M.: Challenges and Solutions in Enterprise Computing. Enterprise Information Systems 2(4) (2008)
148. Shankar, A., Louis, S., Dascalu, S., Hayes, L., Houmanfar, R.: User-Context for Adaptive User Interfaces. In: Proc. 12th Intl. Conf. Intelligent User Interfaces (January 2007)
149. Sharma, S.: The New Way of Business. IEEE Internet Computing 14(1) (2010)
150. Shevade, B., Sundaram, H., Xie, L.: Modeling Personal and Social Network Context for Event Annotation in Images. In: Proc. 7th ACM/IEEE-CS Conf. on Digital Libraries (2007)

151. Shishkov, B., Warnier, M., Van Sinderen, M.: On the Application of Autonomic and Context Aware-Computing to support Home Energy Management. In: Proc. 10th Intl. Conf. on Enterprise Info. Sys. (2010)

152. Shishkov, B.: Methodological Support for the Design of Enterprise Information Systems with SDBC, Towards Distributed, Service-Oriented, and Context-Aware Solutions. In: Proc. 3rd Intl. Workshop on Enterprise Sys. and Tech. (2010)

153. Shishkov. B., Van Sinderen, M.: Service-Oriented Coordination Platform for Technology-Enhanced Learning. In: Proc. 3rd Intl. Workshop on Enterprise Sys. and Tech. (2009)

154. Shishkov, B., van Sinderen, M., Verbraeck, A.: Towards Flexible Inter-enterprise Collaboration: A Supply Chain Perspective. In: Proc. 9th Intl. Conf. on Enterprise Info. Sys. (2009)

155. Shishkov, B., van Sinderen, M., Quartel, D.: SOA-Driven Business-Software Alignment. In: IEEE Intl. Conf. on e-Business Engineering (2006)

156. Shu, W.: Web Engineering Principles and Techniques. Idea Group Inc., London (2005)

157. Spohrer, J., Maglio, P.P., Bailey, J., Gruhl, D.: Steps Toward a Science of Service Systems. IEEE Computer 40(1) (2007)

158. Tan, B., Tang, N., Forrester, P.: Application of QFD for e-Business Planning. Production Planning & Control 15(8) (2004)

159. Tanev, S., durchev, P., Milyakov, H., Ruskov, P., Allen, S., Bailetti, T.: Value Co-creation in Open Source Firms and Beyond. In: Open Source Innovation Workshop, Strasbourg, France (February 2010)

160. Tapscott, D.: Grown Up Digital. McGraw-Hill, New York (2009)

161. Tarasewich, P.: Issues in Mobile e-Commerce. Communications of the Association for Information Systems 8 (2002)

162. Tian, Y., Srivastava, J., Huang, T., Contractor, N.: Social Media Computing. IEEE Computer 43(8) (2010)

163. Toffler, A.: The Third Wave – The rise of the Prosumer. Goldmann Publishers (1983)

164. Toffler, A.: The Third Wave: A Classic Study of Tomorrow. Bantam Books (1984)

165. Torrone, P.: Kryptonite Evolution 2000 U- Lock hacked by a Bic pen. engadget blog post (2004)

166. Tsagkani, C.: Business Process Flexibility: Evaluation Criteria and Guidelines. In: Proc. Intl. Conf. on e-Business (ICE-B 2010) (July 2010)

167. Ueki, Y.: E-Business Innovation and Customs Renovation. Executive Report. Chile Division of International Trade (2003)

168. Unger, T., Mietzner, R., Leymann, F.: Customer-defined Service Level Agreements for Composite Applications. Enterprise Information Systems 3(3) (2009)

169. Unhelkar, B., Ginige, A.: A Framework to Derive Holistic Business Transformation Processes. In: Proc. Intl. Conf. on e-Business (ICE-B 2010) (July 2010)

170. Vallecillo, A., Hernández, J., Troya, J.M.: Object Interoperability. In: Yu, H.-J., Demeyer, S. (eds.) ECOOP 1999 Workshops. LNCS, vol. 1743, pp. 1–21. Springer, Heidelberg (1999)

171. Vernadat, F.B.: Technical, Semantic and Organizational Issues of Enterprise Interoperability and Networking. Annual Reviews in Control 34(1) (2010)

172. Vernadat, F.B.: Enterprise Modeling and Integration: Principles and Applications. Chapman & Hall (1996)

173. Vlachopoulou, M.: E-Business Trends Notes. University of Macedonia (2009)

174. Wang, F., Zeng, D., Hendler, J., Zhang, Q., Feng, Z., Gao, Y., Wang, H., Lai, G.: A Study of the Human Flesh Search (HFS) Search Engine. IEEE Computer 43(8) (2010)

175. Wen, Z., Zhou, M., Aggarwal, V.: Context-Aware, Adaptive Information Retrieval for Investigative Tasks. In: Proc. 12th Intl. Conf. Intelligent User Interfaces (January 2007)
176. Whinston, A.: Economics of Electronic Commerce. Pearson Education, Inc. (1997)
177. Wikipedia (2010),
      http://en.wikipedia.org/wiki/Platform_technology
178. Wikipedia (2010),
      http://en.wikipedia.org/wiki/Context_awareness
179. Xiao, L., Wang, Y., Shen, D., Acero, A.: Learning with Click Graph for Query Intent Classification. ACM Trans. for Info. Sys. 28(3) (2010)
180. Yang, H., Lay, Y., Tsao, W., Lay, J.: The Impact of the Internet on Social Anxiety and Learning Adaptability for Young Adult Internet Users. In: Proc. Intl. Conf. on e-Business (ICE-B 2010) (July 2010)
181. Yardi, S., Poole, E.: Patterns of Personalization in an Online Tech Support Board. In: Proc. 4th Intl. Conf. on Communities and Technologies (2009)
182. Yoon, C., Lee, K.: A Measurement Instrument for Individual Information Competency in an Enterprise Information Enviornment. In: Intl. Conf. on e-Business, ICE-B 2010 (2010)
183. Yu, Q., Liu, X., Bouguettaya, A., Medjahed, B.: Deploying and managing Web services. The VLDB Journal 17 (2008)
184. Zachman, J.: A Framework for Information Systems Architecture. IBM Systems Journal 26(3) (1987)
185. Zaščerinska, J., Ahrens, A.: e-Business Applications in Engineering Education. In: Proc. Intl. Conf. on e-Business (ICE-B 2010) (July 2010)
186. Zeiris, E., Ziema, M.: SOA Based e-Business Systems Design. In: Proc. Intl. Conf. on e-Business (ICE-B 2010) (July 2010)
187. Zhao, V., Liny, W., Liuy, K.: Behavior Modeling and Forensics for Multimedia Social Networks: A Case Study in Multimedia Fingerprinting. IEEE Signal Processing Magazine 26(1) (2009)
188. Zunjarwad, A., Sudaram, H., Xie, L.: Contextual Wisdom: Social Relations and Correlations for Multimedia Event Annotation. In: Intl. Conf. on Multimedia (September 2007)
189. Marques Pereira, C., Sousa, P.: A Method to Define an Enterprise Architecture Using the Zachman Framework. In: Proc. of the 2004 ACM Symp. on Applied Computing (2004)
190. Winter, R., Fischer, R.: Essential Layers, Artifacts, and Dependencies of Enterprise Architecture. In: Proc. of the 10th IEEE Intl. EDOC Enterprise Computing Conf. Workshops (2006)
191. Dai, Q., Kauffman, R.J.: Business Models for Internet-based B2B Electronic Markets. International Journal of Electronic Commerce 6(4) (2002)
192. Barros, A.P., Dumas, M.: The Rise of Web Service Ecosystems. IT Prof. 8(5) (2006)
193. Buyya, R., Shin Yeo, C., Venugopal, S.: Market-oriented Cloud Computing: Vision, Hype, and Reality for Delivering IT Services as Computing Utilities. In: Proc. of the 10th IEEE Intl. Conf. on High Performance Computing and Communication (2008)
194. The Open Group. The Open Group Architecture Framework - Part II (Architecture Development Method). Version 8.1.1, Document G063 (2006)
195. Frankel, D.S., et al.: The Zachman Framework and the OMG's Model Driven Architecture. Business Process Trends, White Paper (2003),
      http://www.bptrends.com/

196. Favre, J.-M.: CaCOphoNy: Metamodel-driven Software Architecture Reconstruction. In: Proc. 11th Working Conf. on Reverse Engineering (2004)

197. Fui-Hoon Nah, F., Lee-Lau, J., Kuang, J.: Critical Factors for Successful Implementation of Enterprise Systems. Business Process Management Journal 7(3) (2001)

198. Pateli, A.G., Giaglis, G.M.: A Framework for Understanding and Analysing eBusiness Models. In: Proc. 16th Bled eCommerce Conference (2003)

199. Mutschler, B., Bumiller, J., Reichert, M.U.: Designing an Economic-driven Evaluation Framework for Process-oriented Software Technologies. In: Proc. 28th Intl. Conf. on Software Engineering, ICSE 2006 (2006)

200. Wieringa, R.J., Gordijn, J., van Eck, P.A.T.: Value-Based Business-IT Alignment in Networked Constellations of Enterprises. In: Proc. 1st Intl. Workshop on Requirements Engineering for Business Need and IT Alignment (REBNITA 2005) (2005b)

201. Mantovaneli Pessoa, R., van Sinderen, M., Quartel, D.: Towards Requirements Elicitation in Service-oriented Business Networks Using Value and Goal Modelling. In: Proc. 4th Intl. Conf. on Software and Data Technologies (ICSOFT 2009) (2009)

202. Zlatev, Z., Wombacher, A.: Consistency between e^3-value Models and Activity Diagrams in a Multi-Perspective Development Method. In: Meersman, R., Tari, Z. (eds.) OTM 2005. LNCS, vol. 3760, pp. 520–538. Springer, Heidelberg (2005)

203. Fatemi, H., van Sinderen, M., Wieringa, R.: Value-Oriented Coordination Process Modeling. In: Hull, R., Mendling, J., Tai, S. (eds.) BPM 2010. LNCS, vol. 6336, pp. 162–177. Springer, Heidelberg (2010)

204. Ilayperuma, T., Zdravkovic, J.: Exploring Business Value Models from the Inter-organizational Collaboration Perspective. In: Proc. 2010 ACM Symp. on Applied Computing (2010)

205. Schuster, R., Motal, T., Huemer, C., Werthner, H.: From Economic Drivers to B2B Process Models: A Mapping from REA to UMM. In: Abramowicz, W., Tolksdorf, R. (eds.) BIS 2010. LNBIP, vol. 47, pp. 119–131. Springer, Heidelberg (2010)

206. Johannesson, P., et al.: Enterprise Modelling for Value Based Service Analysis. In: Strina, J., Persson, A. (eds.) PoEM 2008. 15, vol. LNBIP, pp. 153–167. Springer, Heidelberg (2008)

207. Choi, S.-Y., Whinston, A., Stahl, D.: Economics of Electronic Commerce. Macmillan Computer Publishing (1997)

208. Friedman, D., Steed, A., Slater, M.: Spatial Behaviour in Second Life. In: Pelachaud, C., Martin, J.-C., André, E., Chollet, G., Karpouzis, K., Pelé, D. (eds.) IVA 2007. LNCS (LNAI), vol. 4722, pp. 252–263. Springer, Heidelberg (2007)

209. Gavras, A., et al.: Future Internet Research and Experimentation: The FIRE Initiative. ACM SIGCOMMM Computer Communication Review 37(3) (2007)

210. Welbourne, E., et al.: Building the Internet of Things using RFID. IEEE Internet Computing 13(3) (2009)

211. Crowley, J.L., Reignier, P., Coutaz, J.: Context Aware Services. In: True Visions – The Emergence of Ambient Intelligence. Springer, Heidelberg

212. Picinelli, G., Di Vitantonio, G., Mokrushin, L.: Dynamic Service Aggregation in Electronic Marketplaces. Computer Networks 37(2) (2001)

213. Kutvonen, L., Metso, J., Ruokolainen, T.: Inter-Enterprise Collaboration Management in Dynamic Business Networks. In: Chung, S. (ed.) OTM 2005. LNCS, vol. 3760, pp. 593–611. Springer, Heidelberg (2005)

214. Sun, W., et al.: Software as a Service: Configuration and Customization Perspectives. In: Proc. IEEE Congress on Services, Part II. IEEE Computer Society (2008)

Part I

Data Communication Networking

Static Analysis of Routing and Firewall Policy Configurations

Miroslav Sveda, Ondrej Rysavy, Gayan de Silva, Petr Matousek, and Jaroslav Rab

Brno University of Technology, Brno 612 66, Czech Republic
sveda@fit.vutbr.cz
http://www.fit.vutbr.cz/~sveda/

Abstract. Network design that meets customer's security requirements needs careful considerations when configuring routing and filtering rules. This paper deals with an approach to security analysis based on reachability calculations in dynamically routed networks. The contribution consists of proposing routing abstract model that enables to extend existing reachability analysis approaches to obtain a finer approximation. This approximation captures the effect of routing on packets forwarding. Thus in the combination with reachability calculations based on packet filtering analysis it provides valuable information for a network designer on possible security issues in designed network.

1 Introduction

Fundamental steps in network design consist of definition and implementation of routing and access control mechanisms. Network designers are seeking such configurations that would best implement customers requirements, while considering the limits of underlining technologies. The goal is to provide reliable network services as requested. With growing complexity of network designs the task of configuration implementation, maintainance and modification becomes a challenge for network administrators. It is widely understand that network misconfigurations together with device failures stand behind the most of network outages. Implementation of supportive tools that can identify potential configuration problems to the network design process can valuably aid network designers and administrators.

Particularly difficult task is a configuration of firewall rules. Based on analysis of real configuration files, Wool reports on possible threats of incorrectly configured firewalls [25] and provides suggestions for improving the quality of firewalling rules. One of the observations made concerns about the complexity and size of firewall rulesets. He points out difficulty of creating errorless complex firewall configurations. Although Wool considers only a small set of relatively obvious errors, the survey demonstrates that a ruleset having 1000 items includes more than 8 errors in the average.

The paper focuses on the area of automatic analysis of a network that consists of L3 devices (hosts, routers, firewalls etc.) connected by links and, optionally, with firewall rules applied on them. Based on the network configuration and considering dynamic behavior of the network, we can ask questions like "Is this network protected against P2P connections?", "What packets can be delivered to the given host?", "Is this WWW

M.S. Obaidat, G.A. Tsihrintzis, and J. Filipe (Eds.): ICETE 2010, CCIS 222, pp. 39–53, 2012.
© Springer-Verlag Berlin Heidelberg 2012

service accessible under every state of the network?", or "What can cause the unreachability of the important bussiness service?".

Of course, those questions can be partially answered by scanning and testing tools (ping, nmap), or vulnerability assessment tools (Nessus). However, testing can analyze the network only in immediate state, which means in practice, for a fixed configuration. When the topology is changed, the response of the network can be different. In our work we explore how security and safety properties can be verified under every network configuration by employing principles known from program and computer system verification. The model checking [9] is a technique that explores all reachable states and verifies if the properties are satisfied over each possible path to those states. Model checking requires specification of a model and properties to be verified. In our case, the model of network consists of hosts, links, routing information and access control lists. Specifications of properties have form of security policy descriptions expressible in a formal language.

1.1 Our Contribution

Our approach is close to the work by Xie et al. [27], J. Burns [3], and Bera, Ghosh and Dasgupta [6]. Unlike these works we build a model that includes both static and dynamic behavior, i.e. firewall rules and routing information, see [24]. In this model, the verification of reachability properties can be made. In comparison to Ritchey's work (Ritchey and Ammann, 2000) we do not focus on hosts vulnerability and their resistance to attacks, but on stability of services in dynamic networks.

Main contribution of this paper consists in a method that integrates the effect of routing to reachability analysis based on evaluation of distributed access control lists. Contrary to work by Xie et al. [27], where routing is modeled by extending filtering with route related rules, we developed a split model in which the routing information is analyzed from the network wide perspective. The information from routing analysis is employed in reachability analysis implemented by existing methods. This paper is an extension of our previous work published in [22].

1.2 Structure of the Paper

In section 2, we review the state of the art in the area of automatized configuration analaysis of routing and filtering. In section 3, we provide backgrounds and fundamental definitions for the rest of the paper. In section 4, we present overview of our novel approach to routing modeling and analysis. In section 5, we discuss the issue of packet filter represetnation. In section 6, we review the method for analysis of security policies in network models and examine couple of subtle issues in more detail. The paper concludes in section 7, in which we give a summary and present the possible future work.

2   State of the Art

Research in the area of network security and vulnerability detection has been conducted since the beginning of the Internet. Many papers concentrate on detection of vulnerabilities of hosts and their protection against the network attack, see e.g. [23], [30], or [20].

In [28], an automatic deduction of network security executed in Prolog is introduced. The authors define reasoning rules that express semantics of different kinds of exploits. The rules are automatically extracted from the OVAL scanner and the CVE database [17].

Another approach is an automatic generation of network protection in the form of firewall rules as shown in [4]. The security policy is modeled using Model Definition Language as the first step. Then, the model of a network topology is translated into firewall-specific configurations. These configuration files are loaded into real devices (firewalls).

Ritchey and Ammann in [19] explain how model checking can be used to analyze network vulnerabilities. They build a network security model of hosts, connections, attackers and exploits to be misused by the attacker. Security properties are described by temporal logics and verified using the SMV model checker. However, their goal is different from ours. They verify if hosts on the stable network are vulnerable to attacks. In our case we concentrate on dynamically changing networks and reachability of their nodes.

In 1997, Guttman defined a formal method to compute a set of filters for individual devices given a global security policy [12]. To achieve a feasibility, the network is abstracted such that only network areas and border routers occur in a model. This decision reflects naturally the real situation as internal routers usually do not participate in data filtering. Similarly, data flow model is defined in terms of abstract packets, which are described by abstract source and destination addresses and service type. An algorithm computes a feasibility set of packets that can pass all filtering rules along the path. The rectangle abstraction of packet representation makes the procedure practical and efficient.

Yan et.al have developed a tool called FIREMAN [29], which allows to detect misconfigurations in firewall settings. The FIREMAN performs symbolic model checking of the firewall configurations for all possible IP packets and along all possible data paths. The underlaying implementation depends on a Binary Decision Diagram (BDD) library, which efficiently models firewall rules. This tool can reveal intra-firewall inconsistencies as well as misconfiguration that leads to errors at inter-firewall level. The tool can analyze Access Control List (ACL) series on all paths for end-to-end connection thus offering network-wide firewall security verification.

Jeffrey and Samak in [14] aims at analysis firewall configurations using bounded model-checking approach. They focus at reachability and cyclicity properties. To check reachability, it means to find for each rule r a packet p that causes r to fire. To detect cyclicity of firewall configuration, it means to find a packet p which is not matched by any rule of the firewall ruleset. They implemented analysis algorithm by translating the problem to SAT instance and showed that this approach is efficient and comparable to tools based on a BDD representation. Similar work was done by Pozo, Ceballos and Gasca [18] who provided a consistency checking algorithm that can reveal four consistency problems called shadowing, generalization, correlation and independency.

Liu et.al developed a method for formal verification and testing of (distributed) firewall rules (see [16] and [10]) against user provided properties. They represent firewall rules in a structure called firewall decision diagram (FDD), which forms an input to a verification algorithm. Another input is a property rule, which describes a property that they want to check, e.g. description of a set of packets that should pass the firewall. By a single traversing an FDD from the root to a leave it is possible to check the given property.

Xie et.al reports in [26] on their extensive work on static analysis of IP networks. They define a framework able to determine lower and upper approximations on network rechability considering filtering rules, dynamic routing and packet transformations. The method computes a set of packets that can be carried by each link. By combination of these sets along the possible paths between two end points, it is possible to determine the end-to-end reachability. The upper approximation determines the set of packets that could potentially be delivered by the network, while the lower approximation determines the set of packets that could be delivered under all possible forwarding states. In their paper, the authors also present a refinement of both upper and lower approximations by considering the effect of dynamic routing.

Bera, Dasgupta and Ghosh (see [7], and [6]) define a verification framework for filtering rules that allows one to check the correctness of distributed ACL implementations against the given global security policy and also to check reliability (or fault tolerance) of services in a network. To check the correctness, the filtering rules are translated to assertions in the form of first order logical formulas. They are together with logical description of global security policy sent to SAT solver that mechanically checks the satisfiability. In the case of an inconsistency, the SAT solver produces a counter example that helps an administrator with debugging ACL rules. To check the reliability, the framework accepts a description of a global security policy, a collection of ACL rules and a network description and computes whether the rules are consistent with the given policy. Policy is understood as a description of service availability with respect to defined network zones. The method used computes first a network access model, which is a directed graph with ACLs assigned to its edges. Next, the service flow graphs (SFG) are generated for all services in the interest, e.g. SFG for ssh traffic. An SFG is a subgraph of the network accesss graph. The fault analysis is performed by computing minimum cuts in all SFGs. These values then represent how many link failures can be tolerated.

3 Backgrounds

In this section, we establish some basic facts and definitions that we use in the development presented in the paper. We first define terminology required to understand the problem formulation and the method proposed. We then describe a graph model for computing reachability. At the end of the section, we define the concept of forwarding states, which captures the dynamics of the network and creates a framework for what-if analysis.

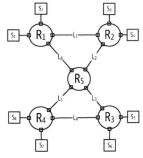

(a) Network Topology

$\mathcal{F}$	Links	$\mathcal{F}$	Links	$\mathcal{F}$	Links
f_{12}^{L}	$L_1 \rightarrow L_2$	f_{12}^{S}	$S_1 \rightarrow S_2$	f_{11}^{SL}	$S_1 \rightarrow L_1$
f_{21}^{L}	$L_2 \rightarrow L_1$	f_{21}^{S}	$S_2 \rightarrow S_1$	f_{11}^{LS}	$L_1 \rightarrow S_1$
$\vdots$	$\vdots$	$\vdots$	$\vdots$	$\vdots$	$\vdots$
f_{54}^{L}	$L_5 \rightarrow L_4$	f_{87}^{S}	$S_8 \rightarrow S_7$	f_{58}^{SL}	$L_5 \rightarrow S_8$
f_{45}^{L}	$L_4 \rightarrow L_5$	f_{78}^{S}	$S_7 \rightarrow S_8$	f_{85}^{LS}	$S_8 \rightarrow L_5$

(b) Filter map

Fig. 1. A Simple Network Example

3.1 Terminology

We assume that networks under analysis consist of intermediate devices (routers) that forward packets through the network according their internal knowledge. We assume that routers can be configured with a mix of static and dynamic routing information. In the present paper, we use the following terms which refer to various routing related concepts:

- *Local Routing Information Base (RIB)* is stored in routing process address space running on a router. Each process has its own RIB, e.g. RIP maintains RIP database. Similarly, *local Forwarding Information Base (FIB)* is a single datatable, which is used by a router to decide where to forward incoming packets.
- *Network RIB/FIB* is a network wide view of routing information. This represents a shared routing knowledge of forwarding devices. Similarly, network FIB represents a global view on routing information that governs forwarding packets in the entire network.
- *Forwarding device* is a network device that actively decides where to forward packets based on its local routing information stored in FIB.
- *Redistribution* stands for copying route information to a target protocol instance, which is done in the scope of a single router.
- *Reachability Set* is a set of packets that can be delivered to the given network location.
- *Routing instance* is a collection of routing processes of the same type on different devices. They share the routing information in order to create the consistent view on (a part of) network.

3.2 Abstract Network Model

The abstract model of the network dealing with routing processes and packet filtering stems from a combination of techniques introduced in [27] and [8]. The network is regarded as a directed hypergraph where vertices are routing devices and edges are communication channels that form abstractions of communication links. In real networks there are other network device then routers. However, every end-point device, such as PC or Web server, can be represented using a router with only one interface, and one outgoing filtering rule representing routing all traffic to a default gateway. Formally, an *abstract network model*, see example in Figure 1, is a tuple $N = \langle R_N, L_N, F_N \rangle$, where

- R_N is a finite set of network devices,
- L_N is a finite set of links between routers, and
- $F_N : L_N \times L_N \to \mathcal{F}$ is a function assigning to each pair of links a filter from the set of filters $\mathcal{F}$.

Filters can have various represetation. For instance, similarly to [26], we can define filters to be reachability sets. A reachability set is a set of all packets that are permited by the filter. There are defined standard operations on such set; thus, it is possible to compute a reachability set over a collection of filters by applying the intersection operation. Benson, Akella and Maltz in [5] showed the symbolic computation of reachability sets based on normalized ACL representation. Other approach, which is used in this paper represents filters as logical formulas, e.g.

$$(dst\_adr \in 10.10.23.0/24 \vee dst\_adr \in 10.10.12.0/24) \wedge proto = udp \wedge dst\_port = 53$$

that allows only IP packets destined for 10.10.23.0/24 and 10.10.12.0/24 subnetworks carrying UDP datagrams with destination port 53. Such representation stands for the characteristic formula of the corresponding reachability set. In section 5, we deal with this representation in more detail.

3.3 Forwarding State

A forwarding state describes a condition of a network determined by a content of network forwarding information base (NFIB). In general, the content of NFIB for the given network depends on the health of devices, state of links, and external routing information pumped into the network.

Consider again the toy network in Figure 1. All routers is running RIP and exchange all information on connected subnetworks. We show how the NFIB depends on the state of links. RIP uses hop count metrics and thus the shortest path from S_1 to S_6 found is $\langle S_1, R_1, L_6, R_5, L_3, R_3, S_6 \rangle$. This path is placed in NFIB. If links L_6 and L_3 were unavailable then NFIB would contain longer path $\langle S_1, R_1, L_1, R_2, L_2, R_5, L_5, R_4, L_4, R_3, S_6 \rangle$. Similarly for other paths we can define NFIB for two forwarding states q and r as follows:

q	S_1	...	S_6	...
S_1	·	...	R_1, L_6, R_5, L_3, R_3	...
⋮	⋮	⋮	⋮	⋮

r	S_1	...	S_6	...
S_1	·	...	$R_1, L_1, R_2, L_2, R_5, L_5, R_4, L_4, R_3$	...
⋮	⋮	⋮	⋮	⋮

It is possible that different combinations of link states or device failures can lead to the same forwarding state. It is because links have different topological importance for packet forwarding. The assesment of links and routers from the viewpoint of their importance on traffic delivery was done, e.g. in [21]. In this paper, we do not deal with packet transformations, which is performed by the network gateways such as NAT gateway or MPLS routers. This would complicated the representation of NFIB and we left it for future work.

4 Routing Approximation

Geoffrey G.Xie et al. in [27] showed that routing information can be added to the static model of the network using additional filtering rules. These filtering rules can be changed as the state of links is changed, so the filtering rules depend on the actual state of the network. In this paper, we present an alternate approach to approximate routing. Instead of simulating routing protocols to find the content of routers' FIBs, we compute the network RIBs and network FIBs directly by using standard graph algorithms.

4.1 Routing Protocols

Routing protocols employ distributive algorithms to compute the common view on a network in each engaged router. In the simplest case, when no customization of routing is applied the routers compute the shortest path to every known destination with respect to the defined metrics. If the network changes its state, which is triggered by, for instance, link or device failure, the routers engage in the process of disseminating updates and computing new local routing tables.

Configuration of dynamic routing protocols can include number of options that affect the distribution of routing data. For instance, configuring passive interfaces prevents a router to send RIP updates through this interface thus the connected routers are not informed about the routing related events. Similarly, using ACL to filter outgoing routing updates can be used to customize the routing information that spreads from the router. Different instances of routing protocols implicitly do not share routing information. Nevertheless, route redistribution can be configured to insert a selected routing information from a source RIB to a destination RIB whithin a router.

A router selects and installs the best route from a collection of local RIBs based on the defined priorities. This route is then used for packet forwarding, which means to determine links used for forwarding packets to their destinations.

4.2 Calculation of Routing Approximation

Our aim is to determine a reachability matrix that would contain all best paths between pairs of destinations in a given forwarding state induced by the current state of links and routers. We use a cost-path pair for representing a forwarding path in the reachability matrix. This reachability matrix corresponds to a network-wide view of the Forward information base (FIB). The calculation is performed in several steps as follows:

1. computation of network RIBs for static routing information,
2. computation of network RIBs for every routing instance, and
3. (repeated) application of the effect of redistribution and selection of the best paths to the network FIB.

Now, we give some details for these computational steps. Generally, in every step we begins with defining an adjacency matrix, which can be obtained directly from the analysis of configuration files. Then, the standard graph algorithm, efor instance, Floyd-Warshall's algorithm [11] with $|V|^3$ time complexity, is applied to get all shortest paths.

Depending on the step, we get either resulting reachability matrix or we need to (iterativelly) perform an additional update operation and a recalculation of RIBs.

Calculation of Static RIBs. A static route configuration is analyzed and the adjacency matrix Adj_S for every destination S is constructed. If router R has defined a static route for destination S such that packets should be forwarded by link L, which connects router Q, then $Adj_S[R, Q] = 1$. A RIB matrix is computed for every unique adjacency matrix. A static reachability matrix for destination(s) S, RIB_S^{Static}, is initialized with adjacency matrix and then the transitive closure is computed. During the compution the usual path concatenation operation is used. A column $RIB_S^{Static}[*, S]$ then defines all possible forwarding paths to the destination S from any node in the network. This matrix defines a reachability graph, which can be discontinued depending on the completeness of information implemented by static routing configuration.

Calculation of Dynamic RIBs. Network RIBs that correspond to dynamic routing protocols is computed using the same techniques but in a different way. Adjacency matrix, Adj_S^P, of routing instance P for each destination S, is determined by analysis adjacency among routing processes within a routing instance. If there are no routing update filters then it is sufficient to consider a single adjacency matrix Adj^P. We will consider the case, in which routing update filters are deployed in the network.

Route update filtering works by regulating the route advertisments sent to neighboring routers and filtering routes advertised by other routers before they are added or updated in the local routing protocol database. Route update filters have only effect on distance vector protocols [1]. In our model, a routing update filter eliminates some adjacencies in an adjacency matrix. Considering the example network. If there is a routing update filter from R_1 to R_2 that denies to propagate information about destination S_2 then $Adj_{S_2}^P$ will have no adjacency from R_2 to R_1. In other words, the adjacency is removed in the opposite order to the effect of routing update filter.

In real world scenario not all networks are filtered or a single filter affects multiple networks. Therefore, we can lower the overall computational complexity by collecting all networks that are treated in the same way, which can be again implemented by grouping networks that have the same adjacency matrix.

Redistribution and Route Selection. The redistribution mechanism is vendor dependend, but most platforms obey two additional rules when doing redistribution: i) The route can only be redistributed if it is installed in routers FIB. ii) Even if a route is redistributed in the routing process with lower AD this new route is not installed into routers FIB. These two rules cause that redistribution is not transitive as pointed out by Le, Xie and Zhang in [15], which requires some additional steps in the reachability computation.

Redistribution configure d on router R_v, which redistributes routing information from RIB_s to RIB_t causes to insert paths at row v of matrix RIB_s to corresponding items in matrix RIB_t if these paths have lower costs and can be found in the network FIB. The impact of redistribution rules is best observable in the process of route selection. The route selection finds the most appropriate information from local RIBs and puts it in the routers FIB. Redistribution then must check whether the information that can be redistributed was selected for FIB to conform with rule i). To satisfy rule ii) the route selection must not choose redistributed network into the FIB.

Among all information in all local RIBs, the router needs to select a single (or a collection of alternate paths for load balancing) route to its FIB. This process is vendor dependent but most often the routing information is prioritized by using administrative distance (AD) measure.

A computation of the network FIB means to implement an abstract route selection process. Informally, the computation proceeds as follows:

1. Take the lowest priority network RIB and copy all information to the network FIB. This will initialize the network FIB.
2. Take a RIB with immediately higher priority and replace paths in the FIB with existing paths in this RIB. This corresponds to the selection of route information with less administrative distance. If there is not path in this RIB then the path from a lower priority RIB remains in the FIB.
3. For each path in the RIB we must also check if this path can replace a suffix in an existing path in the FIB. This means, that if the FIB contains a path $\langle r1, r4, r2, r5, r3 \rangle$ and the RIB contains a path $\langle r4, r7, r8, r9, r3 \rangle$ we should replace the FIBs path with $\langle r1, r2, r4, r7, r8, r9, r3 \rangle$. This replacement corresponds to installation of a route with lower AD in athe router on the existing path.
4. Repeat from step 2 until we process all RIBs.

Information stored in the network FIB (network reachability matrix) can be used to determine paths to all destinations. Forwarding state is uniquely determined by content of the network FIB.

5 Representation of Packet Filters

In this section, we review an existing methods to packet filter representation and develop a simple but efficient method for capturing the semantics of packet filters that is suitable for our network design validation method.

5.1 List-Based Packet Filters

A list-based packet filter (firewalls) consists of rules imposing network security policies ordered by the priority, which depends on the rule's position within the list. Although there may be other kinds of packet filters, we assume the most common case, in which evaluation of packet filters is based on the first match principle. This means that an action of the highest priority rule that matches the analyzed packet is executed.

Each rule is a multidimensional structure. Dimensions are sets of network fields, e.g., source and destination adresses, port numbers, protocol type, or an action field, e.g., accept, deny, redirection. A typical rule can be formally defined as a tuple $\langle src, dst, srv, act \rangle$, where src and dst are set of addresses, srv is a set of services, and act is an action.

Packet filters can suffer from conflicts and dependencies, which complicate its analysis. The goal of packet filter preprocessing is to remove conflicts, redundancies and dependencies such that we avoid the need to evaluate the rules in the imposed order. If the resulting rule set is completely disjoint then it is possible to use a straightforward transformation into logical representation as will be shown at the end of this section. First, we discuss a method to obtain the disjoint rule set from an ordinary rule set.

We discuss the method proposed in [18]. The method consists of two steps. The first step isolates the possibly conflicting rules and figures out their dependencies. Two rules are potentially conflicting, if both rules have different actions and one rule is either subsumed by another or there is an nonempty intersection in one or more dimensions. The result of the first step is a conflicting graph.

The second step analyses the conflicting graph to identify a minimal set of rules that generate inconsistencies with another rules. The result is a collection of two level trees. Each root and leaf pair of trees defines a conflict that needs to be properly characterized to propose a modification that would remove the conflict making these rules independent.

The commonn approach to make the rule independent (disjoint) is to split conflicting rules into more rules and remove conflicting parts. This phase may be followed by merging process in order to optimize the rule set representation as the previous splitting may unecessary increase the rule set size. Note that the similar approach is taken also for redundancy elimination as shown in [2].

5.2 Logical Representations of Rule Sets

Semantics of rule set consisting only of independent rules is invariant to rule ordering. We will use this property to define for each rule set its logical representation. This representation has form of formula of propositional logic in disjunctive normal form.

Recall that filtering rule is a tuple with network fields. In the simplest case it consists of selectors, namely, source address set, destination address set, service set, and the action. A logical formula that is a translation of a simple rule $r = \langle s, d, v, a \rangle$ consists of a conjunction of all selectors. A selector is represented by a predicate that extracts required network fields from some packet p. thus, for rule r the formula is written as follows:

$$src\_adr(p) \in s \wedge dst\_adr(p) \in d \wedge service(p) \in v.$$

A list of possible selector functions in shown in Table 1

We adapt a network-mask convention for representation of a set of continuous addresses. For instance, it allows us to consider 147.229.12.0/24 as a set of addresses ranging from 147.229.12.0 to 147.229.12.255. We can use the standard set operations, e.g.,

Table 1. Network Field Selectors

Function	Description
$dst\_adr(p)$	Destination adress of a packet p.
$src\_adr(p)$	Source address of a packet p.
$dst\_port(p)$	Destination port of udp or tcp datagram carried in packet p.
$src\_port(p)$	Source port of udp or tcp datagram carried in packet p.
$service(p)$	Service of a packet p.

$src\_adr(p) \in 147.229.12.0/24$ or $dst\_adr(p) \in 147.12.28.0/24 \cup 147.12.30.0/24$. The latter can be expanded to $dst\_adr(p) \in 147.12.28.0/24 \vee dst\_adr(p) \in 147.12.30.0/24$, which allows us to use network-mask format for canonical address set representation.

Often, rule sets implicitly assume the existence of a default rule, which has the lowes priority and matches all packets not hitting by the other rules. While the previously described methods cope with default rules transparently, it may cause to split the default rule in a large number of rules appearing in a disjoint rule set. To overcome this issue we ignore the default rule in the process of conflicting rule elimination and consider it again when we compute a logical representation.

A logical representation can be either *positive*, representing all accepted packets or *negative* representing all denied packets. The most commonly, we want to compute a positive representation of rule sets with default deny all rule. In this case we only select all rules with *allow* action and calculate the logical representation for these rules. It completely eliminates the need to take care of the default rule.

6 Analysis of Security Policies

Packet filters implement basic level of security policies in the network. By restricting the accessibility of certain services, computers or subnetworks, we deploy rough but efficient security measures.

Our network model deals only with IP addresses and services or ports. Therefore, the analysis does not reflect hardware or OS attacks. We also don't examine the contents of TCP/UDP packets although it is possible to extend the description to support this. Our primary goal is verify safety or resistance of the network with respect to the effect of dynamic routing. Therefore, our classification includes only basic categories of network security properties. Since it can utilize typical fields from IP, TCP, or UDP headers, namely source/destination IP address and service/port [24], it allows to specify wide range of different communications to be analyzed in the network.

6.1 Reachability Sets

As proposed in [26] the output of reachability analysis and thus the input for consecutive security properties analysis consists of a collection of reachability sets for forwarding paths in an analyzed network. There are various methods to calculate reachability sets. In the following we discuss several issues related to this calculation. We first overview the problem of efficient address representation and rule sets representation. Then, we give an idea of security properties verification and its position with respect to routing analysis and reachability analysis.

Address Scheme. An approach invented by Guttman in [12] deals with *abstract address* scheme. An abstract address is the symbolic name of a host or a subnetwork, which avoids the need to explicitly deal with a huge ip address space, which consists of 2^{32} all unique addresses. An abstract packet consists of an abstract source address, an abstract destination address, a service identification, and a flow orientation, which is either client to server, or server to client. This approach leads to very reasonable complexity in representation depending on the size of a network and mainly on the number of interesting destinations and services. For instance, considering a network with N different distinguished addresses, S different distinguished services, then we get an abstract packet space of size $N^2 \cdot 2S$.

A different approach is to explicitly represent the IP address space by bit variables each for a single bit in the address as used, for instance, by Bera, Ghosh and Dasgupta in [6]. This means that a packet is defined by bit variables $s_1, \ldots, s_{32}$ representing a source address, bit variables $d_1, \ldots d_{32}$ representing a destination address, and a vector of bit variables, $v_1, \ldots, v_n$ of the appropriate length n, representing a service. A flow direction may be modeled separately by a single bit variable or encoded in the service vector. In this way, we have an explicit representation not only for each packet but also for each network set represented in network-mask format.

Rule Sets Representation. Independently on whether we use abstract address representation or explicit representation, we construct logical formula for each rule set as discussed at the end of section 5. Each such formula can be encoded as a SAT instance using the boolean reduction approach, which is defined in detail for explicit address scheme in [7]. If we use the abstract address scheme we model each abstract address by a single boolean variable.

These two approaches thus differ by the number of boolean variables of generated SAT instances. While explicit representation requires the fixed number of variables, the number of variables used by abstract approach depends on the number of abstract addresses. On the other hand, the former may generate a large number of clauses while the latter tends to keep number of clauses smaller. It remains for future work to analyze and compare both approaches from the practical perspective on real scale data.

Verification of Security Policies. Capabilities of used network abstract model allows us to verify security properties that can be expressed in terms of service reachability. Contrary to most of the related work and in the similar way as Xie et al. in [27], we consider a tighter approximation of reachability sets obtained from estimation of routing in a given forwarding state.

In general, our verification method stands for checking whether a service is guaranteed under some assumption on connectivity. This assumption is converted to forwarding state by the method described in section 4. Each forwarding state consists of a set of active forwarding paths encoded in a path reachability matrix (denoted as network FIB). For any forwarding state it is possible to perform reachability analysis to determine the conditions leading to security violations.

In general, the considered analysis method can determine for every path the reachability for the given packet definition. Based on this, it is, for instance, possible:

- to perform security policy verification as proposed by Gutmann [12].
- to verify the access control based security implementations in a similar way as done by Bera, Ghosh and Dasgupta in [6], and
- to compute reachability estimations as shown by Xie at al. in [26].

In general, computing upper and lower bound, which means to consider all paths or finding at least a single path satisfying reachability condition, enables to verify the security policy implementation. However, considering routing effect allows us to find a particular network state in which security policy violation is detected. This gives a network designer refined information that aids him to find the configuration problem. Integration of routing model to the analysis process represents the main contribution of the presented work.

7 Summary

In this paper, we demonstrate the problem of automatic security analysis of IP based computer networks. The presented verification method aims at validating network design against the absence of security and configuration flaws. The network model allows describing effects of static and dynamic routing and access control lists configured on the network devices. The verification technique is based on the encoding problem into SAT instance solved by automatized solvers. Discussed procedure aims at refining of the approximation models proposed in [27],[6], [13], [3], and [16] to include routing effects, which would allow network designers to get an insight to issue of interweaving routing and filtering, and the impact on network security properties. Although not validated on real scale cases, we believe the application of the presented approach is feasible for a large class of network models and properties. Further work is aimed at refining the method to experimental implementation and performing experiments to evaluate its performance and scalability.

Acknowledgements. This project has been carried out with a financial support from the Czech Republic state budget through the CEZ MMT project no. MSM0021630528: Security-Oriented Research in Information Technology, by the Grant Agency of the Czech Republic through the grant no. GACR 102/08/1429: Safety and Security of Networked Embedded System Applications, and by the Brno University of Technology, Faculty of Information Technology through the specific research grant no. FIT-10-S-1: Secured, Reliable and Adaptive Computer Systems. Also, the first co-author was supported by the grant no. FR-TI1/037 of Ministry of Industry and Trade: Automatic Attack Processing.

References

1. Filtering routing updates on distance vector ip routing protocols. Cisco Systems, Document ID:9105 (September 2006)
2. Acharya, S., Wang, J., Ge, Z., Znati, T., Greenberg, A.: Simulation study of firewalls to aid improved performance. In: 39th Annual Simulation Symposium, 2006, p. 8 (2006)

3. Burns, J., et al.: Automatic management of network security policy. In: DARPA Information Survivability Conference and Exposition, pp. 1012–1026 (2001)
4. Bartal, Y., Mayer, A., Nissim, K., Wool, A.: Firmato: A Novel Firewall Management Toolkit. In: IEEE Symposium on Security and Privacy, pp. 17–31 (1999), citeseer.ist.psu.edu/article/bartal99firmato.html
5. Benson, T., Akella, A.: Unraveling the complexity of network management. In: NSDI 2009: Proceedings of the 6th USENIX Symposium on Networked Systems Design and Implementation (2009), http://portal.acm.org/citation.cfm?id=1559000
6. Bera, P., Ghosh, S., Dasgupta, P.: Formal analysis of security policy implementations in enterprise networks. International Journal of Computer Networks and Communications 1(2), 56–73 (2009)
7. Bera, P., Ghosh, S., Dasgupta, P.: Formal Verification of Security Policy Implementations in Enterprise Networks. In: Prakash, A., Sen Gupta, I. (eds.) ICISS 2009. LNCS, vol. 5905, pp. 117–131. Springer, Heidelberg (2009)
8. Christiansen, M., Fleury, E.: An Interval Decision Diagram Based Firewall. In: 3rd International Conference on Networking (ICN 2004). IEEE (February 2004)
9. Clarke, E., Grumberg, O., Peled, D.: Model Checking. MIT Press (1999)
10. Gouda, M., Liu, A.X., Jafry, M.: Verification of distributed firewalls. In: Proceedings of the IEEE Global Communications Conference (GLOBECOM), New Oreleans, Louisiana (November 2008)
11. Gross, L., Yellen, J. (eds.): Handbook of Graph Theory. CRC Press (2004)
12. Guttman, J.D.: Filtering postures: Local enforcement for global policies. In: Proceedings of 1997 IEEE Symposium on Security and Privacy, pp. 120–129. IEEE Computer Society Press (1997)
13. Guttman, J.D.: Filtering postures: Local enforcement for global policies. In: IEEE Symposium on Security and Privacy, pp. 120–129 (1997)
14. Jeffrey, A., Samak, T.: Model checking firewall policy configurations. In: IEEE International Workshop on Policies for Distributed Systems and Networks, pp. 60–67 (2009)
15. Le, F., Xie, G., Zhang, H.: Understanding route redistribution. In: IEEE International Conference on Network Protocols, ICNP 2007, pp. 81–92 (2007)
16. Liu, A.X.: Formal verification of firewall policies. In: Proceedings of the 2008 IEEE International Conference on Communications (ICC), Beijing, China (May 2008)
17. Mitre: Common Vulnerabilities and Exposures Database, http://cve.mitre.org/ (accessed on February 2008)
18. Pozo, S., Ceballos, R., Gasca, R.: Fast algorithms for consistency-based diagnosis of firewalls rule sets. In: Proceedings of the 3rd International Conference on Availability, Reliability and Security, ARES (2008)
19. Ritchey, R.W., Ammann, P.: Using model checking to analyze network vulnerabilities. In: IEEE Symposium on Security and Privacy, Washington, USA (2000)
20. Shahriari, H.R., Sadoddin, R., Jalili, R., Zakeri, R., Omidian, A.R.: Network Vulnerability Analysis through Vulnerability Take-Grant Model (VTG). In: Qing, S., Mao, W., López, J., Wang, G. (eds.) ICICS 2005. LNCS, vol. 3783, pp. 256–268. Springer, Heidelberg (2005), citeseer.ist.psu.edu/749214.html
21. de Silva, G., Sveda, M., Matousek, P., Rysavy, O.: Formal analysis approach on networks with dynamic behaviours. In: Proceeding of the 2nd International Workshop on Reliable Networks Design and Modeling (2010)
22. Sveda, M., Rysavy, O., Matousek, P., Rab, J., Cejka, R.: Security analysis of tcp/ip networks – an approach to automatic analysis of network security properties. In: Proceedings of the International Conference on Data Communication Networking 2010, pp. 5–11. Institute for Systems and Technologies of Information, Control and Communication (2010)

23. Tidwell, T., Larson, R., Fitch, K., Hale, J.: Modeling Internet attacks. In: Proc. of the IEEE Workshop on Information Assurance and Security, West Point, NY (2001)
24. Čejka, R., Matoušek, P., Ráb, J., Ryšavý, O., Švéda, M.: A formal approach to network security analysis. Tech. rep. (2008), http://www.fit.vutbr.cz/research/view_pub.php?id=8572
25. Wool, A.: A quantitative study of firewall configuration errors. Computer 37, 62–67 (2004)
26. Xie, G.G., Zhan, J., Maltz, D.A., Zhang, H., Greenberg, A., Hjalmtysson, G., Rexford, J.: On static reachability analysis of ip networks. In: Proc. IEEE INFOCOM (2005)
27. Xie, G., Zhan, J., Maltz, D., Zhang, H., Greenberg, A., Hjalmtysson, G., Rexford, J.: On static reachability analysis of ip networks. In: INFOCOM, pp. 2170–2183 (2005)
28. Ou, X., Govindavajhala, S., Appel, A.W.: MulVAL: A logic-based network security analyzer. In: Proc. of the 14th USENIX Security Symposium, Baltimore (2005), citeseer.ist.psu.edu/article/bartal99firmato.html
29. Yuan, L., Chen, H.: Fireman: a toolkit for firewall modeling and analysis. In: Proceedings of IEEE Symposium on Security and Privacy, pp. 199–213 (2006)
30. Zakeri, R., Shahriari, H., Jalili, R., Sadoddin, R.: Modeling TCP/IP Networks Topology for Network Vulnerability Analysis. In: 2nd Int. Symposium of Telecommunications, pp. 653–658 (2005), citeseer.ist.psu.edu/749214.html

Threshold Based Multipath Routing Algorithm in Mobile Adhoc and Sensor Networks

Bayrem Triki, Slim Rekhis, and Noureddine Boudriga

Communication Networks and Security Research Lab
University of Carthage, Tunisia
{bayrem.triki,nab}@supcom.rnu.tn, slim.rekhis@isetcom.rnu.tn

Abstract. While communicating nodes in Mobile Adhoc and Sensor Networks (MASNets), need to use multipath routing algorithms to tolerate nodes and links failures, it becomes interesting to let them specify to which extent these paths should be disjoint. Such feature is of high importance as it allows nodes to cope with the sensitivity of the used applications and the variation of the nodes density depending on the network area.

We develop in this paper a new secure multipath algorithm, which allows nodes in MASNet to perform an on-demand discovery and generation of a set of paths, while specifying a disjointness threshold, representing the maximal number of nodes shared between any two paths in the set of the k established paths. The algorithm, which is called Secure Multipath Routing Algorithm for Mobile Adhoc and Sensor Networks (SeMuRAMAS), is adaptive, secure, and uses labels to carry the disjointness-threshold between nodes during the route discovery. A set of security mechanisms, based on the use of Watchdog and digital signature, are used to protect the route discovery process. The conducted simulation estimates the additional overhead, showing the efficiency of the algorithm.

Keywords: k-x-connectivity, Multipath routing, Watchdog, Threshold signature, Mobile Adhoc and Sensor networks.

1 Introduction

In Mobile and Adhoc Networks (MASNets) mobile nodes undergo limiting factors related to the infrastructureless architecture and the dynamic network topology. Maintaining the availability of routes in MASNet during network runtime represents a challenging problem. In fact, they may be easily broken due to nodes mobility, links and nodes failure, and radio interference. In addition, links could have limited bandwidth and network congestions could led to resource starvation in nodes. Multipath routing algorithms were proposed to alleviate nodes these problems[1], making a node able to establish and use simultaneously k paths to the destination[2]. The main objectives of such algorithms is to enforce fault tolerance, load balancing, and end-to-end delivery delay minimization[3]. One the k paths are established, a node sends datagrams redundantly over the alternative paths to enhance the reachability probability[4].

Several multipath routing algorithms were proposed in the literature. For instance, Multipath On-Demand Routing Algorithm (MDR) [5] ensures the establishment of disjoint paths between the source and the destination. It splits the original data packet into

M.S. Obaidat, G.A. Tsihrintzis, and J. Filipe (Eds.): ICETE 2010, CCIS 222, pp. 54–70, 2012.
© Springer-Verlag Berlin Heidelberg 2012

k parts and sends these new sub-packets instead of the whole packet across available paths. The destination, which eventually receive one of the route request messages, will only be aware of the existence of a path. It returns a route reply containing a supplementary field that indicates the number of hops it traveled so far. Each node that receives a route reply, increments the hop count of the message and then forwards the message to the neighbor from which it got the original route request. This solution may cause a lot of overhead in the network. In dynamic multi-path source routing (DMSR) [6], each node must write its bandwidth into forwarded packets in order to find better paths based on the available bandwidth. Best Effort Geographical Routing Protocol (BEGHR) exploits nodes position to forward data, and requires the use of a positioning system such as Global Position Systems (GPS). However, the demands for resources at the different nodes are quite high, which affect battery lifetime. Label-based Multipath Routing (LMR) [7] broadcasts a control message throughout the network for a possible alternative path. It defines a lexicographic total order on the label for each node. The destination should have the minimum label. If a node is a local minimum with respect to its neighbors, it will not have a path to the destination. In this case, it increases its label and reverses some or all of its links. The number of routing paths can be two or more but with relatively long end to end transmission delay.

In MASNets, the mobility of nodes could, not only affect the maximal number of paths that could be established between any source and destination nodes, but also the extent to which these paths are disjoint. The sensitivity of the used applications and the variation of the nodes density from a network location to another, makes it important to extend the multipath routing algorithms so that a new parameter, called disjointness threshold (represent the maximal number of nodes shared between any two paths in the set of the k established paths), will be specified and exploited during the routes discovery to create a trade-off between fault-tolerance and performance.

We develop in this paper a Secure Multipath Routing Algorithm for Mobile Adhoc and Sensor Networks (SeMuRAMAS), which allows nodes in MASNet to perform an on-demand discovery and generation of a set of paths, while specifying both of the number of separate paths k to establish and the disjointness threshold x. A new concept called $k - x$-connectivity is therefore introduced. The algorithm is adaptive, secure, and uses labels to carry the disjointness-threshold between nodes during the route discovery. SeMuRAMAS exploits the watchdog concept to tolerate several types of routing attacks, and uses threshold signature, including the elliptic threshold signature algorithms, to protect the integrity of the exchanged datagrams and prevent attackers from forging routes. The conducted simulation estimates the additional overhead, showing the efficiency of the algorithm.

The paper contribution is sixth-fold. First, the proposed multipath routing algorithm is adaptive according to the network topology. It allows a source node to tune the disjointness threshold to a suitable value before establishing a path and sending data. The value of the threshold may depend on the sensitivity of the message to be sent, or the rate of broken routes during previous communications. Second, thanks to the use of the watchdog mechanism and digital signature, the algorithm is secure. In the WSNs, threshold signature does not require an extensive number of stored keys per sensor node. The technique of sur-signature could be used for the generation of evidences, which could be used by a digital investigation scheme to prove the identity of malicious nodes and trace and analyze the attack. Third, the algorithm is tolerant to a large set of routing attacks such as wormhole. Fourth, SeMuRAMAS takes into consideration the characteristics of Adhoc and wireless sensor networks, in terms of architecture, nodes resources limitation, and categories of attacks. Fifth, the variation of the network topology could make nodes unable to establish multiple disjointness paths to the destination. If the MASNet is used for some application requiring a high level of tolerance to nodes and link failures, by tuning the value of the disjointness threshold, nodes could cope with topology variation and continue benefiting from a degraded level of tolerance. Sixth, in the case of the absence of paths with specified threshold, the proposed algorithm advices the source node about the optimal disjointness value supported by the current MASNet topology to ensure the connectivity between the source and the destination mobile nodes.

The remaining part of the paper is organized as follows. The next section describes the requirements to be fulfilled by a secure and multipath routing algorithm. Section 3 describes the proposed routing algorithm. Section 4, presents security mechanisms used by the proposed algorithm. In Section 5, a validation of the proposed algorithm is addressed. Section 6 presents and discusses simulation results. The last section concludes the work.

2   Requirements of k-x-Connectivity

This section describes the requirements to be fulfilled by a multipath routing algorithm based on the concept of k-x-connectivity.

First, although Adhoc and wireless sensor networks could be infrastructureless-based, and use multihop communication, they may show many differences including in terms of available computational resources, battery energy available on nodes, and security of the area in which the network is deployed. Since the proposed algorithm should be operational on both Adhoc and wireless sensor networks, it should take into consideration those constraints specific to WSN.

Second, the proposed algorithm should be tolerant to attacks on routing protocols. In wormhole attacks, for instance, a node can perform a high-powered transmission of a route request datagram to a non neighbor node, forcing the routing algorithm to include it in the established routing path. This attack makes the malicious node to appear as a highly connected node, while, in reality, it is connected to few number of nodes. In this context, the proposed multipath algorithm should verify that packets are properly forwarded in the networks and identities of intermediate nodes are appended securely to the routing requests. Third, the algorithm should include the generation of evidences regarding the identities and behavior nodes involved during the establishment of the multiple routes. This is of utmost importance if a digital investigation scheme is used to traceback an occurred attack, locate the malicious nodes, and prove the existence of fake routes.

Fourth, it would be better that the algorithm be reactive rather than proactive. In fact, the source node is usually the node that specifies the disjointness threshold value. This value may depend on the sensitiveness of the data to be transmitted from a session to another. . Fifth, the algorithm must be distributed where intermediate nodes should start learning and gathering information regarding potential available path as soon as the route request datagrams propagate. In the case of WSNs, nodes have limited energy, and consequently limited network lifetime, it is essential to share routes computation tasks between nodes. In addition, distributed computation have a better chance to withstand failure in the case of attacks. Sixth, the routing algorithm must preserve the network performance. Especially, the overhead caused by the storage of information regarding potential usable routes, and the distributed computation of the routing paths by intermediate nodes in the networks, should be reduced.

Seventh, If the source node fails to establish a set of paths with the specified threshold value, the algorithm should allow it to receive an indication regarding the minimal disjointness value supported by the current network topology. Such a mechanism will prevent the source node from generating additional failed and overloading the network bandwidth.

3   Description of the Proposed Routing Algorithm

The proposed multipath routing algorithm, SeMuRAMAS, extends the Dynamic Source Routing (DSR) [8] algorithm, which is a reactive routing approach widely used as a basis for a large set of extended routing protocols.

3.1   SeMuRAMAS Phases

This protocol includes two steps: route discovery and route maintenance, which allow to discover and maintain possible multiple paths between any two mobile source node, say S, and destination mobile node, say DM. Especially, in the context of wireless sensor networks, DM should represent the base station.

Route Discovery. This is the mechanism used when S wants to establish a set of paths with DM. Route Request datagrams, say $RReq$, are sent by S when it does not already have a route to DM. The entirely on-demand properties allows SeMuRAMAS to minimize the overhead and specify the path-disjointness threshold value. After receiving list of potential paths, S computes all paths to the destination which satisfy the specified threshold, chooses the list of paths to be used, caches the remaining ones, and starts sending the data. Keeping information regarding unused paths, allows the reaction to routes modification to be rapid and decreases the overhead related to the generation of a new $RReq$.

Route Maintenance. This is the mechanism used by intermediate nodes to let S update the list of paths in use when the network topology changes or some routes are broken due to an attack or sleeping cycles of nodes. This mechanism is based on letting intermediate nodes use the watchdog concept for every packet they forward [9] to detect the identities of misbehaving nodes or detect routes errors. If the next hop appears to be broken, a route error packet, say $RErr$, is generated and sent to S in order to decrease the number of possible path to the destination. S will consider all the path as broken and attempts to use another route that goes over the non responding stored in its cache, which allows to maintain the k-x-connectivity. If none backup route to DM is in the cache, the source node invokes again the Route Discovery mechanism.

3.2 SeMuRAMAS Route Discovery

Six kinds of datagrams are used by SeMuRAMAS during the route discovery:

- Route Request datagram: is the first packet to be broadcasted by a mobile node which wants to establish a multipath route to the destination mobile node. Every intermediate node exploits this datagram to discover incomplete routes in the network. It also appends its identity in the $RReq$ and broadcasts it to its neighbors.
- Route Response datagram: is sent back by the destination mobile node upon reception of the $RReq$. This datagram contains the optimal path and is source routed to the node which generated the $RReq$.
- Notification datagram: is used by the destination node to ask intermediate nodes to forward the information they learned regarding the routes to the source node. The information would have been invisible by the destination mobile node when it received the $RReq$ datagram.
- List forwarding datagram: is used by intermediate nodes to forward the information they stored regarding the existing paths in the network.
- Route Error datagram: is sent by an intermediate node to the source node when it detects a route failure. It also lets the source node update the set of paths it uses to reach the destination mobile node.
- Threshold tuning datagram: is used by an intermediate node to indicate the value by which the threshold should be increased to let the establishment of the requested multiple paths be possible.

Network Discovery. When a mobile node, say $S1$, joins the network, it broadcasts a two-hop HELLO message, which includes its identity and has a Time To Live (TTL) value equal to 2. Any node, say $S2$, which hears the message, includes the identity of $S1$ in its list of one-hop neighbors, sets the TTL value of the HELLO message equal to 1 lower than its received value, and forwards the datagram. Any node, say $S3$, that hears the message includes the identity of $S2$ in its list of one-hop neighbors and $S1$ in its list of two-hop neighbors, sets the TTL value of the HELLO message equal to 1 lower than its received value, and discards the datagram. To be considered as active, every node should periodically send a two-hop HELLO message and follow the above described process. This allows each node to maintain two up-to-date lists. The first is the list of neighbors and the second shows for each neighbor the list of its neighbors. The two lists will support the detection of routing attacks (described later in Section 4).

Route Request Generation and Forwarding. A node which wants to establish a path to the destination mobile node, say MD, initiates the route discovery by generating a $RReq$ datagram to MD, and broadcasting it in the network. Every generated $RReq$ includes a three-tuple information: $\langle Seq, RRec, Dt \rangle$. Seq stands for a sequence number which should be different for every new generated $RReq$. The sequence number together with the IP address of the sender allow to uniquely identify the $RReq$ and associate it to the subsequent generated responses. Dt is the disjointness threshold which is set by the sender to specify the maximal number of nodes that could be shared by any two paths among the set of paths to establish with the destination node. The value of Dt remains unchanged during the forwarding of the $RReq$ to the destination. $RRec$

is a route record which is used to include the path followed by the $RReq$ to reach MD. In fact, when a node in the network receives a copy of this datagram for the first time, it appends its identity to the $RRec$ field, broadcasts it to its neighbors. Every node, say N, including MD, which receives a second copy of the datagram, extracts the content of the $RRec$ field. The latter provides a path from the sender to the node N. The node N will append the content of $RRec$ together with the value of Seq to a list stored locally, entitled RP, which stands for list of Received Paths. Then it discards the datagram.

Route Response Generation and Forwarding. Once different copies of the $RReq$ datagram reach the destination node, the latter will generate a Route Response datagram, say $RRep$, to the source. It includes four-tuple information $\langle Seq, R, RNC, RPBS \rangle$ where Seq represents the value of the sequence number that appeared within the received $RReq$, R is the route, which is composed of the sequence of nodes identities representing the shortest path (between the source and the destination mobile node MD) among those that were received within the different copies of the $RReqs$. RCN stands for the remaining number of common nodes. It is initiated by MD to the value of x received within the $RReq$. This value is decreased by 1 every time the $RRep$ is routed by a node which contains a non empty list of received paths for the same value of the sequence number. The $RRep$ datagram will be source routed to the sender based on the content of R. Moreover a list, say $RPBS$,containing the list of all the routing paths connecting the source node to MD is added to the $RRep$. When the $RRep$ packet is routed to the source, the latter and all intermediate nodes will discover a route to MD, store it in their cache, and use it as an alternative path if some link error will potentially occur. We remind the reader that any different routes requests, to be received by MD may share some nodes. Every route can be written as a series of nodes shared with other routes, followed by a series of distinct nodes.

Notification Datagrams Generation and Forwarding. In the case where the destination mobile node MD has discarded a copy of the $RReq$, it generates a notification datagram, say ND, containing the four-tuple information $\langle Seq, RCN, L, RPBS \rangle$ composed of the sequence number (Seq) and the value of RCN received in the $RRep$, in addition to a list L containing the identities of neighbor nodes from which a received copy of the $RReq$ was previously discarded (i.e., the identities of these neighbors stand for the last nodes in the routing paths provided by RP and related to the sequence number Seq). In the case where the ND is sent by the BS, the list L will be set to the identities of neighbor nodes from which a copy of the $RReq$ was received. $RPBS$ is a list containing the set of routing paths connecting the source node to MD, including the shortest path. These routes are collected from the copies of the $RReq$ received by MD. The notification datagram ND is sent to the source node, broadcasted but treated only by nodes existing in the list L.

In the case where some node X in the network receives the $RRep$, two situations may happen. If X has already discarded at least one copy of the related $RReq$, it forwards it after decreasing the value of RCN and generates an ND containing the four-tuple information $\langle Seq, RCN - 1, L, RPBS \rangle$. If it is not the case, it simply forwards the datagram to its neighbors. When the intermediate node X receives a Notification datagram ND for the first time, two situations may happen. If X has not previously discarded any copy of the related $RReq$, it simply forwards the NP to its neighbors. If X has already discarded at least one copy of the related $RReq$, it forwards it after decreasing the value of RCN and replacing the value of L by the identities of neighbor nodes from which a received copy of the $RReq$ was previously discarded. When X receives a second copy of the ND, it simply discards it. If the value RCN becomes equal to 0 after decreasing it by one, the notification packet will be rejected before sending it.

List Forwarding Datagrams Generation and Forwarding. Every node, which decreases the RCN's value of the Notification Datagram ND, generates a list forwarding datagram containing the sequence number (already received in the ND) and a list obtained from RP (the sequence number associated to RP should be the same as the one received in the ND) after applying two filters, say $F1$ and $F2$, consecutively. The list forwarding datagram is sent to the source node (i.e., the node which initiated the $RReq$). The first filter $F1$ eliminates from RP any path that has more than $RCN - 1$ shared nodes with any path existing in $RPBS$. The second filter $F2$ locates in the output of $F1$ groups of nodes that share more than $RCN - 1$ nodes. It replaces each one of these groups in the RP list by the shortest path. When the source node specifies a disjointness threshold x equal to 0 (i.e., all the discovered paths must be disjoint), the ND will be sent with a value of RCN equal to 0. Intermediate nodes receiving this latter and having an empty RP, should forward the packet to their neighbors. If it is not the case, they drop the notification datagram ND. Each time a node sends its RP list to the source node, it eliminates this list from its memory to preserve storage resources. If there is no additional space in the node memory, a solution consists in using the neighbor memory. Two categories of nodes can be used: nodes with high storage capacity and nodes with limited storage capacity. Each node knows the category of its neighbors. A node with a low storage capacity has the possibility to send parts of the data it stores only to neighbor nodes with high storage capacity. In fact, the receiving node should send back the data to the sender before it goes out of its coverage or sleeps. If the sender memory is still full, the receiving node should find a neighbor node, which is also a neighbor of the sender and has a high storage capacity, transfer the data to that node, and inform the sender about its identity.

Threshold Tuning Datagram Generation and Forwarding. Each time that a mobile node sets the RCN to 0, it executes filters $F1$ and $F2$ of the content of the RP to discard paths exceeding, in terms of shared nodes, the authorized disjointness threshold. The mobile node computes the minimal number of shared nodes, say n, between the remaining paths in the RP and sends this value to the source node within the TTD datagram. This value could be exploited by the source node, in the case where it is unable to establish the set of paths satisfying the requested threshold. In let it determine the best suitable threshold value that could be guaranteed by the network topology. This value will equal be n greater than the last used threshold value.

3.3 Reconstruction of Routes by the Source

The aim of the reconstruction process is to construct k paths satisfying the disjointness threshold x. If several combinations are possible, the sender could select the one which uses the minimal number of shared nodes, or select the one which uses the shortest k possible paths. The first alternative could be chosen if availability is more sensitive than delivery delays. We remind, that x's value specified in the route request $RReq$, has prevented intermediate nodes to forward useless list of paths, which, if assembled together by the source node, would generate routes that include a number of shared nodes higher than what is expected by x.

To reconstruct the set of paths, the following algorithm is executed. Let L_{cp} be the list of complete paths satisfying the threshold x to generate by the algorithm, and L_p be the series of path received in the different list forwarding datagrams sent by intermediate nodes in the network. L_p is a n-tuple of the form $< p_1, ..., p_n >$, where every p_i ($\in L_p$) represents any path of the form of $< S_1, ..., S_{bl} >$, where S_1 represents the identity of the node, which initiated the route discovery, S_2 to S_{bl} represent intermediate nodes and S_{bl} represents the identify of any intermediate node in the network including the destination mobile node MD, which discarded a second copy of the $RReq$ datagram.

Starting with a FIFO queue, say Q, containing the set of paths in $RPBS$ received by MD. Until $Q = \langle \rangle$ or $L_p = \emptyset$, the algorithm executes the following: Let $R = < S_1', ..., S_n' >$, be the first routing path in Q, where S_1' stands for the source node and S_n' stands for MD. Starting from a value of i equal to n, and until i becomes equal to 1 (i.e., i is decreased by 1 in every loop), the algorithms checks for every $p \in L_p$ if $S_i \in R$ corresponds to the last node $S_{bl} \in p$. If it is the case, the source node will generate a path equal to $\langle S_1, ..., S_{bl}, S_{i+1}' ..., S_n' \rangle$, appends it to L_{cp} and Q, and deletes p from L_p. If i becomes equal to 1, the algorithm deletes R from Q. For the particular case where MD has generated an $RPBS$ containing paths which share more than x nodes, the L_{cp} needs to be filtered by keeping the shortest path from those having more than x nodes shared with paths in the $RPBS$. Based on the content of L_{cp}, the source node will be able to select the best combination of paths, in terms of number of hops, satisfying the values of k and x.

if $L_{cp} = \emptyset$, meaning that the request k paths cannot be established while satisfying the threshold x, the source node should have received at least a TTD datagram. It selects the minimal value, say v, from those indicated by the received TTD datagrams. Later, it could generate again a new route discovery where x will be v greater than the last used x value.

3.4   Route Maintenance

A path can fail due to collisions and/or nodes mobility. It is essential to recover broken paths immediately to ensure the reliability of data. After route establishment and during data forwarding, when a node in an established route fails to send the packet to the next hop, or detects that a neighbor is not forwarding the datagram, SeMuRAMAS considers the route as broken and sends a Route Error $RErr$ to the source node to inform it about the identity of the unavailable node. This mechanism is strengthened by applying a watchdog mechanism described in the Section 4. Upon reception of this $RErr$ packet, the source node deletes any alternative route in the k established path that contains the broken node. It tries to replace it by one of the available routes in its cache, and verifies if the set of k paths to use still have, at the maximum possible, x common nodes. If it is not the case, the route discovery step is initiated again.

Lemma 1. *Any two reconstructed paths at the source node do not share a number of nodes higher than the pre-defined disjointness threshold.*

Proof. Assuming that there are two reconstructed paths $p1$ and $p2$ at the source node, the aim is to show that the number of shared nodes between $p1$ and $p2$ does not exceed the pre-defined disjointness threshold, denoted by x. If p_1 and p_2 represent a solution, certainly the first shared node, say s_n, from the destination mobile node to the source node, has received a notification packet. We remind that: (a) each shared node receiving the notification packet or the route response should decrement the value of x and forward this packet with the new value. In addition, the use of filter $F2$ allows , any intermediate node, which receives the value of x, to check if $p1$ and $p2$ do not share more than $x - 1$ nodes from the source node to it. If it is the case, it announces to the source node that $p1$ and $p2$ represent two possible routes which do not share more than x nodes; and (b) each shared node receiving a notification packet with x equal to 1 will discard it after decrementing the value of x to 0. If s_n has received the notification packet, this means that the received value of x is higher than (or equal to) 0. If the number of shared nodes exceeds the x'value, this means that exceeding nodes have received a negative value of x, which is impossible.

Lemma 2. *Given a node, any path in the list of Received Paths RP, related to the same route request, can be described as the concatenation of two series followed by the identity of the node storing the RP list. The first series can be shared by another path in RP while the second series never occurs in another path in the same RP.*

Proof. We remind that a $RReq$ contains the identities of nodes through which the datagram has been routed. During the route discovery, a node broadcasts the $RReq$, and all its neighbors receive a copy. The $RReq$ could follow different paths starting from one node and only a copy of the $RReq$ could be routed through a segment of consecutive nodes. We define for every path in the list of received paths RP two series. This first series is composed of nodes shared with at least a path in the same RP and the second series is formed by nodes which are not involved in any other path within the same RP. We demonstrate the Lemma based on recurrence induction. We consider a path p in RP, which can be written in the form of $p =< S_1, ..., S_i, ..., S_n, >$ as the concatenation of several path segments, where every segment S represents the longest series of nodes that belong to the maximal possible number of paths in the RP.

Every S_i is in the form of $< n_x, ..., n_y >$ where n_y is the node from which the $RReq$ was forwarded to a number of neighbors, say Nn_i ($Nn_i \geq 2$), such that the neighbors in Nn are part of different paths to the node storing the RP. We suppose that the list S_i is shared by Np_i paths in the RP. Therefore, the segment path S_{i+1} will be shared by $Np_i - Nn_i + 1$ paths and we have $Np_{i+1} = Np_i - Nn_i + 1$. This means that the $RReq$ has followed different paths, where every path, which starts with a node in N_n, does not share any node with the next segment $S_{i+1}, ..., S_n$ excepting the node storing the RP list. Roughly speaking, for every i (where $1 \leq i \leq n$) if $Np_i > 1$ the segment S_i will be part of the first series. The same reasoning is applied by recurrence until S_n. Since a node does not forward two copies of the same Route Request Datagram, the segment S_n will inevitably belong to the second series and cannot be empty.

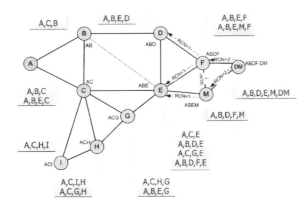

Fig. 1. Response process

3.5 Example Applying k-x-Connectivity

In the example presented in Figure 1, the source node A needs to establish three ($k = 3$) routes to the destination node MD sharing at maximum two nodes between them ($x = 2$). In the proposed topology, it is hard to respect three disjoint paths without tuning the threshold x. A generates and broadcasts a $RReq$ with a disjointness threshold x equal to 2. In the Figure, nodes are represented by circles, and an edge connects two nodes if they are able to directly communicate together. The RP lists stored by each node are represented by rectangles. Node B receives the first packet directly from A and receives a second copy though two other paths which are $< A, C, B >$ and $< A, C, E, B >$. As each time node B drops a duplicated packet, it stores the routing path used by this copy in its RP list, the routing path RP will be equal to $<< A, C, B >< A, C, E, B >>$. The $RReq$ is forwarded to neighbor nodes until it reaches MD on the shortest path $R_{sp} =< A, B, D, F, MD >$.

As shown in Figure 1, based on the number of minimum common nodes RCN which is set to 2 in the Notification Packet ND, the RP lists are only sent by nodes F, M, D and E. In fact, at the response step, when Node F receives the ND from MD, it decreases the value of RCN to 1 and forwards this packet to its neighbors. This node applies the filter $F1$ on its RP list based on the content of the $RPBS$ list received for the destination node. Note that this $RPBS$ contains the two following paths $< A, B, D, F, MD >$ and $< A, B, D, E, M, MD >$. Using the filter $F1$, paths $< A, B, E, F >$ and $< A, B, E, M, F >$, in the RP list of the node F,will be elimi-nated because they have more than $RCN - 1 = 1$ shared node with the $RPBS$. As the RP list of node F is empty, its RP list will be sent back to the source node. When node M receives the NP from MD, it decreases RCN o 1 and applies the two filters $F1$ and $F2$ on its RP list. By applying $F1$, node M, will discard the path $< ABDFM >$ from its RP list, because it has more than $RCN - 1 = 1$ shared nodes with the first path $< A, B, D, F, MD >$ of the $RPBS$ list. When the node M receives a second copy of ND from the node F it will discard it.

When nodes D and E receive ND from node F, they decrease the value of RCN to 0. By applying the two filters $F1$ and $F2$, node D will not send the path $< A, B, E, D >$

stored in its RP list. In fact, the use of filter $F1$ lets node E keep only paths $< A, C, E >$ and $< A, C, G, E >$ in its RP list. However, $< A, C, E >$ and $< A, C, G, E >$ share node C and node E accepts only $RCN - 1 = 0$ common nodes. Therefore, when it applies the filter $F2$, node E is forced to keep only the shortest path it knows, which is $< A, C, E >$. When the node E receives a second copy of the ND from the node M, it discards it. When the neighbors of nodes D and E receive the NP with an RCN set to 0, they discard this packet without sending any information. At the end, the source node A, has a list of paths available to MD which is equal to $L_p = \{< A, C, E >\}$. The $RPBS$, which is extracted from the $RRep$, together with the list of paths L_p will be used to determine the set of routes, characterized by $k = 3$ and $x = 2$, to MD. By applying the reconstruction algorithm described in Subsection 3.3, the final list of reconstructed paths L_{cp} will be equal to: $L_{cp} = \{< A, C, E, F, BS >< A, B, D, F, BS >< A, B, E, M, BS >\}$.

4   Security of SeMuRAMAS

To provide a secure routing algorithm, against a set of attacks, that prepare for the investigation, three main properties should be satisfied. First, nodes should be able to authenticate each others during the process of routes establishment. Datagrams generated with forged information should be discarded before reaching the destination mobile node MD. Second, every node should not only be in charge of generating and forwarding datagrams to MD, but also of controlling the behavior of its neighbors. In this context, the watchdog technique is used to detect nodes that do not forward the datagrams as expected. A node which uses the watchdog technique is able to determine whether its neighbor nodes are forwarding the datagram they receive or not. If the packet is not forwarded within a certain period, this neighbor is considered as malicious[9]. Every node should maintain two lists: a list of one-hop neighbors and a list of two hop neighbors. The two lists are created by letting every node periodically perform a two-hop broadcast of a Hello Message (i.e., by setting the TTL equal to 2). A node, say n_1 which receives a generated Hello message by a node, say n_0, with a TTL equal to 2, appends the identity of n_0 to its list of neighbors, appends it own identity (i.e., n_1), decreases by one the TTL, and forwards the packet. A node, say n_2, which receives a datagram with a TTL equal to 1 from the neighbor node n_1, appends the identity of the sender (i.e., n_0) to its list of two hop neighbors, and marks this node as being reachable through the immediate sender n_1. Third, when a node detects a malicious neighbor, both the source and the destination nodes should be informed.

To protect the routing algorithm against forgery of false routing information, we use a signature scheme to authenticate nodes and guarantee the integrity of the information they exchange. We suppose that, in the case of WSN, every node joining the network is authenticated by the BS. Intermediate verification of packets signature allows discarding compromised packets before they reach the destination nodes, which optimizes the used energy and communication resources, and reduces the overhead of the signature verification process performed by the destination node. During the routes establishment, every node which generates or forwards the $RReq$, appends its identity, the identity of the next receiving nodes, and sur-signs the route record. A node receiving the forwarded message verifies whether the last appended signature is correct, checks if it is the pre-sumed destination, determines the immediate sender (the neighbor node from which the packet is being forwarded) of that datagram and makes sure that it is a neighbor. If it is the case, it appends its identity, the identity of the possible next hops and sur-signs the datagram. In the context of WSN, signature is performed using the elliptic thresh-old signature algorithm provided by [10] is used. It allows to generate for a public key k_{pub}, n associated secret keys $k_{pr_1}, ..., k_{pr_n}$. Every signature created using one of the private keys, say k_{pr_i}, can be checked using k_{pub}. Every node uses its own private key for signature, while the same public key is used by all the other nodes for the purpose of signature verification. In the context of general types of Adhoc networks, where nodes can enter and leave the network at any time perfid, and no resource limitations exist, regular signature can be used. Every node should have its own private and public keys, where a certificate, containing this public key, is delivered by a certification authority. Mobiles nodes will use the certificates of the senders to check the integrity of the signed datagrams. We assume that each mobile node has the ability to contact a certification authority repository to download the certificate of any node in the network.

These techniques increase the resilience to nodes compromise, especially in the con-text of WSN they protect against nodes capture. The protection is done by: (a) using digital signature to authenticate packet content and discarding invalid datagrams (b) using the identification of captured node based on applied watchdog mechanism and intermediate signature; and (c) authorizing x shared nodes in order to be tolerant to the discard of compromised paths involving captured node, which assures that, even when part of the nodes have been captured, the rest of the network remains secure.

In the context of WSN, where threshold signature is used, if a node is duplicated, and its key is used by a malicious node, MD will notice the attack by detecting that the same key was used by several nodes. To do so, MD checks whether two nodes having the same identities have participated in forwarding the $RReq$. If it is not the case, for each signature appended to the $RReq$, the MD determines the identity of the signer node, and verifies whether it could really produce this signature if its private key was used (in the case of WSNs the MD, which is the base station, is assumed to know all the mobile nodes private keys). Note that the use of the public key is not sufficient to authenticate the nodes, because it does not allow detecting whether the same private key was used several times to generate the sur-signed $RReq$. When the BS detects that a node has used the private key of another node, or a node has participated several times in the same $RReq$, it forwards an alert containing the identity of the compromised nodes, asking the remaining nodes in the network to reject any packet sent from that node in the future. When a node receives a second copy of the $RReq$, it signs and stores the received path in the RP list, where each identity, in the received path, is signed by intermediate nodes. If a malicious node wants to modify the RP list, it must use the signatures of all nodes involved in the modified path to re-sign each identity which is impossible. In addition, when an intermediate node eliminates a received RP list instead of forwarding it, the watchdog mechanism used by neighbor nodes will detect such behavior.

SeMuRAMAS is also protected against a set of routing attacks such as the wormhole attack [11], where a malicious node receives packets, tunnels them to another location in the network, and re-send them. In the case of an out-of-band channel establishment, a malicious node may collude with another node, which is typically located near MD, to make the routing paths that go over them, look shorter (in terms of number of hops) than expected. Such behavior could compromise the discovery $k - x$-connected paths. Using the watchdog mechanism and intermediate signature, the wormhole attack will be detected. In fact, a malicious node could forward a packet to non neighbor node using a high powered transmission. Since the node should append its identity and the identity of immediate receivers to the route record and sur-sign them, two situations could happen: (a) If the malicious node, specifies a correct identity of the immediate receiver, the watchdog neighbors, verify the signature in the datagram and detect that the packet was forwarded to a non neighbor node. When the malicious datagram is forwarded to MD, together with the alert generated by the watchdog nodes, the latter could use the signature as an evidence to prove the identity of the malicious node; or (b) the malicious node specifies the identity of a neighbor node when it signs the route record, but forwards the datagram to a non neighbor node. In that case, the neighbor nodes will detect that the node has appended an identity of a non neighbor node, which will receive the packet. The watchdog nodes will broadcast an alert, containing the identity of the malicious node, asking the remaining nodes in the network to reject any datagram sent from that node in the future.

5   Validation of SeMuRAMAS

In SeMuRAMAS, the construction of paths is based on a distributed mechanism where information regarding available links is collected by the BS, or stored by intermediate nodes, and copies of a same datagram are discarded. The correctness of the routes generation is vindicated by the fact that exchanged information are signed and verified by neighbors. In addition, the NDs generated by the destination mobile node MD or by nodes incorporate the disjointness threshold related to the set of the k established paths. Since this value is decreased whenever the ND is forwarded by a node, which maintains a path to the source node, all pairs of paths that have more than x shared nodes will not be generated. This allows that nodes to store and forward only the useful information and reduce the network overhead.

The completeness of SeMuRAMAS is satisfied by the fact that the source node is able to reconstruct all existing and shortest paths to the destination. In fact, SeMuRAMAS broadcasts the $RReq$ over all nodes in the network and makes all the nodes, including MD, able to save all information regarding possible routes from the source node to themselves. In addition, NDs are broadcasted to all neighbor nodes, which have discarded a copy of the $RReq$, to let them send to the source node the list of paths they discovered. Using SeMuRAMAS the network overload may increase depending the number of nodes and the value of the threshold x. Especially, a high number of lists of paths may be generated and the number of list of paths datagrams may increase. The traffic overload will be estimated in the next section. In WSN, if nodes are in sleeping state they will not be involved in the route discovery. If the node changes its state at the end of this process, it will be considered as a novel node joining the network and will be involved in the next route discovery.

The security of SeMuRAMAS is based on the use of watchdog mechanism and digital signature. The watchdog mechanism allows to capture several types of routing attacks including for instance, the wormhole attacks. To efficiently use this mechanism, bi-directional links should be used to communicate between mobile nodes in order to let a node detect whether its neighbor is forwarding the datagram received from another node. False positives may occur if a node detects that its neighbor is malicious because it has not forwarded the datagram, while, in reality, it happens due a collision. False negatives may occur if the state, of some nodes involved in the route to MD, becomes sleeping or runs out of energy. Such node, which is not detected as inactive yet, may be considered as malicious and leads to the generation of false negative alerts.

The values of the two parameters x and k are highly correlated and both of them depend on the node density. Typically, if the source node chooses a high value of k, it should tend to decrease the value of x to guarantee the establishment of all the paths. It is worth to notice that, for a fixed value of k, the more the node density is low, the lower will be the value of x. Conversely, if the nodes density is high, the value of x could increase with regard to the latter situation.

Two particular topologies could reduce considerably the performance of SeMuRA-MAS. The first is obtained when nodes are so close to each other and all of them are located around MD. In this topology, a $RReq$ generated from any node will reach all nodes in the network. As a result, a node could receive the same copy of datagrams from all nodes in the network. The nodes memory will be overloaded due to the highest number of paths to store in the RP list. The second, is obtained when nodes are not deployed with a sufficient number, and most of nodes do not have more than two neighbors. The routing paths to generate will contain a large set of intermediate nodes. While the memory occupation rate in nodes is highly reduced with regard to the previous topology, a multi-path will require a high delay to be established.

6 Simulation Results

6.1 Memory Overhead Estimation

When the $RReq$ datagram is forwarded, every node, which receives a copy, stores the route record in its list of received paths. Since this list is temporary stored within the mobile node memory, we estimate the average number of stored paths in each node in terms of the number of nodes. We consider a network area of 72×72 length units. The nodes communication radius is set to 10 length units and the x's value is set to 2. Based on these values, the optimal number of deployed nodes is given by the following formula:

$$\frac{Total\ Network\ Area}{(3 \times Node's\ Coverage\ Area)}$$

and is approximately equal to $50 \simeq 3 * 72^2/(10^2\pi)$. In this simulation nodes positions are computed using a uniform distribution of random values. The use of uniform distribution is very common as it allows to distribute nodes over the whole network area and ensure a homogeneous coverage [12]. If the nodes would have been deployed in

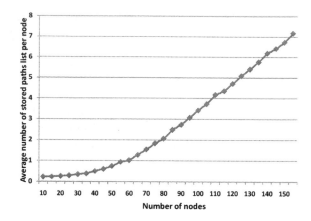

Fig. 2. Influence of nodes density on length of stored paths list

non-flat surface containing valleys, rivers and lakes, the use of another distribution such as normal distribution [13] would be considered.

Figure 2 shows the variation of the average number of stored paths per node, with respect to a number of nodes ranging from 10 to 150. This average is computed during the route discovery phase. It is equal to:

$$\frac{Number\ of\ stored\ paths\ in\ all\ nodes}{Number\ of\ deployed\ nodes}$$

The simulation results indicate that the more the nodes communication radius is, the more will be the memory overhead. Starting from a value of deployed nodes equal to 10, and until this number reaches the optimal value (i.e., 50), the number of received copies of the same $RReq$ increases which slowly increases the number of stored paths in each node. In fact, since the node number is lower than the optimal value, the number of unreachable nodes is important. The node, which do not receive any copy of $RReq$, will have a number of stored paths equal to 0. Starting from a number of nodes higher than 50, all the nodes in the network become reachable and the average of stored paths linearly increases as long as the number of nodes in the network increases.

6.2   Communication Overhead Estimation

In order to estimate the communication overhead generated by SeMuRAMAS, we consider a network area equal to 39×39 length units, which holds a variable number of randomly distributed nodes. The nodes communication radius is set to 10 length units and the value of x is set to 2. Based on these values, the optimal number of deployed nodes is equal to 15. The curve depicted by Figure 3 shows the estimated average time per node required to generate a set of routes satisfying the $k - x$ connectivity scheme, in terms of number of nodes in the network and number of hops separating the source node to the MD. The number of nodes was varied from 5 to 195, and the estimated time was computed for different possible hop values.

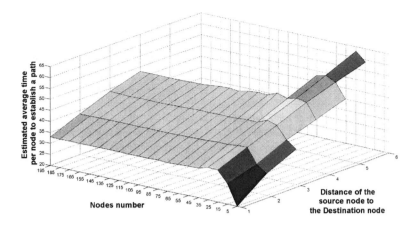

Fig. 3. Influences of nodes density on the overhead and the length of paths

The simulation shows that the estimated average time, per node, to establish a path, initially increases as the number of nodes increases from 5 to approximately 30. In fact, the network becomes more and more covered, and nodes far from the destination mobile node MD become able to establish a path, which increases the average of the estimated time. As the number of nodes becomes far from the optimal value, the estimated average time becomes approximately constant. This is due to the fact, that datagrams generated by the algorithm are always routed through the shortest path. Even during the route establishment phase, the copies of the $RReq$ datagrams arriving to MD, are the ones which were forwarded through the minimal number of nodes. The simulation shows also that the highest values of hops are obtained for a number of nodes ranging from 20 to 35. In fact, since the network is not sufficiently dense, nodes that are far from the MD will require a high number of hops to reach the MD. As the network becomes dense, these nodes become able to reach the MD using shorter paths. Finally, it is also noticed that as the number of hops increases by 1, the estimated average time regularly increases with approximately 5 periods of time due the static value of the waiting and processing time of datagrams in nodes.

7   Conclusions

To let nodes in Wireless Adhoc and Sensor Networks able to use multi-path routing, specifying both of the number of paths that should be available between a source and a destination, and the maximal number of nodes to be shared by these paths, we developed a novel algorithm called SeMuRAMAS. It uses a the concept of watchdogs and digital signature to detect malicious neighbor nodes and authenticate exchanged packets. A simulation is conducted to analyze the memory and communication overhead. Directions for future works will address the estimation of the threshold value depending on the network density and the expected number of paths.

References

1. Li, S., Wu, Z.: Node-disjoint parallel multi-path routing in wireless sensor networks. In: Proceedings of the Second International Conference on Embedded Software and Systems, pp. 432–443 (December 2005)
2. Hanan, S., Michael, S.: k-fault resistance in wireless ad-hoc networks. In: Proceedings of the 2005 Joint Workshop on Foundations of Mobile Computing, pp. 89–96 (2005)
3. Law, Y., Yen, L., Pietro, R., Palaniswami, M.: Secure k-connectivity properties of wireless sensor networks. In: IEEE Internatonal Conference on Mobile Adhoc and Sensor Systems (2007)
4. Almasaeid, H.M., Kamal, A.E.: On the minimum k-connectivity repair in wireless sensor networks. In: The Proceedings of the IEEE International Conference on Communications (ICC), pp. 1–5 (June 2009)
5. Dulman, S., Wu, J., Havinga, P.: An energy efficient multipath routing algorithm for wireless sensor networks. In: IEEE International Symposium on Autonomous Decentralized Systems (ISADS 2003), Pisa, Italy (April 2003)
6. Yang, P., Huang, B.: Multi-path routing protocol for mobile ad hoc network. In: International Conference on Computer Science and Software Engineering (2008)
7. Hou, X., Tipper, D., Kabara, J.: Label-based multipath routing in wireless sensor routing. In: Proceedings 6th International Symposium on Advanced Radio Technologies (ISART 2004), Boulder, CO (March 2-4, 2004)
8. Johnson, D.B., Maltz, D.: Dynamic source routing in ad hoc wireless networks. In: Imielinski, Korth (eds.) Mobile Computing, vol. 353 (1996)
9. Lee, J., Lee, Y., Syrotiuk, V.R.: The performance of a watchdog protocol for wireless network security. International Journal of Wireless and Mobile Computing (May 2007)
10. Sliti, M., Hamdi, M., Boudriga, N.: An elliptic threshold signature framework for k-security in wireless sensor networks. In: 15th IEEE International Conference on Electronics, Circuits and Systems, ICECS 2008 (2008)
11. Triki, B., Rekhis, S., Boudriga, N.: Digital investigation of wormhole attacks in wireless sensor networks. In: Eighth IEEE International Symposium on Network Computing and Applications, nca, pp. 179–186 (2009)
12. Karl, H., Willig, A.: Protocols and Architectures for Wireless Sensor Networks, 1st edn. (2007)
13. Krupadanam, S., Fu, H.: Beacon-less location detection in wireless sensor networks for non-flat terrains. International Journal of Software Engineering and Its Applications 2(3) (July 2008)

The Price of Security: A Detailed Comparison of the TLS Handshake Performance on Embedded Devices When Using Elliptic Curve Cryptography and RSA

Manuel Koschuch, Matthias Hudler, and Michael Krüger

Competence Centre for IT-Security, FH Campus Wien, University of Applied Science
Favoritenstrasse 226, 1100 Vienna, Austria
{manuel.koschuch,matthias.hudler
michael.krueger}@fh-campuswien.ac.at
http://www.fh-campuswien.ac.at/en/research__development/
competence_centre_for_it_security/

Abstract. The Transport Layer Security (TLS) Protocol is the current de-facto standard for secure connections over an insecure medium; it combines asymmetric and symmetric cryptography to achieve authentication, confidentiality and message integrity. The flexibility of the TLS protocol regarding the algorithms used allows it to also run efficiently on mobile devices severely constrained in terms of available memory, computing power and energy. In this work we present a thorough performance evaluation of the TLS handshake process by breaking it down into its individual phases, with a focus on the comparison between the usually applied RSA algorithm and cryptographic primitives based on Elliptic Curve Cryptography (ECC). We are especially interested how the transition to more secure TLS cipher suites (like switching from one-way to mutual authentication or to ephemeral primitives) affects the load that is put on client and server when using RSA and ECC, respectively.

Keywords: Elliptic curve cryptography, Transport layer security, Embedded devices, Sensor networks, Performance evaluation.

1 Introduction

While only several years ago we were mainly used to complete our work using stationary, powerful personal computers, the switch to the long announced "ubiquitous computing" has not only been already made, but almost surpassed all initial speculations; currently we are surrounded by small, portable, mobile devices, which we either interact with knowingly (like PDAs, cellphones or smartphones) or unknowingly (like sensor networks). All these devices, as different as they may be in looks or function, share some common characteristics: they are heavily challenged in terms of available computational power, memory and energy. Especially the latter results in some serious complications when trying to use algorithms or protocols developed for stationary PCs on these mobile devices; yet the need for secure and authenticated communication using these wireless appliances is obvious. So to enable the same level of security present on PCs one has to look at two main parts: the cryptographic calculations performed

M.S. Obaidat, G.A. Tsihrintzis, and J. Filipe (Eds.): ICETE 2010, CCIS 222, pp. 71–83, 2012.
© Springer-Verlag Berlin Heidelberg 2012

by the device have to be implemented in an efficient, memory-saving way. And the exchange of messages during the protocol has to be kept to a minimum, since radio transmissions usually put the biggest load on the constrained energy resources. Especially in the context of Wireless Sensor Networks (WSNs), where a huge (i.e. several thousands) of nodes has to communicate self-sustained for a considerable amount of time, every additional message sent that does not serve the purpose of transmitting data can be considered a waste of precious energy. In this work we look at the asymmetric parts of the Transport Layer Security (TLS) Protocol in detail, especially how many messages have to be exchanged to establish a secure connection, and how an increase in security influences the number of messages and the load on the participating parties. Finally we observe how Elliptic Curve Cryptography (ECC) can be utilized to allow for higher security with lower performance requirements than RSA based solutions can offer. To the best of our knowledge, while the general performance impact of elliptic curve cryptography on the SSL/TLS protocol has been quite thoroughly examined (e.g. [4]), the number of messages and the differences between authentication options has not been extensively treated yet. The remainder of this paper is now structured as follows:

Section 2 introduces Elliptic Curve Cryptography (ECC), and its benefits over RSA when using asymmetric cryptography on constrained devices. Section 3 then gives an overview of the Transport Layer Security (TLS) Protocol, with a focus on the handshake process, which uses asymmetric cryptographic techniques. Section 4 describes the possible cryptographic primitives employed during a TLS handshake in detail, where finally Section 5 summarizes the messages that have to be exchanged by each participating party and the load put onto them, depending on the primitives chosen. Finally, Section 6 gives some concluding remarks and defines the course of our future work.

2   Elliptic Curve Cryptography

An elliptic curve is formed by all the tuples (x, y) satisfying the simplified Weierstrass equation $y^2 = ax^3 + bx + c$, where $a, b \in$ any finite field [5]. For the remainder of this work we focus on prime fields $GF(p)$, containing the integers up to $p - 1$, where p is prime. Thus all arithmetic in $GF(p)$ has to be done modulo p. The points on an elliptic curve, together with a so-called "point-at-infinity" serving as the identity element, form an additive group, with the operations point addition and point doubling, depicted in Figure 1 (a) and (b), respectively, for a curve defined over the real numbers. So a single operation in the elliptic curve group requires several operations in the underlying field, the exact number depending on the calculation method used and the representation of the elements. The basic building block for secure asymmetric cryptographic systems utilizing elliptic curve groups is the assumed intractability of the so-called "Elliptic Curve Discrete Logarithm Problem (ECDLP)". Given two points P and Q on a curve, where Q resulted from adding P k-times to itself (so $Q = k * P$, an operation called "scalar multiplication"), there are no efficient methods known to determine k. It is generally agreed upon that the hardness of solving this problem for a 160-bit underlying finite field is equivalent to solving the integer factorization problem for a 1.024-bit composite number [10,8]. So compared to RSA only a sixth of the bit length is needed to achieve a comparable level of security. This property makes elliptic curves especially

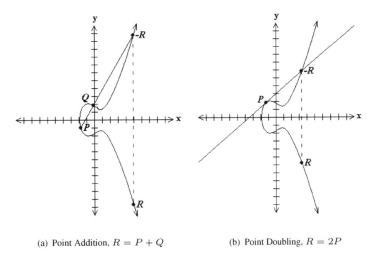

(a) Point Addition, $R = P + Q$ (b) Point Doubling, $R = 2P$

Fig. 1. Operations on an Elliptic Curve Point Group

attractive in the context of resource constrained devices, since it means smaller intermediate values to store, and also smaller signatures and messages to be exchanged [11,12]. In related work we focused on the results achievable by an efficient implementation of elliptic curve primitives for generic fields ([7,6,9]). But when dealing with mobile devices or sensor motes, additional focus has to be on the number and size of messages that have to be exchanged during the execution of a certain cryptographic primitive.

3   Transport Layer Security Protocol

The Transport Layer Security (TLS) protocol, as defined in [3] and extended in [2] and [1], is the current de facto standard for secure, authenticated connections over insecure mediums. It is well researched and defined and, through the use of different ciphersuites that can be negotiated during connection setup, also very flexible and versatile. The protocol basically consists of two parts: an asymmetric one, the handshake part, where authentication of one (or both) of the communicating parties takes place and a shared secret is established. The actual connection is then secured using symmetric techniques to ensure confidentiality and integrity of the exchanged messages. In our work we focus on the asymmetric - the handshake - part, since in the setting of mobile devices, especially sensor motes, usually only small messages are exchanged and so the time needed to perform the asymmetric operations by far outweighs the time needed for the symmetric encryption. The larger the transmitted messages become, the less important the time for the asymmetric part [4].

Figure 2 gives an overview of the most general form of a handshake, where optional messages, that do not have to be exchanged during every handshake, are printed in italics. Usually a session is initiated by the client by sending its *ClientHello* message, presenting the server a list of supported ciphersuites. Such a suite contains information

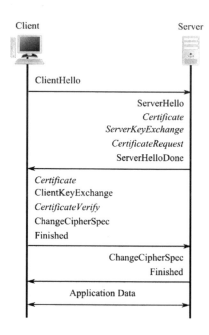

Fig. 2. SSL handshake, optional messages printed *italic*

about the key exchange (ECDH, DH, RSA,...), the signature (DSA, RSA, ECDSA,...), the hash (SHA-1, MD5,...) and the symmetric (3DES, AES,...) algorithm to use during the connection. The server then answers with the *ServerHello* message, containing the ciphersuite selected for this connection. Transmission of the server's certificate in the *Certificate* message is optional, but usual the case, to allow for at least one-way authentication. The *ServerKeyExchange* message is only sent when the chosen key exchange algorithm requires information not present in the server's certificate (for example when using the ephemeral version of the Diffie-Hellman Key Exchange, see Section 4 for details). Likewise, the *CertifacteRequest* is only used when mutual authentication takes place. The server finishes its first bunch of messages with the *ServerHelloDone* message. The client answers with its certificate in the *Certificate* message, if mutual authentication is requested, followed by the information needed by the server to establish the shared secret via the *ClientKeyExchange* message and a signed hash of all messages exchanged thus far in the *CertificateVerify* message to prove possession of the private key associated with the public key in its certificate. Finally, both parties send the *ChangeCipherSpec* and *Finished* messages, where the latter one is already symmetrical encrypted with the exchanged key and contains the hash of all the messages of the entire handshake. The exact number of messages that have to be exchanged and the calculations each party has to perform depends on the selected algorithms, as described in the next Section.

4   Asymmetric Primitives in the TLS Handshake

There are two choices of algorithms that influence the amount of transmission and processing power needed by the parties during a TLS handshake: the algorithm used for key exchange and the one used for signing. The following Subsections give an overview of the most common ones that we investigated in our work.

4.1   Signature Primitives

There are three main algorithms used to sign the exchanged messages:

- The Digital Signature Algorithm/Standard (DSA/DSS)
- The Elliptic Curve Digital Signature Algorithm (ECDSA) and
- The Rivest-Shamir-Adleman Algorithm (RSA)

Algorithms 1 and 2 detail the creation and verification of a DSA signature, respectively. In practice, p is usually selected to be of length 1.024 bits, whereas q and x are usually about 160 bit. Signature generation requires one modular exponentiation with a 160-bit exponent, a modular inversion of a 160-bit number and two modular multiplications of 160-bit factors. Signature verification requires one modular inversion, three modular multiplications and two modular exponentiations, each with 160-bit operands.

Algorithm 1. DSA Signature Generation

Require: Domain Parameters $D = (p, q, g)$, private key x, message m, hash function H
Ensure: Signature (r, s)
1: Select $k \in [1, q - 1]$ at random
2: $T \leftarrow g^k \bmod p$
3: $r \leftarrow T \bmod q$
4: $e \leftarrow H(m)$
5: $s \leftarrow k^{-1}(e + xr) \bmod q$
6: **return** (r, s)

The Elliptic Curve Digital Signature Algorithm (ECDSA) is the elliptic curve implementation of the digital signature algorithm. In addition to an elliptic curve key pair a secure hash function H is needed, whose output is not longer than n. Algorithm 3 describes the signature generation process for ECDSA. Note that the transformation of x to an integer in step 3 can be easily done by just looking at its binary representation, regardless whether the involved field is a prime field or a binary extension field. In addition, calculations in two different finite fields have to be performed: the scalar multiplication involves computation in $\mathbb{F}_q$, but $\bar{x}$ in step 4 is calculated modulo the order n of the base point P. In software implementations this poses not to big a challenge, yet when implementing this algorithm in hardware some additional arrangements have to be made. The entire signature generation process requires one scalar multiplication, one modular inversion and two modular multiplications, usually in the context of 160-bit fields.

Algorithm 2. DSA Signature Verification

Require: Domain Parameters $D = (p, q, g)$, public key $y(= g^x)$, message m, signature (r, s), hash function H

Ensure: ACCEPT or REFUSE message

 1: **if** $r, s \notin [1, q - 1]$ **then**
 2:     **return** REFUSE
 3: **end if**
 4: $e \leftarrow H(m)$
 5: $w \leftarrow s^{-1} \bmod q$
 6: $u_1 \leftarrow ew \bmod q$
 7: $u_2 \leftarrow rw \bmod q$
 8: $T \leftarrow g^{u_1} * y^{u_2} \bmod p$
 9: $v \leftarrow T \bmod q$
10: **if** $v = r$ **then**
11:     **return** ACCEPT
12: **else**
13:     **return** REFUSE
14: **end if**

Algorithm 3. ECDSA Signature Generation

Require: Domain Parameters $D = (q, FR, S, a, b, P, n, h)$, private key d, message m, hash function H

Ensure: Signature (r, s)

 1: Select $k \in [1, n - 1]$ at random
 2: $P_1 \leftarrow k * P = (x_1, y_1)$
 3: Convert x_1 to an integer $\bar{x}_1$
 4: $r \leftarrow \bar{x}_1 \bmod n$
 5: $e \leftarrow H(m)$
 6: $s \leftarrow k^{-1}(e + dr) \bmod n$
 7: **return** (r, s)

Algorithm 4 shows the verification of an ECDSA signature. As in the generation of the signature, calculations with two different moduli are also involved in the verification process. For signature verification, one modular inversion, two modular multiplications and 2 scalar multiplications are required, although the latter can be interleaved and take in fact only negligible longer than a single scalar multiplication.

Finally, Algorithms 5 and 6 show the use of the RSA algorithm for signing: in fact, signing in this context just means encrypting a hash with the private key (usually about 1.024 bits in size), requiring one modular exponentiation with a 1.024-bit exponent. Verification is then done by using the sender's public key (usually in the order of magnitude of 16 bits) as the exponent in a modular exponentiation.

4.2   Key Establishment Primitives

As in the case of signature primitives, there are three main algorithms for establishing a shared key:

Algorithm 4. ECDSA Signature Verification

Require: Domain Parameters $D = (q, FR, S, a, b, P, n, h)$, public key Q, message m, signature (r, s), hash function H
Ensure: ACCEPT or REFUSE message
1: **if** $r, s \notin [1, n - 1]$ **then**
2:     **return** REFUSE
3: **end if**
4: $e \leftarrow H(m)$
5: $w \leftarrow s^{-1} \bmod n$
6: $u_1 \leftarrow ew \bmod n$
7: $u_2 \leftarrow rw \bmod n$
8: $X \leftarrow u_1 P + u_2 Q = (x_1, y_1)$
9: **if** $X = \mathcal{O}$ **then**
10:     **return** REFUSE
11: **end if**
12: Convert x_1 to an integer $\bar{x}_1$
13: $v \leftarrow \bar{x}_1 \bmod n$
14: **if** $v = r$ **then**
15:     **return** ACCEPT
16: **else**
17:     **return** REFUSE
18: **end if**

Algorithm 5. RSA Signature Generation

Require: Sender's private key d, Sender's public key (n, e), message m, hash function H
Ensure: Signature s
1: $h \leftarrow H(m)$
2: $s \leftarrow h^d \bmod n$
3: **return** s

- The Diffie-Hellman Algorithm (DH) or its ephemeral variant (DHE)
- The Elliptic Curve Diffie-Hellman Algorithm (ECDH) or its ephemeral version (ECDHE) and
- The RSA algorithm

The basic Diffie-Hellman scheme is as follows:

1. Both entities agree on a finite cyclic group G^1 and a generator g of this group.
2. A chooses a number a, calculates $x = g * a \in G$ and sends x to B.
3. B chooses a number b, calculates $y = g * b \in G$ and sends y to A.
4. A calculates $K' = y^a = (g * b) * a = g * b * a$.
5. B calculates $K'' = x^b = (g * a) * b = g * a * b$.
6. Since the law of commutativity holds, $K' = K''$.

---

[1] Note that it does not matter whether this group is written additive or multiplicative; in the following description the $*$ means application of the group operation a, or b respectively, times. So in a multiplicative group we need to perform an exponentiation, in an additive group a multiplication.

Algorithm 6. RSA Signature Verification

Require: Sender's public key (n, e), message m, signature s, hash function H
Ensure: ACCEPT or REFUSE message
1: $h \leftarrow H(m)$
2: $s' \leftarrow s^e \bmod n$
3: **if** $s' = h$ **then**
4:     **return** ACCEPT
5: **else**
6:     **return** REFUSE
7: **end if**

An attacker knows G, g, x and y, but is assumed to be unable to calculate a from x (or b from y). The same approach is taken for the elliptic curve version of this algorithm, with all exponentiations in the multiplicative group exchanged by scalar multiplications in the group of points on the curve. In the non-ephemeral versions of the protocol, the client usually receives all the information required to calculate the shared secret in the server's *Certificate* message, and sends its share of the secret back in the *ClientKeyEx-change* message. Both server and client have to perform one modular exponentiation (respectively one scalar multiplication). In the ephemeral case of the protocol, fresh values are used for each run, so the server has to generate the (signed) *ServerKeyEx-change* message to transmit these values to the client. The client needs an additional signature verification step, the server needs to generate one signature, and perform one modular exponentiation, or a scalar multiplication in the elliptic curve case. The bene-fit of this protocol variant is that it guarantees *perfect forward secrecy*, meaning that a compromised connection does not influence the security of past transmissions.

In the case of RSA, the client simply generates a secret, encrypts it with the server's public key and sends it back. The client must thus perform a modular exponentiation with a very small exponent, the server has to calculate a modular multiplication with its (considerably larger) private key. The drawback of this approach is that the quality of the secret depends solely on the client.

5   Implementation and Results

In our practical implementation we used the MatrixSSL[2] library extended by our own generic cryptographic library supporting elliptic curves over arbitrary prime and binary extension fields. Implementation details of this library are presented in [6] and [7], in this work we currently only investigated the version without resistance against side-channel attacks. As server we used an AMD Athlon64 X2 5200+ with one physical core deactivated, fixed to 2.7GHz. The role of the client was performed by a 200MHz Compaq iPaq PDA, running Familiar Linux. The PDA was connected to the server using a USB cable, to avoid the influence of network devices like router or switches on the communication. Tables 1 and 2 give the number of high-level operations performed by server and client, respectively, as well as the total number of messages that have to

---

[2] www.matrixssl.com

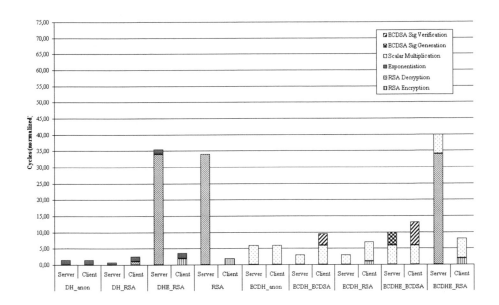

Fig. 3. Breakdown of handshake when one-way authentication is used

be exchanged during a full handshake. It can be observed that the client suffers always more from increased security than the server, in terms of messages to be sent as well as in terms of operations to be performed. Tables 3 and 4 give the cycle count for the individual operations, normalized so that a modular exponentiation with a public RSA (that is, 16-bit) key has a cycle count of one. All elliptic curve operations are performed over a 192-bit prime field, for RSA 1.024-bit moduli are used. Here it becomes obvious that increased security (like using ephemeral Diffie-Hellman) results in a much higher load on the server when using RSA than when using the elliptic curve approach, since the server now has to perform expensive private RSA key operations. For example, where the total load on the server increases by more the twenty-fold when switching to the ephemeral version of Diffie-Hellman combined with RSA signatures, the workload in the elliptic curve version (ECDHE with ECDSA signature) only doubles. This trend is also evident when looking at the client, here the difference when switching to a higher security level (especially when using mutual authentication and thereby requiring the client to also perform private key operations) is even more pronounced as on the server side.

Finally, Figures 3 and 4 give a detailed breakdown of the individual operations performed during the handshake process by server and client, for one-way and mutual authentication, respectively. An interesting fact is the observation that the workload for the client remains almost the same, regardless whether ephemeral or non-ephemeral versions of the algorithms are used. In these cases, the additional load created by the higher security level is put entirely on the server side. The biggest fraction of the key exchange process is taken up by the RSA private key operations, since they are the only one involving the entire 1.024-bit key. In the elliptic curve variants, this operation

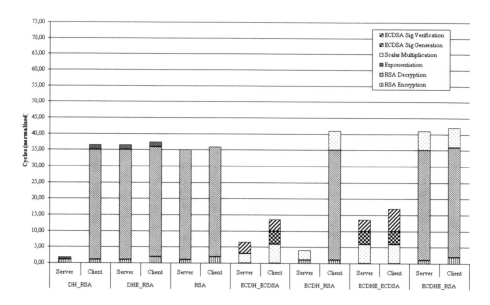

Fig. 4. Breakdown of handshake when mutual authentication is used

does not exist, resulting in a generally lower load put on the participating parties. So these figures suggest that when server load is not an issue, ephemeral versions should be used. For a resource constrained server, on the other hand, the use of elliptic curve operations may still allow for the added security provided by the ephemeral algorithms, which could not be used anymore when RSA based methods are employed. Also when looking at the comparison between one-way and mutual authentication, the additional load put on the client is significantly lower when using ECC compared to the RSA counterpart.

6   Conclusions

We have performed a thorough examination of the TLS handshake with a focus on the number of messages exchanged in relation to the chosen ciphersuites. Especially in the context of constrained, mobile or embedded devices, the number of messages that has to be transmitted to setup a secure connection can have a huge impact on the performance and lifetime of the single appliances. We then observed the influence of higher security on the number of messages and on the load put on the participating parties. Our results indicate that elliptic curve cryptography is not only useful for this special environment due to the smaller memory requirements, but also that the increase in load put on the parties when the security of the connection is heightened, through mutual authentication or the usage of ephemeral variants of the Diffie-Hellman protocol, is significantly smaller when compared to its RSA/DSA counterparts. Future research will now try to bring down the required messages to a bare minimum without sacrificing integrity or authenticity of the connection.

Acknowledgements. The authors are supported by the MA27 - EU-Strategie und Wirtschaftsentwicklung - in the course of the funding programme Stiftungsprofessuren und Kompetenzteams für die Wiener Fachhochschul-Ausbildungen.

References

1. Blake-Wilson, S., Bolyard, N., Gupta, V., Hawk, C., Moeller, B.: RFC 4492: Elliptic Curve Cryptography (ECC) Cipher Suites for Transport Layer Security (TLS) (2006)
2. Blake-Wilson, S., Nystrom, M., Hopwood, D., Mikkelsen, J., Wright, T.: RFC 4366: Transport Layer Security (TLS) Extensions (2006)
3. Dierks, T., Rescorla, E.: RFC 4346: The Transport Layer Security (TLS) Protocol Version 1.1 (2006)
4. Gupta, V., Gupta, S., Chang, S.: Performance Analysis of Elliptic Curve Cryptography for SSL. In: 1st ACM Workshop on Wireless Security, pp. 49–87. ACM, New York (2002)
5. Hankerson, D., Menezes, A., Vanstone, S.: Guide to Elliptic Curve Cryptography. Springer, New York (2004)
6. Koschuch, M., Hudler, M., Krüger, M., Großschädl, J., Payer, U.: Workload Characterization of a Lightweight SSL Implementation Resistant to Side-Channel Attacks. In: Franklin, M.K., Hui, L.C.K., Wong, D.S. (eds.) CANS 2008. LNCS, vol. 5339, pp. 349–365. Springer, Heidelberg (2008)
7. Koschuch, M., Lechner, J., Weitzer, A., Großschädl, J., Szekely, A., Tillich, S., Wolkerstorfer, J.: Hardware/Software Co-Design of Elliptic Curve Cryptography on an 8051 Microcontroller. In: Goubin, L., Matsui, M. (eds.) CHES 2006. LNCS, vol. 4249, pp. 430–444. Springer, Heidelberg (2006)
8. Krasner, J.: Using Elliptic Curve Cryptography (ECC) for Enhanced Embedded Security - Financial Advantages of ECC over RSA or Diffie-Hellman(DH). In: Embedded Market Forecasters, American Technology (2004)
9. Lederer, C., Mader, R., Koschuch, M., Großschädl, J., Szekely, A., Tillich, S.: Energy-Efficient Implementation of ECDH Key Exchange for Wireless Sensor Networks. In: Markowitch, O., Bilas, A., Hoepman, J.-H., Mitchell, C.J., Quisquater, J.-J. (eds.) WISTP 2009. LNCS, vol. 5746, pp. 112–127. Springer, Heidelberg (2009)
10. Lenstra, A.K., Verheul, E.R.: Selecting Cryptographic Key Sizes. Journal of Cryptology 14(4), 255–293 (2001)
11. Potlapally, N.R., Raviy, S., Raghunathany, A., Lakshminarayanaz, G.: Optimizing Public-Key Encryption for Wireless Clients. In: 2002 IEEE International Conference on Communications, vol. 2, pp. 1050–1056. IEEE Press, New York (2002)
12. Ravi, S., Raghutan, A., Potlapally, N.: Securing Wireless Data: System Architecture Challenges. In: 15th International Symposium on System Synthesis (ISSS 2002), pp. 195–200. IEEE Press, New York (2002)

Appendix

This Appendix lists the number of primitive operations for server and client when performing the authentication and key-exchange phase of the SSL/TLS-handshake, normalized cycle numbers for each individual operation, and totals for server and client.

Table 1. Number of High-Level Cryptographic Operations performed by the Server during SSL/TLS-Handshake. Numbers behind "/" indicate mutual authentication.

Key Exchange	# of Messages	RSA Encryption	RSA Decryption	Exponentiation	DSS Sig Generation	DSS Sig Verification	Scalar Multiplication	ECDSA Sig Generation	ECDSA Sig Verification
					Server				
DH_anon	4			2					
DH_DSS	4/5			1		0/1			
DH_RSA	4/5	0/1		1					
DHE_DSS	5/6			2	1	0/1			
DHE_RSA	5/6	0/1	1	2					
RSA	4/5	0/1	1						
ECDH_anon	4						2		
ECDH_ECDSA	4/5						1		0/1
ECDH_RSA	4/5	0/1					1		
ECDHE_ECDSA	5/6						2	1	0/1
ECDHE_RSA	5/6	0/1	1				2		

Table 2. Number of High-Level Cryptographic Operations performed by the Client during SSL/TLS-Handshake. Numbers behind "/" indicate mutual authentication.

Key Exchange	# of Messages	RSA Encryption	RSA Decryption	Exponentiation	DSS Sig Generation	DSS Sig Verification	Scalar Multiplication	ECDSA Sig Generation	ECDSA Sig Verification
					Client				
DH_anon	3			2					
DH_DSS	3/5			2	0/1	1			
DH_RSA	3/5	1	0/1	2					
DHE_DSS	3/5			2	0/1	2			
DHE_RSA	3/5	2	0/1	2					
RSA	3/5	2	0/1						
ECDH_anon	3						2		
ECDH_ECDSA	3/5						2	0/1	1
ECDH_RSA	3/5	1	0/1				2		
ECDHE_ECDSA	3/5						2	0/1	2
ECDHE_RSA	3/5	2	0/1				2		

Table 3. Cycle count for the server to perform the SSL/TLS-Handshake, normalized so that an RSA encryption with a 16-bit exponent needs a count of one. Numbers behind "/" indicate mutual authentication.

Key Exchange	Server cycles							
	# of Messages	RSA Encryption	RSA Decryption	Exponentiation	Scalar Multiplication	ECDSA Sig Generation	ECDSA Sig Verification	Total
DH_anon	4			1.5				1.5
DH_RSA	4/5	0/1		0.75				0.75/1.75
DHE_RSA	5/6	0/1	34	1.5				35.5/36.5
RSA	4/6	0/1	34					34/35
ECDH_anon	4				6			6
ECDH_ECDSA	4/5				3		0/3.5	3/6.5
ECDH_RSA	4/5	0/1			3			3/4
ECDHE_ECDSA	5/6				6	4	0/3.5	10/13.5
ECDHE_RSA	5/6	0/1	34		6			40/41

Table 4. Cycle count for the client to perform the SSL/TLS-Handshake, normalized so that an RSA encryption with a 16-bit exponent needs a count of one. Numbers behind "/" indicate mutual authentication.

Key Exchange	Client cycles							
	# of Messages	RSA Encryption	RSA Decryption	Exponentiation	Scalar Multiplication	ECDSA Sig Generation	ECDSA Sig Verification	Total
DH_anon	3			1.5				1.5
DH_RSA	3/5	1	0/34	1.5				2.5/36.5
DHE_RSA	3/5	2	0/34	1.5				3.5/37.5
RSA	3/5	2	0/34					2/36
ECDH_anon	3				6			6
ECDH_ECDSA	3/5				6	0/4	3.5	9.5/13.5
ECDH_RSA	3/5	1	0/34		6			7/41
ECDHE_ECDSA	3/5				6	0/4	7	13/17
ECDHE_RSA	3/5	2	0/34		6			8/42

Mobile Applications Middleware for File Swapping

Mario A. Gomez-Rodriguez, Victor J. Sosa-Sosa, and Ivan Lopez-Arevalo

Laboratory of Information Technology (LTI), CINVESTAV-Tamaulipas
Parque Científico y Tecnológico TECNOTAM
Km. 5.5 carretera Cd. Victoria-Soto La Marina
C.P. 87130. Cd. Victoria, Tamaulipas, Mexico
{mgomez,vjsosa,ilopez}@tamps.cinvestav.mx
www.tamps.cinvestav.mx

Abstract. Intelligent mobile phones (e.g. smartphones) integrate the functions of PDA (Personal Digital Assistant) in conventional mobile phones. These technologic developments allow them to run applications that generate a large number of files and, as a consequence, require a greater storage capacity. Unfortunately, the storage capacity on these devices has not grown at the pace that mobile applications require. Keeping files in external servers becomes a typical requierement for these type of devices. This paper presents a mobile application midlleware for file swapping. This middleware makes easier transfering files between a mobile device and an external storage server by accessing the best wireless connection (WiFi, GPRS/UMTS) available, considering quality and cost of the service. It is also able to use the Multimedia Messaging Service (MMS) as another option for transferring files. A file swapping application was built on top of this Middleware. This application will detect when the device ran out of local memory and will automatically send selected files from the mobile device to an external storage server, freeing the mobile storage memory. To decide which files should be backed up, it implements several file replacement policies. Results showed that the selection of one replacement policy will be a trade-off between the efficiency of the algorithm and the cost of the wireless service available when a file needs to be backed up.

Keywords: File swapping, Mobile application, Middleware.

1 Introduction

The cell phone is one of the most popular mobile devices. It has constantly evolved since its invention. It's common that current mobile devices have two or more communication interfaces such as USB, infrared, Bluetooth, GPRS and the IEEE 802.11, popularly known as Wi-Fi. Wireless networks improve the utility of portable computing devices, enabling mobile user's versatile communication and continuous access to services and resources of the terrestrial networks. Mobile phones have also been endowed with more computing power. Intelligent mobile phones (a.k.a. smartphones) integrate the functions of PDA (Personal Digital Assistant) in conventional mobile phones. These technologic developments allow current mobile phones to run applications that generate a large number of files and, as a consequence, require a greater storage capacity. Unfortunately,

M.S. Obaidat, G.A. Tsihrintzis, and J. Filipe (Eds.): ICETE 2010, CCIS 222, pp. 84–94, 2012.
© Springer-Verlag Berlin Heidelberg 2012

the storage capacity on these devices has not grown at the pace that mobile applications require. Once a mobile device exceeds its storage capacity, it is necessary to download its files (such as text, images, music, videos, etc.) in an external storage system (e.g., a computer), backing up the information. This process usually limits the mobility because users have to connect their mobile devices to a fixed external storage using a cable (e.g., USB), or through a short-range wireless network such as Infrared or Bluetooth. These storage limitations reduce the mobility and storage capacity of users, particularly in situations when users are travelling and they need more space, for instance, to keep their pictures or videos and there is not available a nearby external storage device. These situations motivate the development of supporting tools that allow files to be exchanged between mobile devices and external storage systems in a transparent way, taking into account LAN or WAN wireless connectivity, cost of the service and available storage. Since there are different mobile devices that work with various computing platforms or operating systems (e.g., Symbian, Blackberry, Windows Mobile, Android, etc.), it is not feasible to develop a proprietary tool for a specific platform, because it would limit its usability. That is why the design of a solution to this problem must include multiplatform considerations that allow better coverage in different mobile devices.

The situations described above were our motivation to build a Mobile Application Middleware (MAM) that can be capable of running on different operating systems and allow mobile applications to send and receive files from an external storage server, connected to Internet through different wireless technologies, taking into account the cost and quality of the service. The MAM was tested by developing a File Swapping Service (FSS) for mobile phones, which offers a service of swapping files between the mobile device and an external storage server in a transparent way. Users of this application perceive a virtual storage space, which is higher than the real memory space included in the mobile device. FSS is similar to a file caching service, reason why it integrates an efficient replacing policy to optimize the file access time.

The rest of the paper is structured as follows. Section II describes related work; some of the systems described in Section II gave technical support to the Mobile Application Middleware (MAM). Section III presents the MAM architecture, which is divided in three main parts: Client-side application layer, Core connection layer and Server-side application layer. In Section IV, a mobile application named File Swapping Service (FSS) is presented. This application was developed as a use case for testing the MAM. Section V includes final comments and mentions ongoing work.

2 Related Work

Mobile file systems like Coda [14,10], Odyssey [13], Bayou [6] and Xmiddle [12], worked with the data sharing-oriented problem in distributed computing environments. This problem could be directly related to the file transfer problem in mobile phones. Although with different focus, all of these systems try to maximise the availability of the data using data replication, each one differing in the way that they maintain consistency in the replicas. Coda provides server replications and disconnected operations; it allows access of data during the disconnection period and focuses on long-term disconnections, which more often occurs in mobile computing environments. Odyssey is the successor of Coda, which has been improved introducing context-awareness and application-dependent behaviors that allow the use of these approaches in mobile computing settings. The Bayou system is a platform to build collaborative applications, its emphasis is on supporting application-specific conflict detection and resolution. It has been designed as a system to support data sharing among mobile users and is intended to run in mobile computing environments. The system use a read-any/write-any replication scheme, thus the replicated data are only weakly consistent. Unlike previous systems, Bayou exploits application knowledge for dependency checks and merges procedures. Lui et al [11] propose a mobile file system, NFS/M, based on the NFS 2.0 and the Linux platform. It supports client-side data caching in order to improve the system performance, reducing the latency during weak connection periods. Atkin et al [1] propose other file system that, like NFS/M, supports client-side caching. Some applications like GSpaceMobile [9] and Emoze [7], enable the file transfer between mobile devices and external storage servers. However, these applications only consider a proprietary storage server.

Boulkenafed and Issarny [5] present a middleware service that allows collaborative data sharing among ad hoc groups that are dynamically formed according to the connectivity achieved by the ad hoc WLAN. These middleware enable to share and manipulate common data in a collaborative manner (e.g, working meet, network gaming, etc.) without the need for any established infrastructure. They implemented their middleware service within a file system in order to evaluate it. The result was a distributed file system for mobile ad hoc data sharing. It is worth mentioning that the performance measurements were done on a platform of ten laptops, and they only use IEEE 802.11b WLAN in ad hoc mode, unlike MAM, which is able to use Wi-Fi, GSM, GPRS or UMTS networks. Belimpasakis et al [2] propose a content sharing middleware for mobile devices using different protocols (UPnP, Atom and WebDAV), providing interfaces for applications, in order to allow 3rd party developers to create applications with sharing capabilities. The middlewares mentioned above make use of both Wi-Fi and GPRS wireless networks. However, they consider neither transferring files through a messaging system like MMS nor the portability issue. We have decided to develop MAM using J2ME, offering portability.

3   Service Architecture

In this section, the MAM architecture is described in more detail. The architecture is mainly divided in three components or layers: Client-side application layer, Core connection layer and server-side application layer. Figure 1 depicts this architecture whose components are presented in the following sub-sections.

3.1   Client-Side Application Layer (API_ESS)

This layer deals with file transferring operations (send/receive) required from mobile applications. One main function is to make transparent the selection of the available wireless connection (WiFi, GPRS or UMTS) or messaging service (MMS) provided by the lower layer (Core) to the mobile application. The main component of the client-side application layer is the External Storage Services Module (API_ESS). This module

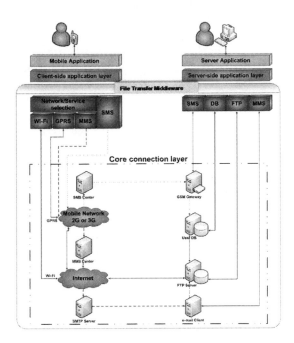

Fig. 1. Layers of the Mobile Application Middleware

offers a set of wrappers for connections with different wireless networks. It uses a connection selector that indicates which wireless network will be used. When connectivity is limited, the connection selector offers the MMS services as the best option for file transferring.

The API_ESS includes both messaging services SMS and MMS. Due to the limitations of SMS (about 150 bytes by message), MMS is the default option chosen by the connection selector.

The API_ESS could include a configuration file that indicates the priorities assigned to the wireless connection services. The first in the list indicates the cheapest service in terms of cost or bandwidth consumption. The API_ESS functions are divided into upper level functions and lower level functions. The upper functions are typically used by mobile applications, e.g., selectRoot( ), retr(file) and stor(file). These functions send and receive files from an external storage service making totally transparent the type of wireless o messaging service used. Lower level functions deal directly with wireless connection and messaging wrappers. Examples of these functions are: autoDetectConnection(), getConnection() and setConnection.

The current implementation of the API_ESS includes the following wrappers:

– *Wi-Fi/GPRS*: It enables to send/request files via the IEEE 802.11 and the GPRS protocols.
– *MMS*: It represents an alternative option for sending and requesting files using the Multimedia Messaging Service (MMS). MMS has to be supported by a mobile phone carrier; otherwise it will not be available. This wrapper will commonly be used when the Wi-Fi and GPRS (or UMTS) networks are not available.

- *SMS-M*: The purpose of this wrapper is to provide mobile applications with one more option for sending information to and/or receiving from the external storage server in future applications. The mobile application FSS uses this wrapper for registering user accounts in a web storage server that is supported by the server-side layer of the MAM.

3.2   Core Connection Layer

This part of the architecture represents the communication services needed by our middleware. It includes modules to deal with the most popular wireless technologies and messaging services. A brief description of these modules is as follows:

- *Center (SMSC)*: The SMSC is responsible for relaying messages between short message entities (SMEs, elements that can send or receive text messages) and store and forward messages, if the recipient SME is not available.
- *MMS Center (MMSC)*: The MMSC is a key element in the MMS architecture, and it is composed of an MMS relay and an MMS server, which are responsible both to store and manage incoming and outgoing multimedia messages. It also ensures interoperability with other messaging systems [4,3] by means of different communication interfaces (e.g., MM3 interface).
- *SMTP Server*: It receives the files that have been sent via multimedia messaging (MMS) to an email account. The data travels across the wireless network available (2.5G or 3G) and are routed by the MMSC to the Internet, then get to our SMTP server. This option is activated when socket connections fail.
- *GSM Gateway*: It receives text messages (SMS) that are sent by the client for complementary services, e.g., to create an account.
- *User DB*: It is an optional database that could contain information of subscribers registered by mobile applications based on MAM.
- *FTP Server*: It is the process responsible for receiving and storing the files. In the FSS application, users have to be registered before obtaining a storage space in the external storage server. Files managed by the FTP Server can come from direct socket connected clients (using a wireless connection) or e-mail clients (using a MMS connection). This server is one of the key parts of the architecture as it controls all the files received in the external storage server.
- *e-mail Client*: This process is used by the server-side layer when the original server-side MMS receiver fails. In this situation, files that are sent by clients using MMS are redirected to a mail box defined in the server-side application layer. The e-mail Client process is in charge of obtaining these files from the indicated mail box using the Post Office Protocol (POP3).

3.3   Server-Side Application Layer (API_ISS)

This layer gives developers an infrastructure (API_ISS) for building a storage server that considers mobile devices. API_ISS includes modules for receiving and sending files through different communication services such as WiFi, GPRS, UMTS and the Multimedia Message Service (MMS). Different types of servers can be implemented using this API. The particular behavior can be customized, for instance, by developing a web storage service or a file sharing storage server. The Internal Storage Service (ISS) module represents the main module included in the API_ISS.

The API_ISS is a module that offers a set of methods, which will be used by server-side applications. It contains functions for managing connections and user accounts as well as functions for receiving and transmitting data through different wireless networks. It includes similar wrappers like those located in the client side application layer. It implements the FTP service, which packs all the methods for transferring and receiving files going to or coming from mobile devices. A file storage server that is developed with the API_ISS could connect with other distributed storage servers building a big virtual disk. This distributed approach allows it to increase its virtual available storage space by integrating the storage space offered by other external storage.

4   Use Case

This section describes a use case for the Mobile Application Middleware (MAM). A mobile application named File Swapping Service (FSS) that uses our MAM was developed. The purpose of FSS is to send files from a mobile phone to an external storage server when the mobile phone runs out of memory. This process is transparent for users that can always see the complete list of files, even when some of them are not physically kept in the memory of the mobile phone. When a file is required by the user, FSS requests the missing file from the storage server using any wireless network available or the MMS service, depending on the service priority defined in the configuration file. Automatic swapping allows mobile devices to free storage space in a transparent way. A web storage server was also developed based on MAM. To use our web storage server, users have to be registered before sending files. The registration process can be done through a SMS message or by filling in a web form. FSS and the MAM were developed using the J2ME platform. The configuration, profile and basic libraries needed for our development are: CLDC 1.1 (Connected Limited Device Configuration 1.1.), MIDP2.0 (Mobile Information Device Profile 2.0), WMAPI 2.0 (Wireless Messaging API 2.0), SATSA-Crypto (JSR 177) and PDA Profile (JSR 75).

Due to the fact that FSS works like a caching system, a file replacement police was included in its implementation. A benchmark based on metrics taken from different real mobile phones was also created. The main metrics were: the average storage space in a mobile phone, the average file size, and the average data transfer rate in wireless LAN and WAN networks such as WiFi y GPRS. Table 1 includes measures taken from different mobile phones and PDAs such as: Nokia5530, 7020, N95 and HP iPAQ HW6945, Blackberry 8220.

A collection of more than 1000 files taken from different mobile phones revealed an average file size of 1.3MB. More of them were of music, photos and videos. Transmitting files of 1.3MB from different mobile phones to an external storage server connected to Internet using WiFi revealed an average time of 8.3s (about 1.3Mb/s). Using GPRS for the same transmissions showed an average time of 148s (about 73Kb/s).

These experiments gave us a realistic average transmission time of wireless networks with different traffic loads. The traffic coming from Internet connections played an important role in these measures. Enriquez [8] made several tests trying to find an optimal

Table 1. Common measures in limited mobile phones and PDAs

Measure	Size
MAX_MEM_SIZE	2GB
MAX_FILE_SIZE	15MB
MIN_FILE_SIZE	469KB
AVG_FILE_SIZE	1.3MB

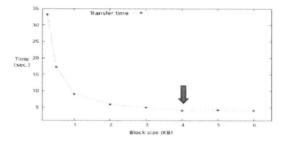

Fig. 2. An optimal transmission block size in a WLAN network

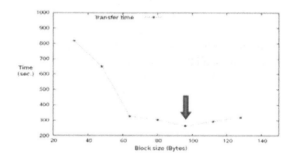

Fig. 3. An optimal transmission block size for a GPRS network

block size for transmitting files between a mobile phone and a data server (PC) using WiFi and GPRS networks, considering different traffic hours. The optimal block size obtained using WiFi was 4KB (Figure 2) and for GPRS was 96B (Figure 3). However, the GPRS transfer rate showed a high variability in hours with high traffic, resulting in many communications errors. Several block sizes were tested with high traffic to observe the GPRS behavior. GPRS showed less variability when a block size of 64B was used, resulting in a better behavior. This stable behavior motivated the use of a block size of 64B in MAM, instead of 96B found in [8].

As we mentioned above, FSS is a mobile application that works like a caching service, reason why it includes a file replacement policy. The main task of a replacement police is to decide which file will be sent to the external storage server to free storage space in the mobile phone memory. In order to find a good replacement policy for FSS, four algorithms were tested. These algorithms were: LRU (Least Recently Used), LFU (Least Frequently Used), LFS (Largest File Size), and SFS (Smallest File Size). As their names indicate, the LRU policy will send the least recently used file to the external

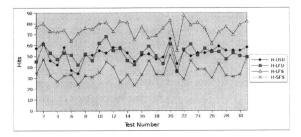

Fig. 4. Average hit ratio obtained by FSS using different replacement polices

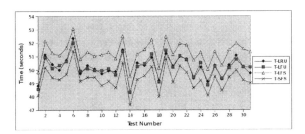

Fig. 5. Average transmission time obtained by FSS using diferrent replacement policies

storage server. LFU will send the least frequently used file, LFS the largest file, and SFS the smallest one. If there is more than one file as the largest or the smallest, a LRU police is applied. A benchmark that reproduces a sequence of send/receive operations, using a group of 120 files with sizes ranging from 512KB to 2.5MB was implemented. Thirty one experiments were carried out with different scenarios. Connections for sending and receiving files were randomly changing between GPRS and WiFi, emulating mobile users.

Figure 4 depicts the behavior of the average hit ratio in FSS using each replacement policy (in 31 experiments). Figure 5 shows the average transmission time.

As we can see, if FSS replaces files based on the largest file size (LFS), it obtains the best hit ratio (almost 8 of 10 files were in the mobile phone memory when they were requested by the user). However, it also obtains the greatest average transmission time, which could be a result of transmitting large files using a GPRS connection at the moment of a miss. These results give us some insights to determine if we should prioritize between the quantity of bytes transmitted and the total time consumption using the network, especially in the GPRS/GSM networks. In most of the cases the wireless communication service is charged based on bandwidth consumption. Figure 6 shows the total bandwidth consumption after running all of the algorithms. These experiments did not show a correlation between the total bandwidth consumption and the average transmission time. Even though the LFU algorithm had low total bandwidth consumption, it did not show low average transmission time. It happened so because most of the time that the mobile application had to send/receive files (using the LRU algorithm) coincided with a GPRS connection.

The evaluations using FSS gave us information for deciding which algorithm could be implemented as part of our Mobile application Middleware (MAM), and to consider

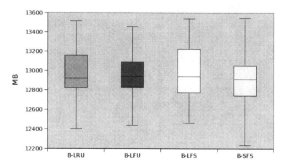

Fig. 6. Total bandwidth consumption obtained by FSS using 4 different replacement policies

if it would be better to include a fixed replacement policy or an adaptive one, considering if the cost of the communication service is based on time or bandwidth consumption. In the current implementation of FSS, users are able to define a cost-based priority list that best fits his or her requirements. This priority list has to be included in a configuration file. Information like depicted in Figure 4, 5 and 6 can help to decide the order of priorities based on the cost of the services in a particular region.

Another important topic considered in FSS was information privacy. This topic becomes an important factor when transmitting files from a mobile phone to an external and public storage server. In cases where the storage server does not offer a private place to keep the user information, FSS can encrypt the files before sending them to the server. In these cases, the external storage server will keep only encrypted files, offering privacy to the information. The encryption process is carried out by using the Java Specification Request 177 (JSR 177, Satsa Crypto). FSS uses the Advanced Encryption Standard (AES), which is a symmetric key algorithm with a key and block size (it could vary) of 128bits. Experiments for evaluating the impact in the transferring time when using encryption were conducted with FSS. The objective was to find out the impact in terms of the cost of extra bandwidth and transferring time needed when encryption is applied. For this experiment, the use of the MMS service as another option (included in MAM) to transfer files was tested. To execute this experiment, our test bed had to be redesigned, because the largest public MMS service provider in Mexico has defined a maximum file size for each MMS message of 100KB. FSS was tested using a group of 100 files with sizes ranging from 80 to 100KB.

Table 2 shows how the encryption process increases the average file transfer time until 3 times in some cases. We can see how WiFi connections are the most affected. This situation is more evident when small files are transmitted. Since GPRS networks

Table 2. Average file transfer time with and without encryption using files with an average size of 90kb

Average File Transfer Time (AFTT)	**Wi-Fi**	**GPRS**	**MMS**
AFTT without Encryption	0.07s	1.23s	32.56s
AFTT with Encryption	0.21s	1.96s	86.12s
Impact Using Encryption	3 times more	1.59 times more	2.64 times more

have a low bandwidth and low transmission rates, the resulting impact of the encryption process is lower. The transmission times obtained from the MMS service showed a high variability, because the public MMS server provider in Mexico does not guarantee real time transmissions.

5 Final Comments

As mobile devices evolve, they require more storage capacity to keep the large amount of files that new mobile applications generate. This paper briefly introduced an Mobile Application Middleware (MAM) for mobile applications. The middleware allows mobile applications to store and request files from an external storage server, taking advantage of available wireless networks and considering issues related to the cost of the service. As a use case, a mobile application that transparently swaps files between a mobile device and an external storage server was developed, increasing storage space in the former. In this application, different file replacement policies were tested. An important parameter that has to be considered when deciding about a replacement policy is the cost of the service. Results obtained in this work showed that it is not a trivial decision to select a specific replacement policy for a mobile device. Mobile devices do not present a correlation between the bandwidth and time consumption because they do not keep the same wireless connection any time. Service costs are usually defined by wireless WAN providers, and could be based on bandwidth consumption or time consumption, criteria that have to be included in the replacement algorithms. MAM is also prepared for transferring files using the Multimedia Messaging Service (MMS), an additional option to be considered for users when connections are limited. Our experiments revealed that the time for transferring encrypted files could rise the original time in a factor of three. This increase is more evident when small files are transmitted using wireless network with high transmission rates.

Acknowledgements. This research was partially funded by project number 51623 from Mix Funds of the National Council for Science and Technology (CONACYT-Mexico) and the Government of Tamaulipas State.

References

1. Atkin, B., Birman, K.P.: Network-aware adaptation techniques for mobile file systems. In: NCA 2006: Proceedings of the Fifth IEEE International Symposium on Network Computing and Applications, pp. 181–188. IEEE Computer Society, Washington, DC, USA (2006)
2. Belimpasakis, P., Luoma, J.P., Börzsei, M.: Content sharing middleware for mobile devices. In: MOBILWARE 2008: Proceedings of the 1st International Conference on MOBILe Wireless MiddleWARE, Operating Systems, and Applications. ICST (Institute for Computer Sciences, Social-Informatics and Telecommunications Engineering), pp. 1–8. ICST, Brussels (2007)
3. Bodic, G.L.: Multimedia Messaging Service. An Engineering Approach to MMS, 1st edn. (2003)
4. Bodic, G.L.: Mobile Messaging Technologies and Services SMS, EMS and MMS. 2nd edn. (2005)

5. Boulkenafed, M., Issarny, V.: A Middleware Service for Mobile Ad Hoc Data Sharing, Enhancing Data Availability. In: Endler, M., Schmidt, D.C. (eds.) Middleware 2003. LNCS, vol. 2672, pp. 493–511. Springer, Heidelberg (2003)
6. Demers, A., Petersen, K., Spreitzer, M., Terry, D., Theimer, M., Welch, B.: The bayou architecture: Support for data sharing among mobile users (1994)
7. Emoze^{TM} (August 2009), http://www.emoze.com/
8. Enríquez, J.A.V.: A vertical handover platform for applications on mobile devices. Master's thesis, CINVESTAV (2009),
    http://www.tamps.cinvestav.mx/sites/default/files/tesis_1.zip
9. GSpaceMobile (March 2009), https://www.ibomobi.com/home/
10. Kistler, J.J., Satyanarayanan, M.: Disconnected operation in the coda file system. ACM Trans. Comput. Syst. 10, 3–25 (1992),
    http://doi.acm.org/10.1145/146941.146942
11. Lui, J.C.S., So, O.K.Y., Tam, T.S.: NFS/M: An Open Platform Mobile File System. In: ICDCS 1998: Proceedings of the The 18th International Conference on Distributed Computing Systems, p. 488. IEEE Computer Society, Washington, DC, USA (1998)
12. Mascolo, C., Capra, L., Zachariadis, S., Emmerich, W.: Xmiddle: A data-sharing middleware for mobile computing. Int. Journal on Personal and Wireless Communications 21(1), 77–103 (2002)
13. Satyanarayanan, M.: Mobile information access. IEEE Personal Communications 3, 26–33 (1996)
14. Satyanarayanan, M., Kistler, J.J., Kumar, P., Okasaki, M.E., Siegel, E.H., David, S.C.: Coda: A highly available file system for a distributed workstation environment. IEEE Transactions on Computers 39(4), 447–459 (1990)

Part II
e-Business

Optimization of a Handwriting Recognition Algorithm for a Mobile Enterprise Health Information System on the Basis of Real-Life Usability Research

Andreas Holzinger[1,2], Martin Schlögl[1,2], Bernhard Peischl[3], and Matjaz Debevc[4]

[1] Medical University Graz, Institute for Medical Informatics (IMI)
Research Unit HCI4MED, A-8036 Graz, Austria
[2] Graz University of Technology, Institute for Information Systems and Computer Media
(IICM), A-8010 Graz, Austria
[3] Graz University of Technology, A-8010 Graz, Institute for Software Technology
[4] University of Maribor, Faculty of Electrical Engineering and Computer Science
SI-2000 Maribor, Slovenia
a.holzinger@hci4all.at, bernhard.peischl@ist.tugraz.at
matjaz.debevc@uni-mb.si

Abstract. Optimizing data acquisition in mobile health care in order to increase accuracy and efficiency can benefit the patient. The software company FERK-Systems has been providing enterprise mobile health care information systems for various medical services in Germany for many years. Consequently, the need for a usable front-end for handwriting recognition, particularly for the use in ambulances was needed. While handwriting recognition has been a classical topic of computer science for many years, numerous problems still need to be solved. In this paper, we report on the study and resulting improvements achieved by the adaptation of an existing handwriting algorithm, based on experiences made during medical rescue missions. By improving accuracy and error correction the performance of an available handwriting recognition algorithm was increased. However, the end user studies showed that the virtual keyboard is still the preferred method compared to handwriting, especially among participants with a computer usage of more than 30 hours a week. This is possibly due to the wide availability of the QUERTY/QUERTZ keyboard.

Keywords: Handwriting recognition, Mobile computer, Human-computer interaction, Usability, Real-life, Health care.

1 Introduction and Motivation for Research

In cases of emergency, rapid patient information collection is very important. This information is most often collected by first aiders (first responders) and paramedics (e.g. Red Cross). Prompt and accurately recorded and well communicated vital patient data can make the difference between life and death [1], [2].

The data acquisition should have as little disruptive effect on the workflow of the emergency responders (rescue staff) as possible. A possible solution for data input can be an mobile application on a lightweight handheld device [3], [4].

M.S. Obaidat, G.A. Tsihrintzis, and J. Filipe (Eds.): ICETE 2010, CCIS 222, pp. 97–111, 2012.
© Springer-Verlag Berlin Heidelberg 2012

Due to the fact that emergencies are usually within difficult physical situations, special attention to the design of information technology for emergencies has to be taken into consideration [5]. A key issue of any such information system is the acquisition of textual information. However, extensive text entry on mobile devices is principally to be avoided and a simple and easy to use interface, in accordance with the proverb: less is more, is a supreme necessity [6].

The basic evidence that entering data onto a mobile device via a stylus is slower, more erroneous and less satisfactory for end users than entering data via a QWERTZ (de) or QUERTY (us) keyboard has been demonstrated in some studies [7], although, on the other hand the use of a stylus is much faster and more accurate than using finger touch [8]. A specific study for "Ambulance Run Reporting" shows good results for acquiring text with a virtual keyboard, while acquiring text by the application of handwriting recognition showed some serious usability problems [4]. Motivated by this previous work, we focus in this work on handwriting recognition and on how to improve its usability – in case of need, also by adaptation of existing handwriting algorithms. Consequently, in this paper we report on real-life experiences and on some improvements achieved by the adaptation of an existing handwriting engine.

2   Theoretical Background and Related Work

A big difficulty of handwriting recognition is that handwritten characters are variable on an individual basis and that these characters are usually separated into alphabets, numerals, and symbols, despite the different characters of the language itself. Although handwriting recognition will benefit in future from improved adaptive and context-sensitive algorithms, improving the user experience of novice end users with the respective technology is possibly the most important factor in enhancing user acceptance [9]. This is even more important in medical or health care contexts, where the difficulty is in the environmental conditions, e.g. if the person is on the move or in a hurry [10]. Whereas the first problem might be solved by the training modus opportunities, in order to adapt the system to the individual handwriting style, the second problem is only solvable by an extremely robust and usable system. Especially in the health care domain, good end user acceptance and usability can only be obtained by providing simple operation (good user guidance), very short response times and low error rates [11].

Basically, there are several methods for handwriting recognition; these belong basically to two distinct families of classification:

I)   Structured and Rule Based Methods

Because of the fuzzy nature of human handwriting, it makes sense to adapt the well known fuzzy logic technique for this purpose [12]. Rather than evaluating the two values as in digital logic, fuzzy terms admit to degrees of membership in multiple sets so that fuzzy rules may have a continuous, rather than stepwise, range of truth of possibility. Therefore non-identical handwritten numerals, from same or different users, can be approximated using fuzzy logic for fast and robust handwriting recognition [13].

II) Statistical Methods

a)   Hidden Markov Modeling (HMM)

The attractiveness of HMM for various pattern recognition tasks is mainly due to their clear and reliable statistical framework. Many efficient algorithms for parameter estimation and model evaluation exist, which is an important prerequisite for their practical implementation for real-life applications [14]. The methods using HMM [15], are based on the arcs of skeleton graphs of the words to be recognized and an algorithm applied to the skeleton graph of a word extracts the edges in a particular order, which is transformed into a 10-dimensional feature vector. Each of these features represent information about the location of an edge relative to four reference lines, the curvature and the degree of the nodes incident to the considered edge. Training of the HMM is done by use of the Baum-Welch algorithm, while the Viterbi algorithm is used for recognition [16], [17].

b) Neural Networks

The methods based on Neural Networks were driven by the emergence of portable, pen based computers. A typical approach is to combine an artificial neural network (ANN), as a character classifier, with a context-driven search over segmentation and word recognition hypotheses [18].

   However, handwriting recognition not only consists of the recognition itself; the data must undergo some preprocessing:

(I) reduce noise;

(II) normalization, and

(III) segmentation.

The last step, the segmentation phase, segments the input into single characters [19]. Writing discrete characters requires no segmentation; this is done by the users themselves [20].

   Another way to improve recognition is to decrease the set of possible alternatives, such as to restrict the set to accepting only lower case letters or digits [21].

   system and their current position within its complexity. However, when striving for a design following the "principle of the least surprise", we are faced with the problem that designers and developers rarely are able to predict exactly what the end users really expect (remember Steve Krug [22]: "Don't make me think!").

   Efficiency and User Satisfaction were derived. Task Effectiveness (TES) determines how correctly and completely the goals have been achieved in the context.

3 Related Work

To date only a few studies considered handwriting recognition on mobile devices and very few in the health care domain.

A very early work by Citrin et al. report very general on the usage of a pen on a flat surface of a LCD unit (scribing and tapping). They reported that with the maximum rate of 100 selections of direction per second for pen, scribing may produce strokes with the speed of 300 (100×3) bps. However, no more results were found [23].

MacKenzie showed that the recognition accuracy for a set containing upper and lower case letters was lower than for a set containing just lower case letters [24].

Chittaro evaluated a system for recording data on a system during a running ambulance drive, having first responders as participants. Text entry via virtual keyboard and handwriting recognition (MS Transcriber – Calligrapher) were also performed. Text entering by handwriting was considered very laborious and difficult by the users (Mean 3.8, Var 6.6), while entering text by use of the virtual keyboard was quite easy (Mean 7.2, Var 1.8). (0=Hard, 9=Easy). Furthermore, they emphasized the bad usability of entering text by using handwriting recognition. Most words were wrongly recognized and there were enormous problems in correcting those wrongly recognized words [4].

4 Methods and Materials

The aim of our study was to increase the performance of available handwriting recognition by improving accuracy and error correction following solid usability engineering methods [25].

We focused on separate character recognition, since the correction of a single letter, at the moment of false recognition, can be made more naturally, and efficiently, than attempting to correct or delete a single letter within a recognised word.

Due to limited space, there could be some problems inputting long words. Therefore, only one character at a time can be written and recognized.

4.1 Experimental Device

The device used for the prototype was an Asus MyPad A626 PDA (Personal Digital Assistant). This device is equipped with an anti-glare touch screen display. For typing on the touch screen, a stylus is used.

The technical specifications of this device are as follows:

CPU Marvell XScale, 312MHz; Operating System: MS Windows® Mobile™ 6; Memory: 256MB Flash ROM and 64 MB SDRAM; Display: 3.5" Brilliant TFT LCD, 65k full-colours, anti-glare, 16-bit display QVGA, 240 x 320 px touch screen; Weight: 158g; Physical dimensions: 117 mm x 70.8 mm x 15.7cm.

4.2 Dialog Design

The light green area (see figure 1) within the writing sections defines the optimal size for handwritten lowercase characters of 80 points [26].

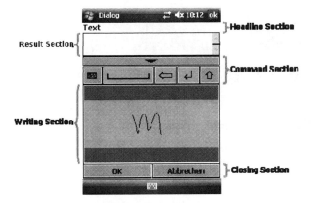

Fig. 1. Design of the handwriting dialog

4.3 Handwriting Recognition

We used the SDK of the handwriting recognition engine Calligrapher (in MS Windows® Mobile Transcriber) in the version 6.0 [26]. This SDK makes it possible to define single character recognition. We can handle the results and a custom timeout (after which time the recognition starts) can be defined.

4.3.1 Adaptive Timeout

A handwritten character consists of one or more strokes. The recognition starts after the character is finished. The system has to await a timeout before starting recognition because the system doesn't know whether the character consists of just one or more strokes. A stroke is defined as the writing from pen down to pen up [20].

Because of the different writing speeds of each user, this timeout has to be calculated for each user. Therefore, the system stores the last ten times which elapse between two strokes.

$$T = \frac{\sum_{i=1}^{11} s(i)}{11} * \frac{X}{100}$$

Fig. 2. Calculation of timeout T [sec]

Figure 2 shows how the timeout is calculated every time a timeout is requested; $s(1)$ is the last calculated average time between strokes, $s(2)..s(11)$ are the last ten stored times between strokes. X is a factor, in this experimental setting X is 200. The result T is the timeout in seconds.

4.3.2 Correction Intervention

Calligrapher SDK 6.0 doesn't adapt recognition on users' handwriting because of the use of static Fuzzy-Neuronal Nets [27].

There are problems with some user's style of writing letters – the user writes a letter (e.g. an "a") but the recognition engine recognizes another letter (e.g. figure 3).

A recognition result is a list of possible characters and its weight (maximum 5 entries). Every time the same letter is wrongly recognized for a user (as in Figure 2), the lists returned by the recognition are similar.

Fig. 3. Written "a" but not recognized as "a", instead as "ir"

These lists (characters and its weight) with its representing letter are stored. Each of them is called schema. During writing, the recognition result will be compared to the stored schemas as follows (see example in Figure 4).

For each stored schema:

Characters from the result list and the list of the schema are compared. If the result list consists of 2 or 3 characters, at least 2 have to match to the stored schemas lists characters. (2 of 2, 2 of 3). If there are 4 or 5 characters in the result list, at least 3 have to match (3 of 4, 3 of 5). This means, the resulting list is validated to the list of the schema. If the list is valid according to the list of the schema, the average deviation between these matching characters is calculated.

Inputted list			Stored Schema's list		Deviation
u	52		k	41	4
n	47		M	35	0
k	37		n	31	16
M	35		h	26	
A	22		m	22	
Validity: 3/5 → VALID					
Average Deviation (16+0+4)/3:					6

Fig. 4. Example of a list comparison

The representing letter of the schema with the lowest average deviation will be put in first place of the recognition result.

4.3.3 Calibration

The calibration is designed to collect user specific data for each letter. This data contains weights, which present every character explicitly. Also, schemas of wrongly recognized letters (Chapter 3.3.2) are collected. The system prompts the user to input a letter.

If the result list of the recognition has the prompted letter in first place, the weight will be stored for this letter. In the calibration phase, at least 2 weights will be stored for each letter.

If not, the result list will be stored as a schema with the prompted letter as a representing letter. In the calibration phase, a maximum of 10 schemas for each letter is stored.

This calibration is done once for each user. A continuous calibration is also done during writing in the handwriting recognition dialog, saving weights and schemas for correctly recognized letters (but not for deleted letters).

4.3.4 Other Interventions on Recognition Results

To avoid side effects, the intervention described in Chapter 3.3.2 is only made when the weight of a recognized letter is less than the average weight for this letter (average of the weights for this letter collected by calibration).

Other interventions are made to avoid potential. problems with highly confusable pairs such as "r" and "v" [21]. (I) While writing a word, only letters and punctuation marks are valid, recognized results. (II) Just deleted letters (with BACKSPACE) are not valid, recognized results for the next recognition (III) Special handling for "O" and "0" as first letter of a word or number.

4.4 Experiment

The real life environment is mostly a seat in an ambulance car (refer to figure 5). To avoid negative effects on ambulance responder's work, the experiment is done in their recess in the ambulance service rooms, simulating the circumstances (sitting in a car) by doing the experiment sitting on a chair, holding the PDA in their hand, without laying down the elbows on e.g. an armrest. [28] shows that simulating environments gives almost the same results.

Fig. 5. Participants from the ambulance service during experiments in real life

Participants were people who work as ambulance officers (professionals, volunteers and former civilian service). No previous experience with mobile computers was required. They were asked to fill out a background questionnaire to obtain data about their age, education and use of computers. The prototype for the experiment is divided into two parts, one for virtual keyboard based text input, and the other for handwriting recognition input. Within these two parts, the users have the opportunity to become familiar with the input methods. After that, the user has to input a given text to the experimental dialog (for measuring the accuracy). Due to measuring the accuracy, text entry is done as text copy [29]. This text consists of 13 German words (94 characters without spaces, 106 with spaces). After the keyboard based experimental dialog, the calibration of the handwriting is done. Speed in wpm, words per minute [24, 30] and the accuracy of the handwriting recognition are measured and calculated. At the end, a feedback questionnaire is filled out by the user. Some questions are based on the study of Chittaro [4]. Every single test user conducted the procedure outlined in Figure 6.

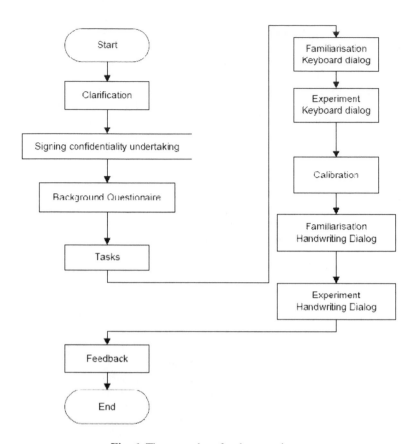

Fig. 6. The procedure for the experiment

5   Results

The participants of the experiment were professional (9) and volunteer (8) first responders of the Austrian Red Cross, one student of medicine and three others (because everyone could be a volunteer first responder, not only medical students). 10 were experienced on a PDA or a mobile phone with touch screen, while 11 had no experience with touch screens.

Their ages ranged from 20 to 85 years. Two elderly people (68 and 85 years) were chosen. The reason for this was, that we wanted to gain insight into the behaviour and performance of somebody who had never before used a QWERTY/QUERTZ keyboard or a PC in their life before. The average use of a PC was 12.3 years, using a PC 31 hours in average per week. 11 participants used a PC ≤ 30 hours a week, while 10 participants used a PC for more than 30 hours. One of the 21 participants was left-handed. All participants had normal or corrected to normal eyesight and none suffered of any kind of colour blindness.

5.1 Accuracy

Overall		≤ 30 weekly usage		> 30 weekly usage	
Mean	Var	Mean	Var	Mean	Var
99.1	6.28	100	11.5	99.06	1.44

Fig. 7. Table: Accuracy inputting text with virtual keyboard [%]; all participants, participants ≤ 30 hours and above

Overall		≤ 30 weekly usage		> 30 weekly usage	
Mean	Var	Mean	Var	Mean	Var
89.25	34.3	91.43	30.20	88.00	37.34

Fig. 8. Table: Recognition accuracy [%] of handwriting recognition; all participants, participants ≤ 30 hours and above with interventions

Overall		≤ 30 weekly usage		> 30 weekly usage	
Mean	Var	Mean	Var	Mean	Var
84.66	57.6	86.99	79.15	83.33	38.21

Fig. 9. Table: Recognition accuracy [%] of handwriting recognition; all participants, participants ≤ 30 hours and above without interventions

The participants using a PC ≤ 30 hours a week include the two elderly people.

The 85 year old participant has an accuracy of 89.2% for inputting text with the virtual keyboard and a recognition accuracy of 80.1% with interventions and 65.6% without interventions.

The 68 year old participant had an accuracy of 100% for inputting text with the virtual keyboard and a recognition accuracy of 95% with interventions and 90.8% without interventions.

The 85 years old participant has an accuracy of 89.2% for inputting text with the virtual keyboard and a recognition accuracy of 80.1% with interventions and 65.6% without interventions.

The 68 year old participant has an accuracy of 100% for inputting text with the virtual keyboard and a recognition accuracy of 95% with interventions and 90.8% without interventions.

5.2 Speed

Participants using a PC ≤ 30 hours a week include two elderly people. The 85 year old participant wrote 2.87 wpm with the keyboard and 2.82 wpm with handwriting recognition. The 68 year old participant wrote 4.88 wpm with the keyboard and 4.17 wpm with handwriting recognition.

Overall		≤ 30 weekly usage		> 30 weekly usage	
Mean	Var	Mean	Var	Mean	Var
13.17	27.7	12.88	29.46	13.43	18.29

Fig. 10. Table: Words per minute virtual keyboard; all participants, participants ≤ 30 hours and above

Overall		≤ 30 weekly usage		> 30 weekly usage	
Mean	Var	Mean	Var	Mean	Var
8.44	4.59	8.11	5.37	8.71	1.95

Fig. 11. Table: Words per minute handwriting recognition; all participants, participants ≤ 30 hours and above

5.3 User Questionnaire

Overall	**Mean**	**Var**
Keyboard		
Inputting Data (+4=easy, -4=difficult)	3.0	2.6
Correction of wrong inputted data (+4=easy, -4=difficult)	4.0	2.8
Handwriting		
Inputting Data (+4=easy, -4=difficult)	2.0	4.9
Correction of wrongly input/recognized data (+4=easy, -4=difficult)	3.0	1.4
Did the recognition slow down your writing (+4=no, -4=yes)	0.5	9.2
I would prefer (+4=handwriting, -4=keyboard)	-2.5	7.9
Basic Information		
Use of colour is (+4=useful, -4=useless)	2.0	2.5
The handwriting recognition positively surprised me (+4=yes, -4=no)	2.5	7.1
Characters on the PDA are easy to read (+4=yes, 4=no)	4.0	3.9

Fig. 12. Overall results of user questionnaire

Weekly computer usage [hours]	**Mean (<=30)**	**Var (<=30)**	**Mean (>30)**	**Var (>30)**
Keyboard				
Inputting Data	3.5	1.4	3.0	3.7
Correction of wrongly input data	4.0	1.7	3.5	4.5
Handwriting				
Inputting Data	2.5	4.2	0.5	3.8
Correction of wrongly input/recognized data	4.0	0.5	2.5	1.8

Fig. 13. Results of user questionnaire for weekly usage of computer ≤ 30 hours and above

Did the recognition slow down your writing	2.5	8.4	-0.5	8.2
I would prefer	-1.5	2.0	-2.5	4.9
Basic Information				
Use of colour	2.0	2.5	1.5	2.6
The handwriting recognition positively surprised me	4.0	7.7	0.0	4.7
Characters on the PDA are easy to read	4.0	4.6	4.0	3.2

Fig. 13. (*Continued*)

5.4 Timeout

Figure 14 outlines the timeout for each user during the experiment described previously. The figure lists the optimized timeout for each of our test users. Most notably, the optimal timeout for the majority of our test users is between 200 and 250 milliseconds. The algorithm is capable of adapting the timeout to slow as well as to fast writers (e.g. user 19 is a rather slow writer whereas user 5 is the fastest one).

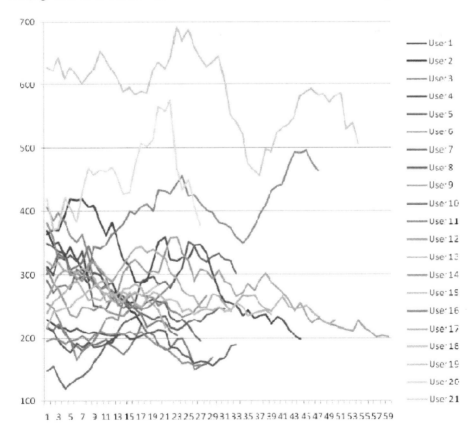

Fig. 14. Timeout adaption for each user

6 Discussion and Lessons Learned

Entering text with the virtual keyboard (Mean 3.0, Var 2.6) was easier for the participants than with handwriting (Mean 2.0, Var 4.9). However, compared to the study of [4], we could reach an significant improvement by inputting data with handwriting. Interestingly, inputting data by handwriting recognition was rated easier by participants who use computers less than or equal to 30 hours a week than by participants with extensively more use (Mean 2.5; Var 4.2; against Mean 0.5, Var 3.8 of virtual keyboard). Also, the correction on the handwriting recognition dialog was rated easier (Mean 4.0, Var 0.5; against Mean 2.5, Var 1.8; of virtual keyboard). Participants with a computer usage of more than 30 hours a week preferred the virtual keyboard (Mean -2.5, Var 4.9) more than the other participants (Mean -1.5, Var 2.0). This could be a result of hardly any handwriting during work and much more typing text on classical keyboards (QWERTZ or QUERTY). Consequently, the two elderly participants were included in this study, in order to obtain data regarding participants who never used any computer or handheld device. The elderly participants were the only ones who provided a complete preference to the handwriting recognition in contrast to the virtual keyboard. This is also clearly visible in the results for these participants, although both groups have quite comparable results in wpm for the virtual keyboard and the handwriting text input.

This is an interesting result; however, it is not of practical relevance, since there are hardly any people left – at least amongst people able to volunteer as a first responder – without experience on computer keyboards. Today, from elementary school on, children get used to work with computers by using the QWERTZ or QUERTY keyboard.

Nevertheless, our interventions on the basis of the results of the handwriting recognition, finally paid off in an significant improvement on the recognition accuracy (over all participants a better accuracy of Mean +4.39%, Var 9.54).

These interventions can also be useful for the improvement of other handwriting recognition engines, due to the fact that our interventions were only made on the results of the engine, achieving better accuracy. The use of a handwriting recognition engine with a higher accuracy than e.g. Calligrapher, in combination with our demonstrated interventions, may even improve the overall accuracy. Our methods on operating on the results of the handwriting recognition engine operate context independent. Using a dictionary to add the likelihood of upcoming characters may improve the accuracy in that part of the problem regarding confusable pairs, such as "r" and "v". Because of typing in characters one by one, a word completion feature could be added to handwriting recognition too. This also would increase the writing speed.

7 Conclusion and Future Outlook

Although much research in the field of handwriting recognition has been done, recognition algorithms still do not 100 % achieve the high prospects of the users. Handwriting is very individual to every person and identifying characters is still very hard – as long time ago described by [31]. This paper demonstrated operations on the result of a recognition engine. Replacing the engine used in this experiment (Calligrapher) with a better recognition engine with higher accuracy can improve the result on accuracy due to the fact that accuracy is the most important parameter for the acceptance. Users rate an accuracy of 90% to 95% to be a very poor recognition rate. Users will accept only accuracies more than 97% (3 wrong recognized items out of 100 inputs). LaLomia [32], [33] let users write specified text to a system, which immediately interpreted the input with randomly occurring errors. The randomly generated accuracy ranged from 90% to 99%. After reviewing the errors, the users rated the acceptability; exclusively recognition accuracy over 97% was acceptable. Because of typing in characters one by one, a word completion feature could be added to the final implementation, however, in the last years, mobile devices and the usage of such devices changed rapidly. Nowadays, many people, especially younger people are connected to social networks, including Facebook, especially by using their smart phones – where today the user interface consists of a touch screen. Data acquisition is mostly realized with improved, intelligent virtual keyboards. Such intelligent keyboards e.g. with implementation of a regional error correction [34]. Often they are connected with tactile feedback for touch screen widgets [35] which can improve performance and usability of virtual keyboards on small screens. Handwriting is taught from elementary school on and nearly everyone learns handwriting at school. Therefore, handwriting recognition is a very important technology for input interfaces of mobile computers. However, today, even children get used to the QWERTY layout keyboard from elementary school. Consequently, interface designers can assume that nearly everyone is experienced in using a QWERTY layout keyboard.

Because of the higher user acceptance of current uncomfortable virtual keyboards compared to handwriting recognition, future developments and projects should focus on data acquisition based on intelligent, comfortable virtual keyboards.

Acknowledgements. This study was performed with support of FERK-Systems. We cordially thank the engineering team for their continued and effective industrial support of this work. The research was partially funded by the Austrian Research Promotion Agency (FFG) within one „Innovationsscheck Österreich".

References

1. Holzman, T.G.: Computer-human interface solutions for emergency medical care. Interactions 6(3), 13–24 (1999)
2. Anantharaman, V., Han, L.S.: Hospital and emergency ambulance link: using IT to enhance emergency pre-hospital care. International Journal of Medical Informatics 61(2-3), 147–161 (2001)
3. Baumgart, D.C.: Personal digital assistants in health care: experienced clinicians in the palm of your hand? The Lancet 366(9492), 1210–1222 (2005)
4. Chittaro, L., Zuliani, F., Carchietti, E.: Mobile Devices in Emergency Medical Services: User Evaluation of a PDA-Based Interface for Ambulance Run Reporting. In: Löffler, J., Klann, M. (eds.) Mobile Response 2007. LNCS, vol. 4458, pp. 19–28. Springer, Heidelberg (2007)
5. Klann, M., Malizia, A., Chittaro, L., Cuevas, I. A., Levialdi, S.: HCI for emergencies. In: CHI 2008 Extended Abstracts on Human Factors in Computing Systems, pp. 3945–3948 (2008)

6. Holzinger, A., Errath, M.: Mobile computer Web-application design in medicine: some research based guidelines. Universal Access in the Information Society International Journal 6(1), 31–41 (2007)
7. Haller, G., Haller, D.M., Courvoisier, D.S., Lovis, C.: Handheld vs. Laptop Computers for Electronic Data Collection in Clinical Research: A Crossover Randomized Trial. Journal of the American Medical Informatics Association 16(5), 651–659 (2009)
8. Holzinger, A., Höller, M., Schedlbauer, M., Urlesberger, B.: An Investigation of Finger versus Stylus Input in Medical Scenarios. In: Luzar-Stiffler, V., Dobric, V.H., Bekic, Z. (eds.) ITI 2008: 30th International Conference on Information Technology Interfaces, pp. 433–438. IEEE (2008)
9. MacKenzie, I.S., Chang, L.: A performance comparison of two handwriting recognizers. Interacting with Computers 11(3), 283–297 (1999)
10. Holzinger, A., Hoeller, M., Bloice, M., Urlesberger, B.: Typical Problems with developing mobile applications for health care: Some lessons learned from developing user-centered mobile applications in a hospital environment. In: Filipe, J., Marca, D.A., Shishkov, B., Sinderen, M. v. (eds.) International Conference on E-Business (ICE-B 2008), pp. 235–240. IEEE (2008)
11. Holzinger, A., Geierhofer, R., Searle, G.: Biometrical Signatures in Practice: A challenge for improving Human-Computer Interaction in Clinical Workflows. In: Heinecke, A.M., Paul, H. (eds.) Mensch & Computer: Mensch und Computer im Strukturwandel, Oldenbourg, pp. 339–347 (2006)
12. Gader, P.D., Keller, J.M., Krishnapuram, R., Chiang, J.H., Mohamed, M.A.: Neural and fuzzy methods in handwriting recognition. Computer 30(2), 79–86 (1997)
13. Shi, B., Li, G.: VLSI Neural Fuzzy Classifier for Handwriting recognition (2006)
14. Plotz, T., Fink, G.A.: Markov models for offline handwriting recognition: a survey. International Journal on Document Analysis and Recognition 12(4), 269–298 (2009)
15. Marti, U.V., Bunke, H.: Using a statistical language model to improve the performance of an HMM-based cursive handwriting recognition systems. In: Hidden Markov Models: Applications in Computer Vision, pp. 65–90. World Scientific Publishing Co., Inc. (2002)
16. Bunke, H., Roth, M., Schukattalamazzini, E.G.: Off-Line Cursive Handwriting Recognition Using Hidden Markov-Models. Pattern Recognition 28(9), 1399–1413 (1995)
17. Xue, H.H., Govindaraju, V.: Hidden Markov models combining discrete symbols and continuous attributes in handwriting recognition. IEEE Transactions on Pattern Analysis and Machine Intelligence 28(3), 458–462 (2006)
18. Yaeger, L.S., Webb, B.J., Lyon, R.F.: Combining Neural Networks and Context-Driven Search for On-Line, Printed Handwriting Recognition in the Newton. In: Orr, G.B., Müller, K.-R. (eds.) NIPS-WS 1996. LNCS, vol. 1524, pp. 275–298. Springer, Heidelberg (1998)
19. Plamondon, R., Srihari, S.N.: On-Line and Off-Line Handwriting Recognition: A Comprehensive Survey. IEEE Transactions on Pattern Analysis and Machine Intelligence 22(1), 63–84 (2000)
20. Tappert, C.C., Suen, C.Y., Wakahara, T.: The State of the Art in On-Line Handwriting Recognition. IEEE Transactions on Pattern Analysis and Machine Intelligence 12(8), 787–808 (1990)
21. Frankish, C., Hull, R., Morgan, P.: Recognition accuracy and user acceptance of pen interfaces. In: Conference on Human Factors in Computing Systems, pp. 503–510 (1995)
22. Krug, S.: Don't Make Me Think: A Common Sense Approach to Web Usability. New Riders, Indianapolis (2000)

23. Citrin, W., Halbert, D., Hewitt, C., Meyrowitz, N., Shneiderman, B.: Potentials and limitations of pen-based computers. In: Proceedings of the 1993 ACM Conference on Computer Science, pp. 536–539 (1993)
24. MacKenzie, I.S., Nonneke, B., Riddersma, S., McQueen, C., Meltz, M.: Alphanumeric entry on pen-based computers. International Journal of Human-Computer Studies 41(5) (1994)
25. Holzinger, A.: Usability Engineering for Software Developers. Communications of the ACM 48(1), 71–74 (2005)
26. Phatware: Calligrapher SDK 6.0 Developer's Manual (2002)
27. Strenge, M.: Konzepte und Toolkits zur Handschrifterkennung (2005)
28. Kjeldskov, J., Skov, M.B., Als, B.S., Høegh, R.T.: Is It Worth the Hassle? Exploring the Added Value of Evaluating the Usability of Context-Aware Mobile Systems in Field. In: Brewster, S., Dunlop, M.D. (eds.) Mobile HCI 2004. LNCS, vol. 3160, pp. 61–73. Springer, Heidelberg (2004)
29. MacKenzie, I.S., Soukoreff, R.W.: Text Entry for Mobile Computing: Models and Methods, Theory and Practice. Human-Computer-Interaction 17(2), 147–198 (2002)
30. Lewis, J.R.: Input Rates and User Preference for three small-screen input methods: Standard Keyboard, Predictive Keyboard and Handwriting Human Factors and Ergonomics Society (1999)
31. Neisser, U., Weene, P.: A note on human recognition of hand-printed characters. Information and Control 3, 191–196 (1960)
32. LaLomia, M.J.: User acceptance of computer applications with speech, handwriting and keyboard input devices. Posters and short talks of the, SIGCHI Conference on Human Factors in Computing Systems, pp. 58–58 (1992)
33. LaLomia, M.: User acceptance of handwritten recognition accuracy. In: Conference Companion on Human Factors in Computing Systems, pp. 107–108 (1994)
34. Kwon, S., Lee, D., Chung, M.K.: Effect of key size and activation area on the performance of a regional error correction method in a touch-screen QWERTY keyboard. International Journal of Industrial Ergonomics 39(5), 888–893 (2009)
35. Koskinen, E., Kaaresoja, T., Laitinen, P.: Feel-good touch: finding the most pleasant tactile feedback for a mobile touch screen button. In: Proceedings of the 10th international conference on Multimodal interfaces, pp. 297–304 (2008)

A Social Location-Based Emergency Service to Eliminate the Bystander Effect

Andreas Geyer-Schulz, Michael Ovelgönne, and Andreas C. Sonnenbichler

Karlsruhe Institute of Technology, Institute of Information Systems and Management
Kaiserstrasse 12, 76131 Karlsruhe, Germany
{andreas.geyer-schulz,michael.ovelgoenne,
andreas.sonnenbichler}@kit.edu
http://iism.kit.edu/em

Abstract. The availability of inexpensive smartphones with GPS units and the ability to run 3rd party software facilitated the rapid emergence of a large number of location-based services (LBS). While LBSs are mostly developed for supporting travel and navigation related application scenarios, in this contribution we want to motivate the use of mobile devices for personal safety services. The problem of getting help in a crowd has been addressed by research in social psychology for more than 30 years. Obstacles in the social help process have been summarized in the concept of the bystander effect. This contribution aims to show how a LBS can overcome these obstacles by activating the social group of a victim. We discuss features of an emergency alert service that notifies nearby contacts of a victim of the incident and guides them to the victim so that they can provide help. Furthermore, we will discuss several ways to develop an emergency alert service as an industrial product which infers the social closeness of service participants from different sources of data. Also, we will discuss and compare approaches for the system design we considered while implementing a prototype. A feasibility assessment indicates that this service will actually provide benefits in practice.

Keywords: Emergency recommender, Social network analysis, Bystander effect, Privacy.

1 Introduction

On Saturday, the 12th of September 2009, 50-year old Dominik Brunner was brutally murdered in a Munich S-Bahn station [42]. The attack on Dominik Brunner was observed by 15 passengers [44] and transmitted and recorded by his mobile-phone on the open police emergency channel [43].

This tragic incident reminds social psychologists of the murder of Kitty Genovese on March 13th, 3:20, 1964 in Queens, New York. Kitty Genovese was stalked, stabbed, and sexually assaulted near her own apartment building. During the attack on her she screamed and broke free twice. 38 of her neighbors witnessed the attack, but no one intervened. After 45 minutes one man called the police, but at this point in time Kitty Genovese was dead.

M.S. Obaidat, G.A. Tsihrintzis, and J. Filipe (Eds.): ICETE 2010, CCIS 222, pp. 112–130, 2012.
© Springer-Verlag Berlin Heidelberg 2012

This incident motivated the study of social processes in emergency situations by Darley and Latané [21] and it points to the short-comings and problems of real emergency response organizations and their management which only very recently have become the object of scientific research e.g. [46], [13], [5], and [7]. The mobile phone of the victim transmitting and recording to the end confirms Palen and Liu's thesis of the increasing availability of ICT and its use in an emergency by citizens and also their observation, that the traditional hierarchical command-and-control reporting system of emergency response organizations may not be adequate and "does not include built-in considerations for the important roles that members of the public play as participants" [33, p. 729]. Public participation in emergencies and disasters is active and altruistic. First responders are often not the trained professionals of an emergency response organization who are sent to the incident, but the people from the local and surrounding communities. They provide first-aid, transport victims to the hospital, and begin search and rescue [33, pp. 728-729]. In the case of Dominik Brunner we may speculate whether a fast activation of his social community parallel to the emergency call could have saved his life.

The paper starts with a short review of the social processes which Darley and Latené have identified as obstacles for helping in emergencies in section 2. These obstacles have become known as the bystander effect: The more bystanders, the less likely the victim will receive help. We address the bystander effect by a social emergency alert service and discuss how social emergency alert services may help in improving these processes in emergency settings by activating the nearby members of the victim's social network.

For the process of giving and receiving help, we propose to monitor social interactions and to identify the social groups of the victims and to locate the nearest members of the social group of the victim in an emergency for notification purposes. In section 3 we present details on the social emergency alert service for getting help in a crowd and in section 4 we discuss implementation variants of realizations of such services based on readily available technology by the telecommunication and Internet industry.

In section 5 we will discuss two system designs that emerged from our work on a prototype of the emergency alert service.

The identification of social groups from social networks will be addressed in section 6.

Section 7 of this paper aims at assessing the chances that the social emergency alert service presented has in reality. For this purpose, a first attempt is made to answer three questions which play a crucial role for the success of a social emergency alert service:

1. Has the victim in an emergency a chance to transmit a request for help?
2. Is someone of his social network nearby?
3. Will this person really help?

2   The Unhelpful Crowd: Five Steps to Helping in an Emergency

The murder of Kitty Genovese in 1964 in Queens, New York, in front of 38 witnesses who did not interfere led Darley and Latané to start investigating the social psychological processes at work in this incident. Their research revealed that the more bystanders,

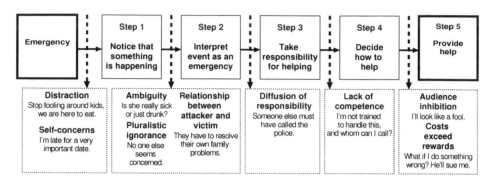

Fig. 1. The social help process: 5 steps leading to assistance

the less likely the victim will be helped. This is the *bystander effect*: The presence of others inhibits helping. One of the reasons for this is the diffusion of responsibility [10]. Darley and Latané [21] provided a careful analysis of the process of emergency intervention shown in figure 1. Unfortunately, many obstacles to helping must be overcome. At each step, however, psychological factors are at work which explain why people fail to help:

1. **Noticing.** The presence of others distracts attention from the victim. People who live in big cities may filter out people lying on sidewalks or screams (stimulus overload [24]).
2. **Interpreting.** People must interpret the meaning of what they perceive. Their perception may be ambiguous: Cries of pain may be taken for laughter, hypoglycemia may be taken for drunkenness (e.g. [6], [34]). A perceived relationship between attacker and victim may lead the observers to think that everything is OK [40]. If an emergency happens, the most powerful information available is often what other people do. However, if everybody looks on everybody else to get clues on what to do, the whole group is suffering from pluralistic ignorance and everybody concludes that help is not needed (e.g. [25], [26]).
3. **Take Responsibility.** When help is needed, who is responsible for providing it? The diffusion of responsibility means that people belief that others will or should help. The effect usually is strengthened by anonymity and considerably reduced by a reduction in psychological distance. Groups with members who know each other are more helpful than strangers. See e.g. [15], [36], [3].
4. **Decide How to Help.** Bystanders are more likely to offer direct help if they feel competent to perform the actions required (e.g. [38], [8]).
5. **Provide Help.** Some people may feel too embarrassed to provide help in a public setting (audience inhibition). However, when people think they will be scorned by others for failing to provide help, the presence of an audience will increase their helpful actions. See [37]. In addition, potential helpers – especially when uncertain about their capability to help – tend to weight the risks of helping against the reward of helping andreas – because of costs exceeds rewards – remain passive.

In addition, a series of other variables have a high influence on helping behavior as experiments in social psychology have shown: Time pressure reduces the tendency to help (e.g. [9], [2]). Group membership and empathy and attractiveness interact: empathy is a positive predictor for help for in-group members, whereas attractiveness works for out-group members [45]. Group membership positively influences help for in-group members, and the group boundaries can be shifted by proper priming [22]. Group status and group identification influence the willingness of receiving help [28].

But what can you do to receive help in a crowd? Try to counteract the ambiguity of the situation by making it clear that you need help, and try to reduce the diffusion of responsibility by addressing a specific individual for help, keep eye contact, point or direct requests (e.g. [27], [39]). Consistent with this is a recent study of P. Markey [23] of people in Internet chat rooms: If the number of individuals is large in a chat room, individuals react slower to a plea for help. However, addressing a specific individual by his name leads to considerably faster help and eliminates this effect.

Research on the bystander effect in social psychology showed that even weak social links matter and increase the chance of a victim to receive help considerably. This fact is the main motivation to send alerts to the geographically close members of the victim's social group.

The asymmetric perception of social links (e.g. [19]), the role of weak ties, and the cultural norms of the community play a major role in the formation of the social group of the victim. The asymmetric perception of social links implies that a person may not be really aware of possible helpers in his loose social contacts. Taken together with cultural norms, even professional acquaintances are potential helpers. The role of weak ties for networks has been studied by M. Granovetter ([18] and [17]). In the context of information diffusion on open jobs Granovetter observed that "it is remarkable that people receive crucial information from individuals whose very existence they have forgotten" [18, p. 14]. This is an indication that an explicit list of emergency contacts provided by the subscriber of such an emergency service will considerably limit the effectiveness of such a service, because of these social phenomena.

3   A Social Emergency Alert Service

As a consequence of the problem of getting help in a crowd we propose a social emergency alert service (EAS) that identifies nearby members of the social group of the victim and notifies them about the victim's need for help and the victim's location. With this service we aim to activate the locally available social network of the victim and to eliminate the bystander effect.

The UML sequence diagram depicted in figure 2 shows the generic process in an emergency incident. It is designed on a high-level, abstract way allowing a variety of industrial implementations. We will address this issue in section 4.

An emergency notification is submitted by the victim by starting an application on his mobile device (LaunchEmergenyApplication in figure 2) e.g. by pressing the help-button shown in figure 5. The application retrieves the current geo-position. Both, the ID of the emergency caller and his geo-location are then transmitted to the emergency alert service (Emergency Alert Service in figure figure 2).

For discovering the most likely person to help in the victim's social network, his social network has to be known and possible helpers identified (Social Group

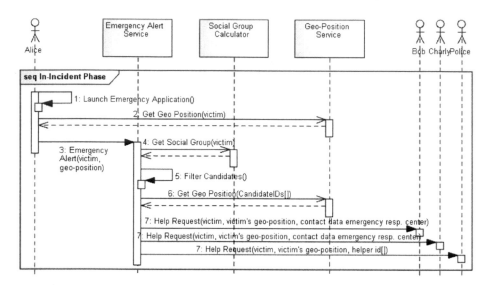

Fig. 2. Sequence diagram of a generic social emergency alert service (in-incident phase)

`Calculator` in figure 2). The network is either built from social interaction data from e-mail, sms, phone, and mobiles where the number of interactions is taken as an indication of social nearness or from social web sites as for example Facebook or Xing. However, the number of social interactions may be ambiguous as a recent incident [35] of a woman threatened by her former husband with Googles Buzz has shown: So the possibility to check for such unwanted relations must be provided for the participants of the emergency alert service (`Filter Candidates` in figure 2). Usually social networks tend to be very large. As emergencies are often time-critical, it might take too long to process such a network on-the-fly. Therefore, the network is generated and updated regularly for all service subscribers. To find out which persons in the social network are likely to help, a clustering of the network is performed. Details for this clustering are addressed in section 6.

Next, the current geo-position of the candidates is retrieved from a geo-position service (`GetGeoPositionofCandidates` in figure 2). The alert service uses the geo-data as a filter on the victim's social group to find out, who of the possible helpers is locally close enough. Section 7 deals with details of having at least one member of the victim's social group in range.

The possible helpers in range and the emergency response center are informed about the emergency situation of the victim (several invocations of `HelpRequest` in figure 2). All possible helpers in range are informed simultaneously. The victim's name, his geo-location and the shortest route as well as the contact data for the emergency response center are provided.

Finally, possible helpers and the emergency response experts at the police's emergency response center may communicate, because of the information forwarded by the emergency alert service (not shown in figure 2). This facility has the potential of providing expert guidance to the socially close first responders on the scene. However, it also reveals the identity of potential helpers to the emergency response center. The privacy impact of this must be addressed for such a service.

In section 2 obstacles to the five steps leading to assistance have been described. The emergency alert service presented addresses these obstacles directly:

1. The *distraction* obstacles can be avoided by noticing, that an emergency incident takes place: Clear signal words are part of the personal message to the helpers. This makes it obvious, an emergency case is happening and this is made clear to the helper.
2. *Self concerns* are also addressed by the service: Since the potential helper is directly addressed and others know this from the incident protocol, social and legal norms lead to pressure to help.
3. *Ambiguity* is by-passed by the clear and unmistakable help request sent to the helpers.
4. As this message is personal, *pluralistic ignorance* is eliminated. Experimental evidence for the elimination of pluralistic ignorance in internet chat rooms is provided by P. Markey [23].
5. The *relationship between attacker and victim* can not lead the helper to overlook the emergency event, because of the unambiguous emergency message.
6. *Diffusion of responsibility* is also reduced, since the emergency alert message is directly and personally addressed to the helper. Because of this, he is responsible and because of the incident protocol, others will know this and hold him responsible.
7. *Lack of competence* may be addressed by providing fast expert backup for helpers from the police emergency response center.
8. Expert guidance of how to help also addresses the problems of *audience inhibition* and *costs exceed rewards*.

4   Implementation Variants

In this section we present implementation examples how the *Emergency Alert Service* can be implemented in an industrial environment.

4.1   Emergency Alerting

To be able to use the service, the user has to possess a mobile device (e.g. a mobile phone). He can then subscribe to the service. In case of an emergency, he starts an application on his mobile device. Of course, the start of the application must be made simple and fast, as we do not expect it likely that the victim is able to deal with complex applications in an emergency situation. For the implementation third-party platforms like Android can be used. Android [1] is a mostly free and open-source OS platform developed and driven by the Open Handset Alliance [29]. Further platforms like Apples iPhone may be supported as well. Special mobile devices combined with body-sensors, e.g. for elderly people, linking the start of the application to a hardwired button can be offered.

4.2   Geo-Position Service

Geo-positions of both the victim and all possible helpers of the victim's social network need to be calculated. Many of todays mobile phones are able to calculate their geo-position by GPS (Global Positioning System). The service Google Latitude is an example for a service that users can publish their current geo-position and share it with friends. If a mobile device does not include such a feature, several alternative techniques have been described and implemented. Even speed vectors can be calculated (for example [20,4]). By this, the expected geo-position of somebody moving in a train can be found out.

4.3   Acquiring Social Network Data and Identifying Possible Helpers

For discovering the most likely person to help in an emergency case the social network has to be known. We present three possible realizations.

The social network can be built by monitoring outgoing and incoming calls on the mobile device of the subscriber. The emergency alert application running on the mobile device collects this call data, pools it and regularly (e.g. once a week) transmits it via HTTP to the social group service (see figure 2). There the call logs of all service subscribers are combined and the communication network is generated: Telephone numbers are represented as nodes, the calls are weighted ties. Each call strengthens a tie. The advantage of this solution is, that the network is independent from the telephone provider. It works depending just on the emergency alert application. The disadvantage is, that the calculated social network consists only of subscribers and their direct connections. Ties between non-subscribers can not be observed technically.

Alternatively not the mobile devices monitor the calls, but connection records from telephone providers are used. Connection records are stored for billing purposes. In the European Union a directive forces the provider to save call logs from six months up to two years [12]. These connection data can be used to calculate the social networks. Every connection is represented by a tie between the calling parties (more concrete, their telephone numbers) as nodes. Of course, the resulting network will be huge. In section 6 we will discuss a clustering algorithm that is able to process such huge datasets. Other scalable algorithms exist (e.g. [31,30]). The advantage of this solution is, that much more network data can be collected so that the problem of missing links is smaller. On the other hand this alternative can only be realized if the calling logs are available to the emergency alert provider. As we do not expect network providers to give such information away, the most likely approach for this alternative is, if the network provider is identical with the emergency alert service provider. The provider can then use the service as an additional opt-in feature. Another disadvantage is, that one network provider will probably not exchange network or call log data with other providers. By this the social network is limited to the customers of the provider plus their direct links.

As an additional feature of both alternatives address books in the customers' devices can be used to group telephone numbers. Different telephone numbers of one person can be combined and fused to one node in the social network.

A third approach to build the social network is to cooperate with existing online social network platforms. Data from Facebook, LinkedIn, Myspace can be used.

The advantage of this solution is, that no subscriber or network provider boundaries exist. The disadvantage is, that people tend to accept more 'friends' in social platforms than they would accept offline. Additionally, most of these platforms do not weight their ties, so that the strength of a connection is unknown.

In practice all three alternatives used to build a social network as discussed above can be complemented with a list of emergency contacts provided by each subscriber and, if available, with a list of dedicated helpers for an event or for a community. In a German small rural community, the community's voluntary fire-fighters are an example of such a community. We expect, that people in the same social group are likely to help each other.

5 System Design

In section 4 critical parts of an emergency alert service have been discussed. Now, we turn to the system as a whole and discuss important issues of the system architecture and the communication protocols. We will present and discuss two approaches for the system architecture. The first approach is a centralized architecture where all system logic and data are provided by a server. The second approach is less centralized and compared to the first approach some system logic and most user-location data are shifted from the server to the mobile clients. A detailed presentation of this prototype can be found in [32].

To evaluate and improve the designs we implemented prototypes of them. Software components for the mobile clients have been developed for a Motorola Milestone smartphone which is running the Android operating system. Server side components have been implemented as Servlets running within an Apache Tomcat environment.

5.1 Centralized Architecture

In figure 3 the system design for an alert service with a centralized architecture is shown (with the geo-position cache). Figure 4 depicts the corresponding communication protocol between the emergency alert service server components and the client software running on mobile devices.

Each subscriber is identified by his unique telephone number (ID). In the *Pre-Incidence Phase* each subscriber continuously submits location updates to the *GPS Cache* (step 1). We use a *GPS Push Service* running as background service on the Android smart phone to transmit the GPS coordinates via REST to the *GPS Cache*. The transmission is done on a regular basis, e.g. every 10 minutes and if the position changed by more than 10 meters. The *GPS Cache* stores the latest transmitted geo-position of each subscriber in a database. The second background service running on the mobile device is the *Communication Capture Service*. This service monitors all in-going and outgoing calls and messages. The communication data is collected in a local cache. Once a day the smart phone submits the cached communication data via SOAP to the *Communication Collector* (step 2). The *Social Group Calculator* pulls new data from the *Communication Collector* on a daily basis. It builds a communication network, identifies social groups and stores the results in a database (step 3).

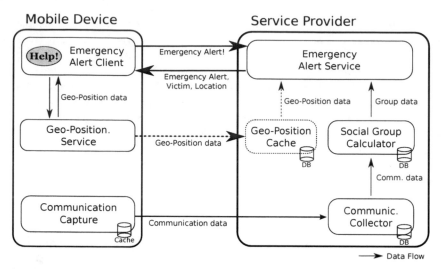

Fig. 3. Architecture of the Emergency Alert Service. All boxes and arrows depicted in solid lines are components of the centralized (5.1) and the privacy-aware (5.2) system design. The Geo-Position Cache and its ingoing and outgoing data flow is depicted in dashed lines as this part becomes unnecessary in the privacy-aware system design.

In the *In-Incident Phase* the user in need (in our example this is Alice) starts a home-screen widget on her smart phone (see figure 5). An emergency alert is transmitted via REST to the *Emergency Alert Service* (step A). The service pulls the helpers' candidate list from the *Social Group Provider* for Alice via OSGi (step B). For each candidate the *GPS Cache* is searched for the latest geo-position data of the candidate (step C). If close enough, a MMS is sent out to the helper with information about the victim and the victims geo-position (depicted on a map).

Note, that figure 4 is restricted to a proper emergency alert. False alerts can be revoked by a similar process (not shown in figure 4) which is password protected. However, pragmatically a set of passwords is provided which act as silent signals. A small solution consists of three passwords, the first signaling a false alarm, the second signaling that the victim is forced to revoke the alarm, and the third that there is danger for the helpers.

5.2   Privacy-Aware Architecture

The architecture presented in Section 5.1 has two major drawbacks, both related to the continuous location transmission. The first is related to the energy consumption, the second to privacy concerns. See section 5.3. To solve both issues we propose an alerting protocol that works without continuous location transmission to a server (see figure 6). This modification of the centralized approach requires to transfer some of the system logic to the mobile devices.

The privacy-aware architecture is shown in figure 3 (now without geo-position cache). The privacy-aware protocol is designed as follows (see figure 6). In the pre-incident phase only communication data is collected. The in-incident phase starts when a victim

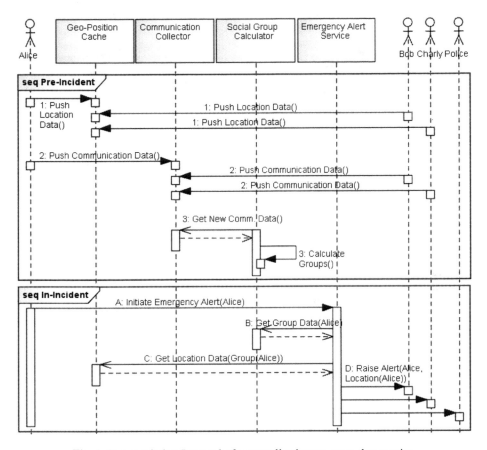

Fig. 4. Communiction Protocol of a centralized emergency alert service

presses the alert button. An initiate-alert notice is sent to the *Emergency Alert Service* (step A) and the victim's phone determines its position (step B). The initiate-alert notice makes the server retrieving the social contacts of the victim (step D) and sending a prepare-for-alert to all of them (step E). The prepare-for-alert message is a system internal message hidden from the user. This message is sent to decrease the overall time needed to inform a potential helper as the communication is initiated while the victim's GPS unit still determines its geo-position. Now, the phones of all social contacts determine their positions (step F). When the position of the victim has been determined and sent to the *Emergency Alert Service* (step G), it is broadcasted to the social contact's phones (step H). The phones of the potential helpers will have acquired their own positions by now and check their distance to the victim (step I). When a client has decided that the distance gives a chance to provide help, it retrieves further guidance information from the *Emergency Alert Service* (step K) and notifies the user.

While knowledge about the social relations of the service participants has still to be processed centrally to identify social groups and to send alert messages to the correct recipients, the server gets only location information from a user who has sent a help request. As the devices of all users do not continuously determine their positions and

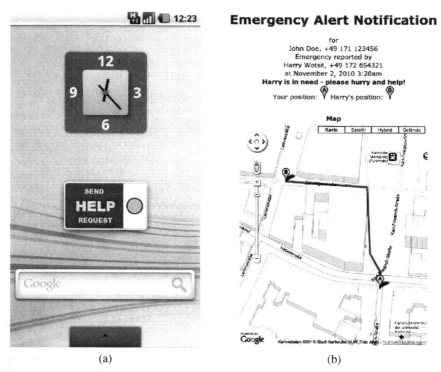

(a)   (b)

Fig. 5. Alert widget on an Android homescreen (a) and alert notification for potential helpers (b)

send location updates to the server, alerts have to be sent to all potential helpers regardless of their current position. Whether a user is close enough to provide help has to be decided by the clients.

5.3   Discussion of Design Variants

The centralized system design with the continuous transmission of location updates has two drawbacks. First, continuously determining and transmitting the current position will drain the battery of a smartphone in a few hours. Tests showed that the service drains the battery of our test device in about 10 hours (5 minutes update interval) when the phone is not used otherwise. The service accounted for more than 80% of the energy consumption. Even on more power-efficient devices the battery life will be unacceptable short - especially when considering that the phone will be used, too. A second problem with the centralized approach is that attracting users will be hard because potential participants of the service might not sign-up because of privacy concerns. A geo-position log is able to reveal a lot – beside spare time activities and favorite shops certainly also personal habits that people want to keep private.

However, a central geo-position cache has also some advantages. A central location database might be desireable for additional security functionalities. For example, a widget that displays the distance to the nearest social contact could convey a sense of security. A geo-position cache also increases the robustness of the system. While the

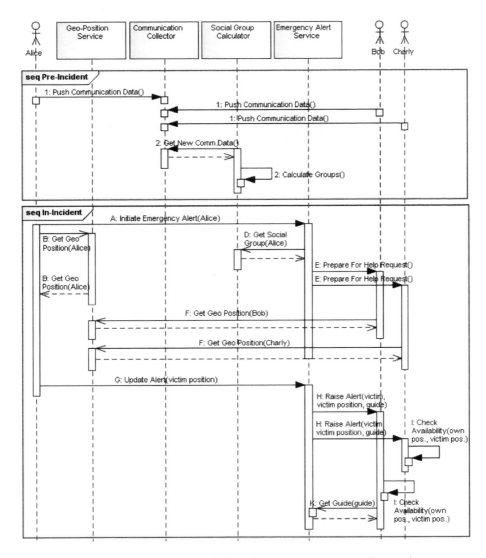

Fig. 6. Communiction Protocol of a privacy-aware emergency alert service

phone signal is often very well even within buildings or narrow streets the GPS signal might not suffice to determine the geo-position. The last-known position (e.g. the position before entering a building) would be helpful in those cases.

6   Identifying Social Groups by Clustering Social Networks

Calling persons willing to help is crucial for the proposed system but their identification is not trivial. Communication networks or 'friend' networks of online social network sites usually contain many links that do not result from close personal relations. Links may connect business partners or co-workers. On social network sites people 'friend' others they rarely know. Therefore, identifying social groups is an approach to separate close personal contacts from other distant contacts that are less willing to help in a case of emergency.

The appropriate cluster algorithms depend on the network that needs to be analyzed. All algorithms need to be highly efficient as the mentioned networks are huge (several million vertices). From communication data weighted networks could be created where an edge connects caller and the callee respectively sender and receiver of a text message. The edges can be weighted by the number of calls or messages. Walk context clustering is a suitable method for this kind of network. It generates overlapping clusters and can reflect that people have several groups of close contacts (family, friends, neighbors) that are almost not connected with each other.

6.1 Walk Context Clustering

Walk context clustering consists of two stages (see algorithm 1). In the walk stage, a set of restricted random walks is generated by starting a number of walks at each vertex and repeatedly choosing the following vertices randomly among those vertices that are linked by an edge which has a higher weight than the previously taken one (see figure 7).

Algorithm 1. Walk context clustering

Data: undirected, weighted graph $G = (V, E)$, constant p
▼ **Walk generation**
 $walkSet \leftarrow \emptyset$;
 forall the $v \in V$ **do**
  for $counter \leftarrow 1$ to p **do**
   $walk \leftarrow (i)$; $last \leftarrow 0$; $i \leftarrow v$;
   while $N = \{x | \omega_{ix} > last\} \neq \emptyset$ **do**
    $j \leftarrow$ random element of N;
    $last \leftarrow \omega_{ij}$;
    append j to walk w;
    $i \leftarrow j$;
   end
   $walkSet \leftarrow walklist \cup walk$;
  end
 end

Data: walkSet ws, vertex v, level l
▼ **Cluster Construction**
 $cluster \leftarrow \emptyset$;
 forall the $w \in ws | v \in w \wedge pos(v, w) > l$ **do**
  forall the $x \in w | pos(x, w) > l$ **do**
   $cluster \leftarrow cluster \cup x$;
  end
 end

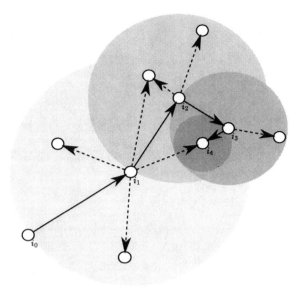

Fig. 7. Narrowing search space for successive vertices of the restricted random walk algorithm. The walks terminates when no neighbor is within the search space. Solid arrows symbolize used transitions. Dashed arrows symbolize links to possible successors that have not been chosen by the random process.

In the cluster construction stage, clusters get generated from the walks. Walk context clustering assigns a vertex to the cluster of another vertex if both are part of the same walk. A level parameter l specifies the fraction of vertices at the beginning of a walk that are disregarded. The later a pair of vertices appears in a walk the stronger is their connection. The interesting feature of walk-context clustering is that the closeness of two persons can be measured by the maximal level that assigns one person to the cluster of the other one.

A recently developed database-backed update algorithm for the walk stage maintains asymptotically optimal clusters in near real-time (< 0.2 sec for a single update on graphs with approximately 500000 nodes and 20 million edges) [14].

7   Assessment of Benefits

7.1   Ability to Transmit Request for Help

Emergency situations can result of various incidents, e.g. crime, accidents, medical emergencies. By their nature, accidents happen unexpected and sudden. Some medical emergencies as heart attacks do as well. The ability to make an emergency call in these cases will depend on the physical condition of the person in need.

For victims of violent crime their ability to send an emergency signal depends on the progress of crime. In 25%, respectively 22%, of the robberies analyzed by Smith [41] instant violence or attempts to snatch property don't give the opportunity to call for help. However, in 37% of the robberies the offender approached the victim and demanded money or valuables without immediate violence. In many cases later victims

Table 1. Average number of other persons of same social group connected to same cellular tower for 1000 randomly selected persons and points of time

	Day (6am-6pm)		Evening (6pm-11pm)		Night (11pm-6am)	
	Group	Others	Group	Others	Group	Others
09/2004	1.16	3.74	1.17	2.73	0.95	1.51
10/2004	1.33	3.12	1.29	3.4	1.14	1.82
11/2004	2.2	3.18	1.53	2.16	1.76	1.03

were also aware of an upcoming threat. In those cases it would be possible to send an emergency message.

7.2   Chance for Nearby Help

The helpfulness of the proposed system depends on the availability of close social contacts in the proximity of the site of the emergency. The actual number of persons in ones proximity in general and the number of close contacts with a particular motivation to help will surely depend on several factors, e.g. place and time.

To gain insight into the availability of potential help the MIT reality mining experiment [11] provides an interesting data set. For this experiment a group of 100 persons (75 students or faculty of the MIT Media Laboratory and 25 students of the MIT Sloan Business School) has been equipped with smart phones with special software applications preinstalled. These applications recorded phone numbers of incoming and outgoing calls, text messages, and the id of the cellular tower the phones were connected to during one academic year.

The phone call and text message data from the reality mining data set can be used to construct a communication network. Based on the assumption that the communication intensity of two people reflects the closeness of their relation, social groups can be identified by clustering this weighted network. The availability of nearby help from within the social group of a person in need can be estimated by the number of persons from the same social group whose phones are connected to the same cellular tower as the person in need.

For three consecutive months all communication prior to the specific month has been used to build an undirected, weighted communication network. The edge weights are the number of communication events (calls, text messages). This network has been clustered by the walk context cluster algorithm with the level parameter set to 0.8. The generated clusters had an average size of about 5.

The MIT reality mining data set contains a history of time-stamped connection records of the participating persons. For each month 1000 connection records have been randomly selected. Then, for each person in a connection record the number of persons of his social group who have been connected to the same cellular tower at the same time has been counted. This simulation showed that on average more than one close fellow student was available for help at any time (see table 1). E.g. for September 2004 the probability of having at least one person from one's social group in the proximity was 78% - independent of time of the day.

This is just a basic assessment for a particular group of people that has several shortcomings. Due to the lack of more detailed data it was not possible to assess if other social contacts than fellow students were available for help. Proximity could just be estimated by radio cells which have a radius of a few hundred meters in urban areas and a radius up to about 35 km in rural areas. But it is fair to regard the results as an indication that people living in urban areas will usually have at least one of their social contacts in their proximity.

7.3   Chance to Actually Receive Help

Once a request for help has been transmitted to a potential helper in the proximity of the site of the emergency the chance to actually receive help depends on the willingness and the ability of the informed persons to get to that place. The ability to get to a specific site can be supported in various ways. For example a map and route directions could be displayed together with the emergency message. The research of Markey [23] showed that also in computer-mediated communication settings help requests that were directed to specific persons had a high probability to receive fast response and the bystander effect was virtually eliminated.

8   Conclusions

In this paper a novel emergency alert service has been introduced which addresses all obstacles to providing help identified in the social emergency intervention process discussed in section 2. The service is designed to reduce psychological barriers that result in a bystander effect and inhibit effective help for persons in need. The analysis of emergency situations and whereabouts of persons in relation to their respective social group suggest that the described service can actually provide a benefit in practice. A first prototype of this service is currently under development.

The main emphasis of this paper is on the reduction of the bystander effect. However, the following challenges which are beyond the scope of this paper are examples of what must be addressed thoroughly for concrete industrial service offerings:

1. Legal Issues. The service raises e.g. the problem that potential helpers become liable to help and failure to do so may be prosecuted.
2. Privacy. The service should be designed in order to minimize the intrusion of privacy of service-subscribers.
3. Emergency dialog: The emergency dialog could be further automated e.g. by providing an automatic classification of the incident type.
4. Geo-positioning problems. Geo-positioning is still problematic in large buildings, tunnels, subterranean areas (e.g. subway). Enhancements could be based e.g. by embedding geo-position senders in such structures or by image recognition techniques which exploit public geo-coded images of such spaces.

Acknowledgments.   The research leading to these results has received funding from the European Community's 7th Framework Program FP7/2007-2013 under grant agreement n°215453 – WeKnowIt.

This contribution is a revised and extended version of the paper presented at ICE-B 2010, the 2010 International Conference on e-Business in Athens, Greece [16].

References

1. Android, http://www.android.com/
2. Batson, C.D., Cochran, P.J., Biederman, M.F., Blosser, J.L., Ryan, M.J., Vogt, B.: Failure to help when in a hurry: Callousness or conflict? Personality and Social Psychology Bulletin 4, 97–101 (1978)
3. Baumeister, R.F., Chesner, S.P., Sanders, P.S., Tice, D.M.: Who's in charge here? Group leaders do lend help in emergencies. Personality and Social Psychology Bulletin 14, 17–22 (1995)
4. Borkowski, J., Lempiainen, J.: Practical network-based techniques for mobile positioning in UMTS. EURASIP J. Appl. Signal Process. 2006, 149–149 (2006)
5. Chen, R., Sharman, R., Rao, H.R., Upadhyaya, S.J.: Coordination in emergency response management. Communications of the ACM 51(5), 66–73 (2008)
6. Clark, R., Word, L.E.: Why don't bystanders help? Because of ambiguity? Journal of Personality and Social Psychology 24, 392–400 (1972)
7. Comfort, L.K., Kilkon, K., Zagorecki, A.: Coordination in rapidly evolving disaster response systems: The role of information. American Behavioral Scientist 48(3), 295–313 (2009)
8. Cramer, R.E., McMaster, M.R., Bartell, P., Dragna, M.: Subject competence and the minimization of the bystander effect. Journal of Applied Social Psychology 18, 1133–1148 (1988)
9. Darley, J.M., Batson, C.: "From Jerusalem to Jericho": A study of situational and dispositional variables in helping behavior. Journal of Personality and Social Psychology 27(1), 100–108 (1973)
10. Darley, J.M., Latané, B.: Bystander intervention in emergencies: Diffusion of responsibility. Journal of Personality and Social Psychology 8(4), 377–383 (1968)
11. Eagle, N., Pentland, A.: Reality mining: Sensing complex social systems. Personal and Ubiquitous Computing 9, 1–14 (2005)
12. EU: Directive 2006/24/EC of the European Parliament and of the Council on the retention of data generated or processed in connection with the provision of publicly available electronic communications services or of public communications networks and amending Directive 2002/58/EC (March 2006)
13. Faraj, S., Xiao, Y.: Coordination in fast-response organizations. Management Science 52(8), 1155–1169 (2006)
14. Franke, M., Geyer-Schulz, A.: An update algorithm for restricted random walk clustering for dynamic data sets. Advances in Data Analysis and Classification 3(1), 63–92 (2009)
15. Garcia, S.M., Weaver, K., Moskowitz, G.B., Darley, J.M.: Crowded minds: The implicit bystander effect. Journal of Personality and Social Psychology 83, 843–853 (2002)
16. Geyer-Schulz, A., Ovelgönne, M., Sonnenbichler, A.: Getting help in a crowd – a social emergency alert service. In: Proceedings of the International Conference on e-Business (ICE-B), pp. 1–12 (2010)
17. Granovetter, M.: The strength of weak ties: A network theory revisited. In: Marsden, P.V., Lin, N. (eds.) Social Structure and Network Analysis, ch. 5, pp. 105–130. Sage Publications, Inc., Beverly Hills (1982)
18. Granovetter, M.S.: The strength of weak ties. The American Journal of Sociology 78(6), 1360–1380 (1973)
19. Hoser, B., Geyer-Schulz, A.: Eigenspectral analysis of hermitian adjacency matrices for the analysis of group substructures. The Journal of Mathematical Sociology 29(4), 265–294 (2005)
20. Kikiras, P., Drakoulis, D.: An integrated approach for the estimation of mobile subscriber geolocation. Wireless Personal Communications 30(2), 217–231 (2004)

21. Latané, B., Darley, J.: The Unresponsive Bystander: Why doesn't he help? Appleton-Century-Crofts, NY (1970)
22. Levine, M., Prosser, A., Evans, D., Reicher, S.: Identity and emergency intervention: How social group membership and inclusiveness of group boundaries shape helping behavior. Personality and Social Psychology Bulletin 31(4), 443–453 (2005)
23. Markey, P.M.: Bystander intervention in computer-mediated communication. Computers in Human Behavior 16, 183–188 (2000)
24. Milgram, S.: The experience of living in cities. Science 167, 1461–1468 (1970)
25. Miller, D.T., McFarland, C.: Pluralistic ignorance: When similarity is interpreted as dissimilarity. Journal of Personality and Social Psychology 53, 298–305 (1987)
26. Monin, B., Norton, M.: Perceptions of a fluid consensus: Uniqueness bias, false consensus, false polarization, and pluralistic ignorance in a water conservation crisis. Personality and Social Psychology Bulletin 29, 559–567 (2003)
27. Moriarty, T.: Crime, commitment, and the responsive bystander: Two field experiments. Journal of Personality and Social Psychology 31, 370–376 (1975)
28. Nadler, A., Halabi, S.: Intergroup helping as status relations: Effects of status stability, identification, and type of help on receptivity to high-status group's help. Journal of Personality and Social Psychology 91(1), 97–110 (2006)
29. Open Handset Alliance, http://www.openhandsetalliance.com/
30. Ovelgönne, M., Geyer-Schulz, A.: Cluster cores and modularity maximization. In: IEEE International Conference on Data Mining Workshops, ICDMW 2010, pp. 1204–1213. IEEE Computer Society (2010)
31. Ovelgönne, M., Geyer-Schulz, A., Stein, M.: Randomized greedy modularity optimization for group detection in huge social networks. In: SNA-KDD 2010: Proceedings of the 4th Workshop on Social Network Mining and Analysis. ACM, New York (2010) (to appear)
32. Ovelgönne, M., Sonnenbichler, A.C., Geyer-Schulz, A.: Social emergency alert service - a location-based privacy-aware personal safety service. In: NGMAST 2010. Proceedings of the 2010 Fourth International Conference on Next Generation Mobile Applications, Services and Technologies, pp. 84–89. IEEE Computer Society (2010)
33. Palen, L., Liu, S.B.: Citizen communication in crisis: Anticipating a future of ICT-supported public participation. In: CHI 2007 Proceedings, pp. 727–736. ACM (2007)
34. Piliavin, I.M., Piliavin, J.A., Rodin, J.: Costs, diffusion, and the stigmatized victim. Journal of Personality and Social Psychology 32(3), 429–438 (1975)
35. Rungg, A.: Privatspäre 2. 0. Financial Times Deutschland, p. 25 (February 17, 2010)
36. Rutkowski, G.K., Gruder, C.L., Romer, D.: Group cohesiveness, social norms, and bystander intervention. Journal of Personality and Social Psychology 44, 545–552 (1983)
37. Schwartz, S.H., Gottlieb, A.: Bystander anonymity and reaction to emergencies. Journal of Personality and Social Psychology 39, 418–430 (1980)
38. Shotland, R.L., Heinold, W.D.: Bystander response to arterial bleeding: Helping skills, the decision-making process, and differentiating the helping response. Journal of Personality and Social Psychology 49, 347–356 (1985)
39. Shotland, R.L., Stebbins, C.A.: Bystander response to rape: Can a victim attract help? Journal of Applied Social Psychology 10, 510–527 (1980)
40. Shotland, R.L., Straw, M.K.: Bystander response to an assault: When a man attacks a woman. Journal of Personality and Social Psychology 34, 990–999 (1976)
41. Smith, J.: The nature of personal robbery. Home Office Research Study 254, Home Office Research, Development and Statictics Directorate (2003)
42. Spiegel Online: Beaten to death in broad daylight - germany shocked by brutal commuter train murder (2009), http://www.spiegel.de/international/germany/0,1518,649134,00.html

43. Spiege Online: Notruf-Mitschnitt belegt Brutalität der S-Bahn-Prügler (September 2009),
    http://www.spiegel.de/panorama/gesellschaft/
    0,1518,656858,00.html
44. Spiegel Online: Tödlicher Angriff: Mehrere Menschen beobachteten Münchner S-Bahn-Attacke (September 2009),
    http://www.spiegel.de/panorama/justiz/0,1518,649288,00.html
45. Stürmer, S., Snyder, M., Omoto, A.M.: Prosocial emotions and helping: The moderating role of group membership. Journal of Personality and Social Psychology 88(3), 532–546 (2005)
46. Yuan, Y., Detlor, B.: Intelligent mobile crisis response systems. Communications of the ACM 48(2), 95–98 (2005)

Part III

Optical Communication Systems

Converged Optical Networks for Multimedia Distribution and Data Services in Hospitality Environments

Iñigo Artundo, David García-Roger, and Beatriz Ortega

Optical and Quantum Communications Group, iTEAM, Universidad Politécnica de Valencia (UPV), Camino de Vera s/n, 46022 Valencia, Spain
{iiarmar,dgarro,bortega}@iteam.upv.es

Abstract. Current hospitality networks are already lagging behind in terms of broadband adoption and high-speed online offered services, and they might not be able to cope with the increasing bandwidth demands required to distribute high-definition video traffic. We propose the use of a converged optical network adapted to the specific needs of the hospitality environment, providing a future-proof and easy to manage solution based on optical fiber wiring, together with radio-over-fiber techniques for wireless access. For short distance installations with reduced transmission losses, the use of plastic optical fiber will significantly lower the infrastructure costs. We use detailed full-system simulations to analyze the validity of such infrastructure to provide a unified, pervasive and future-proof all-optical solution. Bandwidth loads in excess of 5 Gb/s have been detected on the architecture, while being able to serve high-definition TV channels with ultra low latencies.

Keywords: Optical networks, in-Building hospitality networks, IPTV, Plastic optical fiber, Radio-over-fiber.

1 Introduction

The recent growth of demand for higher bandwidth in hospitality buildings (hotels, hospital, residences, etc.) comes from the exploding connectivity of devices and systems sharing data, the high-tech customization of guestroom technology (video streaming to TV and other devices, on-demand movies, high-speed Internet access, online gaming, voice-over-IP and videoconferencing, e-commerce and billing of the resort's services), and the increasingly pervasive mobile access to information [1]. Moreover, remote guest/staff control of room temperature and lighting (including energy management policies), electronic door locks, or other hotel services will only add to the number of connected and managed devices. Emerging technologies will strongly affect network performance and medium/long-term strategies to meet guest demands while still requiring consistent quality of service and experience [2].

The deployment of mixed physical technologies on the network infrastructure (coaxial, Cat.5e/6, phone wire) results in large capital investment in equipment purchase, installation and maintenance. Moreover, the common electrical cabling used poses limitations in diameter, weight, terminations and electromagnetical interference. One growing approach to simplify network design, installation and management costs

M.S. Obaidat, G.A. Tsihrintzis, and J. Filipe (Eds.): ICETE 2010, CCIS 222, pp. 133–144, 2012.
© Springer-Verlag Berlin Heidelberg 2012

is the use of converged networks, both wired and wireless, using a single cable for backbone and in-room wiring to carry all communications for guestrooms as well as for staff systems. Here, the larger bandwidth of fiber over copper links becomes evident in high-density hospitality buildings, where user aggregation reduces installation and operation costs. Moreover, recent developments on Plastic Optical Fiber (POF) [3] and Radio-over-Fiber (RoF) transmission allow for low-cost and competitive converged all-optical architectures [4].

In this paper, we study future requirements and performance in hospitality environments when introducing high-definition video services through converged optical networks. In Section 2 we identify the design boundaries of such scenario through a statistical analysis of TV channel blocking, and Section 3 proposes a future-proof fiber-based optical architecture that provides wired and wireless services, with the limitations on the span of such network thoroughly described. Finally, Section 4 introduces full-system simulations of this architecture to analyze network response over intensive video traffic, depending on the floor distribution capacity. This allows the exploration of the concept of flexible optical resource allocation to cope with temporal limitations and cover specific hospitality services in a dynamic way.

2 Previous Works

Previous works have attempted to measure the impact of technological investment in hotels [5], reaching the conclusion that there is a significant productivity impact when the exploitation of the network and its integration with the infrastructure are strategically optimized, with architectures adapted to the business and its operations.

Similar converged optical architectures have been proposed recently but mostly for generic in-building scenarios. For example, [6] examines the transmission of uncompressed High-Definition TV (HDTV) under Ethernet passive optical networks (EPON) making use of the polarization diversity technique to improve reception sensitivity and increase the anti-interference capacity of the in-building wireless transmissions. [7] showcases a 600 Mb/s radio-over-fiber architecture able to integrate simultaneously Ultra-Wide-Band (UWB), wireless and WiMAX signals over 1 km of silica fibre using reflective electro-absorption transceivers, and similarly, [8] proposes multi-band generation and transmission of all these wireless signals through photonic frequency tripling, demonstrating a testbed able to deliver uncompressed 1.5 Gb/s HDTV video signals over silica fiber and free-space links.

Regarding the use of plastic fiber for RoF transmission, integrated multimedia transmission has been already demonstrated in [9] on a home level, with a network delivering various signals (Ethernet, digital terrestrial or satellite TV, wireless) on graded-index POF, and very high bit rates - up to 16 Gb/s - have been achieved by using techniques such as orthogonal frequency-division multiplexing [10].

However, none of the architectures reviewed to date addresses the specifics of the hospitality networks, nor tries to provide a fully-converged optical solution for the complex structured cabling systems commonly used in these commercial infrastructures.

3 Future Video Bandwidth Requirements

In hospitality installations, IP television (IPTV) networks are quickly substituting traditional RF video systems due to its lower installation and maintenance costs, and the possibility to integrate other interactive hospitality services [11]. IPTV systems use a single type of data connection for television, data and telephony services, benefiting from the use of a single set of cabling. They commonly receive TV channels from either cable television or satellite connections, and they may also introduce receiver antennas to get free local broadcast channels. A key feature for the upgrading of hospitality TV systems to support IPTV is the use of a hybrid solution that can combine simulcast television content (analogue and digital distribution) with multicast and unicast IPTV channels.

However, high-definition IPTV distribution faces specific challenges in the hospitality scenario. The number of channels that must be available to guests tends to be higher than in residential deployments, as overcoming geographic boundaries is desirable for travellers. Video-on-Demand (VoD) is highly promoted, as it offers relatively high margins and is a large part of the hospitality TV service revenues, but it puts an additional demand on temporal extra bandwidth requests. As an example, in Table 1 bandwidth demands for the distribution of high-definition IPTV channels are consisting of different Digital Subscriber Lines (xDSL) to the building and Fast Ethernet or wireless in-door access, and will even become worse when extra video streams like security cameras or higher bitrate video services, like 3D TV (up to 24 Mb/s) are also included.

Table 1. Bandwidth requirements to support hospitality IPTV

External WAN	Maximum bitrate (Mb/s)	Average Throughput (Mb/s)	%	HDTV channels (6 Mb/s/ch)	Full HDTV channels (12 Mb/s/ch)
ADSL	8.2	8*	97.5%	1	0
ADSL2+	24.6	21.8*	88.6%	2	1
VDSL2	250	68*	27.2%	11	5
Gigabit Ethernet/GEPON	1000	941.5	94.1%	156	78
GPON	2500	2488	99.5%	414	207
10Gigabit Ethernet/10GEPON	10000	9415	94.1%	1569	784
In-Building LAN					
Fast Ethernet	100	94.2	94.1%	16	7
Gigabit Ethernet	1000	94.5	94.1%	156	78
WiFi 802.11g	54	10-22	18-40%	1-3	0-1
WiFi 802.11n (2.4/5 GHz)	150/ 600	65-260/ 135- 540	21-86%/ 22-90%	10-43/ 22-90	5-21/ 11-45

* Obtained from empirical measurements over 2500 m [12]. VDLS2 average is calculated theoretically for this same distance.

To analyze the designs boundaries of a common hospitality video distribution network, we will first focus on calculating the blocking probabilities for each TV channel under a standard xDSL-driven IPTV installation. Using the models proposed by [13], the blocking probability $B(i)$ for channel i will be given by Equations (1-3), with

B_{Proc} the blocking probability due to limited processing capability of a Digital Sub-scriber Line Access Multiplexer (DSLAM), and $B_{Link}(i)$ the blocking probability due to insufficient link capacity from a DSLAM to an edge router:

$$B(i) = B_{Proc} + (1 - B_{Proc}) \cdot B_{Link}(i) \quad , \tag{1}$$

$$B_{Proc} = \frac{\dfrac{(s-1)!}{(s-1-n)!n!} \cdot \rho_{DSLAM}^{n}}{\sum_{h=0}^{n} \dfrac{(s-1)!}{(s-1-h)!h!} \cdot \rho_{DSLAM}^{h}} \tag{2}$$

$$B_{Link}(i) = (1 - P(i)) \cdot B_{Engset}(i) \quad . \tag{3}$$

In these equations, s corresponds to the number of users per DSLAM, n is the channel replication capabilities of the DSLAM, and ρ_{DSLAM} is the ratio between guest arrivals and departures to the DSLAM, according to a Poisson distribution.

$$P(i) = 1 - \frac{1}{e^{\rho_i} - B_{Engset}(i) \cdot e^{\rho_i} + B_{Engset}(i)} \quad , \tag{4}$$

$$B_{Engset}(i) = \frac{\dfrac{1}{m!} \cdot \dfrac{d^m \left[\prod_{k=1}^{K} \dfrac{q_k + p_k z}{q_i + p_i z} \right]}{dz^m} \Bigg|_{z=0}}{\sum_{j=0}^{m} \dfrac{1}{j!} \dfrac{d^j \left[\prod_{k=1}^{K} \dfrac{q_k + p_k z}{q_i + p_i z} \right]}{dz^j} \Bigg|_{z=0}} \quad . \tag{5}$$

$P(i)$ represents the probability of channel i to be 'on', as shown in Equation (4), with ρ_i as the ratio between guest arrivals and departures to channel i. $B_{Engset}(i)$ described in Equation (5) is the probability that the link from the DSLAM to the edge router is con-sumed by m channels other than the requested channel i. If we consider C as the link capacity coming into the building, and C_0 the channel bitrate (depending on the com-pression coding), we can calculate how many $m = C/C0$ of the K offered channels can be transmitted simultaneously to N guests using M DSLAMs in peak usage hours, which normally correspond to a 41% guests connected between 16:00 and 22:00 [14]. We will consider a single DSLAM for 180 guests. Channel switching rates are distrib-uted with decreasing exponential popularity, according to a realistic distribution [14].

We will consider a non-blocking situation when $B(i) < 10^{-8}$ for all popular chan-nels. Video bitrates depend on the encoding, 3 Mb/s for SDTV using MPEG2 or 1.6 Mb/s with MPEG4, and 12 Mb/s and 6 Mb/s accordingly for HDTV. In this case, the minimum non-blocking number of channel replications per DSLAM would be $n = 65$, although we will consider a more realistic value of $n = 120$. Table 2 shows the maxi-mum available channels and minimum incoming link capacity for different IPTV channel bitrates.

Table 2. Maximum available channels and minimum incoming link capacity

TV Channel bitrate (C_0)	K_{Max} for $C = 1000$ Mb/s	C_{Min} for $K = 500$ ch
1.6 Mb/s	674 ch	750 Mb/s
3 Mb/s	357 ch	1410 Mb/s
6 Mb/s	174 ch	2830 Mb/s
12 Mb/s	85 ch	5560 Mb/s

If we set the link capacity to $C = 1$ Gb/s, there is a clear limitation on the number of non-blocking HDTV channels that can be available. Considering a future offer in the order of 500 channels, the link capacity quickly scales up over the gigabit range due to fragmented channel viewing, limiting the use of traditional coax or twisted pair approaches. Figure 1 shows (a) the channel blocking probability for the same scenario in the case of 200 HDTV channels at 6 Mb/s bitrate, and (b) a future scenario with much larger bitrate channels (e.g. 3DTV) at 24 Mb/s bitrate. It can be clearly seen that only the two most popular channels are absolutely blocking free, and as channel popularity decreases (higher channel index), blocking can raise even four orders of magnitude.

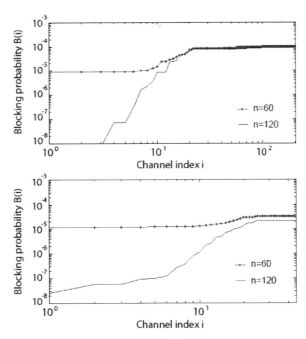

Fig. 1. Channel blocking probability for (a) $K = 200$ HD-MPEG4 channels, and (b) $K = 44$ large bitrate (e.g. 3DTV) channels

For a higher bitrate, blocking due to channel capacity can happen even for the most popular channels. When reducing n to 60 processing limitations quickly appear at the DSLAM for all channels alike.

If we now consider a Gigabit Passive Optical Network (GPON) link capacity of $C = 2.5$ Gb/s, when using HD-MPEG4 encoding we would be able to access 446 channels in a non-blocking way for this same scenario. In case of having wireless IPTV distribution, with links up to $C = 600$ Mb/s, we could transmit blocking-free only 103 channels. Of course, the number of channels will be reduced in a practical implementation depending on bandwidth reservations for management and other extra services. Technical feasibility for newer wireless HD at 60 GHz over POF has been proven [15], but it is still not clear the commercial support for those services.

4 Converged Optical Cabling

The proposed optical architecture, shown in Fig. 2a, consists of a router that connects to the external service/content providers through and optical access network, either Fiber-to-the-Building GPON or EPON connection. The building backbone from the basement router to the different floors is done through single mode fiber (SMF), and floor distribution is done through step-index plastic optical fiber (SI-POF), as shown in Fig. 2a. The use of POF will significantly lower the installation costs of the infrastructure in terms of cabling, connectoring, transceivers and tools. Wireless access will be provided by a Distributed Antenna System (DAS), consisting of multiple Remote Antenna Units (RAUs) capable of transporting frequencies from 800 to 2500 MHz, including 2.5G/3G mobile standards and 802.11/16 data and building automation wireless signals, through the SMF backbone.

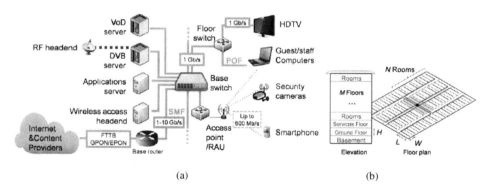

(a)   (b)

Fig. 2. (a) Converged optical network architecture, and (b) building elevation and floor plans

To study the feasibility of such optical infrastructure, a transmission analysis is done first. Maximum floor link lengths will be mainly limited by the high transmission loss of SI-POF. The design boundaries then will be given by the transmission losses for a generic building geometry, as shown in Fig. 2b. Here, M corresponds to the number of floors with rooms, N the number of rooms per corridor side, C the number of corridor sides, H the floor height, L the room length, W the room width, and L_0 the initial length from the floor switch to the first room considered to be always 4 m). In each floor, a double SI-POF cable will be installed to each room to provide two wall plugs (for data access and an IPTV device). If POF transmission is simplex, the cable will contain then two fibers. The basic floor distribution includes a central hallway with connections to security video-cameras and RAUs.

The transmission losses for SI-POF are considered to be $L_T = 0.16$ dB/m at 650 nm, and 0.09 dB/m at 510 nm. High-quality POF connectors (e.g. EM-RJ, SMI) introduce a loss $L_C = 0.75$ dB and tight bends (around 5 mm radius) can introduce losses of $L_B = 1.5$ dB per bend. Therefore, the maximum distance for any floor link will be given by Equation (6), the minimum transmission losses for the longest POF link calculated by Equation (7), and the power margin for each POF link given by Equation (8), with P_T and P_R the transmitter and receiver power respectively, in dBm:

$$D_{POF\_Max} = L_0 + N \cdot W + \left\lfloor \frac{C}{4} \right\rfloor , \qquad (6)$$

$$L_{Min} = D_{POF\_Max} \cdot L_T + L_C + L_B , \qquad (7)$$

$$PM = P_T - L_{Min} - P_R . \qquad (8)$$

Considering a link with a standard Light Emitting Diode (LED) with a transmitted power of $P_T = -3$ dBm and a PIN photoreceiver with a sensitivity of $P_R = -19$ dBm, two connectors (1.5 dB) and six tight bends (9 dB), the maximum transmission loss per link would be 5.5 dB. However, recent Gigabit POF photoreceivers are reaching sensitivities of up to -30 dBm, and higher quality connectors can have losses as low as 1.1 dB, so the power margin and the corresponding maximum distances are expected to be augmented in the following years.

Figure 3 shows the link transmission loss for different room configurations. Up to 30 m² room sizes, the POF links will be able to span up to 5 rooms in each corridor side without significant power loss. This would be enough to cover an average hotel with 20 rooms per floor ($N = 5$, $C = 4$). If using green LEDs, their lower attenuation would allow extending the reach to more than 10 rooms per corridor side. For the backbone RoF transmission, as the bandwidth of SI-POF is limited to only 500 MHz·Km, either SMF or GI-POF with bandwidth of 2500 MHz·Km, would be needed. Maximum link lengths in this case, considering the full span of the building, would be $D_{RoF\_Max} = (M+3) \cdot H$, and considering the same power budget, for an average hotel floor height of 4 m, this would mean a maximum GI-POF link span of 12 floors. For longer heights, low loss silica fiber links would be mandatory for keeping the power budget.

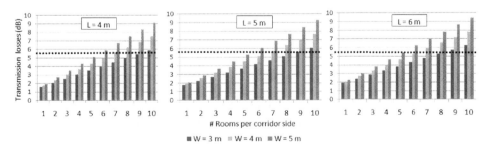

Fig. 3. POF transmission losses depending on the room length, width and number of rooms per corridor

5   Hospitality Data Traffic

To study future network demands of hospitality environments under this converged optical architecture, we have simulated the whole infrastructure presented in Section 3 under OPNET™ Modeler.

An average 4-floor hospitality resort is considered, with 45 rooms per floor plus 45 staff computers making a total of 225 users while in full occupancy. This distribution mirrors a typical medium size hotel or a small hospital. The main building backbone is modeled to be 100 m SMF links running Gigabit Ethernet, and floor distribution is done through POF to wall plugs and through the RAUs for the wireless access. Average POF link lengths range from 6 to 50 m, and are considered to run Gigabit Ethernet, although Fast Ethernet links have been modeled as well for comparison.

Guest and staff users and devices have been profiled daily in time following future application usage distributions [16], and several services have been included in the analysis as shown in Table 3 and Fig. 4.

Table 3. Application profile definition

Application	BW (Mb/s)	Duration (s)	Repetition (s)
Web browsing*	1-100	Exp(600)	Exp(600)
Email	1	Exp(60)	Exp(600)
Database access	0.5	Uni(300)	Uni(300-600)
VoIP	0.096	Exp(600)	Exp(1800)
Videoconference	4	Exp(600)	Exp(7200)
File transfer	100	Exp(300)	Exp(1800)
IPTV	6-24	Exp(7200)	Exp(21600)

*Includes also video browsing, social networking and immersive online games and environments.

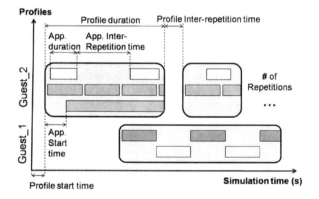

Fig. 4. Guest profile definition

The traffic model for each application follows a typical Ethernet medium access protocol, and with page or transaction inter-arrival times following exponential distributions. No data prioritization has been applied, considering all services as best effort. Application duration and their repetition rate are modeled through uniform and exponential distributions as shown in Table 3, and guest profiles are modeled under a low

(0.5), medium (1) and high (2) usage factor over these values, with application and guest start times modeled through the OPNET *Random Number Generator (PRNG)*, based on the operating system's `random()` implementation.

We performed daytime simulations to see the dynamic evolution of traffic as users connect their devices into the network, and to obtain peak bandwidth demands, which will be dominated by the heavy video traffic. As daily TV usage begins early in the morning, we can see in Fig. 5 the bandwidth demands per floor, quickly over passing the Fast Ethernet limit of 100 Mb/s. Making use of Gigabit Ethernet seems mandatory to avoid congestion if intensive video traffic (HDTV or high resolution videoconferencing) is considered. This might be critical when telemedicine applications are considered. The similarity among floors in the bandwidth traces over the random statistical variability is due to the identical guest profiling used per floor to simplify design and simulation time, and future work intends to add further detail to such guest distribution.

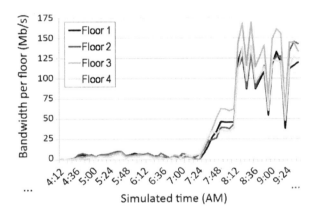

Fig. 5. In-building data traffic at morning time

Figure 5 also depicts the self-similar nature of Ethernet traffic (either internal or external), exhibiting a bursty behavior which looks similar to itself on different time scales. Statistically, temporal high variability can be captured by traffic models with long-range dependences, that is, autocorrelation exhibiting power-law decay with a minimum number of parameters [17].

The outgoing traffic is represented in Fig. 6, with an initial network loading phase of 20 min as the average load of video streams is reached on the building. As shown in the figure, the aggregated bandwidth served by the exit router to the access network is no less than 450 Mb/s and up to 800 Mb/s, for Fast and Gigabit Ethernet floor distributions. The ten fold speed difference between both internal configurations does not impact proportionally the external traffic, as most of the data will be coming from the remote IPTV servers, and only local distribution will be significantly boosted in the second configuration.

As a way to measure the responsiveness of the system, we will use the channel switching time of the hospitality IPTV system. The channel switching time (or zapping delay) can be defined as the time difference between the user asking for a channel change by pressing a button on the remote control and the display of the first frame of the requested channel on the TV screen. In analog TV, channel change is around 100 ms since it only involves the receiver tuning to a new carrier frequency, demodulating the analog signal and displaying the picture on the screen. IPTV channel switching times can be higher due to delay factors [18], like digital video decompression and buffering, IP network related issues (frame encapsulation, IGMP group joining, congestion, etc.) and content management (paid subscription channels, parental filtering, etc.). Fast switching IPTV systems are expected to have zapping delays of less than a second. To make our study more general, we will only consider the network components of the channel switching delay, as video codification and content management greatly depends on the specific IPTV implementation.

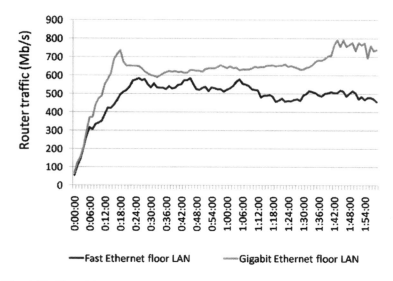

Fig. 6. Traffic exiting the building from the basement router to the access network

In Fig. 7 we see the influence of full HDTV data streams (12 Mb/s per channel) over the channel switch requests (the zapping delay). We observe that, under a gigabit Ethernet network, this value still falls far from the margin of 125 ms limit for seamless zapping time, but over slower connections, delay quickly builds up and can degrade user experience and congest the remaining data network. For the same situation, but considering all users streaming high-definition WebTV video (6.3 Mb/s) instead of IPTV, or high-definition videoconferencing (4.3 Mb/s), there would be an average frame delivery delay of 2.74 ms under a Fast Ethernet network, or only 0.38 μs under a Gigabit Ethernet one. The saturation point hence will be reached for a larger number of video streams allocated in the network, which will again depend on their temporal and spatial distribution, and their correlation with the additional data traffic.

We can conclude that the presented architecture remains valid for the services evaluated and still holds enough margins to cope with spikes due to seasonal trade show attendance or an increase in holiday travelling. Moreover, dynamic network load balancing on the optical domain can spread future demands over all available physical media, avoiding traffic surges, server bottlenecks, connectivity losses and downtimes. Considering specially the RoF distribution system, more wireless and mobile capacity can be allocated to an area (e.g. conference hall) during peak times and then re-allocated to other areas when off-peak (e.g. guestrooms in the evenings). This obviates the requirement for allocating permanent capacity, which would be a waste of resources in cases where traffic loads vary frequently and by large margins. Future explorations on the hospitality scenario will include the dynamic use of different optical wavelengths through reconfigurable Wavelength Division Multiplexing (WDM).

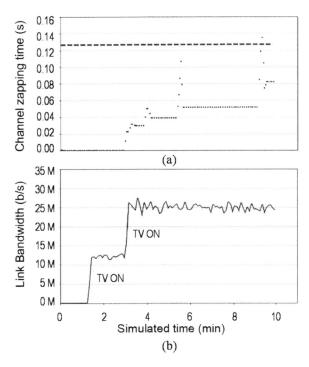

Fig. 7. (a) Channel zapping delay correlated to (b) bandwidth consumption in a Fast Ethernet POF link

6 Conclusions

We have mapped the requirements for high-definition video distribution on hospitality environments, identifying bandwidth demands of more than 5 Gb/s. Thus, fiber emerges as the most appropriate cabling solution, and thus we propose a low-cost and future-proof converged optical network based on silica and plastic fiber. Such cabling infrastructure would be limited to 12 floors with 20 rooms each, and full network simulations have verified seamless transmission of HD video streams, with TV channel switching times of less than 125 ms.

Acknowledgements. This work was supported by the EC 7th Framework Program: Architectures for fLexible Photonic Home and Access networks (ALPHA), ICT CP-IP 212 352, and OPNET Technologies, Inc. University Research Program.

References

1. Cisco Systems whitepaper: Hyperconnectivity and the Approaching Zettabyte Era (2009)
2. Inge, J.: Getting it Together: Technology trends in the hospitality industry. Hosp. Upgrad. Mag., 14–26 (2009)
3. Nespola, A., et al.: High-Speed Communications over Polymer Optical Fibers for In-Building Cabling and Home Networking. IEEE Photonics J. 2, 347–358 (2010)
4. Gomes, N.J., et al.: Radio-over-fiber transport for the support of wireless broadband services. J. Opt. Netw. 8, 156–178 (2009)
5. Sigala, M., et al.: ICT Paradox Lost? J. of Travel. Res. 43, 180–192 (2004)
6. Xu, K., et al.: Enabling RoF Technologies and Integration Architectures for In-Building Optical–Wireless Access Networks. IEEE Photonics J. 2, 102–112 (2010)
7. Walker, S., et al.: Wireless Broadband Service Delivery via Optical In-Home Converged Networks. In: Proc. of the IEEE Photonics Soc. Annu. Meet., pp. 612–613 (2009)
8. Jia, Z.: Wireless High-Definition Services over Optical Fiber Access Networks. In: Proc. of the 18th Int. Conf. on Wirel. and Opt. Commun., pp. 48–51 (2009)
9. Guillory, J.: Multiservice & multiformat home network based on a low cost optical infrastructure. In: Proc. of the ECOC, pp. 1–2 (2009)
10. Yu, J.: 16Gbit/s Radio OFDM Signals over Graded-Index Plastic Optical Fiber. In: Proc. of the ECOC, pp. 1–2 (2008)
11. Held, G.: Understanding IPTV. Auerbach Publications, Informa Telecoms & Media (2006)
12. Kagklis, D., et al.: A comparative Performance Evaluation of the ADSL2+ and ADSL Technologies. GESTS Int. Trans. on Comp. Sci. and Eng. 19, 1–6 (2005)
13. Lu, Y., Kuipers, F.A., Janic, M., Van Mieghem, P.: E2E Blocking Probability of IPTV and P2PTV. In: Das, A., Pung, H.K., Lee, F.B.S., Wong, L.W.C. (eds.) NETWORKING 2008. LNCS, vol. 4982, pp. 445–456. Springer, Heidelberg (2008)
14. SKO Dutch Audience Research Foundation 2008 Annual report, http://www.kijkonderzoek.nl
15. Jian, W., Liu, C., Chien, H.-C., Fan, S.-H., Yu, J., Wang, J., Dong, Z., Yu, J., Yu, C., Chang, G.-K.: QPSK-OFDM radio over polymer optical fiber for broadband in-building 60GHz wireless access. In: Proc. of the Opt. Fiber. Commun (OFC) Conf., pp. 1–3 (2010)
16. ALPHA FP7 Project: End-user future services in access, mobile and in-building networks, Public D1.1 deliverable (2008)
17. Riedi, R.H., Willinger, W.: Towards an improved understanding of network traffic dynamics. In: Self-similar Network Traffic and Performance Evaluation, pp. 507–530. Wiley (2000)
18. Uzunalioglu, H.: Channel change delay in IPTV systems. In: Proc. of the 6th IEEE Conf. on Consum. Commun. and Netw., pp. 206–211 (2009)

Part IV
Security and Cryptography

Differential Resynchronization Attacks on Reduced Round SNOW 3G$^{\oplus}$

Alex Biryukov, Deike Priemuth-Schmid, and Bin Zhang

University of Luxembourg, Luxembourg
{alex.biryukov,deike.priemuth-schmid,bin.zhang}@uni.lu

Abstract. The stream cipher SNOW 3G designed in 2006 by ETSI/SA-GE is a base algorithm for the second set of 3GPP confidentiality and integrity algorithms. In this paper, we investigate the resynchronization security of a close variant of SNOW 3G, in which two modular additions are replaced by xors and which is called SNOW 3G$^{\oplus}$. It is shown that the feedback from the FSM to the LFSR is crucial for security. Given a pair of *known* IVs, the cipher without such a feedback is extremely vulnerable to differential known IV attacks with practical complexities (2^{57} time and 2^{33} keystream). With such a feedback, it is shown that 16 out of 33 initialization rounds can be broken by a differential *chosen* IV attack. This is the first public evaluation result for this algorithm.

Keywords: Stream ciphers, SNOW 3G, Differential, Resynchronization attack.

1 Introduction

The SNOW 3G stream cipher is the core of the 3GPP confidentiality and integrity algorithms UEA2 and UIA2, published in 2006 by the 3GPP Task Force [3]. Compared to its predecessor, SNOW 2.0 [2], SNOW 3G adopts a finite state machine (FSM) of three 32-bit words and 2 S-Boxes to increase the resistance against algebraic attacks by Billet and Gilbert [1]. Full evaluation of the design by the consortium is not public, but a survey of this evaluation is given in [4]. SNOW 3G$^{\oplus}$ (in which the two modular additions are replaced by xors) is also defined and evaluated in [4]. The designers and external reviewers show that SNOW 3G has remarkable resistance against linear distinguishing attacks [5,6], while SNOW 3G$^{\oplus}$ offers much better resistance against algebraic attacks.

In this paper, we present the first attempt of cryptanalysis of SNOW 3G in the public literature. We show that the feedback from the FSM to the LFSR during the key/IV setup phase is vital for the security of this cipher, since we can break a version without such a feedback with two *known* IV's in 2^{57} time, 2^{33} data complexity and for an arbitrary number of the key/IV setup rounds! We then restore the feedback and study SNOW 3G$^{\oplus}$ against differential chosen IV attacks. We show attacks on SNOW 3G$^{\oplus}$ with 14, 15 and 16 rounds of initialization with complexities $2^{42.7}$, $2^{92.2}$ and $2^{124.2}$ respectively.

This paper is organized as follows. We give a description of SNOW 3G and SNOW 3G$^{\oplus}$ in Section 2. The known IV attack on SNOW 3G$^{\oplus}$ without the FSM to LFSR feedback is presented in Section 3 and the differential chosen IV attack on SNOW 3G$^{\oplus}$ with the feedback is presented in Section 4. Finally, some conclusions are given in Section 5.

M.S. Obaidat, G.A. Tsihrintzis, and J. Filipe (Eds.): ICETE 2010, CCIS 222, pp. 147–157, 2012.
© Springer-Verlag Berlin Heidelberg 2012

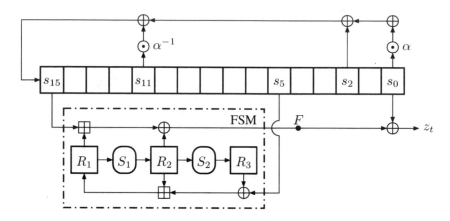

Fig. 1. Keystream generation of SNOW 3G

2   Description of SNOW 3G and SNOW 3G$^\oplus$

SNOW 3G is a word-oriented synchronous stream cipher with 128-bit key and 128-bit IV, each considered as four 32-bit words vector. It consists of a linear feedback shift register (LFSR) of sixteen 32-bit words and a finite state machine (FSM) with three 32-bit words, shown in Figure 1. Here '$\oplus$' denotes the bit-wise xor and '$\boxplus$' denotes the addition modulo 2^{32}. The feedback word of the LFSR is recursively computed as

$$s_{15}^t = \alpha^{-1} \cdot s_{11}^{t-1} \oplus s_2^{t-1} \oplus \alpha \cdot s_0^{t-1} \ ,$$

where α is the root of the $GF(2^8)[x]$ polynomial $x^4 + \beta^{23}x^3 + \beta^{245}x^2 + \beta^{48}x + \beta^{239}$ with β being the root of the $GF(2)[x]$ polynomial $x^8 + x^7 + x^5 + x^3 + 1$. The FSM has two input words s_5^t and s_{15}^t from the LFSR and is updated as

$$R_1^t = R_2^{t-1} \boxplus (R_3^{t-1} \oplus s_5^{t-1}) \qquad R_2^t = S_1(R_1^{t-1}) \qquad R_3^t = S_2(R_2^{t-1}) \ ,$$

with the output word $F^t = (s_{15}^t \boxplus R_1^t) \oplus R_2^t$, where S_1 and S_2 are 32-bit to 32-bit S-boxes defined as compositions of 4 parallel applications of two 8-bit to 8-bit small S-boxes, S_R and S_Q, with a linear diffusion layer respectively. Here S_R is the well known AES S-box and S_Q is defined as $S_Q(x) = x \oplus x^9 \oplus x^{13} \oplus x^{15} \oplus x^{33} \oplus x^{41} \oplus x^{45} \oplus x^{47} \oplus x^{49} \oplus 0x25$ for $x \in GF(2^8)$ defined by $x^8 + x^6 + x^5 + x^3 + 1$. If we decompose a 32-bit word B into four bytes $B = B^0 \| B^1 \| B^2 \| B^3$ with B^0 being the most and B^3 the least significant bytes, then for $i = 1, 2$, the S-boxes are

$$S_i(B) = MC_i \cdot (S_R(B^0), S_R(B^1), S_R(B^2), S_R(B^3))^T \ ,$$

where MC_1 is the AES mix-column for S_1 over $GF(2^8)$ defined by $x^8 + x^4 + x^3 + x + 1$ and MC_2 is the similar operation for S_2 over $GF(2^8)$ defined by $x^8 + x^6 + x^5 + x^3 + 1$.

SNOW 3G is initialized with the key $K = (k_0, k_1, k_2, k_3)$ and the $IV = (IV_0, IV_1, IV_2, IV_3)$ as follows. Let $\mathbf{1}$ be the all-one word, the LFSR is initialized as follows.

$$
\begin{array}{llll}
s_{15} = k_3 \oplus IV_0 & s_{14} = k_2 & s_{13} = k_1 & s_{12} = k_0 \oplus IV_1 \\
s_{11} = k_3 \oplus \mathbf{1} & s_{10} = k_2 \oplus \mathbf{1} \oplus IV_2 & s_9 = k_1 \oplus \mathbf{1} \oplus IV_3 & s_8 = k_0 \oplus \mathbf{1} \\
s_7 = k_3 & s_6 = k_2 & s_5 = k_1 & s_4 = k_0 \\
s_3 = k_3 \oplus \mathbf{1} & s_2 = k_2 \oplus \mathbf{1} & s_1 = k_1 \oplus \mathbf{1} & s_0 = k_0 \oplus \mathbf{1}
\end{array}
$$

The FSM is initialized with $R_1 = R_2 = R_3 = 0$. Then run the cipher 32 times with the FSM output F xored to the feedback of the LFSR and no keystream generated. After this, the cipher is switched into the keystream generation mode, but the first keystream word is discarded. Hence, there are 33 initialization rounds. The keystream word generated at clock t is $z^t = s_0^t \oplus F^t$. If we replace the two modulo additions in SNOW 3G by xors, we get SNOW 3G$^\oplus$.

3   Known IV Attack on SNOW 3G$^\oplus$ without FSM to LFSR Feedback

In this section, we consider a known IV attack on SNOW 3G$^\oplus$ without the FSM to LFSR feedback, in which the attacker has access to two keystreams corresponding to (K, IV_a) and (K, IV_b), where IV_a and IV_b are arbitrary known IVs. This attack works for any number of key/IV setup rounds.

Let $R_{i,a}^t$ and $R_{i,b}^t$ be the individual values in the FSM register R_i at clock t, then we have

$$
\Delta R_1^t = R_{1,a}^t \oplus R_{1,b}^t \qquad R_{2,a}^t = S_1(R_{1,a}^{t-1}) \qquad R_{2,b}^t = S_1(R_{1,b}^{t-1})
$$

$$
\Delta R_2^t = R_{2,a}^t \oplus R_{2,b}^t = S_1(R_{1,a}^{t-1}) \oplus S_1(R_{1,b}^{t-1}) \triangleq \overset{\text{out}}{\Delta} S_1(\Delta R_1^{t-1}) .
$$

During the keystream generation, we have the following equations for the differences at clock t

$$
\Delta z^t = \Delta s_{15}^t \oplus \Delta R_1^t \oplus \Delta R_2^t \oplus \Delta s_0^t \qquad \Delta R_2^t = \overset{\text{out}}{\Delta} S_1(\Delta R_1^{t-1})
$$

$$
\Delta R_1^t = \Delta R_2^{t-1} \oplus \Delta R_3^{t-1} \oplus \Delta s_5^{t-1} \qquad \Delta R_3^t = \overset{\text{out}}{\Delta} S_2(\Delta R_2^{t-1}) .
$$

The differences in the LFSR part propagate linearly and are completely predictable.

The main procedures of our attack are: assume that at time t we have $\Delta R_1^t = 0$. From the linear evolution of the difference in the LFSR and the keystream difference equations, we deduce potential differences in the other FSM registers at different times. Knowing the input-output difference for the S-boxes, deduce few possibilities for the actual values of the FSM registers. Combine the knowledge of the FSM state with that of the keystream to get linear equations on the LFSR state. Collect enough equations to get a solvable linear system which will recover the state of the LFSR. By the invertibility of the cipher, run it backwards to find the 128-bit secret key K.

Assume $\Delta R_1^t = 0$. If this is not true, we just take the next clock and so on. If we try this step 2^{32} times, then it will happen with a good probability. Denote the time that

$\Delta R_1 = 0$ by $t = 1$. Then $\Delta R_1^1 = 0$, $\Delta R_2^2 = 0$ and $\Delta R_3^3 = 0$. From the keystream equation at $t = 1$, we know ΔR_2^1; similarly we know ΔR_1^2, from which we can derive ΔR_3^1, as shown below. Hereafter, we denote the known difference value by Δk_i.

clock t	ΔR_1	ΔR_2	ΔR_3
1	0	Δk_1	Δk_3
2	Δk_2	0	
3			0

At $t = 3$, we have

$$\Delta R_3^2 \oplus \Delta R_2^3 = \Delta z^3 \oplus \Delta s_{15}^3 \oplus \Delta s_5^2 \oplus \Delta s_0^3 .$$

By the notations introduced before, we have

$$\overset{\text{out}}{\Delta} S_2(\Delta k_1) \oplus \overset{\text{out}}{\Delta} S_1(\Delta k_2) = \Delta k_4 . \tag{1}$$

Here we have $\frac{2^{28} \cdot 2^{28}}{2^{32}} = 2^{24}$ pairs satisfying (1). (In the two 8-bit S-boxes, there are at most 2^7 possible output differences for any fixed input difference.) To enumerate the possible pairs, we proceed as follows. First rewrite (1) as

$$\begin{pmatrix} \overset{\text{out}}{\Delta} S_R(\Delta k_2^0) \\ \overset{\text{out}}{\Delta} S_R(\Delta k_2^1) \\ \overset{\text{out}}{\Delta} S_R(\Delta k_2^2) \\ \overset{\text{out}}{\Delta} S_R(\Delta k_2^3) \end{pmatrix} = \begin{pmatrix} \overset{\text{out}}{\Delta} S_Q(\Delta k_1^0) \\ \overset{\text{out}}{\Delta} S_Q(\Delta k_1^1) \\ \overset{\text{out}}{\Delta} S_Q(\Delta k_1^2) \\ \overset{\text{out}}{\Delta} S_Q(\Delta k_1^3) \end{pmatrix} \oplus \begin{pmatrix} p_0^{\text{msb}} \\ p_1^{\text{msb}} \\ p_2^{\text{msb}} \\ p_3^{\text{msb}} \end{pmatrix} \oplus MC_1^{-1} \cdot \begin{pmatrix} \Delta k_4^0 \\ \Delta k_4^1 \\ \Delta k_4^2 \\ \Delta k_4^3 \end{pmatrix} ,$$

where p_i^{msb} ($i = 0, 1, 2, 3$) denotes a byte polynomial which contains only the most significant bits of all the four $\overset{\text{out}}{\Delta} S_Q$ values. For a detailed explanation, please see Appendix 5. Thus we can fulfill the enumeration byte by byte. For the first row, we need the value of $\overset{\text{out}}{\Delta} S_Q(\Delta k_1^0)$, which has 2^7 possibilities and three more bits for p_0^{msb}. Then we check whether the value computed at the right side of the equation is a correct value for $\overset{\text{out}}{\Delta} S_R(\Delta k_2^0)$. This would cost 2^{10} steps and we will obtain 2^9 solutions for this equation. For the next three equations, since we already know the leading bits, we only have 2^6 possibilities left in each byte equation, which yields the same time complexity and 2^5 solutions. To get the solution of the word equation, we have to combine the corresponding byte solutions and get $2^9 \cdot 2^5 \cdot 2^5 \cdot 2^5 = 2^{24}$ solutions, which needs about $2 \cdot 2^{24} = 2^{25}$ words of memory. Now, the states of the FSM are as follows.

clock t	ΔR_1	ΔR_2	ΔR_3		clock t	ΔR_1	ΔR_2	ΔR_3
1	0	Δk_1	Δk_3	next part $\rightarrow$ reduction	1	0	Δk_1	Δk_3
2	Δk_2	0	(2^{24})		2	Δk_2	0	(2^{20})
3	(2^{24})	(2^{24})	0		3	(2^{20})	(2^{20})	0
4					4	(2^{20})	(2^{20})	

Each possible value of ΔR_2^3 results in a possible value of ΔR_1^4. At $t = 4$, we have

$$\Delta R_2^3 \oplus \Delta R_2^4 = \Delta z^4 \oplus \Delta s_{15}^4 \oplus \Delta s_5^3 \oplus \Delta s_0^4 .$$

Replacing the difference ΔR_2^4 with the S-Box representation, we receive

$$\Delta R_2^3 \oplus \overset{\text{out}}{\Delta} S_1(\Delta R_1^3) = \Delta k_5 \ .$$

Let $\Delta R_1^3 = c^0 \| c^1 \| c^2 \| c^3$, $\Delta R_2^3 = a^0 \| a^1 \| a^2 \| a^3$. Expanding this equation to the byte form, we get

$$\begin{pmatrix} \overset{\text{out}}{\Delta} S_R(c^0) \\ \overset{\text{out}}{\Delta} S_R(c^1) \\ \overset{\text{out}}{\Delta} S_R(c^2) \\ \overset{\text{out}}{\Delta} S_R(c^3) \end{pmatrix} = MC_1^{-1} \cdot \begin{pmatrix} a^0 \\ a^1 \\ a^2 \\ a^3 \end{pmatrix} \oplus MC_1^{-1} \cdot \begin{pmatrix} \Delta k_5^0 \\ \Delta k_5^1 \\ \Delta k_5^2 \\ \Delta k_5^3 \end{pmatrix} \ .$$

We have to insert all the 2^{24} possible pairs of $(\Delta R_2^3, \Delta R_1^3)$ and verify the value $\overset{\text{out}}{\Delta} S_R$ for the single bytes. This results in a time complexity of 2^{24}. There are $\frac{2^{24} \cdot 2^{28}}{2^{32}} = 2^{20}$ entries satisfy this equation. This means we have 2^{20} sequences $(\Delta R_3^2, \Delta R_1^3, \Delta R_2^3, \Delta R_1^4, \Delta R_2^4)$ left. For each of them, we know the input-output difference of S_1 at clock 2 and 3. Thus, we can recover $(2 \cdot \frac{126}{127} + 4 \cdot \frac{1}{127})^4 = 16.51$ sorted pairs of values for S_1. This means that we have $\frac{16.51}{2} = 8.255$ possible values for ΔR_3^4. Looking at clock 5, we have $\Delta R_2^4 \oplus \Delta R_3^4 \oplus \overset{\text{out}}{\Delta} S_1(\Delta R_1^4) = \Delta k_6$. We can rewrite this equation into byte form and check the 2^{20} remaining sequences by the byte equations. There are $\frac{2^{20} \cdot 8.255 \cdot 2^{28}}{2^{32}} \approx 2^{19.05}$ possible sequences left and the complexity is about $2^{20} \cdot 8.255 = 2^{23.05}$. This identification of the individual values in the FSM for both keystreams has to be repeated for the next 9 clocks. Each step will have a lower time complexity than the one before and will reduce the possible number of differences. The time complexity for all 10 steps together is $\sum_{i=0}^{9} 2^{20} \cdot (\frac{2^{27}}{127^4})^i \cdot \frac{2^{31}}{127^4} = 2^{24.1}$ and the number of sequences left is $2^{20} \cdot (\frac{2^{27}}{127^4})^{10} = 2^{10.5}$. Then we insert the individual values of the FSM into the keystream generation equations and the FSM update equations to get a linear system of the LFSR initial states. This would need a time complexity of $2^{10.5} \cdot 2^{10} = 2^{20.5}$ steps. The overall time complexity is

$$2^{32} \cdot [2^{10} + 2^{24} + \sum_{i=0}^{9} (2^{20} \cdot (\frac{2^{27}}{127^4})^i \cdot \frac{2^{31}}{127^4})] = 2^{57.1} \ .$$

The memory requirement is 2^{25} words and the keystream is of length 2^{33} words.

4   Differential Chosen IV Attacks on Reduced-Round SNOW 3G$^\oplus$

Now we look at the full SNOW 3G$^\oplus$ (with the feedback). We consider a differential chosen IV attack scenario. Assume that we have two 128-bit IVs differing only in the most significant word IV_0, which gives the difference in s_{15} of the LFSR. As mentioned below in Section 4.2 and Section 4.3, we can restrict the difference to a single byte of IV_0 in order to reduce the complexity of our attacks. Denote this difference by Δd. Then until round 10, this difference will not affect the FSM. In round 11, the known Δd enters the FSM word R_1.

4.1 Reduced Initialization of 12 Rounds

Since all the differences in the FSM are 0, there are no differences fed back into the LFSR. Thus the differences in the LFSR are all known. Our knowledge of differences in the FSM is shown below. We try to compute the unknown values ("?"s) in this table.

round	clock s	$\Delta R1$	$\Delta R2$	$\Delta R3$
11	-1	Δd	0	0
12	0	Δd	?	0
	1	?	?	

From the keystream equation $\Delta z^0 = \Delta s_{15}^0 \oplus \Delta R_1^0 \oplus \Delta R_2^0 \oplus \Delta s_0^0$, where $\Delta R_1^0 = \Delta d$, we get ΔR_2^0, which gives us immediately ΔR_1^1 and also ΔR_2^1 from the next keystream equation. Therefore, we have only one known sequence ($\Delta R_1^{-1} = \Delta d$, $\Delta R_2^{-1} = \Delta R_3^{-1} = 0$, $\Delta R_1^0 = \Delta d$, $\Delta R_2^0, \Delta R_3^0 = 0$, $\Delta R_1^1, \Delta R_2^1$). Now we know the input and output difference of S_1: $\Delta d = \Delta R_1^{-1} \rightarrow S_1 \rightarrow \Delta R_2^0$. Thus, we switch from the differences of the FSM words to the individual values of them, similar to the procedures explained in Section 3. The time complexity is $10 \cdot \frac{2^{31}}{127^4} = 2^{6.4}$ steps. Afterwards we insert the individual values of the FSM into the keystream generation equations and the FSM update equations to get a linear system of the LFSR initial states with a complexity of 2^{10}. We use the keystream equation of clock 12 to check the candidates. The total time complexity is $2^{6.4} + 2^{10} = 2^{10.1}$ steps, the memory complexity is small and the known keystream is only 12 words for each IV.

4.2 Reduced Initialization of 13 Rounds

Here we extend the attack above by one more round. In the 13 round case, since all the differences in the FSM until now are either 0 or the known Δd, no unknown difference was fed back into the LFSR. Thus, the differences in the LFSR values are known. We compute "?"s in the following table as follows.

round	clock s	ΔR_1	ΔR_2	ΔR_3
11	-2	Δd	0	0
12	-1	Δd	?	0
13	0	?	?	

From Δz^0 and ΔR_1^0, we have

$$\Delta z^0 = \Delta s_{15}^0 \oplus \Delta R_2^{-1} \oplus \Delta s_5^{-1} \oplus \Delta R_2^0 \oplus \Delta s_0^0 \ ,$$

which is

$$\Delta R_2^{-1} \oplus \Delta R_2^0 = \Delta z^0 \oplus \Delta s_{15}^0 \oplus \Delta s_5^{-1} \oplus \Delta s_0^0 \ .$$

Then we replace the differences at the left side with their S-Boxes description, denote the known part at the right side with k_0 and get the equation

$$\overset{\text{out}}{\Delta} S_1(\Delta d) \oplus \overset{\text{out}}{\Delta} S_1(\Delta d) = \Delta k_0 \ . \tag{2}$$

Multiplying by MC_1^{-1}, we get the byte form equation

$$
\begin{pmatrix} \overset{\text{out}}{\Delta} S_R(\Delta d^0) \\ \overset{\text{out}}{\Delta} S_R(\Delta d^1) \\ \overset{\text{out}}{\Delta} S_R(\Delta d^2) \\ \overset{\text{out}}{\Delta} S_R(\Delta d^3) \end{pmatrix} \oplus \begin{pmatrix} \overset{\text{out}}{\Delta} S_R(\Delta d^0) \\ \overset{\text{out}}{\Delta} S_R(\Delta d^1) \\ \overset{\text{out}}{\Delta} S_R(\Delta d^2) \\ \overset{\text{out}}{\Delta} S_R(\Delta d^3) \end{pmatrix} = MC_1^{-1} \cdot \begin{pmatrix} \Delta k_0^0 \\ \Delta k_0^1 \\ \Delta k_0^2 \\ \Delta k_0^3 \end{pmatrix},
$$

We can check these four byte equations in $4 \cdot 2^7 = 2^9$ steps. The number of solutions will be $\frac{2^{28} \cdot 2^{28}}{2^{32}} = 2^{24}$ pairs of $(\Delta R_2^{-1}, \Delta R_2^0)$. We have 2^{24} sequences $(\Delta R_1^{-2} = \Delta d, \Delta R_2^{-2} = \Delta R_3^{-2} = 0, \Delta R_1^{-1} = \Delta d, \Delta R_2^{-1}, \Delta R_3^{-1} = 0, \Delta R_1^0, \Delta R_2^0)$. Again, we switch from the differences of the FSM words to the individual values of them by using the input and output difference of S_1: $\Delta d = \Delta R_1^{-2} \rightarrow S1 \rightarrow \Delta R_2^{-1}$. The time complexity of this step is $\sum_{i=0}^{9} 2^{24} \cdot (\frac{2^{27}}{127^4})^i \cdot \frac{2^{31}}{127^4} = 2^{28.09}$. In the end, we have $2^{24} \cdot (\frac{2^{27}}{127^4})^{10} = 2^{14.45}$ difference sequences left. The memory complexity is $2^{25} \cdot 10 \cdot 3 = 2^{29.91}$ words. We then insert the individual values of the FSM into the keystream generation equations and the FSM update equations to get a linear system of the LFSR initial states. This would need a time complexity of $\frac{2^{294}}{127^{40}} \cdot 2^{10} = 2^{24.45}$. The overall time complexity is

$$
2^9 + \sum_{i=0}^{9} \left(2^{24} \cdot (\frac{2^{27}}{127^4})^i \cdot \frac{2^{31}}{127^4} \right) + \frac{2^{294}}{127^{40}} \cdot 2^{10} = 2^{28.2}
$$

steps. The memory complexity is $2^{29.91}$ words and the keystream is of length 12 words for each IV.

If we restrict the known arbitrary difference Δd to a word with three bytes equal to zero and only one non zero byte, we can reduce our attack complexity considerably. We then have only one pair $(\Delta R_2^{-1}, \Delta R_2^0)$ of difference left, as in the attack on 12 rounds explained in Section 4.1. In this way, we will have the same time complexity $2^{10.1}$ and the memory requirement is small. The keystream will be of 12 words for each IV.

4.3   Reduced Initialization of 14 Rounds

Nearly all the differences in the LFSR are known, the only unknown difference is ΔR_2^{-2}, which was fed back into the LFSR, the remaining differences are either 0 or the known Δd. We guess the individual value $R_{1,a}^{-3}$ for the first pair (K, IV_a) with complexity of 2^{32}. From the value $R_{1,a}^{-3}$, we get with $\Delta R_1^{-3} = \Delta d$ the value $R1_b^{-3}$ for the second pair (K, IV_b). Furthermore we obtain $R_{2,a}^{-2}, R_{2,b}^{-2}, R_{3,a}^{-1}, R_{3,b}^{-1}$. We denote the known difference ΔR_2^{-2} with Δk_0, the linear dependent ΔR_1^{-1} with Δk_1 and ΔR_3^{-1} with Δk_2. This gives the following differences for the FSM.

round	clock s	ΔR_1	ΔR_2	ΔR_3
11	-3	Δd	0	0
12	-2	Δd	Δk_0	0
13	-1	Δk_1	?	Δk_2
14	0	?	?	

From

$$\Delta z^0 = \Delta s_{15}^0 \oplus \Delta R_1^0 \oplus \Delta R_2^0 \oplus \Delta s_0^0 \ ,$$

we insert the update equations for ΔR_1^0 and ΔR_2^0 and receive

$$\Delta z^0 = \Delta s_{15}^0 \oplus \overset{out}{\Delta} S_1(\Delta d) \oplus \Delta k_2 \oplus \Delta s_5^{-1} \oplus \overset{out}{\Delta} S_1(\Delta k_1) \oplus \Delta s_0^0 \ ,$$

which gives

$$\overset{out}{\Delta} S_1(\Delta d) \oplus \overset{out}{\Delta} S_1(\Delta k_1) = \Delta z^0 \oplus \Delta s_{15}^0 \oplus \Delta k_2 \oplus \Delta s_5^{-1} \oplus \Delta s_0^0 \ .$$

We denote the known right part by Δk_3, multiply the equation with MC_1^{-1} and rewrite it in byte notation as

$$\begin{pmatrix} \overset{out}{\Delta} S_R(\Delta d^0) \\ \overset{out}{\Delta} S_R(\Delta d^1) \\ \overset{out}{\Delta} S_R(\Delta d^2) \\ \overset{out}{\Delta} S_R(\Delta d^3) \end{pmatrix} \oplus \begin{pmatrix} \overset{out}{\Delta} S_R(\Delta k_1^0) \\ \overset{out}{\Delta} S_R(\Delta k_1^1) \\ \overset{out}{\Delta} S_R(\Delta k_1^2) \\ \overset{out}{\Delta} S_R(\Delta k_1^3) \end{pmatrix} = MC_1^{-1} \cdot \begin{pmatrix} \Delta k_3^0 \\ \Delta k_3^1 \\ \Delta k_3^2 \\ \Delta k_3^3 \end{pmatrix} .$$

Then we check this equation line by line for each byte in $4 \times 2^7 = 2^9$ steps. The number of solutions will be $\frac{2^{28} \cdot 2^{28}}{2^{32}} = 2^{24}$ pairs of $(\Delta R_2^{-1}, \Delta R_2^0)$. Again, we switch from the differences of the FSM words to the individual values of them by using the input and output difference of S_1: $\Delta R_1^{-2} \rightarrow S_1 \rightarrow \Delta R_2^{-1}$. Since we start with 2^{24} sequences, we have completely the same procedure as in the attack on 13 rounds of initialization and thus the same complexities. The overall time complexity is the same as that in 13 rounds of initialization for each guess of $R1_1^{-3}$, which gives

$$2^{32} \cdot \left[2^9 + \sum_{i=0}^{9} \left(2^{24} \cdot (\frac{2^{27}}{127^4})^i \cdot \frac{2^{31}}{127^4} \right) + \frac{2^{294}}{127^{40}} \cdot 2^{10} \right] = 2^{60.2} \ .$$

The memory requirement is $2^{29.91}$ words and the keystream is of length 12 words for each IV.

If we restrict the known difference Δd to only one byte in IV_0, we can reduce our attack complexity to $2^{42.7}$ with similar procedures as above. The corresponding memory complexity is 2^9 words and the keystream is of 12 words for each IV.

4.4 Reduced Initialization of 15 Rounds and 16 Rounds

Nearly all the differences in the LFSR are known, only two unknown differences ΔR_2^{-3} and ΔR_2^{-2} were fed back into the LFSR, the remaining differences are either 0 or the known Δd. We guess the individual values of $R_{1,a}^{-4}$ and $R_{1,a}^{-3}$ for the first pair (K, IV_a) with complexity of 2^{64}. From the value $R_{1,a}^{-4}$ and $\Delta R_1^{-4} = \Delta d$, we get the values of $R_{1,b}^{-4}, R_{2,a}^{-3}, R_{2,b}^{-3}, R_{3,a}^{-2}, R_{3,b}^{-2}$. Denote the known difference ΔR_2^{-3} by Δk_0, ΔR_1^{-2} by Δk_1 and ΔR_3^{-2} by Δk_2. From $R_{1,a}^{-3}$ and $\Delta R_1^{-3} = \Delta d$, we get the values of $R_{1,b}^{-3}, R_{2,a}^{-2}, R_{2,b}^{-2}, R_{3,a}^{-1}, R_{3,b}^{-1}$. Again, we denote the now known difference ΔR_2^{-2} by

Δk_3, ΔR_1^{-1} by Δk_4 and ΔR_3^{-1} by Δk_5. This gives the following differences for the FSM.

round	clock s	$\Delta R1$	$\Delta R2$	$\Delta R3$
11	-4	Δd	0	0
12	-3	Δd	Δk_0	0
13	-2	Δk_1	Δk_3	Δk_2
14	-1	Δk_4	?	Δk_5
15	0	?	?	

We have now the same starting point as that of the attack on 14 initialization rounds. We proceed in the way as explained there. Since we guessed one more word in the beginning of the attack, the time complexity becomes

$$2^{32} \cdot 2^{60.2} = 2^{92.2} \ .$$

The memory complexity remains $2^{29.91}$ words and the keystream is of length 12 words for each IV.

In the 16 rounds case, we guess one more word and then proceed as that of the attack on 15 rounds. The time complexity is

$$2^{32} \cdot 2^{92.2} = 2^{124.2}$$

and the memory complexity remains $2^{29.91}$ words and the keystream is of length 12 words for each IV.

The summary of our results is given in Table 1.

Table 1. The summary of our results on SNOW 3G$^{\oplus}$

attack	keystream	time	memory
SNOW 3G$^{\oplus}$ without feedback	2^{33}	$2^{57.1}$	2^{25}
SNOW 3G$^{\oplus}$ with feedback			
12 rounds	24	$2^{10.1}$	small
13 rounds with 1 byte difference Δd	24	$2^{10.1}$	small
14 rounds with 1 byte difference Δd	24	$2^{42.7}$	2^9
15 rounds	24	$2^{92.2}$	$2^{29.91}$
16 rounds	24	$2^{124.2}$	$2^{29.91}$

5 Conclusions

In this paper, we have shown *known* IV and *chosen* IV resynchronization attacks on SNOW 3G$^{\oplus}$. We can attack arbitrary many key/IV setup rounds of SNOW 3G$^{\oplus}$ if there is no feedback from FSM to LFSR. With such feedback, we show key recovery attacks on up to 16 rounds of initialization and use only a few keystream words. Our results indicate that about half of the initialization rounds of SNOW 3G$^{\oplus}$ might succumb to chosen IV resynchronization attacks. The remaining security margin however is quite significant and thus these attacks pose no threat to the security of SNOW 3G itself.

References

1. Billet, O., Gilbert, H.: Resistance of SNOW 2.0 Against Algebraic Attacks. In: Menezes, A.J. (ed.) CT-RSA 2005. LNCS, vol. 3376, pp. 19–28. Springer, Heidelberg (2005)
2. Ekdahl, P., Johansson, T.: A New Version of the Stream Cipher SNOW. In: Nyberg, K., Heys, H. (eds.) SAC 2002. LNCS, vol. 2595, pp. 47–61. Springer, Heidelberg (2003)
3. ETSI/SAGE. Specification of the 3GPP Confidentiality and Integrity Algorithms UEA2 & UIA2. Document 2: SNOW 3G Specification, version 1.1 (September 2006), http://www.3gpp.org/ftp/
4. ETSI/SAGE. Specification of the 3GPP Confidentiality and Integrity Algorithms UEA2 & UIA2. Document 5: Design and Evaluation Report, version 1.1 (September 2006), http://www.3gpp.org/ftp/
5. Nyberg, K., Wallén, J.: Improved Linear Distinguishers for SNOW 2.0. In: Robshaw, M.J.B. (ed.) FSE 2006. LNCS, vol. 4047, pp. 144–162. Springer, Heidelberg (2006)
6. Watanabe, D., Biryukov, A., De Cannière, C.: A Distinguishing Attack of SNOW 2.0 with Linear Masking Method. In: Matsui, M., Zuccherato, R. (eds.) SAC 2003. LNCS, vol. 3006, pp. 222–233. Springer, Heidelberg (2004)

Appendix

We want to simplify the equation

$$\overset{\text{out}}{\Delta} S_2(\Delta k_1) \oplus \overset{\text{out}}{\Delta} S_1(\Delta k_2) = \Delta k_4 \ .$$

The main difficulty is that S_1 and S_2 use the same Mix-Column matrix but over two different fields $GF(2^8)$. At first we rewrite this equation in the byte notation as

$$
MC_2 \cdot \begin{pmatrix} \overset{\text{out}}{\Delta} S_Q(\Delta k_1^0) \\ \overset{\text{out}}{\Delta} S_Q(\Delta k_1^1) \\ \overset{\text{out}}{\Delta} S_Q(\Delta k_1^2) \\ \overset{\text{out}}{\Delta} S_Q(\Delta k_1^3) \end{pmatrix} \oplus MC_1 \cdot \begin{pmatrix} \overset{\text{out}}{\Delta} S_R(\Delta k_2^0) \\ \overset{\text{out}}{\Delta} S_R(\Delta k_2^1) \\ \overset{\text{out}}{\Delta} S_R(\Delta k_2^2) \\ \overset{\text{out}}{\Delta} S_R(\Delta k_2^3) \end{pmatrix} = \begin{pmatrix} \Delta k_4^0 \\ \Delta k_4^1 \\ \Delta k_4^2 \\ \Delta k_4^3 \end{pmatrix} .
$$

Then multiplying this equation with the inverse matrix MC_1^{-1}, we get

$$
MC_1^{-1} \cdot \left(MC_2 \cdot \begin{pmatrix} \overset{\text{out}}{\Delta} S_Q(\Delta k_1^0) \\ \overset{\text{out}}{\Delta} S_Q(\Delta k_1^1) \\ \overset{\text{out}}{\Delta} S_Q(\Delta k_1^2) \\ \overset{\text{out}}{\Delta} S_Q(\Delta k_1^3) \end{pmatrix} \right) \oplus \begin{pmatrix} \overset{\text{out}}{\Delta} S_R(\Delta k_2^0) \\ \overset{\text{out}}{\Delta} S_R(\Delta k_2^1) \\ \overset{\text{out}}{\Delta} S_R(\Delta k_2^2) \\ \overset{\text{out}}{\Delta} S_R(\Delta k_2^3) \end{pmatrix} = MC_1^{-1} \cdot \begin{pmatrix} \Delta k_4^0 \\ \Delta k_4^1 \\ \Delta k_4^2 \\ \Delta k_4^3 \end{pmatrix} .
$$

If we expand the matrix multiplications and have a look at the byte vectors, it shows that the first entry of the first vector contains the byte $\overset{\text{out}}{\Delta} S_Q(\Delta k_1^0)$ and a byte polynomial containing only the most significant bits of all four $\overset{\text{out}}{\Delta} S_Q$ values. We denote this polynomial with p_0^{msb}. The other three rows have similar structures, but with different polynomials p_i^{msb} ($i = 1, 2, 3$). Therefore we can rewrite the equation to

$$
\begin{pmatrix} \overset{\text{out}}{\Delta} S_R(\Delta k_2^0) \\ \overset{\text{out}}{\Delta} S_R(\Delta k_2^1) \\ \overset{\text{out}}{\Delta} S_R(\Delta k_2^2) \\ \overset{\text{out}}{\Delta} S_R(\Delta k_2^3) \end{pmatrix} = \begin{pmatrix} \overset{\text{out}}{\Delta} S_Q(\Delta k_1^0) \\ \overset{\text{out}}{\Delta} S_Q(\Delta k_1^1) \\ \overset{\text{out}}{\Delta} S_Q(\Delta k_1^2) \\ \overset{\text{out}}{\Delta} S_Q(\Delta k_1^3) \end{pmatrix} \oplus \begin{pmatrix} p_0^{\text{msb}} \\ p_1^{\text{msb}} \\ p_2^{\text{msb}} \\ p_3^{\text{msb}} \end{pmatrix} \oplus MC_1^{-1} \cdot \begin{pmatrix} \Delta k_4^0 \\ \Delta k_4^1 \\ \Delta k_4^2 \\ \Delta k_4^3 \end{pmatrix} .
$$

We denote by m_0 the most significant bit of the value $\overset{\text{out}}{\Delta} S_Q(\Delta k_1^0)$ and with m_1 the most significant bit of the value $\overset{\text{out}}{\Delta} S_Q(\Delta k_1^1)$ as well as m_2 for $\overset{\text{out}}{\Delta} S_Q(\Delta k_1^2)$ and m_3 for $\overset{\text{out}}{\Delta} S_Q(\Delta k_1^3)$. Then the polynomials p_i^{msb} $i = 0, \ldots, 3$ are

$$
\begin{aligned}
p_0^{msb} = &\,(m_1 \oplus m_3)x^7 + (m_0 \oplus m_1)x^6 + (m_2 \oplus m_3)x^5 + (m_1 \oplus m_2)x^4 \\
&+ (m_0 \oplus m_2)x^2 + (m_1 \oplus m_2)x + (m_0 \oplus m_1 \oplus m_2 \oplus m_3)
\end{aligned}
$$

$$
\begin{aligned}
p_1^{msb} = &\,(m_0 \oplus m_2)x^7 + (m_1 \oplus m_2)x^6 + (m_0 \oplus m_3)x^5 + (m_2 \oplus m_3)x^4 \\
&+ (m_1 \oplus m_3)x^2 + (m_2 \oplus m_3)x + (m_0 \oplus m_1 \oplus m_2 \oplus m_3)
\end{aligned}
$$

$$
\begin{aligned}
p_2^{msb} = &\,(m_1 \oplus m_3)x^7 + (m_2 \oplus m_3)x^6 + (m_0 \oplus m_1)x^5 + (m_0 \oplus m_3)x^4 \\
&+ (m_0 \oplus m_2)x^2 + (m_0 \oplus m_3)x + (m_0 \oplus m_1 \oplus m_2 \oplus m_3)
\end{aligned}
$$

$$
\begin{aligned}
p_3^{msb} = &\,(m_0 \oplus m_2)x^7 + (m_0 \oplus m_3)x^6 + (m_1 \oplus m_2)x^5 + (m_0 \oplus m_1)x^4 \\
&+ (m_1 \oplus m_3)x^2 + (m_0 \oplus m_1)x + (m_0 \oplus m_1 \oplus m_2 \oplus m_3)
\end{aligned}
$$

Modelling Uncertain and Time-Dependent Security Labels in MLS Systems[*]

John A. Clark[1], Juan E. Tapiador[1], John McDermid[1], Pau-Chen Cheng[2],
Dakshi Agrawal[2], Natalie Ivanic[3], and Dave Slogget[4]

[1] Deparment of Computer Science, University of York, York, U.K.
{jac,jet,jam}@cs.york.ac.uk
[2] IBM Thomas J. Watson Research Center, New York, NY, U.S.A.
{pau,agrawal}@us.ibm.com
[3] US Army Research Laboratory, Maryland, MD, U.S.A.
nivanic@arl.army.mil
[4] Logica CMG, London, U.K.
dave.sloggett@logicacmg.com

Abstract. Traditional multi-level security (MLS) systems associate security clearances with subjects, security classifications with objects, and provide a clear decision mechanism as to whether an access request should be granted or not. Many organisations, especially those in the national security and intelligence arena, are increasingly viewing the inflexibility of such models as a major inhibitor for missions where there is a need to rapidly process, share and disseminate large quantities of sensitive information. One reason for such inflexibility is the fact that subject and object labels are fixed assessments of sensitivity, whereas in practice there will inevitably be some uncertainty about the potential damage caused if a document falls into the wrong hands. Furthermore, the operational reality of many modern systems dictates a temporal element to the actual sensitivity of an object. In this paper we propose to model both security labels and clearances as time-varying probability distributions. We provide practical templates to model both uncertainty and temporally characterised dependencies, and show how these features can be naturally integrated into an access control framework based on quantified risk.

Keywords: Information sharing, Multi-level security, Risk based access control.

1 Introduction

There is a recent concern about the inability of many organisations, particularly those in the national security and intelligence arena, to rapidly process, share and disseminate

---

[*] This research was sponsored by the U.S. Army Research Laboratory and the U.K. Ministry of Defence and was accomplished under Agreement Number W911NF-06-3-0001. The views and conclusions contained in this document are those of the authors and should not be interpreted as representing the official policies, either expressed or implied, of the U.S. Army Research Laboratory, the U.S. Government, the U.K. Ministry of Defence or the U.K. Government. The U.S. and U.K. Governments are authorized to reproduce and distribute reprints for Government purposes notwithstanding any copyright notation hereon.

M.S. Obaidat, G.A. Tsihrintzis, and J. Filipe (Eds.): ICETE 2010, CCIS 222, pp. 158–171, 2012.
© Springer-Verlag Berlin Heidelberg 2012

large quantities of sensitive information. The JASON Report [10] has reinforced the view that the inflexibility of current access control models is a major inhibitor when dealing with dynamic and unpredictable environments. As an example, in the "Navy Maritime Domain Awareness Concept" paper disseminated by the US Navy in 2007 [11] it is recognised that non-traditional operations (e.g. when facing irregular opponents who employ asymmetric methods) generally require access to information historically unavailable to decision-makers, as well as sharing intelligence at all classification levels with other partners. Given that tasks such as sharing and disseminating information play a fundamental role in supporting informed decision making, such organisations are increasingly resorting to various ad hoc means to surpass these "cumbersome" authorisation policies (e.g., granting "temporary" authorisations for high-sensitive objects; or, as mentioned in [10], to follow the line of the old saying "it is better to ask for forgiveness rather than for permission").

An earlier paper [3] has pointed out one major danger of such practices: they result in an unaccountable risk of information leakage. Access control is essentially about balancing risk and benefit, and a static specification of such tradeoffs is not optimal in a dynamic environment. The work in [3] addresses this issue by making access control much more flexible. The model, known as Fuzzy MLS, is based on a *quantification* of the risk associated with every access request. Information flows are determined by particular policies, which replace the classical binary "allow/deny" decisions by a more flexible mechanism based on these risk estimators and measures of risk tolerance. Interested readers can find further details on Fuzzy MLS in [3] and the extended version [4].

In this paper we address two additional questions related to risk-based access control models: uncertainty and time variation of the security labels. We motivate our approach below.

1.1 Time and Sensitivity

The traditional model of multi-level security (MLS) associates security clearances with subjects, security classifications with objects, and provides a clear decision mechanism as to whether an access request should be granted or not. Thus for example, the "no read-up rule" of Bell and La Padula (BLP) model dictates that a read request should be granted only if the subject clearance dominates the object classification. The intuition behind this (and behind the corresponding "no-write down" rule) is sound. However, such rules encode for a pre-determined calculation of risks and benefits, and in many modern networking situations will preclude effective operations that can be justified on a risk basis when the specifics of the context are taken into account. Some situations demand that higher risks be taken for the sake of operational benefit. In a recent policy statement, US Director of National Intelligence Mike McConnell on 15 September 2008 said that the principal goal for risk management of any intelligence agency such as the CIA or the NSA should be to protect the agency's ability to perform its mission, *not just to protect its information assets*. One practice that certainly impedes the ability of an organisation to dispatch its responsibilities is inappropriate classification of data. The perils of underclassification are obvious; overclassification is a readily explicable outcome. But overclassification does not actually solve the problem it intends to; rather it leads to a variety of 'workarounds' and informal practices that simply take risk-based decision making outside procedural control [10], effectively sweeping the issue under the carpet. Assessment of risk is an *input* into the decision making process, and it should not define the outcome under all circumstances. Closer examination of modern applications reveals further assumptions that underpin traditional MLS based access control. We shall address these in turn.

In implementations of traditional MLS models the default assumption is that the sensitivity of an object does not change over time. This principle is generally known as *tranquility* and was introduced in the BLP model to formally ensure that certain security properties hold over time[1]. For many application scenarios this clearly does not hold. In a military scenario the identified terrorist target of an air-strike is clearly vastly more sensitive an hour before the strike than it is one hour after the strike (when the fact it has been bombed will generally be apparent to all). In contrast, the name of any pilot involved in the strike may remain sensitive for a considerable period of time. Similarly, in a commercial environment, treasury decisions on setting interest rates must be released in a controlled fashion at pre-specified times to avoid unfair market advantages. In a highly mobile tactical situation a soldier's current location may be highly sensitive, but his location yesterday will usually be less sensitive. Similar arguments hold for subject clearances. Thus, for example, a subject entering enemy territory may have his/her clearance temporarily downgraded until coming back to a safer location.

Modern collaborative operations will generate a significant amount of classified data and there would appear to be a need to prevent a general drift towards significant overclassification. More sophisticated practices will need to be adopted to ensure appropriate information usage in current times. Overclassification will make appropriate information sharing harder in almost any plausible access control scheme. Innovative risk benefit tradeoff handling approaches have been proposed to handle the inflexibility of traditional MLS, such as budget-based schemes (e.g. as suggested by [10]). The price a requester pays for an access will increase with the estimate of the consequent risk, which will be inflated if the sensitivity label is too conservative. Thus, to give such innovative schemes the best chances of allowing rational risk-based decision making we must ensure that the underlying labelling accurately reflects the current sensitivity.

We clearly need also to take the time-variant nature of sensitivity into account. Traditionally this would be achieved by trusted subjects downgrading information at an appropriate time. This is a plausible approach for small numbers of documents where manual consideration can be given. However, the emergence of data-rich MANET environments forces us to reconsider this approach and ask: can we usefully model the time-varying nature of sensitivity in a principled yet practical way? In this paper we suggest some means by which this can be achieved.

1.2 Uncertain Security Levels

The traditional MLS model simply assumes that objects can be classified with an appropriate label reflecting the damage that may result from it falling into the wrong hands.

---

[1] To be precise, the tranquility principle states that neither a subject clearance nor an object label must change while they are being referenced. *Strong tranquility* interprets this as that security levels does not change at all during normal operation, whilst *weak tranquility* allows changes whenever the rules of a given security policy are not violated [1].

There is general acceptance that such assignments are best guesses, and typically reflect the *order of magnitude* of the damage that might result. This is indeed a valuable construct, but in practice it will be very difficult to foresee all the implications of informational release. In particular, the value of a piece of information to an adversary may depend on what other information he has already. But in general we do not know what the enemy knows; this alone should cause us to pause and appreciate the inherent uncertainty in assigned labels. The same is applicable to the reliability of individuals (subjects). In many situations it may be impossible to assess with sufficient precision the degree of trustworthiness of a subject. Consider for example a scenario where a military operation needs the involvement of police officers and some civilians. People in these two groups ought to be provided with security clearances in order for them to have access to data. But the usual procedures employed for granting clearances in the military context (i.e., investigation of the subject's background, etc.) might simply not be affordable here.

In summary, the traditional MLS model is too strict to consider any form of uncertainty, either on the security labels or on the subjects' clearances. As pointed out in [10], this limitation is particularly troublesome in multilateral and coalitional operations, where we are often required to deal with new partners in an agile, yet controlled, way. In this paper we suggest that, in principle, both security labels and users' clearances should be modelled as a probability distribution, and provide practical and plausible choices for such distributions.

1.3   Overview

In Sections 2 and 3 we provide practical templates to model time variation and uncertainty in security labels. The proposed scheme is based on the use of Beta distributions, which provides us with a suitable means to model, through parameterisation, a broad range of specifications. In Section 4 we discuss how these features can be integrated into the Fuzzy MLS access control scheme. We stress, however, that this is merely a convenient example and that the approach could be applied to other risk- or trust-based access control schemes. In Section 5 we show how the notions introduced before can be also extended to contextual information (e.g., location) considered in access-control decisions. In Section 6 we discuss how our approach relates to similar works. Finally, Section 7 concludes the paper by summarising our major contributions and pointing out some avenues for future research.

2   Modelling Uncertainty

We choose to model uncertainty in sensitivity labelling via a continuous stochastic distribution. This does not mean that sensitivities are communicated to the end users in continuous form, rather that our decision-making infrastructure uses such distributions. Sensitivity label assignment requires judgement. Some judgements will be more uncertain than others and our modelling approach must cater for such sophistications. We recall that judgements will be approximate in any case and so approximate but practical models will suffice.

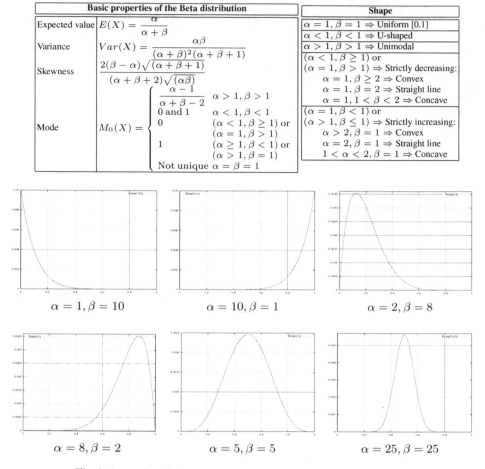

Basic properties of the Beta distribution		Shape

Expected value $E(X) = \dfrac{\alpha}{\alpha + \beta}$

Variance $Var(X) = \dfrac{\alpha\beta}{(\alpha + \beta)^2(\alpha + \beta + 1)}$

Skewness $\dfrac{2(\beta - \alpha)\sqrt{(\alpha + \beta + 1)}}{(\alpha + \beta + 2)\sqrt{(\alpha\beta)}}$

Mode $M_0(X) = \begin{cases} \dfrac{\alpha - 1}{\alpha + \beta - 2} & \alpha > 1, \beta > 1 \\ 0 \text{ and } 1 & \alpha < 1, \beta < 1 \\ 0 & (\alpha < 1, \beta \geq 1) \text{ or} \\ & (\alpha = 1, \beta > 1) \\ 1 & (\alpha \geq 1, \beta < 1) \text{ or} \\ & (\alpha > 1, \beta = 1) \\ \text{Not unique} & \alpha = \beta = 1 \end{cases}$

Shape:
$\alpha = 1, \beta = 1 \Rightarrow$ Uniform [0,1]
$\alpha < 1, \beta < 1 \Rightarrow$ U-shaped
$\alpha > 1, \beta > 1 \Rightarrow$ Unimodal
$(\alpha < 1, \beta \geq 1)$ or
$(\alpha = 1, \beta > 1) \Rightarrow$ Strictly decreasing:
    $\alpha = 1, \beta \geq 2 \Rightarrow$ Convex
    $\alpha = 1, \beta = 2 \Rightarrow$ Straight line
    $\alpha = 1, 1 < \beta < 2 \Rightarrow$ Concave
$(\alpha = 1, \beta < 1)$ or
$(\alpha > 1, \beta \leq 1) \Rightarrow$ Strictly increasing:
    $\alpha > 2, \beta = 1 \Rightarrow$ Convex
    $\alpha = 2, \beta = 1 \Rightarrow$ Straight line
    $1 < \alpha < 2, \beta = 1 \Rightarrow$ Concave

$\alpha = 1, \beta = 10$ $\alpha = 10, \beta = 1$ $\alpha = 2, \beta = 8$

$\alpha = 8, \beta = 2$ $\alpha = 5, \beta = 5$ $\alpha = 25, \beta = 25$

Fig. 1. Properties of the Beta distribution and some illustrative shapes

Without loss of generality, we shall model sensitivity on a continuous interval $[0, S]$, $S > 0$. We make no committment to any interpretation, except that higher values correspond to higher sensitivity and vice versa. One could easily map traditional sensitivity labels onto this scale, e.g. 0 for PUBLIC, 1 for UNCLASSIFIED, 2 for RESTRICTED, 3 for CONFIDENTIAL, 4 for SECRET, 5 for TOP SECRET, etc. We would wish to allow for symmetric and skewed (both left and right) distributions, and allow different variances to be modelled. The Beta distribution provides a suitable model for our purposes. Beta distributions are defined over the interval [0,1]. For $\alpha, \beta > 0$, the Beta probability density function (pdf) is defined by

$$f(x; \alpha, \beta) = \frac{x^{\alpha-1}(1 - x)^{\beta-1}}{B(\alpha, \beta)} \tag{1}$$

where $B(\alpha, \beta)$ is the beta function

$$B(x, y) = \int_0^1 t^{x-1}(1-t)^{y-1}dt \tag{2}$$

Some useful properties of the Beta distribution along with relevant shapes are sum-marised in Figure 1.

We have now defined the basic Beta distributional family over the interval $[0, 1]$. We extend this to the interval of interest by specifying an offset $\gamma \geq 0$ and an interval length $\lambda > 0$. Within the interval of length λ the distribution will generally be non-zero. The distribution within this interval is a stretched and normalised Beta distribution defined over $[0,1]$. Outside this interval the pdf is zero. This allows us to make statements like "the classification must be at least RESTRICTED but definitely is not TOP SECRET". This does not, of course, preclude working over the full interval range, since γ can be set to zero and λ can be equal to the full sensitivity range. The pdf can be now be defined as follows

$$g(x; \alpha, \beta, \gamma, \lambda) = \begin{cases} f(\frac{x-\gamma}{\lambda}; \alpha, \beta) \ \forall x \in [\gamma, \gamma + \lambda] \\ 0 \qquad\qquad\qquad \forall x \notin [\gamma, \gamma + \lambda] \end{cases} \tag{3}$$

Parameters α, β, γ, and λ can be chosen to provide a suitable pdf. There is some flex-ibility as to how such choices are made. In general γ simply shifts measures such as mean, mode, and median to the right. Parameter λ stretches and serves also to change the variance (multiplication of any random variable by a constant λ causes the variance to decrease by a factor of λ^2). The Beta distribution also allows left and right skewness to be modelled.

2.1 Mapping into Suitable Beta Distributions

The use of Beta distributions is an implementation convenience and is not intended for immediate presentation to the end users. (The average user will not take too well to being asked for parameters to a Beta distribution!) However, we can expect the user to answer plausibly question such as:

- What seems the most appropriate classification of this information (P, U, R, C, S, TS)?
- How confident are you that this classification is correct? Pretty confident or not so confident?
- Is it more likely to be classified too high than too low?
- Is there a time after which this information would cease to be classified as it is? If so, what might be the next classification?

From such questions we can provide a technical mapping to our parametric models.

An alternative to estimate the Beta parameters consists of relying on the opinions provided by a number of individuals[2]. If we assume we can collect a number of samples $x_1, \ldots, x_N$ ($N \geq 2$) regarding the sensitivity of an object, we proceed as follows. We

---

[2] It is not the purpose of this work to provide criteria regarding how to choose such individuals. We simply assume they are personnel with appropriate qualifications to carry out this task.

first compute the sample mean $\bar{x}$ and variance $\bar{v}$ By using the method of moments, parameters α and β can be then estimated as

$$\alpha = \bar{x}\left(\frac{\bar{x}(1 - \bar{x})}{\bar{v}} - 1\right) \tag{4}$$

$$\beta = (1 - \bar{x})\left(\frac{\bar{x}(1 - \bar{x})}{\bar{v}} - 1\right) \tag{5}$$

These estimators can be directly used to define the target distribution. If a more precise estimation is required, we can proceed iteratively as follows. Once α and β are obtained, the estimated distribution is used to generate a sufficiently large number of random samples. These are then presented to the end users, who are asked to remove values considered as definitely wrong. The resulting, "filtered" dataset is used again to produce new estimators for α and β, and the procedure is repeated until convergence is reached.

3   Modelling Time Variation

Above we indicated that a constant label will not reflect the true sensitivity of many aspects of data in a dynamic network environment. The true sensivity of data will exhibit some trajectory. Sensitivity may go down but, in principle, also up. Furthermore, the particular type of trajectory followed will vary with context. But if we are to handle time-variant sensitivity, we must be able to model it in some way that the user accepts as plausibly reflecting operational reality. In this section we provide a variety of simple templates for temporal dependencies of sensitivity whose rationale can be effectively communicated to end-users.

Several templates come to mind when considering temporal dependencies:

1. **Fixed:**
$$class(o, t) = K \; \forall t \geq 0$$

   with $K > 0$ constant. The classification remains constant over time.

2. **Step function:**
$$class(o, t) = K_i \; \forall t \in [t_i, t_{i+1})$$

   with $0 = t_0 < t_1 < \cdots < t_{n-1} < t_n = \infty$ and $K_i > 0$ constants. The classification changes according to some step function. This includes the case where a previously classified object becomes public knowledge after some specified period of time.

3. **Linear decay:**
$$class(o, t) = \max\{0, K \cdot t + K_0\}$$

   with $K < 0$ and $K_0 > 0$ (again K and K_0 constants). This is the simplest case of progressive loss of sensitivity over time.

4. **Exponential decay:**
$$class(o, t) = K \cdot e^{-\alpha t} \; \forall t \geq 0$$

   with $K > 0$ and $\alpha > 0$. This is straightforward case of continuous loss of sensitivity over time.

The above are not intended to be exhaustive. Further fundamental templates can be created and combined as desired. For example, sensitivity might be constant for a while and then decay. Sensitivity may also increase over time: the step function can model increasing sensitivity and further fundamental templates can be created to model it continuously.

We now assume that the sensitivity whose temporal trajectory we have just modelled represents some measured and communicable parameter of a distribution. Next we elaborate on how temporal requirements can be integrated with uncertainty modelling.

3.1 Putting the Two Together

We have now defined simple but plausible templates for the temporal evolution of particular sensitivity descriptors and have indicated how at any particular point in time uncertainty in the sensitivity can be modelled using a stretched and offset Beta distribution. We need to put the two together, and this can be achieved in several ways.

In the most general case, the temporal evolution can be specified by a list of time instants and Beta parameters of the form

$$[t_i, (\alpha_i, \beta_i, \gamma_i, \lambda_i)] \tag{6}$$

for $i = 0, 1, \ldots$. The semantics are clear: sensitivity in the interval $[t_i, t_{i+1}]$ is given by a Beta $g(x; \alpha_i, \beta_i, \gamma_i, \lambda_i)$ as defined in expression (3). This allows us to capture in a simple manner any desired variation in time and uncertainty – see, for example, Figure 2(a).

A more compact form can be provided in some cases. The sensitivity distribution over time can be also defined by a Beta of the form

$$g(x; \alpha(t), \beta(t), \gamma(t), \lambda(t)) \tag{7}$$

This allows us to simultaneously model changes in uncertainty and sensitivity. For example, in Figure 2(a) a Beta with parameters $\alpha = \beta = 3$ is initally shifted 5 positions to the right to model a classification "between 5 (SECRET) and 6 (TOP SECRET), with mean 5.5 and a symmetric shape". The template given by functions $\gamma(t)$, $\alpha(t)$ and $\beta(t)$ allows to:

1. reduce exponentially the sensitivity level of the object: the more time elapsed, the less significant the changes; and
2. reduce progressively the amount of uncertainty and approach a delta function.

Figures 2(b) provide another example where the skewness of the distribution is taken into account. This might be useful, for example, to coach requirements of the form "sensitivity should evolve conservatively, i.e. not allowing too much uncertainty on low security levels".

The above merely constitute some illustrative examples. The scheme is sufficiently general as to accommodate many other temporal templates.

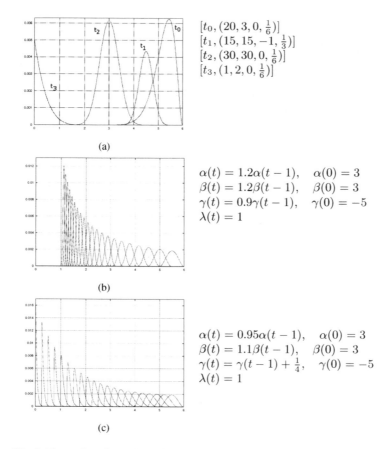

$[t_0, (20, 3, 0, \frac{1}{6})]$
$[t_1, (15, 15, -1, \frac{1}{3})]$
$[t_2, (30, 30, 0, \frac{1}{6})]$
$[t_3, (1, 2, 0, \frac{1}{6})]$

(a)

$\alpha(t) = 1.2\alpha(t-1), \quad \alpha(0) = 3$
$\beta(t) = 1.2\beta(t-1), \quad \beta(0) = 3$
$\gamma(t) = 0.9\gamma(t-1), \quad \gamma(0) = -5$
$\lambda(t) = 1$

(b)

$\alpha(t) = 0.95\alpha(t-1), \quad \alpha(0) = 3$
$\beta(t) = 1.1\beta(t-1), \quad \beta(0) = 3$
$\gamma(t) = \gamma(t-1) + \frac{1}{4}, \quad \gamma(0) = -5$
$\lambda(t) = 1$

(c)

Fig. 2. Examples of templates for time-varying sensitivity with uncertainty. In figures (b) and (c) distributions evolve towards the left, i.e., the rightmost distribution corresponds to the label at time t_0, the next one to t_1, and so on.

4 Integrating Uncertain and Time-Varying Sensitivities with Risk-Based Access Control

We now describe how the templates introduced above can be integrated into an access-control model based on quantified estimators of risk. Altough not covered here, a similar approach could be attempted with trust-based schemes. For the purposes of this paper, we will use the Fuzzy MLS model [3] as a convenient framework. For completeness and readability, we first provide a brief review of the model. Subsequently we show how the proposals above can be integrated within this framework.

4.1   Review of Fuzzy MLS

In [3], *risk*[3] is defined as a function of the "gap" between subject's and object's security level (sl and ol, respectively)

$$risk(sl, ol) = Val(ol) \cdot P(sl, ol) \tag{8}$$

Here $Val(ol)$ is the *estimated value of damage* upon disclosure of the object. The security level is generally considered to represent the order of magnitude of damage, and hence Val is defined as

$$Val(ol) = a^{ol} \tag{9}$$

for some $a > 1$. Note that it is implictly assumed that higher sensitivity corresponds to higher values of the object's security level ol.

The *probability of unathorised disclosure*, $P(sl, ol)$, is defined as a combination of two factors as

$$P(sl, ol) = P_1(sl, ol) + P_2(sl, ol) - P_1(sl, ol)P_2(sl, ol) \tag{10}$$

The first term, $P_1(sl, ol)$, measures the probability that a user with security level sl leaks information of level ol by succumbing to *temptation*. It is defined as a sigmoid of the form

$$P_1(sl, ol) = \frac{1}{1 + exp(-k(TI(sl, ol) - mid))} \tag{11}$$

The term $TI(sl, ol)$, called the *temptation index*, roughly indicates how much a subject with security level sl is tempted to leak information with level ol. It is defined as

$$TI(sl, ol) = \frac{a^{-(sl-ol)}}{M - ol} \tag{12}$$

The intuition for the above formulae can be found in [3]. The number mid in expression (11) is the value of TI that makes P_1 equal to 0.5, and the term k serves to control the slope of P_1. The value of m is the *ultimate object sensitivity*, and the TI approaches infinity as ol approaches M. (The idea here is that access to an object with sensitivity level M or greater should be granted by a human being and not a machine.)

The second component, $P_2(sl, ol)$, is a measure of the *probability of inadvertent disclosure* for information belonging to a given category, regardless of the object's security level. We shall not elaborate on it, as the extensions proposed in this paper do not affect it directly. Please refer to [3] for further details.

4.2   Integrating with Distributions

Fuzzy MLS assumes that both the subject and object labels are static. We can readily incorporate uncertain and time-dependent sensitivities into the risk estimate as follows.

---

[3] This quantifies the risk concerned with the *simple security property* (no read-up) of the Bell-La Padula model. Please see [4] for details about how Fuzzy MLS addresses the concern of the *-property*.

In order to simplify the notation, from now on we will denote by $l_o(x, t)$ the pdf associated with the security level of object o at time t. The variable x indicates the sensitivity and ranges from 0 to S (e.g., in previous examples we used $S = 6$). The same notation will be used for subjects clearances. Thus the pdf of a user s will be denoted by $l_s(x, t)$.

Given a subject s and and object o to be accessed at time t, the temptation index is defined as

$$
\begin{aligned}
TI'(s, o, t) &= \int_0^S \int_0^S TI(x, y) l_o(x, t) l_s(y, t) \mathrm{d}x \mathrm{d}y \\
&= \int_0^S \int_0^S \frac{a^{-(x-y)}}{M - y} l_o(x, t) l_s(y, t) \mathrm{d}x \mathrm{d}y
\end{aligned}
\tag{13}
$$

Expression (16) constitutes the natural extension of the TI to a continuous case, where the index is computed over the entire range(s) of sensitivities given by the Beta distributions. Consequently, the probability of unauthorised disclosure, now denoted $P_1'(s, o, t)$, can be computed as in expression (11), although now using $TI'(s, o, t)$ rather than the previous $TI(sl, ol)$.

Regarding the estimated value of damage, expression (9) can be replaced by

$$
Val'(o, t) = \int_0^S a^x l_o(x, t) \mathrm{d}x
\tag{14}
$$

analogously as it was done for the temptation index.

At a given time t, risk can be computed as before, i.e. weighting the value of damage by the probability of unauthorised disclosure as

$$
risk'(s, o, t) = Val'(o, t) \cdot P'(s, o, t)
\tag{15}
$$

In a practical implementation, previous expressions can be easily replaced by discrete approximations for convenience.

5   Extending Uncertainty to Contextual Information

It is widely recognised that many access control decisions should depend not only on the identities of the subject and object involved, but also on the context where the access will take place. Thus for example, a user might have unconditional access to a document provided he is at the office and the request is done between 9 am and 5 pm. Context information is often assumed to be publicly available. However, when used as an input to an access control decision it should be properly verified or else ensure (e.g., by cryptographic means) its correctness. *Location*, for example, is usually referred as an important factor when dealing with access control decisions. Ensuring that the location provided by the requester is authentic may not always be an easy affair (see e.g. [2,6,12] for some possible solutions). In some scenarios, measures to guarantee the authenticity of the requester's location may not be available, and therefore some uncertainty will be inevitably present on this information. But uncertainty comes from other sources as well. In a battlefield we may want to associate a security label to each location in a map, in such a way that access to information depends, among other attributes, on the requester's current position. Such labels should not be static assessments of sensitivity, for in a dynamic and unpredictable environment the situation around a position is likely to change over time (e.g. if the enemy moves).

Location only constitutes a particular example of contextual information generally taken into account to grant or deny access to information. In the area of risk-based access control, Cheng and Karger [5] have identified multiple contextual factors that may contribute to information leakage. These factors consider security-relevant features of the information systems, communication channels, physical environment and human users. In practical terms, specific measures of such factors are interpreted as *risk indices* which, combined together, contribute to assess the global risk.

The templates introduced above to model uncertainty in labels and clearances can be directly applied to context information, particularly in the form of risk factors. If c is a contextual variable (e.g., location, time), a time-varying probability distribution $l_c(x, t)$ can be associated to c. The domain of x is now specific to c (e.g. coordinates in a 2D battlefield, a time interval). We assume that for each c there exists a function $r_c(x)$ mapping each value of x into $[0, 1]$, and we interpret this as the *risk* incurred by granting access to a request when $c = x$. Uncertainty in c can now be taken into account as before, so the contextual risk introduced by c is given by

$$r'_c(t) = \int r_c(x)^x l_c(x, t) \mathrm{d}x \qquad (16)$$

Expression (15) should be modified so that contextual factors help to modulate the risk purely derived from the MLS model. We propose a multiplicative scheme of the form

$$risk(s, l, c_1, \dots, c_k, t) = risk'(s, o, t) \cdot \prod_{i=1}^{k} r'_c(t) \qquad (17)$$

where $c_1, \dots, c_k$ are contextual variables involved in the decision making.

6   Related Work

The need for access control schemes more flexible than classical approaches has been repeatedly pointed out in recent years, particularly in the context of mobile ad hoc networks. Even though the concept of "risk" is explicitly mentioned by many authors, the great majority of the new models actually rely on a notion of "trust" among parties in order to make access decisions. Trust and risk are indeed related and might be used interchangeably in some contexts, but in an essential sense they are different concepts.

Dimmock *et al* [8,9] explored the relationships between trust, risk and privileges in a trust-based access control setting. Their proposal relies on the idea of granting or denying access depending on the trust it has in the requesting principal and the risk of granting the request. Intuitively, the higher the risk of access, the higher the trust needed in the requester to grant access. In [9] the authors propose a *quantifiable* definition of risk based on the classical combination of cost and likelihood of outcomes. This model is later discarded in [9] due, according to the authors, to the "insufficient expressiveness of the risk metrics to capture all the subtleties conveyed by the trust value". Instead, the policy author is provided with a language to express specific rules to compare trust and expected cost information.

Tuptuk and Lupu discuss in [13] a very similar idea, namely to use risk to determine the level of trust needed to access a resource. For an authorisation to take place, a measure of trust in the requester needs to exceed a given risk threshold. The risk threshold is acknowledged to be dynamic and mainly dependent on the current context. This work, however, assumes that the metric to obtain such a risk is given.

Diep *et al* propose in [7] to make access decisions after a risk assessment of both the request and the context. Risk is estimated for the classical three security properties (confidentiality, integrity and availability), again as a combination of cost and likelihood in a particular context, and then a global risk index is computed.

Though related to the our approach, none of these works explicitly address the notion of risk in an MLS setting.

7   Conclusions and Future Work

Risk-based access control models–and particularly those based on a *quantified* definition of risk, such as Fuzzy MLS–may be of help to address some of the difficulties that classical schemes are experiencing when dealing with dynamic and unpredictable environments. In this paper we have shown how models such as Fuzzy-MLS can be extended to effectively process uncertain and time-varying security specifications. By explicitly expressing sensitivity as a probability distribution, both security labels and clearances are, in a sense, more accurate in their purpose of reflecting real-world situations. We have also shown how these notions can be extended to contextual information.

In future work we will address questions related to the language needed to express authorisation policies based on risk assessment with uncertainty. Fuzzy logic seems a natural candidate for such a purpose.

In Section 6 we have given account of some recent works exploring the idea of using risk to determine the level of trust required to access a resource. The converse seems not to have been so well studied; namely, can we exploit (quantifiable) trust measures to determine risk? Consider for instance the scenario discussed in Section 2.1, where the (distribution associated with the) label of an object is obtained from the opinions of a number of experts. Such inputs might be somehow weighted by a measure of trust on the subject's organisation, agency, expertise, etc. This and other relationships between access control, trust and risk will be explored in future work.

References

1. Bishop, M.: Computer Security: Art and Science. Addison-Wesley (2002)
2. Brands, S., Chaum, D.: Distance-Bounding Protocols. In: Helleseth, T. (ed.) EUROCRYPT 1993. LNCS, vol. 765, pp. 344–359. Springer, Heidelberg (1994)
3. Chen, P.-C., Rohatgi, P., Keser, C., Karger, P.A., Wagner, G.M., Reninger, A.S.: Fuzzy Multi–Level Security: An Experiment on Quantified Risk–Adaptive Access Control. In: 2007 IEEE Symposium on Security and Privacy, pp. 222–230. IEEE Press (2007)

4. Chen, P.-C., Rohatgi, P., Keser, C., Karger, P.A., Wagner, G.M., Reninger, A.S.: Fuzzy Multi–Level Security: An Experiment on Quantified Risk–Adaptive Access Control. IBM Research Report RC24190 (February 2007)
5. Chen, P.-C., Karger, P.A.: Risk Modulating Factors in Risk-based Access Control for Information in a MANET. IBM Research Report RC24494 (February 2008)
6. Denning, D.E., MacDoran, P.F.: Location-based Authentication: Grounding Cyberspace for Better Security. Computer Fraud & Security (2), 12–16 (February 1996)
7. Diep, N.N., Hung, L.X., Zhung, Y., Lee, S., Lee, Y.-K., Lee, H.: Enforcing Access Control Using Risk Assessment. In: Proc. 4th European Conference on Universal Multiservice Networks, pp. 419–424 (February 2007)
8. Dimmock, N.: How Much is 'Enough'? Risk in Trust-based access control. In: IEEE Int. Workshops on Enabling Technologies: Infrastructur for Collaborative Entreprises – Enterprise Security, pp. 281–282 (2003)
9. Dimmock, N., Belokosztolszki, A., Eyers, D., Bacon, J., Moody, K.: Using Trust and Risk in Role-Based Access Control Policies. In: Proc. ACM Symposium on Access Control Models and Technologies (SACMAT 2004), pp. 156–162 (2004)
10. M. C. Jason Program Office. Horizontal Integration: Broader Access Models for Realizing Information Dominance. Technical Report JSR-04-132, The MITRE Corporation, JASON Program Office, Mclean, Virginia (December 2004),
    http://www.fas.org/irp/agency/dod/jason/classpol.pdf
11. Department of the Navy. Navy Maritime Domain Awareness Concept (May 2007),
    http://www.navy.mil/navydata/cno/Navy_Maritime_Domain_
    Awareness_Concept_FINAL_2007.pdf
12. Sastry, N., Shankar, U., Wagner, D.: Secure Verification of Location Claims. In: ACM Workshop on Wireless Security, WiSe 2003 (2003)
13. Tuptuk, N., Lupu, E.: Risk Based Authorisation for Mobile Ad Hoc Networks. In: Bandara, A.K., Burgess, M. (eds.) AIMS 2007. LNCS, vol. 4543, pp. 188–191. Springer, Heidelberg (2007)

Sum Aggregation in Sensor Networks While Preserving Confidentiality and Integrity

Keith B. Frikken[1] and Yihua Zhang[2]

[1] Computer Science and Software Engineering, Miami University, Oxford, Ohio, U.S.A.
[2] Department of Computer Science and Engineering, University of Notre Dame
Notre Dame du Lac, Indiana, U.S.A.
frikkekb@muohio.edu, yihua1023@gmail.com

Abstract. In some sensor network environments there is a need to protect the privacy of the individual readings as well as to ensure the integrity of the aggregated result. Many prior solutions have proposed schemes that protect either privacy or integrity, but very little work has been done on achieving both goals. In this paper, we extend a previously defined splitting scheme to provide privacy and integrity when computing the SUM aggregate. The scheme that we present achieves a usable level of privacy and integrity for the sum aggregation and does not require the usage of expensive cryptography. We also experimentally demonstrate the effectiveness of our techniques.

1 Introduction

Wireless sensor networks have promising applications from military surveillance to civilian usage. In these applications, the base station queries the network and sensor nodes report their values to the base station. In some applications, privacy and integrity are security concerns. For example, if the sensor's individual readings reveal information about specific people, then these values must be protected (even against the base station). Furthermore, as individual nodes may become compromised the base station desires a guarantee about the accuracy of the query result.

A well known technique to extend the lifetime of the network is in-network aggregation. Although this approach reduces the communication overhead and extends the network's operation time, in its most straight-forward implementation it suffers from both privacy and integrity problems (for a detailed survey of security in aggregation see [1]). In terms of privacy, while the base station only receives an aggregated result, the values are now leaked to other nodes(i.e., aggregator nodes) in the network. Also, there are now two integrity threats: i) a node may inflate of deflate its values (and the base station can no longer perform the sanity check on each value) and ii) an aggregator might misrepresent the aggregated value. The work in [4,9] addresses the privacy issue for in-network aggregation, however, all of these works assume that sensors will honestly report their values. Also, many schemes [20,18,10,5,7] address the integrity issue, however, with these approaches a verifying node inevitably learns the sensitive information for the nodes that it verifies. The natural question becomes "Can we design a scheme that achieves both privacy and integrity?"

M.S. Obaidat, G.A. Tsihrintzis, and J. Filipe (Eds.): ICETE 2010, CCIS 222, pp. 172–187, 2012.
© Springer-Verlag Berlin Heidelberg 2012

We propose a scheme for computing the sum aggregate that provably achieves both meaningful privacy and integrity. Our work is built upon the SMART scheme[9], that uses the split-and-merge mechanism. Our main contributions are:

1. We introduce the notion of amplification factor to measure the deviation degree between the reported and the correct aggregate values.
2. We introduce a new privacy notion, k-similarity, that provides "good" enough security. We provide analysis to show that this new notion provides a reasonable level of privacy.
3. We provide a protocol for computing the sum aggregate that achieves both integrity and privacy. The proofs of these claims is omitted due to page constraints. Expensive cryptography is not used in this protocol, which makes it applicable to current sensor technology. Furthermore, the communication is also reasonable.
4. We provide experimental results to demonstrate the effectiveness of our approach.

The rest of this paper is organized as follows: in section 2 we survey related literature. In section 3 we define the problem, and in section 4 we introduce a splitting scheme that performs the sum aggregation. In section 5, we formally define the integrity and privacy goals for splitting schemes. In section 6, we provide a construction that satisfies our goals. In section 7, a series of experiments to test the effectiveness of our constructions is performed. Finally in section 8, we summarize our work and describe future work.

2   Related Work

Initial works[14], [11] in the data aggregation domain share the same assumption that all sensors in the network are honest, and no outsiders attempt to eavesdrop or tamper with the sensor readings. However, in reality, sensors are deployed in unattended or hostile environments which put them at risk in the following ways: i) adversaries interested in the values of individual sensors will either eavesdrop the communication or physically crack the sensors to obtain the sensor readings and ii) adversaries who compromise a fraction of sensors will attempt to mislead the base station to accept a spurious aggregate result or prevent the final aggregate from being reported to the base station. Many schemes have been introduced that address either the privacy or the integrity issue.

There are several protocols [8,16,6,15] that return accurate results in case of node failures. However, these approaches do not consider the presence of malicious nodes that are trying to perturb the aggregation result. A first step in making aggregation protocols resilient against malicious nodes was made in [10,12]; these schemes were secure against a single malicious node. Garofalakis et al introduced a scheme that allowed verification of aggregation results [13] using a cryptographic technique called proof sketches. This scheme allows verification of a wider range of aggregation functions than those considered in this paper. However, this scheme requires the usage of public-key cryptography, while our scheme uses only hash functions and symmetric-key encryption. In [5] and [7], schemes for provably secure hierarchical in-network data aggregation were proposed. These schemes were based on a commit-and-attest mechanism where nodes in the network would commit to the aggregation result and then would verify that their would share was included in the final commitment and that all visible shares were inside the valid range. These schemes fail to achieve privacy, because in the aggregation phase, the intermediate node(aggregator) will learn all private sensor readings sent from its children.

Works presented in [4], [9] are related to privacy preservation. In [4], the author proposed a homomorphic encryption scheme that achieves both the end-to-end privacy and energy-efficient properties. Another work [9] introduced two schemes(CPDA, SMART) to protect individual sensor readings during the aggregation phase. Specifically, in the SMART scheme each sensor conceals its private data by slicing it into pieces, and sends the pieces to different cluster heads in the networks. After receiving all shares, those cluster heads will simply aggregate those shares, and further send the aggregate to the base station. One major problem in these two works[4], [9] is that they did not consider the existence of malicious users who may report illegal values (e.g., values that are outside of the range of legal values). Lacking a mechanism to check the validity of reported values, the integrity will not be guaranteed. Our work is primarily based on analyzing the security characteristics of the SMART scheme, and aims to incorporate both the confidentiality and integrity into this scheme.

Recently, a scheme[19] was proposed to address both of the privacy and integrity issues. In [19], the author applies homomorphic encryption to preserve the privacy, and uses monitoring sensors to detect the abnormal behavior of aggregators. That is, each aggregating node has several monitoring nodes that ensure that the aggregator does not misbehave. However, this does not prevent leaf nodes from intentionally reporting illegal values. In order to preserve privacy, the scheme also requires that neither the aggregating nodes nor the monitoring nodes collude with the base station.

Another scheme, ABBA, [3] was proposed for providing privacy and integrity in sensor aggregation, and utilized an additive checksum to provide integrity. A downside with this approach was that if an adversary corrupted a single node and knows that a certain number of nodes in the network reported a specific value, then it can replace these values with an arbitrary value. This downside limits the applicability of the scheme.

3   Problem Definition

We consider a sensor network with N nodes, denoted by $s_1, \ldots, s_N$. At any given time each sensor node has a value in the range $[0, M]$, where node s_i's value is denoted by v_i. A special node, the base station, will query the network to learn $\sum_{i=1}^{N} v_i$. Limiting the range of values to $[0, M]$ does not limit the applicability of the scheme, because other ranges can simply be scaled to match this type of range.

We assume that there is a special set of nodes, called cluster heads. These cluster heads could either be more expensive tamper-resistant nodes, or can be regular nodes in the network that are identified via a cluster formation process (as in [9]). During deployment (before the adversary compromises nodes), each sensor node discovers its closest C cluster heads. The regular nodes in the network will send information to their closest cluster heads, and then these cluster heads will pass the aggregation information up the aggregation tree to the base station.

We assume that sensor nodes have keys with each other. Specifically, we require that each sensor node has a key with each of its closest C cluster heads. This can be achieved using one of the many well-known key pre-distribution schemes (see [2] for a survey of such schemes). We assume that the base station can perform authenticated broadcast by using a protocol such as μTELSA[17].

The primary security concerns in this paper are:

1. **Integrity.** When using in-network aggregation, there are two potential integrity threats: i) a sensing node is corrupt and reports a value outside of the range $[0, M]$, and ii) aggregating node modifies the results of previous nodes. The scheme in [5] protected against both of these threats, but did not preserve privacy. The work in [19] did not consider the first type of attack, and thus to corrupt the result, an adversary only needs corrupt an individual leaf node. In this paper we focus on preventing this type of attack, but do not address corrupt aggregating nodes. At a high level, we want to prevent nodes from being able to have more influence on the final aggregate than what can be achieved by changing its reported value to something in the range $[0, M]$. However, our techniques can be combined with the technique in [19] to protect against both corrupt reporting nodes and corrupt aggregating nodes.

2. **Privacy.** The value of each sensor node should be private, even from the base station. We assume that the base station and up to t cluster heads are corrupt, and attempt to learn an individual sensor's values. Here "corrupt" means that the cluster heads collude with the base station to reveal the sensor's private data. However corrupt does not mean that the aggregating node lies to the base station (i.e., it does not misrepresent the sensor's private reading, or not warn the base station about illegal shares).

3. **Availability.** We do not consider denial of service attacks in this paper.

4 Sum Aggregation Using Splitting Schemes

In this section, we will review the basic ideas of the SMART [9] splitting scheme that aims to preserve the privacy of each sensor's reading during the sum aggregation. Each sensor hides its private data by slicing it into several pieces, and then it sends each encrypted piece to different cluster heads. After receiving all pieces, each cluster head will calculate the intermediate aggregate result, and further report it to the base station. To explain in details, we will divide this process into three steps: Slice, Mix and Merge.

Step 1("Slice"). Each node s_i, will slice v_i into C shares: $v_i^1, \ldots, v_i^C$. That is $v_i = \sum_{j=1}^{C} v_i^j$. The node sends to each of its C cluster heads one of these values encrypted with the key that it shares with the respective cluster head.

Step 2("Mix"). After receiving all of the shares, the cluster head decrypts all of its values and sums up all of the reported shares. It then sends this aggregate to the base station.

Step 3("Merge"). The base station receives all of the values from the cluster heads and sums up all of these values to obtain the sum of all nodes' values. This value will be $\sum_{i=1}^{N} \sum_{j=1}^{C} v_i^j = \sum_{i=1}^{N} v_i$.

It is important to note that the actual SMART protocol is slightly different from the one above. Specifically, each node sends their shares to a random subset of nodes in the network. Also, the nodes keep one share for themselves, aggregate it with other shares it received. While the SMART protocol intuitively achieves private aggregation for the SUM, there are two main limitations to its initial presentation in [9]. First, no description of how to split the values was given in [9], and second, no formal analysis was given to provide any security guarantees. However, this scheme has the potential to enjoy an additional advantage that was not discussed in [9]; specifically, it can potentially provide integrity in addition to privacy. That is, in the mixing step, the cluster heads can verify that the values are in a valid range; and thus, this could bound the amount a corrupted node can affect the final aggregate. The aims of this paper are to: i) give a specific construction for splitting schemes, ii) provide a formal analysis of the effectiveness of this scheme with regards to privacy and integrity, and iii) demonstrate that the construction provides a meaningful level of privacy and integrity.

5 Formalizing Splitting Schemes

In this section we formalize the desired properties of a splitting scheme, so that it can be used to provide integrity and privacy. Suppose a sensor node has a value v that is in the range $[0, M]$. The node is concerned about the privacy of v so it splits v into integer shares $v_1, \ldots, v_s$ such that $\sum_{i=1}^{s} v_i = v$. The node then reports to each of its cluster heads one of these values. The cluster heads then verify that each share is in a valid range and then aggregate the individual shares. The privacy concern with this approach is that an adversary would obtain some share values (i.e., by corrupting some cluster heads) and then be able to determine information about v. Informally, if the adversary obtains up to some t shares of a value for some threshold t, then the adversary should not be able to determine the value used to generate the shares. What complicates this problem, is the base station goal of data integrity; that is the base station wants to prevent the leaf nodes from inflating or deflating his value too much (i.e., reporting a value outside of the range $[0, M]$). We now formalize some notions about splitting values.

Definition 1. *A splitting scheme is a probabilistic algorithm S that takes as input: i) an upper bound on values M, ii) a value $v \in [0, M]$, and iii) a number of shares s. S then produces output $v_1, \ldots, v_s$ such that $\sum_{i=1}^{s} v_i = v$.*

To simplify the analysis of splitting schemes we will consider only splitting schemes where the distribution for any set of shares is the same as the distribution for any other set of shares. More formally,

Definition 2. *A splitting scheme for s shares, call it S, is called c-symmetric if for all ordered sets $I = \{i_1, \ldots, i_c\}$ and $J = \{j_1, \ldots, j_c\}$ that are subsets of $[1, s]$ and $x_1, \ldots, x_c \in \mathbb{Z}^c$, for all valid choices of M, v, and s $Pr[v_{i_1} = x_1 \wedge \cdots \wedge v_{i_c} = x_c | (v_1, \ldots, v_s) \leftarrow S(M, v, s)] = Pr[v_{j_1} = x_1 \wedge \cdots \wedge v_{j_c} = x_c | (v_1, \ldots, v_s) \leftarrow S(M, v, s)]$.*

To complete this notion, we introduce the following definition:

Definition 3. *A splitting scheme for s shares, call it S, is called symmetric if S is c-symmetric for all $c \in [1, s]$.*

While considering only symmetric splitting schemes simplifies that analysis of our approach, a potential concern with this restriction is that asymmetric splitting schemes may perform better than symmetric splitting schemes. However, this is not the case, because any asymmetric scheme can be converted into a fully symmetric scheme with the same properties. That is, suppose we have an asymmetric splitting scheme, A. To convert A into a symmetric scheme S: S computes a set of shares using A and then randomly permutes these shares. It is straightforward to show that S is a symmetric splitting scheme. Also, if a set of t shares from S reveal information about v, then those same t shares reveal the same information in the original scheme A. Since any asymmetric scheme can be converted into a symmetric scheme with similar properties, limiting our attention to symmetric scheme does not hinder our approach.

The following definition introduces notation used in the rest of the paper with regards to symmetric splitting schemes:

Definition 4. *A symmetric splitting scheme, S for range $[0, M]$ and shares s induces a distribution on $[Min(S, M, s), Max(S, M, s)]$ for each value $v \in [0, M]$. We denote the probability that a share is i given a split value v as:*

$$D_v^{S,M,s}[i] = Pr[v_1 = i | (v_1, \ldots, v_s) \leftarrow S(M, v, s)]$$

5.1   Integrity Goal

The server's integrity concern is that a corrupted sensor may report a value not in the range $[0, M]$. Any splitting scheme will produce shares inside of a specific range, we call the range $[Min, Max]$. Formally,

Definition 5. *The range of a splitting scheme, a share count s and an upper bound M is denoted by $range(S, M, s)$ is $[Min(S, M, s), Max(S, M, s)]$ where*

– *$Min(S, M, s)$ (resp. $Max(S, M, s)$) is the minimum (resp. maximum) share value produced by $S(M, v, s)$ over all possible $v \in [0, M]$ and all possible choices for the randomness for S.*

Since individual cluster heads know the value $range(S,M,s)$, they can verify that the shares that it receives are inside this range. If any of the shares are outside this range, then the cluster head reports the error to the base station. Thus a node can cannot report any value outside of the range $[s \times Min(S, M, s), s \times Max(S, M, s)]$ to the base station. The additional range reporting capability is defined in the following metric:

Definition 6. *The amplification factor of a splitting scheme S for parameters M, s is*

$$\frac{s \times Max(S, M, s) - s \times Min(S, M, s) + 1}{M + 1}$$

Clearly, the goal is to make the amplification factor as close to 1 as possible. In fact, in the absence of the privacy goal, this is trivial. Simply have $s = 1$, and have $S(M, v, s) = v$. However, while this provides amplification factor of 1, it clearly provides no privacy.

5.2   Privacy Goal

The initial privacy goal is that the adversary should not be able to determine the value of the result, when given t of the shares. Since the scheme is symmetric we only consider giving the first t shares to the adversary. We formalize this notion for symmetric splitting schemes in the following experiment:

Definition 7.   Share Indistinguishability Experiment $Exp_A^{M,s,S,t}(k)$

1. *A is given the security parameter 1^k, the values M and s. A chooses two values m_0 and m_1 (both in $[0, M]$).*
2. *A bit b is randomly chosen. $(v_1, \ldots, v_s) \leftarrow S(M, m_b, s)$. A is given $v_1, \ldots, v_t$.*
3. *A outputs a bit b'.*
4. *If $b = b'$, then output 1. Otherwise output 0.*

We denote the advantage of A as $Adv_A^{M,s,S,t}(k) := Pr[Exp_A^{M,s,S,t}(k) = 1] - \frac{1}{2}$. We say that a splitting scheme is cryptographically private if for all probabilistic polynomial time (PPT) algorithms A, $Adv_A^{M,s,S,t}(k)$ is negligible in k. Here, "negligible" has the standard cryptographic definition. That is, a function $f(k)$ is negligible if for all polynomials P and large enough N: $\forall n > N : f(n) < \frac{1}{P(n)}$.

If we ignore the integrity goal, then it is straightforward to achieve cryptographic privacy. Essentially, the algorithm chooses v_1 uniformly from $[0, M * 2^k]$ and sets $v_2 = v - v_1$. We omit a formal proof that this is cryptographically private, but the basic idea is that if v_1 is chosen in the range $[M, (2^k - 1)M]$, then no information is leaked about v, by either of the individual shares. v_1 is not chosen in this range with probability $(2M)/M2^k = \frac{1}{2^{k-1}}$, which is negligible in k. Unfortunately, this scheme has an amplification factor of 2^{k+1}, which clearly provides no meaningful integrity.

Impossibility Result.   As can be seen from the previous two sections, it is possible to achieve either integrity or cryptographic privacy for splitting schemes. The natural question that arises is whether it is possible to achieve both simultaneously. Unfortunately, any splitting scheme with cryptographic privacy has super-polynomial (in terms of the security parameter) amplification factor even if the adversary corrupts only a single share. Due to page constraints we omit the formal proof of this claim, but we formally state the result as follows:

Theorem 1. *Any symmetric splitting scheme, S, with parameters M, and s ($s > 1$) such that $Adv_A^{M,s,S,1}(k) \leq \epsilon$ has an amplification factor $\geq \frac{\sqrt{Ms}}{2(M+1)\sqrt{\epsilon}}$*

A consequence of the above theorem is that if the adversary advantage is negligible in k, then the amplification factor must be super-polynomial. That is, M and s are fixed constants, and the ϵ is in the denominator, so the amplification factor is inversely proportional to the square root of the adversary advantage.

Good Enough Privacy.   The previous impossibility result implies that one of the two constraints must be weakened. In order for a splitting scheme to provide any integrity, the amplification factor must be kept small, and thus the question becomes: "Is there a meaningful notion of privacy that can be obtained that suffers only moderate amplification factor?"

Thus we explore weaker definitions of privacy when $t = 1$ (however this generalizes to other values of t); our fundamental goal is to place some bound on the information gained by an adversary. When considering the amount of knowledge gained from a share, an important factor is that the difference between the two distributions at any point is small relative to the values at those points. Using this as motivation we propose the following definition.

Definition 8. *A symmetric splitting scheme, S, with parameters M, and s provides k-similar privacy if and only if $\forall m_0, m_1 \in [0, M], \forall i \in [Min(S, M, s), Max(S, M, s)]$ either*

i) $D_{m_0}^{S,M,s}[i] = 0$ and $D_{m_1}^{S,M,s}[i] = 0$ or ii) $\dfrac{\min\{D_{m_0}^{S,M,s}[i], D_{m_1}^{S,M,s}[i]\}}{\max\{D_{m_0}^{S,M,s}[i], D_{m_1}^{S,M,s}[i]\} - \min\{D_{m_0}^{S,M,s}[i], D_{m_1}^{S,M,s}[i]\}} \geq k$

Analysis of k-similar Privacy. We are interested in bounding the "information gain" that the adversary has from the captured share. To model this, suppose that the adversary is trying to distinguish whether the node has a value m_0 or a value m_1. Furthermore, the adversary has some background knowledge regarding the likelihood that the value is m_0, and we represent this as probability P. We stress that we do not assume knowledge of value P, but rather we wish bound the information gain for any value of P. Denote as P^i the adversary's probability that the value is m_0 after seeing a single sample with value i. Below, a bound is placed upon the value $|P^i - P|$, which is independent of i.

Theorem 2. *If a splitting scheme satisfies k-similarity, then $|P^i - P| \leq \frac{Q-Q^2}{Q+k}$ where $Q = \sqrt{k^2 + k} - k$*

Proof: For the sake of brevity denote as $p_i = D_{m_0}^{S,M,s}[i]$ and $q_i = D_{m_1}^{S,M,s}[i]$. Now, $P^i = \frac{P \times p_i}{P \times p_i + (1-P) \times q_i}$. We consider two cases: i) $p_i \geq q_i$ and ii) $p_i < q_i$.

Case 1 $p_i \geq q_i$: It is straightforward to show that $P^i \geq P$. Since $\frac{q_i}{p_i - q_i} \geq k$, $q_i \geq \frac{kp_i}{k+1}$. Now, $P^i = \frac{Pp_i}{Pp_i + (1-P)q_i}$, and this value is maximized when q_i is minimized. Thus,

$P^i \leq \frac{Pp_i}{Pp_i + (1-P)\frac{kp_i}{k+1}} = \frac{P}{P + (1-P)\frac{k}{k+1}} = \frac{Pk+P}{Pk+P+(k-kP)} = \frac{Pk+P}{P+k}$. Now $P^i - P \leq$

$\frac{Pk+P}{P+k} - P = \frac{P-P^2}{P+k}$. It is straightforward to show that this value is maximized when $P = \sqrt{k^2 + k} - k$.

Case 2 $p_i < q_i$: A symmetrical argument can be made to case 1.   □

In Figure 1 we plot the the maximal knowledge gain (i.e., $|P^i - P|$) for several value of k. Observe that, as k increases this value decreases rapidly. For example, if a scheme satisfies 7-similarity, then a single sample changes the adversary's belief about the reported value by at most 3.4%, and if the splitting scheme satisfies 10-similarity, the maximum change is 2.4%. Clearly, this is not as strong as the notion of cryptographic privacy, but it may be enough security in some situations.

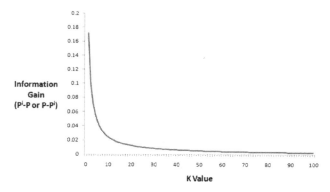

Fig. 1. Relation Between Maximum Information Gain and K Value

6   A Construction

In this section we present a construction for a splitting scheme. Before describing the scheme we introduce a new definition. Define $C_s(T, a, b)$ to be the number of ways to choose s values that sum up to T where all values are in the range $[a, b]$. Note that these C values can be computed using the following recurrence:

1. $C_1(T, a, b) = 1$ if $T \in [a, b]$ and is 0 otherwise.
2. $C_i(T, a, b) = \sum_{j=a}^{b} C_{i-1}(T - j, a, b)$

The main construction is as follows: At a high level, to split a value v among s shares, the splitting scheme takes as a parameter a value N and produces values in the range $[-N, N]$. We discuss how to choose N later, but clearly it is required that $Ns \geq M$. The scheme chooses q as the first share with probability $\frac{C_{s-1}(v-q, -N, N)}{C_s(v, -N, N)}$. It then chooses shares for values $v - q$ using $s - 1$ shares recursively using the same strategy. Before describing the actual construction, we need another building block that chooses a value in a range with the above-specified distribution. This algorithm is given in Algorithm 1, and the details of the construction are provided in Algorithm 2.

Algorithm 1. $CHOOSE(MIN, MAX, v, s)$.
1: **for** $i = MIN$ to MAX **do**
2:    $d_i = \frac{C_{s-1}(v-i, MIN, MAX)}{C_s(v, MIN, MAX)}$
3: **end for**
4: Choose a value $i \in [MIN, MAX]$ according to distribution $d_{MIN}, \ldots, d_{MAX}$
5: **return** i

In Algorithm 2, notice that if the last share does not fall into the range $[-N, N]$, then the algorithm will return FAIL. However, this situation will never happen, because when we set the ith share to v_i it must be possible to obtain $v - \sum_{j=1}^{i} v_j$ using the remaining shares. This follows from the probability of that the ith share is v_i is: $\frac{C_{s-i}(v-\sum_{j=1}^{i} v_j, -N, N)}{C_{s-i+1}(v-\sum_{j=1}^{i-1} v_j, -N, N)}$, which is 0 if it is not possible to obtain $v - \sum_{j=1}^{i} v_j$ with the remaining shares.

Algorithm 2. $SPLIT(M, v, s, N)$.
1: **if** $s = 1$ **then**
2:    **if** $v \in [-N, N]$ **then**
3:        return $< v >$
4:    **else**
5:        return $FAIL$/*This will never happen*/
6:    **end if**
7: **end if**
8: $v_s = CHOOSE(-N, N, v, s)$
9: $< v_1, \ldots, v_{s-1} > = SPLIT(M, v - v_s, s - 1)$
10: return $< v_1, \ldots, v_s >$

This scheme is symmetric and if $N = (k+1)M$ and $s = 3$, then the scheme satisfies k-similarity with an amplification factor of $6(k + 1)$. Due to page constraints we omit the proof of these claims.

- **Computation Overhead.** One concern with this splitting scheme is that its time complexity may not be suitable for a sensor node. Computing the C values is potentially an expensive step. Dynamic programming can be used to compute the C values. We omit the details of the algorithm, but it has complexity $O(s^2 N^2)$, and it is within the sensor's computation capability. That is, the values of s and N are likely to be small enough in practice to make this practical for a sensor node. A storage-computation tradeoff is possible; that is the sensor's can store the various C values.

- **Communication Overhead.** We compare our scheme with both homomorphic encryption[4] and secure aggregation protocol[7] that proposed solutions for solely privacy and integrity respectively. Specifically in our scheme, the congestion occurred in a single node is $O(s)$. The scheme in [4] results in $O(1)$ congestion per node, but only provides privacy. The protocol in [7] has $O(\triangle log N)$ congestion per node, but only provides integrity (Here, $\triangle$ is the maximum degree of aggregation tree).

7 Experiments

In this section we describe various experiments that test the resiliency of the proposed splitting schemes. We initially focus on the case when a single share is compromised (i.e., $t = 1$), but then we consider the case when $t > 1$.

7.1 Resiliency against the Single Share Compromise

Given parameters M, s, and N the level of k-similarity can be computed as follows: Since the scheme is symmetric we need only consider the distribution of the first share. This distribution is computed as in Algorithm 1. Given this distribution it is straightforward to compute the k value by finding the i value in $[-N, N]$ and values m_0 and m_1 in $[0, M]$ that minimize:

$$\frac{\min\{D_{m_0}^{S,M,s}[i], D_{m_1}^{S,M,s}[i]\}}{\max\{D_{m_0}^{S,M,s}[i], D_{m_1}^{S,M,s}[i]\} - \min\{D_{m_0}^{S,M,s}[i], D_{m_1}^{S,M,s}[i]\}}$$

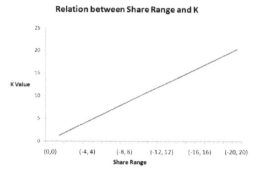

Fig. 2. Relation Between Share Range and K Value

for all values $i \in [-N, N]$. This search can be expedited because this value will be minimized when $m_0 = 0$ and $m_1 = M$ (the proof of this claim is omitted due to page constraints).

We now describe the specific experiments:

- **Relation between Share Ranges and K Value.** In this part, we fix $M = 1$, $s = 3$ and varied N from 1 to 20. Figure 2 shows the k value for each value of N.
- **Comparison between Symmetric and Asymmetric Share Ranges.** The share ranges in the original scheme were symmetric, i.e., $[-N, N]$ but the range of values was not symmetric, i.e., $[0, M]$. In this experiment, we compare the effect of using an asymmetric share range for the shares. We fixed $s = 3$, varied M from 2 to 10, and varied the share range from $[-20, 20]$ to $[-14, 26]$. Figure 3 shows the corresponding k values. It indicates that in most of the cases, the symmetric share range results in the higher k value than the asymmetric ones. For example, when $M = 2$, the share range $[-20, 20]$ leads to 9.83-resilient scheme while the share range $[-14, 26]$ leads to 1.81-resilient scheme.
- **Relation between the Number of Shares and K Value.** The goal of this experiment is to determine the effect of increasing the number of shares. We fixed $M = 1$, varied s from 4 to 7, and determined the minimum N value that was necessary to achieve $k = 10$. Figure 4 shows the k values for the different parameters. It indicates that if the value is split into more number of shares, the corresponding k value increases. This intuitively makes sense because as the number of shares increases the distributions of the shares can become closer. However, it appears that increasing the number of shares will not lead to a significant decrease in amplification factor. Table 1 shows the results. It appears as though the amplification factor is about the same for all values (except $s = 4$). Since increasing the number of shares increases the communication, it appears that if the adversary compromises only a single cluster head, then s should probably be chosen as 3.

7.2 Resiliency against the Collusion Attack

We now consider the case where the adversary has more than one share. We generalize the definition of k-similarity, by looking at the difference in the distributions of t-shares.

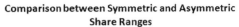

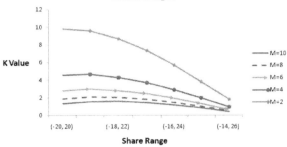

Fig. 3. Relation Between Symmetric and Asymmetric Share Ranges

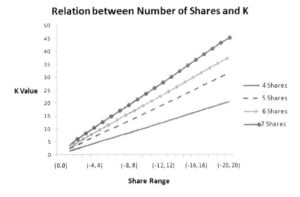

Fig. 4. Relation Between Number of Shares and K Value

Table 1. Amplification Factor for Varied Shares

s	**Minimum N for $k = 10$**	Amplification **Factor**
3	10	30.5
4	10	40.5
5	6	30.5
6	5	30.5
7	4	28.5

Since the scheme is fully symmetric, we need only consider the distribution of the first t shares. To formalize this notion if $t = 2$, then we let $D_{m_0}^{S,M,s}[i,j]$ be the probability that two shares will be i and j when splitting the value m_0. Thus a scheme is k-similar if for all possible share values i and j and values m_0 and m_1:

$$\frac{\min\{D_{m_0}^{S,M,s}[i,j], D_{m_1}^{S,M,s}[i,j]\}}{\max\{D_{m_0}^{S,M,s}[i,j], D_{m_1}^{S,M,s}[i,j]\} - \min\{D_{m_0}^{S,M,s}[i,j], D_{m_1}^{S,M,s}[i,j]\}} \geq k$$

We start with the case where $t = 2$. Given parameters M, s, and N the level of k-similarity can be computed as follows: since the scheme is symmetric we only need to consider the pair distributions of the first and the second share, namely $Pr[s_1 = i \wedge s_2 = j](i, j \in [-N, N])$. The distribution is computed as following:

$$Pr[s_1 = i \wedge s_2 = j] = Pr[s_1 = i|s_2 = j]Pr[s_2 = j]$$

Based on Algorithm 1, we have

$$Pr[s_1 = i|s_2 = j] = \frac{C_{s-2}(v - i - j, -N, N)}{C_{s-1}(v - j, -N, N)}$$

$$Pr[s_2 = j] = \frac{C_{s-1}(v - j, -N, N)}{C_s(v, -N, N)}$$

Therefore,

$$Pr[s_1 = i \wedge s_2 = j] = \frac{C_{s-2}(v - i - j, -N, N)}{C_s(v, -N, N)}$$

Given this distribution it is straightforward to compute the k value by finding the i and j values in $[-N, N]$ and values m_0 and m_1 that minimizes the formula in Definition 10. Similar to Section 7.1, these value will be minimized when $m_0 = 0$ and $m_1 = M$.

- **Relation between Number of Shares and K.** In this part, we fix $M = 1, t = 2$, varied N from 1 to 20, and varied s from 5 to 7. We did not consider s as 3 or 4, because these provide only 0-similarity. To be more specific if $v = 0$ and $s = 3$, then it is possible using the construction that 2 shares are $-N$ and 0 (the 3rd share would be N), but it is not possible to have 2 shares be $-N$ and 0 when $v = 1$ (the 3rd share would need to be $N + 1$, which is not in the value share range).

    Figure 5 shows the results of this experiment. First, observe that it is possible to obtain reasonable values of k for these values. Furthermore, it appears that there is a linear relationship between N and the k value. Specifically, when $s = 5$, the scheme appears to be $.5N$-resilient, when $s = 6$, the scheme appears to be $.67N$-resilient, and when $s = 7$, the scheme appears to be $.88N$-resilient.
- **Relation between Amplification Factor and K.** In this part, we fixed $s = 5$, $t = 2$, varied M from 6 to 10, and varied N from 10 to 200. Figure 6 shows the k value for each pair of N and M values. Again the linear relationship seems to hold, and it appears as though k is linear in the value $\frac{N}{M}$. Similar results hold when s is increased (but these experiments are omitted due to page constraints).

The case when $t > 2$. Due to the page limit, we omit from the manuscript the experiments for when $t > 2$ shares are compromised, but the basic idea is that, we will compute the distributions for the first t shares using the formula $Pr[s_1 = v_1 \wedge s_2 = v_2 \wedge \cdots \wedge s_n = v_n] = \frac{C_{s-n}(v - \sum_{i=1}^{n} v_i, -N, N)}{C_s(v, -N, N)}$, and compute the k value based on Definition 10. Similar results hold in this case, but the number of shares must be increased. That is, it must be that $s > 2t + 1$ in order to have k-similarity for $k > 0$.

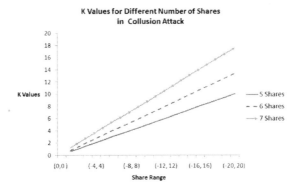

Fig. 5. K Values for Different Number of Shares in Collusion Attack

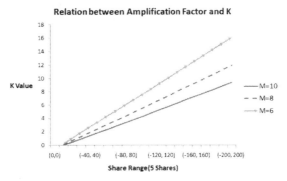

Fig. 6. Relation between Amplification Factor and K value in Collusion Attack

8   Summary and Future Work

In this paper, we introduced a new integrity measure and a new privacy measure, called called k-similarity, which is a weaker notion than cryptographic privacy, but it is still useful in real applications. Furthermore, we built a splitting construction that can achieve both the meaningful privacy and integrity during the SUM aggregation. And finally, we implemented a series of experiments to test the effectiveness of our technique against the adversaries who captured a certain number of shares. There are several problems for future work, including:

1. The splitting scheme currently only protects against leaf nodes reporting false values. While the scheme could be combined with the approach in [19] to protect against malicious aggregator nodes, it would be desirable to create one mechanism that handles both type of integrity violations. For example, is it possible to combine the splitting scheme with the scheme in [5] by using different aggregation trees to obtain similar results.

2. The current scheme doesn't use expensive cryptography (homomorphic encryption, zero knowledge proofs, etc). Is it possible to obtain cryptographic privacy and

constant amplification factor? Or, is there a different approach that does not use expensive cryptography that achieves this result?

3. The analysis in this paper was for the case when $t = 1$. However, there appears to be a linear relationship between the k and N/M. Can this result be formalized and be proven for $t > 1$?

Acknowledgements. The authors would like to thank the anonymous reviewers for their comments and useful suggestions. Portions of this work were supported by Grant CNS-0915843 from the National Science Foundation.

References

1. Alzaid, H., Foo, E., Nieto, J.G.: Secure data aggregation in wireless sensor network: a survey. In: AISC 2008: Proceedings of the Sixth Australasian Conference on Information Security, pp. 93–105. Australian Computer Society, Inc., Darlinghurst (2008)
2. Camtepe, S.A., Yener, B.: Key distribution mechanisms for wireless sensor networks: a survey. Technical report (2005)
3. Castelluccia, C., Soriente, C.: Abba: A balls and bins approach to secure aggregation in wsns. In: WiOpt 2008:Sixth International Symposium on Modeling and Optimization in Mobile, Ad Hoc, and Wireless Networks (2008)
4. Castelluccia, C., Mykletun, E., Tsudik, G.: Efficient aggregation of encrypted data in wireless sensor networks. In: MOBIQUITOUS 2005: Proceedings of the The Second Annual International Conference on Mobile and Ubiquitous Systems: Networking and Services, pp. 109–117. IEEE Computer Society, Washington, DC, USA (2005)
5. Chan, H., Perrig, A., Song, D.: Secure hierarchical in-network aggregation in sensor networks. In: CCS 2006: Proceedings of the 13th ACM Conference on Computer and Communications Security, pp. 278–287. ACM, New York (2006)
6. Chen, J.-Y., Pandurangan, G., Xu, D.: Robust computation of aggregates in wireless sensor networks: distributed randomized algorithms and analysis. In: IPSN 2005: Proceedings of the 4th International Symposium on Information Processing in Sensor Networks, p. 46. IEEE Press, Piscataway, NJ, USA (2005)
7. Frikken, K.B., Dougherty IV, J.A.: An efficient integrity-preserving scheme for hierarchical sensor aggregation. In: WiSec 2008: Proceedings of the First ACM Conference on Wireless Network Security, pp. 68–76. ACM, New York (2008)
8. Gupta, I., van Renesse, R., Birman, K.P.: Scalable fault-tolerant aggregation in large process groups. In: DSN 2001: Proceedings of the 2001 International Conference on Dependable Systems and Networks (formerly: FTCS), pp. 433–442. IEEE Computer Society, Washington, DC, USA (2001)
9. He, W., Liu, X., Nguyen, H., Nahrstedt, K., Abdelzaher, T.: Pda: Privacy-preserving data aggregation in wireless sensor networks. In: 26th IEEE International Conference on Computer Communications, INFOCOM 2007, pp. 2045–2053. IEEE (2007)
10. Hu, L., Evans, D.: Secure aggregation for wireless networks. In: Proceedings of 2003 Symposium on Applications and the Internet Workshops, pp. 384–391 (January 2003)
11. Intanagonwiwat, C., Estrin, D., Govindan, R., Heidemann, J.: Impact of network density on data aggregation in wireless sensor networks. In: ICDCS 2002: Proceedings of the 22 nd International Conference on Distributed Computing Systems, p. 457. IEEE Computer Society, Washington, DC, USA (2002)
12. Jadia, P., Mathuria, A.: Efficient Secure Aggregation in Sensor Networks. In: Bougé, L., Prasanna, V.K. (eds.) HiPC 2004. LNCS, vol. 3296, pp. 40–49. Springer, Heidelberg (2004)

13. Maniatis, P., Garofalakis, M., Hellerstein, J.: Proof sketches: Verifiable in-network aggregation. In: Proceedings of the IEEE 23rd International Conference on Data Engineering (2007)
14. Madden, S., Franklin, M.J., Hellerstein, J.M., Hong, W.: Tag: a tiny aggregation service for ad-hoc sensor networks. SIGOPS Oper. Syst. Rev. 36(SI), 131–146 (2002)
15. Manjhi, A., Nath, S., Gibbons, P.B.: Tributaries and deltas: efficient and robust aggregation in sensor network streams. In: SIGMOD 2005: Proceedings of the 2005 ACM SIGMOD International Conference on Management of Data, pp. 287–298. ACM Press, New York (2005)
16. Nath, S., Gibbons, P.B., Seshan, S., Anderson, Z.R.: Synopsis diffusion for robust aggregation in sensor networks. In: SenSys 2004: Proceedings of the 2nd International Conference on Embedded Networked Sensor Systems, pp. 250–262. ACM Press, New York (2004)
17. Perrig, A., Szewczyk, R., Tygar, J.D., Wen, V., Culler, D.E.: Spins: security protocols for sensor networks. Wireless Networks 8(5), 521–534 (2002)
18. Przydatek, B., Song, D., Perrig, A.: Sia: secure information aggregation in sensor networks. In: SenSys 2003: Proceedings of the 1st International Conference on Embedded Networked Sensor Systems, pp. 255–265. ACM, New York (2003)
19. Roberto, D.P., Pietro, M., Refik, M.: Confidentiality and integrity for data aggregation in wsn using peer monitoring. In: Security and Communication Networks, pp. 181–194 (2009)
20. Yang, Y., Wang, X., Zhu, S., Cao, G.: Sdap: a secure hop-by-hop data aggregation protocol for sensor networks. In: MobiHoc 2006: Proceedings of the 7th ACM International Symposium on Mobile Ad Hoc Networking and Computing, pp. 356–367. ACM, New York (2006)

Stream Cipher-Based Hash Function and Its Security

Yuto Nakano, Jun Kurihara, Shinsaku Kiyomoto, and Toshiaki Tanaka

KDDI R&D Laboratories Inc., 2-1-15 Ohara, Fujimino, Saitama 356-8502, Japan
{yuto,kurihara,kiyomoto,toshi}@kddilabs.jp

Abstract. Stream cipher-based hash function (SCH) is the one of new approachs to construct hash functions. However, the security and the design policy of SCH have not yet been studied sufficiently. In this paper, we analyze the security of SCHs focusing on the stream cipher function. First, we propose a model of SCHs which consist of a pre-computation function and a stream cipher. Then, we show that attacks against a stream cipher can also be threats to SCHs and discuss the security on each phase of SCH; message injection, blank rounds, and hash generation. Finally we derive the necessary conditions on the stream cipher function for an SCH to be secure.

Keywords: Hash function, Stream cipher, Collision resistance, Second preimage resistance, Preimage resistance.

1 Introduction

Standard hash functions MD5 [16] and SHA-1 [15] have been demonstrated that these functions are not collision resistant [18,19]. Many constructions for new hash functions have been presented as alternatives to these ordinary algorithms. Some hash functions such as Boole [17] are based on stream ciphers, and shows that they have good performance on a variety of platforms. A noteworthy advantage of stream cipher-based hash functions is that the algorithm is used not only for generating a hash value but also for encrypting/decrypting data as a stream cipher. We can reduce total costs of implementations for a hash function and a symmetric-key encryption algorithm with a stream cipher-based hash function. Thus, it is a reasonable solution for resource constraint devices.

The general construction of stream cipher-based hash functions (SCHs) was first introduced by Golić [6] as a mode of operation of stream ciphers. An SCH consists of a stream cipher function and an additional function that inputs a message into the internal state of the stream cipher function. Therefore, a model of an SCH consists of a pre-computation function and a stream cipher function. The stream cipher function is a core component of SCHs and an appropriate algorithm is selected from among existing stream cipher algorithms. The pre-computation function is used to absorb the message into the internal state of the stream cipher function. On the other hand, a well developed evaluation design of the security of SCHs is yet to be produced, and design principles of secure SCHs have not been established.

In this paper, we define a stream cipher function that consists of three rounds; message injection, blank rounds, and hash generation. With this function, we show that an attack on the keystream feedback mode and an attack against a self-synchronizing

M.S. Obaidat, G.A. Tsihrintzis, and J. Filipe (Eds.): ICETE 2010, CCIS 222, pp. 188–202, 2012.
© Springer-Verlag Berlin Heidelberg 2012

stream cipher can also be employed as an attack against SCHs. Furthermore, we analyze the security of each phase from an attack perspective. As a result of our work, following criteria can be formulated:

- The size of the internal state is larger than the size the of hash value. $|S| > |H|$ is required for collision, second preimage, and preimage resistance, where $|S|$ is the size of the internal state and $|H|$ is the length of the hash value.1
- The message injection has to be collision resistant. The computational cost of the collision attack against message injection has to be equal to or more than $2^{|H|/2}$, and an adversary is not able to control the internal state of the stream cipher function.
- Blank rounds are preimage resistant. That is, deriving the internal state after message injection by going blank rounds backwardly requires $2^{|H|}$ computational cost. Furthermore, the transition of the internal state is cyclic and its period is more than or equal to $2^{|H|}$.
- The hash value has to be affected by the whole internal state. Suppose that the internal state size is $|S|$ and the hash size is $|H|$, the hash value bit has to be decided by at least an $|S|/|H|$-bit internal state.
- Suppose that an x-bit internal state can be controlled by an x-bit message and this operation does not affect other bits, then the whole internal state can be controlled with an $|S|/x$-bit message. Here we assume that one bit message is xored with n bits of the internal state at equal intervals. Then the adversary can control up to an $|S|/n$-bit internal state. Hence the condition $s(n-1) \geq nh$ is required for a message injection to be collision resistant.

2 Preliminaries

We provide definitions and summarize related works in this section.

2.1 Definitions

Throughout the paper, we use the following notations.

- M: input message
- m_t: input message to the stream cipher function at time t
- S_t: internal state of the stream cipher function at time t
- o_t: output of the stream cipher function at time t
- $|x|$: bit length of x (x can be M, S, H)
- $\oplus$: bitwise exclusive-or
- S_{msg}, S'_{msg}: internal state of stream cipher function after message M or M' are injected, respectively
- S_{blk}, S'_{blk}: internal state of stream cipher function after blank rounds derived from S_{msg} or S'_{msg}, respectively
- Δ_{msg}: internal state difference after message injection $\Delta_{msg} = S'_{msg} - S_{msg}$
- Δ_{blk}: internal state difference after blank rounds $\Delta_{blk} = S'_{blk} - S_{blk}$

2.2 Security Definitions for Hash Functions

Security requirements for hash functions are collision resistance, second pre-image resistance, pre-image resistance [13], and length-extension security. Let M and M' be messages, $|H|$ be hash length, h be a hash function, and the symbol $\|$ be concatenation of data.

Collision Resistance. finding M and M' such that $h(M) = h(M')$ and $M \neq M'$ requires $2^{|H|/2}$ hash operations.

Second Pre-image Resistance. finding M for given M' such that $h(M) = h(M')$ and $M \neq M'$ requires $2^{|H|}$ hash operations.

Pre-image Resistance. finding M from $h(M)$ requires $2^{|H|}$ hash operations.

Length-extension Security. This requirement has been proposed in NIST SHA-3 competition. Given $h(M)$, the complexity of finding (z, x) such that $x = h(M\|z)$ should be greater than or equal to either the complexity of guessing M itself or $2^{|H|}$.

2.3 Related Work

Here we introduce important research related to the construction of SCHs.

Self-synchronizing Stream Cipher. A self-synchronizing stream cipher (SSSC) is one in which the keystream is generated from the secret key and a fixed number of previous ciphertext bits [13]. Let p_t, c_t, and z_t be a plaintext bit, a ciphertext bit, and a keystream bit at time t, respectively. The keystream at time t depends on the secret key K and previous n_{me} ciphertext bits $c_{t-n_{me}}, \ldots, c_{t-1}$, where n_{me} is called *input memory*. The keystream bit is described by

$$z_t = f_c(c_{t-n_{me}}, c_{t-(n_{me}-1)}, \ldots, c_{t-1}, K), \tag{1}$$

where f_c is the function defined by the stream cipher. When the ciphertext is decrypted, the keystream is generated in the same manner as encryption. For the first keystream bit, the previous n_{me} ciphertext bits do not exist. Therefore, n_{me}-bit Initial Vector(IV) has to be defined as $IV = c_{n_{me}}, c_{(n_{me}-1)}, \ldots, c_0$.

Keystream Feedback Mode. Keystream feedback mode is employed in the initialization of many stream ciphers such as SNOW [5]. In the initialization of stream ciphers, an initial key and an IV are loaded into the internal state of the stream cipher. After loading the key and the IV, the stream cipher is clocked a specified number of times. In the initialization process, keystream bits are fed back to the internal state to enable the further diffusion of the key and the IV.

Golić's Construction. Golić [6] showed how to convert a keystream generator into a stream cipher with memory (SCM) mode and how to built hash functions with SCM mode. When a feedback shift register (FSR) based keystream generator is used, SCM mode is easily converted by adding the plaintext bit to the feedback bit of the FSR. The following is the scheme of Golić's construction.

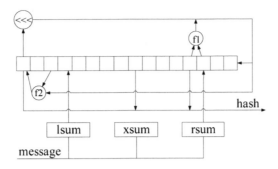

Fig. 1. Schematic of Boole

1. Generate a keystream by feeding back a message into the keystream generator and encrypting the message.
2. Another encryption is applied; this time the ciphertext obtained in step 1. is used in reverse order.
3. Generate a keystream by feeding back a constant value (if possible, set all constants to zero) for αm times, where α is not a large integer.
4. Output the last h successive bits of the keystream obtained in step 3. as the hash value.

In step 1, using a fixed and known key, SCM mode is clocked m times with an m-bit message and the corresponding m-bit ciphertext is memorized. SCM mode is clocked another m times with the m-bit ciphertext in the reverse order in step 2. SCM mode is clocked αm times where α is not a large integer (*e.g.*, three), and the last h successive ciphertext bits (or keystream bits) are output as the hash value.

As the ciphertext in reverse order is used in step 2, this scheme requires an amount of memory that is the same as the message size.

Boole. Boole [17] is a family of hash functions submitted to NIST for SHA-3 competition. The schematic of Boole is shown in Fig. 1. Boole is constructed from a non-linear feedback shift register, input accumulators, and an output filter function. Boole consists of three phases, *i.e.*, an input phase, a mixing phase, and an output phase. The state transition function of the register, referred to as a cycle, transforms state S_t into S_{t+1}.

A message word is input to three word accumulators, and the accumulators are updated in the input phase. Then the register is cycled once. After the input phase, the register is mixed with three accumulators, then the register is cycled 16 times, and the hash value is generated.

ATTACK ON BOOLE. A pre-image attack against Boole is presented by Nikolić [12]. This attack uses the MITM method. The value of ten registers can be determined from the message and the target hash. Therefore the search space is reduced to nine registers. Each register is one byte, hence the complexity of the attack is $2^{\frac{9n}{16}}$.

Boole is vulnerable in two ways: the register value can be determined from the input message and the hash output function is not a one-way function.

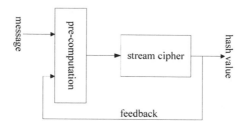

Fig. 2. Model of SCH

A collision attack on Boole is also proposed [12]. Since two Boolean functions used in Boole are not invertible, the collision can be constructed in these functions.

3   Construction of SCHs

In this section we present a general model of SCH, which is shown as Fig.2. An SCH is modeled with two components: a pre-computation function and a stream cipher function. This is the generalized model of the construction of the hash functions based on stream ciphers.

3.1   Components of SCH

A pre-computation function is appended to a stream cipher for constructing an SCH. The pre-computation function is the part which takes an input message and an intermediate hash value as an input and determines the internal state of the stream cipher function. The stream cipher function plays the role of diffusing the message into the internal state. The hash value is a certain length of keystream which is produced by the stream cipher function. Generally, keys and IVs are set to a constant value, usually to zero, and the message is loaded to the internal state of the stream cipher function.

Golić's construction consists of a first-in-last-out (FILO) buffer and a stream cipher. Therefore it is obvious that the FILO buffer should be treated as pre-computation function and the stream cipher is the stream cipher function.

Generally, the pre-computation function requires very few computations; for example, the pre-computation function in Boole is defined as three accumulators; lsum, xsum, and rsum are used to input a message into the non-linear feedback shift register. Hence operations which use these accumulators are defined as the pre-computation function.

3.2   Hash Value Generation

SCHs execute three phases: message injection, *blank rounds*, and hash generation. Here, the message is loaded into the internal state of the stream cipher in the message injection. The blank round is an operation in which the stream cipher function is clocked by feeding back the output without outputting the keystream. This phase is a similar operation to the initialization of the stream cipher. The stream cipher outputs a keystream as a hash value in the hash generation.

We define a stream cipher with a pre-computation function at time t as $f(m_t, S_t, o_t)$. In the stream cipher function, the internal state is updated and the keystream (hash value) is generated from the message, internal state, and feedback of output. The operation can be denoted as:

$$f(m_t, S_t, o_t) \rightarrow S_{t+1}, o_{t+1}. \tag{2}$$

We denote message injection, blank rounds, and hash generation by Eq. (2) as follows:

$$f(m_t, S_t, o_t) \rightarrow S_{t+1}, o_{t+1}, \tag{3}$$
$$f(0, S_t, o_t) \rightarrow S_{t+1}, o_{t+1}, \tag{4}$$
$$f(0, S_t, 0) \rightarrow S_{t+1}, o_{t+1}. \tag{5}$$

The internal state is updated from message, previous state, and feedback of output in the message injection. In blank rounds, the internal state is updated from the previous state, and output. During hash generation, only the previous state is used to update the state and output the hash value.

4   Attacks against SCH

In this section, we consider the relation between attacks against stream ciphers and attacks against SCHs. We also consider general attacks against hash functions to derive secure construction of SCHs.

4.1   Relation to the Attack against a Stream Cipher

Since blank rounds of an SCH and the initialization of stream ciphers have the same structure, chosen IV/key attack against stream ciphers can be applied to the attack against SCH. Wu et al. [20] presented the chosen IV attack against Py [1] and Pypy [2] in which an adversary can find an identical keystream using IVs which have special differences. In the initialization of keystream feedback mode, the internal state is updated after the key and IV setup as follows:

$$f(S_t, z_t) \rightarrow S_{t+1}, z_{t+1}, \tag{6}$$

where S_t and z_t are the internal state and keystream at time t. Blank rounds in an SCH can be denoted as Eq. (4). There is no message to be injected into the internal state during blank rounds, Eq. (4) can be modified as:

$$f(S_t, o_t) \rightarrow S_{t+1}, o_{t+1}. \tag{7}$$

From the Eq. (6) and (7), an attack against keystream feedback mode can be used against blank rounds of an SCH. In the case where the attack proposed by Wu et al. is applied to the SCH, an adversary can find two identical hash values from different messages; this leads to a collision and second preimage attack against SCHs. If there is an attack that reveals the secret key from the keystream, such attack leads to the preimage attack against SCHs.

Blank rounds also have a relation to SSSC. In Eq. (1) c_{t-1} can be considered as an output feedback at time t and $(c_{t-n_{mc}}, c_{t-(n_{mc}-1)}, \ldots, c_{t-2})$ as an internal state. At time $t + 1$, c_t will be fed back and $(c_{t-(n_{mc}-1)}, \ldots, c_{t-1})$ will be the internal state. Let S_t be $S_t = (c_{t-n_{mc}}, c_{t-(n_{mc}-1)}, \ldots, c_{t-2})$, then the generation of the keystream can be denoted as:

$$z_{t+1} = f(S_t, p_t \oplus z_t),$$

and the internal state is updated at the same time:

$$f(S_t, p_t \oplus z_t) \rightarrow S_{t+1}, p_{t+1} \oplus z_{t+1}. \tag{8}$$

Hence an attack against SSSCs can be regarded as an attack against SCHs from Eq. (7) and (8).

An attack against an SSSC which controls the keystream or ciphertext with the fed-back ciphertext should be considered. If there is an attack such that identical ciphertexts can be obtained from different plaintexts, this attack can be converted to the collision attack against SCH. Moreover, if the adversary can set the ciphertext arbitrarily, it is considered to be a second preimage attack.

4.2   Collision Attacks

We consider collision attacks against each phase; the message injection, blank rounds, and the hash generation in an SCH.

Message Injection.   We set the message difference which is canceled after all message bits are input to the internal state in the attack against message injection. Let M and M' be a pair of collision messages. Then for the two internal states S_{msg} and S'_{msg}, $S_{msg} = S'_{msg}$ holds and no input exists except the output feedback after the message injection. Hence $S_{blk} = S'_{blk}$ and $H = H'$ are obtained.

Blank Rounds.   In the collision attack against blank rounds, the difference canceled during the blank rounds is set to the pair of messages. Suppose two internal states S_{blk}, S'_{blk} are obtained after applying blank rounds to S_{msg}, S'_{msg}. The collision attack against blank rounds is successful if $S_{blk} = S'_{blk}$.

First, an adversary searches for a point at which two internal states collide; we call this point c. Once internal states pass point c during j times blank rounds, then the internal states remain the same for the rest of the blank rounds, and this leads to a collision. Set two internal states S_{msg}, S'_{msg} which pass the point c at i-th clock of blank rounds, and derive two messages M, M' from S_{msg}, S'_{msg}. Since the adversary has j choices for i, one point c means j collision pairs.

Hash Generation.   First, an adversary has to find the difference Δ_{blk} which is canceled during $f(0, S_t, 0) \rightarrow S_{t+1}, o_{t+1}$. Second, he has to find the difference Δ_{msg} which leads to Δ_{blk}. Then he derives collision messages M, M' from S_{msg}, S'_{msg}.

Multi-collision Attack.   A. Joux [8] presented a multi-collision attack on iterated hash functions. Constructing 2^t collisions only costs t times as much as an ordinary collision.

4.3 Second Preimage Attacks

As second preimage attacks, attacks on message injection, blank rounds, and hash generation have to be considered.

Message Injection. In the second preimage attack against message injection, an adversary tries to find another message M' which satisfies $S_{msg} = S'_{msg}$ for the given message M. Two internal states derived from two messages are identical and so are the hash values.

Blank Rounds. By applying j clocks of blank rounds internal states S_{blk}, S'_{blk} are obtained from S_{msg}, S'_{msg}. If blank rounds have collision in them, a second preimage attack becomes possible. Similar to the collision attack, an adversary searches for the point c. Given the internal state S_{msg}, and it passes the point c during j clocks of blank rounds, then another internal state S'_{msg} can be found. Thus a second preimage attack against blank rounds can be performed.

Hash Generation. Suppose that h-bit hash is generated and the internal state is updated every one clock of the hash generation. If $|S| > |H|$, then collision occurs by compressing the $|S|$-bit internal state to the $|H|$-bit hash. By using this property, a second preimage attack becomes possible. Specifically, derive internal states S_{blk} and S'_{blk} for given H then a second preimage of M can be found by inverting blank rounds and the message injection.

4.4 Preimage Attacks

Preimage attacks consist of three phases: against the hash generation, blank rounds, and message injection.

In hash generation, since the $|S|$-bit internal state is compressed into the $|H|$-bit hash, it is impossible to derive all bits on S_{blk} only from H.

An adversary tries to invert blank rounds to derive S_{msg} from S_{blk}. Let p be the probability at which all $|S|$ bits of the internal state can be correctly guessed by going through one clock of blank rounds in reverse order. Then the probability to derive S_{msg} from S_{blk} is given as p^j.

The adversary derives the initial state S_0 from the internal state after the message injection S_{msg} in the preimage attack against message injection. Since all bits of S_{msg} are known at this point, it would be possible to guess a message M from S_{msg}.

4.5 Length-Extension Attacks

The adversary has to compute the hash value $x = H(M||y)$ without M. Thus, the adversary tries to obtain S_{msg} or S_{blk} for the message $M||y$ using the hash value $H(M)$.

5 Constructing a Secure SCH

In this section, we propose a construction of an SCH which has collision, second preimage, and preimage resistance.

5.1   Collision Resistance

We discuss collision resistance and collision resistant SCHs.

Collision Resistant SCH. We consider the following three cases as collision attacks against SCHs:

1. Against message injection
   Decide message difference which leads to an identical internal state after all message bits are injected.
2. Against blank rounds
   The internal state difference caused by messages is canceled during blank rounds.
3. Against hash generation
   The difference given by messages goes through blank rounds and is canceled during hash generation.

Theorem 1. *Suppose* $|S| > |H|$. *Given the collision-resistant message injection, SCHs constructed with blank rounds whose period of the transition of the internal state is longer than* $2^{|H|}$ *and hash generation which uses the whole internal state to derive the hash value. Then such SCHs are collision resistant.*

Proof. It is obvious that the condition $|S| > |H|$ is required. SCHs which satisfy lemmas 1, 2, and 3 are secure against case 1, 2, and 3 attacks. Therefore these SCHs are collision resistant.

Lemma 1. *If a message injection has collision resistance, then SCHs can withstand a case 1 attack.*

Proof. If there is a collision attack, which is more efficient than a birthday attack, targeting the internal state after message injection, then an adversary can find two different messages M, M' which have the same internal states $S_{msg} = S'_{msg}$. With two identical internal states after the message injection, internal states during blank rounds and hash generation must be also identical and two hash values collide. Hence message injection has to be collision resistant.

Lemma 2. *If the assumption in Lemma 1 holds and the internal state transition during blank rounds is updated cyclically and has a period of* $2^{|H|}$ *or longer, SCHs are secure against case 1 and 2 attacks.*

Proof. If the internal state transition during blank rounds is cyclic and its period is $2^{|H|}$ or longer, there are at least $2^{|H|}$ candidates for the value of the internal state. Therefore the computational cost required for the collision attack must exceed $2^{|H|/2}$. Furthermore, as the internal state is not compressed in blank rounds, collision resistance of blank rounds is guaranteed.

Hence the assumption of Lemma 1 holds and transition of the internal state in blank rounds has longer period than $2^{|H|}$, SCHs are secure against case 1 and 2 attacks.

Lemma 3. *If assumptions in Lemma 2 hold and the hash value is affected by the whole internal state, SCHs are secure against case 1, 2, and 3 attacks.*

Proof. In the hash generation, if all bits of the internal state affect the hash value, any difference of the internal state is not canceled, and the slight difference of the internal state invokes significant changes in the hash value. This ensures that the hash generation is collision resistant.

Hence if assumptions of Lemma 1 and 2 hold and the hash value is affected by the whole internal state, SCHs are secure against case 1, 2, and 3 attacks.

Condition for a Collision Resistant SCH. Here we discuss how to build a collision resistant stream cipher function which satisfies the condition we presume to prove Theorem 1.

- **Collision Resistant Message Injection**

  Golić's construction updates the internal state of the word size by XORing a message block with feedback of the stream cipher. Generally the word size is the same as the message block size; hence an adversary can fully control the internal state by tweaking the message, due to slow diffusion of the message into the internal state. It is difficult for the message injection phase to be collision resistant, and this is the reason why Golić's construction uses the message twice.

  Boole updates three accumulators during the message injection phase; however, outputs of accumulators to the shift register can be controlled. In order for the message injection phase to be collision resistant, a non-linear function or multiple outputs to the internal state are required. The non-linear function avoids to output the same message difference as injected at the internal state.

  Suppose that an x-bit internal state can be controlled by an x-bit message and this operation does not affect other bits, then the whole internal state can be controlled with $|S|/x$-bit message. Hence multiple bits of the internal state have to be influenced by one bit message. In addition to this, the message needs to be used more than once to avoid the internal state being controlled.

  By fixing the internal state of the stream cipher function, the computational cost of attacks can be reduced. This method is applied by the attack against Boole [14]. Hence the security of an SCH is greatly dependent on whether the adversary can control the internal state or not. We suppose that the message is input into the internal state by xoring with the value in the internal state. Here one bit message is xored with n bits of the internal state at equal intervals. Then the adversary can control up to an $|S|/n$-bit internal state and a computational cost for a collision attack is given by,

$$2^{\frac{|S|-|S|/n}{2}} = 2^{\frac{|S|(n-1)}{2n}} \geq 2^{|H|/2}, \tag{9}$$

$$|S|(n-1) \geq n|H|. \tag{10}$$

  It can be shown that the fewer points that are used in the message injection, the less computational cost is required from Eq. (9). When $n = 1$, the Eq. (10) does not hold. Therefore n has to be equal to or greater than 2.

- **Collision Resistant Blank Rounds**

  Suppose that the transition of the internal state in blank rounds has the period which is longer than $2^{|H|}$. If the internal state after the message injection S_{msg} is different, then the internal state after blank rounds S_{blk} is also different, since the number of blank rounds j ($j < 2^{|H|}$) is independent of the message length. Hence the difference in the internal state is not canceled during blank rounds. The transition of the internal state in blank rounds does not always have the period longer than $2^{|H|}$ in order to satisfy the collision resistance. If the period i of the operations performed in blank rounds is larger than the number of blank rounds j and the transition does not have the collision point of the internal state, then such blank rounds imply collision resistance. In order for blank rounds to have the period longer than $2^{|H|}$, a linear feedback shift register (LFSR) of maximum length sequence can be used as one of option. However LFSRs are vulnerable to correlation attacks, hence other approaches should be considered.

Blank rounds with $i > j$ ensure the collision resistance and second preimage resistance of blank rounds.

– **Collision Resistant Hash Generation**
  The internal state is compressed to derive the hash value in the hash generation. In this process, all bits of the internal state have to affect the hash value, otherwise collisions can occur by putting differences on bits which do not affect the hash value. In order for the hash value to be affected by the whole internal state, more than one bit of the state has to be used to generate a bit of hash value. This can be easily achieved with an n-to-1 filter function. As an example, suppose the internal state size is double the hash size. Then two internal state bits have to be used to generate a 1-bit hash.

Multi-collision Resistance. Here we give a theorem and proof that collision resistant SCHs are secure against multi-collision attacks.

Theorem 2. *Collision resistant SCHs are also multi-collision resistant.*

Proof. Since the internal state size is larger than the hash size. If the internal state of the stream cipher w is large enough, there is no efficient way to find the internal state collision, hence a multi-collision attack does not affect the security of SCHs.

5.2 Second Preimage Resistance

In this section, we consider constructions of second preimage resistant SCHs.

Theorem 3. *Collision resistant hash functions are also second preimage resistant.*

Proof. Generally a collision resistant hash function is also second preimage resistant [13]. A SCH, which satisfies Theorem 1, would be second preimage resistant. Hence collision resistant SCHs imply second preimage resistant SCHs.

5.3 Preimage Resistance

In this section, a preimage attack and preimage resistance will be explained.

Preimage Resistant SCH. Preimage attack against SCH consists of following three steps:

1. Against hash generation
   Find the internal state S_{blk} from the hash value H.
2. Against blank rounds
   Find the internal state S_{msg} from S_{blk}.
3. Against message injection
   Derive the message M from the internal state S_{msg}.

Theorem 4. *If the computational cost of deriving the internal state S_{msg} from S_{blk} is more than $2^{|H|}$, or $|S| > |H|$, then SCHs have preimage resistance.*

Proof. SCHs which satisfy lemmas 4 or 5 are secure against attacks in steps 1 or 2, respectively. When an adversary tries to find a preimage of the message, the adversary has to compute steps 1 to 3, which are described at the beginning of this section. We assumed that $|S| > |H|$ in Theorem 1, therefore step 1 of the attack is infeasible. Hence, collision resistant SCHs imply preimage resistant SCHs.

Lemma 4. *If the internal state size $|S|$ is larger than the hash size, $|S| > |H|$, then the SCH is secure against the step 1 of the attack.*

Proof. The information of $|S| - |H|$ bits of the internal state will be perished by compressing the $|S|$-bit internal state to the $|H|$-bit hash value. Preimage resistance holds because of this property.

Lemma 5. *If blank rounds have preimage resistance, then the SCH is secure against step 2 of the attack.*

Proof. Let the probability of recovering the internal state by inverting one clock of blank rounds be p, then inverting j-clock of blank rounds and recovering S_{msg} from S_{blk} can be denoted as p^j. If $p^j < 2^{-|H|}$ holds, then blank rounds are preimage resistant.

Since S_{msg} is known, it is possible to invert message injection to gain the input message, because we have to assume the case where $|M| > |S|$ as well as the case where $|M| \leq |S|$. Hence, message injection with preimage resistance hardly exists.

Condition for a Preimage Resistant SCH. Here we discuss how to build a preimage resistant stream cipher function which satisfies the condition we presume to prove Theorem 4.

There are two ways for blank rounds to be preimage resistant.

1. Collision occurs during blank rounds.
2. For j-clock blank rounds, $p^j < 2^{-|H|}$ holds, where p is the probability of reverting one-clock of blank rounds and guessing the internal state correctly.

The existence of collision in blank rounds means they are vulnerable to collision and second preimage attacks. Hence, method 2 is appropriate and the stream cipher function has to satisfy $p^j < 2^{-|H|}$ with the probability p and the number of blank rounds j.

The existence of collision is inevitable if the size of the internal state is larger than that of the hash value. However, the collision ensures preimage resistance in the hash generation.

5.4   Length-Extension Security

We give the theorem and proof that a preimage resistant SCH is secure against the length-extension attack.

Theorem 5. *Preimage resistant SCHs are secure against a length-extension attack.*

Proof. In SCHs, the hash value $H(M\|z)$ is computed independently of the hash value $H(M)$, because of blank rounds. If an adversary cannot obtain M from $H(M)$ efficiently, the adversary cannot compute $H(M\|z)$. Thus, an SCH is secure against a length-extension attack, where the SCH has preimage resistance.

6   Discussion

The attack against Boole exploits the fact that an adversary can easily cause collisions of the internal state by tweaking messages. Moreover, it also exploits the fact that the internal state S_{blk} which produces the desired hash value can be derived. In fact, the stream cipher used in Boole does not satisfy our criterion, i.e., "the message injection has to be collision resistant". Thus, this evidence supports the feasibility of our criterion.

Relations to the attacks against stream ciphers also have to be considered. Internal state recovery attacks such as guess-and-determine attacks [3] and correlation attacks [7,11] obtain internal state bits from keystream bits. These attacks can be used for preimage attacks on SCHs. That is, an attacker can obtain internal state bits from the hash value if the stream cipher used for the SCH is vulnerable against an internal state recovery attack. Where we select a stream cipher algorithm for constructing an SCH, it is a mandatory condition that the stream cipher is secure against existing attacks. Recovering the internal state of the stream cipher function from h-bit keystream incurs a computational cost of at least $2^{|H|}$. If there is an attack which recovers the internal state of the stream cipher function with a computation cost of less than $2^{|H|}$ computational cost, this attack can lead to a pre-image attack against the SCH.

Distinguishing attacks [4] are another possible approach for recovering internal state bits. A linear approximation of the nonlinear process is obtained by a distinguishing attack and it is applicable to recovering internal state bits. The internal state bits can be determined to solve a system of linear equations. The attacks require a much longer keystream than the h-bit hash value, hence, it is rarely applied to a pre-image attack on the SCH.

Next, we discuss relationships between two specific attacks on stream ciphers and our criteria for constructing SCHs. Two types of attack as shown in Sect. 4 are relevant to collisions in the blank round. For example, the chosen IV attack against Py and Pypy corresponds to the collision attack against blank rounds in an SCH. In the chosen IV attack against Py and Pypy, identical keystreams can be generated from different IVs. Keystreams correspond to hash values and IVs correspond to internal states. Initialization of Py and Pypy and blank rounds in an SCH are basically the same operations, hence this attack can be applied to collision and second preimage attack against an SCH. From this view-point, we should use a stream cipher that is secure against the attacks when constructing an SCH. Furthermore, security against these attacks is strongly related to our criterion; blank rounds have to be executed as the transition of the internal state has the longer period than $2^{|H|}$.

An attack in which the adversary tries to control the output keystream by inputting a certain ciphertext can be considered to be an attack against an SSSC [9,10]. This type of attacks can be applied to attacks against blank rounds of SCHs as discussed in Sect. 4.1. Hence, the stream cipher functions have to resist this type of attacks in order to be collision and second preimage resistant.

7   Conclusions

In this paper, we introduced a model of SCH, consisting of a pre-computation function and a stream cipher function. Then we defined the stream cipher function with pre-computation as the one which updates an internal state and outputs a hash value from three inputs: a message, an internal state, and feedback. Then we showed that the keystream feedback mode and the self-synchronizing stream cipher are equivalent to SCHs. Therefore, attacks against these stream ciphers can be various attacks against SCHs. Furthermore we described each phase of SCH with the function we defined, and considered attacks against each phase. As a result of our work, the following necessary conditions can be obtained:

- $|S| > |H|$ is required for collision, second preimage, and preimage resistance.
- The computational cost of the collision attack on message injection has to be equal or more than $2^{|H|/2}$, and an adversary is not able to control the internal state of the stream cipher function.
- The internal state transition during blank rounds has a period of at least $2^{|H|}$.
- Deriving the internal state after the message injection by going through one clock of blank rounds in reverse order incurs a computational cost of $2^{|H|}$.
- When one bit message is xored with n bits of the internal state at equal intervals, then the condition $|S|(n - 1) \geq n|H|$ is required for message injection to be collision resistant, where n is the number of bits of the internal state which are xored with one bit message.

In this paper we proposed the conditions for secure SCHs. We showed that conditions for second preimage and preimage resistant SCH are included in the conditions for a collision resistant SCH. Furthermore, the condition for length-extension security is included in the condition for the preimage resistant SCH. Thus, we can focus on the conditions for the collision resistant SCH, when we design the SCH.

References

1. Biham, E., Seberry, J.: Py: A Fast and Secure Stream Cipher using Rolling Arrays. eSTREAM, ECRYPT Stream Cipher Project (2005)
2. Biham, E., Seberry, J.: Pypy: Another Version of Py. eSTREAM, ECRYPT Stream Cipher Project (2006)
3. Bleichenbacher, D., Patel, S.: Sober Cryptanalysis. In: Knudsen, L.R. (ed.) FSE 1999. LNCS, vol. 1636, pp. 305–316. Springer, Heidelberg (1999)

4. Coppersmith, D., Halevi, S., Jutla, C.S.: Cryptanalysis of Stream Ciphers with Linear Masking. In: Yung, M. (ed.) CRYPTO 2002. LNCS, vol. 2442, pp. 515–532. Springer, Heidelberg (2002)

5. Ekdahl, P., Johansson, T.: A New Version of the Stream Cipher SNOW. In: Nyberg, K., Heys, H.M. (eds.) SAC 2002. LNCS, vol. 2595, pp. 47–61. Springer, Heidelberg (2003)

6. Golić, J.D.: Modes of Operation of Stream Ciphers. In: Stinson, D.R., Tavares, S. (eds.) SAC 2000. LNCS, vol. 2012, pp. 233–247. Springer, Heidelberg (2001)

7. Hawkes, P., Rose, G.G.: Guess-and-Determine Attacks on SNOW. In: Nyberg, K., Heys, H.M. (eds.) SAC 2002. LNCS, vol. 2595, pp. 37–46. Springer, Heidelberg (2003)

8. Joux, A.: Multicollisions in Iterated Hash Functions. Application to Cascaded Constructions. In: Franklin, M. (ed.) CRYPTO 2004. LNCS, vol. 3152, pp. 306–316. Springer, Heidelberg (2004)

9. Joux, A., Muller, F.: Loosening the KNOT. In: Johansson, T. (ed.) FSE 2003. LNCS, vol. 2887, pp. 87–99. Springer, Heidelberg (2003)

10. Joux, A., Muller, F.: Chosen-Ciphertext Attacks Against MOSQUITO. In: Robshaw, M.J.B. (ed.) FSE 2006. LNCS, vol. 4047, pp. 390–404. Springer, Heidelberg (2006)

11. Meier, W., Staffelbach, O.: Fast Correlation Attacks on Stream Ciphers. In: Günther, C.G. (ed.) EUROCRYPT 1988. LNCS, vol. 330, pp. 301–314. Springer, Heidelberg (1988)

12. Mendel, F., Nad, T., Schläffer, M.: Collision Attack on Boole. In: Abdalla, M., Pointcheval, D., Fouque, P.-A., Vergnaud, D. (eds.) ACNS 2009. LNCS, vol. 5536, pp. 369–381. Springer, Heidelberg (2009)

13. Menezes, A.J., van Oorschot, P.C., Vanstone, S.A.: Handbook of Applied Cryptography. CRC Press (1996)

14. Nikolić, I.: Preimage attack on Boole-n. The ECRYPT Hash Function (2008), http://ehash.iaik.tugraz.at/uploads/2/2f/Boole.pdf

15. NIST. Secure hash standard. FIPS180-1 (1995)

16. Rivest, R.: The MD5 message digest algorithm. RFC1321 (1992)

17. Rose, G.G.: Design and primitive specification for Boole. submission to NIST (2008), http://seer-grog.net/BoolePaper.pdf

18. Wang, X., Yin, Y.L., Yu, H.: Finding Collisions in the Full SHA-1. In: Shoup, V. (ed.) CRYPTO 2005. LNCS, vol. 3621, pp. 17–36. Springer, Heidelberg (2005)

19. Wang, X., Yu, H.: How to Break MD5 and Other Hash Functions. In: Cramer, R. (ed.) EUROCRYPT 2005. LNCS, vol. 3494, pp. 19–35. Springer, Heidelberg (2005)

20. Wu, H., Preneel, B.: Differential Cryptanalysis of the Stream Ciphers Py, Py6 and Pypy. In: Naor, M. (ed.) EUROCRYPT 2007. LNCS, vol. 4515, pp. 276–290. Springer, Heidelberg (2007)

Flexible Anonymous Subscription Schemes

María Isabel González Vasco[1], Somayeh Heidarvand[2,*], and Jorge L. Villar[2,**]

[1] Univ. Rey Juan Carlos, Madrid, Spain
[2] Univ. Politècnica de Catalunya, Barcelona, Spain
mariaisabel.vasco@urjc.es, {somayeh,jvillar}@ma4.upc.edu

Abstract. We propose a simple and efficient *Subscription Scheme*, allowing a set of users to anonymously pay for and request access to different services offered by a number of service providers. Using an e-cash system in such a scenario, the identity of the user would be hid into the e-coin in order to preserve its anonymity. Providing an additional triggering mechanism that opens this identity in case of double spending, also the service provider will be protected against fraud. Note that in traditional e-cash universality of the coin is required, however, in our scenario, the use of the token is completely determined at issuing time (yet this final aim remains hidden to the issuing authority). This allows for our construction, in which moreover fraud detection here implies no loss of anonymity; as we make access tokens independent of the owner in a quite simple and efficient way. On the other hand, if different usages of the same token are allowed, these are fully traceable by the service providers. An application to e-polling protocols is also given.

Keywords: Anonymous authentication, Blind signatures, Clone detection, Traceability, e-Polling.

1 Introduction

Anonymity in internet transactions is essential to prevent critical personal data to be inadvertently leaked to unwanted people. As an example, an eavesdropper could learn some private information about health, consumer habits or preferences of people if their identity is revealed during internet transactions. However, anonymity could be abused to make criminal acts unlinkable to individuals. To prevent such abuse, in some e-cash protocols the identity of a user can be opened under very special circumstances (*e.g.*, double spending of electronic cash).

In traditional e-coins, the tradeoff between anonymity and fraud-detection (*i.e.*, double spending or over spending) is solved by hiding the identity of the user into the coin and providing an additional triggering mechanism that opens this identity in case of double spending. Hence, fraud detection implies loss of anonymity. This seems to be a somewhat natural solution when universality of the coin is required (*i.e.*, the use of the coin is not determined at the time the coin is generated). Double spending can only be detected (yet not prevented) by the issuer (bank). Otherwise, all merchants would have to collaborate to check for the freshness of every coin.

---

* Partially supported by the Spanish CRM.
** Partially supported by the Spanish research project MTM2009-07694.

M.S. Obaidat, G.A. Tsihrintzis, and J. Filipe (Eds.): ICETE 2010, CCIS 222, pp. 203–219, 2012.
© Springer-Verlag Berlin Heidelberg 2012

Nevertheless, in some real life environments (*e.g.*, online games) the potential damage produced by a dishonest user is very limited, and it is often enough to guarantee some sort of "cloning detection" to prevent overuse of credit vouchers, without providing any identity-escrow mechanism. Indeed, this relaxation allows for simpler and more efficient payment schemes for many concrete applications.

1.1   Our Contribution

In this paper we describe *subscription schemes* which allow a set of users to buy access to a limited set of services, in a perfectly anonymous and efficient way. This access is paid to an issuing authority that dispenses *connection tokens*, which usage is completely determined at issuing time. More precisely, tokens are differentiated in terms of their service providers and validity period (so, time is divided into different time slots). This implies that each service provider can locally and non-interactively take control on the different tokens spent in each time slot, thus rejecting any attempt of token misuse (including over use, incorrect service provider or incorrect time slot).

Following this approach, fraud-detection does not require identification of the owner, and then no loss of anonymity is implied. This will allow for a design in which tokens are independent of any private information identifying the owner in a quite simple and efficient way.

Note that it is reasonable to expect that some information about the user identity will be learned by the issuer agency (as indeed payment is a part of the token issuing protocol). However, it is our goal that this information cannot be linked either to the token itself or to the service the token is intended for. Thus, we will impose that the view of the issuing authority must be independent of the value of the issued token. As a result, no collusion of the issuer agency and one or more service providers will learn any information about the token owner.

Payment is organized in such a way that at the end of a time slot, service providers send the collected tokens to the issuer to be paid for the offered service. Unused tokens can similarly be refunded to the users upon request. Thus, the subscription scheme must ensure that no collusion of users and service providers can forge new valid tokens (not issued by the agency) and they will furthermore not succeed in getting paid more than once for each issued token.

Based on well-known primitives (such as secure blind signatures and encryption schemes) we provide a new simple and practical scheme for handling access policies to on-line services. Our design basically works as follows: Users obtain from an issuing agency some tokens, consisting of a blind signature on a message including a fresh public key (for a signature scheme), the identity of a service provider and a time slot. To access the service, the user signs a random nonce, with respect to the public key contained in the token, and sends it along with the token itself to the service provider. With this simple setting we achieve:

- Perfect user anonymity with respect to the services he purchased (even when some service providers and the issuer collude).
- Unforgeability of tokens by a collusion of dishonest users and service providers.
- Undeniability of purchased services; valid access tokens cannot be repudiated by the issuing authority.

- Efficient token management; time is divided into slots.
- Efficient access to services for users.
- Very flexible access management for the service provider. (Token overuse is not only detected but immediately prevented by the service provider.)

Maybe the main limitation of our scheme resides in the complete traceability of the different accesses with the same token to the same service within the same time slot. However, this behavior is desirable if the service requires storing some settings (like preferences, history, etc.) for each (anonymized) user account.

All in all, our protocol is suitable in many real life scenarios, such as on-line games and service subscriptions (to on-line press, digital libraries, music collections, etc.) and could also be applied to audience control in metering schemes or efficient e-polling schemes.

1.2   Road Map

The paper is organized as follows: we start by briefly reviewing related prior work in Section 2. Then, Section 3 is devoted to the introduction of what we call *Subscription Schemes*, making precise the involved entities, modeling their interaction and defining the security properties we aim at. Our basic construction is described in Section 4. In Section 5, we address some efficiency issues. We also describe some particular scenarios in which no trust on the service providers is required and some hints about how to manage different service access policies in Section 6. In addition, an application of the proposed scheme to e-polling protocols is also given in that section. Since our proposal is based on the use of a blind signature scheme, we give the necessary related definitions in the Appendix.

2   Related Work

Anonymity in commercial transactions (also known in some papers as untraceability) has been firstly introduced by Chaum in the seminal paper on blind signatures [1]. Chaum's *electronic coins* were defined as a value together with a signature from the issuing bank, which was to be withdrawn and spent by the user and subsequently deposited by the shop in the bank (thus, correctness of payment is checked on-line). In that setting, blind signature schemes are introduced as a cryptographic tool to allow the bank constructing electronic coins, in such a way that he will not be able to recognize them later. Hence it will not be able to link a coin with the user that requested it, or identify whether two payments have been made by the same user.

Subsequent work aimed at electronic coins that could be used in an off-line setting. Namely, the shop will only deposit coins every now and then, and if a client paid with the same coin twice, his identity would be revealed. Several solutions based on RSA and Schnorr signatures can be found in [2,3,4].

In some applications, total anonymity of electronic cash is not desirable (for instance, it could be used as an effective method for "whitening" black money). Several proposals for *partial* or *revokable anonymity* can be found in the literature (*e.g.*, [5,6,7]).

In these schemes anonymity may be revoked by a Trusted Third Party under certain circumstances.

Recently, some solutions in the literature with how to prove membership to a group in an anonymous way have been proposed in the context of group and ring signatures (*e.g.*, [8,9]). However, as far as we know, in that scenario no protection against double-use of access credentials has been considered. Damgård *et al.* [10] introduced at Eurocrypt 2006 so called *unclonable group identification schemes*; which allow an honest participant to anonymously and unlinkably authenticate himself as member of a designated group. Moreover, such scheme discloses the identity of any participant that "clones" himself and connects twice with the same keying material. In their paper, Damgård *et al.* give a generic yet inefficient construction. They also describe a concrete instance, which employs some new zero-knowledge techniques. Even though the gain in efficiency is significant, still the resulting scheme is computationally rather expensive. Subsequent work of Camenish *et al.* [11] considers a slightly different goal; each participant should obtain, upon connection with an issuer/authority, enough information to connect k times to a service (anonymously and unlinkably). Again, overusing this private connection information leads to the identification of the fraudulent participant. Their solution, though more practical than that of Damgård *et al.*, is still rather costly—in particular if we look at the number of operations a user has to preform each time he connects—.

Closer to our work, recently, Blanton [12] proposes a subscription scheme which is similar in spirit to our construction; however, no separation between service provider and issuer is made, which in particular forces the service provider to store all access tokens ever presented. Moreover, it is computationally more costly, as each access involves an interactive zero knoledge proof (this however could, as noted by the author, maybe be replaced using recent work of Groth and Sahai [13]). Similarly, Razman and Ruhl [14] put forward a model for subscription-based services which is less flexible than ours; at it, each user obtains a fixed number of accesses to the service, but without expiration date.

3 Subscription Schemes

We start by giving a formal description of what we call a *Subscription Scheme*.

3.1 Involved Entities

Our *subscription scheme* involves different entities, modelled by probabilistic polynomial-time interactive Turing machines:

- A set of *service providers*, $\mathcal{SP} = \{\mathsf{SP}_1, \ldots, \mathsf{SP}_n\}$, each of them offering a concrete service managed according to their own policy. This policy must specify the duration of subscriptions to this service, using as time reference different time slots and possibly, also session identifiers distinguishing different sessions per slot. We assume this providers will never deny access upon request with a valid token.[1]

---

[1] This is quite a natural semi-honest assumption, as it is in their own interest to gain customer loyalty. See Section 6 for some ways to remove this assumption.

– A set of *users*, $\mathcal{U} = \{U_1, \ldots, U_m\}$, which may access some of the services.
– An *issuing authority* IA who certifies all information about the services, and dispense subscription tokens to users upon request (and payment).
– A *trusted third party* TP which will be invoked by a user in case he wants to be refunded for an unused token. This trusted party can also be used to guarantee the fairness of all paying protocols in the system. We may assume the TP is connected with each user via a private and authentic channel.

3.2 Scheme Syntax

Now, the interaction between these entities is specified by the following algorithms and protocols, which define the *subscription scheme*. Here, for simplicity we assume that every token allows the user for a single access to a service. For other access policies (*e.g.*, multiple accesses with the same token) see Section 6.

Start-up Algorithms. They are only run during a set up phase, and provide all involved entities, on the input of the security parameter and other system parameters, with all the public/private key pairs needed for the scheme.

– IAKeyGen. Run once by the IA; it outputs the IA's public/secret keys.
– SPKeyGen. Run once by each service provider SP_j; it outputs the corresponding public/secret keys.
– PublishCatalogue. Run once by the IA; on the input of the public keys and some information from the service providers it outputs an authenticated catalogue (*e.g.*, signed by the IA), including at least all service providers' identifiers and public keys, the service descriptions and access conditions.

Subscription Protocols. We assume that the catalogue of services and the current time slot are always included as common inputs to all protocols. We also assume that all entities are able to verify the authenticity of all public keys. Actually, only IA's public key needs to be certified externally. [2]

– VerifyToken. Run by any party, on the input of a token x a service provider identifier SP and a time slot t it outputs a single bit indicating the validity of x. This auxiliary algorithm will be used in the protocols described below.
– ObtainToken. This protocol is run by a user U and the issuing authority IA. User's private input will include a service provider's name SP and a time slot identifier t' (not necessarily the current one). As private output, U will either receive an error message $\perp$ or a valid token to access the service offered by SP on time slot t', according to the service provider's particular access policy. To ensure this, U might execute VerifyToken at some point.

Typically, an optimistic fair e-cash protocol is involved in this step since at this point the user pays for the service requested. This protocol requires the intervention of a Trusted Party (TP), in order to guarantee its fairness. At this, some information

---

[2] Note that service providers' public keys are included in the catalogue of services, thus they are automatically certified by the IA.

about the identity of the user might be leaked, but the IA shall get no information at all about SP or t'.

Note that the IA will always get the information corresponding to the amount paid by the user in each transaction, but we want that this is the only information he may have in order to link user identities with requested services. Bearing this in mind, in the sequel we may assume all services offered at a given time slot have the same price.

- AccessService. This protocol is run by a user U and a service provider SP. User's private input includes the token, and SP's private input is sk_{SP}.

  User U requests access to the service offered by SP. He gets as output a denial or acceptance message, depending on the validity of the token, and is or not allowed into the service accordingly. As we already noted, tokens recognized as valid will be always accepted by SP. At this, the private output to SP will include some information about U's token, which, if required, could be used as a proof of service in front of the Trusted Party.

Payment Protocols

- Pay. This protocol is invoked by each SP at the end of every time slot, and involves him and the IA. SP sends part of the private outputs collected after successful AccessService executions, including a list of the collected tokens, to the IA, to be paid for the offered service. At the end of the protocol, SP gets paid for the list of tokens and the IA keeps his private output as a receipt of payment, typically involving some function of SP's private keying material and the tokens. Eventually, IA could deny payment. Namely, whenever SP tries to execute the protocol twice in the same time slot, or if some of the tokens are invalid or have been refunded. An optimistic fair e-cash protocol is used here, and the same TP will guarantee the fairness.
- Refund. A user U executes this protocol with the Trusted Party and possibly SP and IA. U's private input includes an unused token, valid for the current time slot and service provider SP. If TP finds that the token is valid and unused, then the user gets refunded (from IA but via TP) for his payment. Both SP and IA will get payment receipts as private output, which SP will use to reject any further attempt to use the refunded token and IA will use to prove TP that the token has been already refunded. Notice that we prefer not to rely on TP's state. Unused tokens not claimed for refund by the user are on the benefit of the IA.

3.3   Security Model

We aim at providing the following properties:

Correctness. If all the involved entities act honestly then: Every service provider SP must grant access to any user U in the execution of AccessService within a time slot t, whenever U uses as private input a token generated by ObtainToken for SP and t. And in all executions of Pay, IA must accept and pay for all tokens collected by SP within a given time slot.

Fairness for the User U*. Recall that, by assumption, a service provider SP will deny service to U* only on input of an invalid token. An adversary corrupting all service providers, any set of users (not including the target user U*) and the IA, has only negligible probability of winning the following game: U*, who acts honestly, runs a polynomial number of instances of the protocol ObtainToken to get tokens for some service providers and time slots. Concurrently, U* runs a polynomial number of instances of AccessService with some of the service providers, and also runs Refund with the Trusted Party giving as private input valid tokens rejected by service providers (this can only happen in case the adversary was able to construct the same token and used it before, exhausting its validity). The adversary wins the game if for a valid token x, a service provider denies access to U* on input x, and moreover, the Trusted Party rejects U*'s execution of Refund against that service provider on the same token x.

Fairness for the Service Provider SP*. Basically, we demand that a service provider will always be paid for all services offered within a given time slot. This is formalized in the following game:

An adversary corrupting a set of users, some service providers (others than SP*) and the IA, has negligible probability of winning the following game: Some corrupt and uncorrupt users run several instances of the protocols ObtainToken and AccessService with SP*, and of Refund against SP*. Moreover, SP* runs several instances of Pay (each one at the end of a different time slot). The adversary wins the game if, impersonating the IA, he denies payment to SP* in a Pay execution, and also convinces the Trusted Party that he already paid SP* in that time slot, or that some of SP*'s tokens are invalid or have been refunded.

Fairness for the Issuing Authority IA. Consider an adversary corrupting a set of users and some (possibly all) service providers. Let n_t be the number of tokens sold by the IA until the end of time slot t, and let n'_t the total number of tokens paid (directly by an execution of Pay or forced by the Trusted Party in Refund) by the IA in all time slots t' such that $t' \leq t$. Then, assuming that a polynomial number of concurrent executions of ObtainToken, AccessService, Pay and Refund on adaptively chosen inputs occur, the probability that $n'_t > n_t$ is negligible. Essentially, fairness for the IA means that the only valid tokens in the system are the ones generated in a successful execution of ObtainToken, and that the IA will never pay twice for a given token. The first condition can be seen as a kind of token unforgeability, while the second requirement relies on the fairness of Refund and Pay protocols, and on the fact that tokens are bound to specific service providers and time slots.

Anonymity for User's Services. Consider the following indistinguishability game between an adversary $\mathcal{A}$, corrupting all parties (*i.e.*, the IA, all users and all service providers) in the system, and a challenger $\mathcal{C}$.

- $\mathcal{A}$ runs Setup and sends to $\mathcal{C}$ all the public information about the users, the service providers and the IA. During the whole game $\mathcal{A}$ may execute polynomially many instances of the ObtainToken and AccessService protocols. In particular $\mathcal{A}$ learns the user's private output of AccessService.

- $\mathcal{A}$ chooses two (possibly equal) service providers' identities, SP_0 and SP_1, and two (possibly equal) user's identities, U_0 and U_1, and sends the choice to $\mathcal{C}$ along with the internal state of U_0 and U_1.
- $\mathcal{C}$ flips a fair coin $b \in \{0, 1\}$ and prepares himself to run two (possibly concurrent) instances of ObtainToken, one as U_0 and the other as U_1, where $\mathcal{A}$ acts as the IA. To that end, $\mathcal{C}$ marks the protocol instance corresponding to U_0 as the target one, and uses as private input (SP_b, t), where t is the only time slot is considered in this game. The other instance's private input is (SP_{1-b}, t). If $\mathcal{C}$ obtains as outputs two valid tokens, we denote by x_b the one from the target instance of ObtainToken, and the other one by x_{1-b}.
- Once the two instances of ObtainToken terminate, if they were both successful $\mathcal{C}$ (concurrently) runs two instances of AccessService, one for token x_0 with $\mathcal{A}$ acting as SP_0, and the other for token x_1 and SP_1.
  Otherwise, if $\mathcal{C}$ failed to obtain the two valid tokens (even if he got one), he does not run any instance of AccessService.
- Eventually, $\mathcal{A}$ ends the game outputting a bit b'.

The probability that $b' = b$ (case in which $\mathcal{A}$ wins the above game) should be non-negligibly greater that $1/2$.

Although the above is only one of the many possible indistinguishability-like definitions related to the anonymity of service, it can be shown that this notion implies the most general possible definition of anonymity. Namely, from the information available to the IA from ObtainToken instances, and to the service providers from AccessService instances, no polynomial time adversary can distinguish any two possible matchings between both sets of instances.

4   A Basic Scheme

The basic scheme uses a public-key encryption scheme ENC, a blind signature scheme $BSig$ (for a summary of the definition and security of blind signatures, see the Appendix), and basic (general purpose) signature scheme Sig. The $BSig$ protocol is linked to a optimistic fair e-cash protocol in order to guarantee that a user gets a valid blind signature if and only if he pays to the signature issuer. This can be typically done by using the e-cash protocol to fairly send the last signer's message in the blind signing protocol. We assume that in case the user does not pay the signer then he does not receive the last message, so no blind signature is generated. Conversely, the user will not pay if the verification of the blind signature fails. To name this dedicated combination of $BSig$ and a fair e-cash protocol, we will often refer to the *modified blind signature scheme*. Our Basic Construction is explained below:

Set Up. Keys for the IA and all service providers are generated and distributed:

- Each service provider SP_j holds a key pair (pk_{SP_j}, sk_{SP_j}) for the encryption scheme ENC, and another key pair for the signature scheme Sig.
- IA generates signing keys (pk_{IA}, sk_{IA}) for $BSig$. It also signs and publishes the catalogue.

– Each SP maintains a list L_{SP} of accepted tokens [3]. Also, IA and each SP maintain a list of tokens paid for through Refund for the current time slot (denoted, respectively R_{IA} and R_{SP}).

Obtain Token. User U wants to buy access to SP's service in (a future) time slot t.

1. U generates a fresh key pair (y, s) for the basic signature scheme Sig.
2. U obtains from IA a valid[4] blind signature $\sigma = \text{BlindSig}(y||\text{SP}||t)$ and pays for it, by means of the modified blind sign algorithm.
3. U stores the token $x = (y, \text{SP}, t, \sigma)$ and s until the end of slot t.

Verify Token. Given a token $x = (y, \text{SP}, t, \sigma)$, any party can verify its correctness by just verifying that σ is a valid blind signature of $m = y||\text{SP}||t$.

Access Service. User U requests access to the service SP on time slot t :

1. U sends an access request message to SP, involving a random nonce ρ.
2. SP generates a random nonce α and forwards it to U.
3. U computes and sends $c = ENC_{SP}(y||\sigma||\tilde{\sigma})$ to SP, where $\tilde{\sigma} = Sig_s(\alpha||\rho)$.
4. SP decrypts c and parses y, σ and $\tilde{\sigma}$.
5. SP checks that σ is a valid signature of $y||SP||t$ and that $\tilde{\sigma}$ is a valid signature of $\alpha||\rho$ with verification key y.
6. SP also checks that σ is not in the refunded token list R_{SP}.
7. SP looks at the access table for previous usages of y [5] and applies the service terms of use to decide acceptance.
8. If all checks are OK, SP allows U into the server and adds a new row $(\alpha||\rho, y, \sigma, \tilde{\sigma})$ to the access table L_{SP}.

Pay. At the end of the time slot, each SP runs the following protocol:

1. SP sends the list of collected (*i.e.*, valid and not refunded) (y, σ) to IA.
2. IA checks whether he paid SP before in the current time slot. If not, IA checks the validity of all the items in the list for the current time slot, and that none of them have been refunded (looking them at R_{IA}), and pays SP for them via the fair e-cash protocol.
3. IA gets as a receipt SP's signature on the time slot identifier t, and keeps it until the beginning of next time slot.
4. SP resets his access table L_{SP} and the refund table R_{SP}, and enters in a lock state until the beginning of the next time slot.

---

[3] Recall that in the above we are assuming for simplicity the access policy to be "one access per token", otherwise this lists would be configured fitting each concrete access policy.

[4] Here, we impose U does have the ability to actually check the validity of the received token, as it is explicited later in VerifyToken.

[5] Checking for σ would be not enough unless the blind signature is strongly unforgeable, as we need that the adversary cannot produce produce a new signature pair (m, σ), even having different signatures on m at hand.

Refund. User U asks the Trusted Party for an unused token refund.

1. U sends TP the (presumably) unused token $x = (y, \mathsf{SP}, t, \sigma)$.
2. TP checks σ and asks SP for a proof of usage or previous refund.
3. If not locked, SP checks for usages of y in table L_{SP} and sends the corresponding entry $(\alpha \| \rho, \tilde{\sigma})$, if it exists. He also checks if σ is in table R_{SP} and if so, sends the corresponding refund receipt.
4. If in either case TP accepts SP's proof (or if SP in locked), then TP aborts.
5. Otherwise, TP asks IA for refund on $(y, \mathsf{SP}, t, \sigma)$.
6. If IA finds in R_{IA} a receipt of previous refund on the token, then TP aborts.
7. Otherwise, TP sends a receipt (TP's signature on `'refunded'` $\|t\| \mathsf{SP} \| \sigma$) to both SP and IA, and sends back the cash to U.
8. SP and IA add σ and the refund receipt to the refund lists R_{SP} and R_{IA}.

4.1 Security Analysis

Let us now argue our generic construction fulfils the properties listed in Subsection 3.3. At this, we are assuming that the underlying blind signatures scheme $BSig$ has the blindness and non-forgeability property, as defined in the Appendix. Moreover, we assume the encryption scheme ENC to be IND-CCA secure. The basic signature scheme Sig is assumed to be existentially unforgeable under chosen message attacks. Finally, we assume the fairness of the optimistic e-cash protocols used in ObtainToken and Pay.

Correctness. It follows trivially from the correctness of the involved tools $BSig$, Sig and ENC, and the e-cash protocols.

Fairness for the User U^*. Note that the adversary will not be able to replay an eavesdropped connection message c from a previous connection, as c involves a signature of the nonce α that can only be used once. Therefore, the adversary will not succeed in a strategy of "exhausting" the usage of a token legitimately obtained by U^*. As a result, the only case in which fairness for user U^* may be violated is that in which for a valid token x, a corrupt service provider denies access to U^* on input a legitimate c constructed from x and, moreover, the Trusted Party rejects U^*'s execution of Refund against that service provider on that same token x. However, the Trusted Party rejects U^*'s execution of Refund only if the adversary $\mathcal{A}$ defined in Section 3.3 shows him a valid pair $(\alpha \| \rho, \tilde{\sigma})$, where α is a session identifier and $\tilde{\sigma}$ is a basic signature on $\alpha \| \rho$, with respect to the verification key y. But this is only possible if either U^* computed $\tilde{\sigma}$ (so he indeed accessed the service) or $\mathcal{A}$ forged that signature.

Fairness for the Service Provider SP^*. Suppose that an honest service provider SP^* and an adversary $\mathcal{A}$ are playing the game corresponding to the present security notion, as described in Section 3.3. Let $L_{\mathsf{SP}^*} = \{(y_k, \sigma_k, \alpha_k \| \rho_k, \tilde{\sigma}_k)\}$ be the contents of SP^*'s access table at the end of a specific time slot t. Notice that each σ_k is a valid blind signature on $m_k = y_k \| \mathsf{SP}^* \| t$, and all m_k are different. At the end of the time slot, SP^* runs Pay with the adversary, who acts as the IA, for list L_{SP^*}. Assume that $\mathcal{A}$ cheats

SP^* and denies payment. Now SP^* complains to the Trusted Party, by sending him the list L_{SP^*}. As SP^* acts honestly, the Trusted Party is convinced about the validity of the collected tokens. Next, the Trusted Party asks A, who acts as the IA, for both a list of receipts for tokens in L_{SP^*} which have been refunded, and a payment receipt for SP^* and current time slot. Since SP^* acts honestly, there are no unused tokens in L_{SP^*}. Hence, the only way A can show a refund receipt for a token in L_{SP^*} is by forging a signature on the token on behalf of the Trusted Party. Indeed, no used token can be refunded, since during the execution of Refund, the Trusted Authority asks SP^* for a proof of usage of the token, and SP^* answers with a valid pair $(\alpha||\rho, \tilde{\sigma})$, so the Trusted Party denies refunding.

On the other hand, A cannot show a payment receipt for the current time slot, and thus the Trusted Party forces him to pay SP^* for all tokens in L_{SP^*}. Indeed, due to the fairness of the e-cash protocol in Pay, A can only show a payment receipt if he forged one (*i.e.*, he forged a signature by either SP^* or the Trusted Party) or if he successfully ran Pay with SP^* before. But the last situation is impossible, as an honest SP^* runs Pay at most once per time slot.

Fairness for the Issuing Authority IA. Consider a successful adversary A who plays the game defined in Section 3.3. Then, we show a forger F, who internally uses A, winning the blind signature unforgeability game against a challenger C, with a non-negligible probability.

Firstly, the challenger C generates, according to the specification of the blind signature scheme, the system parameters and the public key pk_{BSig}, and sends them to a forger F. Next, F completes the public parameters of the subscription scheme (including the public key of the Trusted Party) and the public key of the (honest) IA, and sends this information to A. Now A computes and sends to F the set of public keys of the service providers, and also a description of the corresponding services. F compiles and signs the catalogue of services and send it back to A. Now A, acting as a (dishonest) user, concurrently runs polynomially many instances of BlindSig with F acting as the IA. A can also run a polynomial number of instances of the protocols Refund and Pay. Here, A takes the roles of both the users and the service providers, while F acts as both the IA and the Trusted Party. During the game, F maintains a list of all valid pairs $(m_k = y_k||SP_k||t_k, \sigma_k)$ of blind signatures and messages collected in all executions of Refund and Pay. As a honest IA he also maintains lists of refunded and paid tokens, and the corresponding receipts, for each service provider, which are needed in a proper execution of those protocols. Eventually, A ends the game (with a non-negligible probability of having been paid for more tokens than there were bought). Finally, F sends C the list of collected message/signature pairs, and ends the game. Here we assume that F maintains the list in such a way that all messages in it are different, and that all signatures are valid.

Now, let us see that F will only pay A for valid tokens, and he will never pay twice for the same token. Indeed, in both protocols Refund and Pay the IA checks the validity of the token (*i.e.*, the validity of the blind signature) before paying. On the one hand, F maintains a list of refunded tokens, so that any repeated execution of Refund is rejected; and this list is also used to check for duplicates in Pay. Since F only accepts a single execution of Pay per service provider and time slot, no token can be paid more than once[6].

Finally, due to the fairness of ObtainToken, the only executions of BlindSig accepted by $\mathcal{F}$ come from executions of ObtainToken accepted by $\mathcal{F}$ (*i.e.*, paid by $\mathcal{A}$). Hence, whenever $\mathcal{A}$ is successful, the number of executions of BlindSig accepted by $\mathcal{F}$ is less than the number of message/signature pairs outputted by $\mathcal{F}$, thus breaking the unforgeability of the blind signature scheme.

Anonymity for User's Services. Given a successful adversary $\mathcal{A}$ against the anonymity of the subscription scheme, we show another adversary $\mathcal{B}$ who breaks the blindness of the blind signature scheme by internally using $\mathcal{A}$. Let $\mathcal{C}$ be the challenger for $\mathcal{B}$ in the blindness game.

Firstly, $\mathcal{C}$ generates the system parameters of the blind signature scheme and gives them to $\mathcal{B}$. $\mathcal{B}$ completes the public parameters with the system parameters of the other components in the anonymous subscription system, and send them to $\mathcal{A}$. Then $\mathcal{A}$ generates the public output of the Setup protocol (*i.e.*, public keys for all entities including the public key for the blind signature pk_{BSig} and the signed catalogue of services) and sends it to $\mathcal{B}$. Now, $\mathcal{A}$ selects the target identities: SP_0, SP_1 and U_0, U_1 and sends them to $\mathcal{B}$ along with the internal state of U_1 and U_2. Notice that the internal states in particular include the secret information about user's identities, needed in the e-cash protocol. After verifying the information received from $\mathcal{A}$, $\mathcal{B}$ forwards pk_{BSig} to $\mathcal{C}$. $\mathcal{B}$ also generates two key pairs for the basic signature scheme (s_0, y_0) and (s_1, y_1), and sends $m_0 = y_0\|\mathsf{SP}_0\|t$ and $m_1 = y_1\|\mathsf{SP}_1\|t$ to $\mathcal{C}$, where t is the descriptor of the current time slot.

Now $\mathcal{C}$ flips a fair coin b and starts two instances of BlindSig on m_b and m_{1-b}, notifying $\mathcal{B}$ that the former is the target one. For each instance, $\mathcal{B}$ executes ObtainToken with $\mathcal{A}$ as the IA in the following way: $\mathcal{B}$ forwards all messages corresponding to the signing protocol from $\mathcal{C}$ to $\mathcal{A}$ and from $\mathcal{A}$ to $\mathcal{C}$, and uses the corresponding identity (U_0 for the target instance, and U_1 for the other one) in the e-cash part of the protocol. $\mathcal{B}$ also informs $\mathcal{A}$ that the instance using U_0's identity is the target one. If at the end of the protocols $\mathcal{C}$ gets two valid blind signatures: σ_0 on $m_0 = y_0\|\mathsf{SP}_0\|t$ and σ_1 on $m_1 = y_1\|\mathsf{SP}_1\|t$, then he sends (σ_0, σ_1) to $\mathcal{B}$. Otherwise, $\mathcal{C}$ sends $\perp$ to $\mathcal{B}$. In the first case, as $\mathcal{B}$ holds valid tokens $x_0 = (y_0, \mathsf{SP}_0, t, \sigma_0)$ and $x_1 = (y_1, \mathsf{SP}_1, t, \sigma_1)$, he runs two instances of AccessService: one for x_0 with $\mathcal{A}$ acting as SP_0, and the other for x_1 with $\mathcal{A}$ acting as SP_1. This means that $\mathcal{A}$ receives encryptions of both $(y_0\|\sigma_0\|\tilde{\sigma}_0)$ and $(y_1\|\sigma_1\|\tilde{\sigma}_1)$, for valid $\alpha_0\|\rho_0$ and $\alpha_1\|\rho_1$, along with valid basic signatures of them, $\tilde{\sigma}_0$ and $\tilde{\sigma}_1$, for verification keys y_0 and y_1, respectively. In the second case, no instance of AccessService is executed. In both cases, $\mathcal{A}$ eventually ends the game by outputting a guess bit b', which is forwarded to $\mathcal{C}$ by $\mathcal{B}$.

It is straightforward to see that $\mathcal{B}$ perfectly simulates a challenger for $\mathcal{A}$ in the anonymity game. So $\mathcal{A}$ wins the game with a non-negligible probability, which is equal to the probability that $\mathcal{B}$ wins the blindness game.

---

[6] Reusing a blind signature for two service providers would mean breaking the unforgeability of the signature scheme.

5 Efficient Instances

In the previous sections a generic flexible anonymous subscription scheme has been presented. Here we go further in the efficiency analysis, roughly sketching the cost of concrete instantiations. To implement the scheme we propose using RSA blind signature that is fast and efficient for `ObtainToken` and the hashed ElGamal signature (as modified by Pointcheval and Stern [15]) as the basic general purpose signature scheme Sig used in `AccessService`. ElGamal signing requires 1 exponentiation and verification requires 3. Furthermore, ElGamal key generation (which is required every time a token is generated) only requires one exponentiation. As IND-CCA encryption scheme ENC, we choose RSA OAEP+ [16]. The cost of encryption and decryption is just one exponentiation.

The first RSA blind signature was introduced in [17] but is not secure. The Hashed RSA blind signature, which is secure in the random oracle model, is used instead. It works as follows: Assuming the usual RSA key generation, to get a blind signature on the message m, a receiver chooses a random value r relatively prime to N, computes $M = H(m)r^e$, where H is a suitable hash function, and sends it back to the signer. Then the signer computes $\sigma' = M^d = H(m)^d r$. The blind signature is computed by the receiver as $\sigma = \sigma' r^{-1}$, and it can be verified by the equation $\sigma^e = H(m)$.

Now we compare our protocol with the one by Camenisch et al. [11][7] looking at the efficiency of the corresponding algorithms for buying tokens and connecting to the services. The comparison is summarized in Table 1. Their `ObtainToken` protocol requires 6 exponentiations (3 performed by the user and 3 by the issuer). Using RSA blind signature, the complexity of obtaining a token in our proposal is basically computing 4 exponentiations (3 by the user and 1 by the issuer), which is more efficient. However Hashed RSA blind signature is known to be secure only in the random oracle model, though no known attack against it in the standard model is known. Compared to ours, the protocol `Show` of Camenisch et al. — which is the most efficient, up to our knowledge, proposed so far — calls for 13 exponentiations from the user and 7 from the service provider, when the user connects to a service, while in our `AccessService` protocol only 2 exponentiation is computed by the user, and 5 exponentiations are performed by the service provider, what is far more efficient. This makes our protocol completely suitable in most practical scenarios.

Table 1. Efficiency comparison between Camenisch et al. and our scheme, measured in number of exponentiations

	ObtainToken		AccessService	
	User	Issuer	User	Service Prov.
Camenish et al. [11]	3	3	13	7
Ours	3	1	2	5

---

[7] This scheme is significantly more efficient than that of Damgård et al. [10].

6   Extended Features

6.1   Multiple Accesses per Token

Our description of AccessService can be easily modified to provide full flexibility of the service providers policy. Multiple accesses per token can be implemented if the Service Provider allows more than one record per token in the access table. At this, further precautions should be taken in order to prevent replay attacks, *e.g.*, we can add some structure to the nonce α. Namely, α may be the concatenation of a constant part α_0 and an access counter α_1. Then SP will only accept an access attempt for a signed nonce $\alpha_0 || \alpha_1$, with $\alpha_1 > 0$, if a previous usage of the token shows the value $\alpha_0 || \alpha_1 - 1$. It is straightforward for the SP to apply a limit in the number of accesses per token based on the stored value of α_1. Actually, SP can save memory if he stores only the last usage of each token. Also, timing information can easily be added to the access table in order to apply more complex access policies involving both the number of accesses and the total access time, or the time elapsed from the first access.

On the other hand, if the service is configured in different sessions (*e.g.*, sub-services or groups) per time slot among which users may freely chose, then a (public) session identifier sid can be appended to the nonce α.

Obviously, in case of multiple accesses per token, the protocol Refund should be refined depending on the concrete policy. For instance, the Trusted Party can consider a token unused if no access to the service have been given for that token or one may impose that tokens may be refunded as long as they are not exhausted. Additionally, partial refunds (*i.e.*, refund of the estimated unused part of a token) could be considered. However, this variant has a high cost in terms of efficiency, as the Refund protocol (which is likely to be very costly) will presumably be executed many times.

6.2   Removing Trust on SP

In the basic definition of AccessService we assumed that a Service Provider never denies access to the service if the user shows a valid unused token. However, dropping this assumption may make sense in settings in which client loyalty is not valuable; like services that are only required once and for which potential clients are not in touch with former users. At this, a dishonest SP could collect a valid token and deny access to the user. Then nobody can prevent SP to include this actually unused token in the Pay protocol. Actually, the Trusted Party should not accept any complaint from a user, since a dishonest user could complain just to be refunded on a used token.

In some settings this problem can be circumvented with a small overhead: if, for instance, the service consists of a user connected to a resource (*e.g.*, game, multimedia streaming, chat room, ...) for a long period of time. In such scenario the user can be requested to send his token and a signature on an incremental nonce, as explained above, at a fixed and reasonable rate (say, once every minute). In the worst case, if the Service Provider interrupts the service then he can only prove to the Trusted Party that the used got access during one more minute than the actual access time, which is not a great deal in most applications. Moreover, a user cannot ask for refund on more than the unused time, since the SP holds a user's signature on the nonce used in the last access.

6.3   Application to e-Polling Schemes

E-polling schemes can be seen as basic e-voting schemes with relaxed security requirements [18]. Our anonymous subscription scheme can be transformed into a very simple
e-polling scheme by identifying voters with users, service providers with candidates or
proposal supporters, and the issuing authority with the polling control system.

A voter computes a valid vote by running `ObtainToken` in the subscription scheme.
The identity of the voter is checked in order to ensure that only valid (registered) voters can vote and at most one token is issued to a voter. The candidate supported by
the voter is selected at issuing time (but blindly with respect to the issuer). The vote
is anonymously casted to the supported candidate via the `AccessService` protocol,
who verifies and stores it. After all votes are casted, each candidate sends them back to
the issuing authority to compute the tally. To that end the issuing authority verifies all
the blind signatures contained in the collected votes.

Under the assumption that it is on the interest of the candidate that all valid votes
supporting him are counted, both anonymity and correctness of the result are guaranteed. Furthermore, if the final list of valid votes is published by the issuing authority
then every voter can check whether his vote is in the list. In addition, a voter cannot
vote twice without being detected and candidates cannot modify or forge new votes
without breaking the underlying blind signature scheme.

References

1. Chaum, D.: Blind Signatures for Untraceable Payments. In: Goldwasser, S. (ed.) CRYPTO
   1988. LNCS, vol. 403, pp. 199–203. Springer, Heidelberg (1990)
2. Chaum, D., Fiat, A., Naor, M.: Untraceable Electronic Cash. In: Goldwasser, S. (ed.)
   CRYPTO 1988. LNCS, vol. 403, pp. 319–327. Springer, Heidelberg (1990)
3. Brands, S.A.: Untraceable Off-Line Cash in Wallets with Observers. In: Stinson, D.R. (ed.)
   CRYPTO 1993. LNCS, vol. 773, pp. 302–318. Springer, Heidelberg (1994)
4. Ferguson, N.: Single Term Off-Line Coins. In: Helleseth, T. (ed.) EUROCRYPT 1993.
   LNCS, vol. 765, pp. 318–328. Springer, Heidelberg (1994)
5. Camenish, J., Maurer, U., Stadler, M.: Digital Payment Systems with Passive Anonymity-
   Revoking Trustees. J. of Comp. Security 5, 254–265 (1997)
6. von Solms, S., Naccache, D.: On Blind Signatures and Perfect Crimes. Computers & Security 11, 581–583 (1992)
7. Jakobsson, M., Yung, M.: Revokable and versatile electronic money. In: Proc. of the 3rd
   CCCS, vol. 765, pp. 76–87. ACM Press (1996)
8. Chang, C.C., Hwang, T.: Anonymous proof of membership with ring signature. In: Proc. of
   the 2005 IEEE Int. Conf. on Electro Info. Tech., pp. 5–9 (2005)
9. Fujii, A., Ohtake, G., Hanaoka, G., Ogawa, K.: Anonymous Authentication Scheme for Subscription Services. In: Apolloni, B., Howlett, R.J., Jain, L. (eds.) KES 2007, Part III. LNCS
   (LNAI), vol. 4694, pp. 975–983. Springer, Heidelberg (2007)
10. Damgård, I., Dupont, K., Pedersen, M.Ø.: Unclonable Group Identification. In: Vaudenay, S.
    (ed.) EUROCRYPT 2006. LNCS, vol. 4004, pp. 555–572. Springer, Heidelberg (2006)
11. Camenisch, J., Hohenberger, S., Kohlweiss, M., Lysyanskaya, A., Meyerovich, M.: How to
    win the clone wars: Efficient periodic n-times anonymous authentication. Cryptology ePrint
    Archive, Report 2006/454 (2006) http://eprint.iacr.org/

12. Blanton, M.: Online subscriptions with anonymous access. In: Proc. of the 2008 ACM Symp. on Inf., Comp. and Communications Security, pp. 217–227 (2008)
13. Groth, J., Sahai, A.: Efficient Non-Interactive Proof Systems for Bilinear Groups. In: Smart, N.P. (ed.) EUROCRYPT 2008. LNCS, vol. 4965, pp. 415–432. Springer, Heidelberg (2008)
14. Ramzan, Z., Ruhl, M.: Protocols for anonymous subscripton services. Unpublished manuscript. At the time of writing (2000),
    http://people.csail.mit.edu/ruhl/papers/drafts/
    subscription.pdf/
15. Pointcheval, D., Stern, J.: Provably Secure Blind Signature Schemes. In: Kim, K.-c., Matsumoto, T. (eds.) ASIACRYPT 1996. LNCS, vol. 1163, pp. 252–265. Springer, Heidelberg (1996)
16. Shoup, V.: OAEP reconsidered. J. of Cryptology 15, 223–249 (2008)
17. Chaum, D.: Untraceable Electronic Mail, Return Addresses, and Digital Pseudonyms. Communications of the ACM 24, 84–88 (1981)
18. Bruschi, D., Fovino, I.N., Lanzi, A.: A Protocol for Anonymous and Accurate E-Polling. In: Böhlen, M.H., Gamper, J., Polasek, W., Wimmer, M.A. (eds.) TCGOV 2005. LNCS (LNAI), vol. 3416, pp. 112–121. Springer, Heidelberg (2005)
19. Juels, A., Luby, M., Ostrovsky, R.: Security of Blind Digital Signatures. In: Kaliski Jr., B.S. (ed.) CRYPTO 1997. LNCS, vol. 1294, pp. 150–164. Springer, Heidelberg (1997)
20. Okamoto, T.: Efficient Blind and Partially Blind Signatures Without Random Oracles. In: Halevi, S., Rabin, T. (eds.) TCC 2006. LNCS, vol. 3876, pp. 80–99. Springer, Heidelberg (2006)
21. Okamoto, T.: Efficient blind and partially blind signatures without random oracles. Cryptology ePrint Archive, Report 2006/102 (2006), http://eprint.iacr.org/
22. Pointcheval, D., Stern, J.: Security arguments for digital signatures and blind signatures. J. of Cryptology 13, 361–396 (2000)

Appendix

Blind Signature Schemes

The security of Blind Signatures Schemes was formalized in [15,19]. Here we follow the notation and terminology of [19], however; the definition of blindness below is taken from [20,21][8].

A blind digital signature scheme is a tuple BlindSig $= (S, U, Gen, Ver)$ where Gen, the key generation algorithm, is a probabilistic polynomial time algorithm that on the input of the security parameter k it outputs a key pair (pk, sk), and $Verify$, the verification algorithm, is a deterministic polynomial time algorithm which on the input of (pk, m, σ) it outputs accept/reject. The signer, S, and the user, U, are both interactive polynomially-bounded probabilistic Turing machines, each having the following (separate) tapes: read-only input tape, write-only output tape, a read/write work tape, a read-only random tape and two communication tapes, a read-only and a write-only tape. U and S engage in an interactive protocol for some polynomial number of rounds. At this, S takes as input (pk, sk), and outputs completed/not-completed, while U takes as input pk and a message m, and outputs either an error message $\perp$ or a signature $\sigma(m)$.

---

[8] Basically Okamoto modified a previous definition by allowing the adversary to freely choose the public key and also to act dishonestly during BlindSign executions, without being forced to abort the game.

It must be the case that if both U and S follow the protocol, then S always outputs *completed*, and U outputs $\sigma(m)$ that is always *accepted* by Ver. The following two properties must be achieved in order to consider a Blind Digital Signature scheme secure:

Definition 1. *[Non-forgeability property] Consider the following game between an adversary $\mathcal{A}$ against a blind signature scheme* BlindSig *and a challenger $\mathcal{C}$:*

- $\mathcal{C}$ *runs* Gen *on input 1^k and retrieves (pk, sk), and forwards pk to $\mathcal{A}$*
- $\mathcal{A}$ *as a user engages in polynomially many concurrent protocol executions with $\mathcal{C}$ acting as an honest signer, all with the same keys (pk, sk). Let l be the number of executions accepted by $\mathcal{C}$.*
- $\mathcal{A}$ *outputs a collection of j pairs $(m_i, \sigma(m_i))$, for different messages m_i, so that each pair is accepted by Ver on input pk.*

Then, BlindSig *is* non-forgeable *if for any probabilistic polynomial-time adversary $\mathcal{A}$, the probability, taken over coin-flips of Gen, $\mathcal{A}$ and $\mathcal{C}$, that $j > l$ is negligible in k.*

The above definition corresponds to the notion of security against "one-more" forgery considering parallel attacks from Pointcheval and Stern (see, for instance, [22]).

Definition 2. *[Blindness Property] Consider the following game between an adversary $\mathcal{A}$ against a blind signature scheme* BlindSig *and a challenger $\mathcal{C}$:*

- $\mathcal{A}$ *chooses a valid[9] public key, pk, and two different messages m_0 and m_1 to be signed, and sends all to $\mathcal{C}$.*
- *Now $\mathcal{C}$ flips a fair coin b and starts two instances of* BlindSig *on m_b and m_{1-b}, notifying $\mathcal{A}$ that the former is the target one.*
- *At the end of the protocols, if $\mathcal{C}$ gets two valid blind signatures: σ_0 on m_0 and σ_1 on m_1, then $\mathcal{C}$ sends (σ_0, σ_1) to $\mathcal{C}$. Otherwise, if some of the protocols have been aborted or some of the signatures are not valid, $\mathcal{C}$ sends $\perp$ to $\mathcal{A}$.*
- *Finally, $\mathcal{A}$ ends the game by outputting a guess bit b'.*

Then the corresponding signature scheme fulfills the blindness property if the probability, taken over the choice of b, and the coin-flips of Gen, $\mathcal{A}$ and $\mathcal{C}$, that $b = \hat{b}$ is bounded by

$$\frac{1}{2} + \varepsilon(k),$$

for some negligible function ε.

---

[9] Here 'valid' means one of the possible outputs of Gen.

Proxiable Designated Verifier Signature

Mebae Ushida[1,*], Yutaka Kawai[2], Kazuki Yoneyama[3], and Kazuo Ohta[1]

[1] The University of Electro-Communications, Cho-fu, Tokyo, Japan
[2] The University of Tokyo, Tokyo, Japan
[3] NTT Information Sharing Platform Laboratories, Tokyo, Japan
ushida.mebae@jp.fujitsu.com

Abstract. Designated Verifier Signature (DVS) guarantees that only a verifier designated by a signer can verify the *"validity of a signature"*. In this paper, we propose a new variant of DVS; Proxiable Designated Verifier Signature (PDVS) where the verifier can make a third party (i.e. the proxy) substitute some process of the verification. In the PDVS system, the verifier can reduce his computational cost by delegating some process of the verification without revealing the validity of the signature to the proxy. In all DVS systems, the validity of a signature means that a signature satisfies both properties that (1) the signature is judged *"accept"* by a decision algorithm and (2) the signature is confirmed at it is generated by the signer. So in the PDVS system, the verifier can make the proxy substitute checking only the property (1). In the proposed PDVS model, we divide verifier's secret keys into two parts; one is a key for performing the decision algorithm, and the other is a key for generating a dummy signature, which prevents a third party from convincing the property (2). We also define security requirements for the PDVS, and propose a PDVS scheme which satisfies all security requirements we define.

Keywords: Designated verifier signature, Proxy, Strong unforgeability.

1 Introduction

1.1 Background

Designated Verifier Signature (DVS) was first introduced by Jakobsson, Sako and Impagliazzo [4]. In the DVS system, a signer designates a verifier and only the verifier designated by the signer can verify the validity of a signature.

DVS is useful for a situation where a signer expects that the validity of the signature is confirmed by only specific person and is not confirmed by the others.

We consider the situation of public procedures. The person sends his personal information (a report of one's removal etc.) to the government office. And he hopes that this information cannot be leaked to others. He must generate his signature for this document, but he worries about leaking and being confirmed his personal information. If he uses the DVS, he can inform his personal information to the government and not have to worry about leaking it.

---

* Presently with FUJITSU LABORATORIES LTD.

M.S. Obaidat, G.A. Tsihrintzis, and J. Filipe (Eds.): ICETE 2010, CCIS 222, pp. 220–232, 2012.
© Springer-Verlag Berlin Heidelberg 2012

Another kind of signature where the signer can restrict to verify the validity of the signature is the Undeniable Signature (US) [3]. In the US system, the verifier needs the interaction with the signer to perform the verification. The signer designates the verifier by selecting the person whom the signer interacts with for verification. The third party who does not interact with the signer can not confirm the validity of the signature, and the verifier cannot convince the third party of validity of the signature which the verifier verified before by revealing the records of verification process.

In the US system, the verifier must interact with the signer whenever he verifies the signature. On the other hand in the DVS system, the signer designates the verifier when he generates the signature, and the verifier can verify the validity of the signature at any time without interaction with the signer.

By using Message Authenticate Code (MAC), the prover can also designate the verifier. MAC is also verified the validity without interaction. However the prover and the verifier must share a common secret key before using MAC. In the DVS system, the signer can designate the verifier using only the verifier's public key.

In the DVS system, the validity of a signature is checked by following two procedures: Decision and Distinction. By Decision, the signature is checked whether it is *"accepted"* by the decision procedure. By Distinction, the signature is checked whether it is exactly generated by the signer. In this paper, we call a signature which is accepted by Decision *an acceptable signature*, and a signature which is acceptable signature and generated by the signer *a valid signature*. The meaning of verifying the validity of a signature is confirming that the signature is valid by performing Decision and Distinction.

In the DVS system, the verifier can also generate an acceptable signature. We call such an acceptable signature *a dummy signature*, while we call a signature generated by a signer *an original signature*. Only the original signature must be confirmed as the valid signature. Any third party should be unable to distinguish the original signature from dummy signatures. Even if a third party accepts a signature, he is unable to confirm that the signature is the original signature because it could be a dummy signature. Therefore, a third party is unable to verify the validity of the signature. On the other hand, the verifier can decide whether the signature is the original signature by using his own list of dummy signatures generated by himself. Hence, the verifier cannot convince a third party the validity of the signature.

In several DVS systems [4,8,7,10], anyone can perform the Decision. However, a third party cannot confirm the validity of a signature because he can not perform Distinction. We call those DVS systems *ordinary DVS*. In the ordinary DVS system, a third party can narrow the signer to two candidates. On the other hand, *strong DVS* [9,6,11] in which only the verifier can perform the Decision was proposed. In the strong DVS system, a third party cannot even narrow two signer candidates.

1.2 A Motivating Problem

In a strong DVS system, all processes of the verification can be performed by only a verifier. If one person is designated by large numbers of signers, he must proceed large amount of the task of the verification procedure by himself.

This situation will often occur if the DVS system is applied to the situation of public procedures. In this case, a lot of people would send their documents with DVSs to one government office. Then, the officer must verify large amount of DVSs. Hence, the officer would like to entrust other organizations to some processes of verification.

1.3   Contribution

In order to reduce the computational cost for verification, we will propose Proxiable Designated Verifier Signature (PDVS) where the verifier can make a third party (i.e. the proxy) substitute some process of the verification. In previous DVS systems, if the third party can perform the Decision, but he cannot confirm the validity of a signature. Hence in the PDVS system, the Decision is delegated to the proxy and the verifier performs only the Distinction. If the verifier does not issue any dummy signature for message m, he verifies that (m, σ) is valid immediately when he is reported that (m, σ) is acceptable by the proxy. Hence the verifier can reduce his computational cost.

In previous strong DVS systems [9,6,11], there is only one kind of verifier's secret key which is used for performing the Decision algorithm and for generating dummy signatures. If the verifier gives his secret key in order to delegate the Decision, the proxy can also generate a dummy signature. In this case, the verifier cannot perform the Distinction. Thus in the previous strong DVS systems, the verifier cannot delegate the verification task to the proxy.

Hence in the PDVS system, there are two kinds of verifier's keys; one is a key for performing the Decision and the other is for generating dummy signatures. The verifier can delegate the Decision to the proxy by giving only the secret key for performing the Decision, and the verifier keeps the both of keys; a key for performing the Decision and a key for generating dummy signatures.

Unlike the previous DVS systems, there is the new entity proxy in the PDVS system. Hence we consider the requirements for each position, not only the verifier and the third party but also the proxy. We define security requirements for PDVS scheme by capturing following requirements. (1) The verifier can surely verify the validity of the signature at any time. (2) The proxy can perform the Decision, but cannot generate any acceptable signature. (3) The third party cannot perform even the Decision. We describe the definition of security requirements in Sect 3.2.

In this paper, we formalize PDVS, and define security requirements for PDVS in Sect 3. We propose a concrete PDVS scheme and prove that our PDVS scheme satisfies security requirements we define in Sect 3.2.

1.4   Related Works

In 1996, DVS [4] was first introduced and is the first ordinary DVS. After that, strong DVS [9] was proposed, and several security requirements for DVS was defined [9,6,7].

At the same time, several variants of DVSs were proposed. *multi-DVS* [5] is the DVS where the signer can designate several verifiers in one signature, and the verifiers can verify the signature individually. *Universal DVS* [11,12,2,10] is a system that a basic digital signature can convert a designated verifier signature. *designated proxy signature* (DVPS) [13] is the DVS where the signer can delegate his signing capacity to the third party (i.e. the proxy).

In all of the DVS system which was proposed before, the verifier has to verify the validity of the signature himself.

2   Preliminaries

We will provide several definitions which are building blocks of our PDVS scheme.

Definition 1 (Bilinear Map). *Let $(\mathbb{G},+)$, and $(\mathbb{H},\cdot)$ be two groups of the same prime order q. Let P be a generator of $\mathbb{G}$. A bilinear map is a mapping $e : \mathbb{G} \times \mathbb{G} \to \mathbb{H}$ satisfying the following properties:*

  - *bilinear: $e(aQ, bR) = e(Q, R)^{ab}$, for all $(Q, R) \in \mathbb{G}^2$, and all $(a, b) \in \mathbb{Z}^2$;*
  - *non-degeneration: $e(P, P) \neq 1$;*
  - *computability: there exists an efficient algorithm to compute e;*

Definition 2. *[Prime-order-BDH-parameter-generator] Prime-order-BDH-parameter-generator is a probabilistic algorithm that takes on input a security parameter k, and outputs a 5-tuple $(q, P, \mathbb{G}, \mathbb{H}, e)$ satisfying the following conditions:*

  - *q is a prime with $2^{k-1} < q < 2^k$;*
  - *$\mathbb{G}$ and $\mathbb{H}$ are groups of order q;*
  - *$e : \mathbb{G} \times \mathbb{G} \longrightarrow \mathbb{H}$ is a bilinear map;*

Definition 3 (Computational Diffie-Hellman Assumption). *Let Gen be a Prime-order-BDH-parameter-generator. Let $\mathcal{A}$ be an adversary that takes on input 5-tuple $(q, P, \mathbb{G}, \mathbb{H}, e)$ generated by Gen and $(X, Y) \in \mathbb{G}^2$, and returns an elements of $Z \in \mathbb{G}$. We consider the following random experiments, where k is a security parameter;*

$$\boxed{\text{Experiment } \mathsf{Exp}^{cdh}_{Gen,\mathcal{A}}(k)}$$

$$(q, P, \mathbb{G}, \mathbb{H}, e) \xleftarrow{R} \mathsf{Gen}(k)$$
$$(x, y) \xleftarrow{R} \mathbb{Z}_q^{*2}, X := xP, Y := yP$$
$$Z \leftarrow \mathcal{A}(q, P, \mathbb{G}, \mathbb{H}, e, X, Y)$$
$$\text{Return } 1 \text{ iff } Z = xyP$$

We define the corresponding success probability of $\mathcal{A}$ via

$$\mathsf{Succ}^{cdh}_{Gen,\mathcal{A}}(k) = Pr[\mathsf{Exp}^{cdh}_{Gen,\mathcal{A}}(k) = 1].$$

Let $t \in \mathbb{N}$. CDH is said to be (k, t, ϵ)-hard if no adversary $\mathcal{A}$ running in time t has $\mathsf{Succ}^{cdh}_{Gen,\mathcal{A}}(k) \geq \epsilon$.

Definition 4 (Gap-Bilinear Diffie-Hellman Assumption). *Let* Gen *be a Prime-order-BDH-parameter-generator. Let* $\mathcal{A}$ *be an adversary that takes on input 5-tuple* $(q, P, \mathbb{G}, \mathbb{H}, e)$ *generated by* Gen *and* $(X, Y, Z) \in \mathbb{G}^3$, *and returns an elements of* $h \in \mathbb{H}$. *We consider the following random experiments, where* k *is a security parameter;*

Experiment $\mathsf{Exp}_{Gen,\mathcal{A}}^{gbdh}(k)$

$(q, P, \mathbb{G}, \mathbb{H}, e) \xleftarrow{R} \mathsf{Gen}(k)$

$(x, y, z) \xleftarrow{R} \mathbb{Z}_q^{*3}, X := xP, Y := yP, Z := zP$

$h \leftarrow \mathcal{A}^{DBDH}(q, P, \mathbb{G}, \mathbb{H}, e, X, Y, Z)$

Return 1 iff $h = e(P, P)^{xyz}$

---

where $\mathcal{A}^{DBDH}$ *denotes that the adversary* $\mathcal{A}$ *has access to a DBDH oracle. A DBDH oracle is an oracle that for input* $aP, bP, cP,$ *and* $e(P, P)^d$, *decides whether* $d = abc$ *or not. We define the corresponding success probability of* $\mathcal{A}$ *via*

$$\mathsf{Succ}_{Gen,\mathcal{A}}^{gbdh}(k) = Pr[\mathsf{Exp}_{Gen,\mathcal{A}}^{gbdh}(k) = 1].$$

Let $t \in \mathbb{N}$. *GBDH is said to be* (k, t, ϵ)-*hard if no adversary* $\mathcal{A}$ *running in time* t *has* $\mathsf{Succ}_{Gen,\mathcal{A}}^{gbdh}(k) \geq \epsilon$.

3   Definitions of Proxiable DVS

In this section, we will propose the definition of the PDVS and will several security properties of the PDVS.

3.1   The Models of PDVS Scheme

A PDVS scheme consists of seven algorithms : Let k be a security parameter. Each definition is described as follows.

Common parameter generation (**SetUp**): A probabilistic algorithm, on input k, outputs the public parameters *params*.

Signer's key generation (**SKeyGen**): A probabilistic algorithm, on input *params*, outputs the public and secret signer's key PKs and SKs.

Verifier's key generation (**VKeyGen**): A probabilistic algorithm, on input *params*, outputs verifier's secret key SKv and SKp, and the verifier's public key PKv. SKv is kept by only the verifier. SKp is given to the proxy by the verifier.

Designated signing (DSign): A probabilistic algorithm, on input *params*, message m, signer's secret key SKs and signer's and verifier's public keys PKs, PKv, outputs a original signature σ.

Transcript simulation (TSim): A probabilistic algorithm, on input *params*, message m, verifier's secret key SKv, and signer's and verifier's public keys PKs, PKv, outputs a dummy signature σ'.

Designated verifying 1 (Decision): A deterministic algorithm, on input *params*, message m, a signature σ, public key's PKs, PKv and verifier's secret key SKp, outputs a verification decision, *accept* or *reject*.

Designated verifying 2 (Distinction): A deterministic algorithm, on input *params*, message m, an acceptable signature σ, PKs, PKv, verifier's secret key SKv and the list of dummy signatures which the verifier issued before, outputs a verification decision, *valid* or *invalid*.

3.2 Definitions of Security Properties of PDVS

In this section, we propose definitions of security requirements for the PDVS.

Strong Unforgeability. We point out that *Existential Unforgeability* (EUF) is not sufficient and *Strong Existential Unforgeability* (sEUF) must be satisfied for secure PDVS schemes.

In the PDVS system satisfying EUF but not satisfying sEUF, the proxy is also able to confirm the validity of the signature.

We consider a following strong-forgery-attack. The strong-forgery-attacker generates an acceptable message/signature pair (m, σ^*) from another acceptable message/signature pair (m, σ). Anyone can not distinguish whether (m, σ^*) is generated by formal procedures (DSign or TSim) or the strong-forgery-attack. Such an attacker could exist in the PDVS system satisfying just EUF, because EUF only guarantees that anyone is unable to generate an acceptable (m^*, σ^*) where m^* is different from any acceptable signed message m.

If such a strong-forgery-attacker exists, the following situation occurs. The verifier generates a dummy signature σ_{TSim} for a message m, and issues (m, σ_{TSim}). Then the strong-forgery-attacker can generate a forgery (m, σ^*_{TSim}) by using (m, σ_{TSim}). After that, the signer generates an original signature σ_{DSign} for the message m. In this case, even if the verifier can decide that (m, σ) is acceptable, he cannot confirm where σ is the original signature σ_{DSign} or the forgery σ^*_{TSim}. Then even the verifier is unable to confirm the validity of the signature by the Distinction. So the verifier is unable to issue any dummy signature to confirm the validity of the signature in any cases. In the above situation, the proxy is able to confirm the validity of the signature by performing the Decision, because the acceptable signature is surely the original signature. Hence, if the PDVS does not satisfy sEUF, the proxy is able to confirm the validity of the signature. So, the PDVS must satisfy sEUF.

The PDVS requires that not only an arbitrary third party but the proxy, who has verifier's secret key SKp, is not able to forge a signature.

Definition 5 (Strong Unforgeability). [1] *Let $\mathcal{A}$ be a strong-forgery against adaptive chosen message attack (sEUF-CMA)-adversary against PDVS, Σ_S be the original signing oracle, Σ_T be the dummy signing oracle, and Υ be the distinction oracle* [2] . *Let $\{(m_1, \sigma_1), \cdots, (m_{q_{\Sigma_S}}, \sigma_{q_{\Sigma_S}})\}$ be a set of message and signature pair which is given to $\mathcal{A}$ by oracle Σ_S, $\{(m'_1, \sigma'_1), \cdots, (m'_{q_{\Sigma_T}}, \sigma'_{q_{\Sigma_T}})\}$ be a set of message and signature pair which is given to $\mathcal{A}$ by oracle Σ_T. Let k be a security parameter. We consider the following random experiment:*

Experiment $\mathsf{Exp}_{PDVS,\mathcal{A}}^{seuf-cma}(k)$

$params \stackrel{R}{\leftarrow} \mathsf{Setup}(k)$

$(PKs, SKs) \stackrel{R}{\leftarrow} \mathsf{SKeyGen}(params)$

$(PKv, SKv, SKp) \stackrel{R}{\leftarrow} \mathsf{VKeyGen}(params)$

$(m^*, \sigma^*) \leftarrow \mathcal{A}^{\Sigma_S, \Sigma_T, \Upsilon}(params, PKs, PKv, SKp)$

s.t. $(m^*, \sigma^*) \notin \{(m_1, \sigma_1), \cdots, (m_{q_{\Sigma_S}}, \sigma_{q_{\Sigma_S}})\} \cup \{(m'_1, \sigma'_1), \cdots, (m'_{q_{\Sigma_T}}, \sigma'_{q_{\Sigma_T}})\}$

Return 1 iff $\mathsf{Decision}(params, m^*, \sigma^*, PKs, PKv, SKp) = accept$

We define the success probability of the adversary $\mathcal{A}$ by

$$\mathsf{Succ}_{PDVS,\mathcal{A}}^{seuf-cma}(k) = \Pr[\mathsf{Exp}_{PDVS,\mathcal{A}}^{seuf-cma}(k) = 1].$$

A PDVS scheme is said to be (k, τ, ϵ)-sEUF-CMA secure, if no adversary $\mathcal{A}$ running in time τ has a $\mathsf{Succ}_{PDVS,\mathcal{A}}^{seuf-cma}(k) \geq \epsilon$.

Privacy of Signer's Identity. In the PDVS system, a third party who has only public keys must be unable to confirm whether a signature is acceptable or not. To capture this requirement, we define *Privacy of signer's identity* (PSI) that "there are two possible signers. An adversary sees a signature σ, he is not able to distinguish the signer who generates σ." This condition can be described as follows.

Definition 6 (Privacy of Signer's Identity). *Let $\mathcal{A}$ be a PSI-CMA-adversary against PDVS, Σ_{S_0} and Σ_{S_1} be original signing oracles, Σ_T be the dummy signing oracle, Γ be the Decision oracle, and Υ be the Distinction oracle. Let k be a security parameter. We consider the following random experiment for $i \in \{0, 1\}$.*

---

[1] In the basic digital signature, the security notion of strong unforgeability is proposed by [1]. We define strong unforgeability for the PDVS by adapting strong unforgeability to the PDVS system.

[2] The Decision oracle does not need in this experiment, because the adversary who has SKp can execute the **Decision** by himself.

> Experiment $\mathsf{Exp}^{psi-cma-i}_{PDVS,\mathcal{A}}(k)$
>
> $params \overset{R}{\leftarrow} \mathsf{Setup}(k)$
>
> $(PKs0, SKs0) \overset{R}{\leftarrow} \mathsf{SKeyGen}(params)$
>
> $(PKs1, SKs1) \overset{R}{\leftarrow} \mathsf{SKeyGen}(params)$
>
> $(PKv, SKv, SKp) \overset{R}{\leftarrow} \mathsf{VKeyGen}(params)$
>
> $m^* \leftarrow \mathcal{A}^{\Sigma_{S_0}, \Sigma_{S_1}, \Sigma_T, \Gamma, \Upsilon}(params, PKs0, PKs1, PKv)$
>
> $\sigma^* \leftarrow \mathsf{DSign}(params, m^*, SKsi, PKv)$
>
> Return $i' \leftarrow \mathcal{A}^{\Sigma_S, \Sigma_T, \Gamma, \Upsilon}(params, m^*, \sigma^*, PKs0, PKs1, PKv)$

We define the advantage of the adversary $\mathcal{A}$ by

$$\mathsf{Adv}^{psi-cma}_{PDVS,\mathcal{A}}(k) = |\mathrm{Pr}[\mathsf{Exp}^{psi-cma-0}_{PDVS,\mathcal{A}}(k) = 1] - \mathrm{Pr}[\mathsf{Exp}^{psi-cma-1}_{PDVS,\mathcal{A}}(k) = 1]|$$

A PDVS scheme is said to be (k, τ, ϵ)-PSI-CMA secure, if no adversary $\mathcal{A}$ running in time τ has $\mathsf{Adv}^{psi-cma}_{PDVS,\mathcal{A}}(k) \geq \epsilon$.

Source Hiding. In the PDVS system, anyone except the verifier who has all secret keys must be unable to confirm whether a signature is valid signature or not in order to guarantee that the Distinction is able to be performed by only the verifier. In this paper, *Source Hiding* (SH) means "even if any adversary $\mathcal{A}$ has all secret and public keys, he can not distinguish the original signature from the dummy signature."

It is clear that if a PDVS scheme satisfies SH, $\mathcal{A}$ who has a part of secret keys can not distinguish the original signature from the dummy signature. Thus if a scheme satisfies SH, the proxy can not confirm the validity of the signature.

Definition 7 (Source Hiding). *Let $\mathcal{A}$ be an arbitrary completely source hiding (SH)-adversary against a PDVS scheme. Let k be a security parameter. We consider the following random experiment:*

> Experiment $\mathsf{Exp}^{sh}_{PDVS,\mathcal{A}}(k)$
>
> $params \overset{R}{\leftarrow} \mathsf{Setup}(k)$
>
> $(PKs, SKs) \overset{R}{\leftarrow} \mathsf{SKeyGen}(params)$
>
> $(PKv, SKv, SKp) \overset{R}{\leftarrow} \mathsf{VKeyGen}(params)$
>
> $m^* \leftarrow \mathcal{A}(params, PKs, PKv, SKs, SKv, SKp)$
>
> $r \leftarrow_R \{0, 1\}$
>
> if $r = 1 : \sigma^* \leftarrow \mathsf{DSign}(params, m^*, SKs, PKs, PKv)$
>
> otherwise : $\sigma^* \leftarrow \mathsf{TSim}(params, m^*, SKv, PKs, PKv)$

$$r' \leftarrow \mathcal{A}(params, m^*, \sigma^*, PKs, PKv, SKs, SKv, SKp)$$

Return 1 iff $r' = r$

We define the advantage of the adversary $\mathcal{A}$ by

$$\mathsf{Adv}^{sh}_{PDVS,\mathcal{A}}(k) = |\mathsf{Pr}[\mathsf{Exp}^{sh}_{PDVS,\mathcal{A}}(k) = 1] - \tfrac{1}{2}|.$$

A PDVS scheme is said to be (k, τ, ϵ)-SH-CMA secure, if no adversary $\mathcal{A}$ running time τ has $\mathsf{Adv}^{sh}_{PDVS,\mathcal{A}}(k) \geq \epsilon$.

Non-coincidental Proerty. For message m, if the probability that $\sigma_{DSign} = \sigma_{TSim}$ such that $\sigma_{DSign} \leftarrow \mathsf{DSign}(params, m^*, SKs, PKs, PKv)$ and $\sigma_{TSim} \leftarrow \mathsf{TSim}(params, m^*, SKv, PKs, PKv)$ is non-negligible, the verifier cannot confirm the validity of the signature. Since he cannot confirm that (m, σ_{DSign}) is the original signature because he cannot distinguish (m, σ_{DSign}) from the dummy signature (m, σ_{TSim}) he issued before.

Hence, the PDVS must satisfy the property that the provability that the original signature is identical with the dummy signature is negligible. In this paper, we call this property *Non-Coincidental property* (NCP).

Definition 8 (Non-coincidental Property). *A PDVS scheme is said to be (k, ϵ)-NCP secure, if for any m,*

$$\mathsf{Pr}[\sigma_{DSign} = \sigma_{TSim} | params \leftarrow \mathsf{SetUp}(k);$$
$$(SKs, PKs) \leftarrow \mathsf{SKeyGen}(params);$$
$$(PKv, SKv, SKp) \xleftarrow{R} \mathsf{VKeyGen}(params)$$
$$\sigma_{DSign} \leftarrow \mathsf{DSign}(params, m^*, SKs, PKs, PKv);$$
$$\sigma_{TSim} \leftarrow \mathsf{TSim}(params, m^*, SKv, PKs, PKv)]$$
$$\leq \epsilon.$$

4   Our Proposed PDVS Scheme

In this section, we propose a PDVS scheme satisfying all security requirements which we defined in Sect 3.2.

First, we propose a naive PDVS scheme. But the naive PDVS scheme does not satisfy sEUF. Next, we show a strong-forgery attack for the naive PDVS scheme. Finally, we propose a PDVS scheme which is improved from the naive PDVS scheme and satisfies sEUF and other security requirements.

4.1   Naive PDVS Scheme

Idea. We achieve the naive PDVS scheme by using the bi-DVS scheme proposed by Laguillaumie and Vergnaud [5]. In the bi-DVS, a signer designates two verifiers in one signature. The bi-DVS system does not capture dummy signatures and the validity of the signature is confirmed by only checking the **Decision**. Two verifiers have their own secret key respectively and can execute the **Decision** by using only his secret key [3].

We find that the bi-DVS scheme has a property where a person who has both two verifiers' secret keys can generate an acceptable signature without using signer's secret keys, and such acceptable signature is not distinguished from the signature generated by the signer. That is he can generate a dummy signature. We achieve the PDVS scheme by corresponding a key for performing the **Decision** to one of two verifiers' keys in the bi-DVS and keys for generating dummy signatures to both of two verifiers' keys.

Naive PDVS Scheme. Let k be a security parameter.

SetUp: Let **Gen** be a prime-order-BDH-generator and let $(q, P, \mathbb{G}, \mathbb{H}, e)$ be an output of **Gen**(k). Let $\mathcal{H} : \mathbb{G} \times \mathbb{G} \longrightarrow \mathbb{H}$ be a hash function family and H be a random member of $\mathcal{H}$.

SKeyGen : Pick $a \overset{R}{\leftarrow} \mathbb{Z}_q^*$ and compute $P_A = aP$. The signer's public key PKs is P_A and the secret key SKs is a.

VKeyGen: Pick $b \overset{R}{\leftarrow} \mathbb{Z}_q^*$ and compute $P_B = bP$. Pick $c \overset{R}{\leftarrow} \mathbb{Z}_q^*$ and compute $P_c = cP$. The verifiers' public key PKv is P_B and P_C. The secret keys SKv which the verifier keeps are b and c, and the secret key SKp which the proxy is given by the verifier is c.

DSign : Given a message $m \in \{0, 1\}^*$, pick $(r, l) \overset{R}{\leftarrow} \mathbb{Z}_q^{*2}$, compute $P_{BC} = P_B + P_C$, $u = e(P_B, P_C)^a$ and $M = H(m, u^l)$ and set $Q_A = a^{-1}(M - rP_{BC})$ and $Q_{BC} = rP$. The signature σ of m is (Q_A, Q_{BC}, l).

TSim: Given a message $m \in \{0, 1\}^*$, pick $(r', l') \overset{R}{\leftarrow} \mathbb{Z}_q^{*2}$. Compute $P_{BC} = P_B + P_C$, $u = e(P_A, P_C)^b$ and $M' = H(m, u^{l'})$, and set $Q'_A = r'P$ and $Q'_{BC} = (b + c)^{-1}(M' - r'P_A)$. The dummy signature σ' of m is (Q'_A, Q'_{BC}, l').

Decision : Given m and σ, compute $u = e(P_A, P_B)^c$ and $M = H(m, u^l)$. Finally, check whether $e(Q_A, P_A)e(Q_{BC}, P_{BC}) = e(M, P)$. If it does, return $accept$. Otherwise return $reject$.

Distinction : Given an acceptable message/signature pair (m, σ), check whether $(m = m') \wedge (\sigma = \sigma')$ for any message/dummy signature pair (m', σ') which was issued before. If it does not, return $valid$. Otherwise return $invalid$.

Strong-forgery-attack for Naive PDVS Scheme. We describe the strong-forgery-attack for the naive PDVS scheme.

Select $\epsilon \overset{R}{\leftarrow} \mathbb{Z}_q^*$ for accepted (m, σ), and compute $Q_A^* = Q_A - \epsilon P_{BC}$, $Q_B^* = Q_{BC} + \epsilon P_A$ and output forgery (Q_A^*, Q_{BC}^*, l). Then (Q_A^*, Q_{BC}^*, l) satisfies $e(Q_A^*, P_A)e(Q_{BC}^*, P_{BC}) = e(M, P)$. Therefore anyone can generate forgery (Q_A^*, Q_B^*, l) by using an acceptable message/signature pair.

---

[3] If each of verifiers can generate a dummy signature, the other verifier cannot confirm the validity of the signature. Because if it is so, there are more than two entities who can generate an acceptable signature and the verifier cannot confirm that the signature is generated by the signer. In the bi-DVS system, the validity of the signature is confirmed by only checking the **Decision**. So, each of verifiers can transfer the validity of the signature to a third party. Therefore, to be exact, the bi-DVS is not DVS.

4.2   Proposed PDVS Scheme

Idea. To prevent the strong-forgery attack in Sect 4.1.3, we add a signing procedure for generating a new part of signature ch corresponding to (m, σ). ch is computed only by using signer's or verifier's secret key. A valid signature consists of σ and ch. Even if a third party generates (m, σ^*), he cannot generate ch' corresponding to (m, σ^*). Hence a third party never generates strong-forgery (m, σ^*, ch^*).

PDVS Scheme. Let σ be a signature which is generated by DSign or TSim in the naive PDVS scheme and Σ be a family of σ.

> SetUp: Let be the same as SetUp in the naive PDVS. Besides let $\mathcal{G}: \{0, 1\}^* \times \Sigma \times \mathbb{H} \longrightarrow \mathbb{H}$ be a hash function family and G be a random member of $\mathcal{G}$.
>
> SKeyGen : Pick $(a, a') \xleftarrow{R} \mathbb{Z}_q^{*2}$ and compute $P_A = aP$ and $P_{A'} = a'P$. The signer's public keys PKs are P_A and $P_{A'}$, and the secret keys SKs are a and a'.
>
> VKeyGen: Pick $(b, b') \xleftarrow{R} \mathbb{Z}_q^{*2}$ and compute $P_B = bP$ and $P_{B'} = b'P$. Pick $c \xleftarrow{R} \mathbb{Z}_q^*$ and compute $P_c = cP$. The verifiers' public keys PKv are $P_B, P_{B'}$ and P_C. The secret keys SKv that the verifier keeps are b, b' and c. The secret key SKp that the proxy is given by the verifier is c.
>
> DSign : Given m, generate σ by DSign in the naive PDVS scheme and compute $ch = G(m, \sigma, a'P_{B'})$. The original signature σ_{new} of m is (σ, ch).
>
> TSim: Given m, generate σ' by TSim in the naive PDVS scheme and compute $ch' = G(m, \sigma', b'P_{A'})$. The dummy signature σ'_{new} of m is (σ', ch').
>
> Decision : Let be the same as Decision in the naive PDVS scheme.
>
> Distinction : Given an acceptable message/signature pair (m, σ, ch), if $m \neq m'$ for any m' which was issued with dummy signature before, output *valid*. Else if $(m = m') \wedge (\sigma = \sigma')$ for any message/dummy signature pair (m', σ') which was issued before, output *invalid*. Otherwise check whether $ch = G(m, \sigma, b'P_{A'})$, if it does, output *valid*.

4.3   Comparison

In this section, we compare previous DVS schemes with our proposed PDVS scheme in terms of the computational cost of the verification task for the verifier.

We describe the cost of computing modulo exponentiation as E and the cost of computing pairing calculation as P.

In previous strong DVS systems, Decision is performed only by the verifier. The cost of performing the Decision of the scheme by Saeednia et al. [9] is $3E$, and the scheme by Laguillaumie et al. [5] is $E+4P$.

In our proposed PDVS scheme, the verification cost of the verifier is at most E. But this calculation is performed when only the message/signature pair (m, σ) satisfies $(m = m') \wedge (\sigma \neq \sigma')$ for any (m', σ') which the verifier issued before. In the PDVS system, indeed, the verifier need not issue any dummy signature. In this case, the verifier verifies that (m, σ) is valid immediately when he is reported that (m, σ) is acceptable by the proxy. Hence, in practice, the verification cost of the verifier is very smaller than that of previous DVS systems.

4.4   Security Proofs

Theorem 1 (Strong Unforgeability). *For any sEUF-CMA-adversary $\mathcal{A}$ in the random oracle model, with security parameter k, which has the success probability $\epsilon = Succ_{PDVS,\mathcal{A}}^{seuf-cma}(k)$, and makes q_G queries to the random oracle, q_{Σ_S} queries to the original signing oracle, q_{Σ_T} queries to the dummy signing oracle, q_Υ queries to the Distinction oracle, there exists an adversary $\mathcal{A}$ for CDH which has the advantage $Succ_{Gen,\mathcal{A}}^{cdh}(k)$ upper-bounded by ϵ' such that*

$$\epsilon' \geq \epsilon - \frac{(q_G + q_\Upsilon)(q_{\Sigma_S} + q_{\Sigma_T})}{2^{4k}} - \frac{1}{2^k}.$$

Theorem 2 (Privacy of Signer's Identity). *For any PSI-CMA-adversary $\mathcal{A}$, in the random oracle model, with security parameter k, which has the success probability $\epsilon = Succ_{PDVS,\mathcal{A}}^{psi-cma}(k)$, and makes q_H and q_G queries to the random oracle, q_{Σ_S} queries to the original signing oracle, q_{Σ_T} queries to the dummy signing oracle, q_Γ queries to the Decision oracle, q_Υ queries to the Distinction oracle, there exist an adversary $\mathcal{A}$ for GBDH which has the advantage $Succ_{Gen,\mathcal{A}}^{gbdh}(k)$ upper-bounded by ϵ' such that*

$$\epsilon' \geq \frac{\epsilon}{2} - \frac{q_\Gamma + q_\Upsilon}{2^k} - \frac{(q_H + q_{\Sigma_S} + q_{\Sigma_T})(q_{\Sigma_S} + q_{\Sigma_T})}{2^k} - \frac{(q_G + q_\Upsilon)(q_{\Sigma_S} + q_{\Sigma_T})}{2^{4k}}.$$

Theorem 3 (Source Hiding). *In the PDVS scheme we propose, the following expression holds.*

$$Adv_{PDVS,\mathcal{A}}^{sh}(k) = 0.$$

Due to the lack of space, we will show the proofs of Theorem 1,2 and 3 in the full version of this paper.

Finally, we will show that PDVS satisfies NCP.

We consider the probability that $\sigma = \sigma'$ where $\sigma \leftarrow \mathsf{DSign}(m, SKs, PKv)$, $\sigma' \leftarrow \mathsf{TSim}(m, SKv, SKp, PKs)$ in the random oracle model. We represent an original signature as $\sigma = (Q_A, Q_{BC}, l)$ and a dummy signature as $\sigma' = (Q'_A, Q'_{BC}, l')$. We also denote that $r \in \mathbb{Z}_q^*$ is a random string the signer selects and $r' \in \mathbb{Z}_q^*$ is a random string the verifier selects. $\Pr[\sigma = \sigma'] = \Pr[l = l'] \cdot \Pr[Q_A, Q_{BC} = Q'_A, Q'_{BC} | l = l'] = (q - 1)^{-2}$. Hence, $\Pr[\sigma = \sigma']$ is negligible.

5   Conclusions

In this paper, we proposed concept and definitions of the PDVS that a verifier can delegate some computational cost of the verification to the proxy. We defined new security requirements for the PDVS, and proposed a concrete PDVS scheme. Finally we proved that our PDVS scheme satisfies all security requirements for the PDVS under CDH and GBDH assumptions.

References

1. An, J.H., Dodis, Y., Rabin, T.: On the Security of Joint Signature and Encryption. In: Knudsen, L.R. (ed.) EUROCRYPT 2002. LNCS, vol. 2332, pp. 83–107. Springer, Heidelberg (2002)

2. Baek, J., Safavi-Naini, R., Susilo, W.: Universal Designated Verifier Signature Proof (or How to Efficiently Prove Knowledge of a Signature). In: Roy, B. (ed.) ASIACRYPT 2005. LNCS, vol. 3788, pp. 644–661. Springer, Heidelberg (2005)
3. Chaum, D., van Antwerpen, H.: Undeniable Signatures. In: Brassard, G. (ed.) CRYPTO 1989. LNCS, vol. 435, pp. 212–216. Springer, Heidelberg (1990)
4. Jakobsson, M., Sako, K., Impagliazzo, R.: Designated Verifier Proofs and Their Applications. In: Maurer, U.M. (ed.) EUROCRYPT 1996. LNCS, vol. 1070, pp. 143–154. Springer, Heidelberg (1996)
5. Laguillaumie, F., Vergnaud, D.: Multi-Designated Verifiers Signatures. In: López, J., Qing, S., Okamoto, E. (eds.) ICICS 2004. LNCS, vol. 3269, pp. 495–507. Springer, Heidelberg (2004)
6. Laguillaumie, F., Vergnaud, D.: Designated Verifier Signatures: Anonymity and Efficient Construction from *any* Bilinear Map. In: Blundo, C., Cimato, S. (eds.) SCN 2004. LNCS, vol. 3352, pp. 105–119. Springer, Heidelberg (2005)
7. Lipmaa, H., Wang, G., Bao, F.: Designated Verifier Signature Schemes: Attacks, New Security Notions and a New Construction. In: Caires, L., Italiano, G.F., Monteiro, L., Palamidessi, C., Yung, M. (eds.) ICALP 2005. LNCS, vol. 3580, pp. 459–471. Springer, Heidelberg (2005)
8. Rivest, R.L., Shamir, A., Tauman, Y.: How to Leak a Secret. In: Boyd, C. (ed.) ASIACRYPT 2001. LNCS, vol. 2248, pp. 552–565. Springer, Heidelberg (2001)
9. Saeednia, S., Kremer, S., Markowitch, O.: An Efficient Strong Designated Verifier Signature Scheme. In: Lim, J.-I., Lee, D.-H. (eds.) ICISC 2003. LNCS, vol. 2971, pp. 40–54. Springer, Heidelberg (2004)
10. Shahandashti, S.F., Safavi-Naini, R.: Construction of Universal Designated-Verifier Signatures and Identity-Based Signatures from Standard Signatures. In: Cramer, R. (ed.) PKC 2008. LNCS, vol. 4939, pp. 121–140. Springer, Heidelberg (2008)
11. Steinfeld, R., Bull, L., Wang, H., Pieprzyk, J.: Universal Designated-Verifier Signatures. In: Laih, C.-S. (ed.) ASIACRYPT 2003. LNCS, vol. 2894, pp. 523–542. Springer, Heidelberg (2003)
12. Steinfeld, R., Wang, H., Pieprzyk, J.: Efficient Extension of Standard Schnorr/Rsa Signatures into Universal Designated-Verifier Signatures. In: Bao, F., Deng, R., Zhou, J. (eds.) PKC 2004. LNCS, vol. 2947, pp. 86–100. Springer, Heidelberg (2004)
13. Wang, G.: Designated-verifier proxy signature schemes. In: Security and Privacy in the Age of Ubiquitous Computing. IFIP International Federation for Information Processing, vol. 181, pp. 409–423. Springer, Boston (2005)

Adaptive and Composable Non-interactive String-Commitment Protocols

Huafei Zhu[1], Tadashi Araragi[2], Takashi Nishide[3], and Kouichi Sakurai[3]

[1] Institute for Infocomm Research, A-STAR, Singapore
[2] NTT Communication Science Laboratories, Kyoto, Japan
[3] Department of Computer Science and Communication Engineering
Kyushu University, Fukuoka, Japan
huafei@i2r.a-star.edu.sg, araragi@cslab.kecl.ntt.co.jp,
nishide@inf.kyushu-u.ac.jp, sakurai@csce.kyushu-u.ac.jp

Abstract. In this paper, a non-interactive string-commitment protocol in the common reference string model is presented and analyzed. We show that the proposed (length-flexible) commitment protocol realizes the universally composable security in the presence of adaptive adversaries in the standard computational model assuming that the underlying Paillier's public-key encryption (or Damgård and Jurik's public-key encryption scheme when a lengthflexible property is claimed) is semantically secure and the Damgård-Fazio- Nicolosi's non-interactive protocol is zero-knowledge in the registered public-key model.

Keywords: Non-interactive, String-commitment protocol, Universally composable security.

1 Introduction

Informally, a commitment scheme is a two-party protocol that has two phases: a committing phase, where a receiver of the commitment obtains some information which amounts to a commitment to an unknown value (sealed by a committer), and a reveal phase, where the receiver obtains an opening of the commitment to some value (revealed by the committer). Commitment is an essential building block in many cryptographic protocols, such as zero-knowledge protocols (e.g., [3,18,9]), general functional evaluation protocols (e.g., [18,14]), contract-signing and electronic commerce, and more (see [15,16] for further reference) and has been studied extensively in the past two decades (e.g., [2,20,5,21,1,7]).

Universally composable (UC) commitments guarantee that a commitment protocol behaves like an ideal commitment service, even when concurrently composed with an arbitrary set of protocols. To prove security of a commitment scheme realizes the UC-security in the presence of an adaptive adversary, one must construct an ideal-world adversary such that the adversary's view of a real-life execution of a commitment protocol can be simulated given just the data the adversary is entitled to. That is, to prove the UC-security, a commitment scheme running between a committer P_i and a receiver P_j in an environment $\mathcal{Z}$ must be equivocable and extractable. To simulate the case where

M.S. Obaidat, G.A. Tsihrintzis, and J. Filipe (Eds.): ICETE 2010, CCIS 222, pp. 233–242, 2012.
© Springer-Verlag Berlin Heidelberg 2012

the honest committer P_i sends a commitment c to the receiver P_j in the real-world, an ideal-world adversary S must interpret this fake commitment c as a genuine commitment of a message m (the value m is revealed by the ideal commitment functionality during the reveal phase). As such, the commitment scheme must be equivocable. If the real-world adversary A sends a commitment c to P_j on behalf of the corrupted committer P_i, the ideal-world adversary S must extract the implicit message m which is the explicit input to the commitment functionality. As such, the commitment scheme must be extractable. It follows that a commitment scheme that realizes UC-security in the presence of adaptive adversaries must be equivocable and extractable.

1.1   The State-of-the-Art

The state-of-the-art non-interactive commitment schemes in the universally composable framework are mainly constructed from the following two categories: non-interactive, universally compsosably secure bit-commitment schemes and interactive universally composable string-commitment schemes.

UC-SECURE NON-INTERACTIVE BIT-COMMITMENTS. Canetti and Fischlin [5] have proposed two basic approaches for constructions of non-interactive and universally composable bit-commitment schemes in the common reference string model. The first construction of commitment protocol is based on any trapdoor permutation in the one-time common reference string model. The second construction is based on the existence of claw-free pairs of trapdoor permutations in the reusable common reference string model, where the honest players are assumed that they faithfully erase some parts of their internal randomness (i.e., their commitment scheme works in the internal randomness erasure model). Canetti and Fischlin then proposed an improved bit-commitment scheme based on the Diffie-Hellman assumption in the (randomness) non-erasure model.

Canetti, Lindell, Ostrovsky and Sahai [6] have presented a new universally composable non-interactive bit-commitment protocol that is secure against adaptive adversary based on the existence of enhanced trapdoor permutations in the common reference string model. Their scheme realizes the UC-security in the the multi-session ideal commitment functionality, an extension of the single-session ideal commitment functionality presented in [5]. The Canetti and Fischlin commitment schemes [5] and the Canetti, Lindell, Ostrovsky and Sahai commitment schemes [6] use $\Omega(\lambda)$ bits to commit a bit, where λ is a security parameter. These pioneer works are important from point view of the theoretical research.

UC-SECURE INTERACTIVE STRING-COMMITMENTS. Damgård and Nielsen have presented practical interactive string-commitment protocols in the common reference string model [13]. The Damgård and Nielsen interactive string-commitment protocol realizes the UC-security in the presence of adaptive adversaries but the size of the common reference string grows linearly with the number of participants. Damgård and Groth [10] then proposed an improved commitment scheme with constant common reference string size which is independent with the number of the parties in the commitment protocol.

Camenisch and Shoup [8] have constructed alternative interactive universally composably secure string-commitment protocols in the context of verifiably committed encryptions. Their construction is based on the zero-knowledge proof of an encryption indeed decrypts to a valid opening of a commitment. This construction realizes universally composable security assuming the Diffie-Hellman assumption is hard in the common reference model.

UC-SECURE NON-INTERACTIVE STRING-COMMITMENTS. Very recently, Nishimaki, Fujisaki and Tanaka [23] have proposed an interesting universally composable non-interactive string-commitment scheme based on all-but-one trapdoor functions introduced by Peikert and Waters in STOC 2008 [24]. The idea of their implementation is sketched below: Let Σ =(SKGen, Sign, Veri) be a signature scheme that is secure against adaptive chosen-message attack in the sense of Goldwasser, Micali and Rivest [17]. Let Δ = (EGen, Enc, Dec) be Damgård-Jurik's length-flexible public-key encryption scheme [12]. To commit a message $m \in \mathcal{M}$, a common-reference-string generation algorithm (CRS) invokes the key generation algorithm SKGen of the underlying signature scheme to produce a pair of verification key and signing key (vk^*, sk^*). CRS then invokes the encryption algorithm Enc to produce a ciphertxt $\mathrm{Enc}(vk^*)$ of the public verification key. The common reference string σ is $\mathrm{Enc}(vk^*)$ together with a description of a pair-wise independent hash function $\mathcal{H}$. Given σ and m, a committer S invokes SKGen to generate a new pair of verification and signing key (vk, sk), and then generates a randomized ciphertext C of the message $(vk^* - vk)m$. That is, the committer S invokes the encryption algorithm Enc which takes $(vk^* - vk)m$ as input to produce a ciphertext C (=$\mathrm{Enc}((vk^* - vk)m, r_m)$) with randomness r_m. To simulate the view of the honest committer S, the lossy branch vk^* will be set to vk.

1.2 This Work

This paper studies non-interactive (no interactive communication between a committer and a receiver during the commitment stage) string-commitment schemes in the universally composable framework in the presence of adaptive adversaries. Our non-interactive string-commitment protocol is based on Piallier's homomorphic encryption scheme. Recall that the difficulty to realize the uc-security of a commitment protocol is to provide an efficient method to reach the equivocability and extractability once a common reference string is given.

- To realize the extractability, we allow a simulator to run a key generation algorithm of the Paillier's homomorphic encryption scheme. We allow the simulator to randomly select two ciphertexts K_1 and K_2. The common reference string is defined by (K_1, K_2). Since the simulator knows the trapdoor of the underlying public-key encryption scheme, it follows that the simulator is able to extract the all encrypted messages (including the randomness used to generate the common reference string and extractable keys sketched below).
- To realize the equivocability, we will construct a random key K (=$K_1{}^{r_1} K_2{}^{r_2}$) from the common reference string (K_1, K_2). The random key K is a base to commit a message m in the form $K^m r_m^N \bmod N^2$. The committer P_i then invokes 3-move Σ-protocol and proves the knowledge of (r_1, r_2) to a receiver P_j. Let **PoK** be a transcript of the zero-knowledge derived from the Σ-protocol. The commitment of a string m is denoted by $(K, C, \textbf{PoK})$, where $C = K^m r_m^N \bmod N^2$.

Let $\psi(k, r) = (1 + N)^k r^N \bmod N^2$ be an equivocable key (intuitively, a key is equivocable if it is of from $\psi(0, r)$, i.e., $k = 0$, the randomness r of the equivocable key K is called trapdoor string; a key K is called extractable if it is of form $\psi(k, r)$ ($k \neq 0$)). Let xKey be a set of all extractable keys and eKey be a set of all equivocable keys. The key point to reach the equivocability is that we allow a simulator to select the randomness (r_1, r_2) so that K can be either an extractable key or an equivocable key. In case that K is an extractable key, the simulator is able to extract the implicit input message of a corrupted party. In case that K is an equivocable key, the simulator is able to modify the internal state when an honest party gets corrupted.

We stress that the standard rewinding technique for extracting the knowledge of a zero-knowledge proof is not allowed in the universally composable framework of Canetti [4]. This means that we cannot get the implicit input message m by rewinding a knowledge prover. Fortunately, in our construction, a simulator knows the secret key of the Paillier's encryption scheme and the randomness (r_1, r_2) used to generate K (the base to commit a message m) that are sufficient for the simulator to extract the message m.

We stress that a straight-forward application of a 3-move interactive Σ-protocol results in an interactive string-commitment protocol. A well-known technique for making interactive Σ-protocols non-interactive is the Fiat-Shamir heuristic, where a random challenge string e is computed by the prover as a hash of the statement proved and the first message K. Unfortunately, if the Fiat-Shamir heuristic is applied then the resulting string-commitment protocol works in the random oracle only.

To avoid using of the random oracle model, we will apply the Damgård, Fazio and Nicolosi's method [11] for compiling a class of Σ-protocols into non-interactive zero-knowledge arguments $\widetilde{\Sigma}$, where a verifier is assumed to hold a pair of registered public/secret keys. As a result, our non-interactive string-commitment scheme works in the registered public key model (we refer to the reader [11] for more details).

THE RESULT. We claim that the adaptive and composable non-interactive string-commitment scheme presented and analyzed in this paper reaches the UC-security in the presence of adaptive adversaries in the common reference string model assuming that the underlying Paillier's public-key encryption scheme is semantically secure, and the underlying Damgård-Fazio-Nicolosi's non-interactive protocol is zero-knowledge in the registered public-key model. If the underlying Paillier's public-key encryption scheme is replaced by Damgård-Jurik's length-flexible public key encryption scheme [12], then the non-interactive string-commitment is length-flexible as well.

ROAD MAP. The rest of the paper is organized as follows. In Section 2, security definition of commit schemes is sketched; Our adaptive and composable non-interactive string-commitment scheme is presented and analyzed in Section 3. We conclude our work in Section 4.

2   Preliminaries

This paper works in the universally composable framework of Canetti [4] and assumes that the reader is familiar with the standard notion of UC-security.

THE COMMON REFERENCE STRING MODEL The functionality of common reference string model assumes that all participants have access to a common string that is drawn from some specified distribution $\mathcal{D}$. The common reference string is chosen ahead of the time and is made available before any interaction starts. The common reference string functionality defined below is due to Canetti and Fischlin [5].

Functionality $\mathcal{F}_{\mathsf{crs}}^{\mathcal{D}}$

$\mathcal{F}_{\mathsf{crs}}^{\mathcal{D}}$ proceeds as follows, when parameterized by a distribution $\mathcal{D}$.

- when receiving a message (sid, P_i, P_j) from P_i, let $\mathsf{crs} \leftarrow \mathcal{D}(1^n)$ and send (sid, crs) to P_i, and send $(\mathsf{crs}, sid, P_i, P_j)$ to the adversary, where sid is a session identity. Next when receiving (sid, P_i, P_j) from P_j (and only from P_j), send (sid, crs) to p_j and to the adversary, and halt.

Fig. 1. A description of common reference string functionality

THE COMMITMENT FUNCTIONALITY To capture the notion of reusability, one must define the functionality of multi commitment, de-commitment processes. The commitment functionality defined below is due to Canetti, Lindell, Ostrovsky and Sahai [6].

Functionality $\mathcal{F}_{\mathsf{mcom}}$

$\mathcal{F}_{\mathsf{mcom}}$ proceeds as follows, running with parties $P_1, \ldots, P_n$ and an adversary $\mathcal{S}$

- **Commit Phase**: Upon receiving a value (**commit**, $sid, cid, P_i, P_j, m \in \mathcal{M}$), record the tuple (sid, cid, P_i, P_j, m) and send the message (**receipt**, sid, cid, P_i, P_j) to P_j and $\mathcal{S}$. Ignore any future **commit** messages with the same cid from P_i to P_j.
- **Open Phase**: Upon receiving a value (**open**, sid, cid) from P_i: If a tuple (sid, cid, P_i, P_j, m) was previously recorded, then send the message (**open**, sid, cid, P_i, P_j, m) to P_j and $\mathcal{S}$ and halt; otherwise ignore.

Fig. 2. A description of Functionality $\mathcal{F}_{\mathsf{mcom}}$

Definition 1. *Let $\mathcal{F}_{\mathrm{mcom}}$ be a multi commitment functionality. A protocol π is said to universally composable realize $\mathcal{F}_{\mathrm{mcom}}$ if for any adversary $\mathcal{A}$, there exists a simulator $\mathcal{S}$ such that for all environments $\mathcal{Z}$, the ensemble $\mathrm{IDEAL}_{\mathcal{F}_{\mathrm{mcom}}, \mathcal{S}, \mathcal{Z}}$ is computationally indistinguishable with the ensemble $\mathrm{REAL}_{\pi, \mathcal{A}, \mathcal{Z}}$.*

3   Non-interactive String-Commitment Schemes

We will make use of Paillier's probabilistic public key system [22] to construct non-interactive, universally composable string-commitment schemes in this paper.

3.1 xKeys and eKeys

Borrowing the notations and notions from Damgård and Jurik [12], we define extractable keys (xKeys) and equivocable keys (eKeys) in the context of the Paillier's encryption scheme. Let $\psi(k,r) = (1 + N)^k r^N \bmod N^2$. A key is called equivocable if it is of from $\psi(0, r)$. The randomness r of the equivocable key K is called trapdoor string. A key K is called extractable if it is of form $\psi(k, r)$ ($k \neq 0$). Let xKey be a set of all extractable keys and eKey be a set of all equivocable keys. If the decisional composite residuosity assumption (DCRA) introduced in [22] holds, then elements of form $\psi(0, r)$ cannot be distinguished from the element of the form $\psi(k, r)$, where r is uniformly from Z_N^* and k is any fixed element in Z_N.

3.2 The Damgård-Fazio-Nicolosi's Non-interactive Zero-Knowledge Protocol

A Σ-protocol for a relation R is an interactive proof system Σ for $L_R := \{x \mid \exists w : (x, w) \in R\}$ with the conversation of form (a, e, z), where (a, z) is computed by a prover and e is selected by a verifier. Damgård, Fazio and Nicolosi [11] provide a method for compiling a class of 3-move Σ-protocols into non-interactive zero-knowledge arguments $\widetilde{\Sigma}$. Their method is based on homomorphic encryptions (say, Paillier's encryption scheme) and does not use random oracles. The Damgård-Fazio-Nicolosi's non-interactive zero-knowledge protocol requires that a private/public key pair is set up for the verifier (i.e., it works in the registered public-key model). Below, we sketch the Damgård-Fazio-Nicolosi's compiler:

1. Given an instance (x, w) to prove, a prover P gets a verifier's registered public key pk_V derived from the Paillier's encryption scheme, together with a ciphertext c broadcast by the verifier, where c is an encryption of a random string e (the randomness e is selected and encrypted by the verifier under the public-key pk_V, i.e., $c = \mathcal{E}_{pk_V}(e, r_e)$);
2. the prover P generates the first message a using the randomness r and then computes a randomized ciphertext $Z = \mathcal{E}_{pk_V}(r)c^w$. Finally, the prover sends $(x, (a, Z))$ to the verifier.
3. Upon receiving $(x, (a, Z))$, the verifier decrypts Z to get z ($z = r + ew$ by the correctness) and checks that whether $(x, (a, e, z))$ is valid transcript. If the transcript $(x, (a, e, z))$ is valid then accepts; otherwise, rejects the received transcript.

(due to [11]) Damgård, Fazio and Nicolosi have shown that the non-interactive zero-knowledge protocol $\widetilde{\Sigma}$ is complete and sound in the registered public-key model.

3.3 The Description

The non-interactive string commitment protocol π presented in this section is based on the Paillier's encryption scheme. We stress that if the underlying Paillier's public-key encryption scheme is replaced by Damgård-Jurik's length-flexible public key encryption scheme [12], then the described non-interactive string-commitment is length-flexible. Below, we describe our string-commitment protocol in the context of the Pailler's encryption scheme (the description of string-commitment protocol based on the Damgård-Jurik's is straight-forward and thus omitted).

1. Common-reference-string generation phase: On input a security parameter 1^k, $((p, q), N) \leftarrow \mathbf{Gen}(1^k)$. Let $K_1 \leftarrow (1 + N)^{k_1} r_{k_1}{}^N \bmod N^2$ and $K_2 \leftarrow (1 + N)^{k_2} r_{k_2}{}^N \bmod N^2$, where $k_1 \neq 0$ and $k_2 \neq 0$, i.e., both K_1 and K_2 are xKeys. The common reference string $\sigma = (N, K_1, K_2)$. The trapdoor string τ is (p, q).

2. The committing phase: On input a message $m \in Z_N$, the committer P_i performs the following computations
   - P_i randomly selects $r_1, r_2 \in Z_N$ and computes $K = K_1^{r_1} K_2^{r_2} \bmod N^2$;
   - P_i then invokes the Damgård-Fazio-Nicolosi's non-interactive zero-knowledge argument $\widetilde{\Sigma}$ and proves the knowledge $r_1 \in Z_N$ and $r_2 \in Z_n$ such that $K = K_1^{r_1} K_2^{r_2}$ to P_j. Let **PoK** be a transcript of zero-knowledge argument derived from the Damgård-Fazio-Nicolosi's protocol $\widetilde{\Sigma}$;
   - P_i then computes $K^m r_m^N \bmod N^2$. Let $C = K^m r_m^N \bmod N^2$.
   - Finally P_i sends $(K, \mathbf{PoK}, C)$ to the receiver P_j.

3. The opening phase: Upon receiving $(K, \mathbf{PoK}, C)$ and (m, r_m), the receiver P_j first checks the validity of the received transcript **PoK**. If it is invalid, then outputs $\perp$; otherwise, P_j checks that $C \stackrel{?}{=} K^m r_m^N \bmod N^2$. If the check is invalid, P_j outputs $\perp$, otherwise, it outputs "accept".

This ends the description of the non-interactive string-commitment scheme

3.4   The Proof of Security

Theorem 1. *The non-interactive string-commitment protocol π reaches the UC-security in the presence of adaptive adversaries in the common-reference-string model assuming that the underlying Paillier's public-key encryption scheme is semantically secure, and the underlying Damgård-Fazio-Nicolosi's non-interactive protocol is zero-knowledge in the registered public-key model.*

We describe the ideal model adversary S which comprises the following 6 simulation steps (S. 1 - S. 6):

   - S. 1): At the outset of the simulator S prepares a common reference string σ by invoking the key generation algorithm $\mathcal{K}$ of the underlying Paillier's encryption scheme and outputs (pk', sk'). Given pk', S randomly selects $K_1' \in \mathcal{C}$ and $K_2' \in \mathcal{C}$. Let $\sigma' = (pk', K_1', K_2')$. The trapdoor string τ' is sk'. The simulator keeps τ' secret and broadcasts σ' to all participants.
   - S. 2): If at the some point in the execution the environment $\mathcal{Z}$ writes a message (**commit**, sid, cid, P_i, P_j, m) on the tape of the uncorrupted party P_i, then the ideal world simulator S who cannot read the actual message m, generates a simulated view of the real world committer P_i via the following computations:
     • On input σ', S extracts $(k_1', r_{k_1'})$ and $(k_2', r_{k_2'})$ from the common reference string σ' with the help of the auxiliary string sk'; Note that K_1' and K_2' are chosen uniformly at random. As a result, K_1' and K_2' are xKeys with over-whelming probability.
     • S randomly chooses $r'_1 \in Z_N$ and computes $r'_2 \in Z_N$ from the equation $k'_1 r'_1 + k'_2 r'_2 = 0 \bmod N$; Let $K' = K_1'^{r'_1} K_2'^{r'_2} \bmod N^2$.

- $\mathcal{S}$ then invokes the Damgård-Fazio-Nicolosi's non-interactive zero-knowledge protocol $\widetilde{\Sigma}$ and proves to P_j the knowledge (r'_1, r'_2) such that $K' = K_1'^{r'_1} K_2'^{r'_2}$ mod N^2. Let **PoK$'$** be a transcript of generated by Damgård-Fazio-Nicolosi's non-interactive zero-knowledge protocol $\widetilde{\Sigma}$ for proving the knowledge (r'_1, r'_2) such that $K' = K_1'^{r'_1} K_2'^{r'_2}$ mod N^2;
- $\mathcal{S}$ randomly selects m' and $r_{m'}$ and sets $C' = K'^{m'} \mathcal{E}(0, r_{m'})$.

The simulator $\mathcal{S}$ then tells the real world adversary $\mathcal{A}$ that P_i has sent $(K', \textbf{PoK}', C')$ to P_j.

- S. 3): If at the some point in the execution $\mathcal{Z}$ instructs an corrupted party P_i to open the commitment (**open**, sid, cid, P_i, P_j, m), $\mathcal{S}$ learns m^* via the functionality $\mathcal{F}_{\text{mcom}}$ and then modifies the internal state of $(K', \textbf{PoK}', C')$ such that $(K', \textbf{PoK}', C')$ looks like a genuine commitment of the string $m^* \in Z_N$ from the point view of the environment $\mathcal{Z}$. That is,
  - (equivocation) Since $K' = K_1'^{r'_1} K_2'^{r'_2}$ mod N^2 is an eKey (recall that the simulator randomly selects $r'_1 \in Z_N$ and then computes r'_2 from the equation $k'_1 r'_1 + k'_2 r'_2 = 0$ mod N), the simulator $\mathcal{S}$ must provide (m^*, r_{m^*}) such that $C = K'^{m'} \mathcal{E}_{pk'}(0, r_{m'}) = K'^{m^*} \mathcal{E}_{pk'}(0, r_{m^*})$. This is an easy task since $\mathcal{S}$ knows the trapdoor string sk'.
- S. 4): If the simulated adversary $\mathcal{A}$ lets the corrupted party P_i send (**commit**, sid, cid, P_i, P_j, $(K', \textbf{PoK}', C')$) to an honest party P_j. Given K' and **PoK$'$**, the simulator $\mathcal{S}$ checks the validity of **PoK$'$**. If the check is valid, $\mathcal{S}$ performs the following computations
  - (extraction) $\mathcal{S}$ first extracts k' from K' with the help of the secret key sk'; $\mathcal{S}$ then extracts $k' \times m'$ mod N from C' with the help of the secret key sk'. Finally, $\mathcal{S}$ sends the extracted message m' to the functionality $\mathcal{F}_{\text{mcom}}$.
- S. 5): If $\mathcal{A}$ tells the corrupted party P_i to open a valid commitment C' correctly with message m^*, then $\mathcal{S}$ compares m^* with the previously extracted message m' and stops if they differ; otherwise, $\mathcal{S}$ sends (**open**, sid, cid, P_i, P_j) in name of the party to the functionality $\mathcal{F}_{\text{mcom}}$. If P_i is supposed to decommit incorrectly, then $\mathcal{S}$ also sends an incorrect opening to the functionality.
- S. 6): Whenever the simulated $\mathcal{A}$ demands to corrupt a party, $\mathcal{S}$ corrupts this party in the ideal model and learns all internal information of the party. $\mathcal{S}$ first adapts possible decommitment information about the previously given but not yet unopened commitment of this party, like in the case if an honest party decommitting. After this, $\mathcal{S}$ gives all this adjusted information to $\mathcal{A}$.

This ends the description of the simulator.

We first show that the distribution of public-key pk generated by the protocol π is identical to the public-key pk' generated by the simulator. The random variables (K_1, K_2) in π are xKeys. The random variables (K'_1, K'_2) generated by the simulator are random ciphertetxts. It follows that the distribution of the common reference string $\sigma = (pk, K_1, K_2)$ generated in generated in the protocol π is computationally indistinguishable from the distribution of the common reference string $\sigma' = (pk', K'_1, K'_2)$ generated by the simulator.

We then show that the distribution of the view in the protocol π is computationally indistinguishable from that of the simulation assuming that the Paillier's encryption scheme is semantically secure and the Damgård-Fazio-Nicolosi's non-interactive protocol is zero-knowledge. Let $(K, \textbf{PoK}, C)$ be random variables generated in π and $(K', \textbf{PoK}', C')$ be random variables generated by the simulator. Note that K is an xKey in π (with overwhelming probability) while K' is an eKey in the simulation (with overwhelming probability). Also notice that C is an xKey in π (with overwhelming probability) while C' is an eKey in the simulation (with overwhelming probability). Since the Paillier's encryption scheme is semantically secure, it follows that the random variables (K, C) and (K', C') are computationally indistinguishable. Since the Damgård-Fazio-Nicolosi's non-interactive protocol is zero-knowledge, it follows that the distribution of the random variable $\textbf{PoK}$ and $\textbf{PoK}'$ are identical. As a result, the random variables $(K, \textbf{PoK}, C)$ and $(K', \textbf{PoK}', C')$ are computationally indistinguishable assuming that the Paillier's encryption scheme is semantically secure and the Damgård-Fazio-Nicolosi's non-interactive protocol is zero-knowledge.

Finally, we know that r'_m is computed from the equation $r'^{m'}_k r_{m'} = r^m_k r_m \bmod N$. The distribution of the random variable $(m, r_m))$ in π is identical to the distribution of the random variables generated by the simulator. As such, the distribution of the view $((K, \textbf{PoK}, C)$ and $(m, r_m)))$ generated by the protocol π is computationally indistinguishable to the view $((K', \textbf{PoK}', C')$ and $(m', r_{m'})))$ generated by the simulator. As a result, we know that $\text{IDEAL}_{\mathcal{F}_{\text{mcom}}, \mathcal{S}, \mathcal{Z}} = \text{REAL}_{\pi, \mathcal{A}, \mathcal{Z}}$.

4   Conclusions

In this paper an adaptive and composable non-interactive string-commitment protocol has presented and analyzed. We have shown that the proposed commitment protocol realizes the universally composable security in the presence of the adaptive adversaries in the common reference string model assuming that the underlying Paillier's public-key encryption scheme is semantically secure, and the underlying Damgård-Fazio-Nicolosi's non-interactive protocol is zero-knowledge in the registered public-key model.

References

1. Barak, B., Canetti, R., Nielsen, J.B., Pass, R.: Universally Composable Protocols with Relaxed Set-Up Assumptions. In: FOCS 2004, pp. 186–195 (2004)
2. Blum, M.: Coin Flipping by Telephone. In: CRYPTO 1981, pp. 11–15 (1981)
3. Brassard, G., Chaum, D., Crépeau, C.: Minimum Disclosure Proofs of Knowledge. J. Comput. Syst. Sci. 37(2), 156–189 (1988)
4. Canetti, R.: Universally Composable Security: A New Paradigm for Cryptographic Protocols. In: FOCS 2001, pp. 136–145 (2001)
5. Canetti, R., Fischlin, M.: Universally Composable Commitments. In: Kilian, J. (ed.) CRYPTO 2001. LNCS, vol. 2139, pp. 19–40. Springer, Heidelberg (2001)
6. Canetti, R., Lindell, Y., Ostrovsky, R., Sahai, A.: Universally composable two-party and multi-party secure computation. In: STOC 2002, pp. 494–503 (2002)
7. Canetti, R., Dodis, Y., Pass, R., Walfish, S.: Universally Composable Security with Global Setup. In: Vadhan, S.P. (ed.) TCC 2007. LNCS, vol. 4392, pp. 61–85. Springer, Heidelberg (2007)

8. Camenisch, J., Shoup, V.: Practical Verifiable Encryption and Decryption of Discrete Logarithms. In: Boneh, D. (ed.) CRYPTO 2003. LNCS, vol. 2729, pp. 126–144. Springer, Heidelberg (2003)
9. Damgård, I.B.: On the Existence of Bit Commitment Schemes and Zero-Knowledge Proofs. In: Brassard, G. (ed.) CRYPTO 1989. LNCS, vol. 435, pp. 17–27. Springer, Heidelberg (1990)
10. Damgård, I., Groth, J.: Non-interactive and reusable non-malleable commitment schemes. In: STOC 2003, pp. 426–437 (2003)
11. Damgård, I.B., Fazio, N., Nicolosi, A.: Non-interactive Zero-Knowledge from Homomorphic Encryption. In: Halevi, S., Rabin, T. (eds.) TCC 2006. LNCS, vol. 3876, pp. 41–59. Springer, Heidelberg (2006)
12. Damgård, I., Jurik, M.: A Generalisation, a Simplification and Some Applications of Paillier's Probabilistic Public-Key System. In: Kim, K.-c. (ed.) PKC 2001. LNCS, vol. 1992, pp. 119–136. Springer, Heidelberg (2001)
13. Damgård, I., Nielsen, J.B.: Perfect Hiding and Perfect Binding Universally Composable Commitment Schemes with Constant Expansion Factor. In: Yung, M. (ed.) CRYPTO 2002. LNCS, vol. 2442, pp. 581–596. Springer, Heidelberg (2002)
14. Galil, Z., Haber, S., Yung, M.: Cryptographic Computation: Secure Faut-Tolerant Protocols and the Public-Key Model. In: Pomerance, C. (ed.) CRYPTO 1987. LNCS, vol. 293, pp. 135–155. Springer, Heidelberg (1988)
15. Goldreich, O.: Foundations of Cryptography, vol. 1. Cambridge University Press (2001)
16. Goldreich, O.: Foundations of Cryptography, vol. 2. Cambridge University Press (2004)
17. Goldwasser, S., Micali, S., Rivest, R.L.: A Digital Signature Scheme Secure Against Adaptive Chosen-Message Attacks. SIAM J. Comput. 17(2), 281–308 (1988)
18. Goldreich, O., Micali, S., Wigderson, A.: How to Play any Mental Game or A Completeness Theorem for Protocols with Honest Majority. In: STOC 1987, pp. 218–229 (1987)
19. Goldwasser, S., Micali, S.: Probabilistic Encryption. J. Comput. Syst. Sci. 28(2), 270–299 (1984)
20. Naor, M.: Bit Commitment Using Pseudorandomness. J. Cryptology 4(2), 151–158 (1991)
21. Naor, M., Ostrovsky, R., Venkatesan, R., Yung, M.: Perfect Zero-Knowledge Arguments for NP Can Be Based on General Complexity Assumptions (Extended Abstract). In: Brickell, E.F. (ed.) CRYPTO 1992. LNCS, vol. 740, pp. 196–214. Springer, Heidelberg (1993)
22. Paillier, P.: Public-Key Cryptosystems Based on Composite Degree Residuosity Classes. In: Stern, J. (ed.) EUROCRYPT 1999. LNCS, vol. 1592, pp. 223–238. Springer, Heidelberg (1999)
23. Ryo, N., Keisuke, T., Eiichiro, F.: Efficient Non-Interactive Universally Composable String-Commitment Schemes. In: Pieprzyk, J., Zhang, F. (eds.) ProvSec 2009. LNCS, vol. 5848, pp. 3–18. Springer, Heidelberg (2009)
24. Peikert, C., Waters, B.: Lossy trapdoor functions and their applications. In: STOC 2008, pp. 187–196 (2008)

Dynamic Adaptation of Security and QoS in Energy-Harvesting Sensors Nodes

Antonio Vincenzo Taddeo, Marcello Mura, and Alberto Ferrante

ALaRI, Faculty of Informatics, University of Lugano, via G. Buffi 13, Lugano, Switzerland
{antonio.taddeo,marcello.mura,alberto.ferrante}@usi.ch
http://www.alari.ch

Abstract. Pervasive computing applications have, in many cases, hard requirements in terms of security. In particular when deploying a Wireless Sensor Network (WSN), security and privacy exigences must be accommodated with the small computational power and especially with the limited energy of the nodes. In some applications nodes may be equipped with energy harvesting devices, especially solar cells, to keep their small batteries charged. The presence of an harvesting device, while enabling the use of WSN in more application fields, represents an additional challenge in the design phase. Given the stochastic nature of most energy harvesting sources, optimizing system performance requires the capability to evaluate the current system conditions runtime.

In this chapter we present a runtime mechanism that optimizes network lifetime and quality of service by adapting network security provisions to the current situation in terms of available energy and recharging rate. By applying our algorithm, network lifetime when the harvester cannot collect energy can be prolonged. The algorithm tries to limit power consumption by suitably changing security settings and by lowering the number of unessential messages sent on the network.

Keywords: Security, Priority, Wireless sensor networks, Quality of services, Energy harvesting.

1   Introduction

Wireless Sensor Networks (WSN) are composed of a large number of nodes with sensing, processing, and data communication capabilities. Recent improvements in microelectronic technologies enable the creation of small and inexpensive nodes with limited power consumption. In a typical application scenario, nodes are provided with a local power source which is usually limited and non-replaceable; thus, power consumption requirements represent the utmost constraint for most WSN nodes [1]. Typically, sensor nodes proper communicate over limited distances with a "sink" - usually acting as gateway to some remote systems - which may have less stringent power requirements as it might be equipped with better power sources.

Recently, in [2] it was observed that, in real usage scenarios in which WSN are used for monitoring the environment, nodes cannot be powered just by using small batteries. Energy harvesting becomes an essential feature in this as well as in other contexts

M.S. Obaidat, G.A. Tsihrintzis, and J. Filipe (Eds.): ICETE 2010, CCIS 222, pp. 243–258, 2012.
© Springer-Verlag Berlin Heidelberg 2012

where small batteries cannot provide the needed power for the required time. Different techniques have been explored to harvest energy from the environment [3]; so far, solar energy has been the most exploited energy harvesting resource as the technology is sufficiently mature to provide a suitable quantity of energy for wireless applications. Though, the use of solar energy introduces a further level of uncertainty in the amount of energy available to the system. Energy consumption is, in any WSN, partially deterministic and partially non-deterministic (e.g. due to random components of the wireless protocol and asynchronous alarms). The recharge rate given by a solar source superposes a natural deterministic feature (i.e. day/night, seasons) to a dominant non-deterministic stochastic nature (weather conditions) as well noted in [4]. In particular, the length of the periods in which the insulation is insufficient to guarantee operation of nodes is not known. For this reasons, defining strategies to optimize network operations in such conditions is of primary importance.

Another fundamental factor influencing the design and performance of sensor networks concerns the security of their communications. Security services such as authentication, confidentiality, and availability becomes especially critical for WSNs operating in hostile environments and managing potentially sensible data. Generally, in order to enforce communication security, additional computational resources are required [5]: typically, packet header sizes are incremented, thus inducing a significant increase in the energy spent for communications [6]. Traditional security solutions are designed by using ad-hoc approaches which offer specific protection against certain attacks. However, they rely on the assumption that the operative environment is well-known and essentially static. Moreover, some of these technologies have not been specifically developed for embedded systems; in many cases, their adoption in the pervasive world would be impossible due to high hardware resources requirements [7].

In practice, when designing secure systems, the worst case scenario is considered: the system has to guarantee adequate protection against the strongest possible security attacks that it may face. This is generally in contrast with the typical requirements of resource-constrained devices: mobility, flexibility, real-time configuration, open and dynamic operative environment [8,9]. In this chapter we introduce a new approach to security by relating it to the current system conditions. The best possible security solution, specified within a range of possible choices, is chosen dynamically to optimize both security and lifetime of the system. As discussed in [10,11], evaluating run-time the trade-off between security and consumed energy is not straightforward.

Furthermore, in some scenarios, nodes might require the ability to guarantee the delivery of critical data packets even in presence of scarce resources. For this purpose, a network Quality of Service (QoS) mechanism may be put in place. In our case, the scarce resource is not network bandwidth as in the large majority of cases in which QoS is adopted. Instead, in this context, the scarce resource is energy: when available energy is low and no solar recharge is available, only essential packets should be delivered to preserve the system main functionalities. To this goal, we associate with each packet a priority level and propose a run-time mechanism to manage security and QoS inside WSN nodes equipped with solar panels. The mechanism proposed in our approach provides the unique ability to optimize the trade-off between consumed power and security while providing support for QoS. In our approach, security is being adapted to the energy conditions of the system. At the same time, high-priority packets are processed faster and with higher security.

In Section 2, the related works are presented and the innovation of our work is highlighted. We introduce the main parameters that we considered in the design of our solution and provide details regarding the trade-off mechanism in Section 3. A case study to prove the validity of our approach as well as the simulations results are outlined in Section 4. Security and performances considerations are discussed in Section 5.

2   Related Work

Various task scheduling policies suitable for energy harvesting WSNs nodes were studied in [4,12]; in [13] algorithms for maximizing a function of merit of the devices are proposed. Appropriate voltage/frequency levels selection depending on the available energy is studied in [14] and in [15]. Adaptivity by means of setting different reliability levels depending on the available energy is presented in [16]. Most current studies discuss this subject with the classical approach used for scheduling tasks on a microprocessor: packets are considered as tasks and their schedulability is evaluated by substituting energy to CPU time.

We modify this classical approach by introducing a QoS management mechanism [17] similar to the ones commonly used in conventional networks. Packets might be subdivided into different categories, each one with a different "importance". Most critical packets are prioritized over the others; thus, their probability of being delivered in presence of scarce resources (i.e., a low battery level and no solar recharge) will be higher than the one of low priority packets.

Concerning security aspects, the problem of optimizing resources used for security, yet providing an adequate level of protection, is an hot topic at the moment [18]. In particular, the trade-off between energy and performance requirements of security solutions is of utmost relevance for embedded systems [5]. Each adopted security solution should be a good compromise between factors that are conflicting in nature and finding a good trade-off among these factors is a complex task, especially when it needs to be performed at run-time [10,11]. Our solution is able to dynamically adapt the security settings based on current node energy conditions and according to specific security requirements. Furthermore, it provides the highest possible security (compatible with security requirements) for high-priority packets.

3   Security and QoS Management

In this paper we considered a WSN in which nodes periodically send packets to a sink destination. Packets to be delivered may have security requirements that, depending on the operative context, the system might or might not be able to satisfy. For example, the battery level might be too low to use certain security settings. Therefore, in order to assure a high number of packets transmitted, a change in the security provided must be applied. Moreover, delivery of critical packets must be guaranteed: a priority value is used to mark each packet and to provide such a QoS. Priorities should be carefully assigned to packets at system configuration time: packets that are essential for the network, for example, should be associated to highest priority levels as low-priority packets may, most probably, be delayed indefinitely when available energy is scarce.

Our adaptation mechanism manages QoS and changes the security settings dynamically to maximize the trade-off between the number of packets sent and their security. Such optimizations require to estimate the energy consumption connected with the security processing and the transmission of packets. The security and QoS management process that we propose is based on a set of optimization strategies. The optimizations to be applied depend on a set of parameters related both to the system status and to the characteristics of data packets to be transmitted.

In this section we first describe the considered parameters; then we introduce the optimization process that we have designed.

3.1   Parameters

The system parameter considered in the optimization process is the available energy $E_{available}$; this parameter also includes the contribution of the energy recharge E_{harv} due to the harvesting system.

The characteristics of data packet considered are both related to intrinsic packet characteristics (e.g., their length) and to associated parameters such as their importance (expressed as a priority level) and their required security.

Energy Model. Energy consumption data can be collected only after the corresponding activity happens. Therefore, we introduce a prediction model that gives an indication of the foreseen power costs for packet transmission. The actual consumption is collected after corresponding packets have been sent and is used to have a more precise estimate of available energy.

In most networking protocols a boundary on the amount of time and energy necessary to ensure that a given packet is transmitted does not exist. For example, by using a CSMA algorithm, there may be cases in which the access to the channel cannot be obtained due to channel jamming. For this reason, an average energy for transmitting the packet should be considered instead of the worst case one. The penalty for transmitting multiple times a packet because of errors on the channel is very strong. For this reason our average takes into consideration a number of retrials that depends on the state of the network.

We model the energy needed to process a packet as:

$$E_{packet} = E_{tx} + E_{errors} \tag{1}$$

where, E_{tx} is the energy required to transmit a packet assuming that the channel is always free. Instead, E_{errors} takes into account the energy spent for multiple executions of the CSMA algorithm that are necessary when the channel is found to be busy or when packets need to be retransmitted due to collisions. E_{tx} is composed of: the energy consumed by the CSMA algorithm, E_{csma}; the energy spent for sending the packet, considered as the sum of the energies necessary to send the header of the packet (i.e. E_{header}), the possible increase in the overhead of the packet due to security (i.e.

E_{ovhsec}) and the energy necessary for sending the payload $E_{payload}$. That is:

$$E_{tx} = (E_{csma} + E_{header} + E_{ovhsec} + E_{payload}) \tag{2}$$

In Table 1a the security overhead considered is reported [19]. E_{header}, as well as E_{ovhsec} and $E_{payload}$ depend on the size of the corresponding parts of the packet and on the energy per byte e_b (i.e. transmission power/throughput in bytes). Our methodology does not require any modification of the header different than that modeled by the security components. As a matter of fact, depending on the architectural choices for the node platform, there may also be a relevant contribution to energy budget due to execution of encryption/authentication algorithms as shown in [6]. In this paper, we refer to node platforms that process security through hardware co-processors in which such contribution is negligible.

Following the analysis of the 802.15.4 algorithm done in [19] the other contributions can be refined as:

$$E_{csma} = mode * (E_{idle2rx} + E_{cca}) + E_{twait} \tag{3}$$

Therefore, E_{csma} can be decomposed into the sum of the energies to switch the radio from the idle to the receiving mode ($E_{idle2rx}$) and the energy consumed while receiving the CCA (E_{cca}). These operations are executed once in beaconless mode ($mode = 1$) and twice when beacons are used ($mode = 2$). E_{twait} is the energy consumed, in idle state, while waiting the random time before performing the CCA; we used the worst case value for this parameter.

E_{errors} is composed of two factors:

$$E_{errors} = E_{busy} + E_{re\_tx} = \frac{(K_{busy} * E_{csma} + N_{re\_tx} * E_{tx})}{M_{sent}} \tag{4}$$

the first is the energy spent for executing multiple times the CSMA procedure when the CCA reports that the channel is busy, hence it equals K_{busy} times the energy of a CSMA algorithm. The latter is the energy consumed for retransmitting the entire packet due to channel collisions, that is N_{re_tx} times E_{tx}. Values are meant by the number of packets successfully sent (M_{sent}) in a transmission time slot. Values of these parameters, K_{busy}, N_{re_tx} and M_{sent} has to be computed based on the applicative scenario. They can assume a constant value, if the channel behavior is quite static; or can be computed at run-time, for example, by monitoring the channel conditions and updating proper counters.

Every time a packet is processed and transmitted, the corresponding energy consumption E_{packet} is drawn from the available energy $E_{available}$.

Finally, we introduce an *energy constraint* E_{frame} which is a discrete time derivative of the current energy consumption $E_{available}$:

$$E_{frame} = E_{available}(t) - E_{available}(t-1) \tag{5}$$

This constraint is used to assures that, for each transmission time slot, the variation of the energy required to process a certain number of packets is below the specified threshold E_{frame}. Thus, it is a hard constraint in the maximum energy consumption allowed

Table 1. a) Packet schema. b) Security suites supported by IEEE Std 802.15.4 and their packets overhead [6].

a)

Security Suites			
SuiteID	Description	Service	Overhead [byte]
0	Null	No Security	0
1	AES-CBC-MAC-32		9
2	AES-CBC-MAC-64	Authentication	13
3	AES-CBC-MAC-128		21
4	AES-CTR	Encryption (only)	5
5	AES-CCM-32		9
6	AES-CCM-64	Authentication and Encryption	13
7	AES-CCM-128		21

b)

Packet #	102	$SecReq$	
Size [bytes]	Priority [0, 3]	SecSuite (8bit)	ActiveSuite [0, 7]
50	3	[1,0,1,0,1,1,0]	5

in a transmission slot. The value for E_{frame} can be either constant, (and, therefore, assigned statically at design time) or computed dynamically as a function of the energy currently available. In general, the value assumed by this parameter should be tuned according to the considered scenario.

Packet Characteristics. In our system each packet, with a given payload size, is labeled with an identifier $P_\#$ and it is associated to security requirements as well as to a priority level. These pieces of information are only used by the optimization mechanism and they do not cause any network overhead as they are local parameters. An example is shown in Table 1b.

A *priority* ρ can have values between 1 and 4 (the higher the number, the higher the priority). As mentioned earlier, when energy is scarce, our system will favour high-priority packets. Low priority packets will be delayed indefinitely or discarded if the memory becomes full. The aim of this approach is to preserve as much energy as possible to send essential packets. Non-essential packets might be sent later when harvesting allows the system to recover the battery level.

Security requirements associated to packets are a central parameter in our trade-off mechanism. The security level chosen for each packet impacts both on the associated consumed energy and on the associated computational and network latencies. A secure packet, due to longer packet header and security processing, consumes more energy and takes more time to be managed by the network than a non-secure one [6]. While some packets have mandatory security requirements, others may have softer requirements. Therefore security of such packets can be decided at runtime depending on the current status of the system.

We defined a *security requirements*, $SecReq$, as composed of:

$$SecReq = \langle SecSuite; ActiveSuite \rangle \tag{6}$$

SecSuites is a list of security suites that may be used for the particular packet. *SecSuites* is a bitstream in which every bit corresponds to a different security suite supported by the transmission protocol, the bit is set to 1 if it is possible to use that suite for the particular packet. For example, if we refer to the security suites of the IEEE 802.15.4 wireless standard [20] we need 8 bits to model the entire set, as reported in Table 1a.

ActiveSuite identifies the security suite to be used for processing the given packet. If a change in the security provided is required, the *ActiveSuite* is updated to the new security suite ID. Changes in *ActiveSuite* are allowed within the packet security suites bitstream. Therefore, to have a fixed security suite only one bit should be set in *SecSuites* list. This corresponds to a mandatory security requirement given by, for example, the following tuple: $\langle SecSuite = [0,0,0,1,0,0,0]; \; ActiveSuite = 4 \rangle$. *ActiveSuite* is the index of the 8 bit array of *SecSuite*.

An example of definition of softer packet *SecReq* is shown in Table 1b; the packet with label 102 has a priority value 3 and may support different suites for data protection: 0, 2, 4 and 5. The current active suite is the number 5, that is the suite AES-CCM-32 of Table 1a. If an adaptation is needed, the system may decide to use a different security suite (e.g. *ActiveSuite* = 4) to save energy (because of lower header size overhead).

3.2   Optimization Process

By using the aforementioned parameters our management algorithm optimizes the security of packets while managing QoS and optimizing energy consumption. An optimization strategy is applied by the optimization mechanism to obtain these results.

Optimization Strategies. Different optimization strategies can be defined for different system conditions. An optimization strategy ($\wp$) can be defined as a composition of actions to be performed in order to meet the energy constraint given by E_{frame}.

We designed the strategies with two goals in mind: to maximize the number of high-priority packets that are delivered and to ensure that security requirements of each packet are satisfied. These strategies are optimized to provide to each packet the safest possible suite among the ones specified in *SecSuite*.

We identify the following actions that can be combined within a strategy $\wp$:

- change the *ActiveSuite* security suite used to protect the considered packet, according to the suites specified in *SecSuite*;
- either drop or delay the packet transmission to the next communication slot, according to the priority of the considered packet;
- limit the number of packets to be sent. Such a limitation can be imposed both on predetermined priorities levels or globally on all packets.

QoS may be provided through one of the well known approaches listed in [17], for example by applying *Weighted Fair Queueing* (WFQ) or *Priority Queueing* (PQ).

By combining the aforementioned actions in a strategy, the system can directly change the energy consumption needed to process the packets that are in the send queue with the goal of satisfying the energy constraint given by E_{frame}.

For example, a possible strategy to meet such a constraint may be as follows:

- low priority packets are delayed to successive communication slots;
- other, less energy hungry, security suites are chosen for the remaining packets in queue;
- other packets may be selected for being delayed.

Optimization Mechanism. An adaptation is required when the amount of energy required to transmit λ packets is above the threshold E_{frame}. The adaptation is performed by enforcing a certain strategy $\wp$. The process has been designed by following the Monitor-Controller-Adapter loop [21]. In the monitoring phase, the available energy capacity $E_{available}$ and the λ packets to be delivered to a sink node are measured every transmission time slot. The available energy includes the contributions of the harvested energy E_{harv} obtained through solar cells. Depending on the current energy conditions, it exists a given energy constraint E_{frame} to be respected. Moreover, network conditions are monitored by updating the counters of the Equation 4 (N_{ri_tx}, K_{busy} and M_{sent}) at each transmission time slot. All these monitored information are propagated to the controller module that decides which packets to send and their associated security suites. These information are then propagated to the adapter that organizes packet transmission according to what decided by the controller. Packets are then sent by using conventional network stack.

The controller uses the energy model introduced in Section 3.1 to estimate the energy per packet E_{packet}, and the total energy consumption of the candidate packets. This estimation is used to select packets according to a strategy $\wp$.

A further constraint on the candidate packet selection might be imposed by the current network conditions: for example, it can be set an higher bound for the number of packets that can be transmitted.

In Algorithm 1 we show an example of a selection mechanism used within the controller module to select the optimal packets.

4   Experimental Results

We designed a case study that represents a simple yet realistic case and allows evaluating the performances of our optimization algorithm. In this section we provide a description of this case study; we then describe the simulations we have performed and we show the results we have obtained.

4.1   Case Study

We consider a wireless sensor network composed of 7 nodes. The optimization algorithm is applied at node level, thus, its efficiency does not depend on the number of nodes. Each node is equipped with a digital camera, it acquires an image every 30s and sends it to the central point. Every picture is composed of 160 packets of 90 bytes. Though, it should be noted that the actual dimension of packets depends on the security suite adopted. The application is data intensive for a WSN, having a global application throughput of about 35kbps. This is a classical scenario in many application fields such as, for example, surveillance, traffic monitoring, environment monitoring. Information are usually uniformly spread in pictures. For this reason we divided each picture into five segments. Data of each segment are subdivided into network packets. All the packets belonging to the same segment share the same priority level. Priorities are assigned to each segment by following an uniform distribution. Security requirements of packets (i.e., $SecSuite$ bitstream) are taken from a binomial distribution. Consumption of the packets to be delivered is estimated according to the model specified in Section 3.1. In particular, by considering data collected during previous simulations, we estimate a value of $K_{busy} = 64$, $N_{re\_tx} = 32$ and $M_{sent} = 160$ packets for the parameters of Equation 4.

In this scenario, we considered the IEEE 802.15.4 protocol in Beaconed Mode (i.e., $mode = 2$ in Equation 3). We simulated a star topology, therefore every communication passes through the coordinator. We assume that the coordinator is connected to a power line; the other nodes have limited energy capacity and they are able to harvest solar energy. Considering the fact that charge/discharge cycles are harmful for chemical batteries, we suppose to use a super-capacitor instead of a battery. While this improves time-invariance of the power section, the energy contained in the ultra-capacitor is about one order of magnitude less than the one of a commercial battery. We considered our power section made of a small solar cell that produces at peak about $300mA$, and a super-capacitor of $310Farad$ with slightly more than $400.000mAs$ available. This correspond, for example, to the adoption of a Maxwell BCAP0350 E270 T9 SuperCap. The consumption of the digital camera was considered to be $25mAs$ per picture. E_{frame} has been considered to be a constant value of $3.5mAs$ plus a percentage (0.09%) of the total energy capacity, meant by the number of frames. This value has been chosen to provide a system lifetime, among battery recharges, of roughly 4 days. In conditions of peak solar power, the super-capacitor is fully recharged in less than half an hour.

4.2   Simulations

The case study discussed above has been simulated to verify the effectiveness of our approach. Results show that, while our method does not allow for a decrease of consumed energy, it allows for an optimization of the trade-off among consumed energy, importance of the packets sent, and their security level.

In our case study we adopted the optimization algorithm shown in Algorithm 1. We assumed an approach to QoS similar to Priority Queueing (PQ). With PQ, higher-priority packets are transmitted before lower-priority ones, thus guaranteeing that an higher number of high-priority packets are delivered even in conditions of scarce energy. We considered the following optimization strategy $\wp$: by default, the active security suite for all packets is the $SuiteID = \#0$ (i.e. $NULL$); when the energy consumption of the high-priority packets is below the threshold, their security is increased according to packet security requirements. After the security upgrade, the remaining packets in queue are analyzed in order to consume the residual energy. Instead, if the energy consumption of the high-priority packets is above threshold, the most energy-hungry packets are removed from the list of candidates.

When solar cells are active our optimization algorithm is set to work as if the batteries were fully charged. In these conditions our algorithm is at least not worse than any static setting for security. In fact, in this condition, our optimization algorithm will select the highest security algorithm specified for each class of packets. For this reason in the simulations we focused only on a scenario in which there is no solar recharge for a long period of time, for example due to clouds.

Algorithm 1. $sel\_pos = \text{SELECTOR}(\ E_{frame},\ sub\_set)$

Require: An energy constraint $E_{frame} \geq 0$.
Require: Set of packets (indexes) to analyze, $sub\_set \neq 0$.
Ensure: The optimal set of packets (indexes) to send sel_pos.

1:   $pri\_pos = \text{HIGHPRICANDIDATES}(queue, sub\_set)$
2:   $E_{packet} = \text{GETPACKETSENERGY}(queue, pri\_pos)$
3:   $E_{residual} = E_{frame}$
4:   $E_{consumption} = \sum E_{packet}$
5:   $sel\_pos = [\ ]$
6:   **if** $min\ (E_{packet}) > E_{frame} \mid sel\_pos == [\ ]$ **then**
7:     **return** sel_pos
8:   **else**
9:     **if** $E_{consumption} < E_{frame}$ **then**
10:       $sel\_pos = pri\_pos$
11:       $E_{residual} = E_{residual} - E_{consumption}$
12:       **if** $\text{CHECKSECUPGRADE}(E_{residual}, pri\_pos)$ **then**
13:         $E_{residual} = \text{UPGRADESEC}(pri\_pos)$
14:       **end if**
15:       $sel\_trail = \text{SELECTOR}(E_{residual}, \text{TRAIL}(pri\_pos))$
16:       **return** $sel\_pos = sel\_pos + sel\_trail$
17:     **else**
18:       $new\_pos = \text{REMOVEMAXENERGY}(pri\_pos)$
19:       $sel\_pos = \text{SELECTOR}(E_{residual}, new\_pos)$
20:     **end if**
21:     **return** sel_pos
22:   **end if**

Simulation Environment. The case study has been simulated by using the SystemC network simulator described in [22]. This simulator is capable of emulating node and network operations as well as annotating with μs precision the corresponding power consumption for all the nodes involved. Furthermore, the simulator is capable of managing channel contention and to repeat transmissions when interferences occur.

The simulator is based on an implementation independent model that can be later characterized for practical implementations [19]. The characterization includes the substitution of the actual consumption values for the different activities of the node (e.g., reception and transmission). In [19] it is shown that the power consumption obtained with the simulator is few percent different from the actual data of consumption gathered from real nodes through an oscilloscope. In order to characterize our implementation independent model, we considered that the devices are equipped with the CC2420 radio with a $0dBm$ transmission power and that they use corresponding power levels.

Results. The impact of our method is highlighted by comparing the same scenarios with and without applying the optimizations. In case of no limitations on energy consumption and with no optimization, the system has an operative lifetime of about three days when non energy harvesting is possible. When proper constraints on the consumed

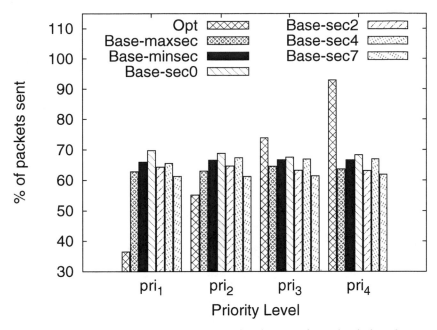

Fig. 1. Comparison of average percentage of packets sent for each priority value

power are set (E_{frame} of Equation 5), the lifetime in the same conditions is increased to four days. In this paragraph we focus on the comparative analysis of various cases in which the energy constraint is set.

Six different configurations have been simulated for comparing different possible situations, one of them in which the optimization methodology was used (*Opt*), and the other five (*Base-**) in which it was not. The last five considered cases are as follows(to cover almost all the cases of Table 1a):

- security is the maximum in the *SecSuite* range specified for each packet (*Base-maxsec*);
- security is the minimum in the *SecSuite* range specified for each packet (*Base-minsec*);
- security is at level *0* for all packets (*Base-sec0*);
- security is at level *2* for all packets (*Base-sec2*);
- security is at level *4* for all packets (*Base-sec4*);
- security is at level *7* for all packets (*Base-sec7*);

Figure 1 shows the percentage of packets of each priority level that the node have been able to send (remaining packets are discarded so to respect energy constraints) in the simulation period when different system configuration are considered. The figure shows that, while a non-optimized node does not guarantee any privilege to high-priority packets, the optimized node does. When no QoS is considered, each packet has the same possibility of being discarded (about 30-40% depending on the case considered). When QoS is used, instead, the probability to be delivered for each packet is proportional to

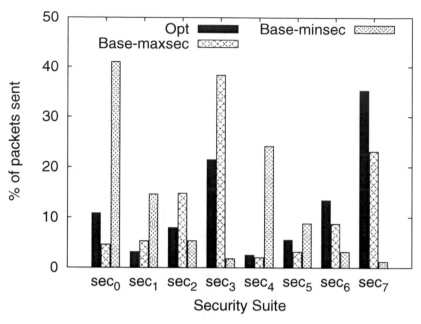

Fig. 2. Comparison of average percentage of packets sent for each security suite

its priority. Highest priority packets are delivered more than 90% of the times; lowest priority packets are delivered about 35% of the times. Obviously, the adoption of a QoS mechanism does not change the total number of packets sent, it only changes the distribution of these packets among the different priority levels.

Figure 2 compares the number of packets sent for each security level when the optimized system and the *Base-maxsec* and *Base-minsec* cases are considered. As it can be seen from the figure, the optimized node tends to maximize the number of packets that are processed by using the security suites number *3* and *7* which are to be considered the most secure ones available. Thus, our optimization system tends to guarantee an higher security level to the packets.

Figure 3 compares the energy per byte spent by the optimized system with the energy spent in all the cases in which the optimization is not used. The optimization allows the system to spend less energy per byte then in the *Base-maxsec* case. It also provides the ability of saving energy with respect to the cases in which security level *2* and security level *7* are always selected (*Base-sec2* and *Base-sec7*). The *Base-minsec* case is of course less energy hungry, but, at the same time, it provides, in average, a lower level of security to packets. The same applies to the *Base-sec4* case.

Figure 4 compares the number of packets sent by the optimized system during the simulation period with the ones sent by the non-optimized systems. The optimized system is able to send an highest number of packets with respect to more energy hungry modes. Obviously, less energy hungry modes are able to send more packets before finishing the battery.

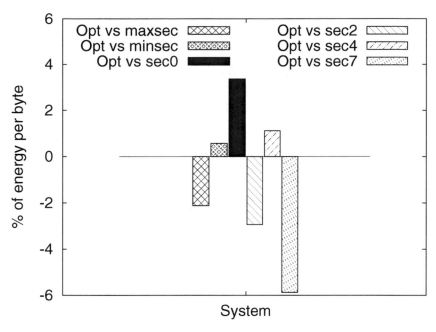

Fig. 3. Comparison of percentage variation of energy per byte consumed by the Optimized system w.r.t the Base System

Summarizing, the results show how our optimization method provides QoS management while obtaining the highest possible level of security that is compatible with the current system parameters.

It should be noticed that our results report the energy consumption of the whole node, even including the sensing part. It is well known that, in these conditions, the energy spent for transmission is not the predominant part of the total energy consumption. Indeed, the portion of energy devoted to communication (not considering the energy used by the infrastructure) is about 10% of the total consumed energy. For this reason the differences in performances among different cases might appear limited, even if they are not. In fact, they are significant if we focus our analysis only to energy related to data transmission.

5 Security and Performances Analysis

In this section we provide an analysis on how our optimization mechanisms influences security and energy consumption.

5.1 Security Analysis

The use of multiple cryptographic algorithms may lower the security of applications. In particular, when weakest algorithms are used, the transmitted data are more exposed

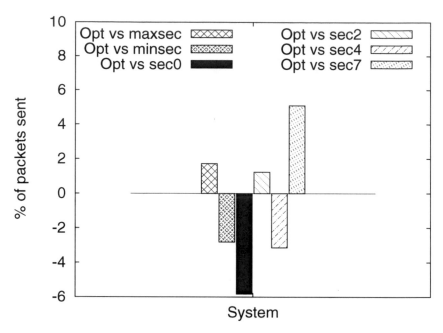

Fig. 4. Comparison of number of packets sent by the Optimized system w.r.t. the Base system

to attacks. Though, our approach tries to provide a reasonable solution for those situations in which device constraints would not give the possibility to provide any (or little) security to applications. Moreover, in our implementation, we considered different crypto-key for each security suite. Thus, an attacker that guessed the key of the weakest algorithm does not have knowledge of the data encrypted by using other cryptographic algorithms.

Aim of our self-adaptation mechanism is to provide the highest possible security level in any instant of time. Degradation of security is only performed if the energy constraints of the system cannot be satisfied. In this particular context, lowering the security of the communication increases the potential of attacks only for a limited quantity of data (i.e., just the ones that are being transmitted in those periods of time).

Possible attacks in which the system can be forced to decrease the security level of applications may also affect our security degradation method. For example, multiple communications requests can be used to drain the battery, thus forcing the system to degrade security. Though, we should consider that our framework performs adaptation of security level based on application security requirements. Therefore, applications are always guaranteed to have the minimum level of protection that they require.

Similar attacks can be used to cause a denial of service by totally draining the battery. Our management of security allows the system to stand longer to these attacks, even though it does not provide a specific protection for them. The best defense against this kinds of attacks would be to have an intrusion detection system installed on the nodes. Though, running such a system, even if simplified, would be too expensive in terms of computational power, memory, and consumed energy.

5.2 Analytical Analysis of Energy Consumption

For our approach to be convenient, the energy spent by exploiting multiple security suites, selected applying our optimizations, must be lower than the energy spent to process all packets by using a single security suite (system without optimizations):

$$E(s_1, p_1) + \delta_{1,2} + E(s_2, p_2) + \ldots + \delta_{n-1,n} + E(s_n, p_n) \leq E(s_n, (p_1, p_2, \ldots, p_n)) \quad (7)$$

where $E(s_i, p_i)$ is the average energy consumption, computed by using Eq. 1, needed to process the packets p_i by the security suite s_i. With $\delta_{i,i+1}$, we identify the energy consumed for switching from suite s_i to s_{i+1} as well as the energy spent for computing the optimization. The costs of applying the optimization are related both to the additional security suites initializations required and to performing the optimization itself.

In our case, since the energy spent for processing each packets depends also on packet size, we can order the suites according to the overhead they introduce, as shown in Table 1a. Thus, we can have: $E(s_1, p_1) \leq E(s_2, p_2) \leq \ldots \leq E(s_n, p_n)$.

By using the mathematical induction theorem, it can be demonstrated that, from the energy stand point, it is convenient to adopt our optimization system if:

$$\sum_{i=1}^{n} \delta_{i,i+1} \leq E(s_n, (\sum_{i}^{n} p_i)) - \sum_{i=1}^{n} E(s_i, p_i) \quad (8)$$

The value of $\delta_{i,i+1}$ depends on different factors: a) the number of security suites available, b) the hardware and software architecture of a node, and c) the switching technique implemented for changing from one suite to another. In some cases, there could be possible to have $\delta_{i,i+1} = \delta_{i+1,i+2} = \ldots = \delta_{n-1,n}$ with further simplification of the above equations.

We did not measure directly the switching costs; instead we proved the validity of Eq. 8 by experiment results, as shown in Section 4. Further improvements may be introduced by optimizing the switching technique.

6 Conclusions and Future Work

In this paper we proposed a novel adaptation mechanism to deal with secure and priority-based transmission of packets in WSNs. This optimization mechanism allows the system to survive long periods in which the energy harvesting adopted might not be able to provide energy. The algorithm, by performing QoS management, provides the ability to privilege important (i.e., high priority) packets when the energy available is scarce. Security settings are changed dynamically to provide the best security compatible with the current system conditions.

Future work include refinement and extension of the methodology proposed and, in particular, the addition of new capabilities such as, for example, changing dynamically the duty cycle of the network and/or the monitoring period.

References

1. Akyildiz, I.F., Su, W., Sankarasubramaniam, Y., Cayirci, E.: Wireless Sensor Networks: a Survey. Computer Networks 38, 393–422 (2002)
2. Alippi, C., Camplani, R., Galperti, C., Roveri, M.: Effective design of WSNs: From the lab to the real world. In: ICST 2008, pp. 1–9 (2008)

3. Roundy, S., Steingart, D., Frechette, L., Wright, P., Rabaey, J.: Power Sources for Wireless Sensor Networks. In: Karl, H., Wolisz, A., Willig, A. (eds.) EWSN 2004. LNCS, vol. 2920, pp. 1–17. Springer, Heidelberg (2004)
4. Moser, C., Brunelli, D., Thiele, L., Benini, L.: Real-time scheduling for energy harvesting sensor nodes. Real-Time Syst. 37, 233–260 (2007)
5. Chandramouli, R., Bapatla, S., Subbalakshmi, K.P., Uma, R.N.: Battery power-aware encryption. ACM Trans. Inf. Syst. Secur. 9, 162–180 (2006)
6. Mura, M., Fabbri, F., Sami, M.: Modelling the Power Cost of Security in Wireless Sensor Networks: the Case of 802.15.4. In: IEEE ICT 2008 (2008)
7. Ferrante, A., Piuri, V., Owen, J.: IPSec Hardware Resource Requirements Evaluation. In: NGI 2005, Rome, Italy, EuroNGI (2005)
8. Keeratiwintakorn, P., Krishnamurthy, P.: Energy Efficient Security Services for Limited Wireless Devices. In: International Symposium on Wireless Pervasive Computing, pp. 1–6 (2006)
9. Großschädl, J., Szekely, A., Tillich, S.: The energy cost of cryptographic key establishment in wireless sensor networks. In: ASIACCS 2007, pp. 380–382. ACM (2007)
10. Chigan, C., Li, L., Ye, Y.: Resource-aware self-adaptive security provisioning in mobile ad hoc networks. In: IEEE WCNC, vol. 4, pp. 2118–2124 (2005)
11. Lighfoot, L., Ren, J., Li, T.: An energy efficient link-layer security protocol for wireless sensor networks. In: 2007 IEEE International Conference on Electro/Information Technology, pp. 233–238 (2007)
12. Moser, C., Thiele, L., Brunelli, D., Benini, L.: Adaptive power management in energy harvesting systems. In: DATE 2007, pp. 773–778 (2007)
13. Moser, C., Chen, J.J., Thiele, L.: Reward Maximization for Embedded Systems with Renewable Energies. In: IEEE RTCSA 2008, pp. 247–256 (2008)
14. Liu, S., Qiu, Q., Wu, Q.: Energy aware dynamic voltage and frequency selection for real-time systems with energy harvesting. In: DATE 2008, pp. 236–241. ACM (2008)
15. Liu, S., Wu, Q., Qiu, Q.: An adaptive scheduling and voltage/frequency selection algorithm for real-time energy harvesting systems. In: DAC 2009, pp. 782–787 (2009)
16. Wang, L., Yang, Y., Noh, D.K., Le, H., Abdelzaher, T., Ward, M.: AdaptSens: An Adaptive Data Collection and Storage Service for Solar-Powered Sensor networks. In: RTSS 2009 (2009)
17. Sean Convery: 49. In: Internetworking Technologies Handbook, 49-1–49-32. Cisco Press (2004) ISBN158705115X
18. Ravi, S., Raghunathan, A., Kocher, P., Hattangady, S.: Security in embedded systems: Design challenges. Trans. on Embedded Computing Sys. 3, 461–491 (2004)
19. Mura, M., Paolieri, M., Negri, L., Fabri, F., Sami, M.: Power Modeling and Power Analysis for IEEE 802.15.4: a Concurrent State Machine Approach. In: CCNC 2007 (2007)
20. Sastry, N., Wagner, D.: Security considerations for IEEE 802.15.4 networks. In: WiSe 2004, pp. 32–42. ACM (2004)
21. Derin, O., Ferrante, A., Taddeo, A.V.: Coordinated management of hardware and software self-adaptivity. Journal of Systems Architecture 55, 170–179 (2009)
22. Mura, M., Sami, M.: Code generation from statecharts: Simulation of wireless sensor networks. In: Proceedings of DSD 2008, Parma, Italy (2008)

Threshold Discernible Ring Signatures

Swarun Kumar[1], Shivank Agrawal[1], Ramarathnam Venkatesan,[2]
Satyanarayana V. Lokam[2], and C. Pandu Rangan[1]

[1] Indian Institute of Technology Madras, Chennai, India
[2] Microsoft Research, Bangalore, India
{swarun.s,shinku100}@gmail.com, {venkie,satya}@microsoft.com,
prangan@iitm.ac.in

Abstract. A ring signature [1] demonstrates that the signer who produced it is among a group A of n people, called a ring. A signer may produce a ring signature on any ring A he is part of, arbitrarily without any setup procedure or the consent of anyone in A. Several extensions of ring signatures have been proposed in literature. *Step out ring signatures* introduced in [2] address the issue of a ring member proving that she is not the original signer of a message, in case of dispute. First we show that the scheme in [2] has several flaws and design a correct scheme and prove formally the security of the same. Then we use the basic constructs of our scheme to design a protocol for a new problem, which we refer to as *threshold discernible ring signatures*. In threshold discernible ring signatures, a group B of t members can co-operate to identify the original signer of a ring signature that involved a group A of n alleged signers, where $B \subseteq A$ and $n \geq t$. This is the first time that this problem is considered in the literature. We formally prove the security of our scheme in the random oracle model and propose various extensions.

1 Introduction

A ring signature [1] demonstrates that the signer who produced it is among a group A of n people, called a ring. A signer may produce a ring signature on any ring A he is part of, arbitrarily without any setup procedure or the consent of anyone in A. Such signatures have been expanded to various applications: deniable ring authentication [3,4], linkable ring signature schemes that allow one to link signatures signed by the same person, short versions of linkable ring signature [5,6]. Furthermore, identity based ring signature schemes, which allow ring construction across different identity-based master domains [7,8,9] and confessible threshold ring signature [10], where the actual signer can prove that she has created the signature, have also been proposed in literature.

The original intent was to keep the real signer anonymous. However in the event of a dispute, a member of the ring A may want to prove that she was not the actual signer of a particular message. A new variant called *step out* ring signature was introduced in [2]; here the real signer can prove that she created the signature, while any one else in the ring can prove that she is not the original signer. Their proposal was an intermediate solution between the classical ring and group signatures, and can be used for instance in e-auction schemes, and this is the only scheme present in the literature. However, our attack presented here shows that their scheme allows a third party, who is not a member

M.S. Obaidat, G.A. Tsihrintzis, and J. Filipe (Eds.): ICETE 2010, CCIS 222, pp. 259–273, 2012.
© Springer-Verlag Berlin Heidelberg 2012

of the ring, to forge a signature on behalf of the ring. In another scenario, we break the anonymity of the signer of a ring signature. We also correct these flaws and provide a modified step out ring signature scheme.

Exposing the identity of the original signer of a ring signature may arise in several other contexts as well. Suppose a petitioner wishes to send a complaint regarding certain government officials on behalf of several people, say the residents of her locality. The signer wishes to remain anonymous in order to prevent harassment from the concerned officials. However, any resident who disagrees with the complaint must have the right to prove that she is not the petitioner. At the same time, a sufficiently large threshold of the residents should be able to discover the identity of the petitioner, in case the complaint was malicious.

Consider a joint bank account scenario, where n people share a single account. Any account holder among these n people is authorized to sign and transact with the bank. The bank will only know that someone among these n people has signed, but will not know the exact identity of the signer. Hence the situation cannot afford a centralized manager. Now, in case of fraud by any one of the n members, any threshold of t people among the n members can cooperate and identify the fraudulent person.

Our Contributions. We perform cryptanalysis on the step out ring signature scheme [2] and identify defects in unforgeability and anonymity. We additionally provide appropriate modifications in order to present a provably secure step out ring signature scheme under the random oracle model.

We introduce the concept of threshold discernible ring signatures, where a threshold of t signers are together capable of finding the identity of the original signer. This may be applied, for example, to situations where a message has been maliciously signed on behalf of a ring of signers and a majority (or a threshold t) of the ring members decide to unmask the original signer of the message. We shall use the basic constructs of our modified step out ring signature scheme to produce a threshold discernible ring signature scheme. We also formally prove the security of our scheme in the random oracle model and propose various extensions.

2   Preliminaries

We shall consider rings with n members, denoted by $\mathcal{U}_1, \cdots, \mathcal{U}_n$. Let p, q be large primes $(p, q >> n)$, $q | p - 1$, and $G = < g >$ be an order q cyclic subgroup of $\mathbb{Z}_p^*$. For the sake of simplicity we shall skip "mod p" if it follows from the context. We assume that user $\mathcal{U}_i$ holds a private key x_i; the corresponding public key is $y_i = g^{x_i}$. The key y_i is publicly available. $\mathcal{H}$ denotes a secure hash function $\{0, 1\}^* \rightarrow \{0, 1\}^k$, where k is a fixed constant. We assume that the following assumptions are fulfilled in G:

Definition 1 - Decisional Diffie-Hellman Assumption. Let G be a cyclic group generated by g of order q. Let $\mathcal{A}^{DDH}$ be an algorithm that has to distinguish $c_0 = (g, g^a, g^b, g^{ab})$ from $c_1 = (g, g^a, g^b, g^c)$ for randomly chosen $a, b, c \in \mathbb{Z}_q$. Let $\mathbf{Adv}_{\mathcal{A}}^{ddh} = |Pr[\mathcal{A}(c_1) = 1] - Pr[\mathcal{A}(c_0) = 1]|$ be called the advantage of $\mathcal{A}$ in breaking the DDH problem.

The DDH assumption holds for G, if advantage $\mathbf{Adv}_{\mathcal{A}}^{ddh}$ is negligible for each probabilistic polynomial-time algorithm $\mathcal{A}$, i.e. $\mathbf{Adv}_{\mathcal{A}}^{ddh} < \epsilon_{ddh}$ where ϵ_{ddh} is negligible.

Definition 2 - Discrete Logarithm (DL) Assumption. Let G be a cyclic group generated by g of order q. Let $\mathcal{A}$ be an algorithm such that on input g^a, where $a \in \mathbb{Z}_q$, $\mathcal{A}$ should output a. Let $\mathbf{Succ}_{\mathcal{A}}^{dl} = Pr[\mathcal{A}(g^a) = a]$ be called the success of $\mathcal{A}$ in breaking the DL problem.

The DL assumption holds in G, if for each probabilistic polynomial-time algorithm $\mathcal{A}$, success $\mathbf{Succ}_{\mathcal{A}}^{dl}$ is negligible, i.e. $\mathbf{Succ}_{\mathcal{A}}^{dl} < \epsilon_{dl}$ where ϵ_{dl} is negligible.

2.1 SKDL Proof of Knowledge

The SKDL proof of knowledge is a signature of knowledge of discrete logarithms defined in [11]. It is based on the Schnorr signature scheme [12]. This signature proves the knowledge of $x : y = g^x$ in the context of a message m. We explain the construction and verification below.

SKDL Construction. The construction $SKDL(g, y, m)$ is described below. It is executed by the prover who possesses $x : y = g^x$. Note that g is a generator of the group G.

1. Pick $r \leftarrow_R \mathbb{Z}_q^*$.
2. Calculate $c = \mathcal{H}(g||y||g^r||m)$.
3. Calculate

$$s = r - cx \qquad (1)$$

The procedure returns the values (c, s).

SKDL Verification. The verification procedure $\mathcal{V}_{SKDL}(g, y, m)$ is executed by the verifier and checks if:

$$c \stackrel{?}{=} \mathcal{H}(g||y||g^s y^c||m)$$

This proves that the prover is aware of discrete logarithm $x = \log_g(y)$ without actually revealing x.

2.2 SEQDL Proof of Knowledge

The step-out ring signature scheme in [2] is based on a *signature of knowledge of equality of discrete logarithms* (SEQDL). Let $g, \hat{g}, \hat{y}_w \in G$ and tuples $(y_1, \cdots, y_n), (w_1, \cdots, w_n) \in G^n$. SEQDL allows a prover to prove in zero-knowledge that $\log_{\hat{g}} \hat{y}_w = \log_g(y_j w_j)$ for some index j, with j not revealed to the verifier.

Preliminaries. Recall that G is an order q cyclic subgroup of $\mathbb{Z}_p^*$ with g as its generator. Let $\mathcal{U}_j$ be a prover who has the following information:

- $Y = (y_1, \cdots, y_n) \in G^n$
- For a specific index j, $\mathcal{U}_j$ knows $x_j : y_j = g^{x_j}$. Note that $\mathcal{U}_j$ is not aware of the discrete logarithms of $y_i \in Y : i \neq j$.
- $W = (w_1, \cdots, w_n) \in G^n$ and $(r_1, \cdots, r_n) \in \mathbb{Z}_q^n$, where $w_i = g^{r_i}$ for all $i = 1, \cdots, n$. Note that unless $\mathcal{U}_j$ is the signer, she is not aware of the discrete logarithms of $w_i \in W : i \neq j$.
- $\hat{g} \in G$, which is randomly chosen by the signer and $\hat{y} = \hat{g}^{x_j + r_j}$.

Using these values, $\mathcal{U}_j$ wishes to convince the verifier that the discrete logarithms $\log_{\hat{g}} \hat{y}_w$ and $\log_g(y_j w_j)$ are equal, with the index j not revealed to the verifier. $\mathcal{U}_j$ achieves this by executing the SEQDL construction algorithm and passing the outputs to the SEQDL verification algorithm. The details are given below:

SEQDL Construction. The SEQDL construction algorithm, run by the $\mathcal{U}_j$, is SEQDL$(\hat{g}, g, x_j, r_j, \hat{y}_w, Y, W, m)$. Typically, the vector W is chosen by the signer. W may be withheld by the signer, distributed only to the other ring members or be made available along with the signature. The construction of SEQDL is as follows:

Algorithm SEQDL$(\hat{g}, g, x_j, r_j, \hat{y}_w, Y, W, m)$

Pick random elements $r \in \mathbb{Z}_q$ and $c_i, s_i \in \mathbb{Z}_q$, for $i \in \{1, \cdots, n\} \backslash \{j\}$.
For all $i \in \{1, \cdots, n\} \backslash \{j\}$, user U_j computes:

$$t_i \leftarrow \hat{g}^{s_i} \hat{y}_w^{c_i}, u_i \leftarrow g^{s_i}(y_i w_i)^{c_i}, t_j \leftarrow \hat{g}^r, u_j \leftarrow g^r \qquad (2)$$

We denote $\overline{Y} = y_1 || \cdots || y_n$, $\overline{W} = w_1 || \cdots || w_n$
Compute:

$$c_j \leftarrow \mathcal{H}(\hat{g}||g||\hat{y}_w||\overline{Y}||\overline{W}||t_1||u_1|| \cdots ||t_n||u_n||m) - \sum_{i<n, i \neq j} c_i \qquad (3)$$

$$s_j \leftarrow r - (x_j + r_j)c_j \bmod q \qquad (4)$$

return $C = (c_1, \cdots, c_n)$, $S = (s_1, \cdots, s_n)$.

SEQDL Verification. Given a signature SEQDL$(\hat{g}, g, x_j, r_j, \hat{y}_w, Y, W, m) = (C, S)$, with parameters $\hat{g}$, g, $\hat{y}_w$, Y, W, and a message m, the verification algorithm $\mathcal{V}_{\text{SEQDL}}(\hat{g}, g, \hat{y}_w, Y, W, C, S, m)$, run by the verifier, checks if:

$$\sum_{i=1}^{n} c_i \overset{?}{=} \mathcal{H}(\hat{g}||g||\hat{y}_w||\overline{Y}||\overline{W}||\hat{g}^{s_1}\hat{y}_w^{c_1}||g^{s_1}(y_1 w_1)^{c_1}|| \cdots$$
$$||\hat{g}^{s_n}\hat{y}_w^{c_n}||g^{s_n}(y_n w_n)^{c_n}||m) \qquad (5)$$

The verifier returns 1 if the above condition succeeds, 0 otherwise. When verification returns 1, the verifier is convinced of the equality of discrete logarithms $\log_{\hat{g}} \hat{y}_w$ and $\log_g(y_j w_j)$ with the index $j \in \{1, \cdots, n\}$ unknown to the verifier.

3   Step Out Ring Signatures

Step out ring signatures (SRS) [2] allow the real signer to prove that she created the signature, while any one else in the ring can prove that she is not the original signer. However, the scheme provided in [2] has several security flaws. We provided the correct modified SRS scheme in section 3.1. In section 3.2, we provide the cryptanalysis of the original scheme in [2].

3.1   Modified SRS Scheme

Let us assume that $\mathcal{U}_j$ is the real signer and $\mathcal{U}_1, \cdots, \mathcal{U}_n$ are all ring members. Let the private and public key of user $\mathcal{U}_i$ be x_i and $y_i = g^{x_i}$ respectively. For our modified Step-out Ring Signatures (MSRS) we have the following procedures.

Signing Algorithm. $\mathcal{S}_{MSRS}(g, \hat{g}, x_j, Y, m)$ is a randomized algorithm that takes generator g and a random element $\hat{g} \in <g>$, $\hat{g} \neq 1$, the secret key x_j, the set of public keys $y_1, \cdots, y_n \subset <g>$ and a message m. It returns a signature σ.

Verification Algorithm. $\mathcal{V}_{MSRS}(\sigma, m)$ is a deterministic algorithm that takes a message m, and a signature σ for m. It returns a bit: 1 or 0 to indicate whether σ is valid, i.e. someone having a public key in a set Y indicated by σ has signed m.

```
Algorithm S_MSRS(g, ĝ, x_j, y_1, ⋯, y_n, m)         Algorithm V_MSRS(σ, m)
  repeat                                               if(V_SKDL(g, w_i, m) = 0,
    r_1, ⋯, r_n ←_R Z_q*                                  for any i = 1, ⋯, n)
    w_i ← g^{r_i} for each i = 1, ⋯, n                  then return 0
  until (y_i w_i ≠ y_j w_j for each i ≠ j)              d ← V_SEQDL(ĝ, g, ŷ_w, y_1, ⋯, y_n,
  ŷ_w ← ĝ^{x_j + r_j}                                       w_1, ⋯, w_n, c_1, ⋯, c_n, s_1, ⋯, s_n, m)
  (c_1, ⋯, c_n, s_1, ⋯, s_n) ← SEQDL(ĝ,               if d = 1
      g, x_j, r_j, ŷ_w, y_1, ⋯, y_n, w_1, ⋯, w_n, m)     then return 1
  Y ← y_1, ⋯, y_n                                       else return 0
  W ← w_1, ⋯, w_n
  σ = (g, ĝ, ŷ_w, Y, W, c_1, ⋯, c_n, s_1, ⋯, s_n,
      {SKDL(g, w_i, m), i = 1, ⋯, n})
  return(m, σ)
```

Confession Algorithm. The confession algorithm verifies whether a member of the ring $\mathcal{U}_j$ has generated the ring signature σ by obtaining σ' from her as shown below. Note that the verifier verifies σ' using $\mathcal{V}_{MSRS}$ because the SKDL's corresponding to W have already been verified in the verification of σ.

We denote $Y' = (y_1', \cdots, y_n')$, $Y'' = (y_1'', \cdots, y_n'')$, $Y''' = (y_1''', \cdots, y_n''')$. The confession record $\sigma' = (g, \hat{g}, \hat{y}, \hat{w}, Y', W, \mathrm{SEQDL}(\hat{g}, g, x_i, r_i, \hat{y}.\hat{w}, Y', W, m))$ is a new signature with the same parameters $g, \hat{g}, W$ as in σ and some new set of potential signers $Y' : Y \cap Y' = \{y_j\}$, where y_j stands at the same position in both sequences.

Step-out Algorithm. The step-out algorithm verifies whether a member of the ring $\mathcal{U}_i$ has not generated the ring signature σ by obtaining (σ'', σ''') from her as shown below. Note that the verifier verifies σ'' and σ''' using $\mathcal{V}_{MSRS}$ because the SKDL's corresponding to W have already been verified in the verification of σ. We define the step-out records σ'', σ''' below:

- $\sigma'' = (g, \hat{g}, \hat{y}'', \hat{w}'', Y'', W, \mathrm{SEQDL}(\hat{g}, g, x_i, r_i, \hat{y}''.\hat{w}'', Y'', W, \tilde{m}))$ - a SRS signature with the same parameters $g, \hat{g}, W$ as in σ and $\hat{y}'' = \hat{g}^{x_i}$, $\hat{w}'' = \hat{g}^{r_i}$, some new set of potential signers Y'', for the control message $\tilde{m}$ = "I have not signed m".
- $\sigma''' = (g, \hat{g}, \hat{y}'', \hat{w}'', Y''', W, \mathrm{SEQDL}(\hat{g}, g, x_i, r_i, \hat{y}''.\hat{w}'', Y''', W, \tilde{m}))$ - a SRS signature for the same control message $\tilde{m}$ with the same $g, \hat{g}, \hat{w}'', W$ and Y''' such that $Y'' \cap Y''' = \{y_i\}$ and y_i stands on the same position in Y'' and Y'''. Moreover, $y_{i_1}'' w_{i_1} \neq y_{i_2}''' w_{i_2}$ for $i_1 \neq i_2$

```
Algorithm C_MSRS(σ, σ', y_j, m)              Algorithm D_MSRS(σ, m, σ'', σ''', y_i, m̃)
  if(the same g, ĝ, ŷ, ŵ, W were used in       if(the same g, ĝ, W were used in σ, σ'', σ'''
      σ and σ') then                               and the same ŷ'', ŵ'' were used
    d_1 ← V_MSRS(σ, m), d_2 ← V_SRS(σ', m)          in σ'', σ''') then
    if(d_1 = d_2 = 1 and {y_j} = Y ∩ Y'          d_1 ← V_MSRS(σ, m), d_2 ← V_SRS(σ'', m̃),
      and y_j stands on position j in Y') then    d_3 ← V_SRS(σ''', m̃)
      return 1 else return 0                      if(d_1 = d_2 = d_3 = 1
  else return 0                                      and {y_i} = Y'' ∩ Y'''
                                                     and y_i stands at the same position
                                                     in Y'' and Y''' and ŷŵ ≠ ŷ''ŵ'') then
                                                     return 1, else return 0
                                                 else return 0
```

3.2   Cryptanalysis of [2]

In the SRS scheme in [2], it is possible without the knowledge of any of the ring members' secret keys, to produce $\hat{y}_w, w_j$ for some j such that $\log_{\hat{g}} \hat{y}_w = log_g(y_j w_j)$. The algorithm $\mathcal{F}_{SRS}$ below shows how this can be done.

$$
\begin{array}{l}
\text{Algorithm } \mathcal{F}_{SRS}(g, \hat{g}, Y, m) \\
\quad \text{repeat} \\
\qquad r_i \leftarrow_R \mathbb{Z}_p^* \text{ for each } i \in \{1, \cdots, n\} \backslash \{j\} \\
\qquad w_i \leftarrow g^{r_i} \text{ for each } i \in \{1, \cdots, n\} \backslash \{j\} \\
\qquad \alpha \leftarrow_R \mathbb{Z}_p^* \\
\qquad w_j \leftarrow g^{\alpha}/y_j \\
\qquad \text{until } (y_i w_i \neq y_k w_k \text{ for each } i \neq k) \\
\qquad \beta \leftarrow_R \mathbb{Z}_p^* \\
\qquad \hat{w} \leftarrow \hat{g}^{\beta}, \hat{y} \leftarrow \hat{g}^{\alpha-\beta}, \hat{y}_w \leftarrow \hat{y}\hat{w} \\
\qquad (C, S) \leftarrow \text{SEQDL}(\hat{g}, g, \alpha - \beta, \\
\qquad\qquad \beta, \hat{y}_w, Y, W, m) \\
\qquad Y \leftarrow y_1, \cdots, y_n \\
\qquad W \leftarrow w_1, \cdots, w_n \\
\qquad \sigma \leftarrow (g, \hat{g}, \hat{y}, \hat{w}, Y, W, C, S) \\
\qquad \text{return } (m, \sigma)
\end{array}
$$

Motivation. In [2], the signer generates a random value r_j, but uses only $x_j + r_j$ in SEQDL. However, there is no proof of knowledge of r_j (or other r_i's) insisted by the verification algorithm. Thus, a forger may set '$x_j + r_j$' arbitrarily without proving that she knows x_j and r_j individually. This is exactly what we did in our forgery algorithm by *reverse engineering* the $(x_j + r_j)$ values.

Notice that in $\mathcal{F}_{SRS}$, α and β chosen in such a way that when $\alpha - \beta$ and β are used as parameters for SEQDL, the algorithm produces the same value that SEQDL would have produced with x_j and r_j. Hence, to fix the above problem, we add SKDL's for w_i's and verify them during verification. $\mathcal{F}_{SRS}$ clearly does not use private information x_j to forge a ring signature. If this were performed by the kth ring member, she can step out using the value r_k and also allow every ring member other than the jth one to step out by releasing the values r_i for each $i \in \{1, \cdots, n\} \backslash \{j\}$.

Anonymity. In the SRS scheme in [2] anonymity can be broken because the signature σ output by the signer contains $\hat{w}$ explicitly as a part of it. In some SRS schemes, the parameters r_i are released together with the signature. Thus a distinguisher simply tests if $\hat{g}^{r_i} \stackrel{?}{=} \hat{w}$ for each $i = 1, \cdots, n$ to identify the original signer. However, notice the verification algorithm needs only the product $\hat{w}\hat{y}$, and not $\hat{w}$ individually. Hence, in MSRS, we provide only the product value $\hat{w}\hat{y}$ as a component of σ, and not $\hat{w}$ or $\hat{y}$ individually. As one can not compute $\hat{w}$ from the product $\hat{w}\hat{y}$, this modification prevents one from breaking anonymity.

3.3   Analysis

Unforgeability. The modified SRS scheme proposed is unforgeable. Our proof requires forking lemma for adaptive chosen message attacks [13] stated as follows:

Forking Lemma. Let $\mathcal{A}$ be a probabilistic polynomial time Turing machine whose input only consists of public data. We denote respectively by q_h and q_s the number of queries that $\mathcal{A}$ can ask to the random oracle and the number of queries that $\mathcal{A}$ can ask to the signer. Assume that, within a time bound T, $\mathcal{A}$ produces, with non-negligible probability ϵ, a valid signature $(m, \sigma_1, h, \sigma_2)$. If the triples (σ_1, h, σ_2) can be simulated without knowing the secret key, with an indistinguishable probability distribution, then, a replay of the attacker $\mathcal{A}$, where interactions with the signer are simulated, outputs two valid signatures $(m, \sigma_1, h, \sigma_2)$ and $(m, \sigma_1, h', \sigma_2')$ such that $h \neq h'$, within a bounded time and non-negligible probability.

The following lemma is about the applicability of forking lemma for the modified step-out ring signatures. The proof is similar to [2] and we omit this due to space constraints.

Lemma 1. Modified SRS signatures can be simulated by a simulator, with oracle access to $\mathcal{H}$, under DDH assumption without knowing the corresponding secret signing key and with distribution probability indistinguishable from SRS signatures produced by a legitimate signer.

We now apply forking lemma in the chosen message attack scenario. The signature σ is written as (σ_1, h, σ_2) where:

$$\sigma_1 = (\hat{g}, \hat{y}_w, W, u_1, \cdots, u_n, t_1, \cdots, t_n),$$
$$\text{where } u_i, t_i \text{ are constructed like in (2)}$$

$$h = (H(\hat{g}||g||\hat{y}_w||\overline{Y}||\overline{W}||u_1||t_1||...||u_n||t_n||m),$$
$$\{H(g||w_i||g^{\tilde{s}_i}w_i^{\tilde{c}_i}||m), i = 1, \cdots, n\}$$

$$\sigma_2 = (C, S, \tilde{c}_1, \tilde{s}_1, \cdots, \tilde{c}_n, \tilde{s}_n)$$

After acquiring two valid signatures (σ_1, h, σ_2) and $(\sigma_1, h', \sigma_2')$, such that $h \neq h'$ and $\sigma_2 \neq \sigma_2'$, the DL solver can compute the $x_i = \log_g(y_i)$ corresponding to the signer whose signature the forger generated.

The solver first computes $\alpha_i = x_i + r_i = (s_i' - s_i)/(c_i - c_i')$ for all $i = 1, \cdots, n$ where $c_i \neq c_i'$, which holds due to equation 4 in SEQDL construction. It then computes $r_i' = (\tilde{s}_i' - \tilde{s}_i)/(\tilde{c}_i - \tilde{c}_i')$ for all $i = 1, \cdots, n$ where $\tilde{c}_i \neq \tilde{c}_i'$, which is evident from equation (1) in SKDL construction. Finally, it computes $x_i' = \alpha_i - r_i'$ for all obtained values of α_i and r_i'. Clearly, if the forger produced a signature by the user with public key y_j, then solver has obtained $x_j' : g^{x_j'} = y_j$.

Hence the solver has the solution to the DL problem $x' = \log_g X$ provided $j = t$. The probability that this happens is $1/n$. Since we assume that the DL assumption holds, the above algorithm must have negligible probability of success, therefore the forger has negligible success probability too.

Anonymity. The anonymity argument in [2] can be readily extended to the proof of anonymity of the modified scheme. As the r_i's are chosen randomly, the SKDLs reveal no additional information about the signer. Also, the proof of anonymity in [2] assumes that the only distinguishing property of two signature tuples of the form $\sigma = (m, g, \hat{g}, \hat{w}, y_1, y_2, w_1, w_2, c_1, c_2, s_1, s_2)$ by two different signers 1 and 2, is that in the former, $\log_g(y_1 w_1) = \log_{\hat{g}}(\hat{y}\hat{w})$ and in the latter, $\log_g(y_2 w_2) = \log_{\hat{g}}(\hat{y}\hat{w})$. However, the fact that the adversary, in scenario 2, may use $r_i = \log_{\hat{g}}(\hat{w})$, when r_i is released along with the signature was not considered. This can be rectified when the product $\hat{y}_w = \hat{y}\hat{w}$ is released with the signature instead of the individual values $\hat{y}, \hat{w}$.

Confession. A confession has a positive outcome only if performed by the original signer of a modified step-out ring signature according to protocol.

Proof. Since $\mathcal{V}_{\text{SEQDL}}(\hat{g}, g, \hat{y}_w, Y, W, C, S, m) = 1$, there exists α such that $g^\alpha \in \{y_1 w_1, \cdots, y_n w_n\}$ and $\hat{g}^\alpha = \hat{y}\hat{w}$. Moreover, if σ' is constructed appropriately and $\mathcal{V}_{\text{MSRS}}(\sigma', m) = 1$, then $g^\alpha \in \{y'_1 w_1, \cdots, y'_n w_n\}$ as well. So $g^\alpha \in \{y_1 w_1, \cdots, y_n w_n\} \cap \{y'_1 w_1, \cdots, y_n w'_n\}$. Since $\{y1, ..., yn\} \cap \{y'_1, ..., y'_n\} = \{y_j\}$, and $y_{i_1} w_{i_1} \neq y'_{i_2} w_{i_2}$ for $i_1 \neq i_2$, we know that $g^\alpha = y_j w_j$, so in this case user $\mathcal{U}_j$ was a creator of σ and $\mathcal{C}_{MSRS}(\sigma, \sigma', y_j, m) = 1$.

Step-Out. A step-out has a positive outcome only if performed by a ring-member of a modified step-out ring signature, other than the original signer, according to protocol.

Proof. It is easy to see that the see that σ''' is a confession that a message $\tilde{m}$ has been signed as σ'' by the user $\mathcal{U}_i : y_i = Y'' \cap Y'''$. Clearly, this user is a member of the ring. We will show that the outcome of the step-out procedure performed by this user is positive. Let us assume that $\mathcal{D}_{\text{MSRS}}(\sigma, m, \sigma, \sigma, y_i, \tilde{m}) = 0$. This happens if $\hat{y}\hat{w} = \hat{y}''\hat{w}''$. As in the proof of Lemma 1, we can see that the signatures σ'' and σ''' guarantee that there exists α' such that $g^{\alpha'} = y_i w_i$ and $\hat{g}^{\alpha'} = \hat{y}''\hat{w}''$. So $\alpha = \log_g(y_i w_i) = \log_{\hat{g}}(\hat{y}''\hat{w}'') = \log_{\hat{g}}(\hat{y}\hat{w}) = \log_g(y_j w_j)$, where $\mathcal{U}_j$ is the signer of σ. We have got that $y_i w_i = y_j w_j$, but this contradicts the assumption about generating secrets r_i and computing w_i during the signing procedure, provided $i \neq j$.

Let us consider the case when an actual signer attempts to step-out. When performing the step-out procedure and generating signatures σ' and σ'', the user $\mathcal{U}_j$ has to generate $y''w'' = g^{x_j + r_j}$. However, this product is the same as in σ, so this would lead to a failure of the test of the step-out procedure.

4   Threshold Discernible Ring Signatures

Threshold discernible ring signatures are ring signatures where a threshold of t signers are together capable of finding the identity of the original signer. This may be applied for example to situations where a message has been maliciously signed on behalf of a ring of signers and a majority (or a threshold t) of the signers decide to unmask the original signer of the message.

We extend the modified step out ring signature scheme from section 3.1 to allow threshold discernibility. The signing algorithm additionally outputs a set of verifiably encrypted shares of the secret $l = \log_g(\hat{g})$. This can be done using verifiable sharing of discrete logarithms [14] and verifiable encryption of discrete logarithms [14,15]. Once l is gathered by any set of t ring members, the original signer is easily found by inspecting for which index i of the ring members, the equation $(y_i w_i)^l = \hat{y}_w$ holds. This is the index of the original signer.

4.1   Preliminaries

We assume the same settings and complexity assumptions as the SRS signature scheme. The algorithm uses a verifiable encryption scheme [14,15,16]. The notations used for this scheme are explained below. We also explain Shamir's secret sharing scheme [1] which is used in the verifiable secret sharing of discrete logarithms [14].

Verifiable Encryption. We denote verifiable encryption of a discrete logarithm $\alpha = \log_g(\beta)$ under public key PK as $VE_{PK}(\alpha : \beta = g^\alpha)$. This denotes the cipher-text created by the *Encrypt* algorithm. The encryption scheme has three algorithms namely:

1. *Encrypt*$(\alpha : \beta = g^\alpha)$: Takes a message α, a public key PK and outputs cipher text $VE_{PK}(\alpha : \beta = g^\alpha)$ where $g, \beta = g^\alpha$ are publicly known.
2. *Decrypt*$(VE_{PK}(\alpha : \beta = g^\alpha))$: Takes a cipher-text $VE_{PK}(\alpha : \beta = g^\alpha)$ and obtains the original message α. This requires the secret key SK.
3. *Verify*$(VE_{PK}(\alpha : \beta = g^\alpha))$: Takes the cipher-text $VE_{PK}(\alpha : \beta = g^\alpha)$ and verifies the zero knowledge proof that the cipher text indeed encrypts α such that $\beta = g^\alpha$.

Shamir's Secret Sharing Scheme. A (t, n) secret sharing scheme is a scheme where a secret d is shared among n users where only a coalition of size at least t can recover the secret. Such a scheme was proposed by Shamir [1] and is explained below. A user $\mathcal{U}_i$ has a well known public parameter $\alpha_{u_i} \in \mathbb{Z}_q$.

Preliminaries. Let q be a large prime ($q >> n$), and $d \in \mathbb{Z}_q$ be the secret to be shared. There are $n \geq t$ users in total.

Share.(d) The dealer chooses a random polynomial $f(x) = d + \sum_{i=1}^{t-1} a_i x^i$, of degree $t - 1$ from $\mathbb{Z}_q[x]$ where the constant term is set to d. The dealer then distributes the secret shares $s_i = f(\alpha_{\mathcal{U}_i})$, to the ith user, for each $i = 1 \cdots n$.

Reconstruct.$((\alpha_{v_1}, s_1), \cdots, (\alpha_{v_{|S|}}, s_{|S|}))$ This process is a simple polynomial interpolation to compute $f(0) = d$. Suppose a coalition $S, |S| \geq t, S = \{v_1, \cdots, v_{|S|}\}$ wants to reconstruct the secret. They can compute the secret polynomial f(x) and the secret by Lagranges polynomial interpolation:

$$f(0) = \sum_{i \in S} y_i \lambda_{i0} \text{ , where } \lambda_{ij}^S = \prod_{j' \in S \setminus \{i\}} \frac{j - j'}{i - j'}$$

The additional requirement to Shamir's secret sharing our scheme requires is that the shared secrets are encrypted and these encrypted portions must still be verifiable.

4.2 Scheme Description

Outline. Let us assume that $\mathcal{U}_j$ is the real signer and $\mathcal{U}_1, \cdots, \mathcal{U}_n$ are all ring members. Let the private and public key of user $\mathcal{U}_i$ be x_i and $(y_i = g^{x_i}, \alpha_i)$ respectively, where $\alpha_i \in \mathbb{Z}_q$. For Threshold Discernible Ring Signatures (TDS) we have the following procedures:

Signing Procedure. $\mathcal{S}_{TDS}$ $(g, x_j, y_1, \cdots, y_n, \alpha_1, \cdots, \alpha_n, t, m)$ is an algorithm that takes generator g, the secret key x_j, the set of public keys $\{y_1, \cdots, y_n\} \subset < g >$, threshold t and a message m. It returns a threshold discernible signature σ.

Verification Procedure. $\mathcal{V}_{TDS}(m, \sigma)$ is an algorithm that takes a message m, and a signature σ for m. It returns a bit: 1 or 0 to indicate whether σ is valid, i.e., someone having a public key in a set Y indicated by σ has signed m, and whether it is indeed threshold discernible by t of the members of the ring.

Threshold Distinguisher Procedure. $\mathcal{T}_{TDS}(m, \sigma)$ is an algorithm that takes a message m, and a signature σ for m, and returns i, the index of the original signer among the public key sequence Y in the signature σ. The algorithm requires inputs by at least t signers among the n members of the ring indicated by σ.

4.3 Signing Algorithm

The signing algorithm verifiably encrypts n shares of the secret $l = \log_g(\hat{g})$, along with the MSRS signature. It performs the sharing by encrypting the values of $t - 1$ degree polynomial function $f(x) = l + \sum_{j=1}^{t-1} f_j x^j$, at n points viz. at $x = \alpha_1, \cdots, \alpha_n$.

4.4 Verification Algorithm

The verification algorithm verifies the MSRS signature as well as the verifiably encrypted shares of the secret l. The verification algorithm must check whether t is an acceptable value based on the required policy. For instance, one may require that $t = \lceil \frac{n}{2} \rceil$.

Algorithm $\mathcal{S}_{TDS}(g, x_j, y_1, \cdots, y_n,$
    $\alpha_1, \cdots, \alpha_n, t, m)$
$f_1, f_2, \cdots, f_{t-1} \leftarrow_R \mathbb{Z}_q^*$
$F_i \leftarrow g^{f_i}, i = 1, \cdots, t-1$
$l \leftarrow_R \mathbb{Z}_q^* \setminus \{1\}$
$\hat{g} \leftarrow g^l$
$s_i \leftarrow l + \sum_{j=1}^{t-1} f_j \alpha_i^j, i = 1, \cdots, n$

$V_i \leftarrow VE_{y_i}(s_i : g^{s_i} = \hat{g} \prod_{j=1}^{t-1} F_j^{\alpha_i^j}), i = 1, \cdots, n$
$\sigma_1 \leftarrow \mathcal{S}_{MSRS}(g, \hat{g}, x_j, y_1, \cdots, y_n, m)$
$\sigma \leftarrow (\sigma_1, \{V_i : i = 1, \cdots, n\},$
    $\{F_i : i = 1, \cdots, t-1\})$
return (m, σ)

Algorithm $\mathcal{V}_{TDS}(m, \sigma)$
if $(\text{Verify}(VE_{y_i}(s_i : g^{s_i} = \hat{g} \prod_{j=1}^{t-1} F_j^{\alpha_i^j})) = 0$
    for any $i = 1, \cdots, n)$
    return 0
return $\mathcal{V}_{MSRS}(m, \sigma)$

4.5 Threshold Distinguisher Algorithm

The threshold distinguisher algorithm requires that at least t of the signers in the ring share their respective s_i's. It is required that each of these s_i's are such that $S_i = \hat{g} \prod_{j=1}^{t-1} F_j^{y_i^j} = g^{s_i}$. Now, using Lagrange's interpolation formula, the function f, hence the value $f(0) = l$, can be computed. Once l is computed, the verifier checks for which value of i, the equation, $(y_i w_i)^l = \hat{y}_w$ holds. This i is the index of the original signer.

Algorithm $\mathcal{T}_{TDS}(m, \sigma)$
    if $(\mathcal{V}_{TDS}(m, \sigma) = 0)$
        then return $\perp$

    Obtain $s_i = Decrypt(VE_{y_i}(s_i : g^{s_i} = \hat{g} \prod_{j=1}^{t-1} F_j^{\alpha_i^j}))$
        from t signers w.l.o.g. $i = 1, \cdots, t$.
    $l \leftarrow Reconstruct((\alpha_0, s_0), \cdots, (\alpha_t, s_t))$
    for $i = 1$ to n
        if $((y_i w_i)^l = \hat{y}_w)$
            then return i
    return $\perp$

4.6   Security

In this section we define the security models for threshold discernible ring signatures and detailed proofs of security. A threshold discernible ring signature (TDS) scheme must follow the following conditions:

Unforgeability. Unforgeability in threshold discernible ring signatures requires that no entity other than a member of the ring must be able to produce a ring signature with non-negligible advantage in polynomial time.

For security proof of unforgeability we formalize the attacks of a forger $\mathcal{F}_{TDS}$ in the chosen-message scenario. We consider the following experiment of running a forger $\mathcal{F}_{TDS}$:

Experiment $\mathrm{Exp}_{\mathcal{F}_{TDS}}$
    for $k = 1$ to q_{max}
        query for (m_k, σ_k), such that $\mathcal{V}_{TDS}(\sigma_k, m_k) = 1$
    let $(m, \sigma) \leftarrow \mathcal{F}_{SRS}(g, \hat{g}, y_1, ..., y_n, m, (m_1, \sigma_1), ...$
        , $(m_k, \sigma_k))$
    if $\mathcal{V}_{SRS}(\sigma, m) = 1$ return 1
    else return 0

Then we define the advantage $\mathrm{Adv}_{\mathcal{F}_{TDS}}$ of the forger. $\mathcal{F}_{TDS}$ as the probability $Pr[\mathrm{Exp}_{\mathcal{F}_{TDS}} = 1]$.

Theorem 1. Threshold discernible ring signatures are secure against forgery, i.e. $\mathrm{Adv}_{\mathcal{F}_{TDS}}$ is negligibly small, provided the DL assumption holds and the underlying verifiable encryption scheme is secure.

Proof. We assume that the underlying verifiable encryption scheme is from [17]. Our proof involves the use of forking lemma defined in section 3.3. We first show the applicability of forking lemma for threshold discernible ring signatures.

Applicability of Forking Lemma. In order to take advantage of the Forking Lemma for attacks in the adaptive chosen-message scenario we show that the threshold discernible ring signature is of the form (σ_1, h, σ_2) and can be simulated without the knowledge of the corresponding secret signing key and with indistinguishable distribution probability.

Lemma 2. Threshold discernible ring signatures (TDS) can be simulated by a simulator, with oracle access to $\mathcal{H}$, under DDH assumption without knowing the corresponding secret signing key and with distribution probability indistinguishable from TDS signatures produced by a legitimate signer.

Proof Sketch. The proof is very similar to the proof of Lemma 1. The key idea is to construct two simulation algorithms S_0 and S_1, where S_0 requires knowledge of the secret signing key x_j and S_1 simulates oracle $\mathcal{H}(\cdot)$ to verify SKDLs and SEQDL correctly. Then we can show that any algorithm which can distinguish between S_0 and S_1 can break the DDH assumption.

Now, we shall construct an adversary that can solve the DL problem by finding $x_i = \log_g y_i$ for some i. Note that the y_i's are supplied to the forger as input. Hence a DL solver attempting to find $\log_g X$ can do so by setting $y_t = X$ for some t. With success probability $1/n$, this is the index of the signer whose signature the forger generates.

Construction of DL Solver. We now apply forking lemma in the chosen message attack scenario (section 3.3). The signature σ is written as (σ_1, h, σ_2) where:

$\sigma_1 = (\hat{g}, \hat{y}_w, W, u_1, \cdots, u_n, t_1, \cdots, t_n, \bar{C}_1, \cdots, \bar{C}_n, F_1, \cdots, F_{t-1})$,

where u_i, t_i are constructed like in (2)

$h = (\mathcal{H}(\hat{g}\|g\|\hat{y}_w\|\overline{Y}\|\overline{W}\|u_1\|t_1\|...\|u_n\|t_n\|m),\ \{\mathcal{H}(g\|w_i\|g^{\tilde{s}_i}w_i^{\tilde{c}_i}\|m),\ i = 1,\cdots,$
$n\}, \{\mathcal{H}(\bar{C}_i, \hat{g}\prod_{j=1}^{t-1} F_j^{\alpha_i^j}, g_i^{\bar{c}_i}\bar{C}_i^{\bar{r}_i}, g^{\tilde{c}_i}(\hat{g}\prod_{j=1}^{t-1} F_j^{\alpha_i^j})^{\bar{r}_i}), i = 1,\cdots,n\})$

$\sigma_2 = (C, S, \tilde{c}_1, \tilde{s}_1, \cdots, \tilde{c}_n, \tilde{s}_n, \bar{c}_1, \bar{r}_1, \cdots, \bar{c}_n, \bar{r}_n)$

After acquiring two valid signatures (σ_1, h, σ_2) and $(\sigma_1, h', \sigma_2')$, such that $h \neq h'$ and $\sigma_2 \neq \sigma_2'$, the DL solver can compute the $x_i = \log_g(y_i)$ corresponding to the signer whose signature the forger generated.

The solver first computes $\alpha_i = x_i + r_i = (s_i' - s_i)/(c_i - c_i')$ for all $i = 1, \cdots, n$ where $c_i \neq c_i'$, which holds due to equation 4 in SEQDL construction. It then computes $r_i' = (\tilde{s}_i' - \tilde{s}_i)/(\tilde{c}_i - \tilde{c}_i')$ for all $i = 1, \cdots, n$ where $\tilde{c}_i \neq \tilde{c}_i'$, which is evident from equation (1) in SKDL construction. Finally, it computes $x_i' = \alpha_i - r_i'$ for all obtained values of α_i and r_i'. Clearly, if the forger produced a signature by the user with public key y_j, then solver has obtained $x_j' : g^{x_j'} = y_j$.

Hence the solver has the solution to the DL problem $x' = \log_g X$ provided $j = t$. The probability that this happens is $1/n$. Since we assume that the DL assumption holds, the above algorithm must have negligible probability of success, therefore the forger has negligible success probability too.

Threshold Anonymity. Threshold anonymity in threshold discernible ring signatures requires that no entity other than a group of at least t ring members must be able to identify the original signer of a ring signature with non-negligible advantage in polynomial time.

Theorem 2. Let $\mathcal{A}_{ATDS}$ be a probabilistic polynomial time algorithm that can distinguish between σ_x, σ_y produced by two different signers for an arbitrary message m by any group of $t - 1$ signers among n signers. Let advantage of $\mathcal{A}_{ATDS}$ be defined as $Adv_{\mathcal{A}_{ATDS}} = Pr[A(\sigma_b) = b]$, where $b \in \{x, y\}$. We say that the scheme provides threshold anonymity, if for any efficient algorithm $\mathcal{A}_{ATDS}$ the value of $Adv_{\mathcal{A}_{ATDS}}$ is at most negligibly greater than $1/n$. The threshold discernible ring signature scheme discussed above has the threshold anonymity property.

Proof: We will show threshold anonymity for the two-member ring scenario. The argument may be extended for larger rings. Let $\mathcal{A}^{ATDS}$ be a probabilistic polynomial time algorithm that can distinguish between $\sigma_0 = \mathcal{S}_{TDS}(g, \hat{g}, x_0, y_0, y_1, \alpha_0, \alpha_1, 2, m)$ and $\sigma_1 = \mathcal{S}_{TDS}(g, \hat{g}, x_1, y_0, y_1, \alpha_0, \alpha_1, 2, m)$ for an arbitrary message m.

Let advantage of $\mathcal{A}^{ATDS}$ be defined as $Adv_{\mathcal{A}^{ATDS}} = Pr[\mathcal{A}(\sigma_b) = b]$, where $b \in \{0, 1\}$. We say that the scheme provides anonymity, if for any efficient algorithm $\mathcal{A}^{ATDS}$ the value of $Adv_{\mathcal{A}^{ATDS}}$ is at most negligibly greater than $1/2$.

We show that breaking anonymity of our scheme is not easier than breaking DDH problem. Namely, we construct an algorithm $\mathcal{A}^{ddh}$ for breaking instances of DDH problem built on the top of any $\mathcal{A}^{ATDS}$. Moreover, we show that $\mathcal{A}^{ddh}$ calls $\mathcal{A}^{ATDS}$ as a sub-procedure a limited number T of times and $Adv_{\mathcal{A}^{ATDS}} = 1 - 1/e > 1/2$. Let us describe the algorithm $\mathcal{A}^{ddh}$. For an instance of DDH problem (g, g^a, g^b, g^c) we will construct simulated signatures σ_i , by the means of simulator S_b described above, and treat this simulations as inputs for algorithm $\mathcal{A}^{ATDS}$. As assumed this algorithm gives 1 for the input of the form (g, g^a, g^b, g^c) for $c = ab$ with probability $Adv_{\mathcal{A}^{ATDS}} = \epsilon > 1/2$. Moreover, we assume that it gives 0 for input of the form (g, g^a, g^b, g^c) for $c \neq ab$ with probability $1/2$.

$$
\begin{array}{l}
\text{Algorithm } \mathcal{A}^{ddh}(g, g^a, g^b, g^c) \\
\quad p_1, \cdots, p_T \leftarrow_R \mathbb{Z}_p^* \\
\quad d_1, \cdots, d_T \leftarrow_R \{0, 1\} \\
\quad m, y_0, y_1 \leftarrow_R \mathbb{Z}_p^* \\
\quad \text{FOR } i = 1 \text{ to } T \ \{ \\
\qquad \text{if } (d_i = 1)\, \sigma_i \leftarrow S_\beta(g, g^{ap_i}, m, y_0, y_1, g, g^{bp_i}, g^{cp_i^2}) \\
\qquad \text{else } \sigma_i \leftarrow S_\beta(g, g^{bp_i}, m, y_0, y_1, g, g^{ap_i}, g^{cp_i^2}) \\
\qquad d_i' \leftarrow \mathcal{A}^{ATDS}(\sigma_i) \\
\quad \} \\
\quad X = \{i \leq T | d_i = d_i'\} \\
\quad \text{if } (X < (\epsilon/2 + 1/4)T) \text{ return } 0 \\
\quad \text{else return } 1
\end{array}
$$

We can consider the above algorithm as T independent Bernoulli trials, where $T = 2/(\epsilon - 1/2)^2$, and with probability of success in each trial equal to $1/2$ if $c \neq ab$, or equal to $\epsilon > 1/2$ if $c = ab$. Therefore $X \sim B(T, \epsilon)$ or $X \sim B(T, 1/2)$.

Let us recall the following well-known variant of Chernoff inequality:

Lemma 2. Let $X \sim B(T, p)$ be a random variable with the binomial distribution. Then $Pr(X > EX + t) \leq exp(-2t^2/T)$ and $Pr(X \leq EX - t) \leq exp(-2t^2/T)$ for any $t > 0$. We analyze probability that the algorithm gives correct answer, if $c \neq ab$. In this case we treat X as a random variable with binomial distribution $B(T, 1/2)$. That probability of failure equals

$$Pr(X > (\epsilon/2 + 1/4)T) = Pr(X > 1/2T + (\epsilon - 1/2)/T)$$

Since $EX = 1/2T$ and $T = 2/(\epsilon - 1/2)^2$, using Lemma 2 this probability equals $Pr(X > EX + (\epsilon - 1/2)/2T) \leq 1/e$. Using exactly the same reasoning we can show that if $c = ab$, then $Pr(X \leq (\epsilon/2 + 1/4)T) \leq 1/e$. Indeed, it is enough to remember that $EX = \epsilon T$ and apply the second inequality in Lemma 2. We can see that for each input $\mathcal{A}^{ddh}$ gives the correct answer with probability exceeding $1 - 1/e > 1$. The runtime of $\mathcal{A}^{ddh}$ is polynomial provided that $\epsilon - 1/2 = 1/poly(n)$. We have constructed an appropriate algorithm for a basic case of a distinguishing two signers, however such an approach can be easily generalized to the case of several potential users. Let us also note that in this analysis only some parameters of the signature were taken into account. One can easily see that rest of them cannot be used for recognizing the real signer since their distribution does not depend on the signer identity and therefore cannot reveal any information on the signer.

5 Extensions

There are several extensions possible to threshold discernible ring signatures:

- **Linkability.** Threshold discernible ring signatures can be made linkable by using the same l for several signatures. In this case, the threshold distinguisher algorithm will identify the original signer across all signatures produced by the signer. In this case, it is very clear if two signatures are produced by the same individual if the term $\hat{g}$ matches across signatures.
- **Confession and Step Out.** Threshold discernible ring signatures can use the same confession and step out algorithms as in MSRS (section 3.1). Hence it can be seamlessly integrated with MSRS.
- **Weighted Thresholds.** In the above scheme we assumed that all users in the ring have equal weight, i.e. any group needs at least t ring members to identify the original signer. We readily extend the scheme by having more verifiably encrypted shares for some privileged users so that they can identify the original signer with a smaller group.

6   Conclusions and Open Problems

Step out ring signatures, introduced in [2], had security flaws. We identified those flaws present in the scheme and fixed them in order to make it secure. We have introduced the new concept of the Threshold discernible ring signature using the corrected version of the step out ring signature and proved security under the DDH assumption in the random oracle model. The problem of finding a scheme which is secure in the standard model remains open. It is also an open problem to accommodate more complex authorization policies for users and groups who want to identify the original signer.

References

1. Rivest, R.L., Shamir, A., Tauman, Y.: How to Leak a Secret. In: Boyd, C. (ed.) ASIACRYPT 2001. LNCS, vol. 2248, pp. 552–565. Springer, Heidelberg (2001)
2. Klonowski, M., Krzywiecki, Ł., Kutyłowski, M., Lauks, A.: Step-Out Ring Signatures. In: Ochmański, E., Tyszkiewicz, J. (eds.) MFCS 2008. LNCS, vol. 5162, pp. 431–442. Springer, Heidelberg (2008)
3. Naor, M.: Deniable Ring Authentication. In: Yung, M. (ed.) CRYPTO 2002. LNCS, vol. 2442, pp. 481–498. Springer, Heidelberg (2002)
4. Susilo, W., Mu, Y.: Deniable Ring Authentication Revisited. In: Jakobsson, M., Yung, M., Zhou, J. (eds.) ACNS 2004. LNCS, vol. 3089, pp. 149–163. Springer, Heidelberg (2004)
5. Tsang, P.P., Wei, V.K.: Short Linkable Ring Signatures for E-Voting, E-Cash and Attestation. In: Deng, R.H., Bao, F., Pang, H., Zhou, J. (eds.) ISPEC 2005. LNCS, vol. 3439, pp. 48–60. Springer, Heidelberg (2005)
6. Au, M.H., Chow, S.S.M., Susilo, W., Tsang, P.P.: Short Linkable Ring Signatures Revisited. In: Atzeni, A.S., Lioy, A. (eds.) EuroPKI 2006. LNCS, vol. 4043, pp. 101–115. Springer, Heidelberg (2006)
7. Cheng, W., Lang, W., Yang, Z., Liu, G., Tan, Y.: An identity-based proxy ring signature scheme from bilinear pairings. In: ISCC 2004: Proceedings of the Ninth International Symposium on Computers and Communications, vol. 2, pp. 424–429. IEEE Computer Society (2004)
8. Awasthi, A.K., Lal, S.: Id-based ring signature and proxy ring signature schemes from bilinear pairings. CoRR (2005)

9. Savola, R.: A requirement Centric Framework for Information Security Evaluation. In: Yoshiura, H., Sakurai, K., Rannenberg, K., Murayama, Y., Kawamura, S.-i. (eds.) IWSEC 2006. LNCS, vol. 4266, pp. 48–59. Springer, Heidelberg (2006)

10. Chen, Y.S., Lei, C.L., Chiu, Y.P., Huang, C.Y.: Confessible threshold ring signatures. In: ICSNC 2006: Proceedings of the International Conference on Systems and Networks Communication, p. 25. IEEE Computer Society (2006)

11. Camenisch, J.: Efficient and Generalized Group Signatures. In: Fumy, W. (ed.) EUROCRYPT 1997. LNCS, vol. 1233, pp. 465–479. Springer, Heidelberg (1997)

12. Schnorr, C.P.: Efficient signature generation by smart cards. J. Cryptology, 161–174 (1991)

13. Catalano, D., Cramer, R., Crescenzo, G., Darmgård, I., Pointcheval, D., Takagi, T., Pointcheval, D.: Provable security for public key schemes. In: Casacuberta, C. (ed.) Contemporary Cryptology, CRM Barcelona. Advanced Courses in Mathematics, pp. 133–190. Birkhäuser, Basel (2005)

14. Stadler, M.: Publicly Verifiable Secret Sharing. In: Maurer, U.M. (ed.) EUROCRYPT 1996. LNCS, vol. 1070, pp. 190–199. Springer, Heidelberg (1996)

15. Camenisch, J., Shoup, V.: Practical Verifiable Encryption and Decryption of Discrete Logarithms. In: Boneh, D. (ed.) CRYPTO 2003. LNCS, vol. 2729, pp. 126–144. Springer, Heidelberg (2003)

16. Camenisch, J., Damgård, I.: Verifiable Encryption, Group Encryption, and Their Applications to Separable Group Signatures and Signature Sharing Schemes. In: Okamoto, T. (ed.) ASIACRYPT 2000. LNCS, vol. 1976, pp. 331–345. Springer, Heidelberg (2000)

17. Bao, F.: An efficient verifiable encryption scheme for encryption of discrete logarithms. In: Schneier, B., Quisquater, J.-J. (eds.) CARDIS 1998. LNCS, vol. 1820, pp. 213–220. Springer, Heidelberg (2000)

18. Klonowski, M., Krzywiecki, L., Kutyowski, M., Lauks, A.: Step-out group signatures. Computing 85, 137–151 (2009)

Universally Composable Non-committing Encryptions in the Presence of Adaptive Adversaries

Huafei Zhu[1], Tadashi Araragi[2], Takashi Nishide[3], and Kouichi Sakurai[3]

[1] Institute for Infocomm Research, A-STAR, Singapore
[2] NTT Communication Science Laboratories, Kyoto, Japan
[3] Department of Computer Science and Communication Engineering
Kyushu University, Fukuoka, Japan
huafei@i2r.a-star.edu.sg, araragi@cslab.kecl.ntt.co.jp
nishide@inf.kyushu-u.ac.jp, sakurai@csce.kyushu-u.ac.jp

Abstract. Designing non-committing encryptions tolerating adaptive adversaries is a challenging task. In this paper, a simple implementation of non-committing encryptions is presented and analyzed in the strongest security model. We show that the proposed non-committing encryption scheme is provably secure against adaptive adversaries in the universally composable framework assuming that the decisional Diffie-Hellman problem is hard.

Keywords: Adaptive security, Decisional Diffie-Hellman assumption, Non-committing encryptions, Oblivious sampling and faking algorithms.

1 Introduction

Informally, a non-committing encryption protocol is an encrypted communication that allows a simulator to open a ciphertext to any plaintext it desires and simulate the real world adversary's view before and after a player is corrupted. Nielsen [15] shows that no non-interactive communication protocol can be adaptively secure in the asynchronous model. Beaver and Haber's protocol [2] realized the functionality of non-commitment encryption schemes in the erasure model and then Beaver [1] proposed a much simpler scheme based on the decisional Diffie-Hellman assumption with expansion factor $O(k)$. The non-committing encryptions presented in [1] and [2] are designed and analyzed in the stand-alone, simulation-based framework.

Canetti, Feige, Goldreich and Naor [6] proposed non-committing encryptions based on so called common-domain permutations. To encrypt 1 bit, $\Theta(k^2)$ public key bits are communicated. Damgård and Nielsen [8] proposed generic constructions of non-committing encryption schemes based on so called simulatable public-key encryption schemes in the universally composable framework. Roughly speaking, a public-key encryption scheme is simulatable if, in addition to the normal key generation algorithm procedure, there is an algorithm to generate a public key without knowing the corresponding secret key. Moreover, it must be possible to sample efficiently a random ciphertext without getting to know the corresponding plaintext. They showed that a non-committing encryption scheme can be constructed from any semantically secure and simulatable public-key system. Although the Damgård and Nielsen's construction [8] is general, the

M.S. Obaidat, G.A. Tsihrintzis, and J. Filipe (Eds.): ICETE 2010, CCIS 222, pp. 274–288, 2012.
© Springer-Verlag Berlin Heidelberg 2012

cost of computation is expensive since one should obliviously generate a pair of public keys to communicate 1-bit in open networks. Later, Zhu and Bao's scheme [17] have proposed alternative implementation of non-commitment scheme based on the notion of oblivious public-key encryptions instantiated by the DDH problem.

Choi, Soled, Malkin and Wee [7] have presented a new implementation of non-committing encryptions based on a weaker notion (called trapdoor simulatable cryptosystems). The idea behind their construction is that − on input a security parameter k, a receiver first generates total $4k$ public keys where the first k public keys are generated by a key generation algorithm of the underlying trapdoor simulatable encryption scheme while the rest $3k$ public keys are generated by an oblivious sampling algorithm. To encrypt a bit b, the sender sends $4k$ ciphertexts of which k are encrypted b and the remaining $3k$ ones are obliviously sampled. Although the non-committing encryption scheme in [7] is at the expense of higher computation and communication of the Damgård and Nielsen's protocol [8], such an implementation is definitely interesting since the subtle failure model in [8] is eliminated (i.e., the scheme presented in [7] is round-optimal) in their framework. Right after this paper, Zhu et al[16,18] have further proposed error-free, multi-bit non-committing encryptions with constant round complexity. The proposed scheme realizes the UC-security in the presence of adaptive adversary assuming that the decisional Diffie-Hellman problem is hard.

1.1 This Work

This paper studies non-committing encryptions in the UC-framework of Canetti. Our implementation is based on the notion of the oblivious transfer protocols first studied by Naor-Pinkas randomizer[12]. We show that the proposed non-committing encryption scheme is provably secure against adaptive adversaries in the universally composable framework assuming that the decisional Diffie-Hellman problem is hard.

AN OVERVIEW OF THE PROTOCOL. The proposed non-committing encryption protocol comprises two phases: a channel setup phase and a communication phase. The idea behind our construction is simple: to set up a secure channel, a sender S first picks a random bit $\alpha \in \{0, 1\}$, and then selects a Diffie-Hellman quadruple e_α and a garbled quadruple $e_{1-\alpha}$ and send (e_0, e_1) to a receiver R. Given (e_0, e_1), the receiver R picks a selection string f_β and a garbled string $f_{1-\beta}$, and then obliviously selects 1-out-of-2 quadruples with the help of the selection string f_β. If e_α is selected, then a secure channel is established; Otherwise, S and R retry the channel setup procedure.

MAIN RESULT. We claim that the non-commitment protocol π depicted by Fig. 2 realizes the universally composable security in the presence of adaptive adversaries assuming that the Decisional Diffie-Hellman problem is hard.

THE PROOF OF SECURITY. We will show that for any real world adversary $\mathcal{A}$ there exists an ideal-world adversary $\mathcal{S}$ such that no environment $\mathcal{Z}$, on any input, can tell with non-negligible probability whether it is interacting with $\mathcal{A}$ and players running π, or with $\mathcal{S}$ and $\mathcal{F}_{SC}^N$ in the ideal execution if the decisional Diffie-Hellman assumption holds. The core technique applied to the security proof is a novel application of oblivious sampling and faking algorithms introduced and formalized by Canetti and Fischlin in [4]. Roughly speaking, an oblivious faking algorithm fake takes $g \in G$ as input and outputs a string $r_g \in \{0,1\}^{2|p|}$. An oblivious sampling algorithm sample takes $r \in_U \{0,1\}^{2|p|}$ as input and outputs an element $r_G \in G$. The oblivious sampling and faking algorithms engaged in the security proof benefit a PPT simulator to generate subgroup elements of $G \subseteq Z_p^*$ uniformly at random and interprets a Diffie-Hellman quadruple e_α as a garbled quadruple $e_{1-\alpha}$. The oblivious sampling and faking algorithms also benefit the simulator to interpret a random selection string as a garbled string. As a result, no environment $\mathcal{Z}$, on any input, can tell with non-negligible probability whether it is interacting with $\mathcal{A}$ and players running π, or with $\mathcal{S}$ and $\mathcal{F}_{\mathrm{SC}}^{\mathcal{N}}$ in the ideal execution if the decisional Diffie-Hellman assumption holds.

EFFICIENCY. Our scheme requires 3 messages to communicate k encrypted bits, where k is the security parameter. The total communication is $O(k)$ Diffie-Hellman quadruples and garbled quadruples and $O(k)$ selection strings and garbled strings and k bits (the communication of the final k bits of the communication depend on the actual messages to be sent). Thus, our universally composably secure non-committing encryption protocol is as efficient as the stand-alone, simulation-based (but the notion of environment is defined in their security definition and the proof of the protocols) protocol by Beaver [1] — the most efficient implementation of non-committing encryptions so far.

2 Non-committing Encryptions: Functionality and Security Definition

The notion of non-committing encryption scheme introduced in [6] is a protocol used to realize secure channel in the presence of an adaptive adversary. In particular, this means that a simulator can build a fake transcript to the environment $\mathcal{Z}$, in such a way that the simulator can open this transcript to the actual inputs, that the simulator receives from the functionality when the parties get corrupted. Let $\mathcal{N}$ be a non-information oracle which is a PPT Turing machine that captures the information leaked to the adversary in the ideal-world. That is, $\mathcal{N}$ is the oracle which takes (Send, sid, P, m) as input and outputs (Send, sid, $P, |m|$). Let ChSetup be a channel setup command which on inputs (ChSetup, sid, S) produces no output and (Corrupt, sid, P) be a corruption command which takes (Corrupt, sid, P) produces no output. The functionality of non-committing encryption secure channels defined below is due to Garay, Wichs and Zhou [10].

Definition 1. *(due to [10]) We call the functionality* $\mathcal{F}_{\mathrm{SC}}^{\mathcal{N}}$ *a non-committing encryption secure channel. A real-world protocol* π *which realizes* $\mathcal{F}_{\mathrm{SC}}^{\mathcal{N}}$ *is called a non-committing encryption scheme.*

3 Non-committing Encryption

In this section, we first describe an implementation of non-committing schemes based on the decisional Diffie-Hellman problem, and then show that the proposed scheme realizes UC-security in the presence of adaptive adversaries [3]. Our protocol is constructed from the oblivious sampling and faking algorithms of Canetti and Fischlin [4] and the

---

The ideal functionality $\mathcal{F}_{SC}^{\mathcal{N}}$

$\mathcal{F}_{NCE}^{\mathcal{N}}$ proceeds as follows, when parameterized by leakage function $\mathcal{N}: \{0,1\}^* \rightarrow \{0,1\}^*$
Channel setup: upon receiving an input (**ChSetup**, sid, S) from party S, initialize the machine $\mathcal{N}$ and record the tuple $(sid, \mathcal{N})$. Pass the message (**ChSetup**, S) to R. In addition, pass this message to $\mathcal{N}$ and forward its output to S;
Message transfer: Upon receiving an input (**Send**, sid, P, m) from party P, where $P \in \{S, R\}$, find a tuple $(sid, \mathcal{N})$, and if none exists, ignore the message. Otherwise, send the message (**Send**, sid, P, m) to the other party $\overline{P} = \{S, R\} \setminus \{P\}$. In addition, invoke N with (**Send**, sid, P, m) and forwards its output (**Send**, sid, P, $|m|$) to the adversary S.
Corruption: Upon receiving a message (**Corrupt**, sid, P) from the adversary S, send (**Corrupt**, sid, P) to $\mathcal{N}$ and forward its output to the adversary. After the first corruption, stop execution of $\mathcal{N}$ and give the adversary S complete control over the functionality.

Fig. 1. A description of non-committing encryption secure channel

Naor-Pinkas randomizer [12]. We assume that the reader is familiar with the the oblivious sampling and faking algorithms of Canetti and Fischlin as well as the Naor-Pinkas randomizer, a cryptographic primitive extensively used in the literature(say, Peikert, Vaikuntanathan and Waters [13] have presented a framework for efficient and composable oblivious transfer based on Naor-Pinkas randomizer. Freedman et. al [9] used the Naor-Pinkas randomizer for constructing keyword search and oblivious pseudo-random functions. Pinkas [14], Lindell and Pinkas [11] and Freedman [9] have successfully applied the Naor-Pinkas randomizer to privacy preserving data mining).

3.1 Description of Non-committing Encryption Scheme

The non-committing encryption protocol comprises two phases: a channel setup phase and a communication phase. To set up a secure channel, S prepares two quadruples e_0 and e_1, where e_α is a Diffie-Hellman quadruple and $e_{1-\alpha}$ is a garbled quadruple, $\alpha \in \{0, 1\}$. S now let a receiver R to choose 1-out-of-2 quadruples. If e_α is selected, a secure channel has been set up between two parties; Otherwise, S and R retry the channel setup procedure. The details of protocol is depicted by Fig. 2.

3.2 The Proof of Security

Theorem 1. *Assuming that the Decisional Diffie-Hellman problem is hard in G, the non-commitment protocol π depicted by Fig. 2 realizes universally composable security in the presence of adaptive adversaries.*

Proof. There are four cases defined in the following proof, depending on when the real world adversary $\mathcal{A}$ makes its first corruption request (and thus the proof is tedious):

- Case 1: the real world adversary $\mathcal{A}$ makes its first corruption request after a secure channel has been set up successfully;
- Case 2: the real world adversary $\mathcal{A}$ makes its first corruption request after the sender S has received R's first message;

Universally Composable Non-committing Encryptions

Initialization: the environment $\mathcal{Z}$ invokes a system key generation algorithm $\mathcal{G}$ which takes security parameter k as input and outputs (p, q, G), where p is a large safe prime number (i.e., $p=2q+1$, q is a prime number) and G is a cyclic group with order q.

Channel setup: To set up a secure channel, a sender S and a receiver R jointly perform the following computations

- On input (p, q, G), S chooses $\alpha \in_U \{0, 1\}$ and performs the following computations
  - S generates a random Diffie-Hellman quadruple $(g_{1,\alpha}, g_{2,\alpha}, h_{1,\alpha}, h_{2,\alpha})$, where $g_{1,\alpha}$ and $g_{2,\alpha}$ are two random generators of G, and $h_{1,\alpha}$ and $h_{2,\alpha}$ are two elements in G such that $h_{1,\alpha} = g_{1,\alpha}^{sk_\alpha} \bmod p$, and $h_{2,\alpha} = g_{2,\alpha}^{sk_\alpha} \bmod p$, where $sk_\alpha \in_U Z_q$. Let $e_\alpha = (g_{1,\alpha}, g_{2,\alpha}, h_{1,\alpha}, h_{2,\alpha})$.
  - S picks a quadruple $(g_{1,1-\alpha}, g_{2,1-\alpha}, h_{1,1-\alpha}, h_{2,1-\alpha}) \in G^4$ uniformly at random. Let $e_{1-\alpha} = (g_{1,1-\alpha}, g_{2,1-\alpha}, h_{1,1-\alpha}, h_{2,1-\alpha})$.
  - S sends (e_0, e_1) to R.
- Upon receiving (e_0, e_1), R checks the conditions $1 \neq g_{i,j} \in G$ and $1 \neq h_{i,j} \in G$ ($i = 1, 2, j = 0, 1$), if any of the conditions are violated, R outputs $\perp$; Otherwise, R performs the following computations
  - R chooses $\beta \in_U \{0, 1\}$ and $s_\beta, t_\beta \in_U Z_q$ and then computes $u_\beta = g_{1,\beta}^{s_\beta} g_{2,\beta}^{t_\beta} \bmod p$ and $v_\beta = h_{1,\beta}^{s_\beta} h_{2,\beta}^{t_\beta} \bmod p$. Let $f_\beta = (u_\beta, v_\beta)$ and $\tau_\beta = (s_\beta, t_\beta)$.
  - R picks $u_{1-\beta} \in G$ and $v_{1-\beta} \in G$ uniformly at random. Let $f_{1-\beta} = (u_{1-\beta}, v_{1-\beta})$.
  - R sends (f_0, f_1) to S;
- Upon receiving (f_0, f_1), parsing f_0 as (u_0, v_0) and f_1 as (u_1, v_1), S checks that $1 \neq u_i \in G$ and $1 \neq v_i \in G$ ($i = 0, 1$), if any of the conditions are violated, S outputs $\perp$; Otherwise, S further checks the condition $v_\alpha \overset{?}{=} u_\alpha^{sk_\alpha} \bmod p$.
  - If $v_\alpha \neq u_\alpha^{sk_\alpha} \bmod p$, S sends $b = 0$ to R and retries the **channel setup** procedure;
  - If $v_\alpha = u_\alpha^{sk_\alpha} \bmod p$, S sends $b = 1$ to R and continues the **message transfer** step below.

Message transfer: On input $m \in \{0, 1\}$ and α, S computes $m \oplus \alpha$. Let $c = m \oplus \alpha$. S then sends c to R. Upon receiving a ciphertext c', R obtains m' by computing $c' \oplus \beta$.

Fig. 2. A description of non-committing encryption protocols

- Case 3: the real world adversary $\mathcal{A}$ makes its first corruption request after S has generated its first message, but before S receives R's first message;
- Case 4: the real world adversary $\mathcal{A}$ makes its first corruption request before any messages are generated.

We show that in each case above there exists an ideal-world adversary S such that no environment $\mathcal{Z}$, on any input, can tell with non-negligible probability whether it is interacting with $\mathcal{A}$ and players running π, or with S and $\mathcal{F}_{SC}^{\mathcal{N}}$ in the ideal execution if the decisional Diffie-Hellman assumption holds.

To simplify the description of a simulator, we omit the explicit description of the non-information oracle $\mathcal{N}$ here and what follows since the non-commitment encryption scheme described in this paper is a well-structured protocol (informally, a well-structured protocol requires the message sizes and the number of rounds are completely determined by the protocol and are independent of the input values or random coins of the parties. For the details definition of well-structured protocol, please refer to [10]). We here and what follows, also omit the explicit checks that the simulator has seen the previous steps of the protocol.

Case 1 – *the first corruption occurs after a secure channel has been set up successfully.* If the real world adversary $\mathcal{A}$ makes its first corruption request after a secure channel has been set up successfully, an ideal world adversary $\mathcal{S}$ must simulate any of the following three cases: 1) the first corruption occurs after R has received c; or 2) the first corruption occurs after S has generated c, but before R receives c; or 3) the first corruption occurs before S generates c. The corresponding simulator $\mathcal{S}$ is described as follows.

- Step 1: $\mathcal{S}$ first picks $g_{i,0} \in_U G$, $g_{i,1} \in_U G$, $sk_0 \in_U Z_q$ and $sk_1 \in_U Z_q$, and then computes $h_{i,0} = g_{i,0}^{sk_0} \bmod p$, $h_{i,1} = g_{i,1}^{sk_1} \bmod p$, $i = 1, 2$. Let $e_0 = (g_{1,0}, g_{2,0}, h_{1,0}, h_{2,0})$ and $e_1 = (g_{1,1}, g_{2,1}, h_{1,1}, h_{2,1})$. $\mathcal{S}$ keeps the auxiliary strings sk_0 and sk_1 secret.
- Step 2: $\mathcal{S}$ then picks $s_i \in_U Z_q$ and $t_i \in_U Z_q$, and computes $u_i = g_{1,i}^{s_i} g_{2,i}^{t_i} \bmod p$, $v_i = h_{1,i}^{s_i} h_{2,i}^{t_i} \bmod p$. Let $f_i = (u_i, v_i)$, $i = 0, 1$. $\mathcal{S}$ keeps the auxiliary strings (s_0, t_0) and (s_1, t_1) secret.
- Step 3: $\mathcal{S}$ outputs a bit b (=1).

Case 1.1 – *the first corruption occurs after R has received c;* If a party $P \in \{S, R\}$ gets corrupted, $\mathcal{S}$ corrupts the corresponding dummy party $\widetilde{P}$ and obtains m. Let $\gamma = m \oplus c$. Following the steps (Step 1, Step 2 and Step 3) above, we further consider subcases below:

Case 1.1.1: If the sender S gets corrupted in the first corruption, $\mathcal{S}$ invokes the faking algorithm **fake** which takes S's internal state r_S as input and interprets e_γ as a Diffie-Hellman quadruple r_{e_γ} associated with the auxiliary string sk_γ and interprets $e_{1-\gamma}$ as a garbled quadruple $r_{e_{1-\gamma}}$. That is, the faking algorithm **fake** interprets $g_{i,j} \in G$ as a string $r_{g_{i,j}} \in \{0,1\}^{2|p|}$ and $h_{i,j} \in G$ as a string $r_{h_{i,j}} \in \{0,1\}^{2|p|}$ ($i = 1, 2, j = 0, 1$). Let $r_{e_\gamma} = (r_{g_{1,\gamma}}, r_{g_{2,\gamma}}, r_{h_{1,\gamma}}, r_{h_{2,\gamma}})$ and $r_{e_{1-\gamma}} = (r_{g_{1,1-\gamma}}, r_{g_{2,1-\gamma}}, r_{h_{1,1-\gamma}}, r_{h_{2,1-\gamma}})$. The auxiliary string sk_γ is associated with r_{e_γ} such that $(r_{g_{1,\gamma}}, r_{h_{1,\gamma}}) \in \mathrm{Dlog}(sk_\gamma)$ and $(r_{g_{2,\gamma}}, r_{h_{2,\gamma}}) \in \mathrm{Dlog}(sk_\gamma)$ (*Note that given a string $r_{g_{i,j}} \in \{0,1\}^{2|p|}$, the corresponding group element $g_{i,j} \in G$ can be efficiently reconstructed by applying the Canetti-Fischlin's sampling algorithm*). $\mathcal{S}$ reveals (r_{e_0}, r_{e_1}), sk_γ and m to $\mathcal{A}$.

If R gets corrupted in the second corruption, $\mathcal{S}$ modifies the receiver's internal state r_R before it is revealed to $\mathcal{A}$. That is, $\mathcal{S}$ first invokes the faking algorithm **fake** which takes R's internal state r_R as input and interprets f_γ ($= (u_\gamma, v_\gamma)$) as a selection string r_{f_γ} ($= (r_{u_\gamma}, r_{v_\gamma})$) associated with the auxiliary string (s_γ, t_γ) and interpreted $f_{1-\gamma}$ ($= (u_{1-\gamma}, v_{1-\gamma})$) as a garbled string $r_{f_{1-\gamma}}$ ($= (r_{u_{1-\gamma}}, r_{v_{1-\gamma}})$). $\mathcal{S}$ reveals (r_{f_0}, r_{f_1}) and (s_γ, t_γ) to $\mathcal{A}$.

Case 1.1.2: When R gets corrupted in the first corruption, $\mathcal{S}$ corrupts the dummy party $\widetilde{R}$ in the ideal world and obtains m. $\mathcal{S}$ then invokes the faking algorithm **fake** which takes R's internal state r_R as input and interprets f_γ as a selection string r_{f_γ} associated with the auxiliary string (s_γ, t_γ) and interprets $f_{1-\gamma}$ as a garbled string $r_{f_{1-\gamma}}$. $\mathcal{S}$ reveals (r_{f_0}, r_{f_1}) and (s_γ, t_γ) to $\mathcal{A}$.

If S gets corrupted in the second corruption, $\mathcal{S}$ corrupts the dummy party $\widetilde{S}$ in the ideal world and obtains m. $\mathcal{S}$ invokes the faking algorithm fake which takes r_S as input and interprets e_γ as a Diffie-Hellman quadruple r_{e_γ} associated with the auxiliary string sk_γ and interprets $e_{1-\gamma}$ as a garbled string $r_{e_{1-\gamma}}$. $\mathcal{S}$ reveals (r_{e_0}, r_{e_1}), sk_γ and m to $\mathcal{A}$.

Case 1.2 – *the first corruption occurs after S has generated c, but before R receives* c; Following the steps (Step 1, Step 2 and Step 3) above, we further consider subcases below:

Case 1.2.1: If S gets corrupted in the first corruption after it has generated c, but before R receives c. $\mathcal{S}$ corrupts the dummy party $\widetilde{S}$ in the ideal world and obtains m. Let $\gamma = c \oplus m$. $\mathcal{S}$ invokes the faking algorithm fake which takes r_S as input and interprets e_γ as a Diffie-Hellman quadruple r_{e_γ} associated with the auxiliary string sk_γ and interprets $e_{1-\gamma}$ as a garbled string $r_{e_{1-\gamma}}$. $\mathcal{S}$ reveals (r_{e_0}, r_{e_1}), sk_γ and m to $\mathcal{A}$.

If the second corruption occurs *before* R receives a ciphertext c' (the received ciphertetxt c' may not be the same as the ciphertext c generated by S since the real-world adversary $\mathcal{A}$ may change the ciphertext c). $\mathcal{S}$ invokes the faking algorithm fake which takes r_R as input and interprets f_γ as a selection string r_{f_γ} associated with the auxiliary string (s_γ, t_γ) and interprets $f_{1-\gamma}$ as a garbled string $r_{f_{1-\gamma}}$. $\mathcal{S}$ reveals (r_{f_0}, r_{f_1}) and (s_γ, t_γ) to $\mathcal{A}$.

If the second corruption occurs *after* R has received a ciphertext c'. The simulator invokes fake which takes r_R as input and interprets f_γ as a selection string associated with the auxiliary string (s_γ, t_γ) and interprets $f_{1-\gamma}$ as a garbled string. Let $m' = \gamma \oplus c'$. $\mathcal{S}$ reveals (r_{f_0}, r_{f_1}), (s_γ, t_γ) and m' to $\mathcal{A}$.

Case 1.2.2: If the receiver R gets corrupted in the first corruption, $\mathcal{S}$ corrupts the corresponding dummy party $\widetilde{R}$ and obtains β. Let $\gamma = \beta$. $\mathcal{S}$ invokes the faking algorithm fake which takes R's internal state r_R as input and interprets f_γ as a selection string r_{f_γ} associated with the auxiliary string (s_γ, t_γ) and interprets $f_{1-\gamma}$ as a garbled string $r_{f_{1-\gamma}}$. $\mathcal{S}$ reveals (r_{f_0}, r_{f_1}) and (s_γ, t_γ) to $\mathcal{A}$.

If the second corruption occurs, $\mathcal{S}$ corrupts the corresponding dummy party $\widetilde{S}$ and obtains m. $\mathcal{S}$ then invokes the faking algorithm fake which takes r_S as input and interprets e_γ as a Diffie-Hellman quadruple r_{e_γ} associated with the auxiliary string sk_γ and interprets $e_{1-\gamma}$ as a garbled string $r_{e_{1-\gamma}}$. $\mathcal{S}$ reveals (r_{e_0}, r_{e_1}), sk_γ and m to $\mathcal{A}$.

Case 1.3 – *the first corruption occurs before S generates c*; Following the simulation steps (Step 1, Step 2 and Step 3) above, we consider the following two subcases:

Case 1.3.1: If the sender S gets corrupted in the first corruption, $\mathcal{S}$ corrupts the corresponding dummy party $\widetilde{S}$ in the ideal world and obtains m. $\mathcal{S}$ picks a random bit $\gamma \in \{0, 1\}$ uniformly at random. Let $\alpha = \gamma$ and $\beta = \gamma$. $\mathcal{S}$ invokes the faking algorithm fake which takes r_S as input and interprets e_γ as a Diffie-Hellman quadruple r_{e_γ} associated with the auxiliary string sk_γ and interprets $e_{1-\gamma}$ as a garbled quadruple $r_{e_{1-\gamma}}$. $\mathcal{S}$ reveals (r_{e_0}, r_{e_1}), sk_γ and m to $\mathcal{A}$.

If R gets corrupted in the second corruption, $\mathcal{S}$ invokes the faking algorithm fake which takes R's internal state r_R as input and interprets f_γ as a selection string r_{f_γ} associated with the auxiliary string (s_γ, t_γ) and interprets $f_{1-\gamma}$ as a garbled string $r_{f_{1-\gamma}}$. $\mathcal{S}$ reveals (r_{f_0}, r_{f_1}) and (s_γ, t_γ) to $\mathcal{A}$.

Case 1.3.2: If the receiver R gets corrupted in the first corruption, S picks a bit $\gamma \in \{0,1\}$ uniformly at random and then invokes the faking algorithm fake which takes r_R as input and interprets f_γ as a selection string r_{f_γ} associated with the auxiliary string (s_γ, t_γ) and interprets $f_{1-\gamma}$ as a garbled string $r_{f_{1-\gamma}}$. S reveals(r_{f_0}, r_{f_1}) and (s_γ, t_γ) to $\mathcal{A}$.

If S gets corrupted in the second corruption, S corrupts the corresponding dummy party $\widetilde{S}$ and obtains m. S invokes the faking algorithm fake which takes r_S as input and interprets e_γ as a Diffie-Hellman quadruple r_{e_γ} associated with the auxiliary string sk_γ and interprets $e_{1-\gamma}$ as a garbled quadruple $r_{e_{1-\gamma}}$. The simulator reveals (r_{e_0}, r_{e_1}), sk_γ and m to $\mathcal{A}$.

Case 2 – *the first corruption occurs after the sender S has received R's first message.* If the real world adversary $\mathcal{A}$ makes its first corruption after the sender S has received R's first message (f_0, f_1), the constructed ideal world adversary S must simulate any of the following three subcases: 1) the first corruption occurs after S has generated b and R has received b; or 2) the first corruption occurs after S has generated b, but before R receives b; or 3) the first corruption occurs before S generates b. We describe the corresponding simulator S below

- Step 1: S picks $g_{i,0} \in_U G$, $g_{i,1} \in_U G$, $sk_0 \in_U Z_q$ and $sk_1 \in_U Z_q$, and then computes $h_{i,0} = g_{i,0}^{sk_0} \bmod p$, $h_{i,1} = g_{i,1}^{sk_1} \bmod p$. Let $e_i = (g_{1,i}, g_{2,i}, h_{1,i}, h_{2,i})$, $i = 1, 2$. S keeps the auxiliary strings sk_0 and sk_1 secret.
- Step 2: S picks $s_i \in Z_q$ and $t_i \in Z_q$ uniformly at random, and then computes $u_i = g_{1,i}^{s_i} g_{2,i}^{t_i} \bmod p$, $v_i = h_{1,i}^{s_i} h_{2,i}^{t_i} \bmod p$. Let $f_i = (u_i, v_i)$, $i = 0, 1$. S keeps the auxiliary strings (s_0, t_0) and (s_1, t_1) secret.

Case 2.1 – *the first corruption occurs after the sender S has received (f_0, f_1) and R has received a bit b.* Following the simulation steps (Step 1 and Step 2) above, we further consider subcases below:

Case 2.1.1 if $b=1$ and a party $P \in \{S, R\}$ gets corrupted in the first corruption, the corresponding simulator can be constructed exactly as that described in Case 1.

Case 2.1.2 if $b=0$ and if the sender S gets corrupted in the first corruption, the simulator S corrupts the corresponding dummy party $\widetilde{S}$ in the ideal world and obtains m. S then chooses a random bit $\gamma \in_U \{0,1\}$. Let $\alpha = \gamma$ and $\beta = 1 - \gamma$. S invokes the faking algorithm fake which takes r_S as input and interprets e_γ as a Diffie-Hellman quadruple r_{e_γ} associated with the auxiliary string sk_γ and interprets $e_{1-\gamma}$ as a garbled quadruple $r_{e_{1-\gamma}}$ and reveals (r_{e_0}, r_{e_1}), sk_γ and m to the real world adversary $\mathcal{A}$.

If the receiver R gets corrupted in the second corruption, S invokes fake which takes r_R as input and interprets $f_{1-\gamma}$ as a selection string $r_{f_{1-\gamma}}$ associated with the auxiliary string $(s_{1-\gamma}, t_{1-\gamma})$ and interprets f_γ as a garbled string r_{f_γ} and reveals (r_{f_0}, r_{f_1}) and $(s_{1-\gamma}, t_{1-\gamma})$ to $\mathcal{A}$.

Case 2.1.3 if $b=0$ and if the receiver R gets corrupted in the first corruption, S picks a bit $\gamma \in \{0,1\}$ uniformly at random and sets $\beta = \gamma$ and $\alpha = 1 - \gamma$. S invokes the faking algorithm fake which takes r_R as input and interprets f_γ as a selection string r_{f_γ} associated with the auxiliary string (s_γ, t_γ) and interprets $f_{1-\gamma}$ as a garbled string $r_{f_{1-\gamma}}$. S reveals (r_{f_0}, r_{f_1}) and (s_γ, t_γ) to $\mathcal{A}$.

If the sender S gets corrupted in the second corruption, the simulator S corrupts the corresponding dummy party $\widetilde{S}$ in the ideal world and obtains m. S then interprets $e_{1-\gamma}$ as a Diffie-Hellman quadruple $r_{e_{1-\gamma}}$ associated with the auxiliary string $sk_{1-\gamma}$ and interprets e_γ as a garbled quadruple r_{e_γ}. S then reveals (r_{e_0}, r_{e_1}), $sk_{1-\gamma}$ and m to $\mathcal{A}$.

Case 2.2 – *the first corruption occurs after S has received (f_0, f_1) and S has generated b but before R receives the bit b.* Following the simulation steps (Step 1 and Step 2) above, we further consider subcases below:

Case 2.2.1 if S gets corrupted in the first corruption and if $b = 1$, S corrupts a dummy party $\widetilde{S}$ and obtains m. S then picks a bit $\gamma \in_U \{0, 1\}$. Let $\alpha = \gamma$ and $\beta = \gamma$. S invokes the faking algorithm fake which takes r_S as input and interprets e_γ as a Diffie-Hellman quadruple r_{e_γ} associated with the auxiliary string sk_γ and interprets $e_{1-\gamma}$ as a garbled quadruple $r_{e_{1-\gamma}}$. S reveals (r_{e_0}, r_{e_1}), sk_γ and m to $\mathcal{A}$.

If the receiver R gets corrupted before R receives the bit b ($=1$) in the second corruption, S invokes fake algorithm which takes r_R as input and interprets f_γ as a selection string r_{f_γ} associated with the auxiliary string (s_γ, t_γ) and interprets $f_{1-\gamma}$ as a garbled string $r_{f_{1-\gamma}}$. S reveals (r_{f_0}, r_{f_1}) and (s_γ, t_γ) to $\mathcal{A}$. If the receiver R gets corrupted after it has received a bit b' (the generated bit might be changed by $\mathcal{A}$) in the second corruption, the corresponding simulator can be constructed exactly as that described in Case 2.1.

Case 2.2.2 if R gets corrupted in the first corruption and if $b=1$, S picks a random bit $\gamma \in_U \{0, 1\}$ and sets $\beta = \gamma$ and $\alpha = \gamma$. S interprets f_γ as a selection string r_{f_γ} associated with the auxiliary string (s_γ, t_γ) and interprets $f_{1-\gamma}$ as a garbled string $r_{f_{1-\gamma}}$. S reveals (r_{f_0}, r_{f_1}) and (s_γ, t_γ) to $\mathcal{A}$

If S gets corrupted in the second corruption, S corrupts the dummy party $\widetilde{S}$ and obtains m. S then interprets e_γ as a Diffie-Hellman quadruple r_{e_γ} associated with the auxiliary string sk_γ and interprets $e_{1-\gamma}$ as a garbled quadruple $r_{e_{1-\gamma}}$. S reveals (r_{e_0}, r_{e_1}), sk_γ and m to $\mathcal{A}$.

Case 2.2.3 If S gets corrupted in the first corruption and if $b = 0$, S corrupts a dummy party S and obtains m and picks a bit $\gamma \in \{0, 1\}$ uniformly at random. Let $\alpha = \gamma$ and $\beta = 1 - \gamma$. S invokes the faking algorithm fake which takes r_S as input and interprets e_γ as a Diffie-Hellman quadruple r_{e_γ} associated with the auxiliary string sk_γ and interprets $e_{1-\gamma}$ as a garbled quadruple $r_{e_{1-\gamma}}$. S reveals (r_{e_0}, r_{e_1}), sk_γ and m to $\mathcal{A}$.

If the receiver R gets corrupted before it receives a bit b' in the second corruption, S interprets $f_{1-\gamma}$ a selection string $r_{f_{1-\gamma}}$ associated with the auxiliary string $(s_{1-\gamma}, t_{1-\gamma})$ and interprets f_γ as a garbled string r_{f_γ}. S reveals the randomness (r_{f_0}, r_{f_1}), $(s_{1-\gamma}, t_{1-\gamma})$ to $\mathcal{A}$. If the receiver R gets corrupted after it has received a bit b', the simulator can be constructed exactly as that described in Case 2.1.

Case 2.2.4 if R gets corrupted in the first corruption and if $b=0$, S picks a random bit $\gamma \in \{0, 1\}$ uniformly at random and sets $\beta = \gamma$ and $\alpha = 1 - \gamma$. S interprets f_γ as a selection string r_{f_γ} associated with the auxiliary string sk_γ and interprets $f_{1-\gamma}$ as a garbled string $r_{f_{1-\gamma}}$. S then reveals (r_{f_0}, r_{f_1}), (s_γ, t_γ) to $\mathcal{A}$. If S gets corrupted in the second corruption, S corrupts $\widetilde{S}$ and obtains m, and then interprets $e_{1-\gamma}$ as a

Diffie-Hellman quadruple $r_{e_{1-\gamma}}$ associated with the auxiliary string $sk_{1-\gamma}$ and interprets e_γ as a garbled quadruple r_{e_γ}. S reveals (r_{e_0}, r_{e_1}), $sk_{1-\gamma}$ and m to $\mathcal{A}$.

Case 2.3 – *the first corruption occurs after the sender S has received (f_0, f_1), but before S generates b.* Following the simulation steps (Step 1 and Step 2) above, S picks a bit $b \in \{0, 1\}$ uniformly at random. We further consider the following subcases

Case 2.3.1 if S gets corrupted in the first corruption and if $b = 1$, the corresponding simulator S can be constructed exactly as that described in Case 2.2.1;

Case 2.3.2 if R gets corrupted in the first corruption and if $b = 1$, the corresponding simulator S can be constructed exactly as that described in Case 2.2.2;

Case 2.3.3 if S gets corrupted in the first corruption and if $b = 0$, the corresponding simulator S can be constructed exactly as that described in Case 2.2.3;

Case 2.3.4 if R gets corrupted in the first corruption and if $b = 0$, the corresponding simulator S can be constructed exactly as that described in Case 2.2.4.

Case 3 – *the first corruption occurs after S has generated its first message, but before it receives R's first message.* If the real world adversary $\mathcal{A}$ makes its first corruption request after S has generated its first message, but before it receives R's first message, an ideal world adversary S must simulate any of the following subcases: 1) the first corruption occurs after R has received (e_0, e_1) and have generated its first message (f_0, f_1) but before S receives it; or 2) the first corruption occurs after R has received (e_0, e_1) but before R generates (f_0, f_1); or 3) the first corruption occurs after S has generated its first message, but before R receives S' first message.

Case 3.1 *if the first corruption occurs after R has received (e_0, e_1) and R has generated (f_0, f_1) but before S receives it.* The corresponding simulator S can be constructed as follows.

- Step 1: S picks $g_{i,0} \in_U G$, $g_{i,1} \in_U G$, $sk_0 \in_U Z_q$ and $sk_1 \in_U Z_q$, and then computes $h_{i,0} = g_{i,0}^{sk_0} \bmod p$, $h_{i,1} = g_{i,1}^{sk_1} \bmod p$, $i = 1, 2$. Let $e_0 = (g_{1,0}, g_{2,0}, h_{1,0}, h_{2,0})$ and $e_1 = (g_{1,1}, g_{2,1}, h_{1,1}, h_{2,1})$. S keeps the auxiliary strings sk_0 and sk_1 secret.
- Step 2: S then picks $s_i \in_U Z_q$ and $t_i \in_U Z_q$, and then computes $u_i = g_{1,i}^{s_i} g_{2,i}^{t_i} \bmod p$, $v_i = h_{1,i}^{s_i} h_{2,i}^{t_i} \bmod p$. Let $f_i = (u_i, v_i)$, $i = 0, 1$. S keeps the auxiliary strings (s_0, t_0) and (s_1, t_1) secret.

Following the simulation steps (Step 1 and Step 2) above, we consider the following subcases:

Case 3.1.1 if S gets corrupted in the first corruption, S corrupts the corresponding dummy party $\widetilde{S}$ in the ideal world and obtains m. S then picks a bit $\gamma \in_U \{0, 1\}$ uniformly at random and sets $\alpha = \gamma$; S invokes the faking algorithm fake which takes r_S as input and interprets e_γ as a Diffie-Hellman quadruple r_{e_γ} associated with the auxiliary string sk_γ and interprets $e_{1-\gamma}$ as a garbled quadruple $r_{e_{1-\gamma}}$. S reveals (r_{e_0}, r_{e_1}), sk_γ and m to $\mathcal{A}$.

If R gets corrupted in the second corruption, S chooses a bit $b \in_U \{0, 1\}$ uniformly at random. We further consider the following cases

- if $b = 1$, then let $\beta = \gamma$. $\mathcal{S}$ invokes the faking algorithm **fake** which takes r_R as input and interprets f_γ as a selection string r_{f_γ} associated with the auxiliary string (s_γ, t_γ) and interprets $f_{1-\gamma}$ as a garbled string $r_{f_{1-\gamma}}$. $\mathcal{S}$ reveals (r_{f_0}, r_{f_1}) and (s_γ, t_γ) to $\mathcal{A}$.

- if $b = 0$, then let $\beta = 1 - \gamma$. $\mathcal{S}$ invokes the faking algorithm **fake** which takes r_R as input and interprets $f_{1-\gamma}$ as a selection string $r_{f_{1-\gamma}}$ associated with the auxiliary string $(s_{1-\gamma}, t_{1-\gamma})$ and interprets f_γ as a garbled string r_{f_γ}. $\mathcal{S}$ reveals (r_{f_0}, r_{f_1}) and $(s_{1-\gamma}, t_{1-\gamma})$ to $\mathcal{A}$.

Case 3.1.2 if R gets corrupted in the first corruption, $\mathcal{S}$ picks a bit $\gamma \in_U \{0, 1\}$ uniformly at random and sets $\beta = \gamma$; $\mathcal{S}$ invokes the faking algorithm **fake** which takes r_R as input and interprets f_γ as a selection string r_{f_γ} associated with the auxiliary string (s_γ, t_γ) and interprets $f_{1-\gamma}$ as a garbled string $r_{f_{1-\gamma}}$. $\mathcal{S}$ reveals (r_{f_0}, r_{f_1}) and (s_γ, t_γ) to $\mathcal{A}$.

If the sender S gets corrupted in the second corruption, $\mathcal{S}$ chooses a bit $b \in_U \{0, 1\}$ uniformly at random. We further consider the following cases

- if $b = 1$, let $\beta = \gamma$. $\mathcal{S}$ invokes the faking algorithm **fake** which takes r_R as input and interprets f_γ as a selection string r_{f_γ} associated with the auxiliary string (s_γ, t_γ) and interprets $f_{1-\gamma}$ as a garbled string $r_{f_{1-\gamma}}$. $\mathcal{S}$ reveals (r_{f_0}, r_{f_1}) and (s_γ, t_γ) to $\mathcal{A}$.

- if $b = 0$, let $\beta = 1 - \gamma$. $\mathcal{S}$ invokes the faking algorithm **fake** which takes r_R as input and interprets $f_{1-\gamma}$ as a selection string $r_{f_{1-\gamma}}$ associated with the auxiliary string $(s_{1-\gamma}, t_{1-\gamma})$ and interprets f_γ as a garbled string r_{f_γ}. $\mathcal{S}$ reveals (r_{f_0}, r_{f_1}) and $(s_{1-\gamma}, t_{1-\gamma})$ to $\mathcal{A}$.

Case 3.2 if the first corruption occurs after R has received (e_0, e_1) but before R generates (f_0, f_1), the corresponding simulator $\mathcal{S}$ can be constructed as follows.

- Step 1: $\mathcal{S}$ picks $g_{i,0} \in_U G$, $g_{i,1} \in_U G$, $sk_0 \in_U Z_q$ and $sk_1 \in_U Z_q$ uniformly at random, and then computes $h_{i,0} = g_{i,0}^{sk_0} \bmod p$, $h_{i,1} = g_{i,1}^{sk_1} \bmod p$, $i = 1, 2$. Let $e_0 = (g_{1,0}, g_{2,0}, h_{1,0}, h_{2,0})$ and $e_1 = (g_{1,1}, g_{2,1}, h_{1,1}, h_{2,1})$. $\mathcal{S}$ keeps the auxiliary strings sk_0 and sk_1 secret.

Following the simulation Step 1 above, we further consider subcases below:

Case 3.2.1 if the sender S gets corrupted in the first corruption, $\mathcal{S}$ corrupts the corresponding dummy party $\tilde{S}$ in the ideal world and obtains m. $\mathcal{S}$ then picks a bit $\gamma \in \{0, 1\}$ uniformly at random and sets $\alpha = \gamma$; $\mathcal{S}$ invokes the faking algorithm **fake** which takes r_S as input and interprets e_γ as a Diffie-Hellman quadruple r_{e_γ} associated with the auxiliary string sk_γ and interprets $e_{1-\gamma}$ as a garbled quadruple $r_{e_{1-\gamma}}$. $\mathcal{S}$ reveals m, (r_{e_0}, r_{e_1}) and sk_γ to $\mathcal{A}$.

- if R gets corrupted before it generates (f_0, f_1) in the second corruption, $\mathcal{S}$ reveals R's internal state r_R to $\mathcal{A}$; The rest of simulation is trivial since both parties have already corrupted.

- if R gets corrupted after it has generated (f_0, f_1) in the second corruption, $\mathcal{S}$ picks a bit $b \in \{0, 1\}$ uniformly at random
  1) if $b = 1$, $\mathcal{S}$ invokes the faking algorithm **fake** which takes r_R as input and interprets e_γ as a Diffie-Hellman quadruple r_{e_γ} associated with the auxiliary string

sk_γ and interprets $e_{1-\gamma}$ as a garbled quadruple $r_{e_{1-\gamma}}$. $\mathcal{S}$ reveals (r_{e_0}, r_{e_1}) and sk_γ to $\mathcal{A}$.

2) if $b = 0$, $\mathcal{S}$ invokes the faking algorithm **fake** which takes r_R as input and interprets $e_{1-\gamma}$ as a Diffie-Hellman quadruple $r_{e_{1-\gamma}}$ associated with the auxiliary string $sk_{1-\gamma}$ and interprets e_γ as a garbled quadruple r_{e_γ}. $\mathcal{S}$ reveals (r_{e_0}, r_{e_1}) and $sk_{1-\gamma}$ to $\mathcal{A}$.

Case 3.2.2 if the receiver R gets corrupted in the first corruption, $\mathcal{S}$ simply reveals r_R to $\mathcal{A}$.

- if S gets corrupted before it obtains (f_0', f_1') in the second corruption, $\mathcal{S}$ corrupts the corresponding dummy party $\widetilde{S}$ in the ideal world and obtains m. $\mathcal{S}$ picks a bit $\gamma \in \{0,1\}$ uniformly at random and sets $\alpha = \gamma$. $\mathcal{S}$ invokes the faking algorithm **fake** which takes r_S as input and interprets e_γ as a Diffie-Hellman quadruple r_{e_γ} associated with the auxiliary string sk_γ and interprets $e_{1-\gamma}$ as a garbled quadruple $r_{e_{1-\gamma}}$. $\mathcal{S}$ reveals m, (r_{e_0}, r_{e_1}) and sk_γ to $\mathcal{A}$.
- if S gets corrupted after it has received (f_0', f_1') in the second corruption. We consider the following two cases:
  1) if (f_0', f_1') is not well-defined, i.e., any of the conditions $1 \neq u_i \in G$ and $1 \neq v_i \in G$ ($i = 0$, 1) are violated, $\mathcal{S}$ picks a bit $b \in \{0,1\}$ uniformly at random. If $b = 1$, let $\alpha = \gamma$; if $b = 0$, let $\alpha = 1 - \gamma$. The rest work of simulator is same as that described in Case 2.1.
  2) if (f_0', f_1') is well-defined, i.e., $1 \neq u_i \in G$ and $1 \neq v_i \in G$ ($i = 0$, 1), $\mathcal{S}$ picks a bit $b \in \{0,1\}$ uniformly at random. If $b = 1$, let $\beta = \gamma$; If $b = 0$, let $\beta = 1 - \gamma$. The rest work of simulator is same as that described in Case 2.1.

Case 3.3 if the first corruption occurs after S has generated (e_0, e_1) but before R receives it, the corresponding simulator $\mathcal{S}$ can be constructed as follows.

- Step 1: $\mathcal{S}$ picks $g_{i,0} \in_U G$, $g_{i,1} \in_U G$, $sk_0 \in_U Z_q$ and $sk_1 \in_U Z_q$, and then computes $h_{i,0} = g_{i,0}^{sk_0} \bmod p$, $h_{i,1} = g_{i,1}^{sk_1} \bmod p$, $i = 1, 2$. Let $e_0 = (g_{1,0}, g_{2,0}, h_{1,0}, h_{2,0})$ and $e_1 = (g_{1,1}, g_{2,1}, h_{1,1}, h_{2,1})$. $\mathcal{S}$ keeps the auxiliary strings sk_0 and sk_1 secret.

Following the simulation Step 1 above, we further consider subcases below:

Case 3.3.1 if S gets corrupted in the first corruption, $\mathcal{S}$ picks a bit $\gamma \in \{0,1\}$ uniformly at random and sets $\alpha = \gamma$; $\mathcal{S}$ invokes the faking algorithm **fake** which takes r_S as input and interprets e_γ as a Diffie-Hellman quadruple r_{e_γ} associated with the auxiliary string sk_γ and interprets $e_{1-\gamma}$ as a garbled quadruple $r_{e_{1-\gamma}}$. $\mathcal{S}$ reveals m, (r_{e_0}, r_{e_1}) and sk_γ to $\mathcal{A}$.

- if R gets corrupted before it receives (e_0', e_1') in the second corruption, $\mathcal{S}$ reveals R's internal state r_R to $\mathcal{A}$. The rest of simulation is trivial since both parties have already got corrupted.
- if R gets corrupted after it has received (e_0', e_1'). If (e_0', e_1') is not well-defined, i.e., any of the conditions $1 \neq g_{i,j} \in G$ and $1 \neq h_{i,j} \in G$ ($i = 1, 2, j = 0$, 1) are violated, then $\mathcal{S}$ reveal r_R to $\mathcal{A}$; If (e_0', e_1') is well-defined, i.e., $1 \neq g_{i,j} \in G$ and $1 \neq h_{i,j} \in G$ ($i = 1, 2, j = 0$, 1), $\mathcal{S}$ picks a random bit $\gamma \in \{0,1\}$ and sets $\alpha = \gamma$. The rest work of $\mathcal{S}$ is same as that described in Case 3.2.

Case 3.3.2 if R gets corrupted in the first corruption, S reveals R's internal state r_R to A. If S gets corrupted in the second corruption, we consider the following two cases:

- if (f_0', f_1') has not been received, S picks a random bit $\gamma \in_U \{0, 1\}$ and sets $\alpha = \gamma$. S then invokes the faking algorithm fake which takes r_S as input and interprets e_γ as a Diffie-Hellman quadruple r_{e_γ} associated with the auxiliary string sk_γ and interprets $e_{1-\gamma}$ as a garbled quadruple. S reveals m, (r_{e_0}, r_{e_1}) and sk_γ to the real world adversary A.
- if (f_0', f_1') has been received, and if (f_0', f_1') is not well-defined, the rest work of S is same as that described in Case 3.2; if (f_0', f_1') has been received and if (f_0', f_1') is well-defined, S can be constructed exactly as that described in Case 2.3.

Case 4 *the first corruption occurs before* (e_0, e_1) *has been generated.* If A makes its first request before S generates (e_0, e_1), the corresponding simulator S can be constructed as follows.

Case 4.1 if S gets corrupted in the first corruption, S corrupts the corresponding dummy party $\widetilde{S}$ in the ideal world and obtains m. S reveals its internal state r_S together with its input m to A.

- if R gets corrupted before R generates (f_0, f_1) in the second corruption, S reveals R's internal state r_R to A.
- if R gets corrupted after R has generated (f_0, f_1) in the second corruption, S picks a bit $\gamma \in_U \{0, 1\}$ uniformly at random and sets $\beta = \gamma$. S invokes the faking algorithm fake which takes r_R as input and interprets f_γ as a selection string r_{f_γ} associated with the auxiliary string (s_γ, t_γ) and interprets $f_{1-\gamma}$ as a garbled string $r_{f_{1-\gamma}}$. S reveals (r_{f_0}, r_{f_1}) and (s_γ, t_γ) to A.

Case 4.2 If R gets corrupted in the first corruption, the corresponding simulator S can be constructed as follows.

- Step 1: S picks $g_{i,0} \in_U G$, $g_{i,1} \in_U G$, $sk_0 \in_U Z_q$ and $sk_1 \in_U Z_q$, and then computes $h_{i,0} = g_{i,0}^{sk_0} \bmod p$, $h_{i,1} = g_{i,1}^{sk_1} \bmod p$, $i = 1, 2$. Let $e_0 = (g_{1,0}, g_{2,0}, h_{1,0}, h_{2,0})$ and $e_1 = (g_{1,1}, g_{2,1}, h_{1,1}, h_{2,1})$. S keeps the auxiliary strings sk_0 and sk_1 secret.

Following Step 1 above, S corrupts the corresponding dummy party $\widetilde{R}$ in the ideal world and reveals R's internal state r_R to A. If S gets corrupted in the second corruption, we further consider subcases below:

- if S gets corrupted before R generates (f_0', f_1'), or if S gets corrupted after R has generated (f_0', f_1'), but before S receives (f_0', f_1'), S corrupts the corresponding dummy party $\widetilde{S}$ in the ideal world and obtains m. S picks a random bit $\gamma \in \{0, 1\}$ uniformly at random and sets $\alpha = \gamma$. S invokes the faking algorithm fake which takes r_S as input and interprets e_γ as a Diffie-Hellman quadruple r_{e_γ} associated with the auxiliary string sk_γ and interprets $e_{1-\gamma}$ as a garbled quadruple $r_{e_{1-\gamma}}$. S reveals (r_{e_0}, r_{e_1}), sk_γ and m to A.

- if S gets corrupted after S has received (f'_0, f'_1), we further consider the following two cases:

  - 1) if (f'_0, f'_1) is not well-defined, S picks a random bit $\gamma \in_U \{0,1\}$ and sets $\alpha = \gamma$. S then invokes the faking algorithm fake which takes r_S as input and interprets e_γ as a Diffie-Hellman quadruple r_{e_γ} associated with the auxiliary string sk_γ and interprets $e_{1-\gamma}$ as a garbled quadruple $r_{e_{1-\gamma}}$. S reveals m, (r_{e_0}, r_{e_1}) and sk_γ to $\mathcal{A}$.

  - 2) if (f'_0, f'_1) is well-defined, S further checks $v'_i \overset{?}{=} u'_i{}^{sk_i}$ for $i = 0, 1$. If both indices are invalid, S does the same procedure in the above case and reveals m, (r_{e_0}, r_{e_1}) and sk_γ to $\mathcal{A}$. If there exists an index i satisfied with the check condition, S picks a bit $b \in \{0, 1\}$ uniformly at random. If $b=1$, then let $\alpha = i$. S invokes the faking algorithm fake which takes r_S as input and interprets e_γ as a Diffie-Hellman quadruple r_{e_γ} associated with the auxiliary string sk_γ and interprets $e_{1-\gamma}$ as a garbled quadruple $r_{e_{1-\gamma}}$. S reveals m, (r_{e_0}, r_{e_1}) and sk_γ to $\mathcal{A}$. If $b = 0$, let $\alpha = 1 - i$. S invokes the faking algorithm fake which takes r_S as input and interprets $e_{1-\gamma}$ as a random Diffie-Hellman quadruple $r_{e_{1-\gamma}}$ associated with the auxiliary string $sk_{1-\gamma}$ and interprets e_γ as a garbled quadruple. S reveals m, (r_{e_0}, r_{e_1}) and $sk_{1-\gamma}$ to $\mathcal{A}$.

By the DDH assumption, we know that the distribution of random variable e_γ is computationally indistinguishable from that of $e_{1-\gamma}$. Due to the randomness of Naor-Pinkas randomizer, the distribution of random variable f_γ is computationally indistinguishable from that of $f_{1-\gamma}$. This means that $REAL_{\pi, \mathcal{A}, \mathcal{Z}}$ and $IDEAL_{\mathcal{F}, \mathcal{S}, \mathcal{Z}}$ are computationally indistinguishable in all cases. As a result, the real-world protocol π realizes $\mathcal{F}_{SC}^N$.   □

4   Conclusions

In this paper, a new implementation of non-committing encryptions has been presented and analyzed. We have shown that the proposed non-committing encryption scheme realizes the UC-security in the presence of adaptive adversary assuming that the decisional Diffie-Hellman problem is hard.

References

1. Beaver, D.: Plug and Play Encryption. In: Kaliski Jr., B.S. (ed.) CRYPTO 1997. LNCS, vol. 1294, pp. 75–89. Springer, Heidelberg (1997)
2. Beaver, D., Haber, S.: Cryptographic Protocols Provably Secure Against Dynamic Adversaries. In: Rueppel, R.A. (ed.) EUROCRYPT 1992. LNCS, vol. 658, pp. 307–323. Springer, Heidelberg (1993)
3. Canetti, R.: A new paradigm for cryptographic protocols. In: FOCS 2001, pp. 136–145 (2001)
4. Canetti, R., Fischlin, M.: Universally Composable Commitments. In: Kilian, J. (ed.) CRYPTO 2001. LNCS, vol. 2139, pp. 19–40. Springer, Heidelberg (2001)
5. Canetti, R.: Universally Composable Security: A New Paradigm for Cryptographic Protocols, eprint.iacr.org (December 14, 2005)
6. Canetti, R., Feige, U., Goldreich, O., Naor, M.: Adaptively Secure Multi-Party Computation. In: STOC 1996, pp. 639–648 (1996)

7. Choi, S.G., Dachman-Soled, D., Malkin, T., Wee, H.: Improved Non-committing Encryption with Applications to Adaptively Secure Protocols. In: Matsui, M. (ed.) ASIACRYPT 2009. LNCS, vol. 5912, pp. 287–302. Springer, Heidelberg (2009)

8. Damgård, I., Nielsen, J.B.: Improved Non-committing Encryption Schemes Based on a General Complexity Assumption. In: Bellare, M. (ed.) CRYPTO 2000. LNCS, vol. 1880, pp. 432–450. Springer, Heidelberg (2000)

9. Freedman, M.J., Ishai, Y., Pinkas, B., Reingold, O.: Keyword Search and Oblivious Pseudorandom Functions. In: Kilian, J. (ed.) TCC 2005. LNCS, vol. 3378, pp. 303–324. Springer, Heidelberg (2005)

10. Garay, J.A., Wichs, D., Zhou, H.-S.: Somewhat Non-Committing Encryption and Efficient Adaptively Secure Oblivious Transfer. In: Halevi, S. (ed.) CRYPTO 2009. LNCS, vol. 5677, pp. 505–523. Springer, Heidelberg (2009)

11. Lindell, Y., Pinkas, B.: Privacy Preserving Data Mining. J. Cryptology 15(3), 177–206 (2002)

12. Naor, M., Pinkas, B.: Efficient oblivious transfer protocols. In: SODA 2001, pp. 448–457 (2001)

13. Peikert, C., Vaikuntanathan, V., Waters, B.: A Framework for Efficient and Composable Oblivious Transfer. In: Wagner, D. (ed.) CRYPTO 2008. LNCS, vol. 5157, pp. 554–571. Springer, Heidelberg (2008)

14. Pinkas, B.: Cryptographic Techniques for Privacy-Preserving Data Mining. SIGKDD Explorations 4(2), 12–19 (2002)

15. Nielsen, J.B.: Separating Random Oracle Proofs from Complexity Theoretic Proofs: The Non-committing Encryption Case. In: Yung, M. (ed.) CRYPTO 2002. LNCS, vol. 2442, pp. 111–126. Springer, Heidelberg (2002)

16. Zhu, H., Araragi, T., Nishide, T., Sakurai, K.: Adaptive and Composable Non-committing Encryptions. In: Steinfeld, R., Hawkes, P. (eds.) ACISP 2010. LNCS, vol. 6168, pp. 135–144. Springer, Heidelberg (2010)

17. Zhu, H., Bao, F.: Non-committing Encryptions Based on Oblivious Naor-Pinkas Cryptosystems. In: Roy, B., Sendrier, N. (eds.) INDOCRYPT 2009. LNCS, vol. 5922, pp. 418–429. Springer, Heidelberg (2009)

18. Zhu, H., Bao, F.: Error-free, Multi-bit Non-committing Encryption with Constant Round Complexity. In: Lai, X., Yung, M., Lin, D. (eds.) INSCRYPT 2010. LNCS, vol. 6584, pp. 52–61. Springer, Heidelberg (2011)

Selectively Traceable Anonymous and Unlinkable Token-Based Transactions*

Daniel Slamanig[1] and Stefan Rass[2]

[1] Carinthia University of Applied Sciences, 9020 Klagenfurt Austria
[2] Klagenfurt University, System Security Group, 9020 Klagenfurt Austria
d.slamanig@cuas.at, stefan.rass@syssec.at

Abstract. In this paper we propose an approach that provides a means for users to conduct transactions with a service provider such that those transactions can neither be linked to a specific user nor linked together. However, a service provider can be sure that only authorized users are able to conduct transactions. Our construction combines the concepts of anonymous authentication from public-key encryption, based on a novel paradigm denoted as post-active anonymity, and anonymous as well as unlinkable token based transactions from blind signature schemes. Thereby, this construction takes advantages of both concepts. Furthermore, in privacy-preserving protocols, unconditional anonymity is usually not desirable. Thus, we provide mechanism to revoke the anonymity of misbehaving anonymous users behind transactions in case of suspicion. More precisely, we realize selective traceability using ideas from searchable public-key encryption. This allows revocation of the anonymity of suspicious users along with the identification of all of their transactions without violating the privacy of all remaining users.

1 Introduction

Today, many services and applications are provided via the Internet resulting in advantageous "anytime, anywhere" access for users. However, privacy becomes a major concern, and its protection is challenging in several ways. Ideally, a user is able to conduct transactions with a service provider in a way such that a transaction cannot be assigned to an identity (anonymity), nor may two or more transactions be related to each other efficiently (unlinkability). On the other hand, preserving security for the provider requires that only authorized users are able to consume a service and users can be revoked in case of suspicion (traceability).

Interesting applications are in the field of cloud computing and especially if even seemingly harmless information about the service-usage behavior, e.g. access frequencies, frequencies of transactions, accessed content, can be valuable information for the service or the cloud provider and needs to be protected from those insiders and wiretappers. One illustrative example is within the healthcare domain, where applications allowing the management of very sensitive health-information for everyone via the Internet, so called personal health records, are growing rapidly (e.g. Google Health, Microsoft Health Vault). In this context, such information can reveal a lot about the state of

---

* This is a revised version of the paper [24] which appeared in the proceedings of SECRYPT 2010.

M.S. Obaidat, G.A. Tsihrintzis, and J. Filipe (Eds.): ICETE 2010, CCIS 222, pp. 289–303, 2012.
© Springer-Verlag Berlin Heidelberg 2012

health of a specific person, e.g. access frequencies will correlate with the state of health. Hence, if such information are available for instance to human resource managers, this could massively influence the chances of getting a job.

1.1   Contribution

In this paper we propose an approach to realize anonymous and unlinkable, but authorized service usage based on a combination of anonymous authentication from public-key encryption and one-show tokens obtained from blind signatures. Our approach is especially applicable for services with many users, which dynamically join and leave a service and frequently conduct transactions with a service provider. Furthermore, our proposed construction achieves all aspects discussed in the introduction at very low computational overhead, whilst coming at negligible cost for implementation, as only standard public-key cryptography and state of the art smart cards are used. This is especially of interest, since public-key infrastructures are widely available today.

Our contributions in this paper are manifold. Firstly, we introduce a novel paradigm called post-active anonymous authentication from public-key encryption, which allows us to realize anonymous authentication at the cost of *a single* decryption for users, in contrast to $O(n)$ decryption resp. encryption operations for schemes known so far. Thereby n is the number of users, the so called anonymity-set. Secondly, we introduce a combination of anonymous authentication from public-key encryption and anonymous one-show tokens from blind signatures. Finally, we present several extensions to one-show tokens including fine-grained validity periods and most notable selective traceability. The latter property means, that a trusted traceability authority is able to link all transactions of a suspicious anonymous user as well as identify this user, without violating the privacy of the remaining users.

1.2   Intuition behind Our Construction

In a nutshell, our construction is as follows. A user registers with a service provider by providing a public-key of a public-key encryption scheme and registers with a traceability authority. Additionally, we assume that user's are in possession of a tamper resistant smartcard. The service provider maintains a directory D of these public-keys along with a validity of service usage. Users anonymously authenticate against a subset of users in this directory and if the authentication succeeds they obtain a blind signature for a token. On presenting a valid token-signature pair along with a query for a service, the service provider checks whether the signature is valid, the token was not already used and is valid for the current time-period. If all these checks hold, he responds with the answer to the query. Simultaneously, he issues a blind signature for a new token. Consequently, users can conduct sequences of transactions with the service provider. If suspicion occurs, the service provider can give the token corresponding to a suspicious transaction and the blacklist containing already spent tokens to a traceability authority, who in turn is able to *identify the respective user* and *find all transactions* of this user without violating the anonymity of other users (opening tokens of other users). Note, that all actions of users are anonymous and unlinkable.

2   Related Work

Several token-based approaches have been proposed so far, although having in mind quite diverge applications. The most prominent are anonymous credential systems introduced in [15]. The basic idea is that users are able to obtain credentials (tokens) for different pseudonyms from different organizations and can prove the possession of these credentials without revealing anything more than the fact that they own such credentials. Over the years, there have been proposed different approaches to design anonymous credential systems providing quite different functionalities [21,10,27]. Although anonymous credential systems are very powerful, realizing identity-escrow, limiting the number of showings as well as realizing dynamical joining and revoking of users comes at high computational costs. Furthermore, we do not focus on systems that involve multiple credential (token) issuers and verifiers and are looking for more efficient solutions.

Another class of schemes are multi-coupon (MC) systems [13,16], whereas a MC represents a collection of coupons (or tokens) that is regarded as a single unit. Basically, a user is issued a batch of tokens (which are tied together) and is allowed to spend one token after another in an anonymous and unlinkable fashion. The most sophisticated schemes [13,16] are based on signature schemes that allow users to obtain signatures on (committed) sequences of messages and provide efficient zero-knowledge proofs of knowledge of signatures and properties of signed message elements [11,12]. Although these schemes are conceptually very elegant, they are quite expensive and do not provide (selective) traceability. Recently, a scheme for anonymous subscriptions, based on one of those signature schemes was proposed in [6]. The concept is very appealing and it provides an elegant solution to realize validity-periods of subscriptions using zero-knowledge range proofs, but it does not support (selective) traceability, which is an important feature of our construction. Another construction of [9] focuses on n-times anonymous authentication, which allows to identify a user if he spends more than n tokens within one time-period. However, they also do not focus on selective traceability.

To the best of our knowledge, the only solution to selective traceability so far are traceable signatures [18,19], which are, however, rather of theoretical interest. In conclusion, none of the aforementioned approaches provides an efficient way to realize selective traceability, whereas our construction presented in this paper achieves this goal at a reasonable overall cost.

3   Postactive Anonymous Authentication

In this section we present a novel paradigm for anonymous authentication schemes from public-key encryption (PKE), which we call *post-active anonymous authentication*. Anonymous authentication from public-key encryption and its application is not absolutely new [23,20,28,25], but allows a convenient way for a prover to anonymously authenticate to a verifier providing user-chosen bandwidth-anonymity trade off. More precisely, users can determine on their own the size of the anonymity-set D' (as a subset of all users in D) and consequently determine the bandwidth consumption of the protocol as well as the anonymity level.

3.1 Deterministic from Probabilistic Public-Key Encryption

The notion of deterministic public-key encryption was introduced in [4]. Basically, the idea behind this concept is to turn any probabilistic PKE scheme into a deterministic scheme. One general and efficient construction is the so called "Encrypt-with-Hash" (EwH) construction introduced in [4], which will be discussed subsequently. An EwH scheme is based on a probabilistic PKE scheme and deterministically encrypts a plaintext m by applying the encryption algorithm of the probabilistic scheme, whereas the used random coins ω are not chosen uniformly at random, but are computed as a hash of the public key PK and the plaintext m. Consequently, everybody who knows a message m and a ciphertext c (presumably an encryption of m), can deterministically infer the random coins used for the encryption, i.e. compute $\omega = H(PK, m)$ and $c^* = E_{PK}(m; \omega)$ and check whether the encryption c^* computed by him equals the given ciphertext. If $c^* = c$ holds, they are both encryptions of the same message m. It should be noted that the output of the hash function needs to be suitable for the use as random coins in the respective PKE scheme.

3.2 Anonymous Authentication from Public-Key Encryption

Loosely spoken, the basic idea behind anonymous authentication protocols is that a verifier runs n parallel instances of a challenge-response protocol based on public-key encryption using n distinct public keys with *one anonymous* prover, who represents n "virtual" provers (we call this set the anonymity-set). Recall, in a challenge-response protocol authentication is achieved by demonstrating the ability to correctly decrypt an encrypted challenge. In anonymous authentication, the verifier chooses one challenge r and encrypts it with everyones public-key (of the anonymity-set). In protocol 1, we assume that $u_i \in D'$ and the challenge r from the verifier is a random number of suitable length. Obviously, if u_i is able to provide a response r' such that $r' = r$ holds, the verifier can be sure (with overwhelming probability) that the unknown prover is in possession of at least one secret which corresponds to one of the n public-keys in $D' = ((ID_{u_1}, PK_{u_1}), \ldots, (ID_{u_n}, PK_{u_n}))$.

User u_i SK_{u_i}		Verifier D
$D' \subseteq D, u_i \in D'$	$\longrightarrow$	D'
		$r \in_R \{0,1\}^k$
$\mathbf{c}$	$\longleftarrow$	$\mathbf{c} = (E_{PK_{u_1}}(r), \ldots, E_{PK_{u_n}}(r))$
$r' = D_{SK_{u_i}}(\mathbf{c}[i])$	$\longrightarrow$	$r' \stackrel{?}{=} r$

Protocol 1. Anonymous authentication from PKE

Obviously, the verifier can cheat by encrypting distinct challenges $r_1, \ldots, r_n$ for distinguishing different responders based on the specific challenge. If the encryptions of all ciphertexts in the challenge-sequence are deterministic (such as in textbook RSA or

Rabin's scheme), then u_i may as well encrypt r' using all remaining public-keys to see whether or not the challenges match [23]. This is what we call *trial encryptions*. The same can be done by turning probabilistic public-key encryption schemes into deterministic ones (see section 3.1) as proposed in [25], which is no longer prone to known security flaws of the aforementioned schemes and retains the efficiency. Nevertheless, the computational effort for the user is linear in the size of the anonymity-set in any case and furthermore the user needs to be in possession of all other public-keys. To reduce the computational effort, users could perform trial encryptions only for a reasonably small randomly subsequence of the challenge-sequence resulting in more efficient protocols providing probabilistic anonymity [25]. However, the need for the public-keys of the respective users still remains.

3.3 Postactive Anonymity

The basic idea behind post-active anonymous authentication is that users do not compute trial encryptions anymore, but post their received challenge-sequence along with the signature for the challenge-sequence of the verifier along with the decrypted random challenge to a public bulletin-board. Clearly, this should not be done until the user has authenticated and the challenge is invalidated.

Now, we assume that users help each other and visit the bulletin-board frequently to check whether the verifier behaves honest. This can be done if deterministic PKE schemes (obtained by applying the EwH construction discussed in section 3.1) are used and the challenge (the plaintext) is known. If a user notices that a verifier has cheated, the user can show this transcript to a judge and can convince him that the verifier has cheated. Since the verifier has digitally signed the transcript, he cannot repudiate the cheating behavior. The verifier can still cheat in this scenario and thus identify a single user who authenticates anonymously, but his trustworthiness is in jeopardy as he is likely to be caught.

The beauty of post-active anonymity is that it passes back the full risk to the dishonest verifier: if he attempts to discover an anonymous enquirer, then he takes a high risk of loosing the trust of the community. Postactive anonymity therefore turns honesty into the verifier's most advisable strategy. Furthermore, it should be noted that this paradigm provides a superior feature, namely users may register public-keys of arbitrary cryptosystems and only the verifier needs to support all algorithms (and those users checking entire challenge-sequences). The user solely uses the respective algorithm corresponding to his public-key cryptosystem and furthermore needs to compute *only one* decryption operation. This results in a low and *constant* computational effort, whereas all other known approaches require effort *linear* in the size of D, which can be enormous for large sets of authorized users. However, it should be noted that the size of the ciphertext-sequence grows linear with the size of D, which can be quite large. In these cases, users may randomly choose a subset $D' \subset D$ for their anonymity-set such that the size of the ciphertext-sequence is acceptable (as in protocol 1). For instance, if the PKE scheme is ElGamal [17] on Elliptic Curves $E(\mathbb{Z}_p)$, where p is a prime with $|p| = 192$ bits, then, a choice of the anonymity-set with $|D'| = 100$ will lead to a ciphertext-sequence of ≈ 5 KB, which is reasonably small for practical applications and usually provides sufficient anonymity.

4   Our Approach

To realize anonymous and unlinkable but authorized transactions, we briefly review the concept of blind signatures and provide a generic construction of a protocol for such transactions based on one-show tokens from blind signatures. Thereafter, we introduce our approach by combining post-active anonymous authentication with such one-show tokens. Subsequently, we gradually augment this construction to get

- fine-grained validity periods for tokens,
- selective traceability, and
- a mechanism for preventing resp. detecting cloning attacks.

4.1   Blind Signatures

Blind signatures are a well known cryptographic primitive introduced in [14], which provide a means such that an entity is able to obtain a valid signature on a message without the signer being able to learn anything about the message at the time of signing. More precisely, the signer actually signs a randomly blinded message and the resulting signature can subsequently be unblinded by the originator, whereas the originator obtains a valid signature for the original message. Consequently, the signed message cannot be linked to the originator by the signer. We rely our construction on efficient two-move blind signature schemes. Therefore, we can take the RSA based scheme of [14], which was proven to be secure for the full-domain hash RSA scheme (FDH-RSA) in the random oracle model under the chosen-target-one-more-RSA-inversion assumption [5]. Alternatively, we can take the blind signature scheme form [7] which is based on the BLS signature [8] and is provably secure in the random oracle model under the chosen-target Computational-Diffie-Hellman assumption. Subsequently, we abstract from the concrete protocol and denote the blinding operation of a message m as $\overline{m} = B(m)$ and the unblinding of the signature $\overline{\sigma}$ as $\sigma = B^{-1}(\overline{\sigma})$.

4.2   Anonymous Unlinkable One-Show Tokens

Below, we provide a generic protocol to obtain one-show tokens from a verifier which can be shown to the same party (spent) in an anonymous and unlinkable fashion. The basic idea behind this construction was proposed in [26], however, providing non of the functionalities discussed in this section and not combined with anonymous authentication.

We define a token as a simple data-structure which can be described as a tuple (id_t, id_{sp}, id_s), whereas id_t is a unique token-ID, id_{sp} is an ID of the service provider and id_s may represent an ID of the respective service (the token may be augmented by further elements, e.g. validity-period, as discussed subsequently in this section). In the literature, tokens (as used here) also known as tickets, credentials, coupons, transaction-pseudonyms or a one-time-pseudonyms.

For now, assume that user u_i holds an initial token-signature pair $\mathbf{t_i} = (t_i, \sigma_{t_i})$ from the service provider (also denoted as the verifier V, for short), e.g. the user registers for some service, pays and obtains a signed token $\mathbf{t}_i$. Furthermore, assume that the

User		Service-Provider
$\mathbf{t_i} = (t_i, \sigma_{t_i}), PK$		SK, BL
$\overline{\text{create}\, t_{i+1}}$ $\overline{t_{i+1}} = B(H(t_{i+1}))$		
$(\mathbf{t}_i, \overline{t_{i+1}}, Q_i)$	$\longrightarrow$	$(\mathbf{t}_i, \overline{t_{i+1}}, Q_i)$
		$t_i \overset{?}{\notin} BL$ $V_{PK_V}(H(t_i), \sigma_{t_i}) \overset{?}{=} accept$ $\sigma_{\overline{t_{i+1}}} = S_{SK_V}(\overline{t_{i+1}})$
$(\sigma_{\overline{t_{i+1}}}, R_i)$	$\longleftarrow$	$(\sigma_{\overline{t_{i+1}}}, R_i)$
$\sigma_{t_{i+1}} = B^{-1}(\sigma_{\overline{t_{i+1}}})$ $\mathbf{t}_{i+1} = (t_{i+1}, \sigma_{t_{i+1}})$		

Protocol 2. Simple Blind Signature-Based Transactions (SBSBT)

service provider generates a key-pair with suitable parameters for issuing blind signatures, with public-key PK_V and private-key SK_V. The generic protocol for conducting anonymous and unlinkable transactions with V is illustrated in protocol 2. In order to make the tokens one-time-usage-only, the verifier maintains a blacklist BL to blacklist already seen tokens and discard tokens upon seeing them again. Assume now that user u_i wants to authorize a query Q_i to the service provider. In order to obtain a new signed token for another transaction, u_i computes a blinded token $\overline{t_{i+1}} = B(H(t_{i+1}))$, whereas H denotes a suitable collision resistant cryptographic hash function and t_{i+1} represents a new token. User u_i sends $(\mathbf{t}_i, \overline{t_{i+1}}, Q_i)$ to the verifier, who checks whether the token is well formed and the ID of t_i is not contained in the blacklist. If this holds, he computes $\sigma_{\overline{t_{i+1}}} = S_{SK_V}(\overline{t_{i+1}})$, i.e signs the blinded token, and sends the resulting signature $\sigma_{\overline{t_{i+1}}}$ along with the result R_i of the query Q_i back to u_i. The user in turn unblinds the signature and obtains $\sigma_{t_{i+1}} = B^{-1}(\sigma_{\overline{t_{i+1}}})$, a valid signature for $H(t_{i+1})$. Consequently, u_i can use $\mathbf{t}_{i+1}$ to authorize a new transaction resp. query Q_{i+1} for some data at the verifier.

4.3 A Combined Approach

The idea is to combine the aforementioned approach to realize one-show tokens with the concept of anonymous authentication. It should be noted that one could use several classes of anonymous authentication schemes for this purpose, e.g. ring signatures [22], group signatures [3], but we will assume that anonymous authentication from public-key encryption (PKE) is used. The combination can be realized as follows:

1. **Registration.** Initially a user u_i registers once to the service provider V (verifier) by providing identifying information ID_{u_i} together with a the user's public-key PK_{u_i}. The verifier adds the user and the public-key to the public directory D of authorized users.
2. **Authentication.** The user anonymously authenticates to the verifier and after a successful authentication the user obtains a blind signature for a token t_0 and thus holds a token-signature pair $\mathbf{t}_0 = (t_0, \sigma_{t_0})$ for a subsequent transaction. Later, the user

posts the challenge-sequence along with the signature and the challenge such that other users can check whether the service provider cheats.

3. **Access.** The user provides t_0 and a new blinded token together with a query to the verifier and obtains a response, which is either a response to the query and a signature on the new blinded token for a subsequent transaction or an indication that the transaction was not authorized.

The register procedure is carried out once for every user. In order to obtain access to the system, a user conducts the authentication procedure with the verifier. Every authentication procedure is connected to a set of subsequent transactions, whereas the number of sequenced transaction is *not* limited by the verifier. Subsequently, we will discuss how a subscription of a user can be terminated, since this is impossible in the aforementioned setting.

4.4   Fine-Grained Validity Periods

A natural and efficient approach to exclude users from being able to conduct further transactions be realized as follows:

– The service provider arbitrarily discretizes the time into time-periods $\Delta_0, \Delta_1, \ldots$ of duration d_{Δ_i} (not necessarily all equal) and assigns a unique random number δ_i to every time-period Δ_i. Observe that the service provider solely publishes δ_i for the current time-period δ_i. More importantly, given all random numbers of previous and the actual time-periods, it is infeasible to compute δ_j for some future time-period.
– The random number δ_i needs to be included into the token by the user, for otherwise the token will be rejected. Hence, we augment our token by an additional element and tokens can now be represented as a tuple $t = (id_t, id_{\mathrm{sp}}, id_s, \delta_i)$. Within a time-period an authorized user can obtain an "initial" token by means of a successful anonymous authentication.
– Service-providers can easily manage the termination of service accesses of a user by removing a user from the directory D. Notice that the termination of service access during a time-period is impossible, but the service provider can easily set the granularity by choosing adequate durations of time-periods.
– Since the validity of tokens is restricted to a specific time-period, the service provider solely needs to blacklist tokens within the actual period. Due to the limited duration, the blacklist size is bounded and previous blacklists can be discarded, which makes the approach entirely practical from this point of view.

4.5   Selective Traceability

Traceability in our context means that a trusted third party (TTP), a so called *traceability authority* (TA), is able to identify the owner of a token as well as it's position within a sequence of transactions conducted by a user. Besides, it is desirable to achieve *selective traceability* for all tokens of the user within a specific time-period Δ_i. This means, that all tokens of a suspicious user can be found without violating the privacy of other users. But it is important that the service provider has no means to revoke the anonymity of honest users by himself. In order to achieve this, we require the user to register a pseudonym γ_{u_i} (which is randomly sampled from an appropriate set) with the TA, and this pseudonym is solely known to the TA and the user's smartcard (and not to the service provider). The tamper resistant smartcard of the user has to maintain an internal counter cnt that is initialized to a fixed user-specific value (which we will discuss below) during every instance of an anonymous authentication protocol and incremented during every generation of a new token.

Basically, the user's smartcard includes additional traceability information e into the token on behalf of the user. Hence, every token t is augmented by an element e and will be a tuple $t = (id_t, id_{sp}, id_s, \delta_i, e)$, where $e = E_{PK_{TA}}(\gamma_{u_i}, \text{cnt}_{u_i}; \omega)$ represents a probabilistic encryption of the tuple $(\gamma_{u_i}, \text{cnt}_{u_i})$ under TA's public-key. Note that ω are the random coins for the probabilistic encryption algorithm, which will be discussed below. After computing a token, the smartcard increments the counter cnt_{u_i} for the next token. In order to avoid partial knowledge about the plaintext we choose user- and time-period-specific start values of counters by computing the initial value of cnt_{u_i} denoted as cnt_{init} (which is initialized during every anonymous authentication) based on a suitable pseudorandom function. Working in the random oracle model, we can use a suitable cryptographic hash function H and compute the initial value as $\text{cnt}_{\text{init}} = H(\gamma_{u_i}, \delta_j)$ which provides us an initial counter value that depends on the pseudonym and on the current time-period.

Tracing of Single Showings: it is obvious that in case of suspicion the respective token (which is maintained by the service provider in his blacklist) can be given to the TA, which in turn can decrypt e and obtain the pseudonym of the user. Consequently, the identity corresponding to the user's pseudonym can be returned to the service provider. To prevent this user from being able to conduct any future transaction, the service provider has to remove the respective user from his directory D used for authentication. Consequently, this user will no longer be able to conduct anonymous authentications with the system. In this setting, the TA is very powerful, since it can identify all users behind all transactions. However, we assume that the TA is trusted and only provides "necessary" information to the service provider if and only if the service provider can credibly argue that fraud or misuse has happened. It should be noted, that in order to decrease the trust, we could share the private-key of the TA among a set of TA's and perform threshold-decryption to reveal the identity of a user.

Efficient Selective Traceability: in order to protect the privacy of other (innocent) users and to reduce the amount of workload for the TA, we propose a novel way to achieve selective traceability. Trivially, the TA could realize this feature by decrypting all remaining tokens in the blacklist and picking out those of the suspicious users. However, we want to protect the privacy of the remaining users and go the other way round. Essentially, the TA re-encrypts potential escrow information of the user and searches the blacklist for these potential values. How this is achieved will be discussed in the following. The TA knows the counter value cnt_{act} and the pseudonym of the user by decrypting the escrow information e of the suspicious token. Since the TA also knows that the counter is incremented during the creation of a new token and knows the value for the current time-period δ_j, it is able to compute the starting value of the user as

$\mathrm{cnt}_{\mathrm{init}} = H(\gamma_{u_i}, \delta_j)$. Consequently, the TA has to look for tokens in the counter-interval $[\mathrm{cnt}_{\mathrm{init}}, \mathrm{cnt}_{\mathrm{act}} + k]$, where k is some positive integer. Basically, the TA looks k tokens ahead from the start, since it cannot determine the actual number of transaction of the suspicious user within his "session". The concrete choice of k mainly depends on the application, however, when assuming that transactions are distributed uniformly among users we could take $k = \overline{|BL|}/|D|$, where $\overline{|BL|}$ represents the arithmetic mean of the sizes of all previous blacklists.

Now, we need a method for the TA to actually find the respective tokens within the blacklist. This can be easily achieved by converting the probabilistic public-key encryption scheme used by the TA into a deterministic one, e.g. by applying the EwH construction. We apply exactly this strategy to the construction of the escrow information e. More precisely, we construct the random coins ω for the encryption algorithm as $\omega = H(PK_{TA}, (\gamma_{u_i}, \mathrm{cnt}_{u_i}))$, whereas PK_{TA} is TA's public-key. Algorithm 1 illustrates how the TA realizes selective traceability when given a suspicious token and the blacklist of the service provider.

Algorithm 1. Selective Tracing

Input: A suspicious token $\tilde{t} = (t, e)$, the value δ of the current time-period, a parameter k, a blacklist BL and a key-pair (PK_{TA}, SK_{TA}) of a public-key encryption algorithm.
Output: A sequence $T = (\tilde{t}_1, \ldots, \tilde{t}_n)$ of transactions.

1: $(\gamma, \mathrm{cnt}_{\mathrm{act}}, \delta) \leftarrow D_{SK_{TA}}(e)$
2: $\mathrm{cnt}_{\mathrm{init}} \leftarrow H(\gamma, \delta)$
3: $pos \leftarrow 0$
4: **for all** $i = \mathrm{cnt}_{\mathrm{init}}$ to $\mathrm{cnt}_{\mathrm{act}} + k$ **do**
5:     $\omega_i \leftarrow H(PK_{TA}, (\gamma, i))$
6:     $e_i \leftarrow E_{PK_{TA}}(\gamma, i; \omega_i)$
7:     $\tilde{t}_i \leftarrow \mathrm{searchBL}(e_i, BL)$
8:     **if** $\tilde{t}_i \neq$ null **then**
9:         $T[pos] \leftarrow \tilde{t}_i$
10:         $pos \leftarrow pos + 1$
11:     **end if**
12: **end for**
13: **return** T

The algorithm $\mathrm{searchBL}$ simply searches the blacklist BL for tokens with escrow information e_i. By realizing the strategy discussed above, the workload of the TA can be decreased significantly. If we denote the size of the interval $[\mathrm{cnt}_{\mathrm{init}}, \mathrm{cnt}_{\mathrm{act}} + k]$ by m, we achieve $O(m)$ encryption operations over $O(n)$ decryption operations in the trivial case, since we can assume that $m \ll n$ holds. Note, that the service provider does not really need to transmit the blacklist to the TA. It is sufficient to send the suspicious token t, the value of the current time-period and the parameter k. The TA can extract γ and compute $\omega_i = H(PK_{TA}, (\gamma, i))$, $\mathrm{cnt}_{\mathrm{init}} \leq i \leq \mathrm{cnt}_{\mathrm{init}} + k$. Consequently, the TA computes $e_i = E_{PK_{TA}}(\gamma, i; \omega_i)$ and sends $\mathbf{e} = (e_0, \ldots, e_k)$ to the service provider. Now, the service provider performs a local search on his blacklist. Furthermore, it should be noted that by means of this approach, the TA would not even have the possibility to violate the privacy of other users.

4.6   Enforcing Traceability

A very simple attack to circumvent the traceability property is as follows. Assume that the smartcard performs the identity-escrow on behalf of the user and assume further that the user behaves malicious, i.e. wants to hinder the TA to identify him in case of fraud or misuse. Therefore, assume that a user is currently conducting transactions and obtains a response R along with the blind signature $\sigma_{\bar{t}}$ for the new token from the service provider in the first step (it could, however, also be the initial transaction). The user passes the signature to his smartcard, which in turn computes $\sigma_t = B^{-1}(\sigma_{\bar{t}})$, generates a new blinded token $\bar{t}'$ (including the traceability information e) and passes the tuple $(t, \sigma_t, \bar{t}')$ to the user. Although $\bar{t}'$ is well-formed, the malicious user can easily replace $\bar{t}'$ with another blinded token $\bar{t}''$ that is nearly well-formed. More precisely, the token is well-formed, except for the traceability information (which could either be chosen at random or represents the encryption of some random value).

The conceptually most straightforward approach to solve this problem is letting the smartcard encrypt the tuple $(t, \sigma_t, \bar{t}')$ under a service provider's public-key of a secure public-key encryption scheme. Consequently, the user will never have access to a tuple of the form (t, σ_t), which would allow him to conduct a transaction with a replaced "self-constructed" non-traceable new blinded token t''. However, the public-key of the service provider needs to be stored in the smartcard in an authentic fashion. Otherwise, a malicious user can easily mount a person-in-the-middle attack by providing some arbitrary public-key (for whom the corresponding private-key is known to the user) to the smartcard. Consequently, the user can decrypt the ciphertext and obtain a tuple $(t, \sigma_t, \bar{t}')$ which he can modify to $(t, \sigma_t, \bar{t}'')$ and send this tuple encrypted under the service provider's public-key.

4.7 Cloning Protection

The drawback of fine-grained validity periods is that it is potentially susceptible to what we call the *cloning-attack*. Loosely spoken, this attack means that a fraudulent authorized users may obtain valid token-signature pairs that he can make available to a set of unauthorized users. These users, the so called *clones*, are consequently able to anonymously conduct a sequence of transactions with the service provider within the respective time-period, although they are not authorized to do so. Note that this attack remains possible when the smartcard only gives the ciphertext of the tuple $(t, \sigma_t, \bar{t}')$ to the user. However, the attack is somewhat reduced, since the clone will solely be able to conduct a *single* transaction. By applying counters cnt as discussed in section 4.6, this attack is easily detected. Therefore, the service provider only has to search for identical escrow values e in his blacklist.

- If a user u_i gives away his encrypted tuple $(t_0, \sigma_0, \bar{t}_1)$ to a clone and the clone spends the token, the entry in the blacklist will contain traceability information $e_0 = E_{PK_{TA}}(\gamma_{u_i}, \text{cnt}_{u_i}; \omega)$, whereas $\omega = H(PK_{TA}, (\gamma_{u_i}, \text{cnt}_{u_i}))$ and $\text{cnt}_{u_i} = H(\gamma_{u_i}, \delta_j)$.
- If the user authenticates again within the same time-period, the traceability information e_0' of the token t_0' will be identical, since the counter is reinitialized to $\text{cnt}_{u_i} = H(\gamma_{u_i}, \delta_j)$.

Hence, if the service provider detects such a cloning attack (tokens where $e_i = e_j$ for some $i \neq j$), he can give both entries of the blacklist to the TA to revoke the anonymity of the misbehaving user. It should be noted, that this could be problematic in case of broken connections. The service provider could have different strategies for handling this, whereas we briefly sketch two of them below.

Upon presenting exactly the same token multiple times, the service provider may re-send the response to the query Q attached to the respective token t. However, that incidence should be indicated by *not* attaching a query, whenever re-showing a token, as this query has been submitted anyway. Still, a request to re-send the answer should come with the token, in case the query did not make it through in the first instance. However, if neither is done, and a known token t with a new (different to the previous) query Q' ($\neq Q$) is coming in, then the verifier should become wary and start tracing. This ensures robustness of the protocol as well it creates a simple mechanism to detect piracy

Alternatively, the service provider could realize some kind of glitch-tolerance, by defining some threshold K of "clone-activity", which need to be reached before revoking users.

5   Security Analysis

In this section we will discuss the threat model and investigate the security of the proposed construction. Therefore, we assume that users communicate their messages to service providers over a communication channel that provides perfect anonymity and unlinkability of exchanged messages, as it is the case with all interactive protocols providing such features.

5.1   Adversary and Threat Model

We assume that the manufacturer of the smart cards is trustworthy and hence the smart cards are tamper resistant and do not contain any backdoors, Trojan horses, etc. Furthermore, users are assumed to be dishonest (active adversaries), i.e. will actively try to fool the service provider resp. authorize unauthorized users, which is a reasonable assumption for real-world scenarios. Service-providers are honest-but-curious, i.e. follow the protocol specification but use any gathered information in order to try to identify anonymous users. However, service providers can also be active adversaries, but only with respect to the anonymous authentication protocol.

5.2   Anonymous Authentication

For the used anonymous authentication protocol we require anonymity, correctness, unforgeability and unlinkability, which can be proven to hold for existing protocols [25,20]. However, the known definitions of anonymity and unlinkability are less formally ensured in the *post-active anonymity* setting. Clearly, anonymity can be broken if the verifier encrypts distinct random challenges, which consequently can restore linkability too. However, it is equally obvious that a cheating verifier acts completely on his own risk, as the community will accuse him of being dishonest. In that case, the service will not be used any more, and a cheating verifier could loose more than he could win. The correctness and unforgeability properties are retained, since solely trial encryptions are omitted. Finally, it should be noted that when using standard anonymous authentication [23,25,20], we obtain security with respect to existing definitions, however, at substantially higher costs.

5.3   Security of Our Construction

In our investigation of the security of the construction we investigate the anonymity of transactions, the unlinkability of transactions and the unforgeability of tokens. We inspect every property below and sketch the ideas:

Transaction Anonymity. Every token showing integrates the issuing of a new token. Hence, we first need to look at the token which is shown, and afterwards look at the blinded token, which is signed by the verifier. The anonymity of the token t shown reduces to inspecting the escrow information e. The anonymity follows from two observations concerning the escrow information e. Firstly, [4] prove that for any at least IND-CPA secure probabilistic public-key encryption that is converted into a deterministic one (by applying the EwH construction), it holds that an adversary provided with encryptions of plaintexts drawn from a message-space of high min-entropy (which is clearly the case, since we encrypt randomly chosen pseudonyms along with a value obtained by evaluating a pseudorandom function on this value) will have negligible advantage in computing any information about the plaintexts. Hence, the so obtained deterministic public-key encryption scheme provides the required security guarantees and can be seen as a computationally hiding commitment. Secondly, the pseudonyms of users are sampled at random from a large enough space and are solely known to the TA and the user's smart cards (which are assumed to be tamper-proof). Consequently, any adversary can solely guess the respective pseudonym of a user. By choosing the space for the pseudonyms accordingly large, this probability can be made negligible. The anonymity of the blinded token follows from the properties of the blind signature scheme.

Unforgeability. Since the smartcard solely gives ciphertexts of tuples $(t, \sigma_t, \overline{t}')$ to the users, a user would need to forge a signature from the verifier. However, this means that a user would need to existentially forge a signature with respect to the signature scheme underlying the blind signature scheme. Thus, if the used blind signature scheme is secure this is intractable.

Unlinkability. The unlinkability of the issuing and showing of a token t reduces to the blindness property of the used blind signature scheme. Hence, there is no way for the signer to relate the issuing and showing of a token. Furthermore, we need to look at the unlinkability of different showings, which means that it cannot be decided whether a set tokens was shown by the same user. Therefore, our argumentation is similar to that used for the transaction anonymity property. Let us assume without loss of generality that we have two tokens t and t'. Only e and e' contain information about the user. However, as already discussed in context of transaction anonymity e and e' are computationally hiding commitments.

6 More Fine-Grained Authorization

One drawback of the approach presented in this paper is that we cannot realize a fine-grained access control for resources connected to services. However, this can be solved by using partially blind signatures [1,2] instead of blind signatures. Loosely spoken, in a partially blind signature scheme, a receiver blinds a message m, obtains $\overline{m} = B(m)$ and sends $\overline{m}$ to the signer. The signer computes a partially blind signature $\overline{\sigma} = S_{SK_S}(\overline{m}, \text{info})$, which includes a common information info and sends $\overline{\sigma}$ to the receiver. The receiver unblinds $\overline{\sigma}$ by computing $\sigma = B^{-1}(\overline{\sigma})$, can verify whether the common information info was included and obtains a valid signature σ for the tuple (m, info). Note, that the message m is entirely unknown to the signer. We can use them as follows: the service provider defines the set of privileges P (which are connected to resources of services) and during registration privileges are assigned to users. By choosing the anonymity set according to required privileges (users which have the same privileges) an encoding of these privileges can be integrated by means of common information info into the blinded token. Hence, when presenting the token, the service provider can decide whether a query Q will be authorized or not. It should be noted, that anonymity and unlinkability are preserved.

Acknowledgements. The authors would like to thank the anonymous referees of SE-CRYPT 2010 for their valuable feedback as well as Christian Stingl and Peter Schartner for discussions and comments on early drafts of this work.

References

1. Abe, M., Fujisaki, E.: How to Date Blind Signatures. In: Kim, K.-c., Matsumoto, T. (eds.) ASIACRYPT 1996. LNCS, vol. 1163, pp. 244–251. Springer, Heidelberg (1996)
2. Abe, M., Okamoto, T.: Provably Secure Partially Blind Signatures. In: Bellare, M. (ed.) CRYPTO 2000. LNCS, vol. 1880, pp. 271–286. Springer, Heidelberg (2000)
3. Ateniese, G., Camenisch, J., Joye, M., Tsudik, G.: A Practical and Provably Secure Coalition-Resistant Group Signature Scheme. In: Bellare, M. (ed.) CRYPTO 2000. LNCS, vol. 1880, pp. 255–270. Springer, Heidelberg (2000)
4. Bellare, M., Boldyreva, A., O'Neill, A.: Deterministic and Efficiently Searchable Encryption. In: Menezes, A. (ed.) CRYPTO 2007. LNCS, vol. 4622, pp. 535–552. Springer, Heidelberg (2007)
5. Bellare, M., Namprempre, C., Pointcheval, D., Semanko, M.: The One-More-RSA-Inversion Problems and the Security of Chaum's Blind Signature Scheme. J. Cryptology 16, 185–215 (2003)
6. Blanton, M.: Online Subscriptions with Anonymous Access. In: ASIACCS 2008, pp. 217–227. ACM (2008)
7. Boldyreva, A.: Threshold Signatures, Multisignatures and Blind Signatures Based on the Gap-Diffie-Hellman-Group Signature Scheme. In: Desmedt, Y.G. (ed.) PKC 2003. LNCS, vol. 2567, pp. 31–46. Springer, Heidelberg (2002)
8. Boneh, D., Lynn, B., Shacham, H.: Short Signatures from the Weil Pairing. Journal of Cryptology 17(4), 297–319 (2004)
9. Camenisch, J., Hohenberger, S., Kohlweiss, M., Lysyanskaya, A., Meyerovich, M.: How to Win the Clone Wars: Efficient Periodic n-Times Anonymous Authentication. In: CCS 2006, pp. 201–210. ACM (2006)

10. Camenisch, J., Lysyanskaya, A.: An Efficient System for Non-transferable Anonymous Credentials with Optional Anonymity Revocation. In: Pfitzmann, B. (ed.) EUROCRYPT 2001. LNCS, vol. 2045, pp. 93–118. Springer, Heidelberg (2001)
11. Camenisch, J., Lysyanskaya, A.: A Signature Scheme with Efficient Protocols. In: Cimato, S., Galdi, C., Persiano, G. (eds.) SCN 2002. LNCS, vol. 2576, pp. 268–289. Springer, Heidelberg (2003)
12. Camenisch, J., Lysyanskaya, A.: Signature Schemes and Anonymous Credentials from Bilinear Maps. In: Franklin, M. (ed.) CRYPTO 2004. LNCS, vol. 3152, pp. 56–72. Springer, Heidelberg (2004)
13. Canard, S., Gouget, A., Hufschmitt, E.: A Handy Multi-coupon System. In: Zhou, J., Yung, M., Bao, F. (eds.) ACNS 2006. LNCS, vol. 3989, pp. 66–81. Springer, Heidelberg (2006)
14. Chaum, D.: Blind Signatures for Untraceable Payments. In: CRYPTO 1982, pp. 199–203. Plemum Press (1982)
15. Chaum, D.: Security without identification: Transaction systems to make big brother obsolete. Commun. ACM 28(10), 1030–1044 (1985)
16. Chen, L., Escalante, A.N., Löhr, H., Manulis, M., Sadeghi, A.R.: A Privacy-Protecting Multi-Coupon Scheme with Stronger Protection Against Splitting. In: Dietrich, S., Dhamija, R. (eds.) FC 2007 and USEC 2007. LNCS, vol. 4886, pp. 29–44. Springer, Heidelberg (2007)
17. El Gamal, T.: A Public Key Cryptosystem and a Signature Scheme Based on Discrete Logarithms. In: Blakely, G.R., Chaum, D. (eds.) CRYPTO 1984. LNCS, vol. 196, pp. 10–18. Springer, Heidelberg (1985)
18. Kiayias, A., Tsiounis, Y., Yung, M.: Traceable Signatures. In: Cachin, C., Camenisch, J.L. (eds.) EUROCRYPT 2004. LNCS, vol. 3027, pp. 571–589. Springer, Heidelberg (2004)
19. Libert, B., Yung, M.: Efficient Traceable Signatures in the Standard Model. In: Shacham, H., Waters, B. (eds.) Pairing 2009. LNCS, vol. 5671, pp. 187–205. Springer, Heidelberg (2009)
20. Lindell, Y.: Anonymous Authentication - Preserving Your Privacy Online. In: Black Hat 2007 (2007)
21. Lysyanskaya, A., Rivest, R.L., Sahai, A., Wolf, S.: Pseudonym Systems (Extended Abstract). In: Heys, H.M., Adams, C.M. (eds.) SAC 1999. LNCS, vol. 1758, pp. 184–199. Springer, Heidelberg (2000)
22. Rivest, R.L., Shamir, A., Tauman, Y.: How to Leak a Secret. In: Boyd, C. (ed.) ASIACRYPT 2001. LNCS, vol. 2248, pp. 552–565. Springer, Heidelberg (2001)
23. Schechter, S., Parnell, T., Hartemink, A.: Anonymous Authentication of Membership in Dynamic Groups. In: Franklin, M.K. (ed.) FC 1999. LNCS, vol. 1648, pp. 184–195. Springer, Heidelberg (1999)
24. Slamanig, D., Rass, S.: Anonymous But Authorized Transactions Supporting Selective Traceability. In: 5th International Conference on Security and Cryptography, SECRYPT 2010, pp. 132–141. SciTePress (2010)
25. Slamanig, D., Schartner, P., Stingl, C.: Practical Traceable Anonymous Identification. In: SECRYPT 2009, pp. 225–232. INSTICC Press (2009)
26. Stubblebine, S.G., Syverson, P.F., Goldschlag, D.M.: Unlinkable Serial Transactions: Protocols and Applications. ACM Trans. Inf. Syst. Secur. 2(4), 354–389 (1999)
27. Verheul, E.R.: Self-Blindable Credential Certificates from the Weil Pairing. In: Boyd, C. (ed.) ASIACRYPT 2001. LNCS, vol. 2248, pp. 533–551. Springer, Heidelberg (2001)
28. Xi, Y., Sha, K., Shi, W., Schwiebert, L., Zhang, T.: Probabilistic Adaptive Anonymous Authentication in Vehicular Networks. J. Comput. Sci. Technol. 23(6), 916–928 (2008)

An Encryption Scheme for a Secure Policy Updating

Luan Ibraimi[1], Muhammad Asim[2], and Milan Petković[2,3]

[1] Faculty of EWI, University of Twente, The Netherlands
[2] Philips Research Eindhoven, The Netherlands
[3] Faculty of Mathematics and Computer Science
Eindhoven University of Technology, The Netherlands

Abstract. Ciphertext policy attribute based encryption is an encryption technique where the data is encrypted according to an access policy over attributes. Users who have a secret key associated with a set of attributes which satisfy the access policy can decrypt the encrypted data.

However, one of the drawbacks of the CP-ABE is that it does not support updating access control policies without decrypting the encrypted data. We present a new variant of the CP-ABE scheme called ciphertext policy attribute based proxy re-encryption (CP-ABPRE). The proposed scheme allows to update the access control policy of the encrypted data without decrypting the ciphertext. The scheme uses a semitrusted entity called proxy to re-encrypt the encrypted data according to a new access control policy such that only users who satisfy the new policy can decrypt the data. The construction of our scheme is based on prime order bilinear groups. We give a formal definition for semantic security and provide a security proof in the generic group model.

Keywords: Proxy re-encryption, Attribute-based encryption, Access policy, Attribute-based proxy re-encrypion.

1 Introduction

Recent studies explore the use of cryptographic techniques to enforce access control policies. Ciphertext policy attribute based encryption (CP-ABE) schemes allow the data to be encrypted according to an access control policy over a set of descriptive attributes (e.g. doctor and nurse). Once the data is encrypted, it can be safely stored in an un-trusted server such that everyone can download the encrypted data (even a malicious user), but only users who have the right secret key associated with a set of attributes which satisfy the access policy can decrypt. Therefore, when the data is encrypted using a CP-ABE, access policy moves with the data and there is no need for the use of other entities, such as access-control managers, to enforce access control policy. For instance, Bob can encrypt his health data according to the access policy $p_1 = [Bob\ OR\ (GP\ AND\ Hospital\ 1)]$, and upload encrypted data to an un-trusted Personal Health Record (PHR) server. Only users who have attributes Bob or GP and $Hospital\ 1$ can decrypt the ciphertext, so neither the server itself nor an unauthorized person can decrypt the ciphertext.

Despite numerous advantageous features of the CP-ABE schemes compared to the traditional access control technologies, CP-ABE schemes does not support updating

M.S. Obaidat, G.A. Tsihrintzis, and J. Filipe (Eds.): ICETE 2010, CCIS 222, pp. 304–318, 2012.
© Springer-Verlag Berlin Heidelberg 2012

access control policies. The only way is to decrypt the data and then re-encrypt it according to a new access control policy. Following the above example, if Bob wants to change the access control policy from p_1 to $p_2 = [Bob\, OR\, (GP\, AND\, (Hospital\, 1\, OR\, Hospital\, 2))]$ (in order to hear a second opinion from a GP from $Hospital$ 2), Bob has to re-encrypt his data according to p_2. A naive solution for Bob to re-encrypt his data would be to send to the PHR server his secret key. Once the PHR server receives the secret key, it decrypts the data and then use the CP-ABE scheme to re-encrypt the data according to the new policy p_2. However , the drawback of this approach is that the server accesses sensitive plain data. To avoid this drawback Bob might perform by himself the re-encryption process. Therefore, Bob has to download the encrypted data from the PHR server, decrypt the data locally using his secret key, and then re-encrypt the data using the CP-ABE scheme. The drawback of this approach is that Bob has to be online during each re-encryption process which is not very efficient both from the communication and processing point of view.

Our Contribution. To overcome the aforementioned drawbacks of the CP-ABE schemes, we propose a ciphertext policy attribute based proxy re-encryption (CP-ABPRE) scheme. In the proposed scheme Bob has to compute only once the re-encryption key $rk_{p_1 \rightarrow p_2}$ which is used by a semitrusted entity called proxy (i.e. PHR server) to update all ciphertexts encrypted according to policy p_1 into ciphertexts encrypted according to policy p_2. The proxy is a semitrusted entity in the sense that it does not have access to the plain data. However it needs to perform re-encryption computations, and also has to stop performing these computations when Bob (the delegator) who generated the re-encryption key $rk_{p_1 \rightarrow p_2}$ does not want to re-encrypt future ciphertexts associated with the access policy p_1. One of the distinctive features of the proposed scheme is that it is collusion resistance, the feature which is lacking in almost all the proxy re-encryption schemes in the conventional public key cryptography. The collusion resistance feature implies that even if the proxy and delegate collude they cannot generate a new secret key. In general, the scheme is useful for dynamic environments where the access policy which controls access to the data changes frequently (e.g. personal health record systems).

The construction of our scheme is based on prime order bilinear groups. The size of the ciphertext depends on the size of the access policy and the size of the user secret key depends on the number of attributes that the user possesses. We give a formal definition for semantic security and provide a security proof in the generic group model.

1.1   Related Work

Proxy Re-encryption. In a proxy re-encryption scheme, introduced by Mambo and Okamoto [14], a proxy is a semitrusted entity which can transform an encryption computed under Bobs' (delegator) public key to an encryption computed under Alices'(delegatee) public key. The proxy is a semitrusted entity i.e. it is trusted to perform only the ciphertext re-encryption, without knowing the secret keys of Bob and Alice, and without having access to the plain data. Blaze, Bleumer and Strauss [3] introduced the notion of "atomic proxy functions" - functions that transform ciphertext corresponding to one key into ciphertext corresponding to another key without revealing any information about the secret decryption keys or plain data. However the scheme presented in [3] is bidirectional where one re-encryption key can be used to transform ciphertext from the delegator to the delegatee and vice versa, and is useful only for the scenarios where the trust relationship between involved parties is mutual. To overcome this situation Jakobsson [12] and Zhou et al. [19] proposed a quorum-controlled protocol where a proxy is divided into many components. Dodis and Ivan [11] propose a number of unidirectional proxy re-encryption for El-Gamal, RSA and IBE scheme, where the delegator's secret key is divided into two shares: one share for the proxy and one share for the delegatee. The drawback of the proposed schemes is that they are collusion-unsafe, i.e. if the proxy and the delegatee collude then they can recover the delegator's secret key. Matsuo [15] and Green and Atteniese [8] propose the identity-based proxy re-encryption scheme, where the encrypted data under the public key generated by delegators' identity is re-encrypted to an encrypted data under the public key generated by delegatees' identity.

Attribute-based Encryption. Sahai and Waters [17] introduce the concept of Attribute-Based Encryption (ABE) where a ciphertext and user secret key are associated with a set of attributes. ABE relies on the presence of a trusted authority (TA) who is in possession of a master key which is used to generate secret keys of users. A user can decrypt the ciphertext if the user secret key has the list of attributes specified in the ciphertext. In CP-ABE [2,5,10] the user secret key is associated with a set of attributes and a ciphertext is associated with an access control policy over a list of attributes. The decryptor can decrypt the ciphertext if the list of attributes associated with the secret key satisfies the access policy. In Key-Policy Attribute-Based Encryption (KP-ABE) [7] the idea is reversed and the secret key is associated with an access control policy over a list of attributes and the ciphertext is associated with a list of attributes. The decryptor can decrypt the ciphertext if the list of attributes associated with the ciphertext satisfy the access policy associated with the secret key.

Attribute-based Encryption and Proxy Re-encryption. Guo et al. [9] propose a proxy re-encryption scheme based on the Goyal et al. [7] KP-ABE scheme. The proposed scheme can transform a ciphertext associated with a set of attributes into a new ciphertext associated with another set of attributes.

Lliang et al.[13] proposed an attribute-based proxy re-encryption scheme. The Lliang et al. scheme is based on the Cheung and Newport CP-ABE scheme [5] and it inherits the same limitations that [5] has: it supports only access policies with AND boolean operator, and the size of the ciphertext increases linearly with the number of attributes in the system.

1.2 Organization

The remainder of this paper is organized as follows. Section 2 provides background information. In Section 3 we give a formal definition of the Ciphertext-Policy Attribute-Based Proxy Re-Encryption scheme (CP-ABPRE) and its security model. Section 4 describes the construction of the CP-ABPRE scheme. The last section concludes the paper.

2   Background – Bilinear Groups

The scheme presented in section 4 is based on pairings over groups of prime order. Let $\mathbb{G}_0$ and $\mathbb{G}_T$ be two multiplicative groups of prime order p, and let g be a generator of $\mathbb{G}_0$. A pairing (or bilinear map) $\hat{e} : \mathbb{G}_0 \times \mathbb{G}_0 \rightarrow \mathbb{G}_T$ satisfies the following properties [4]:

1. Bilinear: for all $u, v \in \mathbb{G}_0$ and $a, b \in \mathbb{Z}_p^*$, we have $\hat{e}(u^a, v^b) = \hat{e}(u, v)^{ab}$.
2. Non-degenerate: $\hat{e}(g, g) \neq 1$.

$\mathbb{G}_0$ is said to be a bilinear group if the group operation in $\mathbb{G}_0$ and the bilinear map $\hat{e} : \mathbb{G}_0 \times \mathbb{G}_0 \rightarrow \mathbb{G}_T$ can be computed efficiently. Note that the map is symmetric since $\hat{e}(g^a, g^b) = \hat{e}(g, g)^{ab} = \hat{e}(g^b, g^a)$.

3   Ciphertext-policy Attribute-Based Proxy Re-Encryption (CP-ABPRE)

A CP-ABPRE scheme extends CP-ABE scheme by adding a proxy component to the existing components: the trusted authority (TA) and users. Another extension has been made to the number of algorithms. CP-ABPRE uses the RKGen algorithm to generate a re-encryption key and $\mathsf{Re - Encrypt}$ algorithm to re-encrypt the ciphertext, in addition to the four algorithms of CP-ABE scheme: Setup, KeyGen, Encrypt, Decrypt.

Definition 1. *A CP-ABPRE scheme is a tuple of six algorithms* (Setup, KeyGen, Encrypt, Decrypt, RKGen, Re − Encrypt):

- Setup(λ) run by the trusted authority (TA), the algorithm on input of the security parameter λ outputs the master secret key MK, and the master public key PK which is distributed to users.
- KeyGen(MK, ω) run by the trusted authority (TA), the algorithm takes as input a set of attributes ω identifying the user, and the master secret key MK, and it outputs a user secret key SK_ω associated with the set of attributes ω.
- Encrypt($m, p_1,$ PK) run by the encryptor, the algorithm takes as input a message to be encrypted m, an access policy p_1 over a list of attribute which specifies which combination of attribute the decryptor needs to posses in order to obtain m, and the master public key PK. The algorithm outputs the ciphertext CT_{p_1} associated with the access policy p_1.
- RKGen($\mathsf{SK}_\omega, p_1, p_2,$ PK) run by the delegator, this algorithm takes as input the secret key SK_ω, the access policies p_1 and p_2, and the master public key PK. The algorithm outputs a unidirectional re-encryption key $\mathsf{rk}_{p_1 \rightarrow p_2}$ if SK_ω satisfies p_1, or an error symbol $\perp$ if ω does not satisfy p_1.
- Re − Encrypt($\mathsf{CT}_{p_1}, \mathsf{rk}_{p_1 \rightarrow p_2}$) run by the proxy, this algorithm takes as input the ciphertext CT_{p_1} and the re-encryption key $\mathsf{rk}_{p_1 \rightarrow p_2}$, and outputs the ciphertext CT_{p_2} associated with the access policy p_2.
- Decrypt($\mathsf{CT}_{p_i}, \mathsf{SK}_\omega$) run by the decryptor, the algorithm takes as input the ciphertext C_{p_i} and the secret key SK_ω, and output a message m if ω satisfies p_i, or an error symbol $\perp$ if ω does not satisfy p_i .

Security Model. In the following we present the game-based security definition (security model) of the CP-ABPRE scheme. Informally, the security model guarantees that: a) an user (adversary) who does not have enough attributes to satisfy the access policy p^* of the ciphertext cannot learn any information about the plaintext being encrypted, b) two users cannot combine their attributes to extend their decryption power, for instance two users cannot combine their secret keys and decrypt a ciphertext associated with p^* if none of users secret keys satisfy p^*, and c) the proxy and an user cannot combine the re-encryption key and the secret key in order to compute a new secret key. Therefore in the security game, played between the adversary $\mathcal{A}$ and the challenger (the challenger simulates the game and answers $\mathcal{A}$'s queries) we allow $\mathcal{A}$ to compromise users secret key except the secret keys which satisfy the challenge access policy p^*. In addition, $\mathcal{A}$ is allowed also to compromise proxy keys or re-encryption keys with the following restriction:

- $\mathcal{A}$ is not allowed to ask secret key queries for the attribute set ω which satisfies p_2 if $\mathcal{A}$ has a re-encryption key $\mathrm{rk}_{p^* \to p_2}$. The reason for this restriction is that $\mathcal{A}$ can use the re-encryption key to re-encrypt the challenge ciphertext associated with p^* to a ciphertext associated with p_2 and decrypt the re-encrypted ciphertext using his secret key which satisfies p_2. In the sequel we will refer to p_2 as a challenge derivative access policy if $\mathcal{A}$ has the re-encryption key $\mathrm{rk}_{p^* \to p_2}$.

At one point of the security game $\mathcal{A}$ gives to the challenger two messages and the challenge access policy p^*, and the challenger return to $\mathcal{A}$ a ciphertext of one of the two messages encrypted under p^*. $\mathcal{A}$ has to guess which of the messages was encrypted. If the guess is correct, then $\mathcal{A}$ wins the game. Formally the security game is defined as follows:

1. Setup. The challenger run $\mathsf{Setup}(\lambda)$ to generate $(\mathsf{PK}, \mathsf{MK})$, and gives PK to $\mathcal{A}$.
2. Phase1. $\mathcal{A}$ performs a polynomially bounded number of queries:
   - $\mathsf{Keygen}(\omega_j)$. $\mathcal{A}$ asks for a user secret key for any attribute set ω_j. The challenger returns SK_{ω_j} to $\mathcal{A}$.
   - $\mathsf{RKGen}(p_1, p_2)$. $\mathcal{A}$ asks for a re-encryption key for $\mathrm{rk}_{p_1 \to p_2}$, where $p_1 \neq p_2$. The challenger runs $\mathsf{SK}_\omega = \mathsf{Keygen}(\omega_j)$ such that SK_ω satisfies p_1, and returns $\mathrm{rk}_{p_1 \to p_2}$ to $\mathcal{A}$.
3. Challenge. $\mathcal{A}$ sends to the challenger two messages m_0, m_1 and the challenge access policy p^*. $\mathcal{A}$ is not allowed to chose a challenge access structure p^* if it has made the following queries in Phase1:
   - $\mathsf{Keygen}(\omega_j)$ queries such that SK_{ω_j} satisfies a challenge access structure p^*.
   - $\mathsf{Keygen}(\omega_j)$ queries such that SK_{ω_j} satisfies any challenge derivative access policies.
   - $\mathsf{RKGen}(p_1, p_2)$ queries if $\mathcal{A}$ previously has issued $\mathsf{Keygen}(\omega_j)$ such that SK_{ω_j} satisfies p_2 and p_1 is a challenge derivative access policy.

   The challenger selects $b \in_R (0, 1)$ and returns $\mathsf{CT}_{p^*} = \mathsf{Encrypt}(m_b, p^*, \mathsf{PK})$.
4. Phase2. $\mathcal{A}$ can continue querying Keygen and RKGen. $\mathcal{A}$ is not allowed to make queries specified in the Challenge phase.
5. Guess. $\mathcal{A}$ outputs a guess b', where $b' \in (0, 1)$.

Definition 2. *A CP-ABPRE scheme is said to be secure against adaptive chosen plain-text attack (IND-CPA) if any polynomial-time adversary $\mathcal{A}$ has only a negligible advantage in the CP-ABPRE game, where the advantage is defined to be $|\Pr[b' = b] - \frac{1}{2}|$.*

4   Construction of CP-ABPRE Scheme

Before introducing the scheme, we briefly explain the structure of the access policy associated with the ciphertext. In our scheme an access control policy is a monotonic boolean formula of conjunction and disjunctions of attributes. The TA in the Setup phase defines the universe of all attributes Ω. An example of the universe of all attribute can be $\Omega = \{A, B, C, D, F\}$, and an example of an access policy can be $p_1 =$ (A ∧ B) ∨ (C ∧ D) where $\{A, B, C, D\} \in \Omega$.

Assigning Values to Attributes in the Access Policy. To enforce the access policy in such a way that only users who satisfy the access policy can decrypt the ciphertext, in the encryption phase, the encryptor encrypts the data according to the access policy. Therefore, the encryptor in the encryption phase picks a secret value s and shares it according to the access policy under which the data is encrypted. We use Benaloh and Leichter [1] secret sharing scheme to share s. The scheme [1] works as follows:

- Transforms an access policy p_1 into an access tree τ and set the value of the root node of τ to be s. Then, recursively for each non-leaf node do the following:
    - If the symbol is ∨, set the values of each child node to be s.
    - If the symbol is ∧, for each child node, except the last one, assign a random value s_i where $1 \le s_i \le p - 1$, and to the last child node assigns $s_t = s - \sum_{i=1}^{t-1} s_i \mod p$.

For example, to share s according to the access policy $p_1 =$ (A ∧ B) ∨ (C ∧ D), the Benaloh and Leichter [1] secret sharing scheme works as follows: a) assign s to OR (∨) operator, b) assign s to two AND (∧) operators and c) assign shares s_A to A, s_B to B, s_C to C and s_D to D, such that $s = s_A + s_B$ and $s = s_C + s_D$.

Policy Evaluation. To decrypt a ciphertext, a user secret key SK_ω associated with a set of attributes ω has to satisfy the policy $p_1 =$ (A ∧ B) ∨ (C ∧ D) associated with the ciphertext. In the example, if $\omega = \{A, B\}$ then the policy is satisfied since $s = s_A + s_B$. This can be verified by substituting the attributes in $\omega \cap p_1 = \{A, B\}$ (attributes which appear in ω and p_1) by true, and attributes in $p_1 \setminus \omega = \{C, D\}$ (attributes which appear in p_1 but not appear in ω) by false. We say that the user satisfies the policy if $p_1 =$ (true ∧ true) ∨ (false ∧ false) evaluates to true.

4.1   The Scheme

In this section we describe the construction of the proposed CP-ABPRE scheme. The scheme consists of the following algorithms:

1. Setup(λ). The setup algorithm selects a bilinear group $\mathbb{G}_0$ of prime order p and generator g, and the bilinear map $\hat{e} : \mathbb{G}_0 \times \mathbb{G}_0 \rightarrow \mathbb{G}_T$. Next to this, the algorithm

generates the list of attributes in the system $\Omega = \{a_1, a_2, ..., a_k\}$, picks randomly $\alpha, \beta, f, x_1, x_2, \cdots, x_k \in \mathbb{Z}_p^*$, and sets $T_j = g^{x_j}$ $(1 \leq j \leq k)$. Note that for each $a_j \in \Omega$ $(1 \leq j \leq k)$ there is an $x_j \in \mathbb{Z}_p^*(1 \leq j \leq k)$. The algorithm also defines the function $H_1 : \mathbb{G}_T \to \mathbb{G}_0$. The public key is published as:

$$\mathsf{PK} = (g, \hat{e}(g, g)^{(\alpha+\beta)}, g^f, \{T_j\}_{j=1}^k, H_1).$$

The master secret key consists of the following components:

$$\mathsf{MK} = (\alpha, \beta, f, \{x_j\}_{j=1}^k).$$

2. KeyGeneration(MK, ω). The key generation algorithm takes as input the attribute set ω which characterize the user. For each user the algorithm picks at random $r \in \mathbb{Z}_p^*$ and computes the secret key SK_ω which consists of the following components:

$$\mathsf{SK}_\omega = (D^{(1)} = g^{\alpha-r},$$
$$\{D_j^{(2)} = g^{\frac{r+\beta}{x_j}}\}_{a_j \in \omega}).$$

3. Encryption(m, p_1, PK). To encrypt a message $m \in \mathbb{G}_T$, under the access policy p_1 over the set of attributes from Ω, the encryption algorithm picks at random $s \in \mathbb{Z}_p^*$ and assigns s_i values to attributes in p_1 (s_i values are shares of s and are generated using the Benaloh and Leichter [1] secret sharing scheme). The resulted ciphertext consists of the following components:

$$\mathsf{CT}_{p_1} = (C^{(1)} = g^s$$
$$C^{(2)} = m \cdot \hat{e}(g, g)^{(\alpha+\beta)s}, C^{(3)} = g^{fs},$$
$$\{C_{j,i}^{(4)} = g^{x_j s_i}\}_{a_j \in p_1}).$$

4. RKGen($\mathsf{SK}_\omega, p_1, p_2, \mathsf{PK}$): The algorithm outputs a re-encryption key which is used by the proxy to update the ciphertext associated with p_1 to a ciphertext associated with p_2. Let $\omega' \subseteq \omega$ be the smallest set which satisfies the access policy p_1. The algorithm first parses SK_ω as $(D^{(1)}, \{D_j^{(2)}\}_{a_j \in \omega})$, picks at random $l, x' \in \mathbb{Z}_p^*$, it sets $(g^f)^{x'} = g^x$ and computes the re-ecnryption key $\mathsf{rk}_{p_1 \to p_2}$ which consists of the following components:

$$\mathsf{rk}_{p_1 \to p_2} = (\hat{D^{(1)}} = D^{(1)} \cdot g^l,$$
$$\hat{D^{(2)}} = \mathsf{Encryption}(g^{x-l}, p_2, \mathsf{PK}),$$
$$\hat{D^{(3)}} = g^{x'} = g^{\frac{x}{f}},$$
$$\hat{D_j^{(4)}} = \{D_j^{(2)}\}_{a_j \in \omega'}.$$

Note: Note that the message g^{x-l} encrypted in this phase belongs to the group $\mathbb{G}_0$, while the message m encrypted in the Encryption phase belongs to the group $\mathbb{G}_T$. The encryption of g^{x-l} is done in the same way as the encryption of m with a small change on the computation of $C^{(2)}$. The only purpose for this change is to keep g^{x-l} in group $\mathbb{G}_0$. So, in encrypting m in the Encryption phase the $C^{(2)}$ had the form:

$$C^{(2)} = m \cdot \hat{e}(g,g)^{(\alpha+\beta)s}$$

for a random $s \in \mathbb{Z}_p^*$. In encrypting g^{x-l} in the RKGen phase the $C^{(2)}$ has the form:

$$C^{(2)} = g^{x-l} \cdot H_1(\hat{e}(g,g)^{(\alpha+\beta)z})$$

where z is a random element in $\mathbb{Z}_p^*$. All the other components are computed in the same way as in the Encryption phase.

5. $\mathsf{Re-Encrypt}(\mathsf{CT}_{p_1}, \mathsf{RK}_{p_1 \to p_2})$. The algorithm parses CT_{p_1} as $(C^{(1)}, C^{(2)}, C^{(3)},$ $\{C_{j,i}^{(4)}\}_{a_{j,i} \in p_1})$, and $\mathsf{RK}_{p_1 \to p_2}$ as $(D^{(1)}, D^{(2)}, D^{(3)}, \{D_j^{(4)}\}_{a_j \in \omega'})$, and computes the following:

(a) In the first step, for every attribute $a_j \in \omega'$, it computes the following:

$$I^{(1)} = \prod_{a_j \in \omega'} \hat{e}(\hat{D}_j^{(4)}, C_{j,i}^{(4)}) = \prod_{a_j \in \omega'} \hat{e}(g^{\frac{r+\beta}{x_j}}, g^{x_j s_i})$$
$$= \hat{e}(g^{r+\beta}, g^s)$$

(b) In the second step it computes the following:

$$I^{(2)} = \hat{e}(C^{(1)}, \hat{D}^{(1)}) \cdot I^{(1)}$$
$$= \hat{e}(g^s, g^{\alpha-r} \cdot g^l) \cdot \hat{e}(g,g)^{(r+\beta)s}$$
$$= \hat{e}(g^s, g^{\alpha+\beta} \cdot g^l)$$

(c) In the third step it computes the following:

$$I^{(3)} = \frac{C^{(2)}}{I^{(2)}} = \frac{m \cdot \hat{e}(g^s, g^{\alpha+\beta})}{\hat{e}(g^s, g^{\alpha+\beta} \cdot g^l)}$$
$$= \frac{m}{\hat{e}(g^s, g^l)}$$

$$\hat{C}^{(2)} = \hat{e}(C^{(3)}, \hat{D}^{(3)}) \cdot I^{(3)}$$
$$= \hat{e}(g^{sf}, g^{\frac{x}{f}}) \cdot \frac{m}{\hat{e}(g^s, g^l)}$$
$$= m \cdot \hat{e}(g^s, g^{x-l})$$

(d) In the fourth step it sets:

$$\hat{C}^{(1)} = C^{(1)}.$$
$$\hat{C}^{(3)} = \hat{D}^{(2)}.$$

The algorithm outputs the re-encrypted ciphertext, which consists of the following components:

$$\mathsf{CT}_{p_2} = (\hat{C}^{(1)}, \hat{C}^{(2)}, \hat{C}^{(3)}).$$

6. Decrypt(CT_{p_i}, SK_ω): The decryption algorithm takes as input the ciphertext C_{p_i} and secret key SK_ω. It checks if the secret key SK_ω related to the attribute set ω satisfies the access policy p_i. If not, then it outputs $\bot$.

   (a) If ω satisfies the access policy p_i and C_{p_i} is a regular ciphertext, then the decryption algorithm performs the following:

   i. In the first step, the algorithm chooses the smallest set $\omega' \subseteq \omega$ which satisfies the access policy p_i and parses C_{p_i} as $(C^{(1)}, C^{(2)}, \{C_{j,i}^{(4)}\}_{a_j \in p_i})$, and SK_ω as $(D^{(1)}, \{D_j^{(2)}\}_{a_j \in \omega})$.

   ii. In the second step, for every attribute $a_j \in \omega'$, it computes

   $$Z^{(1)} = \prod_{a_j \in \omega'} \hat{e}(D_j^{(2)}, C_{j,i}^{(4)})$$
   $$= \prod_{a_j \in \omega'} \hat{e}(g^{\frac{r+\beta}{x_j}}, g^{x_j s_i})$$
   $$= \hat{e}(g^{r+\beta}, g^s)$$

   iii. In the third step, it computes

   $$Z^{(2)} = \hat{e}(D^{(1)}, C^{(1)}) \cdot Z^{(1)}$$
   $$= \hat{e}(g^{\alpha-r}, g^s) \cdot \hat{e}(g^{r+\beta}, g^s)$$
   $$= \hat{e}(g, g)^{(\alpha+\beta)s}$$

   iv. In the final step, the message is obtained by computing

   $$m = \frac{C^{(2)}}{Z^{(2)}}$$

   (b) If ω satisfies the access policy p_i and C_{p_i} is a re-encrypted ciphertext, then the decryption algorithm performs the following:

   i. In the first step it parses C_{p_i} as $(C^{\hat{(1)}}, C^{\hat{(2)}}, C^{\hat{(3)}})$

   ii. In the second step it recovers the message in the following way:

   $$m = \frac{C^{\hat{(2)}}}{\hat{e}(C^{\hat{(1)}}, \mathsf{Decrypt}(C^{\hat{(3)}}, \mathsf{SK}_\omega))}$$

   Note: The operation $\mathsf{Decrypt}(C^{\hat{(3)}}, \mathsf{SK}_\omega) = g^{x-l}$ (where g^{x-l} is part of the group $\mathbb{G}_0$) is done in similar way as $\mathsf{Decrypt}(C_{p_i}, \mathsf{SK}_\omega) = m$ (where m is part of the group $\mathbb{G}_T$) explained under (a). The only change is under (iv) where g^{x-l} is computed as:

   $$g^{x-l} = \frac{C^{(2)}}{H_1(Z^{(2)})}$$

   while m was computed as:

   $$m = \frac{C^{(2)}}{Z^{(2)}}$$

In the following, we presents the properties of our proposed scheme:

- **Uni-directional.** The re-encryption key $rk_{p_1 \to p_2}$ only allows the proxy to re-encrypt ciphertexts encrypted under the policy p_1 into ciphertexts encrypted under policy p_2, and not the other way around. For instance, the re-encryption key $rk_{p_1 \to p_2}$ can be used to re-encrypt ciphertexts associated with a policy $p_1 = [Patient \; AND \; Bob]$ into ciphertext associated with a policy $p_2 = [General \; Practitioner \; (GP)]$. The idea is that a GP should access his patients' health data, however individual patients should not be able to access GPs' data since GP possess data from different patients.
- **Non-Interactive.** The re-encryption key $rk_{p_1 \to p_2}$ is computed by the delegator without any interaction with the delegatee, the TA authority or the proxy. To compute $rk_{p_1 \to p_2}$, the delegator uses his secret key and the master public key. Therefore the delegator remains off-line while computing the re-encryption key and the proxy perform re-encryption process to update (or re-encrypt) ciphertext without any interaction with the delegator.
- **Key Optimal.** The delegator and the delegatee don't need to store extra secrets in addition to their original secret keys associated with a set of attributes, regardless of how many delegations he/she gives (or accepts).
- **Non-transitivity.** The proxy cannot re-delegate the decryption rights. Alternatively it can be said that the proxy cannot combine re-encryption keys to create new delegations. For example, proxy cannot construct a re-encryption key $rk_{p_1 \to p_3}$ from other two re-encryption keys $rk_{p_1 \to p_2}$ and $rk_{p_2 \to p_3}$ under it possession.
- **Collusion Safe.** The proxy and the delegatee cannot combine their secrets in order to derive a new secret key. For example, the proxy should not be able to combine the re-encryption key $rk_{p_1 \to p_2}$ where $p_1 = [GP \; AND \; Hospital \; 1]$ and $p_2 = [GP \; AND \; (Hospital \; 1 \; OR \; Hospital \; 2)]$ with delegatee's who has a secret key associated with attributes $\{GP, Hospital \; 2\}$ in order to compute a delegator's secret key which is associated with the attributes $\{GP, Hospital \; 1\}$. Collusion safeness also implies that two users cannot combine their secret keys in order to extend their decryption power. For instance, Alice who has a secret key associated with attributes $\{Nurse, Hospital \; 1\}$ should not be able to combine her secret key with Charlie who has a secret key associated with the attributes $\{GP, Hospital \; 2\}$ and be able to decrypt a ciphertext encrypted under the policy $p = [Nurse \; AND \; Hospital \; 2]$ which cannot be satisfied neither by Alice nor by Charlie.
- **Multi-User Decryption.** In existing proxy re-encryption, once the proxy performs the re-encryption, the delegator losses the decryption power, thus the delegator cannot use his secret key to decrypt the re-encrypted data. The reason is that the mapping ciphertext-public key is one-to-one, which implies that one ciphertext can be decrypted only by one secret key, thus after the re-encryption is performed only the delegatee has a power to decrypt the ciphertext. One can argue that the proxy can keep a copy of the original ciphertext and enable the delegator to decrypt the original ciphertext. However, this solution requires for the proxy to keep the original ciphertext for each re-encrypted data.

CP-ABPRE scheme has a property which allows the delegator to generate a re-encryption key in such a way that that the delegator does not loose his decryption power after the proxy performs the re-encryption, and the re-encrypted ciphertext can be decrypted by many users whose secret key satisfies the access policy. As an example, suppose there is an encrypted data according to the policy $p_1 = [(A \ AND \ B) \ OR \ (C \ AND \ D)]$. Bob has a secret key $SK_{\omega_{Bob}}$ associated with a set of attributes $\omega_{Bob} = \{A, B, F\}$. Since Bob satisfy the access policy p_1, Bob is capable to compute a re-encryption key that can update the access policy p_1 into another policy p_2. If Bob updates the access policy p_1 into p_2, where $p_2 = [C \ AND \ F]$ then Bob looses his decryption power because Bob does not satisfy the access policy p_2. However, Bob can retain his decryption power by creating a policy $\widetilde{p} = p_1 \ OR \ p_2$.

- **Multi-User & Single-User Delegation.** In CP-ABE schemes many users may have a secret key with an attribute sets that may satisfy access policy associated with ciphertext. Hence many users can compute the re-encryption key as they satisfy the access policy. However, this property may not always be of potential interest and might become a security threat in some scenarios. In practice we can overcome this threat by defining attributes that are unique to an individual, in addition to the attributes that may be possessed by multiple users. For example, consider Alice who has a secret key SK_{Alice_ω} associated with a set of attributes $\omega = \{Alice, Patient\}$ (Alice is an individual attribute which can be possessed solely by Alice and Patient is an attribute which can be possessed by many users), and a ciphertext encrypted under an access policy $p_1 = [Alice \ AND \ Patient]$. It is obvious that only Alice satisfies the access policy p_1 and only Alice can compute the re-encryption key $rk_{p_1 \rightarrow p_2}$, for any p_2.

A full security proof of the scheme is given in Generic Group Model in Appendix 5.

4.2   Efficiency

The size of the secret key SK_ω depends on the number of attributes the user possess and consists of $|\omega| + 1$ group elements in $\mathbb{G}_0$, where $|\omega|$ is the cardinality of ω. The size of the ciphertext C_p depends on the size of the access policy p and has $|p| + 1$ group elements in $\mathbb{G}_0$, and 1 group element in $\mathbb{G}_T$. The size of the re-encryption key $rk_{p_1 \rightarrow p_2}$ depends on ω' which is the smallest set which satisfies p_1 and has $|\omega'| + 1$ group elements in $\mathbb{G}_0$.

5   Conclusions and Future Work

In this work we present a new proxy re-encryption scheme in the CP-ABE setting. The scheme is unidirectional and allows a user (the delegator) to change dynamically the access policy associated with the ciphertext, without necessarily decrypting the ciphertext. To reduce computations performed at the delegators' side and to avoid the need for the delegator to be online all the time, the delegator computes a re-encryption key and delegates the power to the proxy to update the access control policy associated with ciphertext.

There are two interesting open problems. First, it would be interesting to hide the access control policy from the semi-trusted proxy and from the user who decrypts the data since in our scheme the access policy has to be in clear in order for the user who decrypts the data to apply the right attributes to satisfy the access policy associated with the ciphertext. Second, we leave as an open problem to provide a security proof in the standard model where the problem of breaking the scheme is reduced to a well-studied complexity-theoretic problem.

References

1. Benaloh, J., Leichter, J.: Generalized Secret Sharing and Monotone Functions. In: Gold-wasser, S. (ed.) CRYPTO 1988. LNCS, vol. 403, pp. 27–35. Springer, Heidelberg (1990)
2. Bethencourt, J., Sahai, A., Waters, B.: Ciphertext-policy attribute-based encryption. In: Shands, D. (ed.) Proceedings of the 2007 IEEE Symposium on Security and Privacy, pp. 321–334. IEEE Computer Society, Washington, DC, USA (2007)
3. Blaze, M., Bleumer, G., Strauss, M.: Divertible Protocols and Atomic Proxy Cryptography. In: Nyberg, K. (ed.) EUROCRYPT 1998. LNCS, vol. 1403, pp. 127–144. Springer, Heidelberg (1998)
4. Boneh, D., Franklin, M.: Identity-Based Encryption From the Weil Pairing. In: Kilian, J. (ed.) CRYPTO 2001. LNCS, vol. 2139, pp. 213–229. Springer, Heidelberg (2001)
5. Cheung, L., Newport, C.: Provably secure ciphertext policy ABE. In: Proceedings of the 14th ACM Conference on Computer and Communications Security, pp. 456–465. ACM (2007)
6. ElGamal, T.: A public key cryptosystem and a signature scheme based on discrete logarithms. IEEE Transactions on Information Theory 31(4), 469–472 (1985)
7. Goyal, V., Pandey, O., Sahai, A., Waters, B.: Attribute-based encryption for fine-grained access control of encrypted data. In: Proceedings of the 13th ACM Conference on Computer and Communications Security, pp. 89–98. ACM (2006)
8. Green, M., Ateniese, G.: Identity-Based Proxy Re-Encryption. In: Katz, J., Yung, M. (eds.) ACNS 2007. LNCS, vol. 4521, pp. 288–306. Springer, Heidelberg (2007)
9. Guo, S., Zeng, Y., Wei, J., Xu, Q.: Attribute-based re-encryption scheme in the standard model. Wuhan University Journal of Natural Sciences 13(5), 621–625 (2008)
10. Ibraimi, L., Tang, Q., Hartel, P., Jonker, W.: Efficient and Provable Secure Ciphertext-Policy Attribute-Based Encryption Schemes. In: Bao, F., Li, H., Wang, G. (eds.) ISPEC 2009. LNCS, vol. 5451, pp. 1–12. Springer, Heidelberg (2009)
11. Ivan, A., Dodis, Y.: Proxy Cryptography Revisited. In: Proceedings of the Network and Distributed System Security Symposium. The Internet Society (2003)
12. Jakobsson, M.: On Quorum Controlled Asymmetric Proxy Re-Encryption. In: Imai, H., Zheng, Y. (eds.) PKC 1999. LNCS, vol. 1560, pp. 112–121. Springer, Heidelberg (1999)
13. Liang, X., Cao, Z., Lin, H., Shao, J.: Attribute based proxy re-encryption with delegating capabilities. In: Proceedings of the 4th International Symposium on Information, Computer, and Communications Security, pp. 276–286. ACM (2009)
14. Mambo, M., Okamoto, E.: Proxy cryptosystems: delegation of the power to decrypt ciphertexts. IEICE Transactions on Fundamentals of Electronics, Communications and Computer Sciences 80(1), 54–63 (1997)
15. Matsuo, T.: Proxy Re-encryption Systems for Identity-Based Encryption. In: Takagi, T., Okamoto, T., Okamoto, E., Okamoto, T. (eds.) Pairing 2007. LNCS, vol. 4575, pp. 247–267. Springer, Heidelberg (2007)
16. Rivest, R.L., Shamir, A., Adleman, L.: A method for obtaining digital signatures and public-key cryptosystems. Communications of the ACM 21(2), 126 (1978)
17. Sahai, A., Waters, B.: Fuzzy Identity-Based Encryption. In: Cramer, R. (ed.) EUROCRYPT 2005. LNCS, vol. 3494, pp. 457–473. Springer, Heidelberg (2005)

18. Shoup, V.: Lower Bounds for Discrete Logarithms and Related Problems. In: Fumy, W. (ed.) EUROCRYPT 1997. LNCS, vol. 1233, pp. 256–266. Springer, Heidelberg (1997)
19. Zhou, L., Marsh, M.A., Schneider, F.B., Redz, A.: Distributed blinding for ElGamal re-encryption. In: Proceedings of 25th IEEE International Conference on Distributed Computing Systems, pp. 815–824. IEEE Computer Society (2005)

Appendix

Security Proof in Generic Group Model

We provide a security proof in the generic group model, introduced by Shoup [18]. The model relies on the fact that it is hard to find the discrete logarithm in a group (including a group with bilinear pairing) when the order of the group is a large prime number. In this model group elements are encoded as unique random strings, in such a way that the adversary $\mathcal{A}$ can manipulate group elements using canonical group operations in $\mathbb{G}_0$ and $\mathbb{G}_T$ and cannot test any property other than equality. Thus a cryptographically secure group provides no mathematical properties of its group other than its group structure.

Theorem 1. *The advantage of any adversary $\mathcal{A}$ in the security game receiving at most q group elements from queries it makes to the oracles for computing group operation in $\mathbb{G}_0$ and $\mathbb{G}_T$, pairing operation $\hat{e}$ and from the interaction with the CP-ABPRE security game is bounded by $O(\frac{q^2}{p})$.*

Proof. Following the arguments from the proof in [2], we bound the advantage of $\mathcal{A}$ in a modified game in which the challenge ciphertext is either $C^{(1)} = \hat{e}(g,g)^{(\alpha+\beta)s}$ or $C^{(1)} = \hat{e}(g,g)^{\theta}$, instead of giving a challenge ciphertext as defined in the security game of Section 3 as $C^{(1)} = m_b \cdot \hat{e}(g,g)^{(\alpha+\beta)s}$ where $b \in (0,1)$. We show that $\mathcal{A}$ cannot distinguish which game is playing. Then we show that there is no $\mathcal{A}$ which has a non-negligible advantage in a modified game, so there is no $\mathcal{A}$ with has a non-negligible advantage in the security game of Section 3, either. Note that if there is an $\mathcal{A}$ that has advantage ϵ in the security game of Section 3 then there can be another adversary which has advantage $\frac{\epsilon}{2}$ in the modified security game.

We will write $\gamma_0(x) : \mathbb{Z}_p^* \to \{0,1\}^{\lceil \log p \rceil}$ as a random encoding for the group element $g^x \in \mathbb{G}_0$, and $\gamma_1(x) : \mathbb{Z}_p^* \to \{0,1\}^{\lceil \log p \rceil}$ as a random encoding for group element $\hat{e}(g,g)^x \in \mathbb{G}_T$. Each random encoding is associated with a rational function (a function written as a division of two polynomial functions). Let f be a rational function over the variables $\{\alpha, \beta, \theta, s, s_{\tilde{\imath}}, \{x_j\}(1 \leq j \leq k), r, f, l\}$, where each variable is an element picked at random in the scheme. $\mathcal{A}$ receives the following encodings from the interaction with the simulator in the security game:

- Components generated by the Setup algorithm:
  1. $\gamma_0(1)$ representing the group generator g.
  2. $\gamma_0(f)$ representing the group element g^f.
  3. $\{\gamma_0(x_j)\}(1 \leq j \leq k)$ representing $\{T_j = g^{x_j}\}_{j=1}^k$.
  4. $\gamma_1(\alpha + \beta)$ representing $\hat{e}(g,g)^{\alpha+\beta}$.
- Components generated by the KeyGen oracle in Phase1 and Phase2 of the security game. Let ω be the attribute set for which $\mathcal{A}$ asks for e secret key.

1. $\gamma_0(\alpha - r)$ representing $D^{(1)} = g^{\alpha-r}$.
2. $\{\gamma_0(\frac{r+\beta}{x_j})\}_{a_j \in \omega}$ representing $\{D_j^{(2)} = g^{\frac{r+\beta}{x_j}}\}_{a_j \in \omega}$.

- Components generated by the RKGen oracle in Phase1 and Phase2 of the security game. Let RKGen(p_1, p_2) be the re-encryption query used to re-encrypt messages encrypted under the access policy p_1 into messages encrypted under the access policy p_2. Let ω' be the set of attributes that satisfy the access policy p_1.
  1. $\gamma_0(\alpha - r + l)$ representing $D^{\hat{(1)}} = g^{\alpha-r+l}$.
  2. $\gamma_0(z)$, $\gamma_0(R)$, $\gamma_0(fz)$ and $\{\gamma_0(x_j z_{\hat{i}})\}_{a_{j,\hat{i}} \in p_2}$ representing

     $$D_j^{\hat{(2)}} = \text{Encryption}(g^{x-l}, p_2, \text{PK}).$$

  3. $\gamma_0(x')$ representing $D^{\hat{(3)}} = g^{x'} = g^{\frac{x}{f}}$.
  4. $\{\gamma_0(\frac{r+\beta}{x_j})\}_{a_j \in \omega}$ representing $\{D_j^{\hat{(4)}} = g^{\frac{r+\beta}{x_j}}\}_{a_j \in \omega'}$.

- Components generated by the Encryption oracle in the Challenge phase of the security game. Let $\mathcal{A}$ asks for a challenge for messages $m_0, m_1 \in \mathbb{G}_T$ and the access policy p^*.
  1. $\gamma_0(s)$ representing $C^{(1)} = g^s$.
  2. $\gamma_1(\theta)$ representing $C^{(2)} = \hat{e}(g, g)^\theta$.
  3. $\gamma_0(fs)$ representing $C^{(3)} = g^{fs}$.
  4. $\{\gamma_0(x_j s_{\hat{i}})\}_{a_{j,\hat{i}} \in p^*}$ representing $\{C_{j,\hat{i}}^{(4)} = g^{x_j s_{\hat{i}}}\}_{a_{j,\hat{i}} \in p^*}$.

$\mathcal{A}$ uses the group elements received from the interaction with the simulator to perform generic group operations and equality tests.

- Queries to the oracles for group operation in $\mathbb{G}_0$ and $\mathbb{G}_T$. $\mathcal{A}$ asks for multiplying or dividing group elements represented with their random encodings, and associated with a rational function. The oracle returns $f + f'$ when $\mathcal{A}$ asks for multiplying f and f', or $f - f'$ when $\mathcal{A}$ asks for dividing f and f' (Note that $\mathcal{A}$ knows only the encodings of f and f').
- Queries to the oracle for computing pairing operation $\hat{e}$. $\mathcal{A}$ asks for pairing of group elements represented with their random encoding and associated with a rational function. The oracle returns $f f'$ when $\mathcal{A}$ asks for pairing f and f'.

We show that $\mathcal{A}$ cannot distinguish with non-negligible advantage the simulation of the modified game where the challenge ciphertext is set $C^{(2)} = \hat{e}(g, g)^\theta$, with the simulation of the real game where the challenge ciphertext would have been set $C^{(2)} = \hat{e}(g, g)^{(\alpha+\beta)s}$.

First, we show the $\mathcal{A}$'s view when the challenge ciphertext is $\gamma_1(\theta)$. Following the standard approach for security in generic group model, $\mathcal{A}$'s view can change when an unexpected collision happen due to the random choice of the formal variables $\{\alpha, \beta, \theta, s, s_{\hat{i}}, \{x_j\}_{1 \le j \le k}, r, f, l\}$ chosen uniformly from $\mathbb{Z}_p^*$. A collision happen when two queries evaluate to the same value. For any two distinct queries the probability of such collision happen is at most $O(q^2/p)$. Since for large p the probability of such collision is negligible we ignore this case.

Second, we show what the adversaries view would have been if the challenge ciphertext had been set $\gamma_1((\alpha + \beta)s)$. Again, $\mathcal{A}$ view can change when a collision happen, such that the values of two different rational functions coincide. We show that $\mathcal{A}$ cannot

Table 1. Possible queries into $\mathbb{G}_T$

1	$\alpha + \beta$	t_j
$(\alpha - r)s$	$(r + \beta)s_i$	$\frac{r+\beta}{x_j}s$
fz	xs	x
$s(\alpha - r) + (r + \beta)s_i$	$r + \beta$	$(r + \beta)s_i$
$x_j s_i$	$(\alpha - r)(x_j s_i)$	z
$\alpha - r \pm (r + \beta)s_i$	$s(\alpha - r + l)$	R
$(\alpha + \beta) \pm s$	$(\alpha - r + l)$	

make a polynomial query which would be equal to $(\alpha + \beta)s$, and therefore a collision cannot happen. In table 1 we list possible queries that $\mathcal{A}$ can make into $\mathbb{G}_T$ using the group elements received from interaction with the simulator in the security game.

As is shown in table 1 (the highlighted cell), $\mathcal{A}$ can pair s with $\alpha - r$, and $\frac{r+\beta}{x_j}$ with $s_i x_j$, and then sum the results to get $s(\alpha - r) + \sum_{a_i \in \omega} rs_i + \sum_{a_i \in \omega} \beta s_i$. In order to get only $(\alpha + \beta)s$, $\mathcal{A}$ has to create polynomial requests to cancel sr and to compute βs. We observe that $\mathcal{A}$ to obtain βs and sr has to pair $\frac{r+\beta}{x_j}$ with $s_i x_j$. From the table 1 we can see that $\mathcal{A}$ can construct a query polynomial of the form:

$$\underbrace{s\alpha}_{A} - \underbrace{sr}_{B} + \sum_{a_i \in \omega} \underbrace{rs_i}_{C} + \sum_{a_i \in \omega} \underbrace{\beta s_i}_{D}$$

However $\mathcal{A}$ cannot construct a query polynomial of the form $(\alpha + \beta)s = \alpha s + \beta s$ if $\mathcal{A}$ does not have a secret key which satisfies the access policy. First, there must be at least one rs_i missing (there must be one ciphertext component $g^{x_j s_i}$ for which $\mathcal{A}$ does not have a secret key component $g^{\frac{\beta+r}{x_j}}$ to pair, therefore $\mathcal{A}$ cannot cancel x_j), therefore $\mathcal{A}$ cannot reconstruct rs under the term C, and as a sequence cannot cancel term B and C. Second, there must be at least one βs_i missing, hence $\mathcal{A}$ cannot reconstruct βs under the term D. As a result of the above analysis, we conclude that $\mathcal{A}$ cannot make a polynomial query which has the form $(\alpha + \beta)s$.

Machine Learning for the Detection of Spam in Twitter Networks

Alex Hai Wang

The Pennsylvania State University, Dunmore, PA 18512, U.S.A.
hwang@psu.edu

Abstract. The rapidly growing online social networking sites have been infiltrated by a large amount of spam. In this paper, I focus on one of the most popular sites Twitter as an example to study the spam behaviors. To facilitate the spam detection, a directed social graph model is proposed to explore the "follower" and "friend" relationships among users. Based on Twitter's spam policy, novel content-based features and graph-based features are also proposed. A Web crawler is developed relying on Twitter's API methods. A spam detection prototype system is proposed to identify suspicious users on Twitter. I analyze the data set and evaluate the performance of the detection system. Classic evaluation metrics are used to compare the performance of various traditional classification methods. Experiment results show that the Bayesian classifier has the best overall performance in term of F-measure. The trained Bayesian classifier is also applied to the entire data set to distinguish the suspicious behaviors from normal ones. The result shows that the spam detection system can achieve 89% precision.

1 Introduction

Online social networking sites, such as Facebook, LinkedIN, and Twitter, are one of the most popular applications of Web 2.0. Millions of users use online social networking sites to stay in touch with friends, meet new people, make work-related connections and more. Among all these sites, Twitter is the fastest growing one than any other social networking sites, surging more than 2,800% in 2009 according to the report [1]. Founded in 2006, Twitter is a social networking and micro-blogging service that allows users to post their latest updates, called *tweets*. Users can only post text and HTTP links in their tweets. The length of a tweet is limited by 140 characters.

The goal of Twitter is to allow friends communicate and stay connected through the exchange of short messages. Unfortunately, spammers also use Twitter as a tool to post malicious links, send unsolicited messages to legitimate users, and hijack trending topics. Spam is becoming an increasing problem on Twitter as other online social networking sites are. A study shows that more than 3% messages are spam on Twitter [2]. The trending topics are also often abused by the spammers. The trending topics, which displays on Twitter homepage, are the most tweeted-about topics of the minute, day, and week on Twitter. The attack reported in [3] forced Twitter to temporarily disable the trending topic and remove the offensive terms. I also observed one attack on February 20, 2010 as shown in Figure 1.

M.S. Obaidat, G.A. Tsihrintzis, and J. Filipe (Eds.): ICETE 2010, CCIS 222, pp. 319–333, 2012.
© Springer-Verlag Berlin Heidelberg 2012

Fig. 1. A Twitter Trending Topic Attack on February 20, 2010 (The offensive term is shown in the red rectangle and is censor blurred)

Twitter provides several methods for users to report spam. A user can report a spam by clicking on the "report as spam" link in the their homepage on Twitter. The reports are investigated by Twitter and the accounts being reported will be suspended if they are spam. Another simple and public available method is to post a tweet in the *"@spam @username"* format where *@username* is to mention the spam account. I tested this service by searching "@spam" on Twitter. Surprisingly the query results show that this report service is also abused by both hoaxes and spam. Only a few tweets report real malicious accounts. Some Twitter applications also allow users to flag possible spam. However, all these ad hoc methods require users to identify spam manually and depend on their own experience.

Twitter also puts effort into cleaning up suspicious accounts and filtering out malicious tweets. Meanwhile, legitimate Twitter users complain that their accounts are mistakenly suspended by Twitter's anti-spam action. Twitter recently admitted to accidentally suspending accounts as a result of a spam clean-up effort [4].

In this paper, the suspicious behaviors of spam accounts on Twitter is studied. The goal is to apply machine learing methods to automatically distinguish spam accounts from normal ones. The major contributions of this paper are as follows:

1. To the best of our knowledge, this is the first effort to automatically detect spam on Twitter;
2. A directed graph model is proposed to explore the unique "follower" and "friend" relationships on Twitter;
3. Based on Twitter's spam policy, novel graph-based features and content-based features are proposed to facilitate the spam detection;
4. A series of classification methods are compared and applied to distinguish suspicious behaviors from normal ones;
5. A Web crawler is developed relying on the API methods provided by Twitter to extract public available data on Twitter website. A data set of around 25K users, 500K tweets, and 49M follower/friend relationships are collected;

6. Finally, a prototype system is established to evaluate the detection method. Experiments are conducted to analyze the data set and evaluate the performance of the system. The result shows that the spam detection system has a 89% precision.

The rest of the paper is organized as follows. In Section 2 the related work is discussed. A directed social graph model is proposed in Section 3. The unique friend and follower relationships are also defined in this part. In Section 4, novel graph-based and content-based features are proposed based on Twitter's spam policy. Section 5 introduces the method in which I collect the data set. Bayesian classification methods are adopted in Section 6 to detect spam accounts in Twitter. Experiments are conducted in Section 7 to analyze the labeled data. Traditional classification methods are compared to evaluate the performance of the detection ssystem. The conclusion is in Section 8.

2   Related Work

Spam detection has been studied for a long time. The existing work mainly focuses on email spam detection and Web spam detection. In [5], the authors are the first to apply a Bayesian approach to filter spam emails. Experiment results show that the classifier achieves a better performance by considering domain-specific features in addition to the raw text of E-mail messages. Currently spam email filtering is a fairly mature technique. Bayesian spam email filters are widely implemented both on modern email clients and servers.

Web is massive and changes more rapidly compared with email system. It is a significant challenge to detect Web spam. [6] first formalized the Web spam detection problem and proposed a comprehensive solution to detect Web spam. The TrustRank algorithm is proposed to compute the trust scores of a Web graph. Based on computed scores where good pages are given higher scores, spam pages can be filtered in the search engine results. In [7], the authors based on the link structure of the Web proposed a measurement Spam Mass to identify link spamming. A directed graph model of the Web is proposed in [8]. The authors apply classification algorithms for directed graphs to detect real-world link spam. In [9], both link-based features and content-based features are proposed. A basic decision tree classifier is implemented to detect spam. Semi-supervised learning algorithms are proposed to boost the performance of a classifier which only needs small amount of labeled samples in [10].

For spam detection in other applications, the authors in [11] present an approach for detection of spam calls over IP telephony called SPIT in VoIP system. Based on the popular semi-supervised learning methods, an improved algorithm called MPCK-Means is proposed. In [12], the authors study the video spammers and promoters on YouTube. A supervised classification algorithm is proposed to detect spammers and promoters. In [13], a machine learning approach is proposed to study spam bots detection in online social networking sites using Twitter as an example. In [14], the authors collected three datasets of the Twitter network. The Twitter users' behaviors, geographic growth pattern, and current size of the network are studied.

3 Social Graph Model

In this work, Twitter is modeled as a directed graph $\mathcal{G} = (\mathcal{V}, \mathcal{A})$ which consists of a set $\mathcal{V}$ of nodes (vertices) representing user accounts and a set $\mathcal{A}$ of arcs (directed edges) that connect nodes. Each arc is an ordered pair of distinct nodes. An arc $a = (i, j)$ is directed from v_i to v_j which stands for the user i is *following* user j. Following is one of the unique features of Twitter. Unlike most other online social networking sites, following on Twitter is not a mutual relationship. Any user can follow you and you do not have to approve or follow back. In this way, Twitter is modeled as a directed graph.

Since there may or may not be an arc in either direction for a pair of nodes, there are four possible states for each dyad. Four types of relationships on Twitter are defined as follows:

Follower. represents the people who is following you on Twitter. In this paper, follower in Twitter's graph model is defined as:

Definition 1. *Follower: node v_j is a* follower *of node v_i if the arc $a = (j, i)$ is contained in the set of arcs, $\mathcal{A}$.*

Based on the definition, followers are the incoming links, or *inlinks*, of a node. Let the set $\mathcal{A}_i^I$ denote the inlinks of node v_i, or the followers of user i.

Friend. is defined as the people whose updates you are subscribed to. In other words, friends are the people whom you are following. I give a formal definition of the friend relationship in graph model as follows:

Definition 2. *Friend: node v_j is a* friend *of node v_i if the arc $a = (i, j)$ is contained in the set of arcs, $\mathcal{A}$.*

Friends are the outgoing links, or *outlinks*, of a node. Let the set $\mathcal{A}_i^O$ denote the outlinks of node v_i, or the friends of user i.

Mutual Friend is a novel relationship on Twitter. If two users are following each other, or are the friends of each other, the relationship between these two users is mutual friend. A formal definition of the mutual friend relationship on Twitter is defined as follows:

Definition 3. *Mutual Friend: node v_i and node v_j are* mutual friends *if both arcs $a = (i, j)$ and $a = (j, i)$ are contained in the set of arcs, $\mathcal{A}$.*

Since a mutual friend is your follower and friend at the same time, the set of mutual friends is the intersection of the set of friends and the set of followers. If let $\mathcal{A}_i^M$ denote the set of mutual friends of node v_i, the following holds: $\mathcal{A}_i^M = \mathcal{A}_i^I \cap \mathcal{A}_i^O$.

Stranger are two users if there is no connection between them. A formal definition is as follows:

Definition 4. *Stranger: node v_i and node v_j are* strangers *if neither arcs $a = (i, j)$ nor $a = (j, i)$ is contained in the set of arcs, $\mathcal{A}$.*

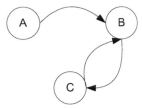

Fig. 2. A simple Twitter graph

Fig. 3. Twitter Social Graph

A simple Twitter social graph example is shown in Figure 2 where user A is following user B, and user B and user C are following each other. Based on our definitions, user A is a follower of user B. User B is a friend of user A. User B and User C are mutual friends. User A and user C are strangers.

Based the directed social graph model proposed above, a real Twitter social graph is shown in Figure 3. 20 random users and their followers and friends are collected from Twitter's public timeline and the figure is drawn using Pajek software [15].

4   Features

In this section, the features extracted from each Twitter user account for the purpose of spam detection are introduced. The features are extracted from different aspects which include graph-based features and content-based features. Based on the unique characteristics of Twitter, novel features are also proposed in this section.

4.1   Graph-Based Features

One important function of twitter is that you can build your own social network by following friends and allowing others to follow you. Spam accounts try to follow large mount of users to gain their attention. The twitter's spam and abuse policy [16] says that, "if you have a small number of followers compared to the amount of people you are following", it may be considered as a spam account.

Four features, which are the number of friends, the number of followers, the number of mutual friends and the reputation of a user, are computed to detect spam from this aspect. According to the social graph model proposed in Section 3, the *indegree* $d_I(v_i)$ of a node v_i, which is the number of nodes that are adjacent to node v_i, stands for the feature of the number of followers. The feature of the number of friends is represented by the *outdegree* $d_O(v_i)$ of a node v_i, which is the number of nodes that are adjacent to v_i. The set of mutual friends is the intersection of the set of friends and the set of followers. I use the number of mutual friends as another graph-based feature.

Furthermore, a novel feature, *reputation*, is proposed to measure the relative importance of a user on Twitter. The reputation R is defined as the ratio between the number of friends and the number of followers as:

$$R(v_i) = \frac{d_I(v_i)}{d_I(v_i) + d_O(v_i)} \tag{1}$$

Obviously if the number of followers is relatively small compared to the amount of people you are following, the reputation is small and close to zero. At the same time the probability that the associated account is spam is high.

4.2   Content-Based Features

Duplicate Tweets. An account may be considered as a spam if you post duplicate content on one account. Usually legitimate users will not post duplicate updates.

Duplicate tweets are detected by measuring the Levenshtein distance [17] (also known as edit distance) between two different tweets posted by the same account. The Levenshtein distance is defined as the minimum cost of transforming one string into another through a sequence of edit operations, including the deletion, insertion, and substitution of individual symbols. The distance is zero if and only if the two tweets are identical.

A typical Twitter spam page is shown in Figure 4. As can be seen, spammers often include different *@usernames* in their duplicate tweets to avoid being detected. This is also an efficient way to spam legitimate users, since Twitter automatically collects all tweets containing your *@username* for you. The example in Figure 4 also shows that spammers include different *#topics* and "http" links in their duplicate tweets. Because of the URL shortening service, such as bit.ly, the different "http" links may have the same destination. Based on these reasons, when the Levenshtein distance is calculated between different tweets, I clean the data by stopping the words containing "@", "#", "http://", and "www." in the tweets. In other words, the username information, topic information, and links are ignored. Instead only the content of the tweets is considered. As shown in Figure 4, the duplicate tweets are circled in the same color rectangles, although they have different *@username, #topic*, and links.

Fig. 4. A Twitter spam page (Duplicate tweets are circled in the same color rectangles)

After cleaning the data, the pairwise Levenshtein distance is calculated in the user's 20 most recent tweets. If the distance is smaller than a certain threshold, it is counted as one duplicate. In this paper, the threshold is set to zero, which means two tweets are considered as duplicate only when they are exactly the same.

HTTP Links. Malicious links can spread more quickly than ever before because of Twitters lightning-fast communications platform. Twitter filters out the URLs linked to known malicious sites. However, a great vulnerability is the presence of shorten URLs. Twitter only allows users to post a short message within 140 characters. URL shortening services and applications, such as bit.ly, become popular to meet the requirements. Shorten URLs can hide the source URLs and obscure the malicious sites behind them. As a result it provides an opportunity for attackers to prank, phish, and spam. While Twitter does not check these shorten URLs for malware, it is considered as spam if your updates consist mainly of links, and not personal updates according to Twitter's policy.

The number of links in one account is measured by the number of tweets containing HTTP links in the user's 20 most recent tweets. If a tweet contains the sequence of characters "http://" or "www.", this tweet is considered containing a HTTP link.

Replies and Mentions. A user is identified by the unique username and can be referred in the @*username* format on Twitter. The @*username* creates a link to the user's profile automatically. You can send a reply message to another user in @*username+message* format where @*username* is the message receiver. You can reply to anyone on Twitter no matter they are your friends/followers or not. You can also mention another @*username* anywhere in the tweet, rather than just the beginning. Twitter automatically collects all tweets containing your username in the @*username* format in your replies tab. You can see all replies made to you, and mentions of your username.

The reply and mention are designed to help users to track conversation and discover each other on Twitter. However, this service is abused by the spammers to gain other user's attention by sending unsolicited replies and mentions. Twitter also considers this as a factor to determine spamming. The number of replies and mentions in one account is measured by the number of tweets containing the "@" symbol in the user's 20 most recent tweets.

Trending Topics. Trending topics are the most-mentioned terms on Twitter at that moment, in this week, or in this month. Users can use the hashtag, which is the # symbol followed by a term describing or naming the topic, to a tweet. If there are many tweets containing the same term, that helps the term to become a trending topic. The topic shows up as a link on the home page of Twitter as shown in Figure 1.

Unfortunately, because of how prominent trending topics are, spammers post multiple unrelated tweets that contain the trending topics to lure legitimate users to read their tweets. Twitter also considers an account as spam "if you post multiple unrelated updates to a topic using the # symbol". The number of tweets which contains the hashtag # in a user's 20 most recent tweets is measured as a content-based feature.

5   Data Set

To evaluate the spam detection methods, a real data set is collected from Twitter website. First I use Twitter's API methods to collect user's detailed information. Second, because no Twitter API method could provide information of a specific unauthorized user's recent tweets, a Web crawler is developed to extra a specific unauthorized user's 20 most recent tweets.

5.1   Twitter API

First I use the *public_timeline* API method provided by Twitter to collect information about the non-protected users who have set a custom user icon in real time. This method can randomly pick 20 non-protected users who updated their status recently on Twitter. Details of the user, such as IDs, screen name, location, and etc, are extracted. At the same time, I also use social graph API methods *friends* and *followers* to collect detailed information about user's friends and followers, such as the number of friends, the number of followers, list of friend IDs, list of follower IDs, and etc. The *friends* and *followers* API methods can return maximum 5,000 users. If a user has more than 5,000 friends or followers, only a partial list of friends or followers can be extracted. Based on the observation, the medians of the number of friends and followers are around 300, so this constraint does not affect the method significantly.

Another constraint of Twitter API methods is the number of queries per hour. Currently the rate limit for calls to the API is 150 requests per hour. This constrain affects the detection system significantly. To collect data from different time and avoid congesting Twitter, I crawl Twitter continuously and limit 120 requests per hour per host.

5.2   Web Crawler

Although Twitter provides neat API methods for us, there is no method that allows us to collect a specific unauthorized user's recent tweets. The *public_timeline* API method

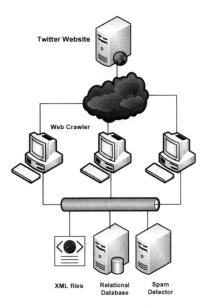

Fig. 5. Twitter Spam Detection System

can only return the most recent update from different non-protected users (one update per user). The *user_timeline* API method can return the 20 most recent tweets posted from an authenticating user. The recent tweets posted by a user are important to extract content-based features, such as duplicate tweets. To solve this problem, a Web crawler is developed to collect the 20 most recent tweets of a specific non-protected user based on the user's ID on Twitter.

The *public_timeline* API method is first used to collect the user's IDs of 20 non-protected users who updated their status recently. Based on the user's IDs, the Web crawler extracts the user's 20 most recent tweets and saves it as a XML file.

A prototype system structure is shown in Figure 5. Currently 3 Web crawlers extract detailed user information from Twitter website. The raw user tweets are stored as XML files. Other user information, such as IDs, list of friends and followers, are saved in a relational database. The graph-based features are calculated at the same time and stored in the relational database. The XML files are parsed and the content-based features are calculated. The results are saved in the relational database.

Finally, I collect the data set for 3 weeks from January 3 to January 24, 2010. Totally 25,847 users, around 500K tweets, and around 49M follower/friend relationships are collected from the public available data on Twitter.

6   Spam Detection

Several classic classification algorithms, such as decision tree, neural network, support vector machines, and k-nearest neighbors are compared. The naïve Bayesian classifier outperforms all other methods for several reasons. First, Bayesian classifier is noise robust. On Twitter, the relationship between the feature set and the spam is non-deterministic as discussed in Section 4. An account cannot be predicted as spam with certainty even though some of its features are identical to the training examples. Bayesian classifier treats the non-deterministic relationship between class variables and features as random variables and captures their relationship using posterior probability. While other methods cannot tolerate this kind of noisy data or confounding factors, such as decision tree.

Another reason that Bayesian classifier has a better performance is that the class label is predicted based on user's specific pattern. A spam probability is calculated for each individual user based its behaviors, instead of giving a general rule. Also, naïve Bayesian classifier is a simple and very efficient classification algorithm.

The naïve Bayesian classifier is based on the well-known Bayes theorem:

$$P(Y|X) = \frac{P(X|Y)P(Y)}{P(X)} \qquad (2)$$

The conditional probability of $P(Y|X)$ is also known as the posterior probability for Y, as opposed to its prior probability $P(Y)$.

Each Twitter account is considered as a vector X with feature values. The goal is to assign each account to one of two classes Y: spam and non-spam. The big assumption of naïve Bayesian classifier is that the features are conditionally independent, although research shows that it is "is surprisingly effective in practice" without the unrealistic independence assumption [18]. With the conditional independence assumption, we can only estimate each conditional probability independently, instead of trying every combination of X.

To classify a data record, the posterior probability is computed for each class:

$$P(Y|X) = \frac{P(Y) \prod_{i=1}^{d} P(X_i|Y)}{P(X)} \qquad (3)$$

Since $P(X)$ is a normalizing factor which is equal for all classes, we need only maximize the numerator $P(Y) \prod_{i=1}^{d} P(X_i|Y)$ in order to do the classification.

7   Experiments

To evaluate the detection method, 500 Twitter user accounts are labeled manually to two classes: spam and non-spam. Each user account is manually evaluated by reading the 20 most recent tweets posted by the user and checking the friends and followers of the user. The results show that there are around 1% spam accounts in the data set. The study in [2] shows that there is probably 3% spam on Twitter. To simulate the reality and avoid the bias in the crawling and label methods, additional spam data are added to the data set. I search "@spam" on Twitter to collect additional spam data. Only a small percentage of results report real spam. I clean the query results by manually evaluating each spam report. Finally the data set is mixed to contain around 3% spam data.

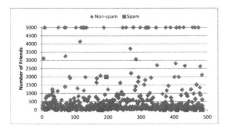

(a) The Number of Friends (The maximum number of friends is 5,000 which is the maximum return value of Twitter *friends* API method)

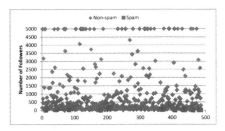

(b) The Number of Followers (The maximum number of followers is 5,000 which is the maximum return value of Twitter *followers* API method)

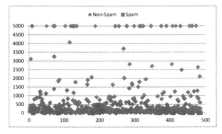

(c) The Number of Mutual Friends (The maximum number of mutual friends is 5,000 which is the maximum return value of Twitter *friends* and *followers* API method)

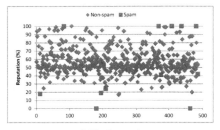

(d) The Reputation

Fig. 6. Graph-based Features

7.1 Data Analysis

Graph-based Features. Figure 6 show the graph-based features proposed in Section 4.1. The number of friends for each Twitter account is shown in Figure 6(a). Twitter spam policy says that "if you have a small number of followers compared to the amount of people you are following", you may be considered as a spam account. As can be seen, not all spam accounts follow a large amount of user as we expected, instead only 30% of spam accounts do that. The reason is that Twitter allows users to *mention* or *reply* any other user in their tweets. In other words, the spammers do not need to follow legitimate user accounts to draw their attention. The spammers can simply post spam tweets and *mention* or *reply* another user in the @username format in the tweets. These tweets will appear on the user's replies tab whose username is mentioned. In this way, the spam tweets are sent out without actually following a legitimate user. The results show that this is an efficient and common way to spam other users as shown in Figure 4.

Figure 6(b) shows the number of followers for each Twitter account. As we expected, usually the spam accounts do not have a large amount of followers. But still I can find there are some spam accounts having a relatively large amount of followers. They may achieve that by letting other spam accounts to follow them collusively or lure legitimate users to follow them.

The number of mutual friends is shown in Figure 6(c). The spam accounts can have relatively large amount of mutual friends. As I explained above, the spammers may lure the legitimate users to follow them to avoid detection. Also, another common way to

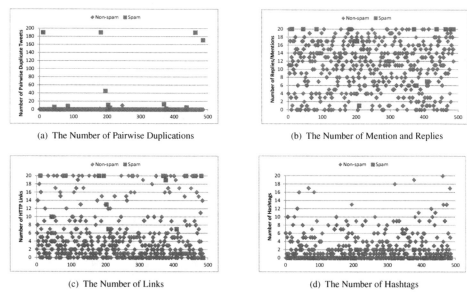

(a) The Number of Pairwise Duplications   (b) The Number of Mention and Replies

(c) The Number of Links   (d) The Number of Hashtags

Fig. 7. Content-based Features

promise "more followers fast" or exchange following relationship to legitimate users. In this way, the spammers can easily get large amount of followers. This kind of spamming is prohibited on Twitter.

The reputation for each Twitter account is shown in Figure 6(d). Surprisingly I find that some spam accounts have a 100% reputation. The reason is as mentioned above that the spam accounts do not have to follow a legitimate user to send malicious tweets. Because of this, some spam accounts do not have a friend ($d_O(v_i) = 0$). However, the reputation feature shows the abnormal behaviors of spam accounts. Most of them either have a 100% reputation or a very low reputation. The reputation of most legitimate users is between 30% to 90%.

Content-based Features. The content-based features proposed in Section 4.2 are shown in Figure 7. Twitter spam policy indicates that "multiple duplicate updates on one account" is factor to detect spam. The number of pairwise duplication in a user's 20 most recent tweets is shown in Figure 7(a). As expected, most spam accounts have multiple duplicate tweets. This is an important feature to detect spam. However, as shown in the figure, not all spam accounts post multiple duplicate tweets. So we can not only depend on this feature to detect spam.

The number of mentions and replies is shown in Figure 7(b). As expected, most spam accounts have the maximum 20 "@" symbol in their 20 most recent tweets. This indicates that the spammers intend to mention or reply legitimate users in their tweets to gain attention. This will lure legitimate users to either read their spam messages or even click the malicious links in their tweets.

Figure 7(c) shows the number of links in each user's 20 most recent tweets. The results show that most spam accounts have the maximum 20 links in their 20 most recent tweets. In other words, each tweet contains a link for most spam accounts. However, the results also show that some legitimate users also include links in all tweets. The reason is that some companies join Twitter to promote their own web sites. Usually they will include a link to their own web page in each of their tweets.

Finally, Figure 7(d) shows the number of "#" tag signs in each user's 20 most recent tweets. Although spamming Twitter trend topics is reported in news, I cannot find that spammers attack trend topics in the dataset. The reason is that this kind of attack usually occur in a very short period of time and does not happen constantly on Twitter. It is difficult for us to capture their trace. It does not mean that this kind of attack is not common or not even exist.

7.2 Evaluation

The evaluation of the overall process is based on a set of measures commonly used in machine learning and information retrieval. Given a classification algorithm, I consider its confusion matrix:

		Prediction	
		Spam	Not Spam
True	Spam	a	b
	Not Spam	c	d

where a represents the number of spam examples that were correctly classified, b represents the spam examples that were falsely classified as non-spam , c represents the number of non-spam examples that were falsely classified as spam, and d represents the number of non-spam examples that were correctly classified. I consider the following measures: precision, recall, and F-measure where the precision is $P = a/(a + c)$, the recall is $R = a/(a + b)$, and the F-measure is defined as $F = 2PR/(P + R)$. For evaluating the classification algorithms, I focus on the F-measure F as it is a standard way of summarizing both precision and recall.

All the predictions reported in this paper are computed using 10-fold cross validation. For each classifier, the precision, recall, and F-measure are reported. Each classifier is trained 10 times, each time using the 9 out of the 10 partitions as training data and computing the confusion matrix using the tenth partition as test data. I then average the resulting ten confusion matrices and estimate the evaluation metrics on the average confusion matrix. The evaluation results are shown in Table 1. The naïve Bayesian classifier has the best overall performance compared with other algorithms, since it has the highest F score.

Finally, the Bayesian classifier learned from the labeled data is applied to the entire data set. As mentioned in Section 5, information about totally 25,817 users was collected. It is nearly impossible for us to label all the data. Instead I only manually check

Table 1. Classification Evaluation

Classifier	Precision	Recall	F-measure
Decision Tree	0.667	0.333	0.444
Neural Networks	1	0.417	0.588
Support Vector Machines	1	0.25	0.4
Naïve Bayesian	0.917	0.917	0.917

the users who are classified as spam by the Bayesian classifier. 392 users are classified as spam by the detection system. I check the spam data by manually reading their tweets and checking their friends and followers. The results show that 348 users are real spam accounts and 44 users are false alarms. This means that the precision of the spam detection system is $89\% = 348/392$.

8 Conclusions

In this paper, I study the spam behaviors in a popular online social networking site, Twitter. To formalize the problem, a directed social graph model is proposed. The "follower" and "friend" relationships are defined in this paper. Based on the spam policy of Twitter, novel content-based and graph-based features are proposed to facilitate spam detection. Traditional classification algorithms are applied to detect suspicious behaviors of spam accounts. A Web crawler using Twitter API methods is also developed to collect real data set from public available information on Twitter. Finally, I analyze the data set and evaluate the performance of the detection system.

The results show that among the graph-based features, the proposed reputation feature has the best performance of detecting abnormal behaviors. No many spam accounts follow large amount of users as we expected. Also some spammers have many followers.

For the content-based features, most spam accounts have multiple duplicate tweets. This is an important feature to detect spam. However, not all spam account post multiple duplicate tweets and some legitimate users also post duplicate tweets. In this way we can not only rely on this feature. The results also show that almost all spam tweets contain links and reply sign "@".

Finally, several popular classification algorithms are studied and evaluated. The results show that the Bayesian classifier has a better overall performance with the highest F score. The learned classifier is applied to large amount of data and achieve a 89% precision.

References

1. Opera: State of the mobile web (2009), http://www.opera.com/smw/2009/12/
2. Pear Analytics: Twitter study (2009),
   http://www.pearanalytics.com/wp-content/uploads/2009/08/
   Twitter-Study-August-2009.pdf
3. CNET: 4chan may be behind attack on twitter (2009),
   http://news.cnet.com/8301-13515_3-10279618-26.html
4. Twitter: Restoring accidentally suspended accounts (2009),
   http://status.twitter.com/post/136164828/restoring-
   accidentally-suspended-accounts
5. Sahami, M., Dumais, S., Heckerman, D., Horvitz, E.: A bayesian approach to filtering junk e-mail. In: AAAI Workshop on Learning for Text Categorization (1998)
6. Gyöngyi, Z., Garcia-Molina, H., Pedersen, J.: Combating web spam with trustrank. In: VLDB 2004: Proceedings of the Thirtieth International Conference on Very Large Data Bases, VLDB Endowment, pp. 576–587 (2004)

7. Gyongyi, Z., Berkhin, P., Garcia-Molina, H., Pedersen, J.: Link spam detection based on mass estimation. In: VLDB 2006: Proceedings of the 32nd International Conference on Very Large Data Bases, VLDB Endowment, pp. 439–450 (2006)
8. Zhou, D., Burges, C.J.C., Tao, T.: Transductive link spam detection. In: AIRWeb 2007: Proceedings of the 3rd International Workshop on Adversarial Information Retrieval on the Web, pp. 21–28. ACM, New York (2007)
9. Castillo, C., Donato, D., Gionis, A., Murdock, V., Silvestri, F.: Know your neighbors: web spam detection using the web topology. In: SIGIR 2007: Proceedings of the 30th Annual International ACM SIGIR Conference on Research and Development in Information Retrieval, pp. 423–430. ACM, New York (2007)
10. Geng, G.G., Li, Q., Zhang, X.: Link based small sample learning for web spam detection. In: WWW 2009: Proceedings of the 18th International Conference on World Wide Web, pp. 1185–1186. ACM, New York (2009)
11. Wu, Y.-S., Bagchi, S., Singh, N., Wita, R.: Spam detection in voice-over-ip calls through semi-supervised clustering. In: DSN 2009: Proceedings of the 2009 Dependable Systems Networks, pp. 307–316 (2009)
12. Benevenuto, F., Rodrigues, T., Almeida, V., Almeida, J., Gonçalves, M.: Detecting spammers and content promoters in online video social networks. In: SIGIR 2009: Proceedings of the 32nd International ACM SIGIR Conference on Research and Development in Information Retrieval, pp. 620–627. ACM, New York (2009)
13. Wang, A.H.: Detecting Spam Bots in Online Social Networking Websites: A Machine Learning Approach. In: Foresti, S., Jajodia, S. (eds.) Data and Applications Security and Privacy XXIV. LNCS, vol. 6166, pp. 335–342. Springer, Heidelberg (2010)
14. Krishnamurthy, B., Gill, P., Arlitt, M.: A few chirps about twitter. In: WOSP 2008: Proceedings of the First Workshop on Online Social Networks, pp. 19–24. ACM, New York (2008)
15. Nooy, W.d., Mrvar, A., Batagelj, V.: Exploratory Social Network Analysis with Pajek. Cambridge University Press, New York (2004)
16. Twitter: The twitter rules (2009),
    http://help.twitter.com/forums/26257/entries/18311
17. Levenshtein, V.I.: Binary codes capable of correcting deletions, insertions and reversals. Soviet Physics Doklady 10, 707–710 (1966)
18. Rish, I.: An empirical study of the naive bayes classifier. In: IJCAI Workshop on Empirical Methods in AI (2005)

Part V

Signal Processing and Multimedia Applications

Deformable Multi-object Tracking Using Full Pixel Matching of Image

Hisato Aota, Kazuhiro Ota, Yuichi Yaguchi, and Ryuichi Oka

Department of Computer and Information Systems, University of Aizu
Tsuruga, Aizu-Wakamatsu, Japan
aoyan0510@gmail.com, {m5131125,d8101109,oka}@u-aizu.ac.jp

Abstract. We propose a novel method for the segmentation of deformable objects and the extraction of motion features for tracking objects in video data. The method adopts an algorithm called two-dimensional continuous dynamic programming (2DCDP) for extracting pixel-wise trajectories. A clustering algorithm is applied to a set of pixel trajectories to determine a shape of deformable objects each of which corresponds to a trajectory cluster. We conduct experiments to compare our method with conventional methods such as KLT tracker and SIFT. The experiment shows that our method is more powerful than the conventional methods.

1 Introduction

Tracking and segmentation of moving objects in video are very important for many tasks, such as video surveillance and event inference. Humans are the principal actors in daily activities, or locomotion (e.g., walking, running and standing), and so human motion is a key class within the field of computer vision. Many approaches for object tracking and segmentation have been proposed. These differ from each other primarily in the way they approach the problem. Approaches depend on such aspects as the target objects, context and environment in which tracking is performed and the end use for which tracking information is being sought. Yilmaz[1] declared object tracking as the problem of estimating the trajectories of objects that are moving continuously in an image sequence from initial frame to end frame. In addition, the estimation must maintain a consistent division of objects in the continuous image sequence with segmentation. It must be also able to provide object information such as area, orientation or shape. In previous methods, continuous trajectories can only be generated by detecting objects, which makes it hard to track objects from data. The difficulty of this problem is the difficulty of fixing units of trajectories in time-sequential images. The problem becomes even more difficult when the movement trajectories are extracted from the object area with inadequate region detection. Much of the previous research concentrated on extracting objects from background areas. We felt that an alternative method based on pixel tracking would not be as restricted as the previous methods.

In our laboratory, we developed a method named two-dimensional continuous dynamic programming (2DCDP), which can define full pixel correspondences between two images. By using this approach, it became possible to extract trajectories of all the

M.S. Obaidat, G.A. Tsihrintzis, and J. Filipe (Eds.): ICETE 2010, CCIS 222, pp. 337–349, 2012.
© Springer-Verlag Berlin Heidelberg 2012

pixels in an initial frame in time-sequential images. Next, to extract effective trajectory groups from these, we used two strategies. The first is to remove the trajectories of background pixels, and the second is to cluster the trajectories that are not removed and to group similar trajectories. The goal of our work is to prove that our proposed method can track and segment moving objects without object detection or recognition, and without pre-knowledge of the state of an object, its motion or environmental factors such as people walking nonlinearly or complex human motions. To prove the method's benefits, we demonstrate an effective full-pixel matching method and connect its outputs. Experimental results indicate that it is possible to extract pixel trajectories of objects and segment them by clustering trajectories.

2   Related Work

Many methods for object tracking have been proposed. Examples include tracking methods with pre-knowledge of an object's state, using Haar-like features[2], HOG features or mean-shift colour features using a statistical classifier (boosting) detector[3] [4][5]. In addition, Mikami[6] proposed a memory-based particle filter(M-PF), which can visually track moving objects that have complex dynamics. It provided robustness against abrupt head movements and recovered quickly from tracking failure caused by occlusions. Yamashita's[7] proposed tracking method with a soft decision feature (EHOG) and online real boosting improved tracking performance in scenes with human poses and posture changes.

Deterministic methods for point correspondence using object tracking based on feature points define a cost of associating each object in frame $t - 1$ to a single object in frame t by using a set of motion constraints. Rabaud[8] developed a highly parallelized version of the KLT tracker[9] that combined graph cuts and RANSAC clustering and was able to count objects in crowds. Sugimura[10] proposed a human tracking method with trajectory-based clustering with a gait feature by KLT corresponding points and Delaunay triangulation. Tsuduki[11][12] used mean-shift searching to track a point based on the information obtained by a SIFT [13], and obtained a better tracking performance than KLT because a SIFT feature is invariant to changes caused by rotation, scaling, and illumination.

3   System Overview

In this section, we describe each system for this proposed method. First, 2DCDP extracts full pixel corresponding points between frame of t and $t + 1$. Then connecting corresponding points with outputs of all frames by 2DCDP, it generate full pixel trajectories. Then thresholding trajectories, it divides trajectories into two groups which is moving objects trajectories and background trajectories. Finally, divided trajectories are extracted and its of moving objects are extracted by incremental clustering(Figure1).

3.1   2DCDP Algorithm

2DCDP[14] is an extension of CDP[15] to 2D correlation, and is an effective algorithm for full-pixel matching (Figure 3). The pixel coordinates of the input image S and reference image R are defined by:

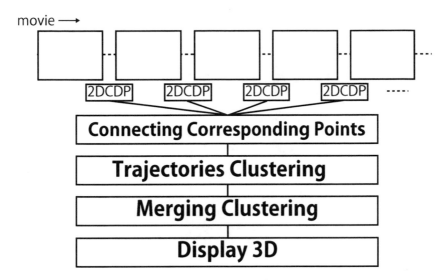

Fig. 1. Proposed Work Flow

$$S \triangleq \{(i,j)|1 \le i \le I, 1 \le j \le J\} \tag{1}$$

$$R \triangleq \{(m,n)|1 \le m \le M, 1 \le n \le N\} \tag{2}$$

The pixel value at location (i,j) of the input image S_p is $S_p(i,j) = \{r,g,b\}$, and the pixel value at location (m,n) of the reference image R_p is $R_p(m,n) = \{r,g,b\}$, where r, g, and b are normalized red, green, and blue values respectively, and $(0 \le \{r,g,b\} \le 1)$. We define the mapping $R \to S$, $(m,n) \in R$ and $(\xi(m,n),\eta(m,n)) \in S$ by $(m,n) \implies (\xi(m,n),\eta(m,n))$, set the end location for pixel matching as $\hat{i} = \xi(M,N)$, $\hat{j} = \eta(M,N)$ and the point $(\hat{i},\hat{j})$ as a nomination of the spotting point that is determined at the $M + N - 1$th iteration of the proposed algorithm. Next, we set the local distance $d(i,j,m,n)$ as the difference value between $S_p(i,j)$ and $R_p(m,n)$, and set $w(i,j,m,n)$ as the weighted value of each local calculation. In this implementation, the local distance is defined as $d(i,j,m,n) = (S_p(i,j) - R_p(m,n))^2$, and weights are set to 1 for all paths (Figure 5). The accumulated local minimum $D(i,j,m,n)$ is used to evaluate the decision sequence, and is defined as:

$$D(\hat{i},\hat{j},m,n) =$$
$$\frac{1}{W} \min_{\xi,\eta} \{\sum_{m=1}^{M} \sum_{n=1}^{N} w(\xi(m,n),\eta(m,n),m,n)$$
$$d(\xi(m,n),\eta(m,n),m,n)\} \tag{3}$$

Then $\xi^*(m,n)$ and $\eta^*(m,n)$ are used to represent the optimal solutions in $\xi(m,n)$ and $\eta(m,n)$ respectively, where W is the optimal accumulated weight $W = \sum_{m,n} w(\xi^*(m,n),\eta^*(m,n),m,n)$. To ensure continuity and monotonicity, $K(m,n) = \{\xi(m-1,n),\eta(m-1,n)\}$ and $L(m,n) = \{\xi(m,n-1),\eta(m,n-1)\}$ are used to define the sets of points that are movable in the i and j directions in the input image, taken from the

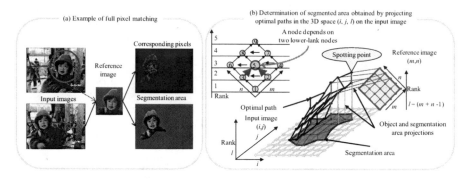

Fig. 2. Full pixel matching overview. (a) An example of full pixel matching; (b) Optimal paths are able to explain a 3D space (i, j, l) in the input image. l is the rank used in the expression $l = m + n - 1$.

movements in the m and n directions in the reference image. The following equation defines the relationship between two corresponding pixels $(m - 1, n - 1)$ and (m, n) (see Figure 4):

$$(\xi(m - 1, n - 1), \eta(m - 1, n - 1)) \in$$
$$K(m, n) \otimes L(m - 1, n) \cap L(m, n) \otimes K(m, n - 1) \qquad (4)$$

Here, the operator $\otimes$ represents the connection between a set of points on the left and a set of points on the right. To calculate the accumulated local distance, each accumulated local minimum $D(i, j, m, n)$ is derived from two previous accumulated local minima $D(i', j', m-1, n)$ and $D(i'', j'', m, n-1)$. In this way, we define the rank $l = m+n-1$, as shown in Figure 2 (b), to calculate the accumulated local minimum smoothly. Note that, for the accumulation and back-tracking, 2DCDP selects two local paths to check the connection of the four points (m, n), $(m - 1, n)$, $(m, n - 1)$, and $(m - 1, n - 1)$ that form a quadrangle (Figure 4).

3.2   Connecting Corresponding Points

To extract the trajectories of the pixels in the first frame, we showed that frame (i_k, j_k) at time t and frame (m_k, n_k) at time $t + 1$ are the points that correspond by 2DCDP. Therefore, the correspondence points in the following frame are derived for all the pixels in the first frame, and the following frame is processed similarly, the trajectory of the first-frame pixels in the time sequence of images can be determined. However, if both (i_a, j_a) and (i_b, j_b) at time t correspond to (m_c, n_c) at time $t + 1$, they are connected. As a result, the number of trajectories decreases.(Figure7)

3.3   Filtering Trajectories for Clustering

In order to erase stationary trajectories, we calculate spatial moving length for each trajectory. The length is determined by the parameter mxy which is defined by $mxy = \max\left(\max_i x_i - \min_i x_i, \max_i y_i - \min_i y_i\right)$, where a trajectory is represented

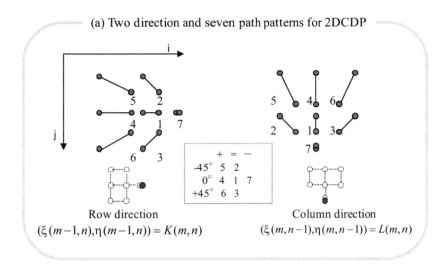

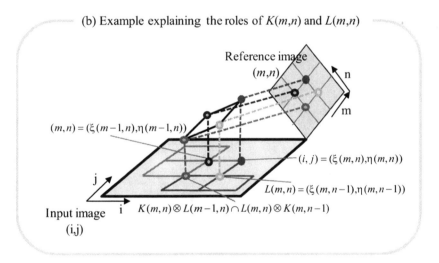

Fig. 3. Two directions and seven paths for selecting optimal path to accumulate value

Fig. 4. One case (linear matching) among the possible cases for optimal matching of local images, which include many different cases of nonlinear optimal matching of local areas

by a location sequence, $(x_1, y_1), (x_2, y_2), ..., (x_p, y_p)$. We introduce a threshold value T. The trajectory with a larger length T is erased for clustering. The parameter T is determined by a heuristic method to each time-sequential image.

3.4 Trajectory Clustering

Incremental clustering is based on the basic sequential algorithm scheme [16]. It finds and determines trajectories that have smaller distances than the threshold value

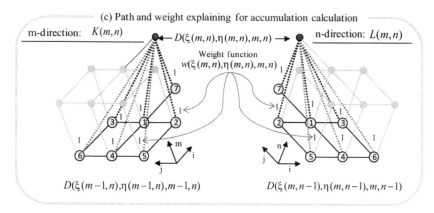

Fig. 5. Seven-path map and weight. All weights w are set to 1 in implementation, but this can be changed.

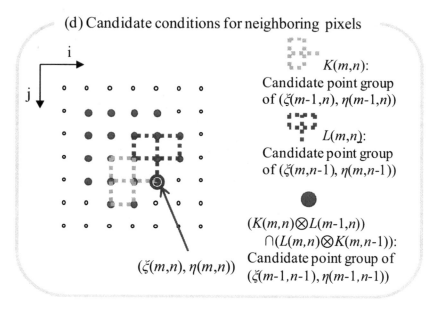

Fig. 6. Each i and j direction can connect seven candidate pixels as (a) and (c). 2DCDP selects the node that has a minimal accumulation value from among these paths, but a node has depending on only two lower-rank nodes.

between their trajectories and the cluster-center trajectory. Then, it calculates the object-centred trajectory of each cluster. These clusters include only trajectories that match the threshold.

(1) The first cluster includes the first trajectory in the threshold ranges.

(2) The Euclidean distance between the cluster-center trajectory and the newly found trajectory is calculated. Using Euclid norm the distance between trajectories,

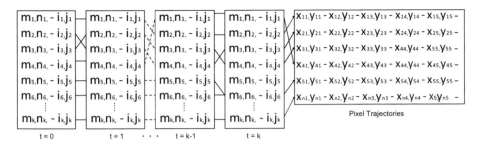

Fig. 7. Connecting corresponding points

$m = 1$
$C_m = \{x_1\}$
For $i = 2 to N$
  - **IF**$(d(x_i, C_k) \geq \Theta)$**AND**$(m \leq q) then$
    $m = m + 1$
    $C_m = \{x_i\}$
  -**Else**
    $C_k = C_k \cup \{x_i\}$
    update mean of C_k.
  -**End** $\{IF\}$
-**End**$\{For\}$

Fig. 8. Algorithm for Incremental Clustering

$C(i) = (c_i x_1, c_i y_1), (c_i x_2, c_i y_2) \dots (c_i x_k, c_i y_k)$ and $C(j) = (c_j x_1, c_j y_1), (c_j x_j, c_2 y_2)$
$\dots (c_j x_k, c_j y_k)$, is defined by:

$$d(i, j) = ||C(i) - C(j)|| \tag{5}$$

(3) A new cluster is created if a newly found trajectory is not within a radius of the centered trajectory within which clusters were created before. Otherwise, the newly found trajectory is included in the nearest cluster.

(4) Whenever a trajectory is included in a cluster, the cluster-center trajectory is re-calculated as an average of members' trajectories. This incrementally increases the size of the cluster. The algorithm repeats (1)-(4), and ends when the last trajectory is processed.(Figure7, 9).

3.5 Merging Clusters

A cluster, may be separated into two or more clusters during the distance calculation of incremental clustering, and so the clusters are merged in post-processing. If the calculated distance of the average trajectory of two clusters stays constant or decreases, the two clusters are considered to form one. k is the frame number. Using Euclid norm the distance between $cluster1$ and $cluster2$ average trajectories, describes $Center(i) = (c_i x_1, c_i y_1), (c_i x_2, c_i y_2) \dots (c_i x_k, c_i y_k)$ and $Center(j) = (c_j x_1, c_j y_1), (c_j x_j, c_2 y_2)$
$\dots (c_j x_k, c_j y_k)$, is defined by:

$$d(i, j) = ||Center(i) - Center(j)|| \tag{6}$$

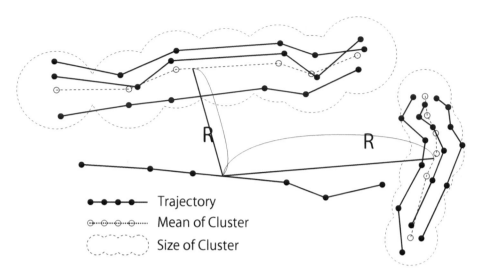

Fig. 9. Incremental Clustering

4 Experiments

4.1 Experiment Specification

Machine Environment. The computer used for the experiments was a Dell Precision (CPU.Xeon 3.16 GHz Dual CPU processors; memory, 64 GB DDRAM; operating system, CentOS and a 300 GB HDD). The video camera was a Cannon IXY DIGITAL 920 IS.

Data Sets. Our research was tested on four different datasets that we prepared. The video frame rate was 10 fps. Because of the computer memory limitation, images used in the experiments were resized to low resolution using Lanczos filter. The datasets were as follows.

- Three people walking in different directions. Frame count is 107 and he image size is 200*150. T is 50.
- Two people walks difference nonlinearly by each direction . Frame number is 183. Image size is 200×150. T is 30.
- Arms moving simultaneously. Frame count is 98, image size is 200×150. T is 40.
- Roller coaster with water splash. Frame count is 17. Image size is 288×192. T is 20.

4.2 Results

Below are illustrations of the conditioned trajectories for times t_0 to t_n for each data set(Figure. 10–13). Note that, the amplitude of the z-axis has been changed for convenience. Each different color indicates a different object corresponding to a cluster.

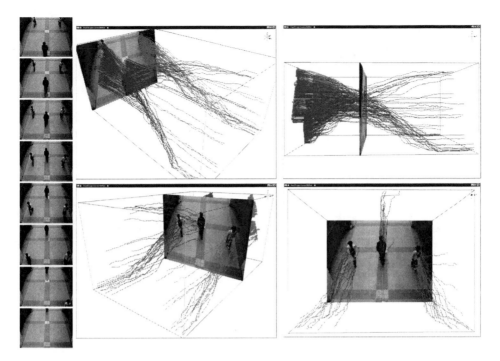

Fig. 10. Result of Experiment 1. Three persons are well separated.

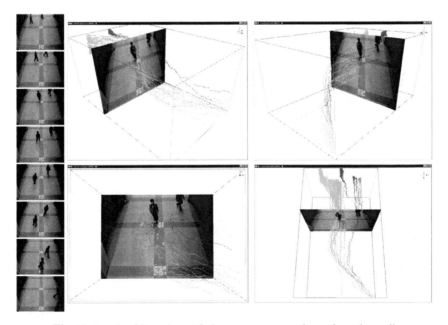

Fig. 11. Result of Experiment 2. It can extract complex trajectories well.

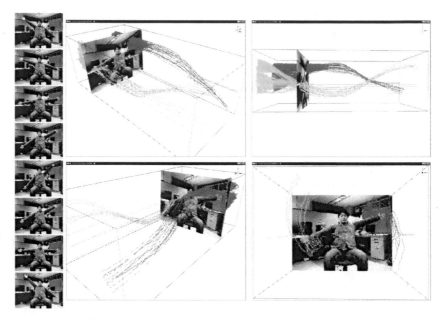

Fig. 12. Result of Experiment 3. Two arms are separated.

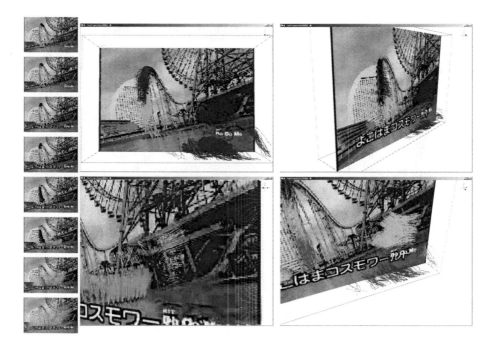

Fig. 13. Result of Experiment 4. Roller coaster, water splash and water surface are well separated.

4.3   Comparison with KLT Tracker and SIFT Tracker

Figure(14) shows the corresponding points and trajectories in 3D space in which z-axis represents time. The corresponding points, which are generated by KLT and SIFT, appear discontinuously and the number of them less than that of 2DCDP, for those reasons, trajectories of those corresponding points cannot be generated by adapting connecting system. In this comparison, we used Stan Birchfield's KLT[17] and Rob Hess's SIFT[18] implementations.

4.4   Discussion

In these experiments, density trajectories of simple or complex movements could be acquired even with low-resolution time-sequential images. The proposed method is effective even for different movements by two or more objects. Moreover, even if the movement changed during the sequence, trajectories could still be extracted. Even when

KLT

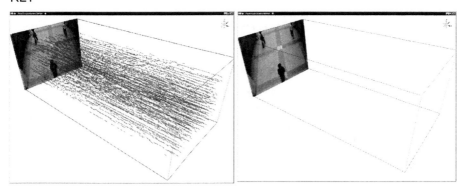

SIFT

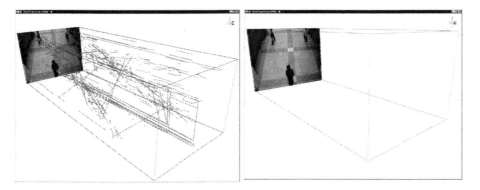

Fig. 14. Comparing with KLT Tracker and SIFT. Corresponding points of KLT and SIFT are plotted to the left figure, and trajectories of those coresponding points are plotted to the right figure by adapting connecting system.

objects have varying texture and edges such that features cannot be detected, the proposed method can still acquire trajectories for corresponding points. We also showed that the proposed method is more effective than methods based of feature points such as KLT or SIFT, because 2DCDP can identify many more accurate corresponding points than KLT Tracker or SIFT Flow(Figure14). Furthermore, our method also finds trajectories even for nonlinear, complex, and detailed movement such as wave splashes and the surface of the water.(Figure13).

5   Conclusions

We have created a novel framework for extracting motion features from time-sequential images in a few steps. We also developed an optimal full-pixel matching method called two-dimensional continuous dynamic programming (2DCDP) that achieved image recognition that supports segmentation for free and full pixel matching. We applied 2DCDP to object tracking and utilized data for corresponding points provided by 2DCDP as input for extracting pixel trajectories and could compute density trajectories of moving objects. We were able to extract trajectories and segment objects from various type of motion with low resolution over many frames. Finally, we validated advantages of the proposed method (2DCDP + trajectory Clustering).

6   Future Work

The present approach has not considered occlusion and decreasing trajectories. Therefore, when objects appear in succession on the screen, the trajectory of a rear object is integrated into that of a front object. Because only a few pixels represent the object trajectories are integrated over time, and so the number of trajectories decreases. If the resolution of the time-sequential images increases so that the number of pixels forming the target object is increased, many trajectories can be calculated more accurately. Further, the time space is divided and clusters can re-form in each time space, and so the decrease in number of trajectories can be reduced if the clustering results are merged through the time axis. It is also necessary to remove outlier noise trajectories to improve the accuracy.

This method is applicable for background detection and subtraction from video captured by a moving camera. By analysing a vector field and extracting the majority 2DCDP vector, our method can divide background and foreground. It is able to apply a presumption of camera motion. The majority vector field is the background, which can be removed to target moving objects. Our experiments indicate that we can also consider applying the method to gesture recognition and to novel human interface such as lip reading and expression recognition.

Acknowledgements. I express my gratitude to members of the Image Processing Laboratory for their cooperation in experiments.

References

1. Yilmaz, A., Javed, O., Shah, M.: Object tracking: A survey. ACM Computing Surveys (CSUR) 38(4) (2006)
2. Viola, P.: Rapid object detection using a boosted cascade of simple features. In: Proc. of IEEE CVPR 2001, pp. 511–518 (2001)
3. Mochiki, R., Katto, J.: Human tracking by particle filter using haar-like feature. In: Proc. of the IEICE General Conference 2007, vol. 2, p. 121 (2007)
4. Nakagawa, H., Habe, H., Kidode, M.: Efficient prior acquisition of human existence by using past human trajectories and color of image. Technical report of IEICE. PRMU 108(484), 305–312 (2009)
5. Takeuchi, D., Ito, Y., Yamashita, A., Kaneko, T.: Multi-viewpoint person tracking based on face detection of arbitrary pose and mean-shift algorithm. ITE Technical Report 33(11), 69–72 (2009)
6. Dan, M., Kazuhiro, O., Junji, Y.: Memory-based particle filter for face pose tracking robust under complex dynamics. In: Proc. of IEEE CVPR 2009, pp. 999–1006 (2009)
7. Takayoshi, Y., Hironobu, F., Shihong, L., Masato, K.: Human tracking based on soft decision feature and online real boosting. In: Proc. of MIRU 2008, pp. 12–19 (2008)
8. Rabaud, V., Belongie, S.: Counting Crowded Moving Objects. In: Proc. of IEEE CVPR 2006, vol. 1, pp. 705–711 (2006)
9. Shi, J., Tomasi, C.: Good features to track. In: Proc. of IEEE Conference on CVPR 1994, pp. 593–600 (1994)
10. Sugimura, D., Kitani, K.M., Okabe, T., Sato, Y., Sugimoto, A.: Tracking people in crowds based on clustering feature trajectories using gait features and local appearances. In: Proc. of MIRU 2009, pp. 135–142 (2009)
11. Tsuduki, Y., Fujiyoshi, H., Kanade, T.: Mean shift-based point feature tracking using sift. IPSJ SIG Technical Reports 49(6), 101–108 (2007)
12. Yuji, T., Hironobu, F.: A method for visualizing pedestrian traffic flow using sift feature point tracking. In: Proc. of IEEE PSIVT 2009 (2009)
13. Lowe, D.G.: Distinctive image features from scale-invariant keypoints. Int. Journal of Computer Vision 60(2), 91–110 (2004)
14. Yaguchi, Y., Iseki, K., Oka, R.: Optimal Pixel Matching between Images. In: Wada, T., Huang, F., Lin, S. (eds.) PSIVT 2009. LNCS, vol. 5414, pp. 597–610. Springer, Heidelberg (2009)
15. Oka, R.: Spotting method for classification of real world data. The Computer Journal 41(8), 559–565 (1998)
16. Gonzalez, R.C., Woods, R.E.: Digital Image Processing, 2nd edn. Prentice-Hall International (2001)
17. Stan, B.: KLT: an implementation of the kanade lucas tomasi feature tracker, http://www.ces.clemson.edu/stb/klt/index.html
18. Hess, R.: Sift feature detector, http://web.engr.oregonstate.edu/~hess/

A Multi-sensor System for Monitoring the Performance of Elite Swimmers

Tanya Le Sage, Axel Bindel, Paul Conway, Laura Justham, Sian Slawson,
James Webster, and Andrew West

Wolfson School of Mechanical and Manufacturing Engineering, Loughborough University
LE11 3TU, Loughborough, U.K.
{T.Le-Sage,A.Bindel,P.P.Conway,L.Justham,S.E.Slawson,
J.M.F.Webster,A.A.West}@lboro.ac.uk

Abstract. A comprehensive system is required to monitor numerous variables of a swimmer's performance. Current methods of analysis do not offer solutions which record and analyse multiple performance parameters simultaneously. The research presented in this paper provides an overview of an integrated system which has been developed to monitor several components of a swimmer's start, free swimming and turn concurrently. The integrated system is comprised of a wearable wireless sensor, vision components, force platform, pressure pad, LED markers and audio communication.

Keywords: Swimming, Components, Integrated system, Signal processing.

1 Introduction

An integrated system is required to monitor multiple components of a swimmer's performance simultaneously. Research up to date does not provide a solution for recording and analysing several parameters concurrently. Past studies do not focus on multi-modal data analysis, thus providing limited feedback to coaches with regards to a swimmer's performance.

Competitive swimming can be broken down into three sections: the start, free swimming and the turn. The start phase is defined as the distance to the 15m mark in the race, which coincides with the break start rope and is the maximum distance a swimmer can travel underwater, as per the FINA rules. Maglischo [1] stated that starts account for approximately 10% of the total time in swimming events of 50m length and for approximately 5% in those of 100m. Researchers have found that through consistent dive practice an elite swimmer can reduce their total race time by a minimum of 0.10s [1] [2]. At the elite level, this improvement could represent the time difference between a first and third place in a sprint event [3] [4].

Current analysis of free swimming does not occur in real-time and is often a time consuming process. The four competition strokes in swimming are front crawl, butterfly, backstroke and breaststroke [5]. Additionally, the four strokes can be combined to form an individual medley (IM). Front crawl and backstroke rely on a windmill action using the arms. Butterfly and breaststroke use symmetric arm movements instead. There are two types of turn used in swimming; the open turn and

M.S. Obaidat, G.A. Tsihrintzis, and J. Filipe (Eds.): ICETE 2010, CCIS 222, pp. 350–362, 2012.
© Springer-Verlag Berlin Heidelberg 2012

the tumble turn [1]. The open turn is used in butterfly and breaststroke and the tumble turn is used during front crawl and backstroke. In short-course events, turns comprise up to one-third of the total race time [6]. The longer the event, from 50 to 1500m, the more significant the turns become [7].

Research presented in this paper details the development of an integrated sensor system, which allowed presentation of meaningful information to coaches and their swimmers in a training environment. The users of the integrated system can be defined as the people, groups or companies who interact with the software and control it directly, and those who use the products (e.g. information, results) of the system [8]. In this example the users are subdivided into the coach, swimmer and biomechanist. The swimmer is the object being monitored and the coach and biomechanist provide feedback to the swimmer based on their performance. The functional requirements of the user were determined, through interviews with elite athletes and their coaches. The requirements can be seen in Fig. 1.

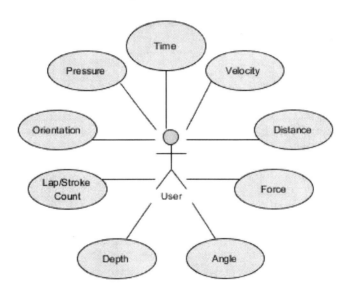

Fig. 1. Functional requirements of the user, for an integrated monitoring system

The user needs were broken down into nine different segments: *time, velocity, distance, force, angle, depth, count, orientation* and *pressure* measurements. The swimmers, coaches and biomechanists all identified time measurement as of primary importance. The users required time and distance measurements for the individual and cumulative laps swum by the swimmers. They also recognised the intrastroke (within one full stroke cycle) and interstroke (across numerous stroke cycles) time, velocity and distance measurements to be of primary importance. A count was required to identify the number of laps and strokes completed by each swimmer. The take-off angle and the angle upon entry into the water were considered of secondary importance. The take-off angle can be defined as the angle between a line from the hip to the toes and between the toes and horizontal plane at take off [9]. Maximum force and depth during the start phase were also identified as secondary requirements.

The contact pressure and foot orientation were deemed important factors affecting turn performance.

2 Related Work

The majority of methods used to analyse swimming technique are vision-based systems. Quintic is an example of vision-based software where the analyst uses a pre-recorded video file and then manually digitises key occurrences within the recording [10]. The disadvantage of this and other vision systems are the parallax errors introduced by the use of video cameras, inaccurate measurements due to light reflections on the water surface and the large amount of time it takes to process the data. Manual digitisation is a time consuming process and does not allow real-time feedback to the coaches or swimmers. The process provides limited quantitative data and requires operator expertise. There is inherent variability within the results due to the reliance of human judgment and expertise.

Force measurement platforms are an additional technology used for measuring swimmer performance. Force data can be integrated with video data during the block phase (time from the start trigger to leaving the block) of the dive to enable more complete analysis [11].

Accelerometer sensor devices have also been developed for use in a swimming environment. An example of this was presented by Davey [12], where a system was developed using a tri-axis accelerometer to monitor stroke technique. Ohgi used a similar system to measure wrist acceleration of swimmers [13]. Both systems used a data logging accelerometer system to capture the data, which meant that the data could not be viewed in real time. These existing systems focus on post processing that again increases the analysis time significantly and subsequently coaches are unable to offer immediate feedback to the swimmers based on these data. Neither case used a wireless sensor network (WSN) to allow data to be captured from multiple swimmers, nor an integrated system to allow full analysis of the stroke technique.

Research presented within this paper, carried out at Loughborough University, UK, was concerned with the development of a component based integrated system for monitoring elite athletes in the water. The main results of the initial feasibility study are presented in this paper. This study considered a variety of different sensing and measurement devices and an integrated system was constructed to capture the data. The integrated system comprised of a WSN, real time audio communications to the swimmer, a vision analysis system using real-time image processing, an underwater camera and a force measurement platform. The WSN was chosen due to its ability to transmit and feedback data in real-time. It also allowed multiple swimmers performances to be analysed simultaneously. Furthermore it was possible to synchronize the network with other data capture methods used within the integrated system. The high-speed and underwater cameras were used because of their ability to provide the coach with visual information with regards to the athletes' performance. This made analysing the data from the accelerometer and the force platform much simpler. The audio communications were chosen because they allowed the coach to feedback information to the swimmer in real-time, based on the data gathered.

The WSN was designed with a star topology. A number of nodes communicated with a poolside personal computer (PC) via an "Access Point" that collated the wireless data transmissions from the wireless nodes and had a hardwired connection to the PC. A trigger function was implemented onto the sensor node to allow synchronised processing of data obtained from all components. A Butterworth filter and signal processing algorithms to extract the relevant swimming features were embedded onto the node, which allowed the coach to extract useful data with regards to each individual swimmer's performance in real time [14].

3 Methodology

The force measurement system was used to augment the information available from a high speed camera and the WSN during the start process. The force measurement system was comprised of a start platform instrumented with four Kistler force transducers (9317B) sampling at 100Hz [15]. The force measurement platform was used to ascertain the following parameters:

- Horizontal force
- Vertical force
- Time: to first movement, to back foot leaving, to front foot leaving, overall block time
- Centre of pressure

A high-speed camera and a WSN were synchronised with the force measurement platform using a TTL trigger function. The function was implemented in the embedded programming of the node which sent an interrupt to the access point (AP) when the trigger was enabled. Sending a TTL signal to a port on the AP triggered the system. The embedded code initialised the trigger, starting the trigger on the rising edge of the signal. The integrated system can be seen in Fig. 2 and has been used to determine the characteristics of an accelerometer trace based on the data gathered from the high speed video camera and force plate.

The camera used was a Photron SA1 colour camera with a 1024x1024 resolution, sampling at 50 frames per second (fps). Automated vision processing was used to track wearable LED markers placed on body key body landmarks, for example, the hip. This was done via spatial thresholding algorithms, developed in Matlab. An underwater bullet CCTV camera sampling at 25 fps was also used. Vision data was used to supplement the data gathered from the WSN, allowing stroke recognition and real-time analysis of the accelerometer signal. The pressure pad used was an RSscan footscan USB plate, Gait Scientific. It measured 1m x 1m with a resolution of >100psi [16].

For many low-g (<2g) inertial sensing applications the signal-to-noise ratio is low and thus any un-modelled error in the physical parameters undermine the effectiveness of the intended application over time [17]. A common method to minimize the errors associated with the accelerometer signal is the use of filtering (see for example [18], [19]). For the current system a low-pass finite impulse response (FIR) filter was implemented to filter out frequencies greater than a pre-defined threshold while retaining the low frequency components [20]. Filtering also reduces the errors associated with integration of a signal, in this case integration of the accelerometer data in order to obtain velocity and double integration to obtain position. Edwards [21] demonstrated that seemingly small aliased content could cause appreciable errors in the integrated waveforms.

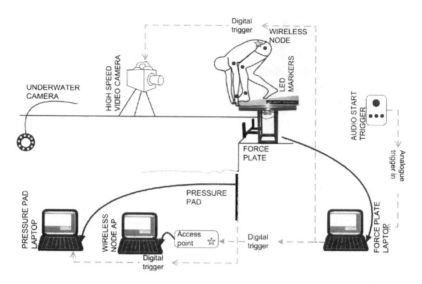

Fig. 2. Integrated system comprised of a wireless sensor node, LED markers, force plate, high speed video camera, underwater camera and a pressure pad

The raw accelerometer values were fed into a real-time Butterworth filter and signal processing equations, which were embedded onto the node. This enabled analysis to take place robustly, in real-time, so that the results could be sent directly from the node rather than sending raw data. This was preferable because the raw data file was large and filled the available bandwidth. A low pass Butterworth filter was chosen to smooth the data collected and to minimize the noise components of the signal. It was chosen over a Chebyshev filter due to its ability to be implemented in real time and embedded on the sensor node. Lap count identification was automatically determined by setting a low filter frequency on the Butterworth filter and using a "zero crossing" algorithm. Signal processing algorithms were developed to analyse filtered data, including a "zero crossing" algorithm to determine the stroke durations and stroke rates, which were identified to be the variables of most interest to the end users. Pulse analysis of the filtered data was also calculated and used to determine the rise and fall times of each stroke. Circular buffers were used to allow real-time implementation of the filter and signal processing algorithms.

A wireless audio communication module was attached to the swimmer and a UART interface to the host device was used to configure the module operation and then transfer data between the host and the communication end-point via the wireless interface. Once the devices were connected the coach used the microphone input to provide feedback to the swimmer (who wore earphones attached to the wireless module) on their performance throughout their training. The module transmitted wirelessly up to a depth of 10cm over a distance of more than 50m underwater.

A system breakdown can be seen in Table 1. In order to satisfy the user needs for the start phase a WSN, force platform, high speed camera, underwater camera and LED markers were employed. The WSN was used to ascertain the acceleration of the swimmer during the dive. It was also used to determine the angle of entry into the water. The force platform was incorporated to supplement this information, providing statistics surrounding the horizontal and vertical forces of the swimmer as well as the block time. The high speed camera and underwater camera were used to track the velocity and position of the swimmer. The LED markers were used to enhance this process, providing an automatic tracking system. During free swimming the wireless sensor depicted lap count, stroke count and stroke rates in real-time, using algorithms which were embedded onto the wireless sensor [14]. The high speed camera provided intrastroke and interstroke velocity and distance. The audio communication allowed the coach to provide feedback to the swimmer throughout the course of the training.

The WSN, underwater camera, pressure pad and LED markers were integrated to monitor the swimmer during the turn; the WSN. The WSN was used to give an estimate of the orientation of the swimmer. The underwater camera was used to track the velocity and position of the swimmer. The LED markers were also used to track the swimmer throughout the turn. The pressure pad determined the position, orientation and pressure of the swimmer's feet on the wall through the individual phases of the turn.

Table 1. Breakdown of the components incorporated in the start, freeswimming and turn

Starts	Free swimming	Turns
WSN	WSN	WSN
Force platform	High speed camera	Underwater camera
High speed camera	Audio communications	Pressure pad
Underwater camera		LED markers
LED markers		

4 Results

Initially the results are used to highlight the implementation of the synchronised system and data capture. The filtering technique used on the synchronised data is then considered. Finally determination and analysis of the stroke characteristics from the filtered data are reviewed.

The TTL trigger function embedded on the sensor node was used to capture data simultaneously from the force measurement platform, the high speed video camera and the sensor node. These data can be seen in Fig. 3. The high speed video was used to supplement the data gathered from the force platform and allowed determination of the key points that occurred during the dive. These key points were the time of hands, back foot and front foot leaving the force platform. The times on the video were correlated with those of the accelerometer data, identifying time to entry (block phase), the point where the stroke was initiated (glide phase) and the time at 15m (where the start officially ends). In addition, the WSN was used to consider elements such as lap count, stroke rate, stroke duration in free swimming and to distinguish the different phases of the turn.

Initially a low pass Butterworth filter was used to cancel the noise in the data and signal processing algorithms were used to ascertain the lap count of the swimmer. A comparison of the raw unfiltered data and the real-time embedded filtered data on 4 lengths of front crawl stroke can be seen in Fig. 4. The raw data was filtered to

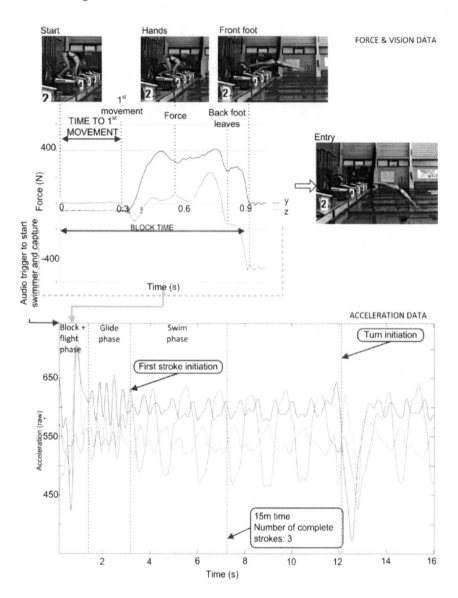

Fig. 3. Integrated system for starts. The components consist of a WSN, force platform, high speed camera, underwater camera and LED markers.

smooth the local maximas and minimas, which occurred as a result of the individual strokes swum by the swimmer. The largest peak in the data was identified as the swimmer's turn at the wall at the halfway point. By setting a threshold the filter and signal processing algorithms were used to pick out the lap count. For these data the four laps were identified.

Different filter parameters were required for the different swimming strokes. In order to retain the peaks in the breaststroke and butterfly data a higher cut off frequency was used. The signal processing technique used for one length of front crawl can be seen in Fig. 5. It was found that pre processed data could be analysed to establish timing information, stroke count, stroke durations, rise times and fall times.

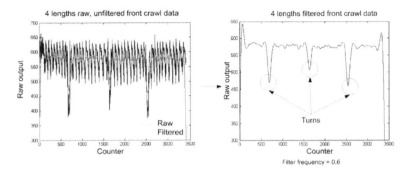

Fig. 4. Butterworth filter on four lengths of front crawl data

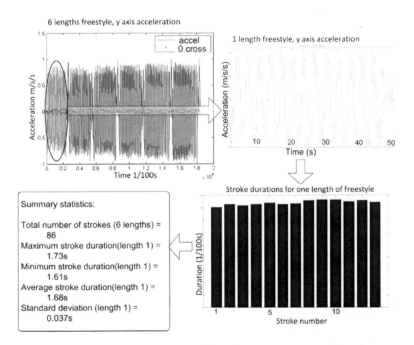

Fig. 5. Analysis of the front crawl stroke using video and accelerometer data

This analysis may then be collated to give an indication of the swimmers performance. Four 100m trials have been analysed to derive all of the discussed parameters, Fig. 6. Automated timing was found to be within 1 second of hand timing on average. Hand timing is undesirable since it is subject to human judgment and variability and cannot be readily scaled to support the monitoring of multiple swimmers in training sessions. Average stroke durations gave an idea of each swimmer's typical stroke and provided a measure to determine if they had changed their technique.

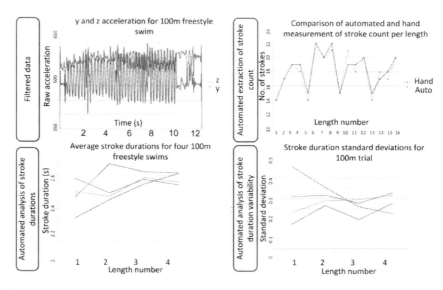

Fig. 6. Summary of free swimming signal processing using video and accelerometer data

The underwater video camera was used to chracterise phases of the turn with the accelerometer data. The x axes represented the forward motion, the y axis the roll of the swimmer laterally and the z axis the vertical movement of the swimmer. On the swimmer's approach to the wall the acceleration in the z axis remained fairly constant. When the swimmer initiated the turn the z axis rotated through 90 degrees, which meant that the x axis experienced the major gravity component and the z axis tended towards zero. When the swimmer turned onto their back the z component experienced a negative contribution from gravity. As the swimmer turned back onto their front the z acceleration returned to fluctuating about 1g. This process can be seen from the video and accelerometer data in Fig. 7.

Using automated vision analysis the LED marker, placed on the hip of the swimmer, was tracked during six turns and the distance from the wall (m) was compared to the depth of foot contact (m). The tracjectory of the swimmer's hip during these turns can be seen in Fig. 8. It has previously been stated that the ideal contact point of the feet on the wall should occur between 0.3m and 0.4m deep [1]. Data from the turns analysed suggests that the swimmer was typically contacting the wall deeper than is considered ideal. It can be seen from the variation of the trajectories that this set was completed by an amateur swimmer, who had little experiencing of tumble turning. Overlaying multiple profiles enables the coach to determine the consistency of a swimmer's turn.

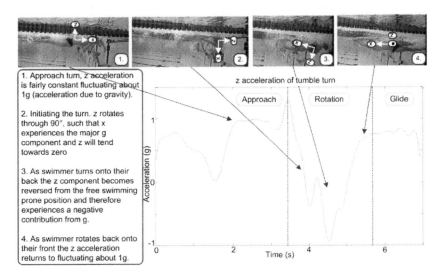

Fig. 7. Integrated system for turns

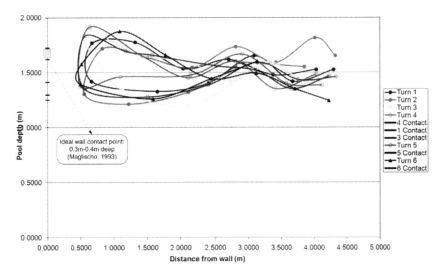

Fig. 8. Path of the hip during a turn, using LED markers to track the position

The pressure pad was used to collect data during five tumble turns. Information with regards to the pressure, contact time, distance of the first foot from the side edge of the pad (horizontal absolute distance) and distance of the top foot from the top edge of the pad (vertical absolute distance) were derived, see Fig. 9. The average contact time for the five turns was determined as 0.31s with a standard deviation of +/- 0.78s. The mean horizontal and vertical absolute distances were 242mm and 286mm respectively.

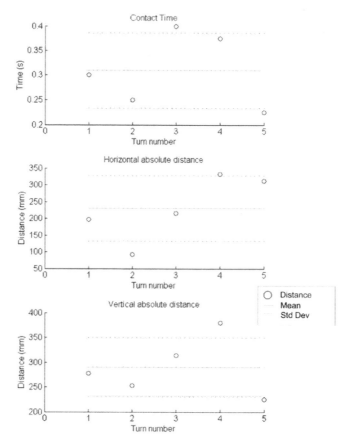

Fig. 9. Data collected by the pressure pad during four tumble turns

5   Conclusions and Future Work

A multimedia system and signal processing techniques for monitoring swimmer performance has been presented in this paper. It provides a significant advantage over current methods used because it allows results from multiple components to be integrated and analysed simultaneously in real-time. The signal processing techniques used on the accelerometer offer feedback to swimmers in real-time and parameters are derived automatically on the sensor node.

An inertial navigation system (INS) will be used in which measurements from embedded accelerometers and gyroscopes will be used to track the position and orientation of a swimmer relative to a known starting point, orientation and velocity. An INS comprising of a tri-axis accelerometer and a tri-axis gyroscope, measuring angular velocity and linear acceleration respectively, will be attached as a strapdown system to a swimmer. By processing signals from these devices it is possible to track the position and orientation of a device [22]. The output of the gyroscope provides the attitude of the swimmer. Strapdown navigation equations will be used to combine the accelerometer and gyroscope data, compensating for the effect of gravity on the system. The output will then be integrated twice (once in order to obtain velocity, and again in order to obtain position).

The results from the IMU will then be fed into an extended Kalman filter. The Kalman filter combines noisy sensor outputs to estimate the state of a system with uncertain dynamics [23]. The noisy sensors in this research will be INS accelerometers and gyroscopes. The system state includes position, velocity and attitude rate of the swimmer. It also includes the accelerometer and gyroscope biases and scale factors. The uncertain dynamics includes unpredictable disturbances of the swimmer, for example, waves in the water. A GPS receiver may be used to calibrate the system initially (before the swimmer enters the building), increasing the accuracy of the initial error predictions.

The integrated system will be presented in a graphical user interface (GUI) thus allowing the coaches and swimmers to visualise the results with ease, allowing unique insight into the skill and performance capabilities of elite swimmers. Further testing is required using the pressure pad and simultaneously tracking of the position of the swimmer using the LED markers, because at present these two components of the system have not been linked together.

References

1. Maglischo, E.W.: Swimming fastest. Human Kinetics (2003)
2. Blanksby, B., Nicholson, L., Elliott, B.: Biomechanical analysis of the grab, track and handle swimming starts: an intervention study. Sports Biomechanics 1 (2002)
3. Cossor, J.M., Blanksby, B.A., Elliott, B.C.: The influence of plyometric training on the freestyle tumble turn. Journal of Science and Medicine in Sport 2, 106–116 (1999)
4. Breed, R., McElroy, G.: A biomechanical comparison of the grab, swing and track starts in swimming, vol. 39, pp. 277–293 (2000)
5. Maglischo, E.W.: Swimming Even Faster. Mayfield Publishing Company (1993)
6. Prins, J., Patz, A.: The influence of tuck index, depth of foot-plant, and wall contact time on the velocity of push-off in the freestyle flip turn. In: Xth International Symposium on Biomechanics and Medicine in Swimming (2006)
7. Tourny-Chollet, C., Chollet, D., Hogie, S., Papparodopoulos, C.: Kinematic analysis of butterfly turns of international and national swimmers. Journal of Sports Sciences 20, 383 (2002)
8. Sharp, H., Finkelstein, A., Galal, G.: Stakeholder identification in the requirements engineering process. In: Proceedings of Tenth International Workshop on Database and Expert Systems Applications, DEXA 1999, Florence, Italy, pp. 387–391 (1999)
9. Galbraith, H., Scurr, J., Hencken, C., Wood, L., Graham-Smith, P.: Biomechanical comparison of the track start and the modified one-handed track start in competitive swimming: an intervention study. Journal of Applied Biomechanics 24, 307–315 (2008)
10. Quintic Consultancy Ltd
11. Slawson, S.: A novel monitoring system for training of elite swimmers. Loughborough (2010)
12. Davey, N.P.: An accelerometer-based system for elite athlete swimming performance analysis. In: Proceedings of SPIE, Sydney, Australia, pp. 409–415 (2005)

13. Ohgi, Y.: Microcomputer-based acceleration sensor device for sports biomechanics -stroke evaluation by using swimmer's wrist acceleration. In: Proceedings of IEEE Sensors 2002, vol. 1, pp. 699–704 (2002)

14. Le Sage, T., Bindel, A., Conway, P., Justham, L., Slawson, S., West, A.: Development of a real time system for monitoring of swimming performance. Procedia Engineering 2, 2707–2712 (2010)

15. Kistler - sensors for pressure, force, acceleration and torque, http://www.kistler.com (accessed November 10, 2010)

16. RSscan International, http://www.rsscan.com (accessed November 21, 2010)

17. Ang, W., Khoo, S., Khosla, P., Riviere, C.: Physical model of a MEMS accelerometer for low-g motion tracking applications. In: Proceedings of IEEE International Conference on Robotics and Automation, ICRA 2004, vol. 2, pp. 1345–1351 (2004)

18. Koukoulas, T., Young, R.C., Chatwin, C.R.: Quantised phase filters with binary low and high pass amplitude response: the effect of quantisation for scale and rotation input distortions. Optics and Lasers in Engineering 43, 963–976 (2005)

19. Haid, M., Breitenbach, J.: Low cost inertial orientation tracking with Kalman filter. Applied Mathematics and Computation 153, 567–575 (2004)

20. Kuo, S.M., Lee, B.H.: Real-Time Digital Signal Processing,: Implementations, Application and Experiments with the TMS320C55X. Wiley (2001)

21. Edwards, T.S.: Effects of aliasing on numerical integration. Mechanical Systems and Signal Processing 21, 165–176 (2007)

22. Woodman, O.J., Woodman, C.O.J., Woodman, O.J.: An introduction to inertial navigation (2007)

23. Grewal, M.S., Andrews, A.P.: Kalman Filtering: Theory and Practice Using MATLAB. Wiley Interscience (2001)

Maximum a Posteriori Decoding of Arithmetic Codes in Joint Source-Channel Coding

Trevor Spiteri and Victor Buttigieg

University of Malta, Msida, MSD 2080, Malta
{trevor.spiteri,victor.buttigieg}@um.edu.mt
http://www.um.edu.mt/

Abstract. Arithmetic codes are being increasingly used in the entropy coding stage in many multimedia transmission applications. Combining channel coding with arithmetic coding can give implementation and performance advantages compared to separate source and channel coding. In this work, novel improvements are introduced into a technique by Grangetto et al. that uses maximum a posteriori (MAP) estimation for decoding joint source-channel coding using arithmetic codes. The arithmetic decoder is modified for quicker symbol decoding and error detection by the introduction of a look-ahead technique, and the calculation of the MAP metric is modified for faster error detection. These modifications also result in improved performance compared to the original scheme. Experimental results show an improvement of up to 0.4 dB when using soft-decision decoding and 0.6 dB when using hard-decision decoding.

Keywords: Arithmetic coding, Joint source-channel coding, Maximum a posteriori decoding.

1 Introduction

A typical digital communication system includes source coding to remove unwanted redundancy in order to make efficient use of the transmission channel, and channel coding to introduce redundancy in a controlled manner in order to overcome the effects of noise and interference in the transmission of the data, thus increasing the reliability of the system.

Multimedia applications have high data rates so that compression is a very important part of multimedia systems. Multimedia compression methods usually include several stages; lossy compression and quantization techniques are used to remove non-essential features from the source data, then the quantized data is processed by an entropy encoder. Arithmetic coding [1] is a popular form of entropy coding. It represents data more compactly than Huffman coding [2], and adapts better to adaptive data models. The use of arithmetic coding is recently increasing, partly owing to the expiration of key patents that somehow hampered earlier adoption.

Joint source-channel coding techniques are emerging as a good choice to transmit digital data over wireless channels. Shannon's source-channel separation theorem suggests that reliable data transmission can be accomplished by separate source and channel coding schemes [3]. Vembu et al. [4] point out shortcomings of the separation

M.S. Obaidat, G.A. Tsihrintzis, and J. Filipe (Eds.): ICETE 2010, CCIS 222, pp. 363–377, 2012.
© Springer-Verlag Berlin Heidelberg 2012

theorem when dealing with non-stationary probabilistic channels. The bandwidth limitations of the wireless channels, and the stringent demands of multimedia transmission
systems, are emphasizing the practical shortcomings of the separation theorem. In practical cases, the source encoder is not able to remove all the redundancy from the source.
Joint source-channel coding techniques can exploit this redundancy to improve the reliability of the transmitted data.

Joint schemes can also provide implementation advantages. For example, Boyd et
al. [5] proposed a joint source-channel coding technique using arithmetic codes, and
mentioned several advantages, including (a) saving on software, hardware, or computation time by having a single engine that performs both source and channel coding,
(b) the ability to control the amount of redundancy easily to accommodate prevailing
channel conditions, and (c) the ability to perform error checking continuously as each
bit is processed.

For error correction, maximum *a posteriori* (MAP) decoding [6] can be used to estimate the transmitted symbols from the received bits. In MAP decoding, error correction
is achieved by searching for the best path through a decoding tree, and techniques are
required to reduce the complexity of this tree. In the following sections, a MAP decoding scheme by Grangetto et al. [7], which uses a forbidden symbol to detect errors in
arithmetic codes, is described, and novel improvements are presented. The placement
of the forbidden symbol is modified to decrease the delay from the introduction of an
error to detection of the error. The arithmetic decoder is modified for quicker detection
by the introduction of a look-ahead technique. The calculation of the MAP metric is
also modified for faster error detection.

Section 2 contains an overview of arithmetic coding and existing joint source-channel
coding techniques based on arithmetic coding, with particular attention to the maximum
a posteriori (MAP) estimation approach in [7]. These schemes have recently received
greater attention in the literature [8]. Section 3 presents novel improvements to the MAP
joint source-channel coding scheme. Section 4 presents experimental results. Finally,
Sect. 5 draws conclusions.

2   Error Correction of Arithmetic Codes

Arithmetic coding [1] is a method for compressing a message u consisting of a sequence
of L symbols $u_1, u_2, \cdots, u_L$ with different probability of occurrence. Arithmetic coding requires a good source model which describes the distribution of probabilities for
the input symbols. The source model can be static or adaptive. In a static model, the
distribution of probabilities remains fixed throughout the message, that is, it is the same
when encoding the first symbol and when encoding the last symbol. In an adaptive
model, the probability distribution can be updated from symbol to symbol, so the probability distribution used to encode the last symbol may be different from that used to
encode the first symbol.

Arithmetic coding can be thought of as representing a message as a probability interval. At the start of the encoding process, the interval is the half-open interval $[0, 1)$, that
is, $0 \leq x < 1$. For each symbol u_l to be encoded, this interval is split into sub-intervals
with widths proportional to the probability of each possible symbol, and the sub-interval

corresponding to the symbol u_l is selected. This interval gets progressively smaller, so to keep the interval representable in computers, it is normalized continuously [9].

2.1 Error Detection

Arithmetic coding can compress data optimally when the source model is accurate. However, arithmetic codes are extremely vulnerable to any errors that occur [10]. Huffman codes tend to be self-synchronizing, so errors tend not to propagate very far; when an error occurs in a Huffman-coded message, several codewords are misinterpreted, but before long, the decoder is back in synchronization with the encoder [10]. Arithmetic coding, on the other hand, has no ability to withstand errors.

Boyd et al. [5] propose the introduction of some redundancy in arithmetic codes. This is done by forbidding a range from the interval. In common arithmetic coding techniques, the coding interval is doubled when normalization is required [9]. Boyd et al. suggest the interval to be reduced by a factor R each time the interval is doubled, consequently forbidding part of the interval. When this redundancy is introduced, errors can be detected by the decoder when the decoding interval falls within a forbidden part. The delay from the bit error to the detection of an error is shown to be about $1/(1 - R)$.

Instead of rescaling the interval for every normalization interval doubling, Sayir [11] suggests introducing forbidden gaps in the interval. After each source symbol is encoded, the source probabilities are rescaled by a rescaling factor γ, such that on average, $- \log_2 \gamma$ bits of redundancy are added for every source symbol. The gap factor ε is defined to be $\varepsilon = 1 - \gamma$.

2.2 MAP Decoding

The forbidden gap technique is a joint source-channel method for detecting errors in arithmetic codes. To perform error correction, we must first encode the symbols with an encoder that introduces redundancy.

Suppose we have a message $\mathbf{u}$ consisting of L symbols, $u_1, u_2, \cdots, u_L$. We encode this using an arithmetic code into a bit sequence $\mathbf{t}$, which has N bits, $t_1, t_2, \cdots, t_N$. The bit sequence $\mathbf{t}$ is then transmitted over a noisy channel, and the received signal is $\mathbf{y}$. Figure 1 is a block diagram of the encoding and decoding process. The task of the decoder is to infer the message $\hat{\mathbf{u}}$ given the received signal $\mathbf{y}$. If the inferred message $\hat{\mathbf{u}}$ is not identical to the source message $\mathbf{u}$, a decoding error has occurred.

MAP decoding [6] is the identification of the most probable message $\mathbf{u}$ given the received signal $\mathbf{y}$. By Bayes' theorem, the *a posteriori* probability of $\mathbf{u}$ is

$$P(\mathbf{u} \mid \mathbf{y}) = \frac{P(\mathbf{y} \mid \mathbf{u})P(\mathbf{u})}{P(\mathbf{y})}. \tag{1}$$

Fig. 1. Block diagram of the encoding and decoding process

Since $\mathbf{u}$ has L elements and $\mathbf{y}$ has N elements, it can be convenient to work in terms of the bit sequence $\mathbf{t}$ instead of the message $\mathbf{u}$. Since there is a one-to-one relationship between $\mathbf{u}$ and $\mathbf{t}$, $P(\mathbf{t}) = P(\mathbf{u})$. Thus, we can rewrite (1) as

$$P(\mathbf{t}\,|\,\mathbf{y}) = \frac{P(\mathbf{y}\,|\,\mathbf{t})P(\mathbf{t})}{P(\mathbf{y})}. \tag{2}$$

The right-hand side of this equation has three parts.

1. The first factor in the numerator, $P(\mathbf{y}\,|\,\mathbf{t})$ is the *likelihood* of the bit sequence $\mathbf{t}$, which is equal to $P(\mathbf{y}\,|\,\mathbf{u})$. For a memoryless channel, the likelihood may be separated into a product of the likelihood of each bit, that is,

$$P(\mathbf{y}\,|\,\mathbf{t}) = \prod_{n=1}^{N} P(y_n\,|\,t_n). \tag{3}$$

If we transmit $+x$ for $t_n = 1$ and $-x$ for $t_n = 0$ over a Gaussian channel with additive white noise of standard deviation σ, the probability density of the received signal y_n for both possible values of t_n is

$$P(y_n\,|\,t_n = 1) = \frac{1}{\sigma\sqrt{2\pi}} \exp\left(-\frac{(y_n - x)^2}{2\sigma^2}\right) \tag{4}$$

$$P(y_n\,|\,t_n = 0) = \frac{1}{\sigma\sqrt{2\pi}} \exp\left(-\frac{(y_n + x)^2}{2\sigma^2}\right). \tag{5}$$

2. The second factor in the numerator, $P(\mathbf{t})$, is the *prior* probability of the bit sequence $\mathbf{t}$. In our case, this probability is equal to $P(\mathbf{u})$, so that

$$P(\mathbf{t}) = \prod_{l=1}^{L} P(u_l). \tag{6}$$

3. The denominator is the *normalizing constant*. The normalizing constant is the sum of $P(\mathbf{y}\,|\,\mathbf{t})P(\mathbf{t})$ for all possible bit sequences $\mathbf{t}$,

$$P(\mathbf{y}) = \sum_{\mathbf{t}} P(\mathbf{y}\,|\,\mathbf{t})P(\mathbf{t}), \tag{7}$$

such that $\sum_{\mathbf{t}} P(\mathbf{t}\,|\,\mathbf{y}) = 1$.

MAP decoding can be summed up as the process of identifying the message $\hat{\mathbf{u}}$ with the highest probability $P(\hat{\mathbf{u}}\,|\,\mathbf{y})$ given the received signal $\mathbf{y}$. So the problem of decoding arithmetic codes using MAP decoding is a problem of searching for this best $\hat{\mathbf{u}}$ from all possible sequences $\mathbf{u}$. To search for the required $\hat{\mathbf{u}}$, we build a decoding tree. The tree consists of a number of nodes (or states) and a number of edges connecting them. The state may be either the bit state or the symbol state. If we are using the bit state, each edge will represent one bit, and each node will have two child nodes, one corresponding to a '0', and the other corresponding to a '1'. When traversing this tree, going from one state to the next (from one node to its child) happens every time we decode one bit.

If we are using the symbol state, the edges will represent symbols instead of bits, and the number of child nodes depends on the number of possible symbols. This time, going from one state to the next happens every time we decode one symbol.

For arithmetic codes, the size of the decoding tree increases exponentially with the number of symbols in the input sequence. So we have to use techniques to limit our search on some section of the tree; it is not feasible to compute $P(\mathbf{u} \mid \mathbf{y})$ for all possible sequences $\mathbf{u}$.

Guionnet and Guillemot [12] present a scheme that uses synchronization markers in the arithmetic codes. They use two kinds of markers: bit markers and symbol markers. For bit markers, a number of dummy bit patterns are introduced into the bit sequence after encoding a known number of symbols. The number of bits required to encode a number of symbols is not fixed, so these bit markers will occur at random places in the output bit sequence. The decoder then expects to find these bit patterns when decoding, and if the patterns are not found, the erroneous path is pruned from the decoding tree. Alternatively, symbol markers can be used. Instead of inserting a bit pattern, a number of dummy symbols are inserted into the input sequence after a known number of input symbols. As for the bit markers, if the decoder does not find these dummy symbols during decoding, the path is pruned from the decoding tree.

Grangetto et al. [7] present another MAP estimation approach for error correction of arithmetic codes. Instead of bit markers or symbol markers, they use the forbidden gap technique mentioned in Sect. 2.1. The decoding tree uses the bit state, rather than the symbol state. Whenever an error is detected in a path of the decoding tree, that path is pruned. The number of bits N required for the whole sequence is sent as side information. If a path in the tree has N nodes but is not yet fully decoded, the detector prunes the path. Grangetto et al. compare this joint source-channel scheme to a scheme with separate source and channel coders. In the separated scheme, an arithmetic code with $\varepsilon = 0$ is protected by a rate-compatible punctured convolutional (RCPC) code. The RCPC code used was of the family with memory $\nu = 6$ and non-punctured rate $\frac{1}{3}$, proposed by Hagenauer [13]. The comparison indicated an improvement over the separated scheme.

In another paper, Grangetto et al. [14] present an iterative decoding technique that uses an adapted BCJR algorithm [15] for error correction of arithmetic codes.

In this paper, the ideas in [7] are implemented and some novel improvements are introduced. Recall that in MAP decoding, the problem is to find the transmitted sequence $\mathbf{t}$ which has the maximum probability $P(\mathbf{t} \mid \mathbf{y})$, and that this probability can be written as

$$P(\mathbf{t} \mid \mathbf{y}) = \frac{P(\mathbf{y} \mid \mathbf{t})P(\mathbf{t})}{P(\mathbf{y})}. \tag{2}$$

As shown above, the right-hand side of this equation has three parts, the likelihood $P(\mathbf{y} \mid \mathbf{t})$, the prior probability $P(\mathbf{t})$, and the normalizing constant $P(\mathbf{y})$.

The *a posteriori* probability $P(\mathbf{t} \mid \mathbf{y})$ is the decoding metric used, that is, the decoding algorithm tries to maximize this value. In the case of memoryless channels, we can use an additive metric m by taking logs of the decoding metric.

$$m = \log P(\mathbf{t} \,|\, \mathbf{y})$$
$$m = \log P(\mathbf{y} \,|\, \mathbf{t}) + \log P(\mathbf{t}) - \log P(\mathbf{y}). \tag{8}$$

The additive decoding metric m can be split into N parts,

$$m = \sum_{n=1}^{N} m_n \tag{9}$$

where m_n is the part of m due to the nth bit. This is convenient as it enables us to update the metric m for each channel symbol y_n we try to decode. That is, after each bit, we can update the metric m. Combining (8) and (9) gives us

$$m_n = \log P(y_n \,|\, t_n) + \log P(t_n) - \log P(y_n). \tag{10}$$

Notice that the second term on the right-hand side, the prior probability, is not very straightforward to evaluate. We know that $P(\mathbf{t}) = P(\mathbf{u})$, because the transmitted bit sequence $\mathbf{t}$ has a one-to-one relationship with the input symbol sequence $\mathbf{u}$. When decoding a sequence $\mathbf{y}$, for each channel symbol, the decoder will either decode no source symbols, or it will decode one or more source symbols. Suppose that using bit y_n, the decoder decodes the symbols $\mathbf{u}_n$. $\mathbf{u}_n$ is a vector containing I_n source symbols $u_{n,1}, u_{n,2}, \cdots, u_{n,I_n}$. If no symbols are decoded after bit y_n, $I_n = 0$ and $\mathbf{u}_n$ is an empty vector. In any case,

$$\log P(\mathbf{u}_n) = \sum_{i=1}^{I_n} \log P(u_{n,i}). \tag{11}$$

We can approximate (10) as

$$m_n = \log P(y_n \,|\, t_n) + \log P(\mathbf{u}_n) - \log P(y_n). \tag{12}$$

It is worth pointing out that (10) is not exactly the same as (12). Since $P(\mathbf{t}) = P(\mathbf{u})$, we can say that $\sum_{n=1}^{N} P(t_n) = \sum_{n=1}^{N} P(\mathbf{u}_n)$, but this does not mean that $P(t_n) = P(\mathbf{u}_n)$.

The normalizing constant $P(\mathbf{y})$ is difficult to evaluate; (7) indicates that this requires knowledge of all possible bit sequences $\mathbf{t}$, which is not feasible. To solve this problem, Grangetto et al. [7] use an approximation by Park and Miller [16]. The bit sequence contains N bits, so assuming that all 2^N bit sequences are possible, then

$$P(\mathbf{y}) \approx \prod_{n=1}^{N} \frac{P(y_n \,|\, t_n = 1) + P(y_n \,|\, t_n = 0)}{2}. \tag{13}$$

2.3   Hard-Decision and Soft-Decision Decoding

Suppose we have an additive white Gaussian noise (AWGN) channel using binary phase-shift keying (BPSK) modulation with a signal-to-noise ratio E_b/N_0.

For hard-decision decoding the signal y_n can be either 0 or 1. The channel transition probability is

$$P(y_n \,|\, t_n) = \begin{cases} 1 - p & \text{if } y_n = t_n \\ p & \text{if } y_n \neq t_n \end{cases} \tag{14}$$

where p is the probability that a bit is demodulated in error, $p = \frac{1}{2} \operatorname{erfc} \sqrt{E_b/N_0}$. From (13) and (14) it is easy to deduce that

$$P(y_n) = \tfrac{1}{2}, \tag{15}$$

so that (12) becomes

$$m_n = \log P(y_n \,|\, t_n) + \log P(\mathbf{u}_n) + \log 2. \tag{16}$$

For soft-decision decoding, the metric can be found in a similar way. As in the case of hard-decision decoding, suppose we have an AWGN channel using BPSK modulation with a signal-to-noise ratio E_b/N_0. The signal y_n will not be constrained to only two values, 0 and 1. Recall that the probability distribution for y_n is given by (4) and (5). For BPSK modulation and an AWGN channel, $x = \sqrt{E_b}$ and $\sigma = \sqrt{N_0/2}$. As we have done for the hard-decision decoding metric, we can approximate $P(y_n)$ by

$$P(y_n) = \frac{P(y_n \,|\, t_n = 1) + P(y_n \,|\, t_n = 0)}{2}.$$

Using this approximation, from (4) and (5) we can find that

$$\frac{P(y_n \,|\, t_n = 1)}{P(y_n)} = \frac{2 \exp\left(4 \frac{E_b}{N_0} \frac{y_n}{\sqrt{E_b}}\right)}{\exp\left(4 \frac{E_b}{N_0} \frac{y_n}{\sqrt{E_b}}\right) + 1} \tag{17}$$

$$\frac{P(y_n \,|\, t_n = 0)}{P(y_n)} = \frac{2}{\exp\left(4 \frac{E_b}{N_0} \frac{y_n}{\sqrt{E_b}}\right) + 1}. \tag{18}$$

Substituting (17) and (18) into (12) gives us

$$m_n = \begin{cases} \log P(\mathbf{u}_n) + \log 2 + \left(4 \frac{E_b}{N_0} \frac{y_n}{\sqrt{E_b}}\right) & \\ \quad - \log\left[\exp\left(4 \frac{E_b}{N_0} \frac{y_n}{\sqrt{E_b}}\right) + 1\right] & \text{if } t_n = 1 \\ \log P(\mathbf{u}_n) + \log 2 & \\ \quad - \log\left[\exp\left(4 \frac{E_b}{N_0} \frac{y_n}{\sqrt{E_b}}\right) + 1\right] & \text{if } t_n = 0. \end{cases} \tag{19}$$

2.4   Stack Algorithm

Direct evaluation of the MAP metric over all possible bit sequences is not feasible. The size of the decoding tree would grow exponentially with the number of symbols L. To prevent this problem, sequential search techniques are used.

The decoder proposed in [7] uses a search algorithm along the branches of a binary tree. The sequential algorithm used is the stack algorithm [17]. The tree paths are kept in a list ordered by their metric; the path with the best metric is kept at the top of the list.

In each iteration, the best path is removed from the list and replaced by two paths; one assuming $t_n = 0$, and the other assuming $t_n = 1$. These two new paths then have their corresponding metrics updated, and are placed in the list in a way to keep it ordered.

The ordered list has a predefined maximum size M. When there are more then M paths, the paths with the worst metric are removed from the list.

Although the algorithm is called a stack algorithm, because the concept of a stack is useful for describing the algorithm, Jelinek (1969) suggests that storing the paths in a physical stack is not optimal, and that it is preferable to store the paths in random access storage. A physical stack would require a sequential comparison of the metric to insert a path, and relocation of large amounts of data in the required stack position. As an alternative method, Jelinek proposes splitting the stack into a number of buckets, each containing metrics that are close in value.

Figure 2 shows an example decoding tree as it evolves during the decoding process. At the start of the process, there is only one node, node 0, with metric $m_0 = 0$. In each step, the node with the highest metric is split into two nodes, the node to the left assuming $t_n = 0$ and the node to the right assuming $t_n = 1$. Sometimes a path is pruned because one of two conditions occurs: either (a) the decoder detects an error in the path, or (b) the number of nodes in the tree exceeds the limit M, so the worst path is removed from the tree.

3   Improved Error Control

The MAP decoding scheme presented in [7] was implemented and some novel improvements were introduced. To enable a fair comparison, the data encoded during testing is of the same form as that used by Grangetto et al.

3.1   Placing the Forbidden Gap

We have already seen that a forbidden gap can be used to detect errors in arithmetic codes. In [11], the gap is placed at the end of the interval. Ben-Jamaa et al. [18] investigated the placement of the forbidden gap by splitting the forbidden gap into three parts for binary-source arithmetic codes, one part before the first symbol sub-interval, the second between the two sub-intervals, and the third after the second sub-interval. Their results show that the worst performance is obtained when the gap is completely between the two sub-intervals.

3.2   Looking Ahead during Decoding

During regular decoding of arithmetic codes [9], two interval values are maintained, one is the decoding interval, which is the same as the interval produced by the encoder, and the other is the input codeword interval, which depends directly on the bit sequence being decoded. For a symbol to be decoded, the input interval has to lie completely

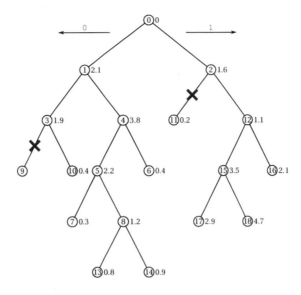

Fig. 2. Example binary decoding tree

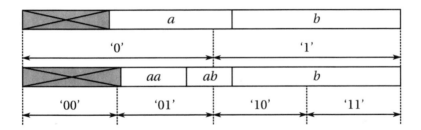

Fig. 3. Looking ahead during decoding

within one of the sub-intervals of the decoding interval. The forbidden gap technique detects an error when the input interval lies completely within a forbidden gap.

When decoding arithmetic codes with a forbidden gap, sometimes we can decode a symbol even though the input interval is not completely within the sub-interval corresponding to the symbol. Consider Fig. 3. The input interval for '0' is not completely within the sub-interval for symbol a, a part of the input interval lies within a forbidden region. But there is only one symbol that can be decoded; no part of the input interval lies within the sub-interval for symbol b, so only symbol a can be decoded. In this case, we can decode symbol a immediately and for the moment assume that the bit sequence is not in error. The sub-interval for a is then further split into three parts: another forbidden region, aa, and ab. If we receive a second '0', the input interval will lie completely within a forbidden region, and an error is detected. Thus, looking ahead during decoding gives two advantages: earlier decoding of symbols, and earlier detection of errors. Table 1 shows the steps performed by the look-ahead decoder for each input bit.

Table 1. Look-ahead decoding steps for one input bit

1: Initially, the input interval is $[l_i, h_i)$,
    the decoding interval is split into S sub-intervals $[l_1, h_1), [l_2, h_2), \cdots, [l_S, h_S)$, and
    t_n is the assumed transmitted bit.

2: **if** $t_n = 0$ **then**

3:     $h_i \Leftarrow (l_i + h_i)/2$

4: **else**

5:     $l_i \Leftarrow (l_i + h_i)/2$

6: **end if**

7: Search for symbols s with their corresponding sub-interval $[l_s, h_s)$ overlapping the
    input interval $[l_i, h_i)$, that is, $l_s < h_i$ and $h_s > l_i$.

8: **if** no matching symbols are found **then**

9:     Flag an error.

10: **else if** only one matching symbol is found **then**

11:     Add found symbol s to the list of decoded symbols.

12:     Scale the region $[l_s, h_s)$ if necessary, scaling $[l_i, h_i)$ in the same way.

13:     Split the scaled $[l_s, h_s)$ into S new sub-intervals $[l'_1, h'_1), [l'_2, h'_2), \cdots, [l'_S, h'_S)$.

14:     $l_1 \Leftarrow l'_1, h_1 \Leftarrow h'_1, l_2 \Leftarrow l'_2, h_2 \Leftarrow h'_2, \cdots, l_S \Leftarrow l'_S, h_S \Leftarrow h'_S$

15:     Go to 7.

16: **else** {more than one matching symbol is found}

17:     Go to 19.

18: **end if**

19: End.

When using look-ahead, the input interval does not need to lie completely within the decoding interval. But since the symbol is decoded, the decoding interval and the input codeword interval have to be normalized, that is, the intervals have to be doubled in size. Since the input interval can be larger than the decoding interval, it is possible for the input interval, denoted by $[l_i, h_i)$ in Table 1, to extend out of the $[0, 1)$ interval. So in the implementation, it is important to cater for the possibility that $l_i < 0$ or that $h_i \geq 1$.

Section 4.1 shows the gain obtained when using this technique in MAP decoding of arithmetic codes.

3.3   Updating the Prior Probability Continuously

In Sect. 2.3, both the metric for hard-decision decoding shown in (14) and the metric for soft-decision decoding shown in (19) have a component for the prior probability $P(\mathbf{u})$. Recall that this component, $\log P(\mathbf{u}_n)$, is calculated using

$$\log P(\mathbf{u}_n) = \sum_{i=1}^{I_n} \log P(u_{n,i}), \qquad (11)$$

where $I_n \geq 0$ is the number of symbols that can be decoded assuming the transmitted bit t_n.

There is another way to calculate the prior probability. In arithmetic coding, the width of the interval is directly related to the probability of the source symbols. Ignoring the forbidden gaps for the moment, we can say that for an input sequence $u_1, u_2, \cdots, u_L$,

$$\text{Interval width} = P(\mathbf{u}) = \prod_{l=1}^{L} P(u_l). \tag{20}$$

In arithmetic coding algorithms, whenever a bit is emitted by the encoder, the message interval is scaled by a factor of $\frac{1}{2}$ [9]. If to encode the input sequence $\mathbf{u}$ with probability $P(\mathbf{u})$ the encoder emits N bits, the interval width is scaled by a total factor of 2^{-N}. Thus,

$$P(\mathbf{u}) \approx 2^{-N} \tag{21}$$

$$\log P(\mathbf{u}) \approx -N \log 2 \tag{22}$$

$$\log P(\mathbf{u}_n) \approx -\log 2. \tag{23}$$

All we have to do to the additive MAP metric to cater for the prior probability is to subtract $\log 2$ for each decoded bit.

In the above, we have ignored the effect of forbidden gaps on the interval width. Compensating for forbidden gaps is not very difficult. Every time there is a forbidden gap, that is, for each symbol encoded or decoded, the interval is reduced by a factor of $(1 - \varepsilon)$. If there are I forbidden gaps,

$$P(\mathbf{u})(1 - \varepsilon)^I \approx 2^{-N} \tag{24}$$

$$P(\mathbf{u}) \approx 2^{-N}(1 - \varepsilon)^{-I} \tag{25}$$

$$\log P(\mathbf{u}) \approx -N \log 2 - I \log(1 - \varepsilon) \tag{26}$$

$$\log P(\mathbf{u}_n) \approx -\log 2 - I_n \log(1 - \varepsilon). \tag{27}$$

Section 4.1 presents experimental results showing the gain obtained when using this improvement in MAP decoding of arithmetic codes.

4 Results

4.1 MAP Decoding

Simulations were preformed to test the MAP decoding algorithms. The source used was similar to that used in [7], to make the comparison fair.

Figure 4 shows the packet error rate (PER) for a static binary source model using hard-decision decoding. The stack size $M = 256$, and the gap factor $\varepsilon = 0.185$. Figure 5 shows the PER for the same conditions using soft-decision decoding.

The performance is improved when the look-ahead technique of Sect. 3.2 is used. When this technique is used, the decoder may detect errors earlier, and it can detect correct symbols earlier as well. When errors are detected early, incorrect paths can be pruned earlier from the decoding tree, reducing the chance that the correct path is removed because of a stack overflow. Detecting symbols early will enable the MAP

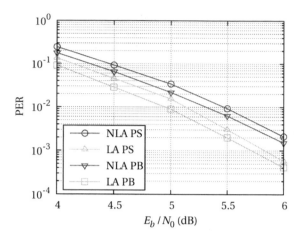

Fig. 4. Performance for MAP hard-decision decoder for static binary model with $M = 256$ and $\varepsilon = 0.185$; without look-ahead (NLA) and with look-ahead (LA); and with $P(\mathbf{t})$ adjusted every symbol (PS) or every bit (PB)

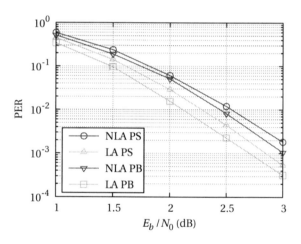

Fig. 5. Performance for MAP soft-decision decoder for static binary model with $M = 256$ and $\varepsilon = 0.185$; without look-ahead (NLA) and with look-ahead (LA); and with $P(\mathbf{t})$ adjusted every symbol (PS) or every bit (PB)

metric to be updated earlier, which can lead to better decoding. The performance is also improved with continuous updating of the prior probability $P(\mathbf{t})$ as described in Sect. 3.3, that is, when $P(\mathbf{t})$ is adjusted every time we decode a bit rather than every time we decode a symbol. The performance is improved most when the techniques are used together.

Figures 6 and 7 show how the PER changes with ε when E_b/N_o is fixed at 5.5 dB for hard-decision decoding and soft-decision decoding respectively. The improved schemes can achieve the error-correction performance of the original scheme using less

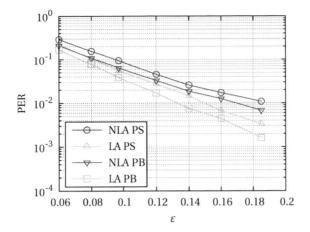

Fig. 6. Performance for MAP hard-decision decoder for static binary model with $M = 256$ and $E_b/N_0 = 5.5$ dB; without look-ahead (NLA) and with look-ahead (LA); and with $P(\mathbf{t})$ adjusted every symbol (PS) or every bit (PB)

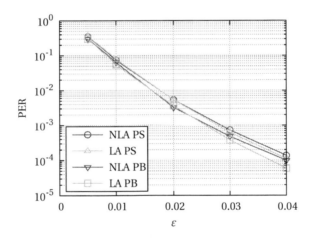

Fig. 7. Performance for MAP soft-decision decoder for static binary model with $M = 256$ and $E_b/N_0 = 5.5$ dB; without look-ahead (NLA) and with look-ahead (LA); and with $P(\mathbf{t})$ adjusted every symbol (PS) or every bit (PB)

redundancy. For example, for a PER of 10^{-2}, the hard-decision decoder for the original scheme needs $\varepsilon = 0.19$, which translates into a code rate of 0.65. For the same PER, the hard-decision decoder for the improved scheme needs $\varepsilon = 0.13$, which translates into a code rate of 0.73.

In all graphs, the plot for the scheme with no improvements, that is with no look-ahead and with the prior probability $P(\mathbf{t})$ updated after every symbol instead of after every bit, is comparable to the plots published in [7].

5   Conclusions

In this paper, a joint source-channel arithmetic MAP decoder proposed in [7] for decoding arithmetic codes with a forbidden symbol transmitted over an AWGN channel was analysed. Novel techniques were introduced to improve the error-correction performance of the code. The arithmetic decoder was improved with a look-ahead technique that enables it to detect errors earlier. When using the MAP decoder, this improves the PER at the cost of a small increase in complexity. The MAP metric calculation was changed by improving the way the prior probability component of the metric is updated, leading to faster updating of the metric and, consequently, to a better error-correction performance. This technique makes the MAP decoder faster as well because the better path in the MAP tree is found earlier. A coding gain of up to 0.4 dB for soft-decision decoding and 0.6 dB for hard-decision decoding was observed for a code rate of $2/3$ and $M = 256$. A number of multimedia applications are using arithmetic coding as the final entropy coding stage, making a joint-source channel coding scheme based on arithmetic coding attractive for wireless multimedia transmission.

References

1. Rissanen, J.J.: Generalized Kraft inequality and arithmetic coding. IBM Journal of Research and Development 20(3), 198–203 (1976)
2. Huffman, D.A.: A method for the construction of minimum-redundancy codes. Proceedings of the IRE 40(9), 1098–1101 (1952)
3. Shannon, C.E.: A mathematical theory of communication. Bell System Technical Journal 27, 379–423 (1948)
4. Vembu, S., Verdù, S., Steinberg, Y.: The source-channel separation theorem revisited. IEEE Transactions on Information Theory 41(1), 44–54 (1995)
5. Boyd, C., Cleary, J.G., Irvine, S.A., Rinsma-Melchert, I., Witten, I.H.: Integrating error detection into arithmetic coding. IEEE Transactions on Communications 45(1), 1–3 (1997)
6. MacKay, D.J.C.: Information Theory, Inference, and Learning Algorithms, ch. 25, pp. 324–333. Cambridge University Press (2003)
7. Grangetto, M., Cosman, P., Olmo, G.: Joint source/channel coding and MAP decoding of arithmetic codes. IEEE Transactions on Communications 53(6), 1007–1016 (2005)
8. Bi, D., Hoffman, M.W., Sayood, K.: Joint Source Channel Coding Using Arithmetic Codes. Synthesis Lectures on Communications. Morgan & Claypool Publishers (2010)
9. Witten, I.H., Neal, R.M., Cleary, J.G.: Arithmetic coding for data compression. Communications of the ACM 30(6), 520–540 (1987)
10. Lelewer, D.A., Hirschberg, D.S.: Data compression. ACM Computing Surveys (3), 261–296 (September 1987)
11. Sayir, J.: Arithmetic coding for noisy channels. In: Proceedings of the 1999 IEEE Information Theory and Communications Workshop, pp. 69–71 (June 1999)
12. Guionnet, T., Guillemot, C.: Soft decoding and synchronization of arithmetic codes: Application to image transmission over noisy channels. IEEE Transactions on Image Processing 12(12), 1599–1609 (2003)
13. Hagenauer, J.: Rate-compatible punctured convolutional codes (RCPC codes) and their applications. IEEE Transactions on Communications 36(4), 389–400 (1988)
14. Grangetto, M., Scanavino, B., Olmo, G., Benedetto, S.: Iterative decoding of serially concatenated arithmetic and channel codes with JPEG 2000 applications. IEEE Transactions on Image Processing 16(6), 1557–1567 (2007)

15. Bahl, L.R., Cocke, J., Jelinek, F., Raviv, J.: Optimal decoding of linear codes for minimizing symbol error rate. IEEE Transactions on Information Theory 20(2), 284–287 (1974)
16. Park, M., Miller, D.J.: Joint source-channel decoding for variable-length encoded data by exact and approximate MAP sequence estimation. IEEE Transactions on Communications 48(1), 1–6 (2000)
17. Jelinek, F.: Fast sequential decoding algorithm using a stack. IBM Journal of Research and Development 13(6), 675–685 (1969)
18. Ben-Jamaa, S., Weidmann, C., Kieffer, M.: Analytical tools for optimizing the error correction performance of arithmetic codes. IEEE Transactions on Communications 56(9), 1458–1468 (2008)

An Ensemble Approach to Improve Microaneurysm Candidate Extraction

Bálint Antal, István Lázár, and András Hajdu

University of Debrecen, Faculty of Informatics, 4010 Debrecen, POB 12, Hungary
{antal.balint,lazar.istvan,hajdu.andras}@inf.unideb.hu

Abstract. In this paper, we present a novel approach to microaneurysm candidate extraction. To strengthen the accuracy of individual algorithms, we propose an ensemble of state-of-the-art candidate extractors. We apply a simulated annealing based method to select an optimal combination of such algorithms for a particular dataset. We also present a novel classification technique, which is based on a parallel ensemble of kernel density estimators. The experimental results show improvement in the positive likelihood rate compared to the individual candidate extractors.

Keywords: Biomedical image processing, Image classification, Pattern recognition, Medical decision-making, Statistics.

1 Introduction

Diabetic retinopathy (DR) is the most common cause of blindness in the developed countries. Microaneurysms (MAs) are early signs of this disease, so the detection of these lesions is essential in the screening process. DR can be prevented and its progression can be slowed down if diagnosed and treated early. A proper medical protocol [1], [2] has been established, but the actual grading required for diagnostics has been performed manually. Manual grading is slow and resource demanding, so several efforts have been made to establish an automatic computer-aided screening system [3], [4]. However, the detection of microaneurysms is still an open issue. Thus, several recent works focus on this problem, including an online challenge for MA detectors [5].

Microaneurysms appear as small circular dark spots on the surface of the retina (see Figure 1). The most common appearance of microaneurysms is near thin vessels, but they cannot actually lie on the vessels. In some cases, microaneurysms are hard to distinguish from parts of the vessel system. For example, the intersections of two thick vessels or a few very thin vessels are rather misleading for the detectors.

In this paper, we propose an ensemble-based approach to MA detection to suppress the errors of individual algorithms. The proposed process consists of three main steps (see also Figure 2): first, we extract MA candidates from fundus images after preprocessing. For this task, we select three state-of-the-art approaches and include a novel one, as well. In the second phase, we combine the results provided by the four candidate extractors and reduce the number of candidates with a voting scheme. The number of required votes and the set of the corresponding candidate extractors is determined

M.S. Obaidat, G.A. Tsihrintzis, and J. Filipe (Eds.): ICETE 2010, CCIS 222, pp. 378–391, 2012.
© Springer-Verlag Berlin Heidelberg 2012

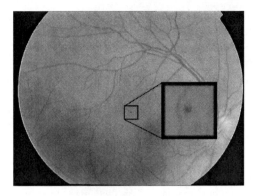

Fig. 1. Fundus image containing a microaneurysm

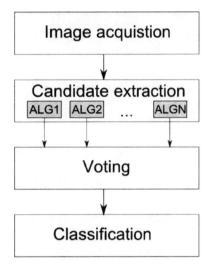

Fig. 2. Steps of microaneurysm detection using an ensemble of candidate extractors

by a simulated annealing algorithm. We also introduce a novel machine-learning based algorithm to classify the candidates.

The rest of the paper is organized as follows. In section 2 we present the MA candidate extractor algorithms to build up an ensemble. The optimal voting scheme of the MA extractor algorithms is described in section 3. In section 4 the results of the ensemble-based system are presented. Finally, some conclusions are drawn in section 5.

2   Microaneurysm Candidate Extraction

Candidate extraction is an effort to reduce the number of objects in an image for further analysis by excluding regions which do not have similar characteristics to microaneurysms. Individual approaches define their own measurement for similarity to extract

MA candidates. In this section, we provide a brief overview of currently popular candidate extractors that will be considered later on in the ensemble system. Namely, we recall Walter et al. [6], the Spencer-Frame method [7] [8] in its original form, and a slightly modified version of [9]. A new approach is also involved, whose development was partly motivated to improve the MA candidate extraction efficiency of the proposed ensemble-based system. As we will see later on, these methods sufficiently diverse to form a successful ensemble.

2.1 Walter et al.

This approach is proposed in [6]. To overcome the imperfections of color fundus images, a contrast enhancement operator is applied as a preprocessing step along with shade correction:

$$[SC(f)] = \begin{cases} \frac{\frac{1}{2}(u_{max}-u_{min})\cdot(f(x)-t_{min})^r}{\left(\mu_f^*-t_{min}\right)^r} + u_{min}, & t \leq \mu_f^* \\ \frac{-\frac{1}{2}(u_{max}-u_{min})\cdot(f(x)-t_{max})^r}{\left(\mu_f^*-t_{max}\right)^r} + u_{max}, & t \geq \mu_f^* \end{cases}$$

where

$$\{t_{min}, \cdots t_{max}\}$$

are the intensity values of the grayscale image,

$$\{u_{min}, \cdots u_{max}\}$$

are the intensity values of the enhanced image, μ_f^* is the mean value of an area opened image and $r \in \mathbb{R}$. The parameter r controls the level of contrast enhancement. Candidate extraction is then accomplished by grayscale diameter closing. That is, the method aims find all sufficiently small dark patterns on the green channel. Let

$$\alpha(X) = \max_{x,\, y\in X} d(x,\, y)$$

be the diameter α of a connected set X with a distance function $d\,(.)$. Let

$$X_t^-(f) = \{x | f(x) \leq t\}.$$

Then, the grayscale diameter closing is defined by the following formula:

$$\phi_\alpha^o = \inf\{s \geq f(x) \,|\, \alpha\left(C_x\left[X_s^-(f)\right]\right) \geq \alpha\}.$$

Then, the candidates are the remaining objects on the image. For an example output, see Figure 3.

2.2 Spencer-Frame

This approach is one of the most popular candidate extractors, originally proposed by [7] and [8]. The algorithm uses shade correction as preprocessing: first, a background

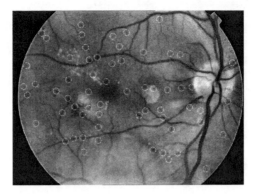

Fig. 3. Candidates extracted by the Walter candidate extractor

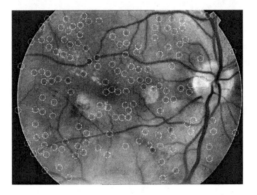

Fig. 4. Candidates extracted by the Spencer-Frame candidate extractor

image i_{bg} is produced by applying a median filter on the green channel of the original image i_{green}. Then, the shade corrected image i_{sc} is established by the following formula:

$$i_{sc} = i_{bg} - i_{green}.$$

The actual candidate extraction is accomplished by subtracting the maximum of multiple morphological top-hat transformations, which is defined as follows:

$$T(f) = f \bullet s - f,$$

where $\bullet$ denotes the morphological closing. For this step, twelve rotated structuring elements were used with a radial resolution of $15\,^\circ$. Then, the vascular map is subtracted from i_{sc} to remove the largest components form the image. As a contras enhancement operator, a 2D Gaussian matched filter is applied on the image. The resulting image is then binarized with a fixed threshold. Since the candidates are not a good representation for the actual lesions, a region growing step is also applied. A slightly modified version of this method is proposed in [10], [11] and [12]. For an example output, see Figure 4.

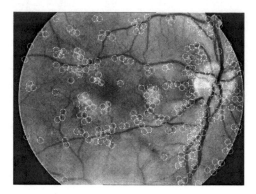

Fig. 5. Candidates extracted by the Circular Hough-transformation based candidate extractor

2.3 Circular Hough-Transformation Based

Based on the idea presented in [9], we established an approach based on the detection of small circular spots in the image. As a preprocessing step, a common biomedical image correction technique, the contrast limited adaptive histogram equalization (CLAHE) is applied [13]. CLAHE is realized in the following way [14]: first, the image is divided into disjoint regions. Then, for each region a histogram and a clipping limit are obtained. After that, all the histograms are redistributed according to the corresponding limit. Finally, the cumulative distribution functions are determined for grayscale mapping. The candidate extraction is obtained by detecting circles on the images. For this purpose we use circular Hough transformation [15]. With this technique, a set of approximately circle-shaped objects can be obtained from the image. The radius of the circles are limited according to the observed size of microaneurysms from a training set. For an example output, see Figure 5.

2.4 Lazar et al.

Besides some popular techniques mentioned so far, we also investigate a new MA candidate extractor developed by our research group.

The green channel of the image is inverted and smoothened with a Gaussian filter. A set of scan lines with equidistantly sampled tangents between -90 ° and +90 ° is fixed. For each direction the intensity values along the scan lines are recorded in a one dimensional array, and the scan lines are shifted vertically and horizontally to process every image pixel of the image. On each intensity profile, the heights of the peaks, and their local maximum positions are used for an adaptive thresholding. The resulting foreground indices of the thresholding process are transformed back to two dimensional coordinates, and stored in a map that records the number of foreground pixels of different directions corresponding to every position of the image. The maximal value for each position equals the number of different directions used for the scanning process. This map is smoothened with an averaging kernel and a hysteresis thresholding procedure is applied. The resulting components are filtered based on their size. For more details, see [16]. For an example output, see Figure 6.

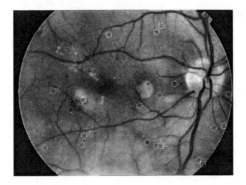

Fig. 6. Candidates extracted by the Lazar candidate extractor

2.5 Diversity of the Candidate Extractors

It is important to use diverse candidate extractors, that is, to reduce the number of false positives efficiently and keep only those candidates on which multiple methods agree. As the most straightforward measure, we aim to raise the the positive likelihood ratio (number of the true positive (TP) / number of the false positive (FP)) [17] using an ensemble.

The pairwise diversity of the classifiers can be measured by the disagreement (D) and double fault (DF) measure, where D, DF $\in [0, 1]$. The disagreement measure sums the cases, where the extractors disagree, but one of them is correct. The double fault measure is the number of candidates, where both extractors agree and both are incorrect. For our aims, a high disagreement and a low double fault measure is the ideal. As it can be seen in Table 1, the selected candidate extractors are quite diverse.

Table 1. Diversity of the candidate extractors

Walter	Spencer	Hough	Lazar	D	DF
x	x			0.73	0.09
x		x		0.77	0.04
x			x	0.49	0.10
	x	x		0.79	0.06
	x		x	0.69	0.14
		x	x	0.74	0.12

3 An Optimal Voting Scheme for Combining the Candidate Extractors

In this chapter, we present a new approach to select the optimal combination of the candidate extractors. First, for the proper comparison of the candidates extracted by the individual approaches, we must preprocess them. Then, we select an optimal configuration for the voting scheme by a simulated annealing algorithm. Finally, the voting is executed using this configuration. Later on, we present some properties of this optimal voting scheme.

3.1   Preprocessing the Candidates

Before letting the individual candidate extractor algorithms vote, we must ensure that there are no candidates too close to each other within the output of an individual algorithm. This issue is addressed by merging them. It is also important to remove any candidates falling on the vessel system. For this purpose, we have detected the vascular system with the algorithm proposed in [18] and removed the candidates falling on vessels.

3.2   Selecting an Optimal Voting Configuration Using Simulated Annealing

The proposed framework aims to find an optimal voting scheme for candidate extractors. This voting scheme determines a subset of the candidate extractors and the number of required votes. Since this problem induces a large search space, we use simulated annealing to find an optimal solution.

Simulated annealing [19] is a widely used global optimization method. This approach is inspired by the annealing in metallurgy. It is effective for large search space problems by using random sampling to avoid stuck in a local minimum. For the optimization, we use the following energy function to be minimized:

$$E = -\frac{TP}{FP},$$

where TP stands for the number of the true, while FP stands for that of the false positive candidates, respectively.

To minimize the target energy E by simulated annealing, each element of the search space S consists of the results sets of a set of candidate extractors $\{ce_1, \dots ce_L\}$ and a required number of votes v ($1 \leq v \leq L$). Each combination occurs in S only once.

The proposed simulated annealing algorithm operates through the following steps:

1. Let T be an initial temperature, T_{min} a minimal temperature, $0 \leq q \leq 1$, $q \in \mathbb{R}$ the temperature change, $S = P\left((\{R_{ce}\}, v)\right)$ the search space, where R_{ce} is the result of the candidate extractor ce, v is the number of required votes and $P(X)$ is the power set of X.
2. Choose $x \in S$ randomly and let $e = E(x)$, $S = S - \{x\}$.
3. Choose $x_i \in S$ randomly and let $e_i = E(x_i)$, $S = S - \{x_i\}$.
4. If $T < T_{min}$ or $S = \emptyset$, then stop.
5. If $e_i < e$, then $x = x_i$, $e = e_i$ and $T = T \cdot q$. Go to step 4.
6. Choose a random number $r \in \mathbb{R}$. If $accept(e, e_i, T, r) = true$, then $x = x_i$, $e = e_i$, where

$$accept(e, e_i, T, r) = \begin{cases} true, & if \ \exp\left(\frac{e-e_i}{T}\right) > r, \\ false, & otherwise. \end{cases}$$

7. Let $T = T \cdot q$. Go to step 4.

Currently, we consider four candidate extractors (that is, $L = 4$ in the algorithm above), but with the use of simulated annealing it can be easily extended to more methods in the future.

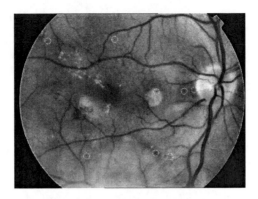

Fig. 7. Result of the voting

3.3 Voting on the Candidates

Each individual candidate extractor algorithm produces an initial set of microaneurysm candidates. Then, we establish a set of final candidates, where these candidates are voted by at least $n \geq 2$ candidate extractors. The voting procedure has the following steps:

1. For each candidate c provided by one of the algorithms, check, whether there is another candidate detected by another algorithm within a distance $r \in \mathbb{R}$ from c.
2. Let sum be the number of candidates satisfying the above proximity criterion and remove all these candidates from their respective initial sets.
3. If $sum \geq n$, then add the centroid of the candidates found by step 2 to the final set.
4. Repeat the procedure until all the initial sets become empty.

The result of the voting for the previously shown example is presented in Figure 7.

3.4 Properties of the Optimal Voting Scheme

Property 1. *The optimal voting scheme selects a subset of the candidate extractors.*

That is, it is not mandatory that all available candidate extractors participate in the voting.

Property 2. *An individually less accurate algorithm can be still useful in an ensemble.*

The optimal voting scheme can make use of some individually less accurate algorithm in certain situations. The results of a simple majority voting with a fixed configuration can be less accurate with a weaker participant.

Property 3. *The use of simulated annealing makes it possible to include a large number of candidate extractors.*

The number of combinations using n candidate extractors is $2^n - 1$ with excluding the empty combination. For a large search space, an approximately optimal solution can also be obtained with simulated annealing by setting a proper annealing schedule in less computational time.

Property 4. *The optimal voting scheme determines the number of required votes from the candidate extractors.*

Thus, the system is more flexible when changing energy functions.

3.5   Candidate Classification

To improve the TP / FP ratio we use a consequent classification step, which is based on certain unique features of microaneurysms. We use a new approach to perform this step, instead of other literature recommendations. The reason to introduce a new classifier is that the existing methods use objects and not single pixels representations to extract features, while our ensemble-based system provides the latter.

Candidates are classified as actual MAs or non-MAs in two steps. First, we train our approach with several fixed size (e.g. 21×21 pixels) subimages for both microaneurysm and random non-microaneurysm examples. Then, for each pixel of the examples, we establish a kernel density estimator for both classes. After the training step, we can classify new instances. We establish a new instance by producing a subimage of the candidate pixel and its neighbourhood with the same size as the training step. The classification procedure is then the following: for each pixel of the instance we compare the probability provided by the kernel density estimators for both classes. Then, the candidate is considered as a microaneurysm if more comparisons confirm that this is a positive example. For the stages of our classifier, see Figure 8.

Formally, the classifier can be described in the following way:
Let

$$E = \{I_1, I_2, \ldots I_m\}$$

an ensemble of classifiers, where

$$I : x \to C, x \in D \subset \mathbb{R}^+$$

and C is a class. In our case,

$$D = \{0, 1, \ldots 255\}$$

and

$$C \in \{C_{MA}, C_{Non-MA}\},$$

where C_{MA} and C_{Non-MA} denotes the class of MAs and Non-MAs, respectively. Let

$$T = \{\langle X_1, c_1 \rangle, \langle X_2, c_2 \rangle, \ldots \langle X_m, c_m \rangle\}$$

be the training dataset, where

$$X_j = \{x_{j1}, x_{j2}, \ldots x_{jn}, \},$$

$$x_{ji} \in D, i = 1 \ldots n, j = 1 \ldots m$$

is a sample and $c_j \in C$ is the corresponding class. We establish n classifier for each element of the samples, where the I_k, $k = 1, \ldots n$ is trained using

$$Y_k = \{x_{1k}, \ldots, x_{mk}\}.$$

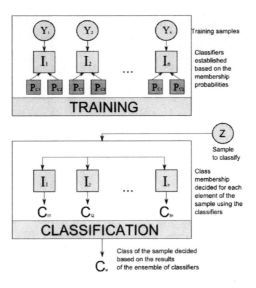

Fig. 8. Stages of classification

Let $f_k(y)$ is the probability density function of Y_k. We establish a kernel density estimator $\hat{f}_{hk}(y)$ to approximate $f_k(y)$:

$$\hat{f}_{hk}(y) = \frac{1}{mh} \sum_{i=1}^{m} K\left(\frac{y - y_i}{h}\right),$$

where $y \in Y_k$, h is a smoothing parameter and K is a Gaussian kernel function (with $\mu = 0, \sigma = 1$):

$$K\left(\frac{y - y_i}{h}\right) = \frac{1}{\sqrt{2\pi}} \exp\left(\frac{-(y - y_i)^2}{2h^2}\right).$$

We establish kernel density estimators for each class, from which the membership probability function $P : D \rightarrow \mathbb{R}$ can be derived. Thus, we define I_k with the following formula:

$$I_k(x) = \operatorname*{argmax}_{C} P(x|C).$$

The final classification for the sample Z by the ensemble O is decided using the following formula:

$$O(Z) = \{C_k | \sum_{i=1}^{m} g_i(C_k) = \max \sum_{i=1}^{m} g_i(C_l)\},$$

$$k, l = 1, \ldots, m,$$

where

$$g_i(C_k) = \begin{cases} 1, & I_i = C_k, \\ 0, & otherwise. \end{cases}$$

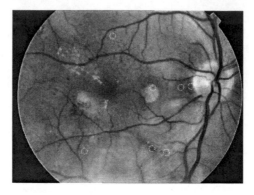

Fig. 9. Result of the classification consequently applied to the output of the voting of the candidate extractors

In our case, the samples are subimages, while the kernel density estimation are based on the pixel intensities.

In Figure 9 we can see the effect of this classification method applied to the previously shown example output. We can see how a large number of FPs has been removed.

4 Results

We have tested our approach on 50 images selected from the Retinopathy Online Challenge database [5]. Currently, it is the only publicly available fundus image database dedicated to measure the accuracy of microaneurysm detectors.

As a result of dynamical selections of algorithms, our ensemble system formed by the Walter, Spencer-Frame and Lazar candidate extractors requiring 3 votes to accept. Our results shows that the ensemble system provides substantially better TP / FP ratio than the individual algorithms. The comparison of our approach can be seen in Table 2.

Table 2. Comparison of microaneurysm candidate extractors

Algorithm	Total	TP	FP	TP / FP
Walter	2831	110	2721	0.040
Spencer-Frame	5821	115	5706	0.020
Hough	15664	94	15570	0.006
Lazar	868	109	759	0.144
Ensemble	165	50	115	0.435

It is also interesting to compare our approach with a state-of-the-art microaneurysm detector. [11] uses a similar candidate extraction algorithm as the Spencer-Frame method, but it relies on a different approach for the final candidate classification. The ensemble-based system outperforms this algorithm (see Table 4) without even classifying the candidates. To validate our classification technique, we compared it to a classifier trained on features collected from [6], [20], [21], [12] and [16]. The complete list of the features can be seen in Table 3. To select the optimal subset of features, we used a

Table 3. Selected features for classification

	Feature	Origin
1.	**area**	[20]
2.	**perimeter**	[20]
3.	aspect ratio	[20]
4.	**circularity**	[20]
5.	**total green intensity**	[20]
6.	**total shade corrected intensity**	[20]
7.	**average green intensity**	[20]
8.	average shade corrected intensity	[20]
9.	normalized green intensity	[20]
10.	**normalized average shade corrected intensity**	[20]
11.	normalized average green intensity	[20]
12.	**normalized average shade corrected intensity**	[20]
13.	compactness	[20]
14.	average Gauss filter response, s = 1	[20]
15.	average Gauss filter response, s = 2	[20]
16.	**average Gauss filter response, s = 4**	[20]
17.	**average Gauss filter response, s = 8**	[20]
18.	**standard deviation Gauss filter response, s = 1**	[20]
19.	**standard deviation Gauss filter response, s = 2**	[20]
20.	**standard deviation Gauss filter response, s = 4**	[20]
21.	**standard deviation Gauss filter response, s = 8**	[20]
22.	maximum correlation coefficient	[20]
23.	**minimum correlation coefficient**	[20]
24.	**average correlation coefficient**	[20]
25.	**major axis length**	[20]
26.	**minor axis length**	[20]
27.	**maximum top-hat**	[6]
28.	mean top hat	[6]
29.	dynamic	[6]
30.	**outer mean**	[6]
31.	outer standard deviation	[6]
32.	**inner mean**	[6]
33.	inner standard deviation	[6]
34.	outer range	[6]
35.	**inner range**	[6]
36.	gray level contrast	[6]
37.	color contrast	[6]
38.	half-range area	[6]
39.	mean red intensity	[21]
40.	mean blue intensity	[21]
41.	standard deviation green intensity	[21]
42.	standard deviation blue intensity	[21]
43.	sqrt (25. * 26.)	[12]
44.	eccentricity	[12]
45.	paraboloid depth	[12]
46.	mean of squared gradient	[12]
47.	45. / 43.	[12]
48.	46. / sqrt(45.)	[12]
49.	ratio of full peaks to the number of scan directions on intersecting scan lines in the specific position	[16]
50.	maximal of width of full peaks on intersecting scan lines	[16]
51.	average peak height	[16]

Table 4. Comparison of the ensemble-based system with an individual microaneurysm detector

Algorithm	Total	TP	FP	TP / FP
Mizutani	225	20	205	0.097
Ensemble	165	50	115	0.435
Ensemble (feature-based classification)	151	48	103	0.467
Ensemble (proposed classification)	106	39	67	0.582

forward feature subset selection technique [22]. The selected subset is showed in bold in Table 3. For classification, we used a kNN classifier. Our novel approach outperforms the feature-based technique as it can be seen in Table 4.

5   Conclusions

In this paper, we have introduced a novel approach for microaneurysm detection which is based on an ensemble-based of several candidate extraction methods. With this technique, we have successfully reduced the number of candidates using a voting scheme. Besides the reduction of the number of false candidates, we have increased the positive likelihood ratio. We have also showed that with a consequent classification step, these results can be improved further. Out method is also easily generalizable in terms of introducing more candidate extractors or classifiers.

Acknowledgements. This work was supported in part by the János Bolyai grant of the Hungarian Academy of Sciences, and by the TECH08-2 project DRSCREEN - Developing a computer based image processing system for diabetic retinopathy screening of the National Office for Research and Technology of Hungary (contract no.: OM-00194/2008, OM-00195/2008, OM-00196/2008). We also acknowledge the Moorefields Eye Hospital, London for their clinical support.

References

1. Harding, S., Greenwood, R., Aldington, S., Gibson, J., Owens, D., Taylor, R., Kohner, E., Scanlon, P., Leese, G.: Grading and disease management in national screening for diabetic retinopathy in england and wales. Diabetic Medicine 20, 965–971 (2003)
2. UK National Screening Committee: National Screening Programme for Diabetic Retinopathy (2009), http://www.retinalscreening.nhs.uk/
3. Abramoff, M., Niemeijer, M., Suttorp-Schulten, M., Viergever, M.A., Russel, S.R., van Ginneken, B.: Evaluation of a system for automatic detection of diabetic retinopathy from color fundus photographs in a large population of patients with diabetes. Diabetes Care 31, 193–198 (2008)
4. Hejlesen, O., Ege, B., Englemeier, K.H., Aldington, S., McCanna, L., Bek, T.: Tosca-imaging developing internet based image processing software for screening and diagnosis of diabetic retinopathy. In: MEDINFO 2004, pp. 222–226 (2004)

5. Niemeijer, M., van Ginneken, B., Cree, M., Mizutani, A., Quellec, G., Sanchez, C., Zhang, B., Hornero, R., Lamard, M., Muramatsu, C., Wu, X., Cazuguel, G., You, J., Mayo, A., Li, Q., Hatanaka, Y., Cochener, B., Roux, C., Karray, F., Garcia, M., Fujita, H., Abramoff, M.: Retinopathy online challenge: Automatic detection of microaneurysms in digital color fundus photographs. IEEE Transactions on Medical Imaging 29, 185–195 (2010)
6. Walter, T., Massin, P., Arginay, A., Ordonez, R., Jeulin, C., Klein, J.C.: Automatic detection of microaneurysms in color fundus images. Medical Image Analysis 11, 555–566 (2007)
7. Spencer, T., Olson, J.A., McHardy, K.C., Sharp, P.F., Forrester, J.V.: An image-processing strategy for the segmentation and quantification of microaneurysms in fluorescein angiograms of the ocular fundus. Computers and Biomedical Research 29, 284–302 (1996)
8. Frame, A.J., Undrill, P.E., Cree, M.J., Olson, J.A., McHardy, K.C., Sharp, P.F., Forrester, J.: A comparison of computer based classification methods applied to the detection of microaneurysms in ophthalmic fluorescein angiograms. Computers in Biology and Medicine 28, 225–238 (1998)
9. Abdelazeem, S.: Microaneurysm detection using vessels removal and circular hough transform. In: Proceedings of the Nineteenth National Radio Science Conference, pp. 421–426 (2002)
10. Niemeijer, M., Staal, J., Abramoff, M.D., Suttorp-Schulten, M.A., van Ginneken, B.: Automatic detection of red lesions in digital color fundus photographs. IEEE Transactions on Medical Imaging 24, 584–592 (2005)
11. Mizutani, A., Muramatsua, C., Hatanakab, Y., Suemoria, S., Haraa, T., Fujita, H.: Automated microaneurysm detection method based on double-ring filter in retinal fundus images. In: Medical Imaging 2009: Computer-Aided Diagnosis. Proceedings of SPIE, vol. 7260, pp. 1N1–1N8 (2009)
12. Fleming, A.D., Philip, S., Goatman, K.A.: Automated microaneurysm detection using local contrast normalization and local vessel detection. IEEE Transactions on Medical Imaging 25(9), 1223–1232 (2006)
13. Zuiderveld, K.: Contrast limited adaptive histogram equalization. In: Graphics gems IV, pp. 474–485 (1994)
14. Reza, A.M.: Realization of the contrast limited adaptive histogram equalization (clahe) for real-time image enhancement. The Journal of VLSI Signal Processing 38, 35–44 (2004)
15. Chen, T.C., Chung, K.L.: An efficient randomized algorithm for detecting circles. Computer Vision and Image Understanding 83, 172–191 (2001)
16. Lazar, I., Antal, B., Hajdu, A.: Microaneurysm detection in digital fundus images. Technical Report 2010/14(387), University of Debrecen, Hungary (2010)
17. Johnson, N.P.: Advantages to transforming the receiver operating characteristic (roc) curve into likelihood ratio co-ordinates. Stastics in Medicine 23, 2257–2266 (2004)
18. Staal, J., Abramoff, M.D., Niemeijer, M., Viergever, M.A., van Ginneken, B.: Ridge-based vessel segmentation in color images of the retina. IEEE Transactions on Medical Imaging 23, 501–509 (2004)
19. Kirkpatrick, S., Gelatt, C.D., Vecchi, M.P.: Optimization by simulated annealing. Science 220, 671–680 (1983)
20. Zhang, B., Wu, X., You, J., Li, Q., Karray, F.: Detection of microaneurysms using multi-scale correlation coefficients. Pattern Recogn. 43, 2237–2248 (2010)
21. Cree, M.J., Olson, J.A., McHardy, K.C., Sharp, P.F., Forrester, J.V.: A fully automated comparative microaneurysm digital detection system. Eye 11, 622–628 (1997)
22. Sondberg-madsen, N., Thomsen, C., Pena, J.M.: Unsupervised feature subset selection. In: Proceedings of the Workshop on Probabilistic Graphical Models for Classification, pp. 71–82 (2003)

Part VI

Wireless Information Networks
and Systems

Modulation-Mode Assignment for SVD-Aided and BICM-Assisted Downlink Multiuser MIMO Transmission Schemes

Andreas Ahrens[1] and César Benavente-Peces[2]

[1] Hochschule Wismar, University of Technology, Business and Design
Department of Electrical Engineering and Computer Science
Communications Signal Processing Group, Philipp-Müller-Straße 14, 23966 Wismar, Germany
[2] Universidad Politécnica de Madrid, E.U.I.T de Telecomunicación
Ctra. Valencia. km. 7, 28031 Madrid, Spain
andreas.ahrens@hs-wismar.de, cesar.benavente@upm.es
http://www.hs-wismar.de
http://www.upm.es

Abstract. Since the capacity of multiple-input multiple-output (MIMO) systems increases linearly with the minimum number of antennas at both the transmitter as well as the receiver side, MIMO systems have attracted a lot of attention for both frequency and non-frequency selective channels and reached a state of maturity. By contrast, MIMO-aided multiple-user systems require substantial further research. In this contribution we jointly optimize the number of multiple-input multiple-output (MIMO) layers and the number of bits per symbol within an iteratively-detected multiuser MIMO downlink (DL) transmission scheme under the constraint of a given fixed data throughput and integrity. Instead of treating all the users jointly as in zero-forcing (ZF) multiuser transmission techniques, the investigated singular value decomposition (SVD) assisted DL multiuser MIMO system takes the individual user's channel characteristics into account. In analogy to bit-interleaved coded irregular modulation, we introduce a MIMO-BICM scheme, where different user-specific signal constellations and mapping arrangement were used within a single codeword. Extrinsic information transfer (EXIT) charts are used for analyzing and optimizing the convergence behaviour of the iterative demapping and decoding. Our results show that in order to achieve the best bit-error rate, not necessarily all user-specific MIMO layers have to be activated.

Keywords: Multiple-Input Multiple-Output (MIMO) system, Wireless transmission, Singular-Value Decomposition (SVD), Extrinsic Information Transfer (EXIT) charts, Bit-Interleaved Coded Modulation (BICM), Iterative decoding, Bit-Interleaved Coded Irregular Modulation (BICIM), Spatial Division Multiplexing (SDM).

1 Introduction

The never ending desire for increasing the available transmission capacities has attracted a lot of research since Shannon's pioneering work in 1948. A possible solution

M.S. Obaidat, G.A. Tsihrintzis, and J. Filipe (Eds.): ICETE 2010, CCIS 222, pp. 395–409, 2012.
© Springer-Verlag Berlin Heidelberg 2012

was presented by Teletar and Foschini in the mid 90's, which revived the MIMO (multiple input multiple output) transmission philosophy introduced by van Etten in the mid 70's [1,2,3].

Bit-interleaved coded modulation (BICM) was designed for bandwidth efficient transmission over fading channels [4,5] and extended to bit-interleaved coded irregular modulation (BICIM) schemes by using different signal constellations and mapping arrangements within a single codeword, offering an improved link adaptation capability and an increased design freedom[6].

Since the capacity of multiple-input multiple-output (MIMO) systems increases linearly with the minimum number of antennas at both the transmitter as well as the receiver side, MIMO-BICM schemes have attracted substantial attention [7,8] and can be considered as an essential part of increasing both the achievable capacity and integrity of future generations of wireless systems [9,10]. However, their parameters have to be carefully optimized, especially in conjunction with adaptive modulation [11]. The well-known water-filling technique is virtually synonymous with adaptive modulation and it is used for maximizing the overall data rate [12,13,14]. However, delay-critical applications, such as voice or video transmission schemes, may require a certain fixed data rate. For these fixed-rate applications it is desirable to design algorithms, which minimize the bit-error rate at a given fixed data rate.

Single-user MIMO-BICM transmission schemes for both non-frequency and frequency selective MIMO channels have attracted a lot of attention and reached a state of maturity [9,15]. By contrast, MIMO-aided multiple-user systems require substantial further research where both multiuser as well as multi-antenna interferences have to be taken into account. Considering the entirety of the antennas of all mobile terminals at one end and the antennas of the base station at the other end of the communication link, state of the art interference cancellation is based on a central signal processing unit, e. g. a central unit at the base station, where joint detection can be applied in the uplink (UL) and joint transmission in the downlink (DL), respectively [16,17,18]. Widely used linear preprocessing techniques such as Minimum Mean Square Error or Zero Forcing (ZF) have attracted a lot of research and have reached a state of maturity, too [19]. Therefore, in this work a SVD-assisted downlink (DL) multiuser MIMO-BICM system is considered, which takes the individual user's channel characteristics into account rather than treating all users channels jointly as in ZF multiuser transmission techniques [20,21,22]. The choice of the number of bits per symbol and the number of activated MIMO layers combined with powerful error correcting codes offer a certain degree of design freedom [23]. In addition to bit loading algorithms, in this contribution the benefits of channel coding are also investigated. The proposed iterative decoder structures employ symbol-by-symbol soft-output decoding based on the Bahl-Cocke-Jelinek-Raviv (BCJR) algorithm and are analyzed under the constraint of a fixed data throughput [24].

Against this background, the novel contribution of this paper is that we jointly optimize the number of activated user-specific MIMO layers and the number of bits per symbol combined with powerful error correcting codes under the constraint of a given fixed data throughput and integrity. Since the "design-space" is large, a two-stage optimization technique is considered. Firstly, the uncoded spatial division multiplexing

(SDM) MIMO scheme is analyzed, investigating the allocation of both the number of bits per modulated symbol and the number of activated MIMO layers at a fixed data rate. Secondly, the optimized uncoded system is extended by incorporating bit-interleaved coded modulation using iterative detection (BICM-ID), whereby both the uncoded as well as the coded systems are required to support the same user data rate within the same bandwidth.

The remaining part of this contribution is organized as follows: Section 2 introduces our system model, while the proposed uncoded solutions are discussed in section 3. In section 4 the channel encoded MIMO system is introduced. The associated performance results are presented and interpreted in section 5. Finally, section 6 provides our concluding remarks.

2   Multiuser System Model

The system model considered in this work consists of a single base station (BS) supporting K mobile stations (MSs). The BS is equipped with n_T transmit antennas, while the kth (with $k = 1, \ldots, K$) MS has $n_{R\,k}$ receive antennas, i.e. the total number of receive antennas including all K MSs is given by $n_R = \sum_{k=1}^{K} n_{R\,k}$. The $(n_{R\,k} \times 1)$ user specific symbol vector $\mathbf{c}_k$ to be transmitted by the BS is given by

$$\mathbf{c}_k = \left(c_{k,1}, c_{k,2}, \ldots, c_{k,n_{R\,k}} \right)^{\mathrm{T}} . \tag{1}$$

The vector $\mathbf{c}_k$ is preprocessed before its transmission by multiplying it with the $(n_T \times n_{R\,k})$ DL preprocessing matrix $\mathbf{R}_k$ and results in the $(n_T \times 1)$ user-specific transmit vector

$$\mathbf{s}_k = \mathbf{R}_k \, \mathbf{c}_k . \tag{2}$$

After DL transmitter preprocessing, the n_T-component signal $\mathbf{s}$ transmitted by the BS to the K MSs results in

$$\mathbf{s} = \sum_{k=1}^{K} \mathbf{s}_k = \mathbf{R} \, \mathbf{c} , \tag{3}$$

with the $(n_T \times n_R)$ preprocessing matrix

$$\mathbf{R} = (\mathbf{R}_1, \mathbf{R}_2, \ldots, \mathbf{R}_K) . \tag{4}$$

In (3), the overall $(n_R \times 1)$ transmitted DL data vector $\mathbf{c}$ combines all K DL transmit vectors $\mathbf{c}_k$ (with $k = 1, 2, \ldots, K$) and is given by

$$\mathbf{c} = \left(\mathbf{c}_1^{\mathrm{T}}, \mathbf{c}_2^{\mathrm{T}} \ldots, \mathbf{c}_K^{\mathrm{T}} \right)^{\mathrm{T}} . \tag{5}$$

At the receiver side, the $(n_{R\,k} \times 1)$ vector $\mathbf{u}_k$ of the kth MS results in

$$\mathbf{u}_k = \mathbf{H}_k \, \mathbf{s} + \mathbf{n}_k = \mathbf{H}_k \, \mathbf{R} \, \mathbf{c} + \mathbf{n}_k \tag{6}$$

and can be expressed by

$$\mathbf{u}_k = \mathbf{H}_k \, \mathbf{R}_k \, \mathbf{c}_k + \sum_{i=1,i\neq k}^{K} \mathbf{H}_k \, \mathbf{R}_i \, \mathbf{c}_i + \mathbf{n}_k , \tag{7}$$

where the MSs received signals experience both multi-user and multi-antenna interferences. In (6), the $(n_{\mathrm{R}\,k} \times n_{\mathrm{T}})$ channel matrix $\mathbf{H}_k$ connects the n_{T} BS specific transmit antennas with the $n_{\mathrm{R}\,k}$ receive antennas of the kth MS. It is assumed that the coefficients of the $(n_{\mathrm{R}\,k} \times n_{\mathrm{T}})$ channel matrix $\mathbf{H}_k$ are independent and Rayleigh distributed with equal variance. The interference, which is introduced by the off-diagonal elements of the channel matrix $\mathbf{H}_k$, requires appropriate signal processing strategies. A popular technique is based on the SVD of the channel matrix $\mathbf{H}_k$. Upon carrying out the SVD of $\mathbf{H}_k$ with $n_{\mathrm{T}} \geq n_{\mathrm{R}}$ and assuming that the rank of the matrix $\mathbf{H}_k$ equals $n_{\mathrm{R}\,k}$, i.e., rank$(\mathbf{H}_k) = n_{\mathrm{R}\,k}$, we get

$$\mathbf{H}_k = \mathbf{U}_k \cdot \mathbf{V}_k \cdot \mathbf{D}_k^{\mathrm{H}} \ , \tag{8}$$

with the $(n_{\mathrm{R}\,k} \times n_{\mathrm{R}\,k})$ unitary matrix $\mathbf{U}_k$ and the $(n_{\mathrm{T}} \times n_{\mathrm{T}})$ unitary matrix $\mathbf{D}_k^{\mathrm{H}}$, respectively[1]. The $(n_{\mathrm{R}\,k} \times n_{\mathrm{T}})$ diagonal matrix $\mathbf{V}_k$ can be decomposed into a $(n_{\mathrm{R}\,k} \times n_{\mathrm{R}\,k})$ matrix $\mathbf{V}_{k\,\mathrm{u}}$ containing the non-zero square roots of the eigenvalues of $\mathbf{H}_k^{\mathrm{H}}\mathbf{H}_k$, i.e.,

$$\mathbf{V}_{k\,\mathrm{u}} = \begin{bmatrix} \sqrt{\xi_{k,1}} & 0 & \cdots & 0 \\ 0 & \sqrt{\xi_{k,2}} & \ddots & \vdots \\ \vdots & \ddots & \ddots & \vdots \\ 0 & 0 & \cdots & \sqrt{\xi_{k,n_{\mathrm{R}\,k}}} \end{bmatrix} \ , \tag{9}$$

and a $(n_{\mathrm{R}\,k} \times (n_{\mathrm{T}} - n_{\mathrm{R}\,k}))$ zero-matrix $\mathbf{V}_{k\,\mathrm{n}}$ according to

$$\mathbf{V}_k = (\mathbf{V}_{k\,\mathrm{u}} \ \mathbf{V}_{k\,\mathrm{n}}) = (\mathbf{V}_{k\,\mathrm{u}} \ \mathbf{0}) \ . \tag{10}$$

Additionally, the $(n_{\mathrm{T}} \times n_{\mathrm{T}})$ unitary matrix $\mathbf{D}_k$ can be decomposed into a $(n_{\mathrm{T}} \times n_{\mathrm{R}\,k})$ matrix $\mathbf{D}_{k\,\mathrm{u}}$ constituted by the eigenvectors corresponding to the non-zero eigenvalues of $\mathbf{H}_k^{\mathrm{H}}\mathbf{H}_k$ and a $(n_{\mathrm{T}} \times (n_{\mathrm{T}} - n_{\mathrm{R}\,k}))$ matrix $\mathbf{D}_{k\,\mathrm{n}}$ constituted by the eigenvectors corresponding to the zero eigenvalues of $\mathbf{H}_k^{\mathrm{H}}\mathbf{H}_k$. The decomposition of the matrix $\mathbf{D}_k^{\mathrm{H}}$ results in

$$\mathbf{D}_k^{\mathrm{H}} = \begin{pmatrix} \mathbf{D}_{k\,\mathrm{u}}^{\mathrm{H}} \\ \mathbf{D}_{k\,\mathrm{n}}^{\mathrm{H}} \end{pmatrix} \ . \tag{11}$$

Finally, the received downlink signal $\mathbf{u}_k$ of the kth MS may be expressed as

$$\mathbf{u}_k = \mathbf{U}_k \mathbf{V}_{k\,\mathrm{u}} \mathbf{D}_{k\,\mathrm{u}}^{\mathrm{H}} \mathbf{R}\,\mathbf{c} + \mathbf{n}_k \ , \tag{12}$$

with the vector $\mathbf{n}_k$ of the additive, white Gaussian noise (AWGN). Taking all MSs received DL signals $\mathbf{u}_k$ into account, the $(n_{\mathrm{R}} \times 1)$ receive vector results in

$$\mathbf{u} = \left(\mathbf{u}_1^{\mathrm{T}}, \mathbf{u}_2^{\mathrm{T}}, \ldots, \mathbf{u}_K^{\mathrm{T}}\right)^{\mathrm{T}} \ . \tag{13}$$

Then, the overall DL signal vector $\mathbf{u}$ including the received signals of all K MSs can be expressed by

$$\mathbf{u} = \mathbf{U}\,\mathbf{V}_{\mathrm{u}}\,\mathbf{D}_{\mathrm{u}}^{\mathrm{H}}\,\mathbf{R}\,\mathbf{c} + \mathbf{n} \ , \tag{14}$$

---

[1] The transpose and conjugate transpose (Hermitian) of $\mathbf{D}_k$ are denoted by $\mathbf{D}_k^{\mathrm{T}}$ and $\mathbf{D}_k^{\mathrm{H}}$, respectively.

with the overall $(n_R \times 1)$ noise vector

$$\mathbf{n} = \left(\mathbf{n}_1^T, \mathbf{n}_2^T, \ldots, \mathbf{n}_K^T\right)^T , \tag{15}$$

the $(n_R \times n_R)$ block diagonal matrix $\mathbf{U}$

$$\mathbf{U} = \begin{bmatrix} \mathbf{U}_1 & \mathbf{0} & \cdots & \mathbf{0} \\ \mathbf{0} & \mathbf{U}_2 & \ddots & \vdots \\ \vdots & \ddots & \ddots & \vdots \\ \mathbf{0} & \mathbf{0} & \cdots & \mathbf{U}_K \end{bmatrix} , \tag{16}$$

the $(n_R \times n_R)$ block diagonal matrix $\mathbf{V}_u$

$$\mathbf{V}_u = \begin{bmatrix} \mathbf{V}_{1u} & \mathbf{0} & \cdots & \mathbf{0} \\ \mathbf{0} & \mathbf{V}_{2u} & \ddots & \vdots \\ \vdots & \ddots & \ddots & \vdots \\ \mathbf{0} & \mathbf{0} & \cdots & \mathbf{V}_{Ku} \end{bmatrix} , \tag{17}$$

and the $(n_T \times n_R)$ matrix $\mathbf{D}_u$ which is given by

$$\mathbf{D}_u = (\mathbf{D}_{1u}, \mathbf{D}_{2u}, \ldots, \mathbf{D}_{Ku}) . \tag{18}$$

In order to suppress the DL multi-user interferences (MUI) perfectly, the DL preprocessing matrix $\mathbf{R}$ has to be designed to satisfy the following condition

$$\mathbf{D}_u^H \mathbf{R} = \mathbf{P} , \tag{19}$$

with the real-valued $(n_R \times n_R)$ diagonal matrix $\mathbf{P}$ taking the transmit-power constraint into account. In order to satisfy (19), $\mathbf{R}$ can be defined as follows

$$\mathbf{R} = \mathbf{D}_u \left(\mathbf{D}_u^H \mathbf{D}_u\right)^{-1} \mathbf{P} . \tag{20}$$

Taking the ZF design criterion for the DL preprocessing matrix into account, the matrix $\mathbf{P}$ simplifies to an $(n_R \times n_R)$ diagonal matrix, i.e. $\mathbf{P} = \sqrt{\beta}\,\mathbf{I}_{n_R \times n_R}$, with the parameter $\sqrt{\beta}$ taking the transmit-power constraint into account. When taking the DL preprocessing matrix, defined in (20), into account, the overall received vector of all K MSs, defined in (14), can be simplified to

$$\mathbf{u} = \mathbf{U}\mathbf{V}_u\mathbf{P}\mathbf{c} + \mathbf{n} . \tag{21}$$

Therein, the $(n_R \times n_R)$ block diagonal matrix $\mathbf{P}$ is given by

$$\mathbf{P} = \begin{bmatrix} \mathbf{P}_1 & \mathbf{0} & \cdots & \mathbf{0} \\ \mathbf{0} & \mathbf{P}_2 & \ddots & \vdots \\ \vdots & \ddots & \ddots & \vdots \\ \mathbf{0} & \mathbf{0} & \cdots & \mathbf{P}_K \end{bmatrix} . \tag{22}$$

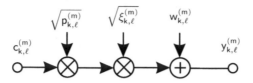

Fig. 1. Resulting kth user-specific system model per MIMO layer ℓ (with $\ell = 1, 2, \ldots, n_{R\,k}$) and per transmitted symbol block m

In (21), the user-specific ($n_{R\,k} \times 1$) vector $\mathbf{u}_k$ can be expressed as

$$\mathbf{u}_k = \mathbf{U}_k \, \mathbf{V}_{k\,u} \, \mathbf{P}_k \, \mathbf{c}_k + \mathbf{n}_k \ , \tag{23}$$

with the user-specific ($n_{R\,k} \times n_{R\,k}$) power allocation matrix

$$\mathbf{P}_k = \begin{bmatrix} \sqrt{p_{k,1}} & 0 & \cdots & 0 \\ 0 & \sqrt{p_{k,2}} & \ddots & \vdots \\ \vdots & \ddots & \ddots & \vdots \\ 0 & 0 & \cdots & \sqrt{p_{k,n_{R\,k}}} \end{bmatrix} . \tag{24}$$

As long as the transmit power is uniformly distributed over the number of activated MIMO layers, the matrix $\mathbf{P}_k$ simplifies to $\mathbf{P}_k = \sqrt{\beta}\,\mathbf{I}_{n_{R\,k} \times n_{R\,k}}$. After postprocessing of the received signal vectors $\mathbf{u}_k$ with the corresponding unitary matrix $\mathbf{U}_k^{H}$, the user-specific decision variables result with $\mathbf{U}_k^{H}\,\mathbf{n}_k = \mathbf{w}_k$ in

$$\mathbf{y}_k = \mathbf{U}_k^{H}\,\mathbf{u}_k = \mathbf{V}_{k\,u}\,\mathbf{P}_k\,\mathbf{c}_k + \mathbf{w}_k \ , \tag{25}$$

or alternatively with $\mathbf{U}^{H}\,\mathbf{n} = \mathbf{w}$ in

$$\mathbf{y} = \mathbf{U}^{H}\,\mathbf{u} = \mathbf{V}_{u}\,\mathbf{P}\,\mathbf{c} + \mathbf{w} \ , \tag{26}$$

where interferences between the different antenna data streams as well as MUI imposed by the other users are avoided [21,22]. The resulting system model is depicted in Fig. 1.

3   Quality Criteria

In general, the user-specific quality of data transmission can be informally assessed by using the signal-to-noise ratio (SNR) at the detector's input defined by the half vertical eye opening and the noise power per quadrature component according to

$$\varrho = \frac{(\text{Half vertical eye opening})^2}{\text{Noise Power}} = \frac{(U_A)^2}{(U_R)^2} \ , \tag{27}$$

which is often used as a quality parameter [23]. The relationship between the signal-to-noise ratio $\varrho = U_A^2 / U_R^2$ and the bit-error probability evaluated for AWGN channels and M-ary Quadrature Amplitude Modulation (QAM) is given by [25]

$$P_{\text{BER}} = \frac{2}{\log_2(M)} \left(1 - \frac{1}{\sqrt{M}}\right) \text{erfc}\left(\sqrt{\frac{\varrho}{2}}\right) . \tag{28}$$

When applying the proposed system structure for the kth user, depicted in Fig. 1, the applied signal processing leads to different eye openings per activated MIMO layer ℓ (with $\ell = 1, 2, \ldots, L$ and $L \leq n_{\text{R}\,k}$ describing the number of activated user-specific MIMO layers) and per transmitted symbol block m according to

$$U_{\text{A}\,k}^{(\ell,m)} = \sqrt{p_{k,\ell}^{(m)}} \cdot \sqrt{\xi_{k,\ell}^{(m)}} \cdot U_{\text{s}\,k}^{(\ell)} , \tag{29}$$

where $U_{\text{s}\,k}^{(\ell)}$ denotes the half-level transmit amplitude assuming M_ℓ-ary QAM, $\sqrt{\xi_{k,\ell}^{(m)}}$ represents the corresponding positive square roots of the eigenvalues of the matrix $\mathbf{H}_k^{\text{H}} \mathbf{H}_k$ and $\sqrt{p_{k,\ell}^{(m)}}$ represents the corresponding power allocation weighting parameters (Fig. 1). Together with the noise power per quadrature component, introduced by the additive, white Gaussian noise (AWGN) vector $\mathbf{w}_k = \mathbf{U}_k^{\text{H}} \mathbf{n}_k$ in (25), the kth user-specific SNR per MIMO layer ℓ at the time m becomes

$$\varrho_k^{(\ell,m)} = \frac{\left(U_{\text{A}\,k}^{(\ell,m)}\right)^2}{U_{\text{R}}^2} . \tag{30}$$

Using the parallel transmission over L MIMO layers, the overall mean user-specific transmit power becomes $P_{\text{s}\,k} = \sum_{\ell=1}^{L} P_{\text{s}\,k}^{(\ell)}$. Considering QAM constellations, the average user-specific transmit power $P_{\text{s}\,k}^{(\ell)}$ per MIMO layer ℓ may be expressed as [25]

$$P_{\text{s}\,k}^{(\ell)} = \frac{2}{3} \left(U_{\text{s}\,k}^{(\ell)}\right)^2 (M_{k\,\ell} - 1) . \tag{31}$$

Combining (30) and (31) together with (29), the layer-specific SNR at the time m results in

$$\varrho_k^{(\ell,m)} = p_{k,\ell}^{(m)} \, \xi_{k,\ell}^{(m)} \, \frac{3}{2\,(M_{k\,\ell} - 1)} \, \frac{P_{\text{s}\,k}^{(\ell)}}{U_{\text{R}}^2} . \tag{32}$$

Assuming that the user-specific transmit power is uniformly distributed over the number of activated MIMO layers, i.e., $P_{\text{s}\,k}^{(\ell)} = P_{\text{s}\,k}/L$, the layer-specific signal-to-noise ratio at the time m, defined in (32), results with the ratio of symbol energy to noise power spectral density $E_{\text{s}}/N_0 = P_{\text{s}\,k}/(2\,U_{\text{R}}^2)$ in

$$\varrho_k^{(\ell,m)} = p_{k,\ell}^{(m)} \, \xi_{k,\ell}^{(m)} \, \frac{3}{L\,(M_{k\,\ell} - 1)} \, \frac{E_{\text{s}}}{N_0} . \tag{33}$$

In order to transmit at a fixed data rate while maintaining the best possible integrity, i.e., bit-error rate, an appropriate number of user-specific MIMO layers has to be used, which depends on the specific transmission mode, as detailed in Table 1 for the exemplarily investigated two-user multiuser-system ($n_{\text{R}\,k} = 4$ (with $k = 1, 2$), $K = 2$, $n_{\text{R}} = n_{\text{T}} = 8$). An optimized adaptive scheme would now use the particular transmission modes, e.g., by using bit auction procedures [26], that results in the lowest BER for each SDM MIMO data vector. However, this would lead to a high signaling overhead. Therefore, in order to avoid any signalling overhead, fixed transmission modes are used in this contribution regardless of the channel quality.

Table 1. Investigated user-specific transmission modes

throughput	layer 1	layer 2	layer 3	layer 4
8 bit/s/Hz	256	0	0	0
8 bit/s/Hz	64	4	0	0
8 bit/s/Hz	**16**	**16**	**0**	**0**
8 bit/s/Hz	**16**	**4**	**4**	**0**
8 bit/s/Hz	4	4	4	4

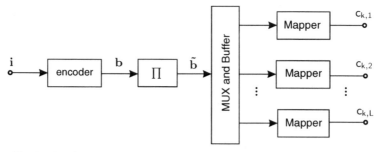

Fig. 2. The channel-encoded kth user-specific MIMO transmitter structure

4   Channel-Encoded MIMO System

The channel encoded user-specific transmitter structure is depicted in Fig. 2. The encoder employs a half-rate nonrecursive, non-systematic convolutional (NSC) code using the generator polynomials $(7, 5)$ in octal notation. The uncoded information is organized in blocks of N_i bits, consisting of at least 3000 bits, depending on the specific QAM constellation used. Each data block $\mathbf{i}$ is encoded and results in the block $\mathbf{b}$ consisting of $N_b = 2\,N_i + 4$ encoded bits, including 2 termination bits. The encoded bits are interleaved using a random interleaver and stored in the vector $\tilde{\mathbf{b}}$. The encoded and interleaved bits are then mapped to the MIMO layers. The task of the multiplexer and buffer block of Fig. 2 is to divide the user-specific vector of encoded and interleaved information bits $\tilde{\mathbf{b}}$ into subvectors according to the chosen transmission mode (Table 1). The individual user-specific binary data vectors are then mapped to the QAM symbols $c_{k,\ell}$ according to the specific mapper used. The iterative demodulator structure is shown in Fig. 3 [27]. When using the iteration index ν, the first iteration of $\nu = 1$ commences with the soft-demapper delivering the N_b log-likelihood ratios (LLRs) $L_2^{(\nu=1)}(\tilde{\mathbf{b}})$ of the encoded and interleaved information bits, whose de-interleaved version $L_{a,1}^{(\nu=1)}(\mathbf{b})$ represents the input of the convolutional decoder as depicted in Fig. 3 [24,9]. This channel decoder provides the estimates $L_1^{(\nu=1)}(\mathbf{i})$ of the original uncoded information bits as well as the LLRs of the N_b NSC-encoded bits in the form of

$$L_1^{(\nu=1)}(\mathbf{b}) = L_{a,1}^{(\nu=1)}(\mathbf{b}) + L_{e,1}^{(\nu=1)}(\mathbf{b}) \ . \tag{34}$$

As seen in Figure 3 and (34), the LLRs of the NSC-encoded bits consist of the receiver's input signal itself plus the extrinsic information $L_{e,1}^{(\nu=1)}(\mathbf{b})$, which is generated

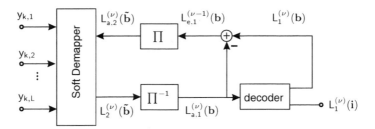

Fig. 3. Iterative demodulator structure

by subtracting $L_{a,1}^{(\nu=1)}(\mathbf{b})$ from $L_1^{(\nu=1)}(\mathbf{b})$. The appropriately ordered, i. e. interleaved extrinsic LLRs are fed back as *a priori* information $L_{a,2}^{(\nu=2)}(\tilde{\mathbf{b}})$ to the soft demapper of Fig. 3 for the second iteration.

5   Results

Assuming predefined QAM constellation sizes, as detailed in Table 1, a fixed total throughput can be guaranteed for each SDM MIMO block regardless of the channel quality.

5.1   Single-User System

Considering a non-frequency selective single-user SDM MIMO link ($K = 1$) composed of $n_T = 4$ transmit and $n_R = 4$ receive antennas, the corresponding calculated BER curves are depicted in Fig. 4 for the different QAM constellation sizes and MIMO configurations of Table 1, when transmitting at a bandwidth efficiency of 8 bit/s/Hz, assuming a Nyquist roll-off factor of 0.5. Assuming a uniform distribution of the transmit power over the number of activated MIMO layers, it turns out that not all MIMO layers have to be activated in order to achieve the best BERs. However, it is worth noting that the lowest BERs can only be achieved by using bit auction procedures leading to a high signalling overhead [26]. Analyzing the probability of choosing a specific transmission mode by using optimal bitloading, as depicted in Table 2, it turns out that only an appropriate number of MIMO layers has to be activated, e. g., the $(16, 4, 4, 0)$ QAM configuration. The results, obtained by using bit auction procedures justify the choice of fixed transmission modes regardless of the channel quality as investigated in the contribution. Besides this, the joint optimization of the number of activated MIMO layers as well as the number of bits per symbol was found to be effective at high SNRs. However, iterative receivers are able to work in a much lower SNR region. Therefore it would be interesting to see how the design criteria change when coding is added to the transmission system.

Using the half-rate, constraint-length $K_{cl} = 3$ NSC code with the generator polynomials of $(7, 5)$ in octal notation, the BER performance is analyzed for an effective throughput of 4 bit/s/Hz based on the best uncoded schemes of Table 1. In addition to the number of bits per symbol and the number of activated MIMO layers, the achievable performance of the iterative decoder is substantially affected by the specific mapping of

Table 2. Probability of choosing specific transmission modes $(K = 1)$ at a fixed data rate by using optimal bitloading $(10 \cdot \log_{10}(E_s/N_0) = 10$ dB$)$

mode	$(64, 4, 0, 0)$	$(16, 16, 0, 0)$	$(16, 4, 4, 0)$	$(4, 4, 4, 4)$
pdf	0.0116	0.2504	0.7373	0.0008

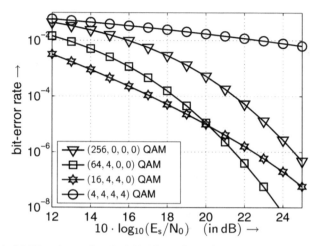

Fig. 4. Uncoded BERs when using the MIMO configurations introduced in Table 1 and transmitting 8 bit/s/Hz over non-frequency selective uncorrelated Rayleigh channels

the bits to both the QAM symbols as well as to the MIMO layers. While the employment of the classic Gray-mapping is appropriate in the absence of *a priori* information, the availability of *a priori* information in iterative receivers requires an exhaustive search for finding the best non-Gray – synonymously also referred to anti-Gray – mapping scheme [5].

A mapping scheme optimized for perfect *a priori* information has usually a poor performance, when there is no *a priori* information. However, when applying iterative demapping and decoding, large gains can be achieved as long as the reliability of the *a priori* information increases upon increasing the number of iterations. As depicted in Fig. 5, the maximum iteration gain can only be guaranteed, if anti-Gray mapping is used on all activated MIMO layers. At the first iteration, using anti-Gray mapping on all MIMO layers results in a lower extrinsic demapper output, compared with layer-specific or Gray mapping schemes (e. g. layer 1: anti-Gray, layer 2 and 3: Gray). However, anti-Gray mapping on all MIMO layers outperforms layer-specific mapping strategies for high *a priori* information. Furthermore, observed by comparing the EXIT chart results of Fig. 5, the overall performance is strongly influenced by the most susceptible MIMO layer, which is here the MIMO layer transmitting 4 bit/s/Hz. Finally, the BER performance is characterized in Fig. 6 based on the best uncoded schemes of Table 1. The information word length is 3000 bits and a random interleaver is applied. The influence of the Gray versus anti-Gray mapping is clearly visible in Fig. 6.

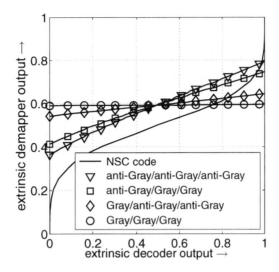

Fig. 5. EXIT chart for an effective throughput of 4 bit/s/Hz and the $(16, 4, 4, 0)$ QAM constellation at $10 \log_{10}(E_s/N_0) = 2$ dB

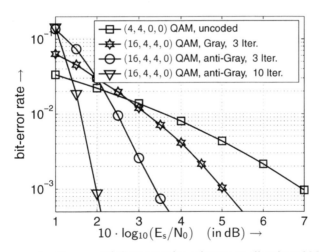

Fig. 6. BERs assuming Gray or anti-Gray mapping schemes on all activated MIMO layers for an effective user throughput of 4 bit/s/Hz

Further improvements in terms of the BER are possible by using unequal power allocation. However, as shown in [23] and [15], unequal power allocation in combination with the joint optimization of the number of activated MIMO layers as well as the number of bits per symbol was found to be effective at high SNRs. However, iterative receivers are able to work in a much lower SNR region, where a power allocation scheme was found to be inefficient.

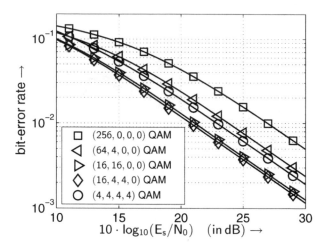

Fig. 7. User-specific BERs when using the transmission modes introduced in Table 1 and transmitting 8 bit/s/Hz over non-frequency selective channels

5.2 Multiuser System

The parameters of the analyzed two-users MIMO system are chosen as follows[2]: $P_{s\,k} = 1\,V^2$, $n_{R\,k} = 4$ (with $k = 1, 2$), $K = 2, n_R = n_T = 8$. The obtained user-specific BER curves are depicted in Fig. 7 for the different QAM constellation sizes and MIMO configurations of Table 1. Assuming a uniform distribution of the transmit power over the number of activated MIMO layers, it still turns out that not all MIMO layers have to be activated in order to achieve the best BERs. This can still be confirmed by analyzing the probability of choosing user-specific transmission modes within the multiuser DL MIMO system by using optimal bitloading [26], as depicted in Table 3. However, based on the higher total throughput within the given bandwidth compared to the single-user system, the gap between the different transmission modes becomes smaller.

Table 3. Probability of choosing user-specific transmission modes ($K = 2$) at a fixed data rate by using optimal bitloading ($10 \cdot \log_{10}(E_s/N_0) = 10$ dB)

mode	$(64, 4, 0, 0)$	$(16, 16, 0, 0)$	$(16, 4, 4, 0)$	$(4, 4, 4, 4)$
pdf	0	0.0102	0.9524	0.0374

Using the half-rate, constraint-length $K_{cl} = 3$ NSC code and comparing the EXIT chart results of Fig. 8, the overall performance is still strongly influenced by the number of activated MIMO layers, suggesting that at low SNR not all MIMO layers has to

---

[2] In this contribution a power with the dimension (voltage)^2 (in V^2) is used. At a real constant resistor this value is proportional to the physical power (in W).

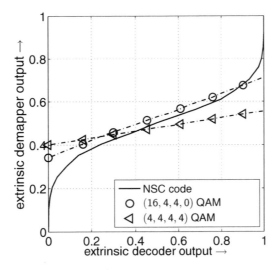

Fig. 8. User-specific EXIT chart for an effective throughput of 4 bit/s/Hz when using anti-Gray mapping on all activated MIMO layers ($10 \log_{10}(E_s/N_0) = 7$ dB) and the half-rate NSC code with the generator polynomials of $(7, 5)$ in octal notation

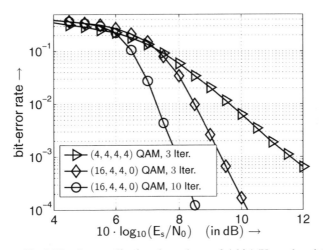

Fig. 9. User-specific BERs for an effective throughput of 4 bit/s/Hz and anti-Gray mapping in combination with different transmission modes and the half-rate NSC code with the generator polynomials of $(7, 5)$ in octal notation.

be activated in order to guarantee an efficient information exchange between the soft-demapper and the corresponding decoder. The user-specific BER performance is given in Fig. 9 and underlines that in order to minimize the overall BER not necessarily all user-specific MIMO layers has to be activated.

6   Conclusions

In analogy to BICIM, we introduced a multi-user MIMO-BICM scheme, where dif-different user-specific signal constellations and mappings were used within a single codeword. The proposed system includes an adaptation of the transmit parameters. EXIT charts are used for analysing and optimizing the convergence behaviour of iterative demapping and decoding.

The choice of the number of bits per symbol and the number of MIMO layers combined with powerful error correcting codes substantially affects the performance of a MIMO system, suggesting that not all MIMO layers have to be activated in order to achieve the best BERs. Here, anti-Gray mapping on all activated MIMO layers seems to be a promising solution for minimizing the overall BER characteristic.

References

1. Telatar, E.: Capacity of Multi-Antenna Gaussian Channels. European Transactions on Telecommunications 10(6), 585–595 (1999)
2. Foschini, G.J.: Layered Space-Time Architecture for Wireless Communication in a Fading Environment when Using Multiple Antennas. Bell Labs Technical Journal 1(2), 41–59 (1996)
3. van Etten, W.: An Optimum Linear Receiver for Multiple Channel Digital Transmission Systems. IEEE Transactions on Communications 23(8), 828–834 (1975)
4. Caire, G., Taricco, G., Biglieri, E.: Bit-Interleaved Coded Modulation. IEEE Transactions on Information Theory 44(3), 927–946 (1998)
5. Chindapol, A., Ritcey, J.A.: Design, Analysis, and Performance Evaluation for BICM-ID with square QAM Constellations in Rayleigh Fading Channels. IEEE Journal on Selected Areas in Communications 19(5), 944–957 (2001)
6. Schreckenbach, F., Bauch, G.: Bit-Interleaved Coded Irregular Modulation. European Transactions on Telecommunications 17(2), 269–282 (2006)
7. McKay, M.R., Collings, I.B.: Capacity and Performance of MIMO-BICM with Zero-Forcing Receivers. IEEE Transactions on Communications 53(1), 74–83 (2005)
8. Müller-Weinfurtner, S.H.: Coding Approaches for Multiple Antenna Transmission in Fast Fading and OFDM. IEEE Transactions on Signal Processing 50(10), 2442–2450 (2002)
9. Kühn, V.: Wireless Communications over MIMO Channels – Applications to CDMA and Multiple Antenna Systems. Wiley, Chichester (2006)
10. Zheng, L., Tse, D.N.T.: Diversity and Multiplexing: A Fundamental Tradeoff in Multiple-Antenna Channels. IEEE Transactions on Information Theory 49(5), 1073–1096 (2003)
11. Zhou, Z., Vucetic, B., Dohler, M., Li, Y.: MIMO Systems with Adaptive Modulation. IEEE Transactions on Vehicular Technology 54(5), 1073–1096 (2005)
12. Krongold, B.S., Ramchandran, K., Jones, D.L.: Computationally Efficient Optimal Power Allocation Algorithms for Multicarrier Communications Systems. IEEE Transactions on Communications 48(1), 23–27 (2000)
13. Fischer, R.F.H., Huber, J.B.: A New Loading Algorithm for Discrete Multitone Modulation. In: IEEE Global Telecommunications Conference (GLOBECOM), London, pp. 724–728 (1996)
14. Park, C.S., Lee, K.B.: Transmit Power Allocation for BER Performance Improvement in Multicarrier Systems. IEEE Transactions on Communications 52(10), 1658–1663 (2004)
15. Ahrens, A., Benavente-Peces, C.: Modulation-Mode and Power Assignment for Broadband MIMO-BICM Schemes. In: IEEE 20th Personal, Indoor and Mobile Radio Communications Symposium (PIMRC), Tokio, Japan (September 13-16, 2009)

16. Meurer, M., Baier, P.W., Weber, T., Lu, Y., Papathanassiou, A.: Joint Transmission: An Advantageous Downlink Concept for CDMA Mobile Radio Systems using Time Division Duplexing. Electronics Letters 36(10), 900–901 (2000)
17. Choi, R.L., Murch, R.D.: A Transmit Preprocessing Technique for Multiuser MIMO Systems using a Decomposition Approach. IEEE Transactions on Wireless Communications 3(1), 20–24 (2004)
18. Joham, M., Utschick, W., Nossek, J.A.: Linear Transmit Processing in MIMO Communications Systems. IEEE Transactions on Signal Processing 53(8), 2700–2712 (2005)
19. Choi, R.L., Murch, R.D.: New Transmit Schemes and Simplified Receivers for MIMO Wireless Communication Systems. IEEE Transactions on Wireless Communications 2(6), 1217–1230 (2003)
20. Liu, W., Yang, L.L., Hanzo, L.: SVD Assisted Joint Transmitter and Receiver Design for the Downlink of MIMO Systems. In: IEEE 68th Vehicular Technology Conference (VTC), Calgary, pp. 1–5 (2008)
21. Ahrens, A., Benavente-Peces, C.: Modulation-Mode and Power Assignment for SVD-assisted and Iteratively Detected Downlink Multiuser MIMO Systems. In: International Conference on Wireless Information Networks and Systems (WINSYS), Athens, Greece, July 26-28, pp. 107–114 (2010)
22. Aust, S., Ahrens, A., Benavente-Peces, C.: Modulation-Mode and Power Assignment for SVD- and GMD-assisted Downlink MIMO Systems. In: 7th IEEE International Conference on Signals and Electronic Systems (ICSES), Gliwice, Poland, September 7-10, pp. 367–370 (2010)
23. Ahrens, A., Lange, C.: Modulation-Mode and Power Assignment in SVD-equalized MIMO Systems. Facta Universitatis (Series Electronics and Energetics) 21(2), 167–181 (2008)
24. Bahl, L.R., Cocke, J., Jelinek, F., Raviv, J.: Optimal Decoding of Linear Codes for Minimizing Symbol Error Rate. IEEE Transactions on Information Theory 20(3), 284–287 (1974)
25. Proakis, J.G.: Digital Communications. McGraw-Hill, Boston (2000)
26. Wong, C.Y., Cheng, R.S., Letaief, K.B., Murch, R.D.: Multiuser OFDM with Adaptive Subcarrier, Bit, and Power Allocation. IEEE Journal on Selected Areas in Communications 17(10), 1747–1758 (1999)
27. Ahrens, A., Ng, S.X., Kühn, V., Hanzo, L.: Modulation-Mode Assignment for SVD-Aided and BICM-Assisted Spatial Division Multiplexing. Physical Communications (PHYCOM) 1(1), 60–66 (2008)

Evaluation of the Performance of Polarization Diversity Estimated from Measurements at One Polarization

Iñigo Cuiñas and Manuel García Sánchez

Universidade de Vigo, Dept. Teoría do Sinal e Comunicacións
Maxwell, s/n 36310 Vigo, Spain
{inhigo,manuel.garciasanchez}@uvigo.es

Abstract. Wireless networks are exposed to deep multipath fading conditions when they are installed in complex indoor environments. A solution to mitigate this situation could be the use of polarization diversity techniques in reception. This chapter explores this possibility, and also presents a procedure to estimate the received cross-polarized power from wide band measurements performed at just one polarization, in the 5 GHz frequency band. After testing up to three different strategies, and once analyzed the results, an improvement of 21% in terms of received power has been detected in rooms presenting strongly multipath events.

Keywords: Diversity, Indoor, Measurements, Polarization, Radio channel, Wireless network.

1 Introduction

The deployment of wireless local area networks is limited, in most situations, by the strong multipath effect that could degrade the performance of the complete communication system. This multipath effect appears as frequency selective fast fading events along the receiver path, when it is moved; or as very low coverage at some locations that could coincide with receiver position. In both situations, the connectivity of the network nodes may be reduced or even unavailable.

The multipath is present in most of the environments where a radio communication system is installed. However, it is at indoor scenarios where the effects of multipath resulted to be more hazardous for the performance of the system. This is the reason why different indoor environments have been used to check the proposal of this chapter.

The work in this chapter is centered in the 5.8 GHz band, one of the assigned to wireless networks [1-3]. Results of several measurement campaigns performed in both line of sight (LoS), non LoS (NLoS), and obstructed LoS (OLoS) indoor environments have been used as a basis to check the options of implementing a solution to reduce the multipath consequences. These data are radio channel responses, with transmitters at fixed locations and receivers measuring along linear paths, as explained in the second section. As we get complex responses, we can analyze the multipath effect, and we can try to reduce the influence of their costs.

M.S. Obaidat, G.A. Tsihrintzis, and J. Filipe (Eds.): ICETE 2010, CCIS 222, pp. 410–423, 2012.
© Springer-Verlag Berlin Heidelberg 2012

Among the various procedures that have been tested to mitigate the multipath consequences, different diversity techniques have been proposed. The general solution of such techniques is to provide two different propagation paths, with almost uncorrelated received signals. Thus, the alternate use of both signals, and the combination between them, provide an output signal with better relation SNR than that obtained with only one standard propagation path.

Diversity techniques could be applied following several strategies: frequency, space, time, angle, polarization, and hybrids that combine some of the previously indicated [4,5].

Among the diversity techniques, the polarization diversity is analyzed along this chapter: two orthogonally polarized signals at the same frequency are used as inputs in the diversity receiver. In this case, the pair of propagation paths is provided by the pair of orthogonal polarizations. This technique has been selected because the indoor environments present both multipath phenomenon and depolarization by transmission and reflection on the walls, ceiling, floor, and so on. Thus, a certain percentage of the transmitted signal would reach the receiver orthogonally polarized. Moreover, the spectrum consumption is reduced compared to frequency diversity, as no new bands are occupied by the second propagation path. Depending on the amount of depolarized signal, the application of polarization diversity at the reception segment could be more or less advantageous.

The depolarization indexes depend on the building material of the wall, specifically on the electromagnetic behavior of the different constructive elements, as previously studied in [6]. Results presented in that paper have been applied in the computation of the improvement by polarization diversity. The information related to depolarization is the aim of the third section.

The proposed computation procedure begins with the data provided by the wide band measurement campaign, which represent the channel response in just one linear polarization. Based on the depolarization indexes induced by each reflection or transmission phenomena, the cross-polarized signal could be obtained by analyzing separately each multipath contribution. The actual copolar contribution and the synthesized cross-polar one are then the inputs of the diversity device, which provides the combination of both contributions. All the procedure to obtain the final signal is explained in detail along section fourth.

Three different strategies are then applied to that couple of signals to be combined into the final result: sum, maximum and average diversity. The performance of the application of such strategies are related and analyzed in section five.

The chapter is organized, then, into six sections. The second section is devoted of the measurements, and the third one is focused on the fundamentals of depolarization indexes. Sections four and five are centered in the results: the fourth on the procedure to compute the cross-polar contributions, and the fifth in the analysis. Finally, the sixth section summarizes the conclusions.

2   Measurements

A large wide band measurement campaign was designed with the aim of obtaining the co-polar response of the radio channel in several indoor environments, both LoS, and OLoS or NLoS. The campaign involved five different environment configurations. The band of interest is centered in 5.8 GHz, as it is focused on propagation aspects for wireless networks.

The measurement system was based on a vector network analyzer (VNA). The wide band condition of the measurements is a key factor in this work, as it allows the transformation from frequency to time domain and, once working in time, also the identification of different multipath contributions. These contributions could then be individually considered when processing the cross-polar response of the channel.

Along the following subsections, the setup used during the measurements, the environments where the experiments were performed, and the applied procedure are described.

2.1   Measurement Setup

As previously commented, the measurement system is based on a VNA Agilent 8510-C, which can perform measurements up to 50 GHz, so far away our needing. Both transmitting and receiving antennas were connected to the ports 1 and 2 of the VNA, which acts as signal generator and as receiver.

The transmitter end was placed in static locations at each environment, whereas the receiving antenna was installed on the top of a engineered mast, which moved the receiver along a linear track, by means of a neverended screw. Figure 1 shows the setup for the receiver.

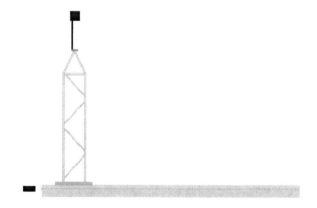

Fig. 1. Receiver setup

This positioning system, which consists of a 2.5 meter long linear table with a millimeter screw along it, improves the precision of the positioning compared to moving the antenna by hand.

Both antennas, Electro Metrics EM-6865, present omni-directional radiation patterns. This kind of pattern is interesting in order to get all the multipath contributions with approximately the same antenna gain, when dealing with receiver end. And this pattern is also important in the transmitter, to generate the maximum amount of multipath components.

The radiation pattern of such antennas was measured within the anechoic chamber of the Radio Systems Research Group, being the 3 dB beam width larger than 50 degree around the horizontal plane, in elevation, at 5.8 GHz. Whereas, the azimuth radiation pattern resulted to be aproximately omnidirectional. Figure 2 depicts the radiation pattern in elevation.

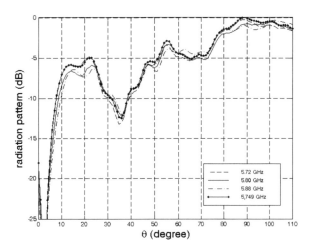

Fig. 2. Radiation pattern at 5.8 GHz, in elevation

2.2   Indoor Environments

Various series of indoor radio channel frequency response were measured in five different environments, some in LoS condition, one in NLoS and the other in OLoS situation. The measurements were taken in research laboratories, with both computers and electronic equipment. The furniture, when it is present, is the typical of this kind of rooms: office tables and chairs, and laboratory benches. The positions of transmitter and receiver are depicted at Figures 3, 4 and 5, at different rooms. During the measurement campaign, the transmitter was fixed at positions Txn, being n a natural number between 1 and 5 devoted to the five environments, and the receiver was moved along the lines labeled as Rxn.

The five environments was selected trying to represent a great variety of rooms: we can compare results at large and small rooms, at furnished and empty places, at square and rectangular spaces, in LoS and NLoS conditions, and so on.

The points and paths labeled as "1" correspond to LoS situation within a large room (more than 100 square meter) and the labeled as "2" to NLoS within the previously commented room and an adjacent saloon. Both plans can be observed at figure 3. The wall that obstructs the propagation channel between both antennas in the second situation is made of bricks and concrete.

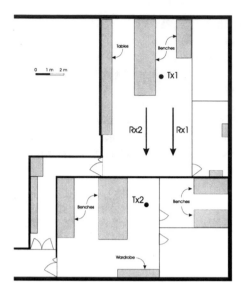

Fig. 3. Map of the measured environments. LoS is situation 1, and OLoS is situation 2

The walls at both rooms are built by bricks and concrete, except the fine line parallel to Rx1, which is made of chip wood, and the upper wall (opposite to the place where the measurements took place) that contains a large window.

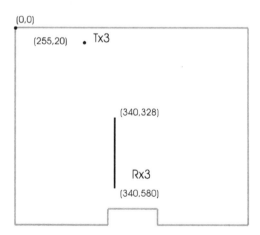

Fig. 4. Map of the measured environments. LoS is defined as situation 1, and OLoS as situation 2.

Figure 4 depicts the third environment, which is again a LoS situation in a smaller square room, with approximately 45 square meters.

The walls of such room are also brick made, except the wall opposite to the transmitter, which contains a large window.

Finally, figure 5 depicts the situation for both fourth and fifth environments. Both are placed in a long room of 36 square meters. Whereas the fourth environment consists of a completely empty room, with perfect LoS conditions, the fifth consists of a furnished office room, in OLoS conditions. When furnished, office equipment was placed within the radio channel: desks, chairs, closets, etc.

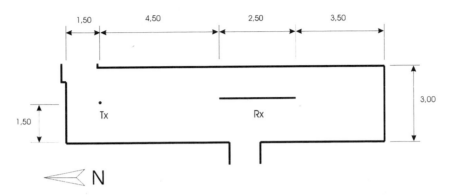

Fig. 5. Map of the fourth and fifth measurement environment

This environment is built by different construction materials: both North and South walls are made of brick, the West wall is made of chip wood in its North half, and brick the South half, and the East wall is brick constructed, but it contains a window.

2.3   Measurement Procedure

The transmitting antenna was kept stationary at a height of 1.8 meter. This height guaranteed that the radiating element was approximately equidistant from floor and ceiling.

The receiving antenna was moved along 2.5 meter long linear paths by means of the automatic positioner. Data were taken every one-eighth of a wavelength [7], which represents a *de facto* standard when measuring radio channels, as adjacent samples are far enough to be uncorrelated and they are near enough to keep all fade events.

At each position, complex frequency responses have been measured in a 160 MHz band around 5.8 GHz, with a resolution of 200 kHz, due to the 801 points in the frequency scan. As a consequence, the sounder resolution in the delay domain is 6.25 ns, while the maximum measurable delay is 5 μs.

The measurements were taken following a procedure "measure-move-stop-measure-..." in order to avoid Doppler effects within the data: the situation is completely static during the time the VNA is acquiring the channel frequency responses.

3   Depolarization

Indoor environments typically present large multipath phenomena, which are the main trouble when planning a wireless network. However, the depolarization induced by transmission of waves across the walls (or by reflection on the walls) is not commonly taken into account during the planning procedure. And it could be useful to improve the performance of the receiving signal if a polarization diversity technique is implemented at the reception end.

This section deals with the fundamentals of depolarisation and the depolarisation indexes used to processing the results.

3.1   Depolarization Phenomenon

A phenomenon associated to reflection, the depolarization that could be generated when a wave beats a flat obstacle, appears to be not so fine defined and modeled as the reflection itself. This phenomenon occurs when a wave is reflected on (or transmitted across) the interface between two propagation media and part of its energy is reflected (or transmitted) orthogonally polarized.

The lack of definition and modeling is probably due to that typical planning tools, as ray-tracing, were initially created to be used at frequencies corresponding to cellular phone or television broadcasting, at which the typical obstacles (walls) are electrically flat enough to provide strong specular reflections. So, there were no interest on depolarization.

At higher frequencies, the electrical size of a given obstacle becomes larger. At 5.8 GHz, as an example, some simulation tools could not work as well as expected, because when a wave reaches an obstacle, several reflection paths are generated in any directions, not only the specular direction [8]. And moreover, the obstacle depolarizes the wave in a certain percentage, which is not commonly considered in such prediction tools.

3.2   Depolarization Indexes

The depolarization index, for any material, at any angle of incidence and any polarization of the transmitted waves is the fraction of the power of this wave that is received in the orthogonal polarization. From this definition, depolarization indexes may be computed by means of a matrix procedure [9].

The depolarization indexes for the reflection mechanism, computed in the specular direction, are summarized in table 1. The values depend on the polarization of the incident wave, which is denoted by "h" when it is horizontal and "v" when vertical. The specular situation is adequate to define very good reflectors, which reflect most of the incident wave towards the opposite direction, being the normal to the surface the axis of symmetry.

Table 1. DI (%) induced by reflection, in the specular direction of observation

Material	Incidence angle (deg)	DIh	DIv
Brick wall	10	0.31 %	0.48 %
	20	0.66 %	0.19 %
	30	0.67 %	0.65 %
	40	0.72 %	0.75 %
Chip wood	10	4.57 %	4.66 %
	20	9.80 %	8.20 %
Stone and concrete facade	10	2.12 %	1.57 %
	20	5.31 %	1.27 %
	30	1.80 %	3.60 %
	40	5.27 %	3.74 %
	50	9.27 %	8.38 %

The results of table 1 indicate that brick wall provides reduced depolarized waves compared to the co-polar reflected waves in the specular direction. The other considered materials provide depolarized waves up to 9.8% compared to the co-polar one.

But when a more complex analysis is expected, as it is the situation of the present chapter, all scattering directions have to be considered, and not just specular one, because the reflector could be randomly located and oriented. With this aim, median depolarization indexes for each material at all pair of angles of incidence and observation are provided in table 2.

Table 2. Median DI (%) induced by reflection

Material	DIh	DIv
Brick wall	23%	30%
Chip wood	18%	18.5%
Stone and concrete facade	4.5%	4%

Once the complete (180 degree) observation arc, not just the specular angles, is introduced, the depolarization indexes grow, and differences between incident polarizations also appear in the brick wall case. The brick wall is the more non isotropic material among the considered, as it presents a clearly oriented structure, whereas the chip wood panel and the stone and concrete facade are the result of the solidification of a mass, which is expected to present a more isotropic behavior. The high median values of depolarization indexes indicate that high depolarized waves could be generated when several scatterers are present in an environment, which is the case of indoor scenarios.

Furthermore, the transmission mechanism across walls induces depolarization. In this case, and focused on the environments under test, the interest is mainly the depolarization by transmission across a brick wall with normal incidence. The measured value for DI at such situation was 9.4 %, considering transmission with vertical polarization.

4   Processing

As measurements have been done following a wide band scheme, information about the multipath components can be obtained from the outcomes. Knowing the multipath scheme, or the power-delay profile (PDP) in the co-polar installation, it is possible to compute a synthetic mirror (another PDP) in the cross-polar domain.

Then, each couple of PDPs (co-polar and cross-polar) could be the input of a diversity block, which provides a new received signal with better performance than just the co-polar one.

The following subsections contain the computation of these cross-polar PDPs as well as the results of applying different diversity techniques at the reception end.

4.1   Effect of the Multipath in the Total Received Power

The receiving antenna at each measuring location is reached by the direct ray, which links the transmitting and the receiving antennas following the shortest path. But that antenna is also reached by several contributions coming from paths generated by reflections on the walls and, perhaps, transmissions across some wall. The received power from each contribution, associated to the time delay relative to the direct ray arrival time, construct the PDP. This profile defines the multipath environment at each reception location.

Commonly, this PDP is shaped by the antenna pattern. In this case, with azimuth omnidirectional antennas, most of the PDP is due to the multipath, and only a few part could be defined by the elevation pattern of the antenna. Consequently, the PDP used along this work could be assumed as the product of the environments where the measurements were performed.

4.2   Computation of Cross Polar Received Power

The measurement outcomes are complex frequency responses between 5.72 and 5.88 GHz, and they have a shape as depicted in figures 6 and 7, which contain the amplitude and the phase respectively.

If only waves following the direct path arrived the receiving antenna, the amplitude of the frequency response would be approximately flat. In fact, it would be locally flat, but it would be smaller at higher frequencies than at lower. The behaviour of the phase would be expected to be linear. Evidently, if we observe figures 6 and 7, the amplitude is not flat and the phase is not linear, which indicates the presence of multipath components.

Applying an inverse fast Fourier transform to each complex frequency response, this can be turned to the time domain, with a resolution of 6.25 ns between adjacent samples. Figure 8 depicts an example.

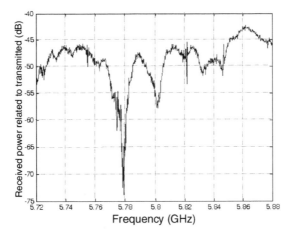

Fig. 6. Example of the amplitude of the complex frequency response

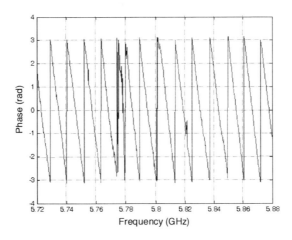

Fig. 7. Example of the phase of the complex frequency response

At this time response, the different contributions after one, two, three, or more reflections can be identified, using an inverse ray tracing procedure. Once the contributions have been classified in terms of the number of reflections on the walls before they reach the receiving antenna, the orthogonal contributions at each delay can be computed.

Firstly, the path followed by each multipath contribution has to be identified, and the walls that generated each reflection or transmission mechanism have to be categorized. Depending on the material that constitutes the wall, the angle of incidence and the frequency, a total depolarization index (TDI) can be obtained. Mean values, used along computation, are summarized in table 3.

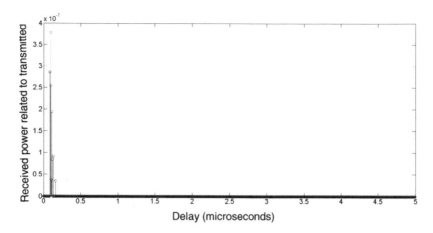

Fig. 8. Example of the amplitude of the time response

The direct path contribution TDI needs a supplementary comment. In LoS conditions, this TDI depends on the depolarization induced by both antennas. In NLoS conditions, and additional depolarization due to the transmission across the wall separating both rooms has to be considered. When dealing with OLoS (furnished) environments, we decided to take into account only the effect of the antennas.

Table 3. Mean TDI (%) at different environments

Environment	Multipath contribution			
	Direct	1 ref	2 ref	3 ref
1, LoS	1.8	0.75	1.5	24.6
2, NLoS	9.4	15.8	24	32.2
3, LoS	1.8	0.75	1.5	24.6
4, LoS	1.8	8.2	16.4	24.6
5, OLoS	1.8	8.2	16.4	24.6

If the total power arriving the receiver antenna at each time delay represents 100%, the co-polar contribution would be (100-TDI)%. The collection of co-polar contributions represent the measured PDP, which is the basis to compute the cross-polar PDP. Obviously, the cross-polar contributions at each delay would be TDI %.

Consequently, the procedure to compute the cross-polar contribution is:

1. Compute the co-polar PDP from the measured frequency response.
2. Calculate the total power at each delay, based on the correspondent TDI.
3. Obtain the cross-polar power at each delay.
4. Combine the collection of delays to obtain the cross-polar PDP.

4.3   Depolarization Phenomenon

Once the co-polar and cross-polar PDPs have been computed at each receiving location, different polarization diversity technique schemes have to be applied to each couple of data.

The three tested combination schemes are:

1. Sum, where the final signal could be the sum of both input signals.
2. Mean, where the final signal is the average of both inputs.
3. Switching, where the diversity device swicths between both channels in order to get the maximum at each instant.

After application of these diversity schemes at all the receiving locations, the results are prepared to be analysed.

5   Results Analysis

The application of diversity techniques provides improvements in the received power signal. Among the three considered schemes, the combination by sum appears to perform better than the other pair, and it offers enhancements as summarized in table 4.

Table 4. Estimation of the mean improvement by polarization diversity at different environments

Environment	Improvement (%)
1, LoS	17.89
2, NLoS	23.29
3, LoS	10.18
4, LoS	18.51
5, OLoS	21.23

Considering each environment separately, the maximum improvement receiving location, the minimum, the mean and the range of improvements along the receiving path can be analysed.

Table 5 contains the data for the environments 1 and 2, which allows the comparison between LoS and NLoS situations within similar rooms. The improvement in terms of received power appears to be larger when there is no line of sight between transmitter and receiver, with a mean of 23.29%. Analysing the maximum and minimum improvements, the application of polarisation diversity appears to be more advantageous in NLoS conditions: the enhancement is, at some points, only 2% in LoS conditions.

Table 6 makes available the data to compare the effect of polarisation diversity at reception as a function of the size of the indoor environment, in LoS conditions (environments 1, 3, and 4). The first comment is that improvements are detected at every room, but the performance of the networks installed in large, and even long, rooms appears to be more enhanced than in small rooms. Besides, the receiving locations where less enhancement has been detected present values under 4%.

Table 5. Comparison between LoS and NLoS

Environment	Improvement (%)			
	Mean	Max.	Min.	Range
1, LoS	17.89	32.28	2.00	30.28
2, NLoS	23.29	37.23	10.38	26.85

Table 6. Comparison among different size rooms

Environment	Improvement (%)			
	Mean	Max.	Min.	Range
1, large	17.89	32.28	2.00	30.28
3, small	10.18	31.94	1.60	30.34
4, long	18.51	56.04	3.46	52.58

Table 7 contains the comparison between furnished (OLoS) and empty (LoS) environments performance. Both data come from the same room, but changing the contents. In presence of furniture, the polarisation diversity technique works better, as it provides larger signal enhancements, even although no obstacles block the line of sight between transmitting and receiving antennas.

Table 7. Comparison between empty (LoS) and furnished (OLoS) situations

Environment	Improvement (%)			
	Mean	Max.	Min.	Range
4, LoS	18.51	56.04	3.46	52.58
5, OLoS	21.23	32.01	5.28	26.73

6   Conclusions

The improvement in the performance of wireless networks by polarization diversity has been estimated from radio channel measurements in the 5.8 GHz band. Measurements at only one polarization were carried out. The cross-polar responses of the channels have been computed from these co-polar data, using depolarization indexes.

The newness of the proposal is the analysis of polarization diversity at several scenarios based in just one polarisation measurements.

Although three possible strategies for implementing the polarization diversity have been taken into account, the main improvements were provided by combination by sum scheme.

The presence of obstacles (when dealing with obstructed line of sight situations), and mainly the absence of line of sight (NLoS situations), leads to larger improvements in the performance provided by the polarization diversity. Even in LoS situations, the improvements are noticeable. They are over 23% in terms of power at NLoS environments, but the minimum mean improvement has been estimated in 10%, which are interesting values for planning.

The proposal of using polarization diversity in reception could be of interest for network designers, mainly in such environments where fading due to multipath is especially deep.

Acknowledgements. This work has been supported by the Autonomic Government of Galicia (Xunta de Galicia), Spain, through Project PGIDIT 08MRU045322PR. The authors would also like to acknowledge Eduardo Cebrián Martínez de Lagos, Mr. Juan Aguilera, and Mr. José Manuel Prado for their help during the measurement campaigns, as well as Mr. José Carlos Fernández Ribao for his help during the data processing.

References

1. Dutta-Roy, A.: Networks for Homes. IEEE Spectrum, 26–33 (1999)
2. IEEE Standard 802.16a-2003: IEEE Standard for Local and metropolitan area networks — Part 16: Air Interface for Fixed Broadband Wireless Access Systems — Amendment 2: Medium Access Control Modifications and Additional Physical Layer Specifications for 2-11 GHz (2003)
3. Eklund, C., Marks, R.G., Stanwood, K.L., Wang, S.: IEEE Standard 802.16: A technical overview of the WirelessMAN air interfaces for broadband wireless acces. IEEE Communications Magazine 40(6), 98–107 (2002)
4. Dietrich, C.B., Dietze, K., Nealy, J.R., Stutzman, W.L.: Spatial, Polarization, and Pattern Diversity for Wireless Handheld Terminals. IEEE Transactions on Antennas and Propagation 49(9) (2001)
5. Turkmani, A.M.D., Arowojolu, A.A., Jefford, P.A., Kellett, C.J.: An Experimental Evaluation of the Performance of Two-Branch Space and Polarization Diversity Schemes at 1800 MHz. IEEE Transactions on Vehicular Technology 44(2) (1995)
6. Cuiñas, I., Sanchez, M.G., Alejos, A.V.: Depolarisation due to scattering on walls in the 5 GHz band. IEEE Transactions on Antennas and Propagation 57(10), 2934–2939 (2009)
7. Dossi, L., Tartara, G., Tallone, F.: Statistical Analysis of Measured Impulse Response Functions of 2.0 GHz Indoor Radio Channels. IEEE Journal on Selected Areas in Communications 14(3), 405–410 (1996)
8. Cuiñas, I., Martinez, D., Sanchez, M.G., Alejos, A.V.: Modelling and measuring reflection due to flat dielectric surfaces at 5.8 GHz. IEEE Transactions on Antennas and Propagation 55(4), 1139–1147 (2007)
9. Cuiñas, I., Sánchez, M.G., Alejos, A.V.: Depolarisation due to scattering on walls in the 5 GHz band. IEEE Transactions on Antennas and Propagation 57(6), 1804–1812 (2009)

Using the OTS/CafeOBJ Method to Formally Specify and Verify the Open Mobile Alliance License Choice Algorithm

Nikolaos Triantafyllou[1], Iakovos Ouranos[1],
Petros Stefaneas[2], and Panayiotis Frangos[1]

[1] School of Electrical and Computer Engineering, National Technical University of Athens
Iroon Polytexneiou 9, Zografou 15780, Greece
[2] School of Applied Mathematical and Physical Sciences
National Technical University of Athens, Iroon Polytexneiou 9, Zografou 15780, Greece
{nitriant,iouranos,pfrangos}@central.ntua.gr,
petros@math.ntua.gr

Abstract. The protection of the distribution of digital contents via mobile networks has been standardized by Open Mobile Alliance (OMA) with the proposition of the OMA Digital Rights Management System. When multiple licenses refer to the same content a decision problem rises as to what license one should use. To solve this decision problem, as part of the OMA DRM system, a License Choice Algorithm is proposed. Here we apply the OTS/CafeOBJ method to specify the above algorithm and verify that it behaves in the expected manner. More specifically we present an equational specification of the License Choice Algorithm as an Observation Transition System (OTS) written in CafeOBJ specification style. CafeOBJ is a powerful new generation algebraic specification language. Finally we verify the following safety property holds: Whenever a license is chosen for a specific content then that license is valid at that specific time, and analyze parts of this verification.

Keywords: CafeOBJ, License choice algorithm, Mobile digital rights systems, OMA-rights expression language, Observational transition systems.

1 Introduction

Digital Rights Management Systems (DRMSs) are apart from a set of cryptographic methods to forbid unauthorized usage, a method for expressing permissions and obligations on a content. A set of such permissions and obligations is called a license. Such licenses are written in languages known as Rights Expression Languages (RELs). The most commonly used such languages today are ODRL [1], XrML [2] and MPEG REL [3].

Open Mobile Alliance (OMA) is an organization created to be the center of mobile service enabler specification work. OMA REL [5] is a digital rights expression language that specifies the syntax and the semantics of rights governing the usage of DRM contents in the OMA DRM system [5]. It is based on ODRL and is defined as a mobile profile of it. Together with the specification of the language, in [5], OMA

M.S. Obaidat, G.A. Tsihrintzis, and J. Filipe (Eds.): ICETE 2010, CCIS 222, pp. 424–438, 2012.
© Springer-Verlag Berlin Heidelberg 2012

proposes an algorithm that comes to lift the burden of the user when he faces the problem of having more than one license that refers to the same content. This algorithm takes into consideration the constraints each license contains, and decides for the user the "best" suited license to use for a desired action on the content. Since this algorithm does not have an official name, we will refer to it for the rest of the paper as the "Choice Algorithm".

Digital Right protected contents are a commodity and as such their success highly depends on their acceptance by the market. DRM systems need to protect the interests of both the publisher and the end user. As a result, licenses intended to work in one manner but end up working differently cause discomfort to both of the parties involved. The end user is dissatisfied because they may end up purchasing a service that does not respond to the advertised manner and the producer might end up losing the consumption control of his contents if the licenses behave unexpectedly.

For these reasons we believe that formal semantics and specification in order to achieve the unambiguous licenses and software that control them, is the key to ensure the success and longevity of these commercial DRM systems. In this paper we formally analyze the Choice Algorithm and verify that it behaves in a correct manner using the Observational Transition System (OTS) / CafeOBJ [4, 6], thus showing both how such techniques can be applied to the field of Mobile DRM and provide at the same time a proof of a fundamental property for the algorithm

The rest of the paper is organized as follows: Section 2 gives a brief introduction to the OTS/CafeOBJ method [12, 13]. In section 3 we describe the Choice Algorithm and its specification as an OTS in CafeOBJ while in section 4 we present the invariant property and the corresponding proof scores. Finally, section 5 concludes the paper.

2   The OTS/CafeOBJ Method

2.1   Observational Transition Systems

An Observational Transition System, or OTS [12, 13], is a transition system that can be written in terms of equations. We assume that there exists a universal states space called Υ and we also assume that each data type we need to use in the OTS, including the equivalence relationship for that data type, has been declared in advance. An OTS S is the triplet $< O, I, T >$ where:

O: is a finite set of observers. Each $o \in O$ is a function $o : \Upsilon \to D$, where D is a data type that may differ from observer to observer. Given an OTS S and two states $u_1, u_2 \in \Upsilon$, the equivalence ($u_1 =_s u_2$) between them wrt. S is defined as $\forall o \in O, o(u_1) = o(u_2)$.

I: is the set of initial states such that $I \subseteq \Upsilon$.

T: A set of conditional transitions. Each $\tau \in T$ is a function $\tau : \Upsilon \to \Upsilon$, such that $\tau(u_1) =_s \tau(u_2)$ for each $u_1, u_2 \in \Upsilon/ =_s$. For each $u \in \Upsilon, \tau(u)$ is called the successor state of u wrt τ. The condition C_τ of τ is called the effective condition. Also for each $u \in \Upsilon, \tau(u) = u$ if $\neg C_\tau(u)$.

Observers and transitions may be parameterized. Generally observers and transitions are denoted as $O_{i_1,...,i_m}$ and $\tau_{i_1,...,i_n}$ respectively provided that $m,n \geq 0$ and there exist data types D_k, D where $k = i_1,...,i_m, j_1,...,j_n$.

2.2 OTSs in CafeOBJ

An OTS S is written in CafeOBJ. The universal state space Y is denoted by a hidden sort, say H. An observer $oi1$, ...,im ☐ O is denoted by a CafeOBJ observation operator. We assume that there exist visible sorts Vk and V corresponding to the data types Dk and D, where $k = i1, ..., im$. The CafeOBJ observation operator denoting $oi1, ...,im$ is declared as follows: bop o : Vi1 ... Vim H -> V. Any state in I, namely any initial state, is denoted by a constant, say $init$, which is declared as follows: op init :-> H.

The initial value returned by $oi1$, ...,im is denoting by the term $o(Xi1$, ..., Xim , $init$) where Xk is a CafeOBJ variable whose sort is Vk, where $k = i1, ..., im$. A transition $\tau j1$, ..., $jn \in T$ is denoted by a CafeOBJ action operator as follows: bop a : Vj1 ... Vjn H -> H with Vk a visible sort corresponding to the data type Dk, where $k = j1, ..., jn$.

Each transition is defined by describing what the value returned by each observer $oi1$, ...,im in the successor state becomes when $\tau j1$, ..., jn is applied in a state u. When $c - \tau j1$, ..., $jn (u)$ holds, this is expressed generally by a conditional equation that has the form ceq o(Xi1,...,Xim, a(Xj1,...,Xjn,S)) = e-a(Xj1,...,Xjn, Xi1,...,Xim, S) if c-a(Xj1,...,Xjn, S) . S is a CafeOBJ variable whose sort is H and Xk is a CafeOBJ variable whose sort is Vk, where $k = j1, ..., jn$. a($Xj1$, ..., Xjn , S) denotes the successor state of S w.r.t. $\tau j1$, ..., jn plus $Xj1$, ..., Xjn . e-a($Xj1$, ..., Xjn , $Xi1$, ..., Xim, S) denotes the value returned by $oi1$, ...,im in the successor state. c-a($Xj1$, ..., Xjn , S) denotes the effective condition $c - \tau j1$, ..., jn . The value returned by $oi1$, ...,im is not changed if $\tau j1,..., jn$ is applied in a state u such that $\neg c - \tau j1, ...jn (u)$, which can be written generally as follows: ceq o(Xi1,Xim, a(Xj1,Xjn,S)) = o(Xi1,Xim, S) if not c-a(Xj1,Xjn, S).

3 The OMA License Choice Algorithm

Because the process of manually choosing which license to use, when dealing with multiple licenses referring to the same contents, may cause discomfort to the user, the following algorithm is proposed by OMA [5]:

1) Only rights that are valid at the given time should be taken into account from the algorithm.

2) Rights that are not constrained should always be preferred over constrained rights.

3) Any right that includes a Datetime constraint, and possibly others, should be preferred over rights that are constrained but do not have such a restriction.

4) If there exist more than one rights with a Datetime constraint, the one with the further in the future End element should be preferred.

5) If there exist a choice between many rights and none of them contains a Date-time constraint the one containing an Interval constraint should be preferred if there exists such.

6) Rights that contain a Count constraint should be preferred after rights that contain a Timed- Count constraint.

This algorithm basically states an ordering on the constraints of the licenses. Based on this ordering, the decision for the best license to use is made between licenses that are valid at the given time, and refer to the desired right.

We will clarify the above algorithm through the use of an example. We assume that Alice has the following two licenses installed in her DRM agent:

License 1: You can listen before the tenth of the month songs A or B one time

License 2: You can listen to songs A or C up to ten times

Notice that the first license contains a datetime constraint, which is stated above as the constraint "*before the tenth of the month*". The right to listen to songs A or B is further constrained using a count constraint stated by "*up to one time*", while the second license contains only a count constraint stated as "*up to ten times*".

We assume the case where Alice decides to use these licenses installed in her DRM agent to listen to song A. The DRM agent is supposed [5] to include an implementation of the above License Choice Algorithm.

When Alice gives the command to listen to song A, the algorithm will search the licenses installed in her DRM agent to find a corresponding right that is valid at that given time based on their constraints, say "*listen song A*", will check the constraints of the "matching" licenses and based on the ordering provided by the OMA Choice Algorithm it will select a license as the best to use the "*listen song A*" right, and finally exercises it. In our example this license will be the first one.

3.1 Basic Data Types

Introducing the OTS model of the OMA Choice Algorithm, we define the basic data types we need to use.

1) *Action*: Defines the data type of an action that a user wants to apply to content, as they are defined by OMA REL.

2) Content: Is the data type that represents the unique identification of a specific content.

3) Use: represents an action enforced to some content. This is defined in our model as $use := action, content$. The only actions allowed by OMA REL are *play*, *display*, *print*, *execute* and *export*.

4) Cons: Defines the data type of the constraints defined by OMA REL.

5) Right, RightSET: define a granted right by a license and a set of such rights respectively. A right is an expression of the form U under C, where U is a Use and C a Cons. RightSET is defined as a super type (Right is a sub sort of RightSET, in CafeOBJ terms) of the data type Right. It has added functionalities such as a "belong" operator (in) and the union of sets. In addition to those,

in the definition of these data types we define operators "check", "belong" and "?". The "check" operator takes a Use and a Right element and checks whether that Use belongs to that Right. The "belong" operator works in a similar way but checks if a Use belongs to a RightSET. Finally the "?" operator takes a RightSET* and returns true or false if the constraints of it hold or not respectively.

6) Lic, LicSET: These data types define a license and a set of licenses respectively. As in Right and RightSET, Lic is a sub sort of LicSET. A Lic is constructed by operator, C about R, where C is a Cons and R is a RightSET. Lics are defined likewise, to capture the fact that in a license written in OMA REL a constraint can apply to a set of rights that can be further more constrained and refer to different contents. LicSET is again defined as a set of Lic data types with the usual set functions. Again, we use the operators "belong", "belongLS", "existLi", "exist" and "?". The "belong" operator determines whether or not a Use element belongs in a Lic element and "belongLS", if a Use element belongs to a set of licenses. The operator "existLi" checks whether there exists a suitable right for a Use element in a license, while "exist"performs the same check for a set of licenses. Finally the "?" operator determines if a license is valid at a given time. As an example of this specification in CafeOBJ, we present the corresponding code for Use data type:

Table 1. Definition of the Use data type

```
mod* USe {pr(ACtion + COntent)

[Use]

op _,_ : Action Cont -> Use {constr}

op none : -> Use

ops play display print execute

export: -> Action

op _ = _ : Use Use -> Bool {comm}

var U : Use

eq (U = U) = true .}
```

3.2 OTS Model and Its Specification

According to the methodology presented in section 3 the hidden state space is denoted by a hidden sort, *[Sys]*.

The observers we will use are: *lics, chosenSet, bestLic, user and valid*. The *lics* observer is specified by the behavioral operator bop lics: Sys -> LicSet and returns the installed licenses on the agent at any given time. The observer *chosenSet* defined in CafeOBJ by the behavioral operator bop chosenSet: Sys -> LicSet denotes the set of licenses that refer to the same content and the same action as the users choice at the current time. The *bestLic* observer defines the most appropriate license to use for a user request according to the OMA Choice Algorithm. This observer is defined in CafeOBJ by the following behavioral operator bop bestLic: Sys -> Lic. The observer *user* denotes the current user request and it is specified in CafeOBJ as bop user: Sys -> Use. Finally the *valid* observer shows whether or not a license is valid at a given time and is denoted as bop valid: Sys Lic -> Bool

The actions we used in order to specify the OMA Choice Algorithm are the following: *request, use, hold, NoHold*.

1) The action *request* is declared through the action operator bop request: Sys Action Cont -> Sys and defines the request by a user to use an action on some content. The transition can only occur if there is such a license in the set of currently installed license of the agent. This is specified using the effective condition for this transition

   ```
   eq c-request(S,A,CONT)=existsLi ((A,CONT); lics(S)).
   ```

2) The action *use* defines the consumption of a usage right on some content. This is denoted by the following action operator: bop _ use _ with _: Sys Use Lic -> Sys. This transition can only occur if the license is valid at that given time, is the best license as that is defined by the Choice Algorithm and finally the usage right about that content belongs to that license. This is defined in CafeOBJ again through the effective condition of the transition rule:

   ```
   eq   c-use(S,A,CONT,L)   =   exist((A,CONT);L)   and   valid
   (S ,L) and (L = bestLic(S)).
   ```

3) *Hold* is used to specify the fact that after the execution of a usage right, that right remains valid, i.e. its constraints are not depleted. This is defined by the action operator: bop hold: Sys Lic -> Sys. Since the only time a usage right can be exercised is if it belongs to the best license, defined by the OMA Choice Algorithm, and for this transition to occur it must remain valid the effective condition of this transition rule is defined as:

   ```
   eq   c-hold(S,L)=(L   in   lics(S))   and   (L)?   and   (L   =
   bestLic(S)).
   ```

4) *NoHold* is the opposite transition of hold. That is after the execution of the usage right, it is no longer valid. This transition is defined in CafeOBJ as: bop NoHold: Sys Lic -> Sys. The only difference with the above effective condition is that for this transition to occur the license must no longer be valid. The effective condition is specified as:

   ```
   eq   c-NoHold(S,L)=(L   in   lics(S))andnot(L)?   and
   (L=bestLic(S)).
   ```

As stated in section 3, a state of an OTS is characterized by the values the observation operators return. Here we present such an example for our specification, for the case of the *NoHold* transition.

In the below table the numbers at the beginning of each line are not part of the code. In line 1 the signature of the effective condition for the transition rule is declared, as a predicate that takes a system state and a license. In line 2 the equation defining the effective condition is declared as: the license belongs on the set of licenses installed in the agent in S, its constraints no longer hold in S and it is the license chosen by the OMA Choice Algorithm in S. In line 3 we declare that the successor state of the application of the NoHold transition is S if the effective condition does not hold.

Table 2. Definition of the NoHold action in CafeOBJ

```
1.op c-NoHold : Sys Lic -> Bool
2.eq c-NoHold(S,L)=(L in lics(S))
and not(L)? and L=bestLic(S)).
3.ceq NoHold(S,L) = S
if not c-NoHold(S,L) .
4.ceq lics(NoHold(S ,L))
= (lics(S) del L) if c-NoHold(S,L) .
5.ceq chosenSet(NoHold(S,L)) = empty
if c-NoHold(S,L) .
6.ceq bestLic(NoHold(S,L))=nil
if c-NoHold(S,L) .
7.ceq user(NoHold(S,L))=none
if c-NoHold(S,L) .
8.ceq valid(NoHold(S,L),L)= false
if c-NoHold(S,L) .
```

Lines 4 to 8 denote the values returned by the observers of the OTS when the No-Hold transition is applied to the arbitrary state S for an arbitrary license L.

In line 4 we declare that the lics observer returns the same set of licenses as the one in S where license L is removed from the set, if the effective condition of the transition holds. In line 5 the observer chosenSET observes the empty set, if the effective condition of the transition holds. In line 6 the observer bestLic observes nil, a dummy license constant that denotes the fact that no license exists. In line 7 the user observer, observes again a dummy use constant to denote that no user choice is made in that state. Finally in line 8 the valid observer for the license L returns false, when the effective condition holds.

4 Verification of the OMA Choice Algorithm

The invariant property that corresponds to the proper function of the algorithm is the following: *Whenever a license is chosen for a given content, then the license is valid at that specific time*. In order to prove such a property, several steps need to be taken [10, 11].

Express the property in a formal way as a predicate, say *invariant pred(p,x)*, where *p* is a free variable for states and *x* denotes other free variables of *pred*.In a module, usually called INV, *pred(p,x)* is expressed in CafeOBJ

```
op inv : H V -> Bool

eq inv(P, X) = pred(P, X).
```

where V the list of visible sorts corresponding to x, P is a CafeOBJ variable for H, the state space and X is a list of CafeOBJ variables for V.

In a proof score we show that our predicate holds at any initial state, say *init*.

```
open INV

red inv(init, x).

close
```

red is a command that reduces a given term by regarding declared equations as left-to-right rewrite rules.

We write a module, usually ISTEP, where the predicate to prove in each inductive case is expressed in CafeOBJ, using two constants p, p' denoting any state and the successor state after applying a transition in the state:

```
op istep : V -> Bool

eq istep(X)=inv(p,X) implies inv(p',X).
```

For each case we write the proof score. It usually looks like the following:

```
open ISTEP

Declare constants denoting arbitrary objects.

Declare equations denoting the case.

Declare equations denoting the facts if necessary.

eq p' = a(p, y).

red istep(x).

close
```

Where y is a list of constants that are used as the arguments of CafeOBJ action operator a, which are declared in this proof score and denote arbitrary objects for the intended sorts. If istep(x) is reduced to true, it is shown that the transition preserves pred(p, x) in this case. Otherwise, we may have to *split the case*, may need some invariants that will be used as lemmas (*lemma discovery*), or we may show that the predicate is not invariant to the system.

Following the procedure presented above several lemmas where required to prove the desired invariant safety property. Their informal description is presented in table 3, where property 1 is the main property.

Here we will present the proof of the invariant 1, the safety property that is, as well as one of the lemmas used to prove it, invariant 2. The formal definition of invariant 1 and 2 in terms of CafeOBJ specification is:

```
op inv1 : Sys Lic -> Bool
eq inv1(S,L) = ((L = bestLic(S)) and not (L = nil) )
implies valid(S,L) .
op inv2 : LicSet Lic Action Cont -> Bool
eq inv2(LS,L,A,C) = ((L = chooseLic(belongLS((A,C);LS)
)) and not (L = nil) ) implies (L in LS) .
```

Table 3. Properties to verify

No.	Informal Definition of Properties to be Proven
1	*Whenever a license is chosen for a given content, then the license is valid at that specific time.*
2	*If a license L is the chosen license by the OMA Choice Algorithm for a given set S and that license exits, i.e. is not nil then L belongs to the set S.*
3	*If the choice made by the OMA choice algorithm for the set R union S, where R is an arbitrary license containing one usage right and S is a set of Licenses, is not R nor is it a choice made solely on S then the chosen license is nil, i.e. not valid license is available*
4	*If the set of licenses contains only a single license, say L and the choice made by the OMA Choice Algorithm is not nil, i.e. there exists a valid license, then the choice is this license L*
5	*If the choice made by OMA Choice Algorithm when the license set contains two licenses L and L' is not nil, and if the choice made is not that made based on the second license L' then the chosen license is L*

Some of the properties presented above are stateless, meaning that they do not depend on the state of our OTS. We can prove such properties in a similar manner, the only difference relies on the fact that the induction does not occur on the states of our OTS but on the complexity of the data types, e.g. on the way a set is constructed. As it can be seen above invariant 2 is a lemma on sets of licenses and as such its proof will be stateless.

We will begin with the proof of invariant 1. In module ISTEP, the following operator denoting the predicate to prove is declared and defined:

```
op istep1 : Lic  -> Bool
eq istep1(l)=inv1(s,l)implies inv1(s',l)) .
```

Using the follow proof passage we prove that the predicate holds for any initial state, say init.

```
open INV
red inv1(init,l).
close
```

This proof passage returns true, so the base case is proven.

Next we write the proof passage for each of the transition rules used in the OTS. For the case of the request, transition rule.

```
open ISTEP

op s' : -> Sys.

op a : -> Action.

op c : -> Cont.

eq s' = request(s,a,c).

red istep1(l).

close
```

The above case returns neither true nor false. In this case we need to split the case to help the CafeOBJ system reduce it. The most natural choice is to split the effective condition of the transition rule based on whether it holds or not.

```
open ISTEP

op s' : -> Sys.

op a : -> Action.

op c : -> Cont.

eq s' = request(s,a,c).

eq c-request(s,a,c) = false.

red istep1(l).

close
```

The above refers to the case that effective condition of the transition is false, that is not c-request(s,a,l) and CafeOBJ returns true. Now that this case is covered we must cover its symmetrical one, i.e. when c-request (s,a,l) is true. This is shown in the following proof passage:

```
open ISTEP

op s' : -> Sys.

op a : -> Action.

op c : -> Cont.

eq s' = request(s,a,c).

eq existsLi((a,c);lics(s)) = true.

red istep1(l).

close
```

Here we replaced the equation c-request(s,a,c)= true with the definition of c-request(s,a,c), that is the equation existsLi((a,c);lics(s)) = true, to help CafeOBJ with the reductions.

In this case CafeOBJ returns again nor true nor false and we need more case splitting based on the returned formula (interactive computer – human proof).

```
open ISTEP

op s' : -> Sys .

op a : -> Action .

op c : -> Cont .

eq s' = request(s,a,c) .

eq existsLi((a,c) ; lics(s)) = true .

eq (l=chooseLic(belongLS((a,c);lics(s)) ))=false.

red istep1(l).

close
```

The above proof passage corresponds to the case existsLi((a,c);lics(s)) ∧ ¬ l=chooseLic (belongLS ((a,c); lics(s))).

This proof passage returns true, so we must continue with the symmetric case once again.

```
open ISTEP

op s' : -> Sys.

op a : -> Action.

op c : -> Cont.

eq s' = request(s,a,c).

eq existsLi((a,c) ; lics(s)) = true.

eq l=chooseLic(belongLS((a,c);lics(s))).

red istep1(l).

close
```

This case corresponds to existsLi((a,c); lics(s)) ∧ l=chooseLic(belongLS((a,c); lics(s)))and CafeOBJ returns again nor true nor false. Once again we need to split the case based on the formula returned by CafeOBJ.

Following this procedure we reach state existsLi((a,c);lics(s)) ∧ l=chooseLic(belongLS((a,c);lics(s))) ∧ ¬ (chooseLic(belongLS((a,c);lics(s)))=nil) ∧ ¬ (chooseLic (belongLS((a,c);lics(s))inlics(s)) where CafeOBJ has returned true to all the symmetrical subcases.

Here CafeOBJ returns nor true nor false again. Normally we would, and can, apply more case splitting, but we notice that these predicates cannot hold simultaneously in our OTS (another example of the interactive proving procedure). So we can use these contradicting predicates to conjuncture a lemma and discard this case. These predicates constitute invariant-lemma 2 we described in table 3 and it is formally defined above.

Using this lemma we can discard this case as is show in the following proof passage:

```
open ISTEP

op s' : -> Sys.

op a : -> Action.

op c : -> Cont.

eq s' = request(s,a,c) .
eq existsLi((a,c) ; lics(s)) = true.

eq l=chooseLic(belongLS((a,c);lics(s))) .

eq (chooseLic(belongLS((a,c);lics(s)))= nil) = false.

eq (chooseLic(belongLS((a,c);lics(s))) in lics(s)) = false.

red inv2(lics(s),l,a,c)implies istep1(l) .

close
```

CafeOBJ returns true for the above proof passage and hence, once we prove lemma 2, this concludes the proof for the request transition rule of our safety property. Applying the same technique, CafeOBJ returned true for all transitions.

We shall continue now with the proof of invariant-lemma 2. As stated above this is a stateless lemma, on sets of licenses so its induction will be conducted on the way such a set is created.

Here the base case consists of checking whether the lemma holds for an empty set. This is achieved by a proof score like the following:

```
            open ISTEP

            op a : -> Action.

            op c : -> Cont.

            red inv2(empty,l,a,c).

            close
```

This proof passage returned true, so now we can continue with checking the induction step. Assuming that the lemma holds for a set s we will check if it holds for the set created by the union of s with an arbitrary license element, that is denoted in our specification as *cons about r*. This can be done with a proof score as follows:

```
open ISTEP

op a : -> Action.

op c : -> Cont.
```

```
op cons :  ->   Cons.

op r   :  -> RSet.

op s   :  -> LicSet.
```

red   inv2(s,l,a,c)   implies   inv2((cons   about
r)s,l,a,c).

```
close
```

In the above proof passage the expression *inv2(s,l,a,c) implies inv2((cons about r)s,l,a,c)*can easily be replaced by *istep2(s,s',l,a,c)* to match the above methodology, though such a replacement is not necessary.

Here CafeOBJ retrurns nor true nor false but a sentence containing the expression *l = (chooseLic(belongL((a,c);(cons about r))belongLS ((a,c);s)))*. So once again we need to apply case splitting in order to continue.

Following the same method as for invariant 1 we reach the case seen below where CafeOBJ has returned true for all the symmetrical sub cases. *l = (chooseLic(belongL((a,c) ;(cons about r)) belongLS((a,c) ;s))) ∧ ¬ (chooseLic(belongL((a,c) ;(cons about r)) belongLS((a,c) ;s))) = nil ∧ ¬chooseLic((belongL((a,c) ; (cons about r))) (belongLS((a,c) ; s))) = cons about r ∧ ¬chooseLic((belongL((a,c) ; (cons about r))) (belongLS((a,c) ; s))) = chooseLic(belongLS((a,c) ; s)) .*

The above case, returns nor true nor false. Once again we conjure a lemma to discard it. This is how lemma three on table three was discovered.

```
open INV

op a : -> Action.

op c : -> Cont.

op cons :  ->   Cons.

op r   :  -> RSet.

op s   :  -> LicSet.
```

eq l = chooseLic((belongL((a,c);(cons about r))) (belongLS ((a,c); s))).

eq (chooseLic(belongL((a,c);(cons about r)))(belongLS
((a,c);s))) = nil) = false.

eq (chooseLic((belongL((a,c);(cons about r)))(belongLS
((a,c);s))) = cons about r) = false.

eq (chooseLic((belongL((a,c);(cons about r)))(belongLS
((a,c);s))) = chooseLic(belongLS((a,c);s))) = false.

red inv3(s,l,a,c,cons,r) implies (inv2(s,l,a,c) implies
inv2((cons about r) s ,l,a,c)).

```
close
```

CafeOBJ returned true for the above proof passage. Thus this together with the proof of invariant-lemma 3 concludes the proof of invariant 2.Where invariant 3 is formally defined in CafeOBJ terms as:

```
eq  inv3(LS,L,A,C,Cons,R)  =   not  (chooseLic(  (belongL(
(A,C)  ;  (Cons about R)))  (belongLS(  (A,C)  ;  LS))  )  = Cons
about R)     and   not  (chooseLic(  (belongL(  (A,C)  ;  (Cons
about R)))  (belongLS(  (A,C)  ;  LS))  )  = chooseLic(  be-
longLS(  (A,C)  ;  LS)  ))     implies  (chooseLic(  (belongL(
(A,C);(Cons about R)))(belongLS(  (A,C);LS))  )  = nil).
```

Finally, all the lemmas presented in table 3 were proven using the same technique and thus our proof concludes.

5 Conclusions and Future Work

We have modeled OMA Choice Algorithm as an Observational Transition System in CafeOBJ, and verified that the algorithm possesses an important invariant property using CafeOBJ system as an interactive theorem prover. We are not the first to use algebraic specification techniques for modeling and verification of Digital Rights Management Systems [17]. This paper is a part of our work in modeling, specification and verification of algorithms and protocols used in mobile settings, using algebraic specification techniques [7, 8].

We have also proposed an abstract syntax for OMA Rights Expression Language in [16]. Some problems for the OMA Choice Algorithm are presented in [9]. More specifically, let us consider the example of section 3. In this example if the user tries to exercise the right *"play song A"* the OMA Choice Algorithm will decide that the best license to use is license A. By doing so, the user is deprived of the right to listen to song B because license A will no longer be valid after the execution of the above right. So, the user ends up losing some of the rights the initial license set contained without exercising them. This malfunction could have been avoided if the OMA Choice Algorithm decided the most fitting license to use for the right *"play song A"* was license B. After the execution of the right the user would retain the rights to play songs A, B and C.

We intend to redesign the OMA Choice Algorithm so that problems like the ones presented in [9] do not occur. The redesign method will include Falsification techniques [15] for CafeOBJ together with the OTS/CafeOBJ method.

References

1. Iannella, R.: Open Digital Rights Language (ODRL) version 1.1 (2002),
   http://odrl.net/1.1/ODRL-11.pdf
2. ContentGuard. XrML 2.0 Technical Overview version 1.0 (2007)
3. Rightscom. The MPEG-21 Rights Expression Language - A Whitepaper (2007),
   http://www.xrml.org/reference/MPEG21_REL_whitepaper_
   Rightscom.pdf
4. Diaconescu, R., Futatsugi, K.: CafeOBJ Report. World Scientific (1998)

5. Open Mobile Alliance. OMA-TS-DRM-REL-V2_ 0-020060303-A (2006),
   http://www.openmobilealliance.org
6. CafeOBJ home page (2009), http://www.ldl.jaist.ac.jp/cafeobj/
7. Ouranos, I., Stefaneas, P., Frangos, P.: An Algebraic Framework for Modeling of Mobile Systems. IEICE Trans. Fund. E90-A(9), 1986–1999 (2007)
8. Ouranos, I., Stefaneas, P.: Verifying Security Protocols for Sensor Networks using Algebraic Specification Techniques. In: Bozapalidis, S., Rahonis, G. (eds.) CAI 2007. LNCS, vol. 4728, pp. 247–259. Springer, Heidelberg (2007)
9. Barth, A., Mitchell, J.C.: Managing Digital Rights using Linear Logic. In: 21th IEEE Symposium on Logic in Computer Science (LICS), pp. 127–136 (2006)
10. Futatsugi, K., Babu, C. S., Ogata, K.: Verifying Design with Proof Scores. In: Meyer, B., Woodcock, J. (eds.) VSTTE 2005. LNCS, vol. 4171, pp. 277–290. Springer, Heidelberg (2008)
11. Futatsugi, K., Ogata, K.: Simulation-based Verification for Invariant Properties in the OTS/CafeOBJ Method. Electronic Notes Theor. Comp. Science 201, 127–154 (2008)
12. Futatsugi, K., Ogata, K.: Some Tips on Writing Proof Scores in the OTS/CafeOBJ Method. In: Futatsugi, K., Jouannaud, J.-P., Bevilacqua, V. (eds.) Algebra, Meaning, and Computation. LNCS, vol. 4060, pp. 596–615. Springer, Heidelberg (2006)
13. Futatsugi, K., Ogata, K.: Proof Scores in the OTS/CafeOBJ Method. In: Najm, E., Nestmann, U., Stevens, P. (eds.) FMOODS 2003. LNCS, vol. 2884, pp. 170–184. Springer, Heidelberg (2003)
14. Diaconescu, R.: Behavioral Coherence in Object -Oriented Algebraic Specification. J. Universal Computer Science 6(1), 74–96 (2000)
15. Ogata, K., Nakano, M., Kong, W., Futatsugi, K.: Induction-Guided Falsification. In: Liu, Z., Kleinberg, R.D. (eds.) ICFEM 2006. LNCS, vol. 4260, pp. 114–131. Springer, Heidelberg (2006)
16. Triantafyllou, N., Ouranos, I., Stefaneas, P.: Algebraic Specifications for OMA REL Licenses. In: Proc: IEEE International Conference on Wireless and Mobile Computing, Networking and Communications, wimob, pp. 376–381 (2009)
17. Xiang, J., Bjørner, D., Futatsugi, K.: Formal digital license language with OTS/CafeOBJ, method. In: IEEE/ACS International Conference on Computer Systems and Applications 2008, pp. 652–660 (2008)

Extended Field Performance Evaluation
of a Gbps FSO Link

J.A.R. Pacheco de Carvalho[1,2], N. Marques[1,3], H. Veiga[1,3],
C.F. Ribeiro Pacheco[1], and A.D. Reis[1,2,4]

[1] U. de Detecção Remota
[2] Dept. de Física
[3] Centro de Informática
Universidade da Beira Interior, 6201-001 Covilhã, Portugal
[4]Dept. de Electrónica e Telecomunicações / Instituto de Telecomunicações
Universidade de Aveiro, 3810 Aveiro, Portugal
{pacheco,nmarques,hveiga,a17597,adreis}@ubi.pt

Abstract. Wireless communications have been increasingly important. Besides
Wi-Fi, FSO plays a very relevant technological role in this context. Performance is crucial, resulting in more reliable and efficient communications. A
FSO medium range link has been successfully implemented for high requirement applications at Gbps. An extended field performance evaluation of this
link has been carried out at OSI layers 1, 4 and 7, through a specifically planned
field test arrangement. Measurements have been made both for powers received
by the laser heads, and TCP, UDP and FTP experiments, resulting in determina-
tions of TCP throughput, jitter, percentage datagram loss and FTP transfer rate.
Corresponding results are presented and discussed. Conclusions are drawn
about link performance.

Keywords: Wireless network, Laser, FSO, Point-to-point link, Performance
measurements.

1 Introduction

Wi-Fi and FSO are wireless communications technologies whose importance and
utilization have been growing.

Wi-Fi uses microwaves in the 2.4 and 5 GHz frequency bands and IEEE 802, 11a,
b, g standards. Nominal transfer rates up to 11 (802.11b) and 54 Mbps (802.11a, g)
are specified [1]. It has been used in ad hoc and infrastructure modes. Point-to-point
and point-to-multipoint configurations are used for both indoors and outdoors, requiring specific directional and omnidirectional antennas. FSO uses laser technology to
provide point-to-point communications e.g. to interconnect LANs of two buildings
having line-of-site. FSO was developed in the 1960's for military and other purposes,
including high requirement applications. At present, speeds typically up to 2.5 Gbps
are possible and ranges up to a few km, depending on technology and atmospheric
conditions. Interfaces such as fast Ethernet and Gigabit Ethernet are used to communicate with LAN's. Typical laser wavelengths of 785 nm, 850 nm and 1550 nm are

M.S. Obaidat, G.A. Tsihrintzis, and J. Filipe (Eds.): ICETE 2010, CCIS 222, pp. 439–446, 2012.
© Springer-Verlag Berlin Heidelberg 2012

used. In a FSO link the transmitters deliver high power light which, after travelling through atmosphere, appears as low power light at the receiver. The link margin of the connection represents the amount of light received by a terminal over the minimum value required to keep the link active: (link margin)$_{dB}$= 10 log$_{10}$ (P/P$_{min}$), where P and P$_{min}$ are the corresponding power values, respectively.

There are several factors related to performance degradation in the design of a FSO link: distance between optical emitters; line of sight; alignment of optical emitters; stability of the mounting points; atmospheric conditions; water vapour and hot air; strong electromagnetic interference; wavelength of the laser light [2]. A redundant microwave link is always essential, as the laser link can fail under adverse conditions. Several studies and implementations of FSO have been reported [3,4]. FSO has been used in hybrid systems for temporary multimedia applications [5].

Performance has been a crucial issue, resulting in more reliable and efficient communications. Telematic applications have specific performance requirements, depending on application. New telematic applications present special sensitivities to performances, when compared to traditional applications. E.g. requirements have been quoted as: for video on demand/moving images, 1-10 ms jitter and 1-10 Mbps throughput; for Hi Fi stereo audio, jitter less than 1 ms and 0.1-1 Mbps throughputs [6].

Several performance measurements have been made for 2.4 and 5 GHz Wi-Fi [7,8]. FSO and fiber optics have been applied at the University Campus to improve communications quality [9-12]. In the present work we have made further investigations on that FSO link for extended performance evaluation at OSI layers 1, 4 and 7.

The rest of the paper is structured as follows: Chapter 2 presents the experimental details i.e. the measurement setup and procedure. Results and discussion are presented in Chapter 3. Conclusions are drawn in Chapter 4.

2   Experimental Details

The main experimental details, for testing the quality of the FSO link, are as follows.

A very high speed full-duplex link at 1 Gbps was planned and implemented, to interconnect the LAN at the Faculty of Medicine building and the main University network, to support medical imaging, VoIP, audio and video traffics [9,10]. Then, a FSO laser link at 1 Gbps full-duplex, over a distance of 1.14 km, was created to interconnect the Faculty of Medicine (FM) building at Pole III and the Sports (SB) building at Pole II of the University (Fig. 1).

We have chosen laser heads from FSONA (Fig. 2) to implement the laser link at a laser wavelength of λ= 1550 nm for eye safety, where allowable laser power is about fifty times higher at 1550 nm than at 800 nm [2]. Each laser head comprised two independent transmitters, for redundancy, and one wide aperture receiver. Each laser had 140 mW of power, resulting in an output power of 280 mW (24.5 dBm). 1000-Base-LX links over OM3 50/125 μm fiber were used to connect the laser heads to the LANs.

For a matter of redundancy a 802.16d WiMAX point-to-point link at 5.4 GHz [13] was available, where data rates up to either 75 Mbps or 108 Mbps were possible in normal mode or in turbo mode, respectively [14]. This link was usable as a backup link for FM-SB communications, through configuration of two static routing entries in the switching/routing equipment [9].

Performance tests of the FSO link were made under generally favourable weather conditions, including both day and night time intervals. The laser heads were set to a data rate mode which was compatible with Gigabit Ethernet. At OSI layer 1 (physical layer), received powers were simultaneously recorded for both laser heads. Data were collected from the internal logs of the laser heads, using STC (SONAbeam Terminal Controller) management software [15]. At OSI layer 4 (transport layer), measurements were made for both TCP connections and UDP communications using Iperf software [16]. In this way network performance results were recorded. Both TCP and UDP are transport protocols. TCP is connection-oriented. UDP is connectionless, as it sends data without ever establishing a connection. For a TCP connection over a link, TCP throughput was obtained. For a UDP communication, we obtained UDP throughput, jitter and percentage loss of datagrams. TCP packets and UDP datagrams of 1470 bytes size were used. A window size of 8 kbytes and a buffer size of the same value were used for TCP and UDP, respectively.

A specific field test arrangement was planned and implemented for the measurements (Fig. 3). Two PC's having IP addresses 192.168.0.2 and 192.168.0.1 were setup as the Iperf server and client, respectively. The PCs were desktop HP computers with 3.0 GHz Pentium IV CPUs running Windows XP, where the server had a better RAM configuration than the client. Each PC was equipped with a 1000Base-T network adapter for connection to a corresponding interface of a C2 Enterasys switch [17]. Each switch had a 1000Base-LX interface which permitted a FSO link through two laser heads, as represented in Fig. 3. The laser heads were located at Pole II and Pole III, at the SB and FM buildings, respectively. The experimental arrangement could be remotely accessed through the FM LAN. In the UDP tests a bandwidth parameter of 300 Mbps was used in the Iperf client. Jitter, which represents the smooth mean of differences between consecutive transit times, was continuously computed by the server, as specified by RTP in RFC 1889 [18]. RTP provides end-to-end network transport functions appropriate for applications transmitting real-time data, e.g. audio, video, over multicast or unicast network services. At OSI layer 7 (application layer) the setup given in Fig. 3 was also used for measurements of FTP transfer rates through FTP server and client applications installed in the PCs. Each measurement corresponded to a single FTP transfer, using a 2.71 Gbyte file. Whenever a measurement was made at either OSI layer 4 or 7, data were simultaneously collected at OSI layer 1. Batch command files were written to enable the TCP, UDP and FTP tests. The results, obtained in batch mode, were recorded as data files in the client PC disk.

3   Results and Discussion

Several data sets were collected and processed from TCP, UDP and FTP experiments, which were not simultaneous. The corresponding results are shown for TCP in Fig.s 4-5, for UDP in Fig.s 6-7 and FTP in Fig.s 8-9. The average received powers for the SB and FM laser heads, mostly ranged high values in the 25-35 µW interval which corresponds to link margins of 4.9-6.4 dB (considering $P_{min}=8$ µW). From Fig. 4 it follows that TCP average throughput (314 Mbps) is very steady, although two small peaks of 13 and 10 Mbps arise for throughput deviation. Fig. 5 illustrates details of TCP results over a small interval. Fig. 6 shows that UDP average throughput (124 Mbps) is fairly steady, having a small steady throughput deviation. The jitter is small, usually less than 1 ms, while percentage datagram loss is practically negligible. Fig. 7 illustrates details of UDP-jitter results over a small interval. Fig. 8 shows that average FTP throughput (345 Mbps) is very steady, having relatively low throughput deviations (10 Mbps, typically). Fig. 9 illustrates details of FTP results over a small interval. It should be noted that, besides CPU and bus performances, transfer rates of the PC's disks are always important in this type of FTP experiments. Higher disk performances lead to increased FTP throughputs. In all types of experiments, given high values of average received powers, the quantities under analysis did not show on average significant variations, even when variations of the received powers were observed. The results here obtained complement previous work by the authors [9-11]. Generally, for our experimental conditions, the FSO link has exhibited very good performances at OSI layers 4 and 7.

Besides the present results, it has been mentioned [12] that we have implemented a VoIP solution, with G.711 and G729A coding algorithms, based on Cisco Call Manager [19]. Tools such as Cisco IP Communicator have been used. VoIP has been working over the laser link without any performance problems. Video and sound have also been tested through the laser link, by using eyeBeam Softphone CounterPath software [20]. Applications using the link continued to be well-behaved.

Fig. 1. View of the 1.14 km laser link between Pole II (SB) and Pole III (FM)

Fig. 2. View of the laser heads at FM (Pole III) and SB (Pole II)

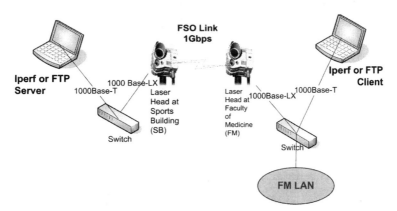

Fig. 3. Field tests setup scheme for the FSO link

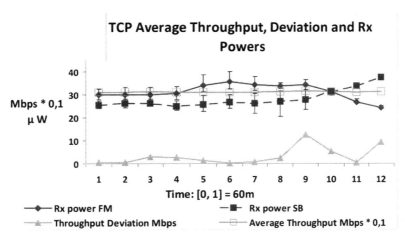

Fig. 4. TCP results

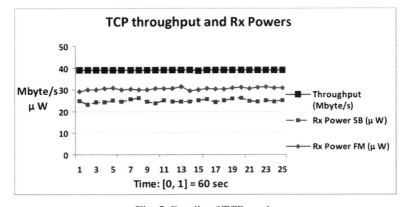

Fig. 5. Details of TCP results

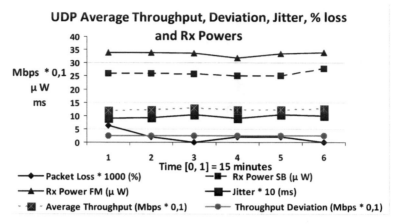

Fig. 6. UDP results; 300 Mbps bandwidth parameter

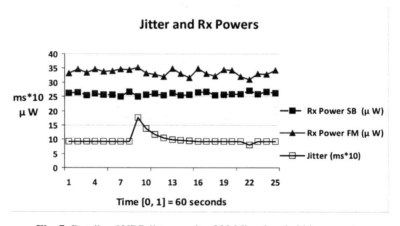

Fig. 7. Details of UDP-jitter results; 300 Mbps bandwidth parameter

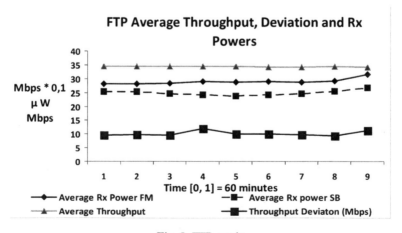

Fig. 8. FTP results

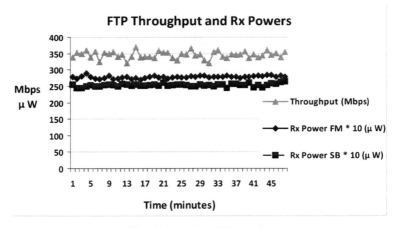

Fig. 9. Details of FTP results

4 Conclusions

A FSO laser link at 1 Gbps has been successfully implemented over 1.14 km along the city, for interconnecting Poles of the University and support high requirement applications.

A field test arrangement has been planned and implemented. Extended performance measurements of the FSO link have been carried out at OSI layers 1, 4 and 7. At OSI layer 1, received powers were simultaneously measured in both laser heads. At OSI layer 4, TCP throughput, jitter and percentage datagram loss were measured. At OSI layer 7, FTP transfer rate data were acquired. Under generally favourable experimental conditions, when the measurements were carried out, the link has shown to be very well behaved, continuing to present very good performances. Applications such as VoIP, video and sound, have again been well-behaved. Further measurements are planned under several experimental conditions, such as environmental and multimedia traffic.

Acknowledgements. Supports from the University of Beira Interior and FCT (Fundação para a Ciência e a Tecnologia)/POCI2010 (Programa Operacional Ciência e Inovação) are acknowledged. We acknowledge Hewlett Packard and FSONA for their availability.

References

1. IEEE Standard 802.11-2007, IEEE Standard for Local and metropolitan area networks-Specific Requirements-Part 11: Wireless LAN Medium Access Control (MAC) and Physical Layer (PHY) specifications, http://standards.ieee.org/getieee802
2. Rockwell, D.A., Mecherle, G.S.: Wavelength Selection for Optical Wireless Communication Systems. In: Proc. SPIE, vol. 4530, pp. 27–35 (2001)
3. D'Amico, M., Leva, A., Micheli, B.: Free Space Optics Communication Systems: First Results From a Pilot Field Trial in the Surrounding Area of Milan, Italy. IEEE Microwave and Wireless Components Letters 13(8), 305–307 (2003)

4. Löschnigg, M., Mandl, P., Leitgeb, E.: Long-term Performance Observation of a Free Space Optics Link. In: Proc. ConTEL 2009-10th International Conference on Telecommunications, Zagreb, Croatia, June 8-10, pp. 305–310 (2009)

5. Mandl, P., Chlestil, C., Zettl, K., Leitgeb, E.: Hybrid systems using Optical Wireless, Fiber Optics and WLAN for temporary multimedia applications. In: Proc. ConTEL 2007-9th International Conference on Telecommunications, Zagreb, Croatia, June 13-15, pp. 73–76 (2007)

6. Monteiro, E., Boavida, F.: Engineering of Informatics Networks, 4th edn. FCA-Editor of Informatics Ld., Lisbon (2002)

7. Pacheco de Carvalho, J.A.R., Gomes, P.A.J., Veiga, H., Reis, A.D.: Development of a University Networking Project. In: Putnik, G.D., Cunha, M.M. (eds.) Encyclopedia of Networked and Virtual Organizations, pp. 409–422. IGI Global, Hershey (2008)

8. Pacheco de Carvalho, J.A.R., Veiga, H., Gomes, P.A.J., Ribeiro Pacheco, C.F., Marques, N., Reis, A.D.: Wi-Fi Point-to-Point Links- Performance Aspects of IEEE 802.11 a,b,g Laboratory Links. In: Ao, S.-I., Gelman, L. (eds.) Electronic Engineering and Computing Technology. LNEE, vol. 60, pp. 507–514. Springer, Netherlands (2010)

9. Pacheco de Carvalho, J.A.R., Gomes, P.A.J., Veiga, H., Reis, A.D.: Wi-Fi and Very High Speed Optical Links for Data and Voice Communications. In: Proc. CISTI 2007-2ª Conferência Ibérica de Sistemas e Tecnologias de Informação, Universidade Fernando Pessoa, Porto, Portugal, June 21-23, pp. 441–452 (2007)

10. Pacheco de Carvalho, J.A.R., Gomes, P.A.J., Veiga, H., Reis, A.D.: Experimental Performance Evaluation of a Very High Speed Free Space Optics Link at the University of Beira Interior Campus: a Case Study. In: Proc. SEONs 2008-VI Symposium on Enabling Optical Network and Sensors, Porto, Portugal, June 20-20, pp.131–132 (2008)

11. Pacheco de Carvalho, J.A.R., Veiga, H., Gomes, P.A.J., Ribeiro Pacheco, C.F.F.P., Reis, A.D.: Experimental Performance Study of a Very High Speed Free Space Optics Link at the University of Beira Interior Campus: a Case Study. In: Proc. ISSPIT 2008-8th IEEE International Symposium on Signal Processing and Information Technology, Sarajevo, Bosnia and Herzegovina, December 16-19, pp. 154–157 (2008)

12. Pacheco de Carvalho, J.A.R., Marques, N., Veiga, H., Ribeiro Pacheco, C.F.F.P., Reis, A.D.: Experimental Performance Evaluation of a Gbps FSO Link: a Case Study. In: Proc. WINSYS 2010- International Conference on Wireless Information Networks and Systems, Athens, Greece, July 26-28, pp. 95–99 (2010)

13. IEEE Standard 802.16-2004, IEEE Standard for Local and metropolitan area networks-Part 16: Air Interface for Fixed Broadband Wireless Access Systems, http://standards.ieee.org/getieee802

14. Alvarion, BreezeNET B-Making Point to Point Connections Fast and Easy (pp. 1-2, 213695 rev. i), http://www.alvarion.com

15. FSONA, SONABEAM Terminal Controller Software User's Guide (pp. 1-98, 95-0282 Rev. H), http://www.fsona.com

16. NLANR, Iperf User Docs, http://dast.nlanr.net

17. Enterasys, Enterasys SecureStack C2-Hardware Installation Guide (pp. 1-78, 9033951-06), http://www.enterasys.com

18. RFC 1889, RTP: A Transport Protocol for Real-Time Applications, http://www.rfc-archive.org

19. Cisco, Cisco Call Manager Version 4.1 (pp. 1–18, 204121.30_ETMG_JM_10.04), http://www.cisco.com

20. CounterPath, eyeBeam 1.5 for Windows User Guide (pp. 1-71), http://www.counterpath.com

Author Index

Agrawal, Dakshi   158
Agrawal, Shivank   259
Ahrens, Andreas   395
Antal, Bálint   378
Aota, Hisato   337
Araragi, Tadashi   233, 274
Artundo, Iñigo   133
Asim, Muhammad   304

Benavente-Peces, César   395
Bindel, Axel   350
Biryukov, Alex   147
Boudriga, Noureddine   54
Bulander, Rebecca   3
Buttigieg, Victor   363

Cheng, Pau-Chen   158
Clark, John A.   158
Conway, Paul   350
Cuiñas, Iñigo   410

Debevc, Matjaz   97
de Silva, Gayan   39

Ferrante, Alberto   243
Frangos, Panayiotis   424
Frikken, Keith B.   172

García-Roger, David   133
Geyer-Schulz, Andreas   112
Gomez-Rodriguez, Mario A.   84

Hajdu, András   378
Heidarvand, Somayeh   203
Holzinger, Andreas   97
Hudler, Matthias   71

Ibraimi, Luan   304
Ivanic, Natalie   158

Justham, Laura   350

Kawai, Yutaka   220
Kiyomoto, Shinsaku   188
Koschuch, Manuel   71

Krüger, Michael   71
Kruslin, Cornelia   3
Kumar, Swarun   259
Kurihara, Jun   188

Lázár, István   378
Le Sage, Tanya   350
Lokam, Satyanarayana V.   259
Lopez-Arevalo, Ivan   84

Marca, David   3
Marques, N.   439
Matousek, Petr   39
McDermid, John   158
Mura, Marcello   243

Nakano, Yuto   188
Nishide, Takashi   233, 274

Ohta, Kazuo   220
Oka, Ryuichi   337
Ortega, Beatriz   133
Ota, Kazuhiro   337
Ouranos, Iakovos   424
Ovelgönne, Michael   112

Pacheco, C.F. Ribeiro   439
Pacheco de Carvalho, J.A.R.   439
Pandu Rangan, C.   259
Peischl, Bernhard   97
Petković, Milan   304
Priemuth-Schmid, Deike   147

Rab, Jaroslav   39
Rass, Stefan   289
Reis, A.D.   439
Rekhis, Slim   54
Rysavy, Ondrej   39

Sakurai, Kouichi   233, 274
Sánchez, Manuel García   410
Schlögl, Martin   97
Shishkov, Boris   3
Slamanig, Daniel   289

Slawson, Sian   350
Slogget, Dave   158
Sonnenbichler, Andreas C.   112
Sosa-Sosa, Victor J.   84
Spiteri, Trevor   363
Stefaneas, Petros   424
Sveda, Miroslav   39

Taddeo, Antonio Vincenzo   243
Tanaka, Toshiaki   188
Tapiador, Juan E.   158
Triantafyllou, Nikolaos   424
Triki, Bayrem   54

Ushida, Mebae   220

van Sinderen, Marten   3
Vasco, María Isabel González   203
Veiga, H.   439
Venkatesan, Ramarathnam   259
Villar, Jorge L.   203

Wang, Alex Hai   319
Webster, James   350
West, Andrew   350

Yaguchi, Yuichi   337
Yoneyama, Kazuki   220

Zhang, Bin   147
Zhang, Yihua   172
Zhu, Huafei   233, 274